Second Edition

The Cold War: A Global History with Documents

Edward H. Judge
Le Moyne College

John W. Langdon
Le Moyne College

Prentice Hall
Boston Columbus Indianapolis New York San Francisco Upper Saddle River
Amsterdam Cape Town Dubai London Madrid Milan Munich Paris Montreal Toronto
Delhi Mexico City Sao Paulo Sydney Hong Kong Seoul Singapore Taipei Tokyo

Executive Editor: Jeff Lasser
Editorial Project Manager: Rob DeGeorge
Editorial Assistant: Amanda Dykstra
Senior Marketing Manager: Maureen Prado Roberts
Marketing Assistant: Marissa O'Brien
Production Manager: Fran Russello
Cover Art Director: Jayne Conte
Cover Designer: Bruce Kenselaar
Manager, Visual Research: Beth Brenzel
Image Cover Permission Coordinator: Karen Sanatar
Cover Art: Popperfoto/Getty Images
Full-Service Project Management: George Jacob / Integra Software Services, Ltd.
Printer/Binder/Cover: RR Donnelley & Sons
Text Font: 10/12 Times

Credits and acknowledgments borrowed from other sources and reproduced, with permission, in this textbook appear on appropriate page within text.

Library of Congress Cataloging-in-Publication Data
The Cold War: a global history with documents/compiled and edited by Edward H. Judge, John W. Langdon.—2nd ed.
p. cm.
Includes bibliographical references and index.
ISBN-13: 978-0-205-72911-1 (alk. paper)
ISBN-10: 0-205-72911-8 (alk. paper)
1. Cold War—Sources. 2. World politics—1945–1989—Sources. 3. World politics—1985–1995—Sources. I. Judge, Edward H. II. Langdon, John W.
D839.3.C57 2011
909.82'5—dc22

2010021200

10 9 8 7 6 5 4 3 2 1

Prentice Hall
is an imprint of

www.pearsonhighered.com

ISBN 10: 0-205-72911-8
ISBN 13: 978-0-205-72911-1

CONTENTS

COLD WAR DOCUMENTS

LIST OF MAPS

PREFACE

The collapse of the USSR in 1991 ended almost half a century of intense international struggle called the Cold War. For those of us who lived through it, the great events, personalities, crises, and conflicts were frightening and familiar aspects of our daily lives. For a new generation of readers, however, they are but dim and distant developments of a bygone era.

This book is meant for both groups. It is, in fact, a combined, revised, and updated edition of our two highly acclaimed Cold War books, *A Hard and Bitter Peace: A Global History of the Cold War* and *The Cold War: A History through Documents.* The former book was designed as a text for Cold War courses and as general reading for those interested in that era. Unlike Cold War texts stressing mainly U.S. history, it provided a *global* perspective, in a clear and engaging narrative style accessible to ordinary readers. The latter book, a wide-ranging collection of Cold War documents, sought both to illuminate the era's great events and to bring them to life in the words of those who were actively involved. We are pleased and satisfied that so many people—teachers, students, and ordinary readers—have used these books and found them helpful in understanding the Cold War.

NEW TO THIS EDITION

We had hoped to publish this second edition sooner, but were engaged for some years in writing our world history textbook, *Connections: A World History* (Pearson Education, 2009). Although that project delayed us, it also enhanced our emphasis on global connections and enabled us to add many new features and improvements to our Cold War coverage.

- *New information and research has been incorporated.* The opening of Soviet archives, publication of Cold War memoirs, and ongoing work of scholars have clarified and expanded our understanding of key decisions, perceptions, and events. How did Soviet and Chinese leaders interact with and view each other? What were Soviet objectives in Berlin and Cuba? How did Reagan's goals and perceptions differ from those of his predecessors? Insights and revelations from archives, memoirs, and scholars, casting light on these issues and numerous others, have been woven into the text of this second edition.
- *We have enhanced the book's global coverage.* Since the end of the Cold War, scholars have focused increasingly on its global impact and on the interaction between the Cold War and the struggles of non-Western nations emerging from Western domination and colonial rule. This second edition thus substantially increases our global coverage.
- *We have expanded and further globalized our document selection.* To support, sustain, and illuminate our enhanced global coverage, we have added a number of documents that deal with the Cold War as it pertained to Asia, Africa, the Middle East, and Latin America.

- *The List of Further Readings has been expanded and updated.* The scholarly literature on the Cold War has virtually exploded since our first editions. Areas such as Soviet foreign and domestic policies, Soviet espionage activities, the policies of the People's Republic of China, and the impact of Cold War rivalries on non-Western nations have been widely and deeply examined. The second edition includes references to numerous significant studies that have enhanced our knowledge of this crucial period.
- *Maps have been revised, updated, and captioned.* Our map program now includes full-color maps inside each cover. Existing maps have been expanded in number and revised to enhance their use as instructional tools. Captions have been added to assist the reader in *learning from* each map rather than simply glancing at it.
- *Marginal notes have been added throughout the book.* Since many younger readers will have no direct familiarity with the Cold War, we have added marginal notes to help them see the "big picture" and to help all our readers understand the significance of the events we describe and the connections among them.
- *The visual program has been thoroughly revised.* We have used Pearson Education's extensive photo archive to replace some photos and add many new ones. In each instance, the educational usefulness of the photograph has been foremost in our minds.
- *We have incorporated suggestions from teachers and professors who have used the first editions.* Our colleagues in the educational world have been generous with their comments and suggestions. Grateful for their insights and their loyalty to our work, we have included many of their ideas in the second edition.

ACKNOWLEDGMENTS

In preparing this work, we have benefited greatly from the reactions and insights of our students, particularly those who have taken our Cold War history courses. We are deeply grateful to them, as well as to the librarians who helped us locate and assemble documents, and to our colleagues and editors—including Joseph Curran, Douglas Egerton, Mark Kulikowski, Larry Eugene Jones, Mark T. Clark, Lawrence H. Madaras, Eleanor McCluskey, Charles Cavaliere, Rob DeGeorge, and Jeff Lasser—who made numerous helpful suggestions. We are especially grateful to our wives, Susan Judge and Janice Langdon, who provided us with patient, good-humored support and helped in countless ways. It is to them, above all, that we are indebted, and it is to them that we lovingly and appreciatively dedicate our work.

Ed Judge and John Langdon

PART I ORIGINS OF THE COLD WAR

1

The Seeds of Conflict

For almost half a century after World War II, the political, social, cultural, and economic life of much of the world was caught up in an intense international struggle called the Cold War. Seen largely as a conflict between the Communist "East," led by the Union of Soviet Socialist Republics (USSR), and the capitalist "West," led by the United States of America, the Cold War was more than a gigantic power struggle between two assertive superpowers. It was also a global rivalry between conflicting perspectives and worldviews, deeply rooted in the different historical experiences and perceptions of those who made up the East and the West. These experiences and perceptions did not cause the Cold War, but they did provide a context that fueled the fears and suspicions of both sides.

THE DOMINANCE OF THE WEST

By the early twentieth century, the West, which included mainly the industrialized nations of Europe and North America, had come to dominate the globe. After centuries of expansion, the powers of Western Europe had gained cultural and economic influence, and often direct political control, over much of the world. In the sixteenth and seventeenth centuries, they conquered and colonized the Americas, displacing the native cultures that had hitherto populated these lands. In the eighteenth and nineteenth centuries, they experienced revolutions in agriculture and industry, providing them with unprecedented wealth and power and with a vast technological edge over non-Western cultures. This wealth and power in turn helped trigger a new wave of imperialist expansion, bringing much of Asia and most of Africa under European rule. Whatever its wisdom and morality, this imperialist expansion seemed to confirm for many in the West the superiority of their institutions and values.

Western powers dominate world by early twentieth century

The West's most cherished institutions and values were those associated with political liberalism, free market capitalism, and Christian religion. Parliamentary assemblies and guaranteed freedoms had become part and parcel of the political terrain in the major Western nations, most of which were moving toward full democracy. Free market economies, although often restricted and regulated in various ways, had become the order of the day, and industrial capitalism seemed to be creating unlimited wealth and opportunities. And although the Christian church was no longer the West's central institution, Judeo-Christian ideals still had a powerful hold on most persons of European descent. It is hardly surprising, then, that Western officials, entrepreneurs, and missionaries sought in various ways to transplant these institutions and ideals to colonial soil and thus "uplift" the colonial peoples by converting them to Western ways.

Western powers impose their values on the non-Western world

But the dominance of the West and the presumed superiority of capitalism, democracy, and Christianity were not universally appreciated. Among non-Western victims of imperialist oppression, there was deep resentment toward Europeans and their institutions. Even in Europe, the sufferings and dislocation occasioned by the growth of industry and empire had led to the emergence of "socialist" movements that sought to alter or overthrow the capitalist system.

THE RISE OF REVOLUTIONARY MARXISM

Prominent among these movements were the Marxists, disciples of the nineteenth century's most influential critic of Western institutions and values. Reacting against the brutalities of industrialization and the sufferings of industrial workers, Karl Marx and his supporters had developed an ideology that served both to explain the success of industrial capitalism and to forecast its eventual destruction. In so doing, they relentlessly attacked the West's most cherished institutions: political liberalism, free market capitalism, and Christian religion.

According to Marxist critique, the history of Western society—and for that matter *any* society—was a history of class conflict. The social class that controlled the means of production, the primary source of economic power and wealth, was in a position to establish and maintain political, cultural, and religious institutions beneficial to itself. For centuries, as a result of the agrarian economy of medieval and early modern Europe, the primary means of production had been the land, and those who controlled it—the landowning aristocracy and landed gentry—had thus been able to dominate political, social, and religious affairs. With the shift to a commercial and industrial economy, however, economic power had passed to an influential new class, the "bourgeoisie," whose wealth was based on capital investment rather than on land. By the end of the nineteenth century, with the rapid growth of an urban industrial economy, the bourgeoisie had become the dominant class in the West. Since it now controlled the means of production, the bourgeoisie established its own institutions, based on free market economics and liberal politics, in most Western countries.

Marxism sees all societies as based on class struggle

From a Marxist perspective, these "bourgeois" institutions were exploitative, designed to perpetuate the bourgeoisie's power over the masses of people. But the Marxists concluded that such institutions were ultimately doomed. The same industrial process that solidified bourgeois control was also creating a new class of people, the urban "proletariat," who owned no property, possessed few rights, and had nothing to sell but their work. Crowded together in squalid factory towns

Marxists say proletarian revolution will overthrow capitalism and subjected to various forms of exploitation and abuse, they would sooner or later become conscious of themselves as an exploited class and join together to rise up against their exploiters, the bourgeoisie. In so doing, it was foreseen, the workers would forcibly sweep away the institutions that oppressed them and establish their own control over the means of production. This process would bring about a "dictatorship of the proletariat," which would eventually develop into a worldwide socialist order based on equality and cooperation. The class struggle would end, social classes would disappear, and nation-states would eventually "wither away."

This Marxist socialist vision had a powerful attraction for many people who were disillusioned with the values and realities of Western society. It opposed the ethic of individualism and competition with one of collectivism and cooperation. It offered a "scientific" explanation for existing inequities and oppression. It held out the prospect that, by organizing themselves for revolutionary action, the downtrodden would eventually be able to settle scores with their oppressors. And it provided a vision of a better society in which conflict and greed would give way to social harmony and economic equality.

By the beginning of the twentieth century, however, the prospects for socialist revolution seemed to be receding in the industrialized West. In country after country, as Marx had foreseen, workers joined together to advance their interests. They discovered, however, that their united actions enabled them to wrestle concessions from industrial capitalists and to gain some influence in parliamentary politics. Labor unions were organized, strikes were initiated, and political parties claiming to represent the workers' interests were formed. Conflict and violence often accompanied these developments, but the typical result was reform, not revolution. Trade unions were legalized, laws were passed protecting workers' rights, and working-class males gained the right to vote. Living standards of the typical worker tended to improve, rather than deteriorate, over time. Capitalists and socialists alike discovered that, once living and working situations improved, workers tended to lose interest in revolution.

These developments occasioned a split in the socialist movement. Some socialists, accepting the new realities, concluded that violent revolution was no longer necessary. "Evolutionary" socialists, such as Jean Jaurès in France and Eduard Bernstein in Germany, argued that the workers and their leaders could bring about a gradual transition to socialism by working within the system, using democratic and parliamentary means. They thus sought to build strong "social democratic" parties and to advance the interests of the workers, sometimes even collaborating with liberal and bourgeois groups. As it attracted large numbers of followers and achieved important successes, socialism in the West started losing its revolutionary edge.

Some socialists say workers can attain goals without revolution

Other socialists, such as France's Jules Guesde, were distressed by these developments. To them, collaboration with the bourgeoisie meant selling out socialist values and compromising socialist goals. From their perspective, no true socialism was possible until the bourgeoisie had been overthrown and the workers (or their representatives) had seized control of the means of production and taken political power. True socialists must strive to radicalize the workers and lead them to revolution, rather than letting them become de-radicalized by economic gain.

Other socialists see revolution as essential

THE TRIUMPH IN RUSSIA OF MARXISM-LENINISM

In the East, where democratic institutions did not exist, socialism remained a radical and revolutionary force. This was particularly true in Russia, the vast "empire of the tsars," which was just beginning to industrialize. In a pamphlet called "What Is to Be Done," published in 1902, the Russian Marxist V. I. Lenin argued that socialists must form a tightly organized party of professional revolutionaries who would serve as the "vanguard of the proletariat," fighting against both the tsarist regime and the emerging capitalist order. To accomplish these goals, Lenin started his own "Bolshevik" movement within the context of Russian socialism.

Lenin builds Marxist Bolshevik party in Russia

Fatefully, despite its internationalist pretensions, Russian Marxism came to incorporate certain nationalistic and imperialistic tendencies that were deeply rooted in Russian culture. It interacted with Slavophilism, the conviction that Slavic ways of thinking and acting were superior to those of the West, to create a form of socialism contemptuous of Western ways and values. And it emulated the Russian Orthodox conception of Moscow as the "Third Rome," the foreordained successor to Rome and Constantinople as the center of civilization, to produce a crusading fatalism convinced that not merely Marxism, but *Russian* Marxism, was the wave of the future. The blending of Marx's philosophy with Russian tradition was thus fraught with consequences for future East–West relations.

Russian Marxists embrace anti-Western attitudes

Meanwhile, Western domination of the globe provided Marxists with fertile new ground for their critique of Western capitalism. Some asserted that Western European expansion was a logical outcome of industrial growth: With their insatiable need for raw materials, markets, and outlets for capital investment, Western nations had asserted economic hegemony, and often political control, over vast areas of the non-Western world. This theme was echoed in 1916 by Lenin, who argued in *Imperialism: The Highest Stage of Capitalism* that empire building was merely an advanced phase of capitalism and that imperialism and capitalism were for all intents and purposes identical. This analysis, although not fully supported by historical evidence, provided a plausible explanation for Western expansionism. More importantly, it became an essential ingredient of "Marxism-Leninism," a revised ideology that appealed to the nationalist aspirations of the victims of imperialism by linking their struggle for "national liberation" with the revolutionary socialist movement. Marxism in time would thus be transformed from an antinationalist movement in which the "workers have no nation" into a pro-nationalist movement urging colonial peoples to fight for national independence from imperialist control.

Marxist-Leninists equate capitalism with imperialism

The crisis of Western capitalism, so staunchly predicted by the Marxists, arrived with a vengeance in 1914. World War I, pitting the Allied Powers (mainly Britain, France, and Russia) against the Central Powers (led by Germany) in a deadly struggle against one another, exposed the horrible dangers of militarism, expansionism, and unbridled nationalism. But it also laid to rest the vision of an "internationalized" proletariat: Marxists watched in dismay as socialist leaders on both sides supported their nations' war efforts and as workers by the millions marched off to engage in combat against other countries' workers.

In Russia, as elsewhere, the war initially hampered the hopes of revolutionary socialists, as workers at first supported the war with patriotic commitment. The prospect of revolution, which had seemed to grow brighter in the years before the war, suddenly dimmed considerably. But as the war dragged on and the humiliation of defeat set in, people in Russia turned increasingly against both their rulers and the war. Early in 1917, a series of stunning events in Petrograd, the Russian capital, resulted in the fall of the tsarist monarchy. But the provisional government that replaced it, failing to comprehend the depth of popular hostility toward the war, sought to continue the conflict. Lenin and his Bolsheviks, seizing the opportunity, called for an end to the provisional government, an end to the war, and redistribution of rural farmland to benefit the Russian peasants. In November, they staged a well-organized coup, seizing power in the name of the "soviets," or workers' councils, that had been formed in the wake of the first revolution.

World War I helps foster Russian Bolshevik revolution

THE SOVIET CHALLENGE AND THE WESTERN RESPONSE

The seizure of power in Russia by revolutionary Marxists sent shock waves throughout the Western world. The immediate concern was military: Lenin's determination to pull Russia out of the war posed a grave threat to the survival of Russia's French and British allies. Their German foes, hitherto forced to fight a two-front war against Russia in the east and Britain and France in the west, would now be free to focus their full force against the West. But in the long run, another concern alarmed Western leaders even more: the avowed Marxist goal of a worldwide socialist revolution that would bring a violent end to free market capitalism and liberal democracy. From their perspective, Bolshevik Russia was an outlaw state, a renegade nation that threatened the very existence of Western civilization.

In 1918, after the new Soviet regime withdrew from World War I, Britain, France, Japan, and America (which had joined the war on the Allied Powers' side in 1917) sent military forces to Russia, allegedly to protect supplies they had previously shipped to the tsarist government, but also hoping to oust the Bolsheviks and get Russia back into the war against Germany. Before long these foreign forces became embroiled in a bitter civil war pitting various anti-Bolshevik groups against the new Soviet regime. This "Allied intervention" in Russia was half-hearted and ineffective, especially after World War I ended with Allied victory later in 1918, and the Bolsheviks' "Red Army" eventually defeated all its "White" opponents in the Russian Civil War (1918–1921). But the fact that the "imperialists" intervened—and kept their armies on Russian soil even after Germany's defeat—left a legacy of bitterness in Russia toward the West.

West intervenes in Russian Civil War against Bolsheviks

Meanwhile a new leader had arisen in the capitalist West. After decades of rapid industrial growth, the United States of America was the world's chief industrial power, its economic output exceeding that of Germany and Britain (the next two leading industrial nations) combined. By remaining neutral for the first two-thirds of the war, while lending money and selling supplies to Europe's belligerent powers, the Americans had further improved their economic standing. After they finally joined the war in April of 1917, their vast resources and fresh troops eventually helped checkmate the exhausted forces of Germany and its allies. Having suffered less and gained more than any other major power, the United States emerged from the war as both a key architect of Allied victory and the world's leading capitalist democracy.

United States emerges as potential Western leader

The United States seemed an ideal candidate for leader of the Western world. A young, vibrant, self-confident nation founded on ideals of popular sovereignty, it had recently become an industrial capitalist giant. It had also acquired a modest overseas empire but had not been a major participant in the scramble for colonies that had tarnished the European powers. Blessed with abundant resources and fertile farmland, and insulated by broad oceans from serious foreign threats, Americans had an almost mystic faith in their economic values and political institutions. Reflecting this faith, their wartime president, Woodrow Wilson, had sought to change the war from an imperialist power struggle into a crusade for democracy and "national self-determination"—the right of each nationality to freely decide its own political status. At the postwar peace conference, which met at Versailles near Paris, he also insisted on the formation of the League of Nations, an organization of the world's nations designed to maintain peace through "collective security"—cooperation among member nations to resolve disputes and act jointly against potential aggressors.

United States opts not to join League of Nations

Americans, however, proved unwilling to follow their president's lead. Fearful of entangling commitments and anxious to preserve American independence in international affairs, the U.S. Senate kept America out of the League of Nations by failing to ratify the Versailles peace settlement. Britain and France, the other two main victors and global powers, did join the League but were wounded by the war and bogged down by problems at home and in their colonies. Strong Western leadership thus did not emerge on either side of the Atlantic.

Meanwhile, Russia's new Bolshevik rulers were creating a new order. They nationalized industries, expropriated capitalists and landowners, and persecuted all opposition. Renamed the Communist Party, they became the sole political power, using a government hierarchy of soviets to rule a new regime they soon came to call the Union of Soviet Socialist Republics (USSR).

Russian-led Communists threaten Western capitalist world

It was in international affairs, however, that the Soviet Communists posed their greatest challenge to the capitalist West. Disparaging traditional diplomacy, they embarked on a global campaign to undermine the capitalist powers and their parliamentary governments. In 1919, they founded the Communist International (or "Comintern"), a worldwide association of Communist parties. Designed to coordinate and control the international Communist movement, it sought to organize and inspire socialist revolutions everywhere. Communist parties acquired a notable following among Western Europe's industrial proletariat, and fear of Communist inroads even elicited a brief "Red Scare" in America. Throughout Asia and Africa, Communists strove to identify with the nationalist aspirations and liberation struggles of colonial peoples who had been subjugated by Western imperialism.

In time, however, as worldwide socialist revolutions failed to materialize, the USSR a started acting like a traditional power with a standard foreign policy.

In 1921, as the Soviets embarked on a "New Economic Policy" that restored some features of a market economy, they signed a trade agreement with Britain. Before long, having temporarily postponed their push for world revolution, they began promoting "socialism in one country" and coexistence with the capitalist world. The West, for its part, came to accept the Soviet state as an unpleasant but unavoidable reality. Several crises in the mid-1920s heightened tensions between East and West but did not destroy the resigned yet wary tolerance that each had developed toward the other.

Failing to spread Communism, Soviets coexist with West

This tolerance was tested by the dramatic events of the 1930s. The Great Depression, beginning with the U.S. stock market crash of 1929, shook the capitalist world to its core. Western leaders turned inward, focusing on domestic problems and seeking to resolve their economic crises, often with limited success. In many countries, socialists on the left and militaristic nationalists on the right won numerous new adherents among the unemployed and disenchanted. In Britain, France, and the United States, democratic and capitalist institutions were strong enough to weather the storm. But in Germany, such institutions were threatened by the rapid growth of the racist and militarist National Socialist (Nazi) movement and the growing strength of the German Communists.

The USSR, meanwhile, experienced its own massive internal crisis. Beginning in 1929, Soviet Communist Party leader Joseph Stalin employed a series of "five-year plans" to bring rapid industrialization and collectivization of agriculture. His goal was to catch up with the West to ensure his regime's survival. But the price of progress was horrendous, as millions of Soviet citizens suffered and died—especially in the brutal civil war and forced famine that accompanied the collectivization of farming in Ukraine. In the West, even admirers of the Soviet system had difficulty defending a regime that slaughtered and starved its own citizens.

Stalin's Soviet regime kills millions in efforts to modernize

THE FAILURE OF COLLECTIVE SECURITY

Events in central Europe nonetheless conspired to create some accommodation between the USSR and the West. In January of 1933, Nazi leader Adolf Hitler was named chancellor of Germany. Within months, he and his supporters declared a national emergency, suspended basic freedoms, and initiated a wholesale assault upon the German Communist Party. The democratic West watched apprehensively as Hitler restructured his country along militarist and racist lines, creating a highly regimented society under a brutal authoritarian regime. The Communist East was equally distressed as the "Führer" and his henchmen launched an international crusade against the "Jewish-Bolshevik menace." Before long, both sides were even more alarmed as Hitler repudiated previous international agreements and began a massive program to rearm and remilitarize his country. Stalin and the Soviets were particularly fearful, since Hitler talked of crushing Communism and gaining "living space" for Germans by expanding to the east.

Rise of Nazi Germany alarms both East and West

At first neither side did much to counter the Nazi threat. The Soviets, consumed by the internal turmoil that accompanied collectivization and needing trade with Germany to sustain their industrialization, continued to do business with the Germans well after the Nazis took power. For a time, they even viewed Hitler's regime as a hopeful harbinger of the decline of the capitalist West. The Western nations, bogged down by the Depression and distracted by domestic woes, offered only feeble protests as Hitler destroyed Germany's democracy and rebuilt its war machine. Many in the West were not totally displeased by the rise of Hitler's "Third Reich," which they saw as a bulwark against Communism.

Soviets seek cooperation with West against Nazi threat

As the German threat became more real, however, leaders on both sides sought to build bridges between East and West. In November of 1933, the Soviet Union and United States finally established full diplomatic relations. The next year, as part of a new foreign policy based on collective security, the USSR joined the League of Nations and pledged to work for peace and disarmament. In May 1935, several months after Hitler renounced the Versailles Treaty and started rearming Germany, the Soviets and French concluded a mutual assistance treaty, agreeing to cooperate if either country was attacked by the Germans. Later that month, the USSR made a similar pact with Czechoslovakia, pledging to assist the Czechs against aggression as long as France (which had committed itself to Czechoslovakia's defense in 1925) also did so.

Western powers fail to counter fascism

But collective security proved elusive. In the fall of 1935, the League of Nations failed to prevent aggression against Ethiopia by Italy, whose Fascist regime combined militaristic nationalism with repressive dictatorship, much like Nazi Germany's. In 1936, when Hitler sent troops into the Rhineland (a west German region around the Rhine River demilitarized by the Versailles Treaty), France and Britain could not agree on an effective response. That same year, when fascist military leaders in Spain began a civil war against its elected left-wing republic, the French, British, and Americans refused to aid the republic, while Italy and Germany sent forces to support the fascists. The Soviets, who did send forces in a futile effort to save the Spanish republic, thus had ample reason to doubt the West's willingness to counter the fascist threat.

Stalin's purges devastate Soviet military

The West, for its part, soon had ample reason to doubt the value of collective security arrangements with the USSR. From 1936 through 1938, the Soviet leadership was decimated by bizarre and terrifying developments that came to be called the Great Purges. Numerous loyal Communists, including former Soviet leaders, were placed on trial, accused of collaborating with the Nazis, forced to make confessions, and executed, while thousands of ordinary people were arrested and imprisoned. Hundreds of military officers, including about 400 of the 700 generals and three of the five field marshals, were imprisoned or shot. Western leaders wondered how they could possibly trust a regime that killed its own supporters and soldiers and how effective the Red Army could be with its leadership destroyed.

Any lingering hopes for collective security vanished in 1938. After Germany annexed Austria in March—again with scant resistance from the West—Hitler demanded territory from his Czechoslovak neighbors. The Sudetenland, a border region inhabited mostly by Germans, was his stated objective, but the Czechs feared he would not stop there. So they called on their French and Soviet allies, both of whom pledged aid under the terms of their existing pacts. The Germans, who were not fully prepared for war in spring of 1938, initially backed off, but Hitler began to plan for an autumn invasion.

In summer, he renewed his demands, and by fall, a new European war seemed imminent. The Soviets called for a firm stand, but the British and French, fearful of being swept into war by the obstinate Czechs, tried to mediate the dispute. They offered concessions, but Hitler simply raised his demands. Finally, on September 29, in a hastily arranged conference at Munich, Britain, France, and Italy agreed to give Hitler the Sudetenland. The Czechs were not invited and the Soviets not even consulted. War was averted, at least for a time, but hopes for collaboration against Hitler were dashed.

Western Power appease Hitler at Munich

It is doubtful that Stalin, who had little capacity for trust, ever placed much confidence in collective security arrangements with the West. But he may have hoped that a war in Europe would work to his advantage by pitting fascists against capitalists in a debilitating carnage, with the USSR remaining on the sidelines. Now he had to face the possibility that the opposite might occur, and the West would choose to sit back and watch as Hitler moved eastward toward the Soviet heartland. This specter became even more haunting in March of 1939, when the Germans occupied much of what was left of Czechoslovakia. Since few Germans lived there, it was clear that Hitler intended to expand into lands well beyond those where German people dwelt.

Stalin fears that West wants Hitler to invade USSR

Meanwhile, the Americans, watching with alarm as Hitler led Germany on a course of militarist expansionism, were too engrossed in their internal affairs to do much to stop the Nazis. Besides, to many Americans, Communism seemed as dangerous as Nazism, and Stalin's regime—with its brutal civil wars, forced famines, and bloody purges—appeared even worse than Hitler's. American leaders, like their Soviet counterparts, were aware of the dangers posed by German militarism. But, deeply distrustful of the Communists and wary of international commitments, they saw little potential or value in collaboration with the USSR.

THE MOLOTOV–RIBBENTROP PACT

Stalin watched warily as Nazi Germany devoured what was left of Czechoslovakia in March of 1939. Poland obviously was next on Hitler's list, to be followed by the USSR itself. Little help could be expected from the West, which seemed only too willing to let Germany move eastward toward the Soviet homeland. Stalin needed peace, at least until the Soviets could rebuild their armed forces from the devastation of his purges. His desperate hope was that Hitler was flexible enough to put ideology aside (as Stalin himself had done in the 1920s, when he decided to build socialism in Russia rather than pursuing a world revolution) and take advantage of alternative means of enhancing German power.

Germany's digestion of Czechoslovakia shocked British prime minister Neville Chamberlain into full awareness that Hitler's word could not be trusted. The Nazi dictator, who had earlier claimed to want only areas (such as Austria and the Sudetenland) populated by ethnic Germans, now stood exposed as hungry for lands peopled mainly by non-Germans. Britain and France responded by issuing a guarantee of Polish independence on 31 March 1939.

Britain and France pledge to back Poland after Hitler takes Czechoslovakia

Hitler was now entangled in a morass of probabilities and possibilities. The guarantee was *probably* a bluff: Britain and France had not fought to defend

Czechoslovakia, which had strong military potential, so why would they fight to defend a weak and almost indefensible Poland? But *possibly* they would, and if so, Germany would be at war with the West several years ahead of Hitler's schedule, which envisioned such a war sometime between 1943 and 1945. He would thus have to rapidly dispose of Poland before dealing with the West.

To invade Poland, Hitler needs Soviet neutrality

Stalin's attitude would be crucial. He *probably* would not intervene to prevent Germany's destruction of Poland, given Soviet military unpreparedness and Russia's lack of love for the Poles. But *possibly* he would, and Hitler could not hope to prevail against Russia, France, and Britain combined. Soviet neutrality was worth purchasing, especially since it might convince Britain and France not to go to war over Poland. After all, they had defeated Germany in 1918 only with American help and a four-year naval blockade that slowly strangled their foe. Now America was neutral, and an agreement with Stalin would make Germany blockade-proof by assuring it unlimited supplies of oil and grain. Foolish indeed would be the British and French to go to war under such conditions for a Poland they could not save.

Whatever the case, Stalin certainly realized that the Anglo-French guarantee of Poland put him in a strong bargaining position. He could play the West off against Germany and take the better offer. On 17 April, the USSR quietly extended feelers toward Berlin. Two weeks later, Soviet Commissar for Foreign Affairs Maxim Litvinov, a Jew and a champion of collective security between East and West, was removed and replaced by Stalin's henchman Viacheslav Molotov. Humorless and inflexible, soon to be nicknamed "Old Stonebottom" for his ability to negotiate for hours without leaving the table, Molotov would handle Soviet diplomacy for most of the next seventeen years. A clever, skillful debater with a habit of stuttering when excited and an unerring eye for the bottom line, he was absolutely devoted to Stalin. Molotov's appointment signaled Berlin that Stalin was willing to talk.

Hitler and the West both court Stalin's support

That summer, the onstage drama of German threats toward Poland was complemented by backstage courtship of Stalin by both Hitler and the West in conditions of controlled panic. If the Soviet dictator had wanted a Western alliance, he would probably have courted Berlin publicly to frighten France and Britain into giving him good terms. Instead, he dealt publicly with the West in order to pressure Hitler. As the Nazi leader's self-imposed late August deadline drew nearer, German foreign minister Joachim Ribbentrop became more and more insistent on reaching an agreement—and Stalin grew more and more coy.

The Western powers could perhaps have negotiated more vigorously, but it is doubtful if such vigor would have made much difference. The Soviets wanted the eastern part of Poland and a free hand in the Baltic States (Estonia, Latvia, and Lithuania), which had been part of the Russian Empire before 1918. By late July, the West had explicitly rejected such terms, for several good reasons. For one thing, the British and French had just guaranteed the independence of Poland. For another thing, they hated and feared Communism and held Soviet military potential in very low esteem. Finally, and most importantly, for the West to give Stalin the lands he wanted would be even more demeaning than appeasement of Hitler at Munich—and Hitler's actions since then had discredited appeasement of *any* dictator.

Hitler, of course, could concede all Stalin wanted, and by 23 August he had done so. The Treaty of Nonaggression between Germany and the USSR, often called the Molotov–Ribbentrop Pact or the Nazi–Soviet Pact, ensured Soviet neutrality at colossal cost. In secret clauses, Germany recognized Soviet spheres of interest in the eastern half of Poland, in Latvia, Estonia, and Finland, and in Bessarabia in southeastern Europe. In exchange for all this territory, Stalin would stay neutral, graciously letting the capitalists and fascists fight each other. Hitler got the worst of the bargain, since Soviet neutrality did *not* deter the British and French from going to war over Poland. If he wanted eventually to invade Russia, he would now have to start from much farther west than the original Russo-Polish frontier. Above all, since Soviet defense of Poland had been doubtful from the outset, he had purchased dearly what he could probably have had for nothing.

Nazi–Soviet Pact assures Hitler of Soviet neutrality

In retrospect, Stalin appears much less a fool than historians have often made him out. The Molotov–Ribbentrop Pact obtained for Russia a breathtaking set of territorial gains and an extensive buffer zone against future German invasion. Had Stalin come to terms with the West, a poorly prepared Russia would quickly have been involved in war with Germany; by concluding an agreement with Hitler, he ensured his country against attack (at least for a time) from the only nation that posed a real threat to its existence. If Stalin was anxious to avoid a German invasion, it made much better sense for him to deal with Hitler than with the West. Of course, he might be mistaken: Hitler might turn on him sooner than he

Pact provides stalin with time and territorial gains

The Molotov–Ribbentrop Pact. Ribbentrop and Stalin look on while Molotov signs the "Nazi–Soviet" nonaggression pact of 23 August 1939. By assuring Hitler of Soviet neutrality if Germany invaded Poland, this treaty set the stage for the outbreak of World War II. It also reinforced the impression in the West that the Soviets were treacherous villains who should not be trusted.

anticipated. Time alone would tell, and in 1939, time—which Stalin badly needed—seemed to be on his side.

Rancor marks Soviet–Western relations at start of World War II

The Molotov–Ribbentrop Pact, of course, horrified and angered the West, confirming its worst fears about Soviet duplicity and treachery. As a result, on the eve of World War II, relations between the Communist East and the capitalist West were no better than they had been twenty years earlier. The two sides had learned to coexist and on occasion had discussed cooperation in the face of a common threat. But these efforts had proven futile, since there was no real basis for long-term accommodation. The Western powers, after all, had forcibly intervened in the Russian Civil War and had often openly condemned the Stalinist regime. And the Communists were still committed to the eventual destruction of the political, economic, and religious institutions most valued in the West. When push came to shove, each side had been willing to betray the other's interests: the West by appeasing Hitler at Munich, the Soviets by signing the Molotov–Ribbentrop Pact. The Cold War did not commence until after World War II, but the seeds of conflict had already been planted by the time that war began.

2

Adversaries and Allies, 1939–1945

On 1 September 1939, having purchased Soviet neutrality with the Molotov–Ribbentrop Pact, Nazi Germany launched a brutal invasion of Poland. Two days later Britain and France declared war on the Third Reich, beginning what was to become history's bloodiest and most devastating war. For the first two years of this conflict, both the USSR and the United States would remain on the sidelines, but by the end of 1941, the actions of the Axis Powers would bring them both into the conflict and help to create the Grand Alliance that would eventually win the war. For the next four years, the Soviets, Americans, and British were allies, united in the collective goal of defeating their common foe, but separated still by a vast chasm in their outlooks, interests, and ideologies.

THE NAZI ONSLAUGHT, 1939–1941

Stalin's willingness to enter into an agreement with Nazi Germany, and his participation with Hitler in the dismemberment of Poland during September–October of 1939, confirmed the West in its negative assessment of the Soviet leadership. With Communist parties throughout the world now cooperating with Nazi expansionism, relations between the Soviet Union and the West were atrocious. This antagonism became obvious during the "Winter War" between the USSR and Finland (October 1939–March 1940). Building on the Molotov–Ribbentrop Pact's concession of primary influence in Finland to the USSR, Stalin moved to protect the land and sea approaches to Leningrad by pressuring the Finns into ceding territory that would give Russia control of the Gulf of Finland. In return he offered less desirable land in Russian Karelia, which was nevertheless twice the size of the areas requested from Finland. Influenced by their long-standing dislike for the Russians, the Finns refused, and the result was a war in which all the advantages seemed to rest with the USSR.

Stalin fails to convince Finland to cede territory to the USSR

At first, the Red Army fared poorly. Overconfidence, mismanagement, and inadequate winter clothing all contributed to a stalemate by December and an astounding Finnish victory in central Finland in January. Fervent sympathy for Finland flourished in the West. Britain and France even went so far as to concoct an incredible scheme by which French forces in Syria would invade the USSR through the Caucasus and link up with an Anglo-French expeditionary force, which would land in Finland and strike directly into the heart of Russia. Fortunately for the British and French, the Soviets rallied and defeated the Finns by 12 March 1940. Had this not occurred, the West would likely have found itself at war with Germany and the USSR at the same time, the results of which could only favor Hitler.

The Soviets defeat the Finns in the "Winter War"

Stalin, victorious despite multiple difficulties, pressed on. The Germans' spectacular defeat of France in June 1940 shattered his hopes that Hitler would be unable to turn east for some time. In June and July 1940, the USSR further secured its borders by annexing the Baltic States and bringing pressure to bear on Romania to cede Bessarabia and Bukovina. Alarmed by this manifestation of Soviet expansionism so close to the Romanian oil fields at Ploesti, from which Germany purchased nearly all of its non-Russian petroleum, Hitler now recalculated his options. With his western flank secured by the defeat of France, he decided in midsummer to pursue his obsession with living space in the east by invading the USSR in 1941. Despite his failure to win the Battle of Britain in the fall of 1940, he proceeded inexorably with these eastward expansion plans.

An operation of such magnitude could not be effectively concealed, even in the days before the deployment of espionage satellites. The Soviet government received numerous warnings of Germany's actual intentions from its agents abroad, from the British and American governments (including, as time grew short, personal messages from British prime minister Winston Churchill and U.S. president Franklin D. Roosevelt), and from a variety of German deserters. Even Richard Sorge, a Communist who had constructed a valuable spy network from his position as a German diplomatic official in Tokyo, weighed in with unequivocal descriptions of the impending attack.

But even the best intelligence is worth little if the consumer chooses to disregard it. Stalin suspected the British of attempting to draw him into war with Germany and may have been so convinced of the value of the Nazi–Soviet accord that he couldn't see any reason for Hitler to destroy it. Alternatively, he may have been whistling past the graveyard, fearful of doing anything to provoke Hitler. His willingness to sign a nonaggression pact with Japan on 13 April points in that direction. Whatever the explanation, on 22 June 1941, as German armored spearheads crashed through inadequate Soviet defense lines, they passed shipments of timber, grain, and oil en route to Germany in final fulfillment of the Molotov–Ribbentrop Pact. Stalin could no longer be neutral; the German invasion transformed his country into the central battleground of World War II.

Stalin disregards Western warnings of the German invasion

Western statesmen, desperate for any form of assistance against Hitler, welcomed Soviet entry into the war. Winston Churchill, long a steadfast anti-Communist, refused to take back anything he had said against the Bolshevik regime. Nonetheless, he promptly offered Moscow all possible assistance, tartly observing that "if Hitler invaded Hell, I would at least make a favorable reference to the Devil in the House of Commons."

Favorable references were one thing and implementation of commitments quite another. British foreign secretary Anthony Eden lost no time in reminding Soviet ambassador Ivan Maisky that the USSR had watched with indifference as Britain fought Germany alone. Terrified that Britain would do the same to Russia, Maisky pressed unceasingly for every possible proof of London's willingness to fulfill Churchill's pledges. The ambassador need not have worried; whatever Britain could give, it would give. But it was pouring money and materials into air defense, and it could not possibly give the Red Army everything it needed.

Britain offers limited aid to Soviet Russia

The United States could do that, but in June 1941 America was still neutral, in fact if not in spirit. The junior senator from Missouri, Harry S Truman, underscored that neutrality on 23 June 1941 with this recommendation: "If we see that Germany is winning we ought to help Russia and if Russia is winning, we ought to help Germany and that way let them kill as many as possible, although I don't want to see Hitler victorious in any circumstances." President Roosevelt was no more infatuated with Communist behavior than Truman, but he saw Hitler as the foremost threat to world peace and security and was thus unwilling to see any of Germany's enemies defeated. American neutrality legislation made the provision of substantial aid difficult until November 1941, when Roosevelt qualified the USSR for lend-lease aid by certifying that its defense against German invasion was vital to the defense of the United States. Once Japan bombed Pearl Harbor on 7 December and Germany followed suit four days later with its own declaration of war, all need for even-handedness passed. What Churchill would call "the Grand Alliance" now became a reality.

The United States enters the war and completes the Grand Alliance

THE GRAND ALLIANCE: ISSUES AND OPERATIONS

As Japanese bombs fell on Hawaii, Anthony Eden was boarding a ship to take him to Russia for a meeting with Stalin. The rough and risky voyage did little to alleviate his stomach flu, and on his arrival on 12 December he was informed that Japan had sunk two of Britain's finest battleships off Malaya. The year 1940 may have been, as Churchill alleged, Britain's "finest hour," but late 1941 was arguably its darkest. Eden had brought with him a bland statement pledging Anglo-Soviet mutual respect and cooperation. He was startled to find that Stalin, perhaps emboldened by Britain's plight, proposed nothing less than British confirmation of all territorial gains made by the USSR under the Molotov–Ribbentrop Pact and subsequent understandings with Germany, including the Soviet annexation of eastern Poland up to the Curzon Line.

Eden was astounded. Acceptance of these Soviet claims would betray what Britain had gone to war to preserve: the independence and territorial integrity of Poland. Churchill complained that Stalin's demands contradicted the Atlantic Charter of August 1941, a British-American agreement (endorsed by the USSR) calling for national self-determination and opposing territorial acquisitions. Churchill told Eden to defer consideration of frontier questions to the end of the war. Stalin, however, angrily replied that it seemed that the Atlantic Charter was directed against the USSR rather than the fascist powers. Eden assured him that this was not so, both in person and indirectly into

Eden's mission to Moscow fails

the microphone he assumed was concealed in his quarters. Grumbling that he preferred the "practical arithmetic" of detailed, precise settlements to the "algebra" of vague, sentimental declarations, the Soviet ruler suggested postponement of a treaty until these questions could be settled.

The failure of Eden's mission revealed two themes that would recur repeatedly in the prehistory of the Cold War. First, the West would continually attempt to soothe Stalin and to relieve his fears of hostility and encirclement. This was futile, both because it could not be done and because it was unnecessary. The Soviet Communists would always be wary of capitalist powers, simply because they were capitalist—and Stalin would always be wary of anyone who was breathing. But this distrust constituted no impediment to an agreement, provided that the terms were spelled out precisely and in detail. Second, Stalin would continue to combine cold-blooded realism with diplomatic audacity. With Hitler at the gates and Soviet losses and needs mounting hourly, he spoke of dividing the spoils of victory as though that victory were assured. He tried to secure Western endorsement of the vast territorial gains he had obtained from Hitler, and then magnanimously accepted extensive military and economic assistance while agreeing in return to defer discussion of his outrageous demands! It was possible to negotiate with Stalin, but it would never be easy, and much of the history of the Grand Alliance revolves around the West's failure to realize how difficult it would be.

The West misreads Stalin's attitudes

Closely linked with the frontier issue was the question of opening a second front in the west to relieve German pressure on the Red Army—which, as Stalin repeatedly reminded his allies, was the only army fighting Hitler in Europe. By the spring of 1942, when Soviet foreign commissar Molotov traveled to London and concluded an Anglo-Soviet treaty that made no reference to territorial concerns, the military situation was desperate. During his subsequent visit to Washington, in fact, Molotov's opposite numbers quipped that he seemed to know only four words of English: "yes," "no," and "second front." His forceful presentation of the catastrophic implications the loss of Ukraine and the Caucasus would have for the Allied war effort inspired Roosevelt to declare that he anticipated the opening of a second front in 1942. No explicit promises were made—and Churchill gave Molotov a memo that forecast a landing in Europe across the English Channel in August or September 1942 but made plain that no irrevocable promise was being given—yet for the moment the question seemed settled to Soviet satisfaction. Westerners who saw Molotov on his return to Moscow described him as "jubilant" (surely one of the few occasions on which so gloomy a diplomat merited that adjective), and Soviet radio began to speak of the impending invasion as a *fait accompli.*

Molotov presses for a second front in Europe

It was not. The British and Americans differed profoundly on the possibility of launching such an undertaking in 1942, and the Americans differed among themselves. Eventually the invasion was postponed until the following year, because to succeed it would require crushing force of a size and scope that could not be assembled quickly. Instead, the Western Allies decided on Operation TORCH, an invasion of French North Africa in 1942.

Western leaders postpone their invasion

To explain matters to Stalin, Winston Churchill traveled to Moscow from12 through 16 August. It was the first meeting between the two leaders, and it was tempestuous. In a technique Stalin would use time and again in the future, a satisfactory opening session was followed by a harsh and unpleasant second day. Molotov reminded Churchill of what he had been told in London and Washington, while Stalin rudely accused the British of being afraid to fight the Germans and pay the blood tax inevitably associated with war. Churchill fought back, at times politely, at times indignantly, pointing out that no promises had been issued and that cogent military reasons argued against a second front in 1942. At the end of a grueling interview, Stalin admitted that he had no choice: He must accept the Allied actions, although he disagreed with them. The atmosphere lightened, and a convivial all-night banquet ended Churchill's visit on the evening of 15 August.

Stalin expresses his outrage to Churchill

Operation TORCH was a success. French North Africa was liberated, and in 1943 German forces were expelled from Libya and Italy was knocked out of the war. It was not an inconsequential operation, although no compelling evidence suggests that it took any German pressure off the Soviet front. A cross-Channel invasion in 1942 would almost certainly have ended in disaster and might have lengthened the war. But the Western–Soviet alliance had been strained. Washington and London still sought to ease Stalin's fears, while Stalin still sought cold, hard commitments instead of honeyed words. Nothing short of a second front would satisfy him, and that would be delayed once again.

In January 1943, Churchill met with Roosevelt at Casablanca in newly liberated Morocco. Stalin too was invited but declined on the grounds that the ongoing battle for Stalingrad, which would soon result in a catastrophic German defeat, demanded his full attention. In his absence, the two Western leaders decided to focus in 1943 on an invasion of Sicily and Italy from North Africa. They met again in Washington in May and agreed to postpone the invasion of France until the following year.

At Casablanca, the Western invasion is postponed again

In early June, then, they informed Stalin of their decision. He was predictably bitter, reviewing the various assurances that he and Molotov had been given regarding a second front. He charged the West with intentionally proceeding in bad faith, an accusation that provoked Churchill into a blistering rebuttal. If it had been the intent of the Western Allies to ease the suspicions Stalin entertained concerning their motivations and intentions, they had been remarkably unsuccessful. The Soviet ruler was interested in actions, not words, and all the Western actions had thus far been concentrated around the Mediterranean.

Throughout the first half of 1943, in fact, Stalin considered other options, including the possibility of a separate peace with Germany. German foreign minister Ribbentrop, anxious to duplicate his feat of August 1939, apparently met Molotov behind Soviet lines in March. Other contacts were made in Scandinavia and Switzerland. The attempts came to nothing, because the two sides had incompatible goals: The Germans sought to retain Ukraine and much of Belorussia, while the Soviets wanted all of that back as well as the Baltic States, Bessarabia, Bukovina, and eastern Poland. Ribbentrop finally concluded that the positions were irreconcilable and spent his time in the late summer of 1944 trying to arrange a meeting with Stalin so that he might shoot him with a fiendishly prepared fountain pen.

Stalin contemplates a separate peace with Germany

Farcical and foredoomed though such negotiations may appear, there is substantial evidence that they were taken very seriously in London and Washington.

It may be that such attention, hopefully leading to a relaxation of the West's attitude toward Soviet territorial gains, was all Stalin sought in the first place. In that case, the failure of the feelers served him well, since the final Soviet victory over Germany brought him acquisitions and influence far more extensive than anything Hitler could have offered him. In any event, as the first full-fledged summit of the three Allied leaders drew near, the British and Americans were on their guard and predisposed to take nothing for granted concerning Soviet participation in the war.

TEHRAN: THE ALLIES PLAN FOR A POST-NAZI WORLD

The Grand Alliance convenes at Tehran

The first "Big Three" meeting of Churchill, Roosevelt, and Stalin took place at Tehran, the capital of Iran, from 28 November through 1 December 1943. The site was selected to accommodate Stalin, who insisted that, owing to the complex military situation, he could not stray far from Russia. The American delegation was housed in the Soviet embassy, where the rooms were filled with electronic as well as multi-legged bugs. Given Roosevelt's predilection for wide-ranging conversations with anyone willing to listen, this arrangement gravely compromised the secrecy of U.S. communications. It could have proven disastrous had the Americans come to Tehran with a clear negotiating position, but this was not the case.

Franklin Roosevelt, the most personable U.S. president of the century, finally got his opportunity to speak with Stalin face to face. In American politics, the president was viewed as an inspirational moral leader whose incorrigible optimism and can-do mentality had brought his nation through the Great Depression and whose "first-class temperament" had enabled him to adjust political differences and solve intractable problems with dexterity. He was also, however, an erratic administrator with a profound dislike for briefing books and a tendency to speak loosely about matters which he understood instinctively rather than intellectually.

Roosevelt proves poorly suited to bargaining with Stalin

These characteristics, so well suited to his job in Washington, placed Roosevelt at a disadvantage in dealing with Stalin. The Soviet ruler was not immune to personal charm and good fellowship, but he was not terribly susceptible to appeals based on moral concerns. He was also far better organized than the president, and he preferred to structure Allied agreements on the bedrock of national interests rather than the shifting sands of leadership personalities. Roosevelt's conduct toward Stalin reflected neither a hopeless naïveté nor the delusive ramblings of a terminally ill man, as his critics would later charge, but rather his standard operating procedure in political matters.

The invasion of Europe is finally scheduled

The disadvantages of Roosevelt's style surfaced quickly. Stalin no doubt expected to confront a united front of English-speaking nations. Instead, Roosevelt seemed intent on demonstrating his independence from Churchill and his ability to construct a friendship with Stalin. From the opening session, the Western disorganization was evident: Stalin asked for Anglo-American plans concerning the upcoming invasion of Europe, only to find that a date had still not been worked out. The issue was fought out openly between the Western delegations as Stalin watched curiously. Indeed, by pointing out that large-scale Soviet attacks in Eastern Europe could be coordinated with an amphibious landing in France, he himself helped to tip the scales in favor of setting a specific timetable for a cross-Channel invasion.

Worse was to follow from the Anglo-American side on the question of Polish borders. Rather than pressing for Soviet concessions, Churchill referred to the Poles in disparaging terms as people who could never be satisfied. He suggested to Stalin that Poland's boundaries be shifted westward, using as an illustration a line of three matches and moving the easternmost one to the westernmost side. Roosevelt, in a separate interview with Stalin, endorsed the westward shift but otherwise said little of substance, depicting the Polish question mainly in terms of his needs to accommodate his Polish American constituency back home.

The Polish question divides the Grand Alliance

Tehran did lay much of the groundwork for postwar conditions. Military plans were completed for Germany's final defeat. An embryonic international organization, which Roosevelt described as "The Four Policemen" (Britain, China, United States, and USSR), was agreed upon in principle. Finland, Poland, and the Baltic States were discussed at length, with final decisions deferred to a future conference. Stalin agreed to eventual Soviet participation in the war against Japan and in return put forth claims to the Kurile Islands, the southern half of Sakhalin Island, and railway and seaport rights in Manchuria. Much of what would later be finalized at Yalta was either decided or foreshadowed at Tehran.

Tehran provides the framework for constructing the postwar world

Everyone left in high spirits. Roosevelt pointed with pride to the many accomplishments of Tehran, and Churchill characterized the atmosphere as one of "friendship and unity of immediate purpose." For the Soviets, things could not have gone much better. An official of the U.S. State Department observed that the Soviet attitude "was that if it could get what it wanted, the United States and Great Britain could take what they wanted, provided it was not something that the Soviet Union wanted." Nothing had surfaced to indicate that this attitude would be unacceptable to the West. There had been disagreements, and some matters had been deferred, but that was to be expected. The world through Stalin's eyes was not a place of unalloyed bliss but a place in which great nations dickered, bartered, and fought over the fates of millions of people. It had been this way for centuries, and if changes were possible in the future, Joseph Stalin did not expect to make them.

Unfortunately, the euphoria of Tehran lasted but a short while. When the conference adjourned, on the evening of 1 December, Europe was still dominated by Adolf Hitler. Allied forces had landed in Italy, but they had found the going rough, and the cross-Channel invasion was still a future projection. In the east, the German army still stood in western Russia and Ukraine, and bitter fighting was taking place around Kiev. It was all well and good to discuss future territorial dispositions in the abstract at Tehran, but when the armies of the Grand Alliance began to evict the Germans from France, Poland, and elsewhere, military considerations and political horse-trading would combine to create an entirely new context for Allied diplomacy.

ALLIED COOPERATION AND CONFRONTATION, 1944

As 1944 began, a sizable source of irritation between the West and the Soviets began to disappear. The long-awaited opening of the second front in northern France at last drew near. To coincide with the western "D-Day" invasion of 6 June 1944, the Soviets planned a major offensive on the eastern front for 22 June, the 132nd anniversary of Napoleon's invasion and the third anniversary of Hitler's. In August, their combined efforts cracked the German defenses, presenting the Grand

Germany is attacked from East and West

Alliance with the heady prospect of victory in the not-too-distant future.

One of the casualties of the combined offensives was the spirit of comradeship that had pervaded Tehran. As the Red Army drove west and captured the city of Lublin on 24 July, the USSR recognized as the official government of Poland a group of Communists and socialists subservient to Moscow. This "Lublin government" maneuvered for power against the "London government," the Polish government-in-exile that had resided in London since the start of the war. As the Red Army approached Warsaw, the London government authorized a revolt by the Polish Home Army, an underground organization of 20,000 soldiers who were hopelessly outnumbered by the Germans and thus dependent for victory on Soviet help. By 1 August, when the uprising began, the Red Army was about ten miles northeast and twelve miles southwest of Warsaw along the Vistula River.

Stalin refuses to help the Polish Home Army in Warsaw

At this point, the Soviets halted and made no further efforts to advance into Warsaw. The London government asked the British to intervene militarily, or at least to drop weapons and supplies from the air. But the closest British and American air bases were in Italy, and given the range of the B-17 bombers then in use in Europe, the planes would have to land on Soviet airfields at Poltava to refuel before returning. The Red Air Force refused to permit such landings, although the Americans were already using the fields for shuttle bombing.

Controversy over Stalin's decision to let the Nazis destroy the Polish Home Army has raged since 1944. Probably it was based on two factors. First, the Red Army had outrun its logistical support; its units were tired and were being opposed by fresh German troops. Second, the Home Army was composed of the wrong kind of Poles: anti-Communists backing the London government. Certainly, it would have been out of character for Stalin to support the action. He had little use for any Poles and was ruthless enough to see his opportunity and profit from it.

Ultimately, the Soviets did let the Americans use Poltava for refueling in mid-September. The Red Air Force even bombed German airfields during the U.S. operations, but few of the supplies reached their targets. In one sense, Stalin's belated support was even more vicious than his original inactivity, for it raised the hopes of the Home Army, encouraged it to break off negotiations with the Germans, and thus assured its eventual extinction.

The Warsaw incident renews Western skepticism of Soviet motives

From a Western perspective, Soviet behavior during the Warsaw uprising was thoroughly reprehensible. It demonstrated clearly the sort of policies Stalin was likely to follow in Eastern Europe once his armies took control. The spirit of Tehran had been modified substantially by the events in Poland, and the survival of the Grand Alliance beyond the end of the war was now in doubt.

Dumbarton Oaks prepares the structure of the United Nations Organization

Still, the Western Allies pressed forward with efforts to create a new world body to replace the League of Nations, which had failed so miserably to prevent World War II. The Dumbarton Oaks Conference, which opened in Washington in the midst of the Polish disaster on 21 August, brought together British, Soviet, and American delegations. They drew up plans for a new organization (later called the United Nations), to include a deliberative General Assembly of all member states and a smaller, more powerful Security Council with the great powers as permanent members. Disputes arose, however, over membership and voting procedures, with the Soviets insisting that all sixteen republics of the USSR should sit in the General Assembly and that each member of the Security Council should have unlimited veto power over any council resolution. The Western powers objected, and final action was postponed until 1945.

Churchill endorsed the harmonious statements issued at Dumbarton Oaks, but he was deeply disturbed by the implications of Soviet actions in Poland. Specifically, he feared the eventual designation of Eastern Europe as a Soviet sphere of influence, and as the conference ended in early October, he and Eden flew to Moscow to meet with Stalin and Molotov. There, without Roosevelt, he attempted to cut a deal with Stalin to guarantee the retention of Anglo-American influence in at least some areas slated for occupation by the Red Army.

Churchill flies to Moscow to bargain with Stalin

Unlike Roosevelt, Winston Churchill had never attempted to build a political career on personal charm and unswerving optimism; on the contrary, he was pugnacious, abrasive, prone to depression, and difficult to work with. A confirmed loner who delighted in taking unpopular stands, he would have gone down in history as a political failure if he had died in 1939 at the age of 64. But like FDR (as President Roosevelt was often called), he could be an inspirational speaker and leader, and his tremendous reserves of moral courage shone through in times of crisis. He was at his best when working in an atmosphere of desperate hardship and mortal danger—like the one he inherited when he became prime minister in May 1940. He would approach Stalin without illusions but with the firmly held conviction that if Britain and Russia were to coexist after the war, total Soviet control of Eastern Europe must be avoided, both for practical and for moral reasons.

At his initial discussion with Stalin, in the presence of Eden and Molotov, Churchill proposed a division of the Balkan peninsula between Soviet and Anglo-American influence, writing down the following percentages:

Stalin and Churchill agree on spheres of influence in the Balkans

Romania:	Russia 90%	UK/USA 10%
Greece:	Russia 10%	UK/USA 90%
Yugoslavia:	Russia 50%	UK/USA 50%
Hungary:	Russia 50%	UK/USA 50%
Bulgaria:	Russia 75%	UK/USA 25%

"I pushed this across to Stalin," Churchill wrote in 1948. "There was a slight pause. Then he took his blue pencil and made a large tick upon it, and passed it back to us. It was all settled in no more time than it takes to set down."

The agreement speaks volumes about the attitudes of Allied leaders late in 1944. Churchill obviously was worried about Soviet expansionism and skeptical of the potential influence of the United Nations. Roosevelt confined his reactions to platitudes about peace in the Balkans—a stance that may have led Stalin to conclude that the United States had little interest in the area. Stalin, it is clear, was still quite willing to haggle over the fate of Eastern Europe and not yet firmly bent on excluding Western influence and imposing Communist regimes throughout the region.

Concerning Poland, Churchill's mission was less productive. He and Stalin were joined by Stanislaw Mikolajczyk, head of the London Polish government. The London Poles insisted on a provisional government in which five parties, including the Communists, would have equivalent representation. Stalin demanded a majority of seats for the Lublin Poles, who like Stalin himself endorsed the Curzon Line (the ethnic boundary suggested as Poland's eastern border in 1919 by British foreign secretary Lord Curzon) as the frontier between Poland and the USSR. To compensate Poland for the territory it would lose, Lublin proposed the shifting of Poland's western boundary to a line roughly configured by the rivers Oder and Neisse (the "Oder-Neisse Line"). Mikolajczyk opposed this arrangement, which would give the USSR the lands it had seized during its collaboration with Nazi Germany in 1939.

The Polish question is deferred again

Days of bickering followed. In the end, Mikolajczyk agreed to try to get his government to accept the Curzon Line and to try to form a government acceptable to the USSR. Churchill told Stalin that unless the London Poles had more than half the seats, the West would never believe that the government was democratic, but Stalin held out for a majority for Lublin. Final action on Poland was deferred for a future conference of the Big Three, to be held in the Crimean resort city of Yalta in February 1945.

THE YALTA CONFERENCE, 4–11 FEBRUARY 1945

Roosevelt insisted on postponing the next Big Three meeting until after his 1944 reelection and his inauguration in January 1945, a stance which accounted in part for Churchill's impatient flight to Moscow in October 1944. Stalin proved similarly immovable concerning the location of the conference, alleging (rather improbably) that his physicians had forbidden him to travel outside the USSR. The choice finally fell on Yalta, a remote Crimean city so inaccessible and unsanitary that Churchill later remarked that a worse site could not have been selected.

To make matters worse, Roosevelt was suffering from a severe sinus infection, untreatable hypertension, and congestive heart failure, conditions made worse by the long trip by ship and plane and the jolting six-hour jeep ride from the airstrip to Yalta. It is little wonder that he looked frail and sick, although there is no evidence that his illness affected his performance. FDR was never at his best at such meetings, and Yalta was no exception.

The Big Three debate the postwar status of Germany

Yalta proved a more organized meeting than Tehran. Military matters were handled first, with Stalin agreeing to delay the Red Army's drive to Berlin in order to coordinate it with a planned Western offensive in March. Discussion then centered on postwar plans for Europe. Hoping to discourage Germany from seeking a separate peace with the West, the Soviet leader demanded that German dismemberment be included in the terms of surrender, but the United States and Britain demurred. Stalin later tried to secure massive reparations payments from Germany, but his overall figure of $20 billion (half of which would go to the USSR) was hotly contested by Britain. Both items were deferred. Churchill made an eloquent case for giving France a zone of occupation in Germany and a seat on the Allied Control Council that would temporarily govern that nation. Stalin was reluctant, but when Roosevelt observed that U.S. troops would be out of Europe within two years of the end of the war, he changed his mind and agreed to these requests, provided that the new French zone be carved out of the British and American zones, leaving the Soviet zone intact. He apparently believed that French participation might prove helpful in the absence of a lengthy U.S. occupation.

Postwar Germany would thus be divided into four occupation zones: British, American, and French sectors in the west and a Soviet zone in the east. Churchill, fearful of a weakened postwar Europe dominated by Moscow, breathed a bit more easily at the prospect of French resurgence.

On 6 February, as the meeting entered its third day, Roosevelt made his first request: that the conference adopt the U.S. proposal on voting procedures in the Security Council of the United Nations. The American version guaranteed the five permanent members' right to veto any motion except those to which they were parties at interest. This was similar to a proposal rejected by the Soviets at Dumbarton Oaks, but this time Stalin agreed, simultaneously signaling his willingness to accept two additional General Assembly seats (for Ukraine and Belorussia) in lieu of the sixteen requested earlier. Somewhat perplexed, the British and Americans concurred, and the conference moved on to the Polish question.

Progress is made on United Nations issues

Roosevelt displayed a lack of concern for the matter, saying that while he hoped the Soviets would make concessions to let the Poles "save face," he would not demand any. Churchill, aware that Britain had gone to war explicitly to secure Polish independence, proved a more formidable advocate. He noted that the Curzon Line had already been conceded as Poland's border with the USSR; in return, the West required free elections and a new provisional government more representative of democratic parties. In reply, the Soviets proposed the Oder-Neisse Line as Poland's frontier with Germany, for the first time specifying the *western* Neisse, which would give the Poles far more German territory than the *eastern* branch of that river. Stalin was willing to enlarge rather than replace the Lublin government and favored general rather than free elections. Stalemate loomed.

Gradually, the conferees nibbled away at the problem. Churchill objected to the western Neisse on the peculiar ground that "it would be a pity to stuff the Polish goose so full of German food that it got indigestion." He may have feared an eventual outbreak of German nationalism in the area. Stalin, graciously declining to develop the goose analogy further, made the outlandish statement that all the Germans had fled the area anyway—at which Admiral William Leahy whispered to Roosevelt, "The Bolshies have killed them all." This astonishing conversation ended with the West rejecting the western Neisse but accepting the addition of an uncertain number of unidentified Poles to the provisional government. On 8 February, Churchill turned to the election issue but failed to commit Stalin to a precise date. Against his better judgment, not wanting to break with Russia on the eve of Germany's collapse, he accepted Stalin's assurances that the Polish people would have the opportunity to express their will. Roosevelt was only too happy to defer final settlement of these issues (Document 1A).

The Polish settlement favors Stalin

Later, many would claim that Poland had been sold out at Yalta, like Czechoslovakia had been betrayed at Munich. Their anger is understandable, but the comparison is invalid. Czechoslovakia was independent in 1938, while Poland in 1945 had been a conquered and occupied nation for more than five years. Hitler was not the ally of Britain and France in 1938, and the German army was not occupying Czechoslovakia during the Munich Conference.

Was Poland betrayed at Yalta?

MAP 1 Territorial Changes and Occupation Zones in Europe, 1945.
In Central and Eastern Europe, World War II brought about major territorial changes. Note that the USSR acquired extensive territories in Eastern Europe, including a large part of prewar Poland, and that Poland was compensated with lands from prewar Germany, while the rest of Germany and Austria were divided into occupation zones.

At Yalta, the British and Americans were in the unenviable position of delicately attempting to wring concessions from Stalin, whose help against Japan they needed badly. Uncomfortably aware of the fact that the USSR had borne the brunt of the fighting against Germany, and recognizing Stalin's intense desire for a Polish government friendly to Moscow, they were reluctant to press him too strongly. Poland was treated shabbily at Yalta, but given the Red Army's occupation of the country and the political and military concerns just mentioned, it is difficult to envision a radically different outcome.

Eventually, the conference moved on to the situation in East Asia. The United States wanted the USSR to enter the war against Japan as soon as possible after Germany's defeat, so that the Red Army could tie down Japan's large Kwantung Army in Manchuria and prevent its use in repelling an Anglo-American invasion of Japan. Stalin needed no convincing: A successful war against Japan would avenge Russia's defeat in the Russo-Japanese War of 1904–1905, establish a powerful Soviet presence in Manchuria, and perhaps earn for Moscow a zone of occupation in Japan itself. Nevertheless, he coaxed substantial territorial concessions out of the Western Allies, including the southern half of Sakhalin Island and all of the Kurile Islands, as well as essential control of Manchuria and Outer Mongolia. Since in East Asia, unlike Eastern Europe, the Red Army was not already in possession of these areas, these Western concessions are open to question. Roosevelt and Churchill, without challenging Stalin's absurd claims that these areas were historically Russian, conceded them willingly in order to obtain Soviet assistance (Document 1B). Both men were resolved on the destruction of the Japanese Empire; their willingness to grant substantial chunks of it to the USSR had less to do with any eagerness to appease Stalin than with their admitted intention to cripple Japan for the foreseeable future.

Roosevelt offers large concessions to gain Soviet support against Japan

The Yalta agreements were signed on 11 February. All three leaders appeared delighted, believing they had made concessions only over unimportant matters and had secured their principal objectives. Churchill had gained the acceptance of France as a great power, so that Britain would not stand alone against Soviet ambitions in Europe. Roosevelt had obtained agreement on the voting procedure in the UN Security Council and had received Stalin's commitment to help defeat Japan. Stalin, while failing to gain acceptance of his German agenda, had nonetheless defended his position in Poland—at least until the next meeting of the Big Three. Each had gotten what he wanted most.

Yalta completes the work of Tehran

Yalta was, at least emotionally, the final celebration of the solidarity of the Grand Alliance. Within a few weeks, as Hitler's empire disintegrated, the defeat of their common enemy and their inability to resolve fully the vexing issues of Soviet security and expansion would shatter the alliance and reveal on the horizon the hazy outlines of the Cold War.

THE IMPACT OF GERMANY'S DEFEAT

After Yalta, Allied military cooperation began to unravel. The Red Army, postponing its advance on Berlin, turned its guns instead on Hungary, Czechoslovakia, Austria, and Denmark. The Anglo-American offensive began on schedule, and at first the going was slow. Then on 7 March, a chance occurrence triggered Stalin's

Churchill, Roosevelt, and Stalin at the Yalta Conference.
The "Big Three" pose for a formal photograph near the end of the Yalta Conference in February 1945. To obtain Soviet participation in the Pacific War against Japan, Roosevelt made several concessions that became highly controversial once they were made public. Stalin was friendly and cooperative at Yalta but later pressed his advantage in Eastern Europe and alienated the British and Americans.

suspicions. At Remagen on the Rhine, American forces poured across the Ludendorff Bridge, which inexplicably had not been dynamited by the retreating Germans. Suddenly the western front began to move, and Stalin, who had explored the possibility of a separate peace with Germany in 1943, now suspected his allies of having secretly arranged the preservation of the bridge so that most of Germany would fall to the West. Simultaneously, SS general Karl Wolff approached American and British agents in Switzerland with an offer to surrender all German forces in Italy. When the Western Allies rejected a Soviet request to be included in these talks, Stalin fired off a series of insulting telegrams to Churchill and Roosevelt, charging bad faith.

The Remagen bridge incident renews Stalin's suspicions

During the same period, Soviet actions in Eastern Europe disturbed the British and Americans. Deputy foreign minister Andrei Vyshinsky, former chief prosecutor at the Moscow Purge Trials of the 1930s, bullied the king of Romania into appointing a cabinet dominated by Communists. Leaders of the Polish Home Army were enticed into coming to Moscow to participate in talks about broadening the provisional government; once there, they were arrested. Churchill and Roosevelt sent stiff notes to the Kremlin (Soviet government headquaters) in early April, referring to the breakdown of the Yalta accords and its implications for Allied unity. Roosevelt, who had been deluged by messages about Soviet misdeeds from W. Averell Harriman, the U.S.

Stalin's actions in Eastern Europe anger Roosevelt

ambassador in Moscow, pounded the arm of his chair and told an aide, "Averell is right. We can't do business with Stalin. He has broken every one of the promises he made at Yalta." Stalin, who believed with some justification that Yalta had given him a free hand in Poland, was likewise suspicious of Anglo-American intentions. Now he was determined to push the Red Army as far to the west as possible while Germany collapsed.

Churchill, convinced that the Red Army was dropping an "iron curtain" across Europe to seal off the Soviet-occupied areas, decided to press Roosevelt to have the United States drive eastward and take Berlin and Prague before the Russians could arrive. But on 12 April, Franklin Roosevelt died in Warm Springs, Georgia, of a massive cerebral hemorrhage. The news reached Moscow in the middle of the night, where Stalin, ever suspicious, wondered if FDR's sudden death might be in any way unnatural. Shaking off the shock, he prepared to deal with Harry Truman, a politician virtually unknown in Moscow.

Roosevelt's sudden death brings Harry Truman to power

Truman, faced with a set of momentous decisions, recognized his own unfamiliarity with the position he now filled. A voracious reader, he briefed himself thoroughly during the next several weeks but considered himself Roosevelt's heir and was determined to fulfill all of his predecessor's promises. He also relied heavily on his existing advisors. Both of these factors left Churchill out on a limb when he tried to convince the new president to have the U.S. Army beat the Red Army to Berlin and Prague. Truman's advisors counseled against mixing military and political considerations, and the U.S. commander, General Dwight Eisenhower, was dead set against spending American lives to take territory that had already been promised to the USSR.

Truman and Molotov clash over Poland

Cooperation in military areas, however, was not matched by political harmony, as Truman relied on his advisors' negative views of Soviet behavior since Yalta. On 23 April, on his way to a San Francisco meeting that would establish the United Nations, Soviet foreign commissar Molotov stopped at the White House to meet the new U.S. president. Truman, who had read all of Harriman's dispatches, told the Soviet diplomat that he was gravely disappointed in Stalin's failure to implement the Yalta agreements on Poland. He characterized Soviet–American relations as "a one-way street" favoring Moscow and curtly dismissed Molotov's diplomatic rejoinder. When Molotov protested that "I have never been talked to like that in my life," Truman (according to his memoirs, but not the interpreter's notes) responded, "Carry out your agreements and you won't get talked to like that." Whatever he actually said, it was apparent that Truman would deal with Stalin more directly and bluntly than had Roosevelt.

Thanks to the Soviet concessions at Yalta on United Nations membership and voting, the San Francisco Conference succeeded in drafting a charter for the new organization. As its members convened on 25 April, Soviet and American soldiers shook hands at Torgau on the Elbe River, cutting Germany in two. With the Red Army fighting in the streets of Berlin, Hitler killed himself on 30 April. When the new German government surrendered, to the British and Americans on the 8th of May and the Soviets on the 9th, American troops stood on soil assigned to the USSR, while Soviet soldiers occupied all of Berlin. Despite Churchill's efforts to have Truman postpone U.S. withdrawal pending satisfactory Soviet conduct in Eastern Europe, the occupied territories were exchanged in July, on the eve of the final Big Three conference in the Berlin suburb of Potsdam.

THE POTSDAM CONFERENCE, 17 JULY–2 AUGUST 1945

Compared with Yalta, the conference at Potsdam was troubling. Roosevelt was gone, and Truman had met neither Churchill nor Stalin. When he did, he was startled to find himself, at 5'9", the tallest and most vigorous of the three. He was also in no mood to take any guff from Stalin. By mid-July Truman had settled into office and was becoming more self-confident. A machine politician from Kansas City, he had fought for everything he had achieved in life, becoming in the process an excellent poker player. His blunt, earthy language made him appear more confrontational than compromising, but just as a poker face conceals the reality of one's hand, Truman's bluntness permitted him to stake out a negotiating position from which he was willing to move, as long as the price was right. He arrived at Potsdam convinced that he held most of the high cards and that Stalin had made big gains at Tehran and Yalta by using transparent bluffs. Harry Truman might make mistakes—but not by underplaying a winning hand.

Truman holds the upper hand at Potsdam

Stalin was unable to arrive until two days after the conference was scheduled to begin; it was later disclosed that he had suffered a mild heart attack. He was increasingly concerned about the behavior of the new American administration. Truman's decision to cut off lend-lease aid to Russia before the ink was dry on the German surrender had disturbed him deeply, even though the Americans had rescinded this decision a few days later in response to an international outcry.

Churchill, at seventy-one, was exhausted, preoccupied, and tormented by the nagging suspicion that his party might have lost the recent British elections. His fears were confirmed in late July when the final results came in. The Labour party swept into office, and its prime minister and foreign minister, Clement Attlee and Ernest Bevin, respectively, replaced Churchill and Eden at Potsdam.

The meetings were tense from the outset. The euphoria of victory, which had bubbled like vintage champagne at Yalta, had long since gone flat. Hitler was dead, Germany was prostrate, and the absence of a common enemy now called into question the future of the Grand Alliance. Stalin pressed for a settlement of the German reparations question, Western confirmation of the Oder-Neisse Line, the dissolution of the London Poles, assignment of Italy's North African colonies as Soviet trustees under the United Nations Trusteeship Council, and Soviet roles in Tangier, Syria, and Lebanon. Truman hoped to settle the Polish question in America's favor, prevent the Soviets from taking reparations from western Germany without providing food for hungry Germans, oust the pro-Communist governments of Romania and Bulgaria, and admit Italy to the United Nations. The British, partly because of their leadership transition, played a secondary role throughout.

Some issues were disposed of easily. Stalin's request for influence in North Africa and the Middle East was never given serious consideration. Similarly, Truman's condemnation of Moscow's heavy hand in Romania and Bulgaria was countered by Stalin's willingness to give the British a free hand in Greece and to concede to the West a fifty-fifty say in Yugoslavia.

The real bargaining started over Germany. Stalin's demand for $10 billion in reparations was finessed by a counterproposal from the newly appointed American secretary of state, James Byrnes, who suggested that each side should take reparations from its own zone. This proposal dismayed the Soviets, who knew that extracting reparations from their largely agricultural eastern sector would provide little of industrial value. Molotov tried to link the reparations issue with the Polish border question, but Byrnes turned the ploy around by offering the Soviets 25 percent of all industrial equipment found in the Ruhr, Germany's bombed-out industrial heartland, provided that Moscow accept the *eastern* rather than the western Neisse as Poland's western frontier. The Soviets were taken aback; bargaining with Roosevelt had been much more pleasant than dealing with Truman and Byrnes.

Byrnes counters Stalin's demand for reparations from Germany

Faced with this situation, Stalin showed a readiness to compromise—and so did Secretary Byrnes. On 30 July, ignoring his British allies, Byrnes offered Molotov a take-it-or-leave-it deal. The Americans would accept the western Neisse after all, defer the question of Italian membership in the United Nations, consider recognizing the governments of Romania and Bulgaria, and grant the Soviets a percentage of usable capital equipment found in the western zones of Germany. In return, the USSR would take reparations from its own zone alone. The Soviets disliked this, but in the end they went along, and an open split was avoided (Document 2).

Stalin's balance sheet at Potsdam was mixed. Most of the items he wanted proved unobtainable, and the Grand Alliance had clearly fallen apart. Still, the damage was limited. At least the West remained willing to bargain, a mode of discourse which the Soviet dictator always found congenial. After all, why should any realistic statesman expect that the wartime alliance would survive Hitler's defeat? The USSR had not been friends with Britain and the United States prior to 1941, and the unraveling of the alliance was merely a return to the *status quo ante bellum*. It did not mean that unrelenting hostility between the Soviets and the West was inevitable.

Potsdam does not make Cold War inevitable

President Truman had also not gotten everything he wanted, especially with regard to Eastern Europe, but he had obtained a number of Soviet concessions and final confirmation of Moscow's readiness to enter the war with Japan. The problem was that he was no longer certain that Soviet entry into the Pacific War would be convenient for the United States. For the Americans had developed a new weapon that could bring Japan to its knees.

DIPLOMACY, DUPLICITY, AND THE ATOMIC BOMB

Rapid advances in physics earlier in the century raised the possibility that splitting the nuclei of heavy atoms could liberate vast amounts of energy and create bombs of awesome destructive force. By 1942, programs to build such a weapon were under way in Germany, Great Britain, Japan, the United States, and the USSR. But only the United States had sufficient wealth, industrial plant, and scientific expertise to carry on such a complex project without endangering its war effort.

By the summer of 1944, the technical problems had been worked out, but it took another year to perfect the components and enrich a sufficient quantity of uranium fuel. At the Yalta Conference, the Americans sought Russian entry into the Pacific War without any firm evidence that the bomb would work. Besides, their priority had been to develop it for use against Germany and not Japan. By the summer of 1945, however, Germany was defeated.

The United States develops atomic bombs

The first atomic bomb was tested successfully at Alamogordo, New Mexico, in the early morning of 16 July 1945. Its explosive yield equated to 18,600 tons of dynamite, the equivalent to a raid of 3,100 B-29 bombers. Truman received the news just as the Potsdam Conference opened on 17 July. A week later, after confirming with Churchill an earlier decision to use the bomb, he informally advised Stalin that the United States now possessed "a new weapon of unusual destructive force." Stalin seemed pleased and expressed his hope that the weapon would be put to good use against Japan, but showed no unusual interest. He certainly knew the general details of the project from Soviet agents such as Klaus Fuchs and Alan Nunn May, who were involved in the U.S. project, but he probably had no idea of how destructive the bomb would be.

Truman discloses the existence of the atomic bomb to Stalin

The United States wasted no time in using the new weapon. The Japanese city of Hiroshima was destroyed on 6 August, followed three days later by the city of Nagasaki. On 8 August, as promised, the Soviet Union declared war on Japan. The Japanese government surrendered on 14 August, ending World War II. Ironically, although many Americans believe that the atomic bombs were solely or primarily responsible for the Japanese surrender, most of the available evidence points to the Soviet declaration of war as the final blow that broke Japan's will to resist.

A view of Hiroshima after the atomic blast of 6 August 1945.

The Japanese manufacturing city of Hiroshima was almost completely obliterated by a single bomb. Called by U.S. president Truman "the greatest thing in history," this was the first atomic bomb to be used in combat. More than 70,000 people died from the blast and the radiation sickness that followed it.

In his memoirs, Truman stated that he decided to drop the bomb in order to save between 500,000 and a million American lives which would have been lost in an invasion of Japan. But this is special pleading after the fact. In reality, Truman made the decision for three reasons. First, he was determined to win the war while losing as few U.S. lives as possible and knew he would be held accountable by the American people if he did otherwise. Second, the government had spent $2.5 billion on the project (an immense sum in those days), and to decide against using the product of that massive effort seemed to make no sense. Finally, Truman was convinced that Soviet entry into the Pacific War would complicate the postwar occupation of Japan; if using the bomb could avoid such complications by forcing a rapid Japanese surrender, so much the better. It also should be noted that both Truman and the bomb's creators saw it simply as a remarkably powerful conventional weapon (Document 3); the idea that it was a hideous device that should never be used was born *after* the horrifying effects of radiation sickness and atomic fallout became apparent.

Truman uses atomic weapons for three reasons

This is not to say that the United States used "atomic diplomacy" at Potsdam. Despite the claims of many "revisionist" historians that Truman bullied the Russians once he knew about Alamogordo, the record tells a different story. Truman behaved in a forceful, blunt manner at Potsdam but that was fully in keeping with his personality and style; he had blustered at Molotov on 23 April, before he knew that the bomb would work. Indeed, the only direct mention of the atomic bomb at the conference came in his casual conversation with Stalin, and that can hardly be construed as intimidation.

Did Truman use "atomic diplomacy" at Potsdam?

After the cataclysmic blasts at Hiroshima and Nagasaki, Stalin embarked on a crash program to create a similar weapon for the USSR. The leader of that project, nuclear physicist Igor Kurchatov, later recalled that Stalin convened a meeting, banged his fist on the table, and ordered: "Comrades, build me a bomb. The Americans have destroyed the balance of power." But even the inception of a nuclear arms race did not mean that Cold War was inevitable. Instead, the Cold War arose out of continuing confrontations in the region that had vexed the Grand Alliance since its inception: Central and Eastern Europe.

A nuclear arms race begins

3

The Formation of the Communist Bloc, 1944–1948

The question of where the Cold War began has long been the subject of controversy. Some scholars contend that it began in the so-called Northern Tier of Iran, Turkey, and Greece. Others think it started in East Asia. But most agree that it originated in Europe, either in Germany (where a temporary military occupation turned into a lasting political division) or in Eastern Europe (where Soviet efforts to establish a buffer zone of friendly nations offended and frightened the West). The German roots of the Cold War will be traced in Chapters 4 and 5, while this chapter will discuss its origins in Eastern Europe.

SOVIET AND AMERICAN OBJECTIVES IN EASTERN EUROPE

Soviet troops occupied much of Eastern Europe as World War II ended. During the latter half of 1944 and early 1945, in its successful campaigns on the eastern front, the Red Army destroyed the German armies controlling this region while paying a terrible price in resources and blood. What they gained, along with the defeat of their mortal enemy, was the power to determine the postwar political character of most of Eastern Europe—and that character, it turned out, was Communist. By 1948, Communist governments were in power in Poland, Czechoslovakia, Hungary, Romania, Bulgaria, Yugoslavia, and Albania, and most of Eastern Europe had become part of a Communist bloc.

Stalin's motives were confusing and complex

The *outcome* of the Soviet liberation of Eastern Europe is well known. But ever since these events transpired, the *intentions* of the Soviet government have been debated. During the first two decades of the Cold War, Western historians usually maintained that Stalin was determined from the beginning to turn Eastern Europe Communist and followed a carefully prepared sequence of steps designed to achieve this. That analysis gave way in the 1970s to an explanation which emphasized Stalin's flexibility and willingness to permit the development of governments like that of Finland, friendly to Moscow and subservient to its foreign policy goals while free to maintain multiparty political systems and capitalist economies. More recent commentaries, such as the one presented here, have tended to accent the interplay of diverse and often conflicting factors in the formulation of Soviet policy.

U.S. ambassador to Moscow W. Averell Harriman believed in 1945 that Stalin was juggling three options for Soviet policy, which might or might not be mutually incompatible. According to Harriman, Stalin wanted to preserve the Grand Alliance after the end of the war, turn Eastern Europe into a buffer zone between the USSR and Germany, and utilize the Communist parties of Western Europe (which had played significant roles in resistance movements against Hitler) to subvert Western governments. The creation of Communist-dominated coalition governments in Eastern Europe may be viewed as an effort to blend these options, ensuring Soviet security while maintaining a positive image for Communism in Western Europe and preserving postwar cooperation within the Grand Alliance. As Vladislav Zubok and Constantine Pleshakov later concluded from documents in Soviet archives, Stalin's initial approach to Eastern Europe was relatively flexible and circumspect, but became increasingly rigid and repressive as his other objectives proved unattainable. The reasons for this may be clarified by a comparison of Soviet objectives in Eastern Europe between 1944 and 1948 with American objectives during the same period.

Harriman identifies three options for Soviet policy

Stalin's government appears to have worked toward the attainment of three objectives in Eastern Europe:

Stalin's three objectives in Eastern Europe

1. *To install governments friendly to the USSR and to Communism.* At first, it was not essential that they be completely controlled by Communists; sooner or later, however, other political parties were expelled or integrated into a "popular front" or "workers' party" entirely dominated by Communists.
2. *To create a buffer zone between the USSR and Germany,* so that in the next war a German invasion of the Soviet Union would begin from much further west than in 1941. Such an invasion would have to move through countries friendly to Moscow and in some cases occupied by Red Army soldiers.
3. *To exploit Eastern European economies for the economic reconstruction of the USSR.* The war had wrecked most of the European portions of the Soviet Union, and rebuilding would require a great deal of time, substantial reparations from Germany, and abundant economic assistance from friendly countries. In return for their liberation from German rule, Moscow's new friends would be expected to provide as much economic support as possible for their exhausted benefactor.

The objectives of the United States and Great Britain were very different:

American and British objectives in Eastern Europe

1. *To enable Eastern European countries to elect democratically any government they chose.* In some nations, like Bulgaria and Czechoslovakia, this might result in the election of Communist governments; in others, like Poland, such a result would be out of the question (as Stalin himself admitted).
2. *To open Eastern European countries to free trade,* thereby helping them to modernize and helping the United States to find markets for its manufactured goods. This had been a guiding principle of U.S. secretary of state Cordell

Hull, who believed that wars began because of economic deprivation and that free trade throughout the world would promote prosperity to such an extent that war would become obsolete.

The problem was that these two sets of objectives were irreconcilable. Washington and London sympathized with Stalin's insistence on a Soviet security zone and did not necessarily object to the formation in Eastern Europe of governments friendly to Moscow. But if such governments could not be elected democratically, the Western Allies would oppose their forcible imposition. Similarly, Soviet economic exploitation of Eastern Europe was incompatible with both the area's economic advancement through free trade and America's desire to expand its foreign markets: Destitute people purchase few consumer goods. Moscow, for its part, feared Western economic penetration of its security zone as greatly as Western European nations feared Communist political penetration. As for democratic elections, the Communist Party of the Soviet Union lacked any commitment to Western-style democracy, preferring instead the Leninist principle of "democratic centralism" (the obligation of all party members to fall in line behind the position articulated by the party leadership majority). Clearly, the seeds of conflict, sown in the misunderstandings and quarrels of the war years, were sprouting in the soil of opposing objectives in Eastern Europe.

Western and Soviet objectives cannot be reconciled

Although Soviet goals in Eastern Europe did not *necessarily* involve the creation of Communist governments, *realistically*, given Western attitudes, the attainment of those goals would be impossible in the absence of such governments. Specifically, the creation of friendly but non-Communist governments such as the one in Finland (often referred to as "Finlandization") would not have allowed Moscow to exploit the economies of Eastern Europe. Congruently, neither of the Anglo-American objectives was *necessarily* anti-Communist, but *realistically* both were. In retrospect, given such firmly held yet discordant goals, it is hard to see how the Cold War could have been avoided.

Why didn't Stalin support rapid takeovers of Eastern European countries by Communist parties advancing in the wake of the Red Army? From his perspective in 1945, the gains implicit in such action (greater efficiency in economic exploitation and guaranteed friendship with the USSR) could well be outweighed by the liabilities of strained relations with America and Britain and alienation of Western European populations which might otherwise prove susceptible to Communism. After all, there was much that the Soviets stood to gain from good relations with the West, including a $6 billion loan they had requested early in 1945 and a favorable reparations settlement which would let them extract substantial resources from Germany. Neither was possible without Western good will. In addition, the forcible Communization of Eastern Europe would certainly provoke resistance, which would refute Stalin's contention that Communist parties there enjoyed widespread public support and force the Red Army to become intimately involved in domestic police work and social control. It was even possible that heavy-handed Soviet tactics would cause direct Western intervention in Eastern Europe, an eventuality that would imperil all of Stalin's objectives in the region and the security of the USSR itself. Faced with such unpleasant ramifications, it was best to proceed cautiously.

Stalin assesses the situation and proceeds cautiously

Stalin's circumspection, regardless of its origins, confused his contemporaries and led to the adoption of different sets of tactics in each of the Eastern European countries. Eventually, however, as relations with the West worsened, Stalin gave up on Western good will and sponsored the creation of "people's democracies" (single-party Communist regimes) throughout Eastern Europe.

POLAND: FROM ONE MASTER TO ANOTHER

It was in Poland that Soviet actions most seriously endangered good relations between Moscow and the West. Germany's invasion of that unfortunate nation had started the war in 1939, and under the terms of the Molotov–Ribbentrop Pact, the USSR was entitled to conquer and occupy several provinces of eastern Poland. Most of the residents of these disputed lands were Ukrainians, who had little love for either Poles or Russians. Once Stalin took these territories in 1939, he meant to retain them, and he informed the British and Americans of that fact as early as 1941. For London, having gone to war with Hitler in order to preserve Polish independence, this was a touchy and troubling matter.

Subsequent Soviet actions offered little reassurance. In the spring of 1943, German military units operating in European Russia unearthed mass graves in the Katyn Forest. Buried in them were more than 10,000 Polish military officers, last seen alive when the Soviets took them into custody in October 1939. Stalin indignantly denied responsibility, but Lavrenti P. Beria, chief of the Soviet secret police, admitted privately to Soviet generals that "a grave mistake" had been made in 1940 concerning the disposition of these prisoners. Not until 1991 did Moscow finally admit publicly that the officers had been murdered while in Soviet custody. Meanwhile the incident further poisoned relations between the USSR and the Poles, who were convinced from the outset of Soviet guilt.

The Katyn Forest Massacre deepens Polish mistrust of the USSR

We saw in Chapter 2 that the Red Army's entry into Poland in 1944 resulted in the creation of the Lublin government as a Communist-dominated rival to the London Poles. Stalin was obviously reluctant to deal with non-Communist Poles; as he would later observe, "Any freely elected government [in Poland] would be anti-Soviet, and that we cannot permit." His posture during the tragic Warsaw uprising enraged the Poles even more and worried the West. By the time the war ended, Polish hatred of Germany had been largely replaced by animosity toward Russia, a fact that made it impossible for the Polish Communist Party to win widespread support from the Polish people.

Ironically, Stalin's oft-repeated contention that it was in Poland's best interest to cultivate good relations with Russia was not devoid of good sense. The decisions of the Big Three concerning Poland's borders could easily be viewed favorably by Warsaw. Before the war, nearly a third of the country consisted of ethnic and religious minorities. Now the border adjustments, coupled with the Nazi slaughter of Polish Jews, turned Poland into an overwhelmingly Roman Catholic and ethnically Polish nation (save for several million Protestant Germans living in western Poland). The country's borders were shortened dramatically and were now far more readily defensible, while Poland's

Arguments favoring Polish friendship with the USSR

pre-1939 landlocked status had been transformed through the acquisition of a Baltic coastline more than 300 miles long. All these gains, of course, were viewed with horror by the Germans, who could be expected to exert every effort in future years to reverse the verdict of Potsdam. Against such actions Soviet friendship provided the surest defense.

Stanislaw Mikolajczyk, leader of the Polish Peasant Party and since 1943 prime minister of the London government-in-exile, apparently hoped that the restraint shown by Stalin in his dealings with Finland could be duplicated in Poland. Since Poland was much more central to Soviet concerns than Finland, it is difficult to explain such optimism. But Mikolajczyk held two high cards. His Peasant Party had been extremely popular between the wars, since it spoke for the farmers of what was then a heavily agricultural country; and in early 1946, the Polish Workers' Party (Communist) was losing members while the Peasant Party, increasingly identified with opposition to Communism, was increasing in size. Properly manipulated, these factors could have lent partial substance to Mikolajczyk's hopes of turning Poland into another Finland.

Mikolajczyk unwisely supports a referendum on frontiers

Unfortunately for Mikolajczyk, his high cards were offset by his own political ineptitude, the presence of the Red Army in Poland, and Stalin's willingness to use intimidation in pursuit of Soviet objectives. The Communists, having been embarrassed by free elections in Hungary in 1945, were reluctant to test the sentiments of the Polish people in an open vote. But their allies, the Polish Socialist Workers' Party, proposed a referendum to legitimize the new frontiers. Mikolajczyk's support for the referendum split the Peasant Party and assured its passage.

Poland joins the Communist bloc

The results encouraged the Communists and Socialists to combine with two smaller parties in a "Democratic bloc" and to schedule elections for January 1947. Those elections were blatantly rigged: Peasant Party supporters were disenfranchised, arrested, or beaten, while ballot boxes across the country were stuffed. The Democratic bloc took more than 80 percent of the votes to the Peasant Party's 10 percent. Mikolajczyk was dropped from the Polish cabinet, and he fled the country in October 1947. In December 1948, the Communists absorbed the Socialists into the Polish United Workers' Party, and Poland became a one-party dictatorship.

Events in Poland intensified the emerging Cold War. The Labour government in Britain, reminded daily by the Tory opposition that Britain had gone to war in 1939 to preserve Polish liberty, was outraged. In 1945, keenly aware of the importance of the Polish-American vote for the Democratic Party in the United States, Roosevelt had impressed upon Stalin the need to avoid actions in Poland that would complicate American political life. In reporting to the Congress after the Yalta Conference, FDR had misled the American people by portraying Moscow and Washington as being in fundamental agreement on the future of Poland. Now, with Harry Truman in the White House and Soviet–American relations deteriorating rapidly, Stalin looked to his own interests and solidified his control over the most important piece of his developing security zone. His actions confirmed British and American opinions of Russian wickedness and intensified the animosity between the former allies.

ROMANIA: EXIT THE MONARCHY

Romania, like Poland, was traditionally hostile to Russia and had fought on the German side after 22 June 1941. But by late summer of 1944, with Germany losing the war, the Romanians decided to switch sides. On 23 August, as the Red Army prepared to invade, King Michael ousted Romania's pro-Axis government and handed Germany a declaration of war. Since the German army was too busy in Poland and France to do anything about it, the gamble paid off, and Michael became a national hero. Stalin, appreciating Romania's strategic significance and hostility toward Moscow, proceeded cautiously, decorating the popular king while authorizing underground activities by Communists like Gheorghe Gheorghiu-Dej and Ana Pauker, who had either resisted Hitler from within or had spent the war in Moscow. Nonetheless, by late 1944 there were fewer than a thousand Communists active in Romania.

In terms of influence, however, the Communists were more important than they appeared. Most of the Romanian army spent the winter of 1944–1945 fighting the Germans in Hungary and Czechoslovakia, giving the Communists a chance to build their strength. The overwhelming power of the Red Army, which moved into Romania in August 1944, likewise played into their hand. In October 1944, the Communists helped form the National Democratic Front (NDF), cooperating with the Social Democrats, the trade unions, and two parties friendly to Communism, the Plowmen's Front (peasants) and the Union of Patriots (business and professional people). Prime Minister Nicolae Radescu, irritated by Communist sponsorship of strikes and demonstrations, angrily denounced Moscow-trained Communists in a speech on 24 February 1945. Stalin reacted at once, dispatching Deputy Foreign Commissar Andrei Vyshinsky to Bucharest, where he bullied King Michael into firing Radescu and accepting an NDF government under the leadership of Petru Groza, the pro-Communist head of the Plowmen's Front. Upon leaving the king's office, Vyshinsky apparently slammed the door with sufficient force to crack the plaster surrounding the frame. This may have convinced Michael to give in, although it is likely that the simultaneous Red Army occupation of Romanian army headquarters and the foreign and defense ministries was even more persuasive.

Communists gain strength in Romania

Groza's government promptly confiscated and redistributed all landed estates in excess of 120 acres, gaining significant popular backing in the process. That autumn, the British and Americans refused to recognize the Groza regime. Michael attempted to exploit this situation to force Groza from power, but his efforts were ignored and he withdrew from public affairs. In his absence, the NDF enjoyed free rein and readily accepted the decision of the Moscow Conference of Foreign Ministers (December 1945) that free elections must be held. After eleven months of street fighting and selective terrorism, the elections were held on 19 November 1946. A combination of bullying tactics and ballot box fraud led the NDF to victory.

The Communists held only a small minority of parliamentary seats, but they enjoyed the support of the Soviet Army and used it skillfully against their coalition partners (in February 1946 the Red Army had been renamed the Soviet Army). In the spring of 1947, they openly accused opposition leaders of complicity with

American imperialism, convicting them and sentencing them to lengthy prison terms. After two years of irrelevance, King Michael abdicated in December 1947 and left the country. Romania thereupon abolished the monarchy and became a "people's democracy," and in March 1948 the Communists absorbed all of their NDF partners. Simultaneously, the headquarters of the Communist Information Bureau (or Cominform, a successor to the Comintern which had been dissolved in 1943) were transferred to Bucharest, the Romanian capital (Documents 10A and 10B).

Romania becomes a "people's democracy"

Britain and the United States played virtually no role in these events. Unwilling to challenge Churchill's 1944 formula giving Britain supremacy in Greece in return for Soviet preponderance in Romania, London kept a discreet silence. Washington protested vigorously and consistently over the lack of free elections in Romania, characterizing Communist behavior as a violation of the Yalta agreements, but the United States was no more willing than Britain to take meaningful action. The Soviet Army controlled the field as Romania passed into the Communist camp.

BULGARIA: THE FRUITS OF FRIENDSHIP WITH RUSSIA

Despite its wartime alliance with Germany, Bulgaria had long looked up to the Russians. Tsarist Russia had liberated it from Turkish rule in the nineteenth century; the Bulgarians used the Cyrillic alphabet, called their rulers "tsars," and were heavily influenced by Russian culture. Unlike Romania, Bulgaria did not participate in the German invasion of the Soviet Union. When the Red Army poured across Bulgaria's frontier with Romania on 8 September 1944, the Bulgarian government at once sued for an armistice, which Moscow quickly accepted. The following day the Soviets installed a coalition government under the Fatherland Front (FF), an anti-German resistance movement with a strong Communist element. Bulgaria then joined in the final assault on Germany. In recognition of these actions, Stalin demanded no reparations from Bulgaria after the end of the war.

Bulgaria demonstrates friendship with Russia

From the beginning, Communists controlled the Ministry of Interior (hence the police) and the local militia. They used this position to purge the government of "German collaborators," killing at least 50,000 officials ranging from cabinet ministers to village councilors. They also used various tactics to intimidate or control other parties, but they ran into serious opposition from Nikola Petkov, leader of a non-Communist party called the Agrarian Union. A staunch friend of Russia, Petkov was nonetheless anti-Communist and tenaciously resisted the maneuverings of the Bulgarian Communists and their Soviet friends. His popularity grew rapidly in the fall of 1945, and in January 1946, Stalin's point man Vyshinsky traveled to Sofia to try to convince Petkov to cooperate with the FF. Soviet persuasion failed, and Petkov remained a powerful anti-Communist rallying point.

Petkov leads a pro-Russian, anti-Soviet party

This tense state of affairs persisted throughout 1946. On 8 September, a plebiscite forced the abdication of seven-year-old Tsar Simeon and proclaimed Bulgaria a republic. Nineteen days later, a constituent assembly was elected to draw up a republican constitution; the FF won more than three-quarters of the seats, but nearly a quarter of its delegates soon defected to the Petkov-led opposition. It appeared that Moscow would be compelled to choose between permitting the emergence of a pro-Russian, anti-Soviet leadership in Sofia and the extinction of that leadership by military force.

Stalin was saved from this unpleasant choice by the United States, which signed a peace treaty with Bulgaria on 10 February 1947 and ratified it on 4 June. This terminated the activities of the Allied Control Commission, which had given London and Washington some say in Bulgarian affairs and had thus given Petkov some leverage. On 5 June, Petkov was arrested as he spoke in parliament; he was tried, convicted of conspiracy, and hanged on 23 September. Eight days later the United States granted diplomatic recognition to the Bulgarian government, now solidly controlled by the Communists. It is difficult to avoid the conclusion that the United States, at loggerheads with the Soviet Union over Greece and Turkey (Chapter 4), had made a calculated decision to write off Bulgaria, just as Churchill had done at Moscow in 1944.

The Control Commission's withdrawal dooms Petkov

HUNGARY: FROM FREE ELECTIONS TO ONE-PARTY RULE

In 1944, the Hungarian leader Admiral Miklós Horthy attempted to cancel his alliance with Hitler and bring Hungary into the war against Germany. Unfortunately, he failed where Romania and Bulgaria succeeded. The plan never got untracked, and Germany ousted Horthy and installed a puppet government. As a result, fighting in Hungary was intense and protracted; when the Red Army finally expelled the Germans early in 1945, Budapest lay in ruins and famine threatened the country.

Stalin's attitude toward Hungary was curiously ambivalent. His Moscow agreement with Churchill granted the Soviet Union preponderant influence there, but Soviet representatives acted with delicacy compared to their conduct in Romania and Bulgaria. There was no systematic purge of collaborators; the provisional government contained only two Communists, in the ministries of trade and agriculture; the Communist platform read like an electoral manifesto from the British Conservative Party; and in November 1945, open, free, and honest elections were held throughout the country. Perhaps Stalin was testing the appeal of Communism in Eastern Europe, or perhaps he was proceeding slowly in Hungary in order to calm Western fears over Soviet conduct in Poland. Certainly, Soviet leaders considered Hungary less strategically significant than either Poland or Romania.

Stalin adopts an ambivalent attitude toward Hungary

Whatever Stalin's motives may have been, the election results were devastating for Moscow. The Smallholders' Party, a rural organization that had dominated Hungary between the wars, swept into power with 57 percent of the vote, while the Communists earned 17 percent, ranking them just behind the Social Democrats. Communist leader Mátyás Rákosi conferred with Stalin in Moscow, then returned to Budapest with the mission of undermining the Smallholders. For the next two years, the battle for Hungary raged behind the scenes. The Communists enjoyed two advantages. The policies of Minister of Agriculture Imre Nagy, a flexible, reform-minded Communist, led to wide-scale redistribution of land to poor farmers and notable increases in Communist popularity. Then, in February 1947, the British and Americans signed a peace treaty with Hungary (as they had with Bulgaria and Romania), thereby ending the authority of

Hungarian Communists lose free elections

the Allied Control Commission and leading to Western recognition of the Hungarian government.

At first it appeared that the Smallholders would be able to keep the Communists at bay. But their position gradually eroded through intimidation and internal political maneuvering. In August 1947, another round of elections gave them 15 percent of the vote, down from 57 percent two years earlier. The Communists became the largest party, despite a relatively unimpressive showing of 22 percent of the vote. Slowly they consolidated their hold on power, building on the presence of the Soviet Army, the apparent inability or unwillingness of the West to intervene, the deepening confrontation between the USSR and the United States over Germany, and the apparent moderation of their leadership. The 1949 elections were contested with a single list of candidates, and in August 1949, Hungary implemented a new constitution and became a "people's democracy."

Communist intimidation moves Hungary into the Soviet bloc

Soviet control over Hungary, however, was incomplete. Nagy proved too liberal for Stalin and was purged in the early 1950s, only to reemerge in 1956 as leader of a popular uprising against Soviet domination. Later, in the 1970s and 1980s, Soviet leaders would tolerate considerable free market economic experimentation by the Hungarian regime of János Kádár. The Hungarian example illustrates the diversity of Soviet tactics in Eastern Europe, just as it underscores the similarity of eventual outcomes: Hungary, despite its internal divergences, was on Moscow's side in the Cold War.

CZECHOSLOVAKIA: A BRIDGE GOES DOWN

Czechoslovakia was the most industrialized country of Eastern Europe and the one with the firmest grievance against Britain and France. Czech president Edvard Beneš, having seen his nation betrayed at Munich, was convinced of the uselessness of Western friendship and the importance of coming to terms with Moscow. Stalin, after all, had been ready to fight at Czechoslovakia's side against Germany in 1938 and, unlike the Poles, neither Czechs nor Slovaks instinctively distrusted Russians. For Beneš, close relations with Moscow would involve no sacrifice of Western values, to which he remained committed; rather, Czechoslovakia would serve as a bridge between East and West, a nation friendly to and willing to do business with both sides. In December 1943, he traveled to Moscow and signed a treaty of alliance with the USSR.

Czechoslovakia seeks close relations with Moscow

After the war, it seemed for a time that the treaty might work. Stalin, aware that the Communist Party was likely to become the strongest in Czechoslovakia and appreciating Beneš's goodwill, realized that free elections might well lead to a Communist-dominated government. This in turn might make it possible to bring Czechoslovakia into the Soviet camp without damaging the Grand Alliance. In May 1946, free parliamentary elections gave 38 percent of the vote to the Communists, who thereby became the largest party and organized a coalition government. For a while, Communist premier Klement Gottwald worked to maintain close economic ties with the West and avoided any persecution of non-Communist parties.

This promising state of affairs ended abruptly in the summer of 1947. When the United States organized the European Recovery Program or "Marshall Plan" (described in Chapter 4), European nations hastened to apply for membership. One of them was Czechoslovakia. The coalition government voted unanimously to take part, only to be denounced by Stalin in July. The Czechs were told to withdraw their acceptance of American aid and instead urged to join in the "Molotov Plan," open to all socialist nations of Eastern Europe. The U.S. objective of free trade clashed openly with the Soviet desire to avoid the overpowering American economy's penetration into the region.

Events moved rapidly. Czechoslovak Communists began to practice the same sort of bullying evident since 1945 in other Eastern European nations. On 20 February 1948, a number of non-Communist cabinet ministers resigned, hoping that the Social Democrats would join them and cause the government to fall. But since the Social Democrats remained in office, the government stayed in power, replacing the departing ministers with more subservient types (Documents 11A and 11B). Foreign Minister Jan Masaryk, son of the founder of the Czechoslovak state, either fell or (more likely) was pushed to his death from an open window during the crisis. Gottwald's government then swiftly turned Czechoslovakia into a one-party state. The bridge between East and West was closed.

Czechoslovakia becomes a one-party state

Despite the pressure exerted by Moscow and the presence of the Soviet Army, the coup of February 1948 appears to have been mainly the work of the Czechoslovaks themselves. The disastrous miscalculation by the minority ministers opened the door for Gottwald to consolidate his power by legal means and to avoid an open confrontation. The coup in Czechoslovakia frightened the West and led to a brief war scare, which was quickly followed by the blockade of Berlin. At the time, many thought that the USSR was preparing for a third world war, but in retrospect it seems that Stalin was simply shoring up his perimeter for the long, twilight struggle of the Cold War.

YUGOSLAVIA: TITO TRIUMPHANT

Nowhere was the diversity of Soviet responses to Eastern Europe more evident than in Yugoslavia. It seems likely that Soviet leaders never understood the situation there, and they certainly mishandled it badly.

Yugoslavia was unpredictable from the moment a coup in Belgrade overthrew a pro-German government in March 1941. An enraged Hitler deferred his offensive against Russia to teach the Yugoslavs a lesson: The Wehrmacht defeated them in eight days and dissolved the multinational state. But Hitler's commitments elsewhere led him to withdraw the German forces before they had destroyed all elements of the Yugoslav army, and some surviving units went underground. For the remainder of the war, they fought not only the Germans but also a volunteer force of Partisans led by Josip Broz (alias Tito), the general secretary of the Yugoslav Communist Party. In a struggle complicated further by British, American, and Soviet aid to conflicting sides, the Partisans eventually caught the country's imagination and played the leading role in defeating the German occupiers by October 1944. Red Army units marched in simultaneously and behaved atrociously, raping women and burning villages throughout northern Yugoslavia. They were quickly withdrawn to fight elsewhere, but Yugoslavs were left with little appreciation for Soviet-style liberation.

Tito's Partisans emerge from the war as heroes

Tito emerged from the conflict with tremendous popularity, based not only upon his victory but also upon his program. A beefy, savvy Croat married to a Serb, he deplored ethnic fragmentation and rivalries, denouncing them as Nazi racism and standing instead for full reunification of the country. This stance was not popular in his native Croatia, where aspirations for independence ran high; but Tito's trump card was his willingness to *practice* national unity as well as to *preach* it. Scrupulously avoiding any hint of ethnic prejudice or preferential treatment, while swiftly constructing an efficient, centralized administration, he won the trust of all Yugoslavs to a degree matched by no one before or since. Indeed, Tito was the only Yugoslav ever who both believed in multinational unity and was able to make it work. He had the touch required to balance a liberal attitude toward cultural multiplicity with a resolute rejection of the divisive pressures such variety can produce.

Tito seeks a centralized, multinational state

From the beginning, Belgrade's relations with Moscow were strained. Tito was so insistent in his territorial demands upon Italy that he provoked a postwar crisis that could have led to war with Britain and America. The Soviets uneasily supported his claims while resenting his dangerous independence. Tito also sent aid to the Communist side in the Greek civil war, an act which embarrassed Stalin, who had assured Churchill that the British would be predominant in Greece and who knew that British and U.S. naval power precluded any significant Soviet gains there. Finally, Tito's plan to build a federation of Balkan states was viewed skeptically by Stalin, who had no desire to see the emergence of a powerful Communist rival.

Even more serious were Yugoslavia's political and economic divergences from Moscow. Tito's government was Communist but not Soviet: It sought to balance the aspirations of ethnic subgroups while constructing a distinctively Yugoslav path to socialism. Moscow expected Yugoslavia, like other Eastern European nations, to increase its production of raw materials and crops so as to help subsidize the USSR's recovery. The horrified Yugoslavs contended that this would condemn them to neocolonial status. Instead, they wanted Moscow to underwrite *their* industrialization program, the success of which would validate their unique path to socialism.

Yugoslavia diverges from the Soviet path to socialism

This was a dagger pointed at Stalin's heart. It was not that Yugoslavia's course was non-Marxist: Tito adopted a Stalinist economic model, emphasizing heavy industry, centralized economic planning, and nationalization of most enterprises. The danger lay in the possibility that Yugoslavia would become more successful economically than the USSR, thereby luring other Eastern European nations along alternative paths to modernization. This would deprive Moscow of the subservience of Eastern European states and prevent it from using those countries as suppliers of raw materials and consumers of low-quality Soviet finished goods. Stalin's chief priority was to *control* Eastern Europe, and that control, achieved in part at the cost of the Grand Alliance, was now jeopardized. Clearly, Tito had to be stopped.

Stalin struck in the spring of 1948. He recalled all Soviet military and civilian advisors from Yugoslavia, orchestrated its expulsion from the Cominform, and organized a trade boycott by all Communist nations (Document 13). Simultaneously, he called on loyal elements within the Yugoslav Communist Party to overthrow Tito and his henchmen. There is no doubt that he fully expected to be successful, observing at the time, "I will lift my little finger and there will be no more Tito!" But even all ten of his fingers, in the form of clenched fists, failed to displace the Yugoslav leader. The boycott was particularly dangerous for Yugoslavia, given its anti-Western activities in Greece; but the United States, sensing an unexpected opportunity to foster dissension inside the Soviet bloc, took up much of the slack. By 1952, one-third of Yugoslavia's imports came from America. Meanwhile, Tito pressed ahead with the development of the "separate Yugoslav path to socialism." He introduced free market factors of supply and demand into Yugoslav industrial production, liberating factories from total dependence on quotas set by a central planning board.

Stalin moves against Tito but fails to oust him

The economic well-being made possible by these reforms and by American imports played a significant role in Tito's survival. His ruthlessness in dealing swiftly with Stalinists within his own party also helped his cause. But three reasons for the failure of Soviet actions against Yugoslavia stand out. First, the immense wartime popularity earned by Tito and the Partisans (reinforced by the atrocious conduct of the Red Army) united the Yugoslavs against Soviet meddling. Second, Tito's solicitude for the aspirations of the country's diverse ethnic groups won him support from all who believed in national unity. Finally, Stalin's own restraint doomed his efforts.

The fact that Yugoslavia was not occupied by the Red Army gave Stalin much less leverage there than in other Eastern European nations. But in 1948, with Britain retreating from empire and the United States, largely disarmed, engaged in efforts to break the Berlin Blockade (Chapter 5), and preoccupied by a four-way presidential election campaign, an invasion of Yugoslavia by Soviet forces would have stood a strong chance of success. It is true that the USSR had no border with Yugoslavia, that the terrain within that country was mountainous and treacherous, and that Yugoslav resistance might have been protracted and ferocious; but none of these factors would have defeated an army that had triumphed over Nazi Germany. The United States, of course, could always threaten to use nuclear weapons, over which it still enjoyed a monopoly, but there was no reason to believe that Washington considered Yugoslavia as vital to Western interests as Berlin.

Stalin refrains from invading Yugoslavia

Perhaps that consideration best explains Stalin's conduct. Berlin was crucial to both sides in the Cold War, but Yugoslavia was not. Once his blows against Belgrade had failed to bring Tito down, Stalin may have reasoned that further action would entail more risks than could be justified by the benefits of success. Indeed, Tito's survival, while it embarrassed the Soviet Union, in no way prevented Stalin from doing what he wanted in Europe. Germany was an altogether different story. And that is where the Cold War began.

4

The Cold War Begins, 1945–1948

The sun that rose over Tokyo Bay on 2 September 1945 illuminated a world order that had changed dramatically since 1939. As the Japanese Empire signed the Instrument of Surrender and followed the Third Reich and the New Roman Empire into history's dustbin, the victors were able to begin the daunting task of keeping the hard-won peace and reorganizing the world. Winning the war had been wrenchingly difficult, but events would soon prove that it had been considerably easier for the Grand Alliance to defeat its enemies than for its members to preserve good relations among themselves in the absence of common foes. It would not be long before the Cold War would take the place of the brutal struggles of World War II.

THE GERMAN QUESTION

In the first half of the twentieth century, Europe's history was in large measure Germany's work. As a unified and immensely powerful nation, it had proven too large and strong for a small continent used to the fragile security offered by a balance of power. The German Empire's belligerent tactics led Europe into war in 1914. The failure of the victorious nations either to deal leniently with Germany or to demolish it perpetuated the German problem after 1919. Hitler's brutal expansionism led to another war in 1939 and created an unlikely opposing coalition of capitalist and Communist powers. When the leaders of the Grand Alliance met between 1942 and 1945, it was easy for them to pontificate about the need to defeat Germany and prevent any return of its power. But it was not easy for them to solve the German problem, and their inability to do so was the principal factor in the development of the Cold War.

The German Question lies at the roots of the Cold War

It wasn't that they didn't try: The conferences at Yalta and Potsdam discussed the German problem at length. Nor did they misunderstand each other; they simply had different objectives. The Americans and British agreed on the necessity for a stringent peace that would greatly reduce German industrial production, provide reparations for the countries victimized by Nazi aggression, and promote political democracy. In 1944, they had toyed with the concept of dismembering Germany, but the Morgenthau Plan for fragmenting the country, approved by both Roosevelt and Churchill, was rejected by their staffs as impractical and as prejudicial to postwar efforts to rebuild all European economies. Soviet objectives differed both in tone and in substance. Stalin was determined to destroy German war-making capacity, primarily by exacting $20 billion in reparations, half of which would go to the USSR. He favored fragmentation of the country, with the industrial heartlands of the Saar and the Ruhr passing under international control. If Germany was to remain a unified nation, it should be crippled and neutralized.

Objectives vary within the Grand Alliance

Both sides agreed that postwar Germany should be divided into zones of occupation, with British and U.S. zones in the west and a Soviet sector in the east. Interestingly, although Stalin at Yalta had opposed an occupation zone for France, Charles de Gaulle's French provisional government adopted positions on Germany similar to those of Moscow. The French wished to dismember and democratize Germany, to internationalize the Ruhr while annexing the Saar and the left bank of the Rhine, and to extract heavy reparations in coal, money, and machinery. For all his alleged shrewdness, Stalin seems to have missed a marvelous opportunity to embarrass the British and Americans by endorsing the French positions.

By the time of the Potsdam Conference, however, the differences had widened. The British and Americans had come to realize that their zones contained most of the Germans, while the Soviet zone contained most of the food. They also decided against dismantling German industry, since destroying Europe's most productive economy would cripple the continent's recovery and make Germany forever dependent on the Allies. They would now speak of reparations only in terms of exchange of West German industrial goods for East German food. The Soviets objected, since a prostrate Europe was consistent with their hopes for the spread of Communism and since they feared the resurrection of German military power that economic recovery would make possible. Under such circumstances, no agreement was possible at Potsdam.

The Potsdam Conference fails to reach agreement on Germany

After the end of the war, the United States, secure in its monopoly of atomic weapons, had nothing to fear from German military strength. American policy henceforth stressed the desirability of a Germany strong enough to resist Soviet expansion and economically healthy enough to anchor a rebuilt, peaceful, and stable Europe. Stalin saw nothing attractive in this scenario and was in no frame of mind to consent to German reunification. So, as time went on, there was no meeting of minds, and the German question continued to bedevil relations between East and West.

POSTWAR ATTEMPTS AT ACCOMMODATION

In September 1945, following Japan's surrender, the foreign ministers of the five permanent members of the UN Security Council (the United States, USSR, Britain, France, and China) convened at London for the first postwar Conference of Foreign Ministers. At Potsdam, it was agreed that such meetings would take place

MAP 2 Divided Germany and Divided Europe, 1945–1955.

In the wake of World War II, Germany and Europe were divided into Western (capitalist) and Eastern (Communist) sectors, separated by what Churchill called the "iron curtain." Although the city of Berlin was 110 miles east of the iron curtain, like the rest of Germany it was divided into U.S., British, French, and Soviet occupation zones, making West Berlin a Western capitalist island in the middle of the Communist sector (see inset map of divided Berlin).

as needed to ease the transition from war to peace. This session was charged with drafting peace treaties between the Grand Alliance and Germany's wartime allies (Bulgaria, Finland, Hungary, Italy, and Romania), but it made little progress. Secretary of State Byrnes arrived with the atomic bomb "in his hip pocket" (as he put it), but if the Americans thought that the Soviets would roll over and play dead, they were mistaken. Foreign Commissar Molotov proved as tough a negotiator as ever, and British foreign secretary Bevin got no further than Byrnes. Britain and America pressed for compliance with the Yalta accords as they understood them: free elections in all Eastern European countries as quickly as possible. Molotov's position was that the Americans had their spheres of influence in Italy and Japan, while the British had theirs in Greece; the Soviet Union would intervene in neither, so the West had no business interfering in Eastern Europe. The Soviets also proposed assuming trusteeship over the former Italian colony of Libya, a move which the West interpreted as an effort to probe in the direction of the Belgian Congo, which contained the world's richest supply of uranium (vital to the construction of atomic bombs).

The conference bogged down and adjourned without agreement. Byrnes returned to Washington shrouded in gloom and uncertain of Soviet intentions. The British were even less pleased: They believed that the Soviets were bent on expansion in the Middle East and Mediterranean and that both the USSR and United States were growing contemptuous of British interests. From the Soviet perspective, Western interest in Eastern Europe was both hypocritical and premature, since the German problem (which Moscow feared most) had not yet been dealt with. Attempting to settle affairs in Eastern Europe before guaranteeing Russia's safety from Germany was bound to increase Stalin's defensiveness. It was not an auspicious beginning for postwar diplomacy.

Disputes plague the London Conference of Foreign Ministers

During the next few months, the Americans tried to develop a sensible policy toward the USSR. Byrnes sent publisher Mark Ethridge and historian Cyril Black to the Balkans on a fact-finding mission. The Ethridge Report, submitted in December, recognized legitimate Soviet concerns in the region but emphasized the imperialistic nature of Moscow's postwar actions there. Simultaneously, the U.S. Congress approved a $3.5 billion loan to Britain, while Soviet requests for $6 billion in credits remained shelved. Byrnes decided to break the stalemate by proposing a December meeting of the Conference of Foreign Ministers in Moscow.

In contrast to London, the Moscow Conference went smoothly, largely because the Balkan question was resolved in favor of the USSR. Romania and Bulgaria would add two non-Communists to their governments, in line with the Soviet interpretation of the Yalta provision for "free elections." Treaties for the Soviet satellites would be drafted at a forthcoming peace conference in Paris. Issues affecting Korea, China, and Japan were also settled, and the Soviets agreed to a joint American-British-Canadian proposal to establish a UN commission to control atomic energy. The sole item on which no agreement was reached concerned the withdrawal of British and Russian troops from Iran—a failure that would have serious consequences. But, on balance, Byrnes was well satisfied, and even Bevin was mildly appeased.

Agreements are reached at the Moscow Conference of Foreign Ministers

A LONG TELEGRAM AND AN IRON CURTAIN

In Washington, however, Byrnes's superior held a different view. Harry Truman had given his secretary of state more discretionary authority than any other in living memory. Byrnes had responded by conducting diplomacy in great secrecy and arranging to present a radio report to the American people on the Moscow Conference without first briefing the president. He had decided against publishing the Ethridge Report before going to Moscow and had not even sent it to the president. Most importantly, his willingness to compromise at Moscow cut against the grain of current thinking in his own State Department and in the Oval Office. Truman, growing increasingly accustomed to his presidential authority, was becoming less tolerant of Byrnes's style and less interested in compromising with what he considered unacceptable Soviet conduct in Eastern Europe.

Truman and Byrnes disagree over U.S. foreign policy

On 5 January 1946, Truman met with Byrnes and made his position clear. Moscow's actions in the Balkans had turned Romania and Bulgaria into police states, and its pressure on Greece, Turkey, and Iran foreshadowed a wave of expansionism in the so-called Northern Tier. Byrnes's conciliation of Stalin at Moscow was not consistent with Truman's view of the interests of the United States, and those interests dictated a firmer American policy toward Stalin; as Truman put it, "I'm tired of babying the Soviets."

That, at least, was Truman's version of events a decade after the fact. Secretary Byrnes vigorously refuted it, plausibly claiming that he would have resigned on the spot had Truman spoken to him that way. Noted Cold War historian Bill Miscamble concludes that, in the mid-1950s, wanting to fortify his anti-Soviet credentials, Truman invented the more sensational details of this story. Certainly his administration did not suddenly change course after January 1946 in dealing with Stalin. Truman, for all his vaunted decisiveness, had been vacillating since April 1945 between conciliation and confrontation with Moscow. In January 1946, in disgust with Soviet conduct in Eastern Europe, he may have swung toward confrontation. But he was a pragmatic politician who knew that changes of course were part of the job and were seldom permanent. America had not yet declared Cold War against the USSR.

Stalin's election speech increases Western concerns

One month after the Truman–Byrnes interview, however, Stalin delivered a speech that nudged the Americans further toward confrontation. In an election speech on 9 February, he reasserted the validity of Marxist-Leninist thought, painted the contrast between capitalism and Communism in vivid colors not used in official Soviet pronouncements since 1941, and blamed the two world wars on conflicts and crises in the capitalist world. The Soviet people must prepare for conflict by tightening their belts yet further and emphasizing the development of heavy industry, as they had in the years before the German invasion (Document 4).

Although Stalin's speech was probably not intended as a declaration of Cold War, it was certainly taken that way in Washington—and Supreme Court justice William O. Douglas even described it as a "declaration of World War III." One week later, the Canadian government disclosed its roundup of a Soviet-sponsored atomic spy ring headed by Canadian scientist Alan Nunn May.

Simultaneously, the Soviet government announced that it would not participate in the International Monetary Fund and the World Bank—a position which made sense to Soviet leaders fearful of capitalist penetration but which baffled Western analysts who knew that immense sums were needed to rebuild the USSR. Perplexed, the U.S. State Department solicited analyses of recent Soviet behavior from its resident experts, including George Kennan, then attached to the U.S. embassy in Moscow.

George Kennan writes the Long Telegram

George Frost Kennan was a moody, introspective Wisconsin Presbyterian with a Princeton degree and nearly two decades of experience as a student of Russian affairs. Highly sensitive, mildly neurotic, and profoundly insightful, his gold-plated analytical abilities would now stamp him as the most influential American foreign service officer of the twentieth century. In reply to Washington's request for reflections on Soviet conduct, Kennan composed an 8,000-word telegram that reached the State Department on 22 February 1946. The "Long Telegram," as it came to be known, situated current Soviet behavior in a Russian mentality dating back centuries. Traditionally suspicious of foreigners and insecure in the face of Western technological superiority, the Russians had long since developed a neurotic outlook on the world (a condition with which Kennan had some personal familiarity). Soviet leaders clothed this worldview in Marxist robes, but these were merely "fig leaves" designed to justify their reprehensible conduct toward their own citizens and their expansionist policies abroad. Stalin's 9 February speech was simply one more attempt to conceal Russian expansionism in the trappings of Marxist theory. Because these attitudes were so deeply rooted in Russian history, the Soviet government could not be reasoned with or mollified; only firm resistance backed by a willingness to use force could convince the Kremlin to back down.

Washington takes a firmer stance against Moscow

Kennan had been saying these things for years. The Long Telegram became important only because Washington was finally ready to listen to such analysis. It transformed Kennan from an obscure diplomat into one of the country's top Soviet experts, but its effects on Truman and his advisors were far more significant. It satisfied their need for a conceptual framework that both explained Soviet conduct and offered a prescription for dealing with Moscow. Within days, all of Washington was talking about it. On 27 February, Republican senator Arthur Vandenberg, one of his party's foremost foreign policy spokesmen, denounced the USSR in a powerful speech in the Senate. The next day Byrnes took up the call for a firmer line toward Moscow in a speech dubbed by wags "The Second Vandenberg Concerto." Derived more from his 5 January discussion with Truman than from Kennan's writing, it nonetheless reinforced the impression the Long Telegram was making throughout the U.S. government.

Churchill's "Iron Curtain" speech is Britain's declaration of Cold War

Just ahead lay the most dramatic event of that turbulent winter. As international tensions intensified, Winston Churchill, since 1945 leader of the Tory opposition to Clement Attlee's Labour government, came to America for a visit. Truman had arranged for him to give an address at Westminster College in Missouri, Truman's home state, on 5 March. Churchill used the podium to deliver a ringing endorsement of joint

Winston Churchill gives the "iron curtain" speech, 5 March 1946.
Churchill, voted out of office in 1945, watched from the sidelines as the Soviet Union consolidated its position in Eastern Europe. In this 1946 speech, with President Truman looking on, Churchill called attention to what he termed an "iron curtain" of Soviet military power imprisoning the Eastern European nations. Stalin took exception to Churchill's call for an English-speaking alliance to oppose Communist expansion, and the two sides drew nearer to Cold War.

Anglo-American action against the Soviet threat, depicting the situation in Eastern Europe in striking language (Document 5A):

> From Stettin in the Baltic to Trieste in the Adriatic, an iron curtain has descended across the Continent. Behind that line lie all the capitals of the ancient states of Central and Eastern Europe. Warsaw, Berlin, Prague, Vienna, Budapest, Belgrade, Bucharest, and Sofia, all these famous cities and the populations around them lie in what I must call the Soviet sphere. . . Whatever conclusions may be drawn from these facts—and facts they are—this is certainly not the Liberated Europe we fought to build up. Nor is it one which contains the essentials of permanent peace.

If Americans could view Stalin's February speech as a declaration of Cold War, it is difficult to consider Churchill's "iron curtain" speech as anything less. As an opposition politician, he did not speak for the British government, but his stature as Britain's wartime leader lent an air of authority to anything he said. Stalin was shocked by the address, referring bitterly to the implicit racism of Churchill's call for an Anglo-American consortium against the Soviets and pointing out the British statesman's interwar anti-Communism (Document 5B). The speech's impact was intensified by the fact that Truman sat on the platform behind Churchill, listening intently and nodding approvingly. The president later claimed that he had not read the address in advance, but this assertion may take its place in a long line of disingenuous remarks by a seasoned politico who knew exactly what he was doing.

Yet Truman himself had not denounced Soviet conduct. While Churchill and Stalin traded insults, he remained above the fray. When the American declaration of Cold War finally came, it would be couched not in terms of a confrontation between capitalism and Communism, nor of the descent of an iron curtain, but of the need to forestall Soviet expansionist ambitions in the Northern Tier (Greece, Turkey, and Iran). Washington's conceptualization of Soviet intentions and actions was being influenced by the pragmatic terminology of George Kennan's Long Telegram.

Truman observes the conflict between Stalin and Churchill

THE CONFRONTATION OVER IRAN

When British and Soviet troops ousted the pro-German Reza Shah Pahlavi and partitioned Iran between them in 1942, they signed a treaty pledging mutual withdrawal of their forces within six months after the end of the war (in the event, no later than 2 March 1946). London pulled out most of its troops by January, but Moscow stalled, demanding oil rights in northern Iran equivalent to those obtained by the British in the south. Simultaneously, the Soviets provoked an uprising by Azerbaijani separatists in the north. By 1 March, when the Soviet government announced that its soldiers would remain in Iran beyond the deadline, those forces were being augmented by additional tanks. Given Soviet behavior in Eastern Europe and recent Soviet pressure on Turkey, events in Iran appeared ominous. Churchill's iron curtain speech, delivered four days after the Soviet announcement, fell on eager ears.

Soviet forces remain in Iran beyond the deadline

Tehran responded by appealing to the Security Council of the United Nations in an effort to force the Soviets to comply with the treaty. Soviet ambassador Andrei Gromyko contended that the UN lacked jurisdiction over the matter and ostentatiously walked out of the session. This gesture, conjuring up recollections of similar Japanese and German actions in the old League of Nations, sent a chill up Western spines and may have had a greater impact on public opinion in America and Britain than the crisis itself. On 6 March, George Kennan delivered a stiff protest to Molotov, signaling that Washington would not remain indifferent to Soviet actions in Iran (Truman later claimed to have sent Stalin an ultimatum, but there is no evidence of this). The crisis deepened over the next fortnight, with widespread reports of Soviet troop movements within northern Iran in the directions of Tehran and Turkey. Washington kept the pressure on at the UN, refraining from bluster and threats and making its position clear while leaving Stalin a face-saving way out if he wished to take it.

The Iran Crisis deepens

By 24 March, Stalin had decided to do just that. Moscow Radio announced troop withdrawals from Iran in accordance with what it termed an "agreement" between Moscow and Tehran. This was actually a unilateral Soviet decision to withdraw within six weeks while proposing a joint Soviet–Iranian oil company, which never came into being. The actual withdrawal was completed by 9 May, and the crisis ended with a significant diplomatic defeat for the Soviet Union. Stalin's decision appears to have been conditioned by an

The USSR withdraws its forces from Iran

American response at once forceful and cautious. Washington did not threaten to intervene in Iran, but Stalin was faced with the prospect of American action in areas of greater concern to him (such as Germany) if the crisis intensified. The Soviet withdrawal seemed to confirm the wisdom of the Long Telegram: If America stood up to the Russians, they would back down. But since Soviet hostility toward the West was rooted in centuries of Russian history, that hostility could not be expected to diminish, and the next crisis would not be long in coming.

THE GERMAN QUESTION REMAINS UNANSWERED

As the Iran confrontation was winding down, the Conference of Foreign Ministers was preparing to convene in Paris. Truman and Byrnes had decided to test Soviet intentions concerning Germany. In addition to the ongoing disputes over reparations and rehabilitation of the German economy, disagreement over the future status of Germany stiffened Soviet resolve to control Eastern Europe and intensified Western distrust of Moscow's ultimate intentions. Now Byrnes returned to an idea that he had floated informally at Potsdam and London: a four-power treaty guaranteeing the demilitarization of Germany for twenty-five years. While removing the greatest threat to Soviet security, such a pact would eliminate any justification for Soviet police-state tactics in Eastern Europe and would assure a long-term American military presence on the continent. It would, as Truman said, "call the Russians' bluff."

Molotov's reaction was noncommittal. Rather than demilitarization, he preferred to speak of "disarmament," a term by which he meant not only the liquidation of German military potential but reparations as well. The U.S. position was that reparations and recovery were incompatible. Byrnes concluded from this that Stalin was more interested in expansion than in security and began to think in terms of a permanent division of Germany. In June, he refused a Soviet offer to connect the opening of negotiations for a large American loan to discussions of the situation in Eastern Europe. One month later, the Americans and British began to combine their occupation zones into one economic unit, called by the eccentric name "Bizonia."

The United States begins to consider a permanent division of Germany

Finally, on 6 September, Byrnes delivered a major speech in Stuttgart to highlight the reversal of America's German policy. He assured the German people that U.S. occupation forces would remain in Germany as long as those of any other nation and explicitly posed the possibility that reunification might not occur. Roosevelt's wartime musings to the contrary, a permanent division of Germany had never become official U.S. policy. Now Truman, Byrnes, and the State Department factored Germany into their newly conceptualized view of Soviet expansionist tendencies and realized that a reunified Germany could fall under Russian domination, particularly since Moscow refused to consider zonal consolidation until its conditions were met. Washington deemed division of the country less objectionable than Soviet control, and Bizonia proved to be the first step down that road.

Byrnes' speech in Stuttgart commits U.S. forces to remain in Germany

The Stuttgart speech was an important milestone in what was coming to be known as the "Cold War." The term was first used in 1945 by the columnist Herbert Bayard Swope and later picked up by nationally syndicated columnist Walter

Lippmann, who used it as the title of his 1947 book. Although the "war" was on, the United States had not yet declared it, and there was still time to draw back from any irrevocable commitments. But time was running out.

THE TRUMAN DOCTRINE

German issues dominated the headlines during the second half of 1946, but the Northern Tier, despite the solution of the Iranian crisis, continued to vex the allies-turned-adversaries. In August, Moscow had begun pressing Turkey for a Soviet military presence in the Dardanelles, the straits controlling access between the Mediterranean and Black seas. The United States, which in 1945 had been willing to consider increased Soviet influence in this area, now saw this as yet another Soviet expansionist threat and responded by sending a stern message to Moscow and warships to the region. In October, faced with American resolve, Stalin dropped his demands, lending further credence to the philosophy contained in the Long Telegram.

The Communist insurgency in Greece intensifies

In Greece, however, the Communist insurgency dating from 1944 intensified, backed secretly by Marshal Tito of neighboring Yugoslavia. And although withdrawing its Dardanelles claim, Moscow continued to suggest revisions in its borders with Turkey and to press for an agreement that would permit Soviet naval vessels unrestricted passage to and from the Black Sea.

All of this worried the British, who were increasingly preoccupied with brushfire insurgencies in their extensive empire on which the sun never set. They decided in early 1947 to cut their losses in areas they were unlikely to hold. India would be given its freedom and partitioned between Hindus and Muslims; the road to Mandalay would be turned over to an independent Burma; Palestine, after an excruciating moral and military struggle, would be partitioned between Jews and Palestinians. Most significantly for Washington, British economic and military assistance to Greece and Turkey could no longer be sustained in the face of a financial crisis so severe that portions of the British Empire were being liquidated. On 21 February, the first secretary of the British embassy called upon Loy Henderson, director of the U.S. State Department's Division of Near Eastern Affairs, and handed him two diplomatic notes.

The documents informed the United States that British aid to Greece and Turkey would be terminated by 1 April 1947. Since it was a Friday afternoon and Secretary of State George Marshall (who had replaced Byrnes after the 1946 congressional elections) was on his way to deliver an address at Princeton University, Henderson took the notes to Undersecretary of State Dean Acheson, who immediately began to work out the implications. With the Dardanelles controversy still fresh in memory and with the Greek civil war going badly for the anti-Communist forces, neither Acheson nor Henderson were in any mood to stall. By 24 February, they had worked out a detailed plan for American assistance to Greece and Turkey and had submitted it for the consideration of Truman and Marshall.

Britain informs the United States that it will end aid to Greece and Turkey

Truman, Marshall, and Acheson made an unlikely trio. The president's lack of higher education never deterred him from surrounding himself with advisors who had enjoyed the intellectual stimulations he had lacked; his self-confidence shone through and enabled him to work with men of great ability without succumbing to either insecurity or defensiveness. He had named George Marshall secretary of state because he had lost confidence in Jimmy Byrnes and because his administration, slipping badly in public esteem after a crushing defeat in the 1946 congressional elections, needed an infusion of highly respected talent. Marshall was neither a genius nor a sage, but he had been America's leading soldier during the past war and had a reputation for unimpeachable integrity. At State, he was fortunate enough to command the services of Dean Acheson, a tall, aristocratic Yalie with a bristling mustache, a caustic tongue, and a magnificently pragmatic and analytic mind. Acheson, who was intolerant of lesser minds (most of the human race) and who had an extremely low boring point, managed to irritate nearly everyone who knew him at one time or another. But he was unflinchingly loyal to Harry Truman, and that devotion, coupled with his considerable abilities, made his arrogance less annoying—at least to the president. Together, these three statesmen would declare Cold War on the Soviet Union and develop a plan for fighting it.

On 27 February, they met with congressional leaders to obtain an informal reading on their plan's prospects. Marshall presented the program in a straightforward, dry

President Truman and his foreign policy team in 1950.

From left to right, we see W. Averell Harriman, former ambassador to the USSR; General George C. Marshall, Secretary of Defense; President Harry S Truman; Dean G. Acheson, Secretary of State; three unidentified men; and General Omar N. Bradley, Chairman of the Joint Chiefs of Staff. This team waged Cold War against the Soviet Union during Truman's final years in office.

manner that left the legislators cold. In desperation, Acheson launched into a passionate oration that compared the United States and USSR to Rome and Carthage. The choice, he said, was between freedom and bondage, between watching the Soviet tide roll over most of the world and taking prudent measures to stop it at once. America's security was at stake. Arthur Vandenberg broke the lengthy silence that followed Acheson's speech: If Truman articulated the problem in those terms, the Congress and the country would support him. Loy Henderson later recalled that Vandenberg was more direct: "Mr. President, the only way you are ever going to get this is to make a speech and scare the hell out of the country."

Acheson phrases the situation in stark terms

Truman did precisely that on 12 March. His style was uninspiring, but his message was forceful and provocative: The United States, which in the last war had become "the great arsenal of democracy," must now assume the financial burden of defending democracy throughout the world (Document 7). Aid to Greece and Turkey cleared Congress in April by margins of two to one, and by the spring of 1949, the U.S.-backed Greek government defeated the Communist insurgency. Kennan was apprehensive about the universal scope of what became known as the Truman Doctrine, but neither Truman, Acheson, nor Marshall ever intended to commit the United States as cosmically as the speech implied. They knew that America had finite resources and that some requests for aid might be insincere efforts to milk Uncle Sam. In the next few years, they refused to dispute the Communist coup in Czechoslovakia and limited the aid provided to Nationalist China. The Truman Doctrine was a response to a perceived threat of Soviet expansion in Europe and the Middle East; as such, it was more limited in scope than Truman seemed to indicate on 12 March.

The Truman Doctrine is the U.S. declaration of Cold War

It was also, of course, the American declaration of Cold War. Truman had bided his time while Stalin and Churchill traded jibes in 1946, but now he would wait no longer. The German question still defied solution; the Eastern European nations were clearly within the Soviet orbit; the Northern Tier, despite Anglo-American diplomatic victories in Iran and the Dardanelles, was still threatened. It was time to block the Communists and defend the West. Those kinds of decisions came easily to Harry Truman.

THE MARSHALL PLAN AND EUROPEAN RECOVERY

Truman's speech recognized no limits on American aid, but George Marshall focused the president's attention on Europe following his return from the Moscow Conference of Foreign Ministers (10 March–24 April). There he had spoken extensively with Stalin and learned that the Soviet leader believed that the final collapse of the European capitalist economies was at hand. Stalin had been predicting this ever since the war's end, but the terrible winter of 1946–1947 and the failure of Britain, France, and Italy to rebound from the war's devastation lent new authority to his words. American diplomats openly predicted that Communists were likely to win free elections in France and Italy in 1948 if economic conditions did not improve. Back in Washington, Marshall formed a Policy Planning Staff at the State Department and charged it with developing policies to counter Soviet expansion. At its head he placed George Kennan, author of the Long Telegram.

Marshall creates the Policy Planning Staff at the U.S. State Department

On 28 April, Defense Secretary Forrestal, who had recommended Kennan for the job, came up with something for him to do. At lunch with Marshall, Forrestal observed that the Soviets were counting on economic despair to turn Europeans toward Communism. The United States, the richest nation on earth, had the goods, food, and money to forestall this looming tragedy. All that was lacking was the will to act and a plan to act on. Marshall turned the matter over to the Policy Planning Staff and requested a solution within ten days—a tall order for a pensive intellectual with a new job, no office, and no staff. Kennan, awed by Marshall's command yet instinctively aware of his chance to make history, assembled the most talented Europeanists available and worked them around the clock. A week later the solution was ready.

Kennan and the Policy Planning Staff design the European Recovery Program

No one person created the Marshall Plan; it was a logical outcome of the Truman Doctrine, and Kennan "simply" put it into appropriate form. He and his staff concluded that its emphasis should be pro-European rather than anti-Communist. The money would come from Washington, but the blueprints for its use would come from the countries themselves. Combining generosity with enlightened self-interest, it would preserve in Western Europe both political freedom and the "open door" for U.S. commerce. Truman bought the concept. Officially named the "European Recovery Program," it would, at his insistence, be known popularly as the "Marshall Plan" (since Truman was disliked in the Republican-controlled Congress that would have to pass the required legislation, while Marshall's prestige transcended party loyalty).

Accordingly, the secretary of state announced the program formally in a commencement address at Harvard University on 5 June (Document 8). Marshall's oratorical abilities compared unfavorably to those of a man reading a telephone directory line by line, and since commencement speeches are generally tolerated rather than listened to, his announcement received indifferent coverage in the press. Intriguingly, it was an open-ended invitation to all European countries, including the USSR and the nations it dominated. Kennan advised Marshall to gamble on Soviet rejection, contending that Communist nations who opened their doors to U.S. trade (and their books to American auditors, as the plan implied) would effectively be relinquishing control over their economies and paving the way for political freedom and the dissolution of the Soviet bloc. Luckily for Kennan the advice proved correct, since Soviet acceptance would have wrecked any chance that Congress would approve the plan. Washington did, however, hold out the hope that some Eastern European nations would enter the program and thereby loosen their ties with Moscow.

Marshall announces the Marshall Plan

On 26 June 1947, representatives of seventeen European nations gathered at Paris for meetings designed to lay the groundwork for the Marshall Plan. Molotov participated but soon withdrew following the rejection of his proposal that each nation should determine its own recovery needs and notify the United States accordingly. Washington insisted on its right to require extensive economic information in return for aid, and this Stalin would not accept. Molotov left the discussions on 2 July; shortly thereafter, the Soviets announced the creation of the "Molotov Plan" for the economic recovery of Eastern Europe and the USSR. Czechoslovakia and Poland, having indicated strong interest in American aid, then announced that they would join the Molotov Plan instead. The

Moscow responds to the Marshall Plan with the Molotov Plan

remaining Western European nations went on to request $17 billion in American aid over a period of four years.

For the Soviets, the Marshall Plan was very dangerous. Not only did it threaten their grip on Eastern Europe, but also it fostered German economic recovery as the basis for a strong Europe, thus raising the specter of a renewed German threat to Soviet security. Stalin responded in September by creating the Communist Information Bureau (Cominform), a mechanism by which he could keep foreign Communist parties in line with Moscow's directives. The wave of strikes sweeping over France and Italy that autumn was orchestrated by the Cominform and seriously damaged the appeal of Stalinism to Western Europe.

Stalin, sensing danger, creates the Cominform

For those nations, of course, the Marshall Plan was, as Ernest Bevin put it, "a lifeline to a sinking man." The devastated economies of "war-torn Europe" could now begin to rebuild. Not everyone was happy about German participation: French premier Georges Bidault begged Marshall to delay German revitalization, or else the French government would lose a confidence vote in the Chamber of Deputies before it could implement the plan! Even the U.S. Congress approached this matter cautiously. Marshall himself had to lay it on the line: "The restoration of Europe involves the restoration of Germany. Without a revival of German production there can be no revival of Europe's economy. But we must be very careful to see that a revived Germany cannot again threaten the European community."

For the United States, secure for the moment in its nuclear monopoly, German restoration posed no threat. For Western Europe, desperate for capital and facing the prospect of Communist victories at the polls in 1948, the risk had to be run. But in the context of the intensifying Cold War, the reactions of Stalin, Bidault, and many members of the U.S. Congress to the rebuilding of Germany illuminate starkly the fateful effects of the failure of the Big Three to come to grips with the German question. In future years, there would be freezes and thaws in the Cold War, but there would be no hope for lasting peace until that question was answered.

The West reluctantly commits itself to German recovery

CONTAINMENT: THE X-ARTICLE

Neither the USSR nor its adversaries expected an answer to the German question in the near future. But for the moment, neither side was anxious to escalate the Cold War. Moscow used the rest of 1947 to shore up its own position, implementing the Molotov Plan, consolidating its hold on Eastern Europe through the Cominform, accelerating its nuclear weapons program, and repressing domestic dissent through the activities of Andrei Zhdanov, one of Stalin's closest associates. Zhdanov's address at the Cominform meeting in Warsaw on 22 September reiterated many of the points made in Stalin's election speech of February 1946, but went much further in dividing the world into two hostile camps. The "Zhdanovshchina," which swept over Russia between September 1947 and Zhdanov's sudden death in July 1948, suppressed any deviation from the party's worldview. One of its most prominent victims was the eminent Soviet economist Evgenii Varga, humbled and eclipsed because of his contention that the final crisis of capitalism was far away and that hopes for the quick collapse of Western economies were misplaced.

The Zhdanovshschina suppresses dissent in the USSR

In Washington, a similar kind of "shoring up" had already begun, although America's own "Zhdanovshchina" of loyalty oaths, committee hearings, spectacular trials, and unprovable McCarthyite accusations was still a few years away. What happened in the summer of 1947 was far more sedate and, in the long run, more significant. Before becoming leader of the Policy Planning Staff, George Kennan had lectured at the National War College (a consequence of his authorship of the Long Telegram). In the fall of 1946, he was one of several professors asked by Secretary of Defense Forrestal to comment on an internal working paper by Edward Willett linking Soviet objectives to Marxist-Leninist principles. Kennan, who felt that Willett overstated the degree of American military expenditure necessary to "contain" Russian expansion, disagreed with the working paper and was promptly asked to write one of his own. The result was a paper entitled "Psychological Background of Soviet Foreign Policy," which went through several drafts before its completion in January 1947.

Kennan never intended the paper to be anything more than a sounding board for discussion within the Navy Department. But after he gave a well-received lecture to the Russian Study Group of the Council on Foreign Relations in January 1947, he was asked by the editor of the council's high-profile journal, *Foreign Affairs*, to submit for publication an article reflecting his views. Since his paper was already written and contained no classified information, he asked the State Department for authorization to publish it. He received permission but was forbidden to use his own name. He therefore signed the article with an "X" and sent it in. It appeared in *Foreign Affairs* in July 1947 under the title "The Sources of Soviet Conduct," just as Kennan arrived in Paris to attend the Marshall Plan meetings.

Kennan's "X-Article" analyzes the sources of Soviet conduct

The X-Article, as it came to be known, turned out to be the most widely discussed publication of the century in the field of international relations (Document 9). *Foreign Affairs* actually reprinted the article in July 1987 on the fortieth anniversary of its original publication. Its notoriety was not attributable to any mystery surrounding its author; Arthur Krock was given a copy of the original working paper by Forrestal, and he disclosed Kennan's identity in his column in the *New York Times*. Indeed, the views expressed in the article were so clearly Kennan's that his use of "X" was futile. The article's importance stemmed rather from the fact that it represented the first public use of the term "containment" as a recommendation for American policy toward the USSR.

Consistent with the Long Telegram, Kennan argued that no variations in U.S. policy could convince the Soviets to trust Washington's intentions. Traditional Russian suspicion of the West, augmented by Marxist-Leninist dogma, was too strong for that. What could and should be done was to realize that Soviet expansion could be "contained by the adroit and vigilant application of counterforce at a series of constantly shifting geographical and political points." Once confronted, the Soviets would back off and apply pressure elsewhere. If they were opposed successfully at every turn, the inability of Marxism to defeat capitalism would place tremendous strains upon the Soviet system, leading either to its self-destruction from internal pressures or to its gradual transformation into a more benign force in international relations.

The X-Article introduces the term "containment"

Kennan was not calling for military confrontation throughout the world, although columnist Walter Lippmann accused him of doing just that. Rather, he proposed a series of political, economic, and diplomatic confrontations, with the use of military force only as a last resort. Given his fears that the Truman Doctrine would lead to unwise American commitments to shaky and insincere regimes, beyond the scope of U.S. military power, he could hardly have argued otherwise. Yet the X-Article, coming so soon after the Truman Doctrine and appearing simultaneously with the Marshall Plan, was widely viewed as the logical blueprint for America's overall approach to the Cold War. The European Recovery Program, indeed, was immediately classified by nearly everyone as the first practical application of the containment theory—an interpretation which perplexed Marshall, who had never read the X-Article.

In 1946, Kennan's Long Telegram had arrived in Washington at precisely the moment when its arguments would fall on receptive ears. Now, in the summer of 1947, the X-Article's appearance provided a coherent rationale for actions that would have been taken by the Truman administration in any case. To maximize the article's impact further, events during the next several months intensified the Cold War and made Kennan's "blueprint" even more necessary to policy makers. On 29 October, Belgium, the Netherlands, and Luxembourg (the "Benelux" nations) built upon their Marshall Plan foundations by announcing plans to form a customs union—the embryonic stage of what would become the European Common Market. One month later, the London Conference of Foreign Ministers deadlocked over reparations and again failed to resolve the German question.

The Benelux countries form a European customs union

Thus, as 1947 drew to a close, the battle lines had been drawn and the strategies set in place that would dominate Cold War policy for the next four decades. Hostility between the Soviet Union and the West, of course, was nothing new. What was unusual, and disturbing, was the increasingly confrontational tone adopted by both sides as they moved incrementally toward a showdown over Germany. By early 1948, no one doubted the Cold War's reality, but how long it would remain cold was by no means certain. Without a resolution of the German question, a third world war loomed as a real possibility.

5

The Battle for Germany, 1948–1952

In 1948, the Cold War grew more ominous. Before that, as relations between wartime allies deteriorated, the international atmosphere became charged with diplomatic declarations and denunciations, as each side maneuvered for power and position within its own sphere. Europe divided into Eastern and Western zones, separated by what Churchill called the iron curtain. There were threats and bluffs aplenty, but no direct military confrontations between the superpowers and relatively little bloodshed.

The Cold War becomes dangerous in 1948

All that began to change in 1948. The next few years brought a Middle East war, the Berlin Blockade, the formation of NATO, the first Soviet A-bomb, the Communist takeover of China, and the outbreak of a brutal conflict in Korea. Only a few years after the end of history's bloodiest war, the world once again became a very dangerous place.

THE CRISES OF EARLY 1948

A series of confrontations and conflicts early in 1948 heightened anxieties and intensified tensions. In February, the Communist coup in Prague consolidated Soviet control over Czechoslovakia, the last hope for neutrality and democracy in Eastern Europe, angering the West and causing fleeting fears of war. That same month an international conference discussing navigational rights on the Danube River established a governing commission limited to states bordering the river itself. This excluded Britain, France, and the United States, but since the USSR and its Eastern European clients were in the majority, their proposal was adopted. The West, having consistently outvoted the Soviet Union in the United Nations and other international committees, now received a dose of its own medicine.

Ironically, the consolidation of Soviet control over Eastern Europe helped expedite the formation of an anti-Soviet military alliance in the West. Influenced by February's developments, Britain and France, along with the Benelux nations

(Belgium, the Netherlands, and Luxembourg), completed their negotiations and signed the Treaty of Brussels on 17 March (Document 12). An explicitly military convention, it created a 50-year alliance providing for social, economic, and military cooperation in the event of armed attack on any of the signatories. It did not identify the USSR as the likely enemy, so that it could be used against Germany if necessary. The five participants established a consultative council to oversee implementation of the treaty, and the council immediately instituted a standing military committee based in London. Contained therein were the seeds of the North Atlantic Treaty Organization that would be created the following year.

The Treaty of Brussels creates a western military alliance

A few months later war broke out in the Middle East, precipitated by the formation of a Jewish state in Palestine. This had been the main goal of the Zionist movement, a worldwide alliance of Jewish nationalists, founded in the 1890s, which promoted Jewish settlement in the Arab lands that had once been Biblical Israel. During World War I, as the British moved into the Middle East, they issued the "Balfour Declaration," asserting their willingness to create in Palestine a "national home for the Jewish people." Once Britain gained a League of Nations mandate over this area, however, its interest in Jewish settlement waned until Hitler's genocide brought the plight of the Jews back to center stage. In 1945, following full public disclosure of the Holocaust, Zionists demanded permission for 100,000 European Jewish refugees to enter Palestine. In deference to the Arab population, however, the British refused and soon found themselves the targets of a Zionist guerrilla war. Frustrated, they referred the matter to the UN, which in November 1947 voted to partition Palestine into Jewish and Arab states. Arab irregulars continued the struggle, but by 14 May 1948, the Jews emerged victorious and proclaimed the State of Israel.

Britain is forced to withdraw from Palestine

Declarations of war soon followed from Egypt, Syria, Lebanon, Transjordan, and Iraq, but their poorly trained and shabbily equipped forces were no match for the Jews. Israel won handily and expanded its territories beyond those allocated by the United Nations. Nearly one million Palestinian Arabs became refugees, and a huge reservoir of resentment was created across the Arab world.

Ironically, the USSR and the United States found themselves on the same side of this question, and both quickly recognized the new Jewish state. The Soviets supported Zionism, not out of affection for the Jews, but out of a desire to embarrass the British and expand their own influence in the region. In the United States, despite some sympathy for the anti-Soviet Arabs and some interest in Mideast oil, there was strong compassion for the Jewish people in light of the Nazi genocide. Still, the hatred and dislocation engendered among Arabs by the formation of Israel provided fertile soil for Cold War confrontations in the not-too-distant future.

Both Moscow and Washington recognize Israel

To further complicate international anxiety, in June of 1948 Stalin provoked his showdown with Tito. The Cominform expelled Yugoslavia, the Soviets withdrew their advisors, and Moscow initiated an economic boycott of the Balkan nation. By this time, however, the world's attention was focused, not on Middle East war or the crisis in Yugoslavia, but on the momentous confrontation between the Soviet Union and the United States over the city of Berlin.

THE BLOCKADE OF BERLIN

The years between 1945 and 1948 witnessed a gradual hardening of the Allied zones of occupation in Germany into what seemed to be a permanent division of that country. In 1946, the Communist and Socialist parties in the Soviet zone had merged to form the Socialist Unity Party (SED), a development which helped consolidate Communist control in the eastern part of Germany. Britain and America ended industrial shipments to the USSR, agreed to revive the economy of western Germany, and created "Bizonia" by merging their two zones of occupation in December 1946. The French, fearing the implications for German reunification, at first refused to permit their zone to join, but their attitude moderated as the Cold War intensified and Marshall Plan aid became available.

The West moves toward the creation of a separate German state

By 1948, the West was ready to consolidate its portion of Germany without further consideration of Soviet views. The London Conference of Foreign Ministers in December 1947 ended with harsh words and complete lack of progress on the German problem. Moscow then initiated a final effort to prevent Western construction of a separate German state. On 20 March 1948, Soviet delegates walked out of the Allied Control Council for Germany, charging the West with undermining four-power administration of the country. Twelve days later the Soviet Army began obstructing traffic between Berlin and the Western occupation zones.

West Berlin appears vulnerable to Soviet pressure

Berlin was an unlikely locale for the first major showdown of the Cold War. Like the country as a whole, the German capital had been divided into zones of occupation in 1945, even though it was located in the heart of Soviet-occupied eastern Germany (see map on page 46). The concept of a divided city enclosed totally within a single zone of occupation was nonsensical and was only intended to be a temporary expedient. The U.S. Army, which might have captured it in 1945 before the Red Army arrived, declined the opportunity. Since the city bore no military significance, and since it was scheduled to be divided anyway, the Americans were only too willing to let the Russians spend the lives necessary to take it. Because it was expected that U.S. troops would be withdrawn from Germany within a few years, the question of Western access to the city did not arise until Secretary of State Byrnes made his 1946 Stuttgart speech promising that U.S. forces would stay in Germany as long as the Soviet Army did. By that time it was too late to rectify the situation, and West Berlin became a permanent hostage, 90 miles behind Soviet lines. Scene of hundreds of spy thrillers and countless real-life intrigues, it would gradually become the quintessential Cold War city, brooding, gray, and heartbreakingly divided—a depressing miniature of a divided Europe and a divided world. But in 1948, it became a major piece in a very dangerous chess game between the Soviet Union and the United States.

Certainly, Stalin viewed Western actions in early 1948 with alarm. The Western decision to proceed independently toward the construction of a West German state threatened the Soviet objective of a permanently weakened Germany. Pressure on Berlin, obviously the most vulnerable spot in the Western position, might force the occupiers to withdraw. In such circumstances, the West would be humiliated, and the creation of a West German state might be indefinitely postponed.

It was, of course, risky business. But Stalin had run risks throughout his life, and this one must have seemed minor. He probably knew that most Western military analysts considered West Berlin untenable in the face of Soviet pressure, and that in the event of a conventional war in Central Europe, the Soviet Army held most of the logistical and numerical trump cards. America was largely demobilized and could not defend western Germany, let alone West Berlin, against a determined Soviet offensive. The Americans, of course, still monopolized the atomic bomb, but 30 months after Hiroshima and Nagasaki, they had made no move to use it against the Great Socialist Motherland. Would they use it to defend Berlin? Why? Which targets would they bomb, and how would they deliver the bombs? Could they be certain that B-29s would not be shot down by Soviet defenses? All in all, it didn't look like a particularly dangerous gamble.

Stalin gambles on a blockade of Berlin

So Stalin made his move, and the Cold War blossomed into outright confrontation. March, April, and May were filled with foreboding, as the Soviets demanded to examine freight and passengers on Western trains making the run to and from Berlin. On 1 June the United States, Britain, France, and the Benelux nations reached a six-power accord on Germany, involving a French decision to join their zone to Bizonia and the drafting of a federal constitution for the three combined sectors. On 18 June, the West announced the abolition of all occupation currencies in West Germany and West Berlin, with a new currency called the deutsche mark replacing them. This removed a major obstacle to rapid German economic recovery. The Soviets responded by setting up their own East zone currency on 23 June, and on the following day, they cut off all road and rail access to West Berlin. The Berlin Blockade had begun.

The British and French, who were skeptical of both the value of West Berlin and the Western ability to run the Russian blockade, deferred to the United States. Counsels in Washington were divided. The American military commander in Germany, General Lucius Clay, suggested that a column of armor and infantry be sent toward Berlin with instructions to fight its way through. He was convinced that the Soviets would back down. But Truman, Marshall, Acheson, and most of official Washington were less sanguine about the prospects. The Soviets could cut bridges before and behind the column, stranding it in hostile territory and making America look ridiculous. Truman on 29 June announced that the United States would remain in Berlin, and news was leaked that sixty B-29s were being hurriedly dispatched to England (Document 14). It caught Moscow's attention, but it didn't invalidate Stalin's reasoning concerning the likelihood of atomic war. If he called Truman's bluff, the Americans would have to fold: The planes were not configured to carry atomic weapons, and their fuel capacity was insufficient to make round trips over Soviet territory. Besides, it would never come to that. Soviet archival sources reveal Stalin's confidence that he could adjust the degree of force deployed around Berlin to avoid war.

The United States decides to remain in Berlin

After several days, it became apparent that the blockade was just that—a blockade, and not the prelude to a military strike. Now a solution presented itself. If West Berlin could be supplied by air, the Soviet Air Force would have to risk war by shooting down American planes in order to maintain the blockade. Since there were three airfields (Tempelhof, Tegel, and Gatow) in West Berlin, it was theoretically possible to fly in enough food and medicine to keep the

The Berlin Airlift frustrates the blockade

An American cargo plane flies into West Berlin during the Berlin Airlift of 1948. Stalin's decision to blockade West Berlin in June 1948 backfired. Rather than withdrawing their forces from the divided and surrounded city, the Americans airlifted food, clothing, and medical supplies to more than two million residents for eleven months. The Berlin Airlift became a symbol of American determination to defend Western Europe against Soviet expansion, and Stalin quietly ended the blockade in May 1949.

city alive. Coal would be a more difficult challenge (early experiments with dropping coal by parachute resulted in substantial air pollution and large quantities of soot on the faces and uniforms of air force observers), but by the fall of 1948, even that was flown in, as C-47 transports landed in Berlin at a rate of one every three minutes. They flew in three carefully limited air corridors from Hamburg, Hanover, and Frankfurt, and Soviet air defenses let them through.

Stalin insisted that his price for calling off the blockade was a reasonable one: agreement by the West to abandon efforts to create a West German state. But he had little leverage. The Soviet effort to starve women and children made the Americans look like heroes. Russian conventional superiority could interdict American land forces, but Stalin had no intention of going to war in the air. Unwilling to authorize the shooting down of American planes, he was forced to let the crisis drag on. As month followed month, it became obvious that his gamble had failed.

THE FORMATION OF NATO AND THE GERMAN FEDERAL REPUBLIC

Stalin's blockade did nothing to retard Western progress toward the creation of a West German state; if anything, it accelerated the process. It also provided the motivation necessary to encourage Western nations to put aside their differences and conclude a peacetime military alliance directed against the Soviet Union. This was the North Atlantic Treaty Organization (NATO), organized in Washington on 4 April 1949 (Document 15). The twelve nations of the alliance (Britain, France, Belgium, the Netherlands, Luxembourg, Italy, Portugal, Denmark, Iceland, Norway, the United States, and Canada) agreed to provide mutual assistance against any aggression occurring in the North Atlantic area and to collaborate closely in matters affecting strategic planning, arms production, and military training. NATO thus committed the United States to the military defense of its allies in Europe. It was unprecedented for the American government to conclude alliances with European powers in peacetime, and its decision to do so in 1949 underscores the severity of the Soviet threat as seen from Washington.

The Berlin Blockade hastens the creation of NATO

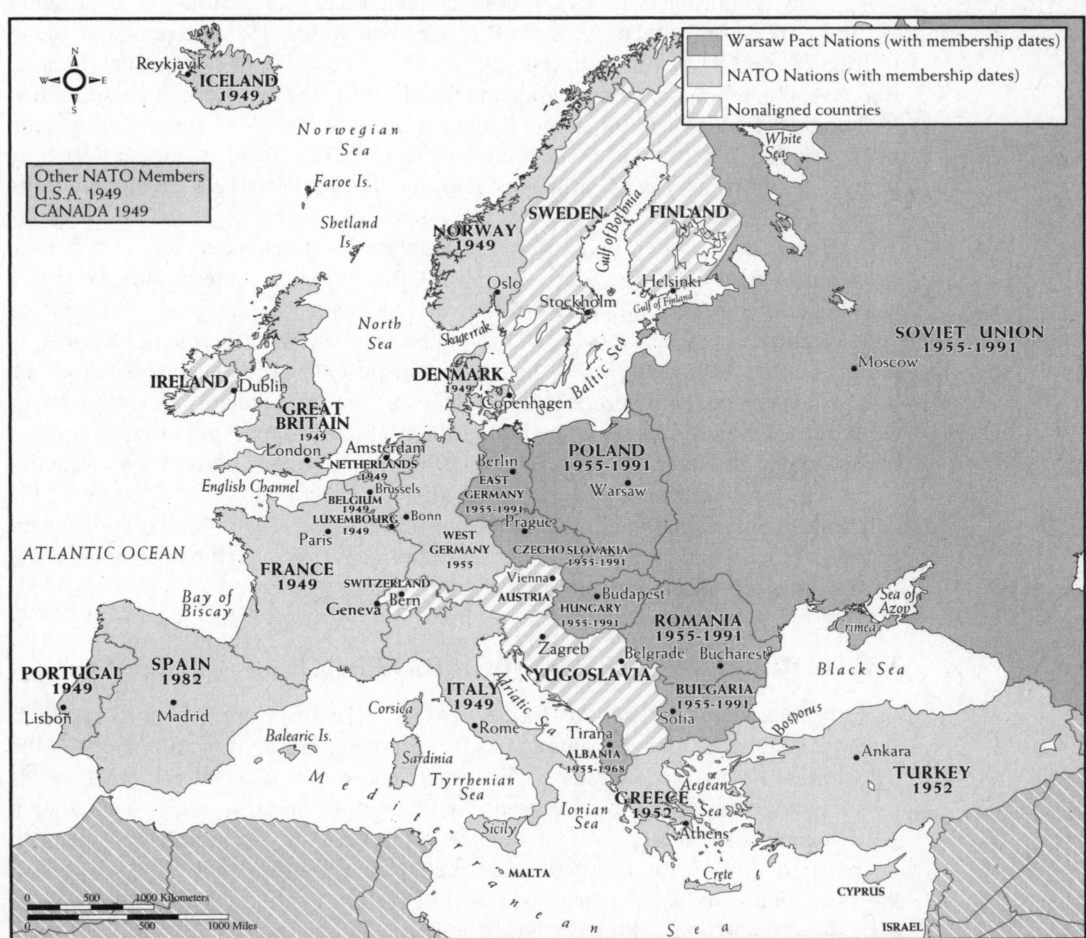

MAP 3 Divided Europe. NATO vs. Warsaw Pact, 1955–1991.

By 1955, only ten years after the end of World War II, Europe was again divided into hostile alliances. Notice that NATO, made up mainly of Western nations led by the United States, expanded by adding new members after it was founded in 1949, while the Soviet-dominated Warsaw Pact remained relatively constant from its founding in 1955 to its dissolution in 1991.

Headquartered in Paris, NATO's first commander was U.S. general Dwight D. Eisenhower. On 20 December 1950, the signatories of the Brussels Treaty (the Western European Union) agreed to merge their military establishment with that of NATO. Moscow responded with categorical denials of any intention to invade Western Europe but with no comparable alliance until the formation of the Warsaw Pact in 1955.

Two German states emerge as the blockade fails

By early 1949, Stalin was ready to acknowledge that the Berlin Blockade had failed. On 19 March, a constituent assembly in the Soviet occupation zone approved a draft constitution for a separate East German state. The following month saw the signing of an Occupation Statute for West Germany by all three Western occupying powers. The statute reserved considerable powers to the occupying authorities, but West Germans gained extensive autonomy. It virtually ended the dismantling of West German industries and removed many restrictions on German industrial activities. The Basic Law of the German Federal Republic was promulgated on 8 May, the fourth anniversary of Germany's surrender. It attempted to duplicate the democratic provisions of the old Weimar Constitution while avoiding repetition of that document's defects. The German Federal Republic, popularly known as West Germany, was officially proclaimed on 23 May, with its capital at Bonn.

Eleven days earlier, on 12 May 1949, the Berlin Blockade quietly ended. Like many subsequent Cold War confrontations, it proved to be counterproductive in that it helped to assure the completion of the very actions it was designed to prevent. In August, the Christian Democratic Union won the first West German elections; its leader, Konrad Adenauer (one of the few living anti-Nazi politicians who had served in a prominent position before Hitler's takeover), became federal chancellor on 15 September. On that same day, the last of the trials of former Nazi officials for war crimes ended in Nuremberg. Germany (at least the western portions) was clearly being transformed from an enemy into an ally of Washington. On 15 December, the new state received its first allotment of Marshall Plan aid. The official establishment of the German Democratic Republic (East Germany) on 7 October completed the formal division of Germany into two separate states.

THE ADVENT OF THE ATOMIC ARMS RACE

The USSR tests an atomic bomb

In early September of 1949, as East and West Germany were consolidating their separate statehood, and as Communists were moving rapidly toward victory in the Chinese Civil War (Chapter 6), an American aircraft detected increased levels of radioactivity over the northern Pacific. Within the next week, further such evidence corroborated the fact that one of the West's worst nightmares had been realized. On 29 August 1949, years sooner than Western leaders had expected, the USSR had conducted a successful test of its first atomic weapon. Before long, both sides would be working on hydrogen bombs, thousands of times more powerful than the earliest atomic devices. The American monopoly had ended, and the nuclear arms race was on.

From the very dawn of the atomic age, it was apparent that nuclear weapons posed a potential threat far greater than any previous weapon. It seemed obvious that

An atomic bomb explodes over Nagasaki, 9 August 1945.
The mushroom cloud that follows an atomic explosion became the symbol of the nuclear arms race between the United States and the Soviet Union. As fusion weapons made fission weapons obsolete, the destructive capacity of nuclear bombs increased geometrically, but this image of a low-yield atomic explosion continued to define atomic warfare in the public mind.

the United States, as possessor of such arms, would have an incalculable advantage in any military exchange with a potential adversary who was not so equipped. This, in turn, made it all but inevitable that other nations would seek to obtain this same technology. Indeed, since 1945 a team of Soviet scientists led by Igor Kurchatov worked secretly on just such a project.

From 1945 until 1949, as the sole possessor of atomic weapons, the United States enjoyed a tremendous advantage in military potential and diplomatic leverage. But its options were by no means unlimited. For one thing, while the United States and its allies demobilized, the Soviets kept significant military forces under arms. For another thing, there was little doubt that sooner or later they were bound to develop a nuclear capability of their own. Finally, the terrifying power of the atomic bomb, and the indiscriminate nature of the devastation it caused, placed very real moral and political constraints upon its use by the United States.

U.S. options are restricted despite its atomic monopoly

Conscious of all these factors, then, and sensitive to world opinion, the Americans sought to devise a policy which would simultaneously internationalize atomic energy, forestall Soviet acquisition of atomic weapons, and prevent a nuclear arms race. Their vehicle was the United Nations Atomic Energy Commission, an agency established in 1946 to monitor the development of nuclear technologies and ensure their peaceful use. In June of 1946, Bernard Baruch, the U.S. representative to this commission, put forth a proposal to place all fissionable materials under international control, to set up an inspection system to make sure that all nations complied, and eventually to destroy all existing atomic weapons (Document 6A). This was, on its face, a very generous proposal, for the United States seemed to be offering to forgo possession of its most powerful and effective weapons.

The Baruch Plan, however, was unacceptable to Moscow. It would have precluded the development of Soviet nuclear weapons, allowed foreign inspectors broad rights of investigation and intrusion into the closed Soviet society, and left the Americans with a permanent monopoly on the technological know-how of producing atomic weapons. It would not have required the United States to destroy its nuclear stockpile until after a system of strict controls and sanctions, enforced by an agency whose actions were not to be subject to any nation's veto, had been put into effect. Furthermore, as the Soviets knew through the work of a secret agent, Washington was secretly collaborating with London in efforts to gain control of the known sources of uranium and thorium and thus effectively monopolize atomic energy. Given all this, it is hardly surprising that the Soviets rejected the plan.

A U.S. plan to internationalize atomic energy fails

The following year, Soviet representative Andrei Gromyko put forth his own proposal, based on Moscow's perception of how disarmament should proceed. The Gromyko Plan called for the destruction of all existing nuclear stockpiles, followed by the implementation of a monitoring system based on periodic inspections of declared weapons facilities (Document 6B). It had no provisions for punishing violations or for unannounced visits to undeclared facilities. The United States, fearful that such a plan would allow the USSR to proceed secretly with its nuclear program, and unwilling to relinquish its nuclear advantage without an ironclad guarantee of Soviet compliance, would have none of this.

The positions staked out by the Baruch and Gromyko plans set the tone for the next several decades of arms control negotiations. To some extent, both the American and Soviet positions were designed as much for public consumption as they were for negotiation, with each side putting forth proposals it expected the other to reject. The United States, fearful that the Soviets would cheat, was unwilling to enter any agreement that did not provide adequate safeguards to ensure that both sides complied or to cut back its weapons production until such safeguards were in place. And the USSR, with its penchant for secrecy and its fear of revealing its strengths and weaknesses to its enemies, was loath to let any outsiders inspect either its arms plants or its military installations.

A nuclear arms race grows out of mutual fears and suspicion

The Soviet atomic blast in August 1949 destroyed any hope of preventing a nuclear arms race, at least for the time being. The Soviet nuclear program was obviously much further along than most Western experts expected, and Moscow clearly had no intention of abandoning its efforts to catch up with the West. And, as the Soviets began building their own atomic stockpile, the Americans abandoned any thought of agreeing to dismantle theirs. In matters of national security, each side preferred to rely on its own devices rather than international agreements, and neither side was anxious to grant the other access to its facilities. The nuclear arms race became the most frightening and ominous aspect of the Cold War, transmitting to that conflict an importance far beyond the policy goals of the leaders of East and West. At the same time, by making all-out war increasingly unthinkable, these horrific weapons placed serious constraints upon the options and exploits of these leaders.

WEST GERMANY'S ROLE IN A STABLE EUROPE

Meanwhile, as the West tried to come to grips with the reality of an adversary armed with nuclear weapons, Moscow stared at a hellish nightmare of its own. A strong German state, politically democratic and economically dynamic, was beginning to arise out of the ashes of war-torn western Germany.

West Germany became such a success story that it is difficult to remember how unlikely that success seemed in 1949. Democracy, after all, had never been the German way. The failure of the Weimar Republic, still fresh in the minds of most, argued against high expectations for the Federal Republic. Books like A. J. P. Taylor's *The Course of German History* (1945) asserted that Germans had a psychological predilection for authoritarian rule; less scholarly works claimed that they were genetically incapable of self-government. Brave indeed were the leaders who were prepared to stake their reputations on the survivability of German democracy.

Many factors combined to assure that, as a popular saying put it, "Bonn is not Weimar." Marshall Plan aid, managed skillfully by Finance Minister Ludwig Erhard, rebuilt the German economy and made possible the *Wirtschaftswunder* (economic miracle), a fifteen-year period of full employment, geometric increases in the gross national product, and unprecedented prosperity. Soviet hostility from the Berlin Blockade through the building of the Berlin Wall in 1961 (Chapter 10) united West Germans behind their government. Equally important was the role played by Adenauer, a crusty, cynical survivor of the concentration camp at Buchenwald who guided the Federal Republic through its first fourteen years. As early as 1919, he had advocated separating the Rhineland from Germany and had envisaged future Franco-German economic cooperation. Nicknamed "Der Alte" (the Old Man), he blended a passionate commitment to democracy with a paternalistic, authoritarian style that many Germans found reassuring. His personification of democratic virtues, combined with his systematic reiteration of the necessity of eventual German reunification (despite his personal misgivings on the subject), provided an indispensable transition between despotism and self-government. By the time he retired at the age of 87 in 1963, the survival of democracy in West Germany was no longer in doubt.

West Germany prospers under Adenauer and Erhard

The new nation quickly involved itself with the flourishing movement toward greater unity in Western Europe. French Foreign Minister Robert Schuman and French Marshall Plan director Jean Monnet proposed in May 1950 the Schuman Plan, designed to integrate the coal and steel industries of the West. One year later it became the European Coal and Steel Community (ECSC), as six nations signed a treaty at Paris: France, Italy, the Benelux nations, and . . . West Germany! Schuman, Monnet, and Adenauer wanted to connect the German and French coal and steel industries so closely that war between the two nations would become not only unthinkable but economically impossible. France's reasons were obvious: With West Germany growing in strength and with Britain preparing to withdraw from the continent, Paris had no choice but to seek some sort of détente with Bonn. Adenauer was equally interested, seeing the French as a valuable counterweight to the USSR. His eagerness to cooperate with Paris, coupled with his assurances that West Germany would never seek to renew Germany's longstanding

West Germany and France move toward cooperation

claims to Alsace and Lorraine, laid the foundations for the astonishing improvement in Franco-German relations that flourished in the 1960s.

France could live and prosper with German economic recovery, but German rearmament was a different story. Shortly after the outbreak of the Korean War (Chapter 7), Washington, fearing a Soviet plan to divert U.S. forces from Korea by causing trouble in Europe, pushed strongly for the creation of a West German military force. French premier René Pleven, hoping to scuttle the idea before it took hold, offered a counterproposal in October 1950: The Pleven Plan, calling for the creation of a multinational European army, composed of small contingents from each nation, as an adjunct to ECSC. Adenauer signed on, hopeful that this European Defense Community (EDC) would, if successful, render further Allied occupation of West Germany superfluous.

France proposes a European Defense Community

The Pleven Plan, despite its eventual failure, reveals some interesting things about the Cold War attitudes of Paris, London, and Bonn. On 27 May 1952, the EDC treaties were signed at Paris by the six signatories of the ECSC. Britain signed an additional protocol pledging to send assistance to any EDC member attacked by any nonsignatory, and both Washington and London swore to consider threats to the EDC as threats to their own security. But the French National Assembly held up ratification, and with Stalin's death and the end of the Korean War in 1953, the need for EDC appeared less urgent. By the summer of 1954, the French defeat in Indochina (Chapter 11) convinced the French army, beaten twice in fourteen years, that to surrender sovereignty over part of its forces would be dishonorable. That sentiment found considerable support in the French Assembly, which after five years of relations with Adenauer was less concerned with a resurgent Germany than with the dangers of delegating sovereignty to a supranational body. As if these were not sufficient nails in EDC's coffin, Britain's consistent refusal to become a direct signatory to the agreement (in keeping with London's fidelity to isolation from the continent), not to mention the lack of any organized political body to control a multinational army, gave the assembly a multitude of pretexts for rejecting France's own proposal in August 1954. The USSR was delighted with what appeared to be a spoke in the wheel of the drive for German rearmament; yet EDC's failure was only the prelude to the admission of West Germany to NATO in 1955, a result which was not at all to Moscow's taste. The German question continued to defy settlement while refusing to go away.

After Stalin's death, France vetoes its own plan

STALIN AND THE GERMAN PROBLEM

After the failure of the Berlin Blockade, Soviet policy toward Germany proceeded along three tracks simultaneously. The first track involved the abandonment of the policy of plunder that Moscow had followed in its zone since 1945. Dismantling had never been particularly profitable: entire German factories, cut into numbered sections and shipped east, sat rusting for months on rail sidings as the Soviet bureaucracy proved incapable of utilizing them. Now it stopped altogether, as Moscow became more interested in rebuilding rather than further destroying the German Democratic Republic, its new client state. If the existence of two Germanies could not be prevented, prudence seemed to dictate that one of them should be strengthened for incorporation into the Soviet system of buffer states.

Track two led through Eastern Europe, as the process of bringing the Soviet satellites into line intensified. By mid-1948, Poland, Czechoslovakia, Hungary, Romania, and Bulgaria were safely within the Russian orbit, while Yugoslavia remained just as safely outside it. As long as any chance existed that the Grand Alliance might yet serve some purpose, Stalin was willing to tolerate non-Communist governments—provided they maintained friendly relations with Moscow. But with the West revitalizing and unifying its zones of Germany, deviation from orthodox Communism was no longer viable. Stalin spent his remaining years in an effort to ensure strict adherence to his wishes through a series of brutal purges and show trials.

Stalin adopts a three-track policy toward Germany

Hungary felt the pinch first with the arrest of Joszef Cardinal Mindszenty in December 1948 following the refusal of the Hungarian Catholic Church to make concessions to the government. Tortured, tried for conspiracy, and sentenced to life imprisonment, Mindszenty was released during a brief uprising in 1956 (Chapter 8) and found refuge in the American legation in Budapest. There he became an international symbol of resistance to Communism until he was permitted to emigrate to the United States in 1971. Similar charges of conspiracy were leveled against Hungarian foreign minister László Rajk in June 1949; his conviction was the signal for a wholesale purge of dissident Communists. That same month, Bulgarian deputy premier Traicho Kostov was arrested and charged with ideological deviation and high treason. With ten of his associates, he was executed in December.

Purges and show trials enforce Communist orthodoxy in Eastern Europe

For two years, possibly because Stalin was distracted by the Korean War, Eastern Europe lay quiet. When another round of purges began in 1952, the targets were predominantly Jewish. The vicious anti-Semitism that characterized Stalin's final year resulted in the liquidation of the Jewish intellectual elite of the Communist parties of Czechoslovakia, Hungary, and Romania. First to fall was Ana Pauker, one of the principal architects of the communist takeover of Romania, purged from the Politburo and Central Committee secretariat in May 1952. That November the former general secretary of the Czechoslovak Communist Party, Rudolf Slánský, was tried with thirteen other party leaders (nearly all Jewish) on charges of treason, espionage, and sabotage. Three were sentenced to life imprisonment; the others, including Slánský, were hanged and cremated. Their ashes were poured into the ruts of a dirt road outside Prague.

Two months later, Stalin announced the discovery of the "Doctors' Plot," an alleged conspiracy by a number of Jewish physicians in the Soviet Union to undermine the health of leading Soviet officials. Shortly thereafter, more than 30 Jewish leaders of the Hungarian Communist Party were purged. There is no telling where all this would have stopped had not Stalin died of a stroke in March 1953. The Eastern European purges terrorized Communist bureaucrats and politicians while cowing them into submission to every directive from Moscow, no matter how trivial its nature. Without question, Stalin's second track succeeded (at least according to his own standards): It provided him with a terrified but unquestioningly loyal Eastern European leadership, ready to serve on the front lines against a reinvigorated and newly dangerous Germany.

Stalin's third and final track targeted Germany itself. On 19 September, a Western communiqué implied that West Germany would soon be contributing directly to NATO defense. The following week, with the Korean War (for the time being) running in favor of the United States, a meeting of Eastern European foreign ministers convened in Prague to discuss the dangers of German remilitarization. This conference issued the Prague proposals: German remilitarization should be forbidden, a unified and neutralized German state should be constructed without delay, and all occupation forces should be withdrawn within one year of the signing of a German peace treaty. East and West Germany would have equal voice on a council charged with creating a new constitution for the entire country. Apparently, Moscow was prepared to make concessions, even to the extent of giving up complete control over East Germany, in order to prevent West German rearmament.

The Prague Proposals suggest a neutralized Germany

The Prague proposals went nowhere. The Truman administration, having come under withering domestic political fire because of earlier concessions to the Soviets in Eastern Europe, was unwilling to rise to Stalin's bait in the midst of the Korean War. Even had Washington been more responsive, there is no guarantee that such negotiations would have succeeded. By its warlike posture and belligerent language, Moscow had consolidated its hold on Eastern Europe while concealing the extent of its military inferiority vis-à-vis the West. But that same conduct had encouraged the West to create a military alliance against Soviet expansion. Stalin, knowing that he had no intention of invading Western Europe (and assuming that Washington must know this as well), probably interpreted NATO as a mechanism designed to roll back Soviet gains in Eastern Europe. Truman, knowing that he had no intention of invading Eastern Europe (and assuming that Moscow must know this as well), saw Soviet opposition to NATO as designed to weaken and subvert Western Europe in preparation for either a military or a peaceful takeover. And so it went: Each side was concerned with not only the *intentions* but the *capabilities* of the other. Intentions, of course, could always change, sometimes with devastating speed. It was prudent to presume that they would and to defend against capabilities. Because of these suspicions, it was impossible in 1950 for the two sides to sit down and negotiate the key issue that divided them and divided Europe: the German problem.

These conditions also destroyed Stalin's final third-track initiative on the German question, launched on 10 March 1952. With the EDC Treaty almost ready for signature and a West German army seemingly about to spring out of the paving stones of Bonn, Molotov dispatched a note proposing four-power talks on German unification. This document went beyond the Prague proposals by declaring that as long as a unified Germany was neutral, Moscow would be willing to permit it to rearm. The note astonished Washington, which rejected it two weeks later, unwilling to jeopardize the fragile EDC in exchange for lengthy, acrimonious, and (in Truman's opinion) probably fruitless negotiations with the Soviets.

Stalin startles the West by suggesting a reunified Germany

Was Stalin serious? Would he have surrendered control over East Germany in exchange for a neutralized, unified state? Adam Ulam believed that the danger of a large German army pointed eastward at a time before the USSR had been able to stockpile many atomic weapons was enough to force Stalin to make serious concessions. He pointed out that any German elections, whether supervised by the United Nations (as Washington expected) or by the four occupying powers (as Moscow wished), would inevitably have led to a non-Communist government. Even if all the East Germans had voted Communist, the West had 75 percent of the population—and the Communist share of the vote there had never reached 10 percent. It is, of course, possible that the Soviet action was, as Vladislav Zubok contends, a carefully orchestrated bluff, designed to derail EDC while bogging the West down in interminable German peace talks.

Washington's rapid rejection, understandable though it was, scuttled any chance of finding out. Although they could not say so publicly, Western leaders were uncomfortable with any prospect of a unified Germany, particularly a neutralized one, since this would deprive them of the advantages conferred by possession of the industrialized, densely populated western sector. Stalin's calling of their bluff was clearly unwelcome. Even had they been willing to discuss the matter, a decision to sit down with Stalin would have been politically hazardous. With anti-Communist hostility high among Americans and a presidential election only eight months away, the prospect of direct talks with the USSR would have frightened any American politician. It would, as Ulam said, be nearly another decade before an American president could say, "Let us never negotiate out of fear, but let us never fear to negotiate."

THE PERSISTENCE OF THE GERMAN PROBLEM

Stalin's three tracks led not to a roundhouse in Berlin but to dimly lit sidings in the remote countryside of Cold War Europe. When he died in March 1953, the face of postwar Europe had been, in essence, fixed for the next 35 years. Eastern Europe was firmly within the Soviet camp, with the exception of Yugoslavia (with which Stalin's successors would bury the hatchet in 1955) and tiny Albania (whose alignment with China against the USSR in the 1960s was more humorous than dangerous). Marshall Plan aid enabled Western Europe to rebuild its economies, and NATO provided it with a Cold War military shield against perceived Soviet ambitions and genuine Soviet capabilities. The legacy of bitterness and distrust between Washington and Moscow was so great that future efforts at détente would be halting, tentative, and unsatisfying. In the midst of it all stood Germany, the only nation (after Austrian reunification in 1955) divided by the iron curtain, a country of barbed wire, watchtowers, guard dogs, minefields, and armies poised to spring across heavily defended borders in defense of the status quo. As the world's attention wandered to Cold War disputes in Asia and the disruptions posed by the triumph of Communism in China, every nation's leadership kept one eye focused on Germany. The German problem had still not been solved, and as long as it persisted, there would be no end to the Cold War.

6

The Communist Revolution in China, 1946–1950

The Cold War's roots and origins were mainly European, with conflicts in Europe dominating its first few years and shaping perceptions and policies on both sides. By mid-1949, however, relative equilibrium had been achieved in Europe. The Soviets had consolidated control over Eastern Europe, and the West had neither the will nor inclination to challenge this control. But the Truman Doctrine, Marshall Plan, Berlin Airlift, and North Atlantic Treaty had helped block further Soviet gains, restoring the West's initiative and confidence.

The illusion of Western success, however, was soon shattered by developments in Asia. On 1 October 1949, Chinese Communist leader Mao Zedong proclaimed in Beijing a new socialist state called the People's Republic of China. The Communist victory in China's civil war, and the establishment of a militant socialist regime in the world's most populous nation, immensely boosted the Communist cause and sent shock waves throughout the Western world.

THE NATIONALISTS AND THE COMMUNISTS

Off and on since the late 1920s, China's Communists had been fighting the Nationalist regime of Jiang Jieshi (Chiang Kai-shek). At various points and in various ways the Soviets had helped China's Communists, and Americans had aided the Nationalists, but neither superpower had been fully engaged, and each was somewhat ambivalent about its Chinese clients.

Nationalists work to unify China in the 1920s

In 1912, following the fall of China's last imperial dynasty, Chinese revolutionary Sun Yixian (Sun Yat-Sen) had founded the National People's Party, the Guomindang (Kuomintang). Dedicated to nationalism and democracy, its fortunes had fluctuated in its early years as China disintegrated into territories ruled by regional warlords. By the 1920s, however, the party had emerged as the leading force in the struggle to reunite China. The Soviets, aligning with this national unification effort, sent agents to China in 1923 to help Sun reorganize and strengthen his movement. Sun's disciple Jiang Jieshi went to Moscow to study

Soviet military techniques and then returned to create a Guomindang army with the help of Soviet advisors. After Sun died in 1925, Jiang led his new army on the Great Northern Expedition of 1926–1928, conquering some warlords and cutting deals with others. By 1928, he had unified much of China under his new Nationalist government, headquartered at Nanjing (Nanking).

Born into a petty noble family, Jiang had chosen a military career and remained at heart a military man. Surrounded by Western advisors, converted to Methodist Christianity, and married to an American-educated Chinese woman whose brother was a wealthy industrialist, he initially seemed to represent a Westernizing democratic trend. But the opportunistic militarism that helped him unify his country did not serve him well as its leader. Distrustful of the masses and uncomfortable with democracy, he soon turned his government into a repressive single-party dictatorship characterized by corruption and reliance on military force.

Communists ally with Nationalists in efforts to unify China

Meanwhile, in 1921, a group of Marxist intellectuals had founded the Chinese Communist Party (CCP), hoping to initiate in China a Soviet-style revolution. Aided by Soviet agents, they had joined the Communist International (Comintern), the Soviet-led organization designed to help spread Communism throughout the world. In 1923, on Comintern orders, the fledgling CCP allied itself with the Guomindang by joining that organization. This arrangement seemed to make sense: From a Marxist-Leninist perspective, the Communists were natural allies of newly emerging nationalist groups in their struggle against Western imperialism.

Nationalists turn on Communists and massacre them in Shanghai

But the Nationalist–Communist alliance did not last. Alarmed by the CCP's growing strength, and fearful that the Soviets were merely using him to pave the way for a Communist takeover, Jiang soon turned against his Communist allies. In 1926, he staged a *coup* in the city of Guangzhou (Canton), arresting some of his Soviet advisors and removing many CCP leaders. The following year, with the tacit support of Western capitalists, he unleashed a reign of terror in Shanghai, using local gangs to slaughter numerous Communists. The Soviets, hoping to remain on good terms with Jiang as China's emerging new leader, insisted that the CCP maintain the alliance in spite of Jiang's persecution, displaying a callous pragmatism that left Chinese Communists distrustful of their Soviet mentors. Jiang, meanwhile, showed no signs of conciliation: In 1931, having consolidated his control over much of China, he launched a series of "extermination campaigns" designed to rid his country of the Communist presence.

Mao emerges as leader of peasant-based Communist movement

In this period the CCP, devastated and decimated, acquired a new leader with a new vision. Mao Zedong, who came from a peasant family in south central China, believed not only in Marxist class struggle but also in the vast untapped potential of the Chinese peasantry. As an early member of the CCP, he did organizational work among urban workers in Shanghai, but finding it frustrating and uninspiring, he returned in 1925 to his native Hunan province to work among the peasants. There he found that they were already forming associations, creating paramilitary organizations, and displaying a revolutionary mentality. He became convinced that, contrary to orthodox Marxist expectations, he could lead a socialist revolution based on the peasants. This conviction, combined with his dynamic leadership skills, his driving and restless intellect, and his unshakable faith in his ability to transform society by mobilizing the masses, would soon make him the dominant figure in Chinese Communism.

Aided by some Soviet advisors, Mao and his comrades set up in south central China a "Soviet Republic" with its own laws, institutions, and primitive army. On four occasions from 1931 through 1933 they fought off Jiang's extermination campaigns, but a fifth campaign was too massive for them to resist. In desperation, in October of 1934, the beleaguered Communists abandoned their territory and began a perilous yearlong flight with the Nationalists in hot pursuit. It came to be called the Long March, one of Communism's most heroic epics. In October 1935, after 6,000 miles of constant danger and struggle, the vestiges of Mao's forces finally made it to the relative safety of Yan'an, a town in northwest China. There, shielded by distance and rugged terrain, they regrouped and reorganized, setting up a simple, egalitarian society among the sturdy peasants of this primitive, arid, inhospitable region.

Long March helps Communists escape Nationalist assault

Although Jiang, still determined to crush the Communists, sent periodic bombing raids against Yan'an, looming war with Japan proved a major distraction. Having forcibly annexed the northeastern Chinese province of Manchuria in 1931–1932, the Japanese military expanded its operations and increased its belligerence. Jiang tried to ignore the Japanese and focus on fighting the Communists, but this effort dismayed his own supporters, and in 1936 he was kidnapped by one of his warlords and forced to form a "united front" with the Communists against Japan. Under Moscow's instructions the CCP agreed, and when the conflict with Japan became an all-out war in 1937, the Nationalists and Communists were once again "allies."

Nationalists and Communists form united front against Japan

Over the next eight years, despite their formal alliance, the Nationalists and Communists battled both Japan and each other. The Communists proved more effective: With their talent for organizing peasants and experience at using guerrilla tactics to stave off Jiang's attacks, they were a painful thorn in the side of Japanese invaders and occupiers. Their bravery, dedication, and focus on reform helped them also to expand their support among the Chinese peasants.

Meanwhile the Guomindang army, committed to conventional warfare, proved no match for the Japanese forces. The Nationalist government, forced to flee from its power base by Japan's conquest of eastern China, survived only by moving its headquarters deep in the interior to Chongqing (Chungking). Riddled with corruption and incompetence, it further alienated peasants by subjecting them to grain requisitions and forced labor. The United States, after joining the war against Japan in 1941, grew increasingly ambivalent about its Nationalist allies. To Americans on the scene, Jiang appeared as a petty dictator who was misgoverning his people, undermining the war effort, and squandering U.S. aid. But to his many supporters in the West, Jiang was still a heroic ally struggling against both Japanese militarism and Marxist-Leninist socialism.

Communists gain support and Nationalists lose it during was against Japan

In the end Japan was defeated, not by Chinese resistance, but by the gross overextension of Japanese forces and by America's massive resources and devastating technology. The United States, therefore, expected to play a leading role in determining the future of postwar China. But the USSR, which joined the war against Japan only in its final stage, was also determined to play a role. As a result, the ongoing conflict between the Chinese Nationalists and Communists soon became part of the emerging Cold War in East Asia.

AMERICAN ATTEMPTS AT MEDIATION

Japan's surrender in 1945 did not bring peace to China. Indeed, as soon as the world war ended, civil war was in the air. The "united front" between Nationalists and Communists had been a hollow façade since 1941, when Nationalist forces attacked the headquarters unit of a key Communist army. By 1945, both sides had begun to position themselves for renewed hostilities once the Japanese were gone. But civil war was delayed by the maneuvering of the superpowers, neither of which had a good grasp on the situation in China.

The Americans, largely unaware of the CCP's strength and its strained relations with Moscow, were anxious to prevent a civil war, fearing it might help the Soviets dominate Communist-controlled parts of China, much as they were imposing their control over Eastern Europe. The United States thus labored to create a Chinese coalition government, trying to restore the "united front" between Nationalists and Communists. Somewhat incongruously, the Americans also gave continued aid and support to their wartime ally, the Nationalist government, which was seeking to crush the Communists and control all of China.

Americans try to avert Chinese civil war after Japan's defeat

Dependent on American aid, the Nationalists played along with the "coalition" charade, even though their overall goal was to destroy the CCP. General Patrick Hurley, the special U.S. emissary in China, arranged face-to-face talks between Jiang and Mao in Chongqing from August to October of 1945. For public consumption, the two agreed to combine their forces and cooperate in supporting human rights and representative government. Seldom have words meant less. Even as the talks went on, both sides were actively fighting for control of northern China.

The Nationalists, with U.S. support, at first gained the upper hand. The Americans ordered Japan's defeated forces to surrender to the Guomindang army everywhere in China but Manchuria, which had been designated at Yalta as a Soviet zone of operations. American ships and planes moved Nationalist troops quickly into China's major cities, and U.S. Marines were sent to northern China to help prevent Communist expansion. When the CCP forces tried to extend control across northern China, the Nationalists ordered Japanese troops still there to forcibly resist them—an effective ploy, but a public relations nightmare. Before long, using such tactics, the Nationalists had gained nominal control over most of China and effective control of almost all its cities and railways. The Guomindang army was three times as large as the CCP's and, thanks to U.S. aid, far better equipped. To all appearances, Jiang Jieshi was once again emerging as master of China.

U.S. support helps Nationalists occupy Chinese cities

But appearances proved deceptive. The Chinese people were disillusioned with the Nationalists, who forfeited much of their remaining support by rampant profiteering in reoccupied cities. By failing to carry out meaningful land reform, moreover, they left open the village gates to the CCP, which had worked assiduously to earn peasant trust. And the Communists, despite their apparent weakness, were not without resources. Having mobilized the northern Chinese countryside against the Japanese, they had established bases there from which they could operate effectively. Having fought Japan more convincingly than the Nationalists, and having implemented land and social reforms in the areas they controlled, the Communists had won the allegiance of the local peasants. Furthermore, the Soviet occupation of Manchuria would enable them to move into that area and gain access to many weapons and supplies left behind by Japan.

Communists and Nationalists in China.
Mao Zedong and Jiang Jieshi (Chiang Kai-shek), bitter lifelong enemies, toast each other in a sham show of solidarity in October 1945. Despite U.S. efforts to mediate, by this time Mao's Communists and Jiang's Nationalists were battling for northern China, a fight that would soon erupt into all-out civil war.

But the Soviets were no more in touch with Chinese reality than the Americans. Stalin, who neither understood nor trusted the CCP, underestimated its potential strength. Ever the cautious pragmatist, he sought simultaneously to help the Chinese Communists and stay on good terms with Jiang. In August 1945, following through on an agreement made at Yalta, he concluded a Treaty of Friendship and Alliance with the Nationalists, ironically giving Moscow a stake in the survival of Jiang's regime. Soviet troops in Manchuria did aid the CCP, allowing its forces to control key positions and help themselves to Japanese equipment. But when American-assisted Guomindang forces defeated the Communists in south Manchuria late in 1945, Stalin once again urged the CCP to cooperate with the Nationalists, assuming they were stronger and thus that Soviet interests would best be served by a new "united front." After withdrawing their last forces from Manchuria in May 1946, the Soviets supplied little aid or support to their Chinese Communist comrades.

Stalin orders CCP to cooperate with Nationalists

The Americans, meanwhile, persisted in their efforts to arrange a Chinese coalition government. General George C. Marshall, wartime U.S. Army chief of staff, was sent to China in December 1945 to negotiate a Nationalist–Communist truce. Using the promise of U.S. aid, coupled with the threat of its withdrawal, he got the Nationalists to agree to a ceasefire early in 1946. The Communists went along, mainly to buy time, but efforts to form a workable coalition foundered. The CCP wanted a share of real power, and Jiang, ever fearful of Communist subversion, refused. U.S. policy vacillated between evenhanded mediation and support for the Nationalists, but in trying to have it both ways, the Americans succeeded at neither. Continued U.S. assistance to the Nationalists undermined Marshall's credibility with the CCP, and his belated embargo on arms shipments to Jiang came too late to restore it. By mid-spring the truce had broken down, and by fall of 1946, a full-fledged civil war was raging in Manchuria. In January 1947, when Marshall returned to Washington to become secretary of state, it was obvious that his mission had failed.

U.S. efforts to avert Chinese civil war fail

THE CHINESE CIVIL WAR

The Nationalists again gained an early advantage in the renewed civil war. Sweeping across northern China in 1946, they captured the major cities, controlled the railways, and even conquered Yan'an, the longtime CCP headquarters. Communist leaders fled, and their sympathizers in the countryside were brutally rooted out by Nationalist soldiers and landlords. Deprived of its main bases, and scattered throughout the countryside, the CCP seemed to have been dealt a crippling blow.

But the Communist setback was less serious than it seemed. As experienced guerrilla warriors, the CCP forces had learned to retreat and avoid direct confrontation when the odds were against them. And having treated the peasantry well in areas they controlled, the Communists could subsequently count on broad popular support. The Nationalists held the cities and railways, but these were like islands and bridges in the midst of a hostile sea. The Guomindang army was widely regarded as an occupying force, much as the Japanese had been, in much of northern China.

Besides, by the time Soviet forces had withdrawn from Manchuria, the CCP had established a power base there. There, as in northern China before, they cultivated the peasants, carried out reforms, and organized the countryside for struggle on their behalf. There, for the first time, they equipped their troops with modern weapons, thanks to the unintended largess left behind by the Japanese. There, if the Nationalists attacked, they were willing to make their stand.

Communists set up power base in Manchuria

By 1947 Manchuria was the main front in the Chinese civil war. Perceiving a chance to destroy the CCP, Jiang committed his best troops to that region, ignoring the danger of overextending his forces and fighting the Communists on their own turf. Under the skillful leadership of General Lin Biao, the Communist "People's Liberation Army" retreated to the northeast, avoiding direct combat and forcing Jiang's army to further extend its lines. Then, in July, Lin began a stunning counterattack, launching a series of raids that divided the Nationalist forces. Jiang, who trusted neither the Manchurian authorities nor his own commanders, insisted on calling all the shots from a distance. He refused to allow a retreat until too late, leaving large elements of his army trapped in Manchurian cities. Although the battle for Manchuria raged until fall of 1948, by late 1947 the Communists had the upper hand.

Nationalists invade Manchuria but Communists counterattack

MAP 4 The Chinese Civil War, 1946–1949.
Early in the Chinese Civil War, the Nationalists, with more modern equipment and a much larger army than the Communists, seemed to have the upper hand. Observe, however, that after an early retreat into Manchuria, the Communists turned the tide in 1948 and drove the Nationalists in 1949 from mainland China to the island of Taiwan, shocking the Western world.

The Manchurian debacle stunned the United States, whose policymakers soon concluded that the Nationalists could no longer win the civil war. Quite wrongly, however, they assumed that the Communists could not win either, due to the size of Jiang's forces and superiority of his equipment. Washington, therefore, braced for a protracted struggle that might split China into Communist and Nationalist entities. Preoccupied with Europe, the Truman administration was unwilling to commit U.S. forces and massive resources to Jiang Jieshi's defense. But neither was it willing to abandon him entirely and face charges of "sellout" from the American "China Lobby." So the United States continued to send aid, pouring in good money after bad.

U.S. aid to Nationalists proves inadequate

The Soviets were no more perceptive than U.S. leaders. Rather than urging the Chinese Communists to follow up their victories, Moscow instead advised them to be cautious and consolidate their position in Manchuria before moving on. Soviet assistance to the CCP remained minimal, and Soviet relations with the Nationalist regime continued unimpaired. As late as summer of 1948, as they confronted each other in Germany over West Berlin, neither superpower expected that the collapse of Jiang's forces was imminent.

But imminent it was. By November 1948 the Communists had conquered Manchuria, winning a decisive victory that added to their momentum. The CCP not only showed that it could beat the best Guomindang forces, it also captured from them large amounts of American-supplied equipment. Communist morale soared, while that of the Nationalists waned, so that some Guomindang troops offered scant resistance while others defected to the Communists. That same year, the Nationalist government imposed an ill-conceived currency reform that accelerated inflation so much that its money became almost worthless. This fiasco cost Jiang his support among China's urban middle classes, destroying the remnants of his political base.

Communists gain momentum as Nationalists retreat

As battle lines moved south, CCP soldiers received aid and sustenance from the peasants, effectively mobilized by the party leaders to hamper the Nationalist forces. In October and November of 1948, a massive battle developed near the Huai River north of Nanjing. The Battle of Huai-hai, as it was known, pitted a half million Communist troops against a similar number of Nationalist soldiers. But hundreds of thousands of peasants aided the CCP, digging miles of tank traps to stop the Guomindang armored units. Jiang Jieshi took command of his troops but could not stave off defeat. When the dust had settled, the Nationalists had lost over 200,000 soldiers and were cut off from units further north. By the year's end, Beijing (which the Nationalists called Beiping) was surrounded by Communist forces; in January of 1949, its Nationalist commander surrendered. China's once and future capital had fallen into Communist hands.

Communists win decisive battles and take Beijing

By early 1949, the Nationalists were in disarray. Their support had evaporated, their armies were losing, and their confidence was gone. Two decades of corruption, incompetence, oppression, and disaster had taken a heavy toll. Jiang himself temporarily "retired," in hopes that a new leader could strike a deal with the CCP, but this effort came to naught. The Communists, now that victory was within their grasp, had no incentive to bargain. Although they were no less authoritarian and brutal than the Nationalists, they were better organized, better led, more idealistic, less corrupt, and more tuned in to the people's needs and concerns. In an earlier era, it might have been said that the "Mandate of Heaven" had passed to Mao Zedong.

THE COMMUNIST VICTORY AND ITS IMPACT

The Communist capture of Beijing in early 1949, following the decisive CCP victories in Manchuria and at Huai-hai, showed the world that the Nationalists were in trouble. By the end of April, Communist troops had crossed the Yangzi

River and captured Nanjing, the Nationalist capital. The next month they seized the great port city of Shanghai. The Nationalist leaders moved south to Guangzhou, where they set up a temporary headquarters, but by October they had fled even there. By May 1950, when the fighting finally ceased, the Communists controlled mainland China.

Nationalists flee to Taiwan as Communists control mainland China

The Nationalists, meanwhile, had fled to Taiwan (also known in the West as Formosa), a large island about 100 miles off the southeast China coast. Here, protected by the distance and eventually by the U.S. Navy's Seventh Fleet, Jiang and his followers regrouped. The Communist victory was thus incomplete: Based on Taiwan, the Nationalist regime continued to exist and to press its claim as China's legitimate government throughout the Cold War.

The Communist victory was momentous nonetheless. In October of 1949, when Mao Zedong proclaimed the formation of the People's Republic of China (Document 17), his new government could claim authority over more than half a billion people. In just a few years, the Communist tide had swept over Eastern Europe and much of East Asia. From the Baltic to the Pacific, from the Arctic Ocean to the South China Sea, a vast landmass with a third of all humanity was under Communist rule. "The East is Red," proclaimed the Chinese Communists, and those words resonated ominously in the Western world.

Loss of China seen as a major U.S. setback

The Chinese Communist victory was a severe setback for the United States, where the Truman administration was soon blamed for "losing China." It came hard on the heels of reports that, in August 1949, the Soviets had tested their first atomic bomb—years ahead of Western expectations. Although the U.S. State Department issued a "White Paper" defending its China policies and exposing the corruption and incompetence of Jiang's regime (Document 16), it also portrayed Mao as a Soviet agent and Communist China as a new Soviet satellite.

Spy scandals and China's fall foster U.S. Red Scare

These developments intensified a "Red Scare" that was sweeping America, fostered by fears of Communist infiltration. Indeed, based on information from Soviet defectors and a highly secret VENONA project that decrypted covert Soviet messages, Western agencies had learned that some key Westerners were Soviet spies. In 1946, Canada revealed that British scientist Alan Nunn May, working with the Manhattan Project that developed America's atomic bomb, had supplied nuclear secrets and materials to the USSR. In the U.S. Congress, a House Un-American Activities Committee then held public hearings looking into claims that Communist agents had infiltrated the U.S. government. In 1948, these hearings produced charges that State Department official Alger Hiss was a Communist, fueling a growing public impression of traitors in high places. The Soviet atomic test and birth of "Red China," coming the next year, added to widespread fears that such traitors were undermining America and its allies.

In January 1950 Klaus Fuchs, another British scientist who had worked on the Manhattan project, confessed to spying for the Soviets, and Alger Hiss was convicted of perjury in connection with charges that he had also done so. The next month Senator Joseph McCarthy of Wisconsin leveled accusations of "Communist conspiracy" at the U.S. government, charging that over 200 Soviet agents worked in

Senator McCarthy in Action.
Flanked by attorney Roy Cohn, Senator Joseph McCarthy points an accusing finger during Senate committee hearings. McCarthy's charges that many U.S. officials were Soviet agents intensified a "Red Scare" in the United States based on fears of Communist infiltration, following the exposure of some Soviet spies and the Communist victory in China. Although McCarthy was eventually discredited, fear of Communism remained a potent force in America throughout the Cold War.

the State Department (Document 19). Although he was later discredited, his initial assertions heightened public fears. Compelled in this atmosphere to reinforce its anti-Communist credentials, the Truman administration refused to grant diplomatic recognition to China's new Communist government and used U.S. influence to ensure that the Nationalists on Taiwan would continue to hold China's United Nations seat. Hence, for the next few decades, America officially pretended that Jiang was still China's ruler.

America comes to support Japan as crucial Cold War ally

Ironically these developments also benefited Japan, the recently defeated enemy of America, China, and the USSR. In 1945, as Japan's occupying power, the United States had set out to demilitarize that country, decentralize its industry, and break up its military–industrial combines, hoping and intending that a revived and refortified Nationalist China would replace Japan as East Asia's main power. But as Chinese Communist victories dissipated these hopes, the Americans came to see Japan an important Cold War partner. They began to focus on Japan's reindustrialization, abandoning efforts to decentralize its economy and helping to transform the island nation into an Asian bastion of industrial capitalism. By 1950, in an astonishing turn of events, Japan was becoming a crucial U.S. ally, while China had become an implacable foe.

STALIN AND COMMUNIST CHINA

China's new Communist leaders, meanwhile, pursued radical policies that reinforced U.S. fears. Emulating the Soviet model, they set up parallel institutions in the government and Communist party, installing party leaders as the dominant figures in the state bureaucracy, trade unions, military, and police. In the cities they organized mass campaigns against merchants, manufacturers, and remnants of the Guomindang. In the countryside they pursued extensive land reforms, complete with a "class struggle" against the former landlords. "Enemies of the people" were identified and persecuted, while a program of "thought reform" was used to modify attitudes and behaviors of people "contaminated" by the former regime. This process, often called "brainwashing," fostered in the West an image of a regime more fiercely totalitarian than the Soviet state. When Mao praised Stalin, and moved toward an alliance with the USSR, the worst fears of the Western world seemed to have been realized.

Communists impose radical reforms in China

But Moscow's joy was much more subdued than Western worries would have warranted. Stalin, in fact, was less than thrilled by the turn of events that brought the Chinese Communists to power. He was used to working with the Nationalists, and his 1945 treaty with them gave him important rights in Manchuria. And Mao, despite his show of allegiance to the aging Soviet dictator, represented a potential rival for leadership of the Communist world. Although the CCP, mindful of its need for assistance from Moscow, had joined in denouncing Tito when he quit the Soviet camp, the memories of the Yugoslav debacle were too fresh in Stalin's mind for him to be happy with a Communist leader not fully under Moscow's control.

Stalin sees Mao as potential rival

During 1949, then, as the Chinese Communists repeatedly routed the Nationalists, Stalin remained largely neutral. He chose not to recognize Mao's regime, either when it took Beijing in January or captured Nanjing in April. Instead he offered to mediate and help form a Nationalist–Communist coalition government. Only in October, after Mao officially declared the People's Republic, did the USSR formally recognize the new regime. By then he could see that America was not going to rescue Jiang and that China's future was in the hands of Mao Zedong.

Even so, when Mao arrived in Moscow in December of 1949 to negotiate a new Treaty of Friendship and Alliance, he was welcomed with less than open arms. China's new leader was greeted not by Stalin but by Foreign Minister Molotov, was referred to in newspapers as "Mr. Mao" rather than "Comrade Mao," and was treated more as a supplicant than a partner. Stalin at first refused to discuss a new Sino-Soviet pact, insisting that his 1945 treaty with Jiang, and the extensive rights it provided the Soviets in Manchuria, must remain in full force. Only after two weeks of standoff did the Soviet ruler relent. Perhaps, as Britain moved toward formal recognition of Mao's regime in January 1950, Stalin grew anxious that his obstinacy might drive China's new rulers into Western arms. Still, the talks were tough, with agreement reached only in February, thanks largely to the efforts of China's adroit and astute premier Zhou Enlai. In the resulting accords (Documents 18A and 18B), the Soviets agreed to give limited credits and aid to their new ally and eventually to give up the railway and seaport rights Jiang had granted them in Manchuria. On this rare occasion Stalin relinquished gains he had earlier obtained.

Soviet and Communist Chinese leaders sign treaty in 1950

So, although the Communist victory in China was a big setback for the West, it was less of a boon to the USSR than Westerners then feared. The affinities between the superpowers and their Chinese clients were in fact more apparent than real. China's Nationalists, it is true, maintained a façade of parliamentary governance, but Jiang's regime was more of a corrupt dictatorship than a Western-style democracy. China's Communists, to be sure, professed allegiance to Marxism-Leninism and Soviet-style socialism, but they were not Soviet puppets. They had come to power on their own, with little support or encouragement from Moscow. And theirs was a peasant revolution, rural and anti-urban, scarcely resembling the proletarian dictatorship envisioned by Marx and Lenin or the industrialized behemoth created by Joseph Stalin.

Tensions remain in Soviet–Chinese relations

The Chinese Revolution, and the superpower involvement therein, set a pattern for Asian and African struggles throughout the Cold War. Indigenous groups, vying for power within their own country, often found it expedient to define their causes in Cold War terms. One side might claim to be a socialist vanguard, or at least a liberation movement fighting Western capitalist imperialism. The other might identify with liberal democracy, or at least with Western opposition to the spread of Communist oppression. By identifying with one side or the other, they were able to lay claim to the moral and material support, and sometimes armed assistance, of the capitalist or socialist camp. As the overall leaders of these camps, the United States and the USSR were frequently drawn into the fray, if for no other reason than to prevent the other side from gaining an advantage. Internal rivalries and power struggles thus became intertwined with the superpower conflict. And the Cold War, which had started mainly in Europe but soon reached a standoff there, increasingly became a global confrontation.

7

The Conflict over Korea, 1950–1953

The Communist victory in China broadened the scope of the Cold War. The American policy of containment had been designed mainly to check the spread of Communism in Europe and Southwest Asia; it was not yet clear how it applied to East Asia. Indeed, the Truman administration's preoccupation with Europe had been a key factor in precluding U.S. military involvement in the Chinese Civil War. American resources were extensive but not unlimited, and conventional strategic wisdom said they must not be diverted to support a land war in Asia. The Soviet Union, likewise absorbed with Europe, had been unwilling to supply substantial aid to its Chinese Communist comrades during their struggle against Nationalist rule.

But Mao's triumph altered these attitudes. Stalin, for all his caution, was compelled by events to make concessions and provide assistance to the People's Republic of China. And the Truman administration, for all its focus on Europe, was so severely wounded by the "loss" of China that it could not tolerate any new extensions of Communist power anywhere. As a result, in 1950, a remarkable series of events propelled the American administration into precisely the situation it had so recently avoided: a land war in Asia against the Chinese Communists. And the Cold War became a shooting war in a country called Korea.

NORTH AND SOUTH KOREA

The Korean peninsula extends from southeast Manchuria like an incomplete land bridge stretching three-fourths of the way to Japan. Only 100 miles from the westernmost Japanese islands, it has a short border with Russia and a long one with China. Partly due to its location at the juncture of these three powers, Korea's affairs were often subject to outside interference.

From 1910 until 1945, in fact, Korea was ruled by imperial Japan. These were difficult years for Koreans. On one hand, the Japanese sought to modernize the peninsula: They built factories, roads, hospitals, and schools; improved sanitation and medicine, and industrialized the Korean economy. At the same time, however, their rule was harsh and repressive. They exploited Korean natural resources, drained off the fruits of Korean labor, and set up a brutal police state to control the Korean people. Living standards fell as Japanese capitalists exploited Korean workers. Japanese landlords increasingly controlled Korean peasants. Korean laws and customs were banned, and Korean newspapers were suppressed. Korea was transformed into a Japanese province called Chosen.

Japan rules and represses Korea, 1910–1945

But Japan's harsh rule helped spawn in Korea a national liberation movement. In 1919, emboldened by Woodrow Wilson's call for national self-determination, a group of Korean intellectuals drafted a "Proclamation of Independence," and the funeral of Korea's last emperor prompted popular demonstrations all over Korea. Japanese authorities brutally suppressed the movement, and Western leaders meeting in Versailles that year ignored it since Japan had been their wartime ally. But it did help lay foundations for a nationalist movement in exile.

As the Japanese cracked down, hundreds of Korean patriots fled their country to plan its liberation. Many went to China, where they established at Shanghai a provisional government in exile that claimed to speak for "Free Korea." Some resettled in the United States, especially in Hawaii. Hoping to win American support for their movement, they espoused Western liberal and nationalist ideals and maintained contact with the Korean émigrés in China. A third group went to Soviet Russia, the only major nation that seemed fully supportive of national liberation movements. Disenchanted with the West, in 1925 they helped create a Korean Communist Party.

Korean émigrés form nationalist and Communist movements

In the 1930s, as Japan moved into Manchuria and then China proper, the prospects for Korean independence grew dimmer. With their economy integrated into Japan's and their land mostly surrounded by Japanese-controlled territory, Koreans became a forgotten people, increasingly forced to speak Japanese and take Japanese names. But in 1941, when Japan went to war against America and Britain, Koreans regained hope: Their oppressors had overreached and sooner or later must fall. Korean morale got a further boost in 1943, when Roosevelt, Churchill, and Jiang Jieshi declared in Cairo that Korea should "in due course" become free and independent after Japan was defeated. Stalin added his assent at Tehran a few weeks later.

Allied Powers pledge to liberate Korea

Unfortunately for the Koreans, Japan's defeat did not bring them full independence. In February 1945, when Allied leaders met again at Yalta, they discussed the possibility of putting postwar Korea under the joint trusteeship of the United States, Great Britain, Nationalist China, and the USSR. They made no arrangements, however, for the liberation or occupation of Korea, and did not include Korea in the secret agreement by which Stalin agreed to join the war against Japan after Germany was defeated. In ensuing months, anticipating a long and difficult struggle to conquer the Japanese islands, the Americans deferred making concrete plans for Korea, effectively consigning it to the Soviet zone of operations. Stalin, who rarely missed a chance to extend his influence, needed no further invitation. On 9 August, the day after his country declared war on Japan, he sent troops to invade both Manchuria and Korea. Within a few weeks, these forces occupied much of Manchuria and northern Korea.

Americans and Soviets divide Korea into postwar occupation zones

The United States, caught off guard by the rapidity of this advance, became concerned that Korea would fall fully under Soviet control. So in drafting General Order No. 1, the surrender instructions issued to the Japanese troops, U.S. officials inserted a provision dividing Korea along the 38th parallel of latitude. Japanese forces north of that line were ordered to surrender to the Soviets; south of it, they were told to submit to the Americans.

Somewhat surprisingly, Stalin accepted this arrangement. He could easily have occupied all of Korea, since the Americans as yet had no presence there, but instead he agreed to divide it with them. Hoping, perhaps, that America might honor his request for a Soviet occupation zone in Japan, he did not press his advantage in Korea. Besides, neither Moscow nor Washington saw the division as permanent; both agreed that Korea should be reunified once the occupation was over. But there was no agreement as to how unification would happen or what sort of regime would run a unified Korea.

Since they were already there, the Soviets could move more quickly. Having at hand a number of Soviet-trained Korean Communists, Moscow simply gave them positions of authority in northern Korea. The Americans, who did not arrive in southern Korea until three weeks after the war ended, ignored a "Korean People's Republic" set up by left-wing nationalists in Seoul, fearing it might be controlled by Communists. Instead, showing manifest insensitivity, they at first tried to run south Korea using Japanese officials. Within months, however, these officials were replaced by Americans, whose job it was to run things until unified rule was established.

Soviets set up Communist regime in North Korea

But unified rule never came. With Cold War tensions rising, Moscow and Washington could not agree on a united government, and the Koreans were soon engaged in a struggle for influence and power. As a result, two separate regimes emerged. In the Soviet-occupied north, a Communist-dominated provisional government was set up in 1947. Its leader was Kim Il-sung (born Kim Song-ju), a young Korean Communist who had taken the name of a legendary guerrilla fighter. Talented and energetic, but ruthlessly ambitious and cruel, he would prove the most durable of all Cold War leaders, maintaining power until his death in 1994. His regime quickly nationalized industry and confiscated landed estates, prompting thousands of people, including many industrialists and landlords, to flee to the south.

Americans help form anti-Communist regime in South Korea

In the south, as hopes for unity faded, the Americans began turning over power to Koreans. The United States avoided outwardly imposing its will, preferring instead to set up a representative assembly, see that elections were held, and then let elected Korean officials set policies. Nevertheless, due partly to U.S. influence and partly to the influx of capitalists and landlords from the north, southern politics came to be dominated by conservative and ultra-nationalistic forces. Their leader was an aging nationalist named Yi Sung-man, known in the West as Syngman Rhee. Having fled Korea in 1911, following the Japanese takeover, the Princeton-educated Rhee had spent decades in exile, living in Hawaii and pushing the cause of Korean independence. An eloquent speaker, effective organizer, and strident anti-Communist, he returned to Korea after the war, created a political party, and conducted a bitter struggle against leftist elements in the south. In summer 1948, after leading his party to victory in South Korean elections, he became president of a new "Republic of Korea," which set up its capital at Seoul. In response, Kim Il-sung and his comrades in the north declared the formation of a "Democratic People's Republic" with its capital at P'yongyang.

The establishment of two separate and hostile Korean regimes pleased no one. Each side talked of eventually uniting the country under its control. In the north, Kim Il-sung moved systematically to eliminate opponents and create a personal dictatorship. With continued Soviet assistance, he also built up his military forces and launched an industrialization drive. In the south Syngman Rhee, faced with widespread left-wing opposition, used martial law and brutal authoritarian methods to quell dissent. His government nonetheless was recognized by the United States and admitted to the UN as Korea's sole representative.

The superpowers, meanwhile, moved to end their occupation. By late 1948, the Soviets withdrew most of their forces, leaving behind a well-equipped North Korean army and a cadre of political advisors and military technicians. The Americans, aware of the north's preponderant strength but unwilling (at that point) to make a permanent military commitment to the south, pulled out their troops the next year. They agreed to provide limited aid to Syngman Rhee's regime, as well as equipment and training for its army. But they avoided a major investment, fearful that Rhee might use it to launch a war against North Korea. At the same time, they purposely left their intentions concerning defense of South Korea ambiguous, gambling that the resulting uncertainty would deter a North Korean attack. They would soon lose this gamble.

Soviets and Americans withdraw occupying forces

THE OUTBREAK OF HOSTILITIES

The end of the Soviet and American occupations left Korea in an unstable situation verging on civil war. Each side staged periodic raids and attacks against the other, and each began preparing for possible combat. In the south, Syngman Rhee vigorously pressed for more U.S. aid, while cracking down even further on dissenters. His popularity was slipping, thanks partly to his repressive policies and partly to the rampant inflation afflicting South Korea's economy. American support for the Seoul regime, moreover, was called into question when Secretary of State Dean Acheson, in a major address on January 12, 1950, outlined an American defensive perimeter embracing Japan and the Philippines but not Taiwan or South Korea (Document 20). The secretary was referring to a global conflict, in which the United States would be unable to defend the last two areas, and not to an invasion of South Korea from the north. His remarks nonetheless cast doubt on U.S. willingness to defend South Korea.

Stalin, who had hitherto urged the North Koreans to be cautious, now began to support their aim of invading the south. Noting that America had not saved Nationalist China, and buoyed by intelligence reports that South Korea did not expect U.S. armed assistance, he met Kim Il-sung in Moscow that spring to discuss military plans. Although unwilling to commit Soviet troops, Stalin supplied Kim with ample arms and ammunition and with extensive Soviet support in planning and preparing an attack. On Sunday, 25 June 1950, with a well-trained and well-equipped army of over 130,000 strong, North Korea launched a massive invasion of the south, counting on a quick victory to preclude U.S. intervention. The Korean War had begun.

With Stalin's backing, North Korea invades South Korea

The Americans at that point were in the midst of reconsidering their overall strategy. Early in 1950, in the wake of the successful Soviet atomic bomb test and the Chinese revolution, President Truman had authorized his National Security Council (NSC) to undertake a secret reassessment of U.S. policy. Its report, known as NSC-68

(Document 21), had been completed in April and reviewed by the president. Portraying the Soviet challenge mainly in military terms, it called for a massive American military effort to counter this global threat. America must build up its conventional and nuclear forces, it asserted, and must be prepared to respond to Communist advances anywhere in the world. Although highly secret and not formally approved until September of 1950, NSC-68 clearly had an impact on U.S. reaction to the Korean crisis.

Thus, although caught off guard by the news from Korea, American officials responded with speed and vigor. President Truman, home in Missouri when the war broke out, rushed back to Washington to confront the crisis. Presuming that the Soviets were behind the attack, and smarting from widespread criticism of the recent debacle in China, he and his advisors quickly concluded that they could not countenance any further extension of Communist control. Both in domestic politics and international relations, they saw their credibility at stake. So on 25 June, within hours of the invasion, at a hastily arranged special session of the UN Security Council, they pushed through a resolution calling for immediate withdrawal of North Korean forces from the south. General Douglas MacArthur, head of the U.S. occupation forces in Japan, was ordered to send in supplies to aid South Korea. Two days later, the United States won Security Council approval of a resolution calling on UN member nations to assist the South Koreans in resisting the invasion from the north (Document 22B).

Americans get UN support for defense of South Korea

Now it was Stalin's turn to be caught off guard. Early in 1950, in protest against the UN refusal to admit Communist China in place of the Nationalist regime, he had withdrawn his UN delegation. He was thus not in a position to counter U.S. maneuvering in the Security Council, and he clearly had not anticipated how swiftly Truman would use the UN to mobilize world opinion and legitimize U.S. military intervention in Korea.

Events in Korea were likewise moving swiftly. Even before the passage of the second UN resolution, Truman had authorized American air and naval power to slow the Communist advance (Document 22A). But South Korean forces, poorly trained and ill equipped, still could not stop the North Koreans. By 28 June 1950, only three days into the war, the Communists had captured Seoul, and it seemed they would soon overrun the entire peninsula. Two days later, following a quick trip to the combat zone, General MacArthur reported that South Korea could not hold out without the aid of U.S. ground forces. Washington, concerned that the invasion was a Soviet tactic to divert Western resources in anticipation of a major thrust elsewhere, had been hesitant to take such a step. On 30 June, however, deciding he could wait no longer, Truman authorized the employment of American troops. The war in Korea thus became an international conflict.

Americans commit forces to defense of South Korea

The big question at this point was how Moscow would react. The Americans' rapid response, and their ability to win UN approval for it, left Soviet leaders with little room for diplomatic maneuvering. On 29 June, they officially disavowed any responsibility for the war and accused South Korea of having started it by invading the north. They also issued a warning against foreign involvement in Korea's internal affairs, declaring their own intention not to intervene. Most importantly, they did not send Soviet forces to augment the North Koreans. At the time, in view of the sweeping successes enjoyed by Kim Il-sung's armies, such assistance hardly seemed necessary. Still, as they would often do during the Cold War, the Soviets showed caution in an international crisis. For all their efforts to extend their influence, when push came to shove they were generally unwilling to risk direct armed conflict between the superpowers.

Soviets back North Korea but do not send forces

THE WIDENING OF THE WAR

In Korea, however, the United States took that risk. Although conducted under the auspices of the UN, the defense of South Korea was largely an American affair. Truman had authorized the use of U.S. forces without awaiting UN approval, and the Americans quickly took the lead in organizing the war effort. On 7 July 1950, when a United Nations Command was created, it was immediately placed under U.S. authority. Although sixteen UN member nations eventually sent forces, the United States provided fully half the ground troops and most of the air and sea power. On 8 July, in a move that proved portentous, Truman appointed General MacArthur commander-in-chief of UN forces in Korea.

During a long and spectacular career, General of the Army Douglas MacArthur had emerged as one of America's leading military figures. Brilliant and vain, eloquent and arrogant, he had led the U.S. Army in the Pacific theater during World War II and had served since then as Supreme Allied Commander in occupied Japan. There, wielding vast powers, he had helped to implement reforms designed to transform imperial Japan into a capitalist democratic bulwark against Communism in Asia. A rigid conservative and staunch anti-Communist, he judged that U.S. policy focused too much on Europe and too little on Asia.

American General MacArthur commands UN forces in Korea

When MacArthur assumed command in Korea, the situation of the South Koreans was desperate. The first several weeks of the war had witnessed a steady string of North Korean victories. The South Korean army was in disarray, unable to regroup and mount an effective resistance. The first American units, arriving in July, were too few and too poorly equipped to be of much help. U.S. air power, which might have been used to slow the attacking forces, was instead directed against strategic targets in North Korea. And, although no mass uprising occurred against Syngman Rhee, many South Korean students and workers at first welcomed the invaders.

By early August, North Korean forces controlled the whole peninsula except for a small southeastern "perimeter" around the city of Pusan. By then, however, the strategic balance was shifting. With their lines extended and increasing harassment from UN tactical warplanes, the North Korean forces found the going much tougher. And they soon found themselves outnumbered: By late August, a steady influx of UN soldiers gave the defenders of South Korea a numerical advantage. The Pusan perimeter, fortified by U.S. tanks and protected by U.S. aircraft, held out against a determined North Korean assault. In early September, the assault came to an end: The North Koreans had fallen short of the quick and total victory they sought.

North Koreans overrun most but not all of South Korea

Meanwhile, the UN Command was planning its own assault. General MacArthur, with vast experience in amphibious operations, had in early July conceived the idea of staging a surprise landing behind enemy lines. By the end of August, his plans were complete. On 15 September, in a daring and spectacular operation, UN personnel began landing at Inchon, a port city on the Yellow Sea located 20 miles from Seoul and 180 miles behind the North Korean lines. The next day, UN troops in the Pusan perimeter launched another offensive. Within two weeks, the South Korean capital had been recaptured, and the Communist forces were in full retreat almost everywhere.

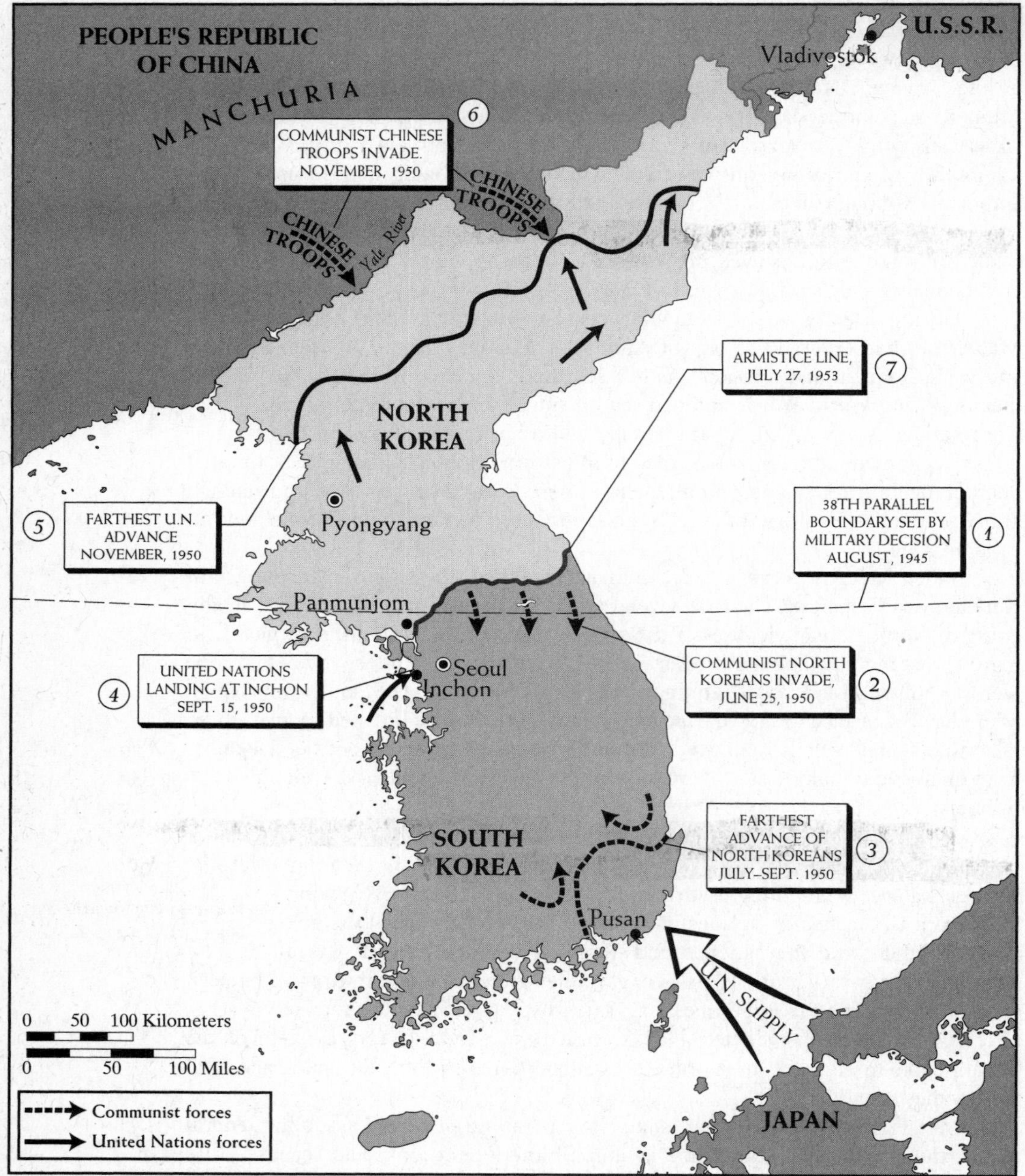

MAP 5 The Korean War, 1950–1953.

Although Korea was divided along the 38th parallel in 1945 (box 1), in June of 1950 Communist North Korea invaded South Korea (box 2), starting the Korean War. After overrunning much of the south (box 3), the North Koreans were driven back (boxes 4 and 5) by a U.S.-led UN coalition, only to have the momentum change again when forces from Communist China came to aid the North Koreans (box 6). Notice that the fighting ended in 1953 with a truce along an armistice line not far from the 38th parallel (box 7).

As the North Koreans fled, the Americans began to expand their original objectives. Instead of simply defending South Korea, they now resolved to move into the north, destroy Kim Il-sung's regime, and unite the entire peninsula under Syngman Rhee's. Late in September, Truman authorized MacArthur to cross the 38th parallel, provided there was no immediate threat of Soviet or Chinese intervention. Early in October, South Korean troops actually traversed the dividing line, while the Americans pressed the UN for approval of their plans to do the same. It came on 7 October, and on that same day, American forces moved into North Korea. The effort to resist aggression was thereby transformed into a campaign to conquer the north.

UN forces land behind Communist lines, then invade North Korea

During the next few weeks, as UN troops pushed deep into North Korea, it looked as if their new goal would be achieved. By 19 October, MacArthur's forces had taken P'yongyang, and they were soon moving north toward the Yalu River that separates Korea from Manchuria. Ignoring counsels of caution from his superiors in Washington, the general pushed on toward what he hoped and expected would be a swift and total victory.

UN forces drive deep into North Korea

The UN invasion of the north, however, placed Stalin and Mao in a situation not unlike the one faced by the United States several months earlier. They had to

Troops in Combat During Korean War.

Difficult conditions and harsh climate complicated combat in the Korean conflict. Note the rugged terrain on which fighting took place and the cold weather battle gear worn by these soldiers in action.

decide whether to watch their comrades fall or to intervene and risk a world war. Stalin, ever cautious, refused to commit his own forces, but he strongly exhorted the Chinese to send theirs.

In early October, after South Korean troops began crossing the 38th parallel, the Chinese leaders tentatively decided to send soldiers into Korea, as long as the Soviets supplied them with weapons and air cover. Then, calling in India's ambassador to China in the middle of the night, Chinese premier Zhou Enlai issued a pointed warning: China would intervene in Korea if non-Korean UN forces invaded the north. When the UN Command, undeterred, went ahead with its invasion, Zhou flew to meet Stalin, who cautiously agreed to provide weapons but said that air support would take time. Within a few weeks, the Chinese were sending troops across the Yalu River, portraying them as "volunteers" sent to aid their North Korean comrades.

Communist China sends "volunteers" to aid North Koreans

Meanwhile, at a dramatic 15 October meeting on Wake Island in the Pacific, MacArthur assured Truman that the war would soon be over and that Chinese forces would be slaughtered if they intervened. Returning to Korea, the general then prepared for a major offensive designed to end the war. But when that offensive finally came, in late November, thousands more Chinese "volunteers" poured in, driving back the UN forces. Desperate evacuation efforts in December averted a UN disaster, but most of North Korea was soon back under Communist control. Once again the momentum had shifted, this time in favor of the Communists.

Combined Communist forces drive back UN forces

MACARTHUR'S DISMISSAL AND THE STALEMATE IN KOREA

Now it was America's turn to face the specter of defeat. At a press conference on 30 November, responding to news of the massive Chinese intervention, President Truman pointedly refused to rule out using nuclear weapons to halt the Communist advance. This implicit threat caused a flap between the United States and its allies, with British prime minister Attlee flying to Washington to secure assurances that the war would remain limited. And, although Truman declared a national emergency in mid-December, his administration was already starting to talk about a cease-fire and looking for ways to cut its losses.

But MacArthur had other ideas. Blaming his reverses on intelligence leaks and restraints on him by U.S. superiors, he demanded the authority to widen the war by blockading Communist China, bombing its industrial sites, and bringing in Nationalist Chinese troops to join the war in Korea. By then, however, the Truman administration had abandoned hopes of unifying Korea and was seeking a way out of the war. MacArthur's demands received little sympathy from U.S. military planners who, as General Omar Bradley would later suggest, saw an invasion of China as "the wrong war, in the wrong place, at the wrong time, and with the wrong enemy." For a few months, MacArthur chafed as Washington moved to keep the war limited and seek a negotiated settlement. Finally, on 24 March 1951, he issued a statement containing a virtual ultimatum to the Chinese, in effect demanding they surrender to him or risk "imminent military collapse."

MacArthur presses to attack Red China but Pentagon resists

Truman saw MacArthur's statement, which contradicted both U.S. and UN policy, as an act of insubordination. Shortly thereafter, when a wire from the general implicitly denouncing the administration's "limited war" policy was read in the U.S. Congress, the president decided he could tolerate no more. On 11 April, in a dramatic and controversial gesture, he dismissed MacArthur from his military command. The move ignited a storm of protest in America, where the president's popularity sank to an all-time low, while the general returned to a hero's welcome of epic proportions. But in Europe, where MacArthur was widely regarded as dangerous and uncontrollable, Truman's move was applauded and Allied fears relieved. And in Asia, where the battles were fought, the terrifying prospect of all-out war was diminished.

Truman dismisses MacArthur, limits war to Korea

Yet the fighting in Korea dragged on. By June of 1951, UN forces had managed to stop the Communist advance, inflict severe casualties on the Chinese and North Koreans, and push them back across the 38th parallel. Rather than pressing their advantage, however, the Americans decided to test the diplomatic waters. George Kennan, the Truman administration's leading Soviet expert, met several times in late May and early June with Soviet UN ambassador Jacob Malik, who was privately hinting that Moscow wanted peace. Then, in a 23 June UN broadcast, Malik gave a speech calling for peace talks in Korea and a cease-fire along the 38th parallel. The UN Command in Korea responded six days later with a broadcast offer to meet with Communist commanders, and on 10 July, discussions began in Kaesong, a city not far from the front.

UN forces stop Communist advance; truce talks begin

The optimism greeting these developments soon vanished. The talks bogged down over various issues, while the fighting continued. Some progress was made in October, when the talks were moved to nearby Panmunjom, but the issue of exchanging prisoners of war remained intractable. Many of the captives held in South Korea balked at going back to Communist rule, so the UN side and the South Koreans would simply not agree to turn them over.

The impasse at the conference table was accompanied by stalemate on the battlefield. With a cease-fire apparently in sight, both sides maneuvered for position, but neither was willing to risk an all-out offensive. Instead they dug in behind heavily fortified lines, fighting occasional battles and carrying on a debilitating war of attrition for two more years. The deadlock was not broken until 1953—and then only after major changes had occurred in superpower leadership.

Truce talks deadlock as war becomes stalemate

CHANGES IN LEADERSHIP IN WASHINGTON AND MOSCOW

The Korean War coincided with a rightward shift among U.S. voters, who in 1952 elected a Republican president for the first time since 1928. Cold War considerations played a key role in the election. In 1948, maintaining the foreign affairs bipartisanship that had prevailed since Pearl Harbor, Republicans had largely refrained from attacking the Truman administration on foreign policy. But Truman's unexpected triumph, followed in 1949 by the Communist victory in China, had undermined this cooperative spirit, and it had since been blown to pieces by Truman's dismissal of General MacArthur and the tactics of Senator McCarthy (Chapter 6).

The presidential campaign of 1952, then, provided a forum for debating U.S. Cold War policy. The Republicans, eager to regain the White House after twenty years of Democratic rule, mercilessly blasted the Truman administration with the pithy slogan, "Korea, Communism, and Corruption." Truman did not seek reelection, and his party's candidate, Adlai Stevenson of Illinois, found it advisable to distance himself from the beleaguered president. Pressure from the "McCarthyites" compelled moderate Republicans, including presidential nominee General Dwight D. Eisenhower, to run on a platform that deplored the "immoral policy of 'containment' which abandons countless human beings to a despotism and godless terrorism." In the course of the campaign, Republicans called for a new policy of "liberation" that would free the "captive nations" behind the "iron curtain." Although Eisenhower privately doubted its wisdom, he publicly embraced this concept, while promising to "go to Korea" and bring that war to "an early and honorable end." Stevenson ran a thoughtful and articulate campaign, but Eisenhower, a highly popular war hero commonly called "Ike," rode into office on a landslide.

Eisenhower elected president having pledged to end Korean War

Despite the fact that he often came across as a simple and loyal soldier, folksy and direct, Dwight David Eisenhower was in fact a complex man who possessed considerable skills as an administrator and a politician. As the wartime commander of Anglo-American forces in Europe, he had acquired valuable experience in dealing with the British, the French, and even the Soviets. Critical of Truman's Cold War approach, which he saw as unsystematically devised in response to a series of crises, and dismayed by the huge costs of military buildup projected in NSC-68, he set out to establish a comprehensive long-term strategy that would protect U.S. interests while balancing the federal budget. In these efforts, he would be assisted by his hard-nosed secretary of state, John Foster Dulles, a prominent international lawyer and foreign affairs expert who saw Communism as a mortal threat and felt that America must seize the Cold War initiative rather than merely reacting to Communist advances.

To some extent, Eisenhower's election reflected a widespread belief among Americans that he and Dulles, by virtue of their toughness and experience, were the ones best suited to deal with Joseph Stalin. But in March of 1953, only six weeks after the new president took office, the Soviet dictator confounded Western expectations one last time. He died.

The last few years of Stalin's reign had been marked by continued tensions, both in the USSR and abroad. The aging dictator, jealous of his powers and neurotically suspicious of even his closest comrades, refused to yield authority even as his faculties declined and his country reaped the bitter harvest of his paranoid policies. In his brutal efforts to secure the Soviet borders and spread Communism in Eastern Europe and Asia, he had frightened his erstwhile allies and enemies into joining forces against him. In relying so heavily on military force, he had saddled his people with history's largest peacetime military establishment. And in seeking so belligerently to prevent "capitalist encirclement," he had awakened in the capitalist world a virulent anti-Communism, thus advancing the careers of Western politicians most hostile to the USSR and ensuring that any Soviet initiative would meet staunch resistance.

Several signs of internal change preceded Stalin's passing. In October 1952, when the Nineteenth Congress of the Soviet Communist Party convened in Moscow, for the first time in memory the keynote speech was given not by Stalin but by Georgi M. Malenkov, the dictator's principal lieutenant and heir apparent. Stalin himself, looking white haired and frail, attended the congress sessions only sporadically. Then, in January 1953, Soviet police arrested a group of Kremlin doctors and charged them with hastening the deaths of high officials and conspiring with Western spies. A new and bloody purge, menacing even Stalin's closest comrades, may have been in the works. But early in March, as tension mounted, the dictator suffered a stroke. His deputies, less than eager to find out what their mentor was planning, may have taken their time in securing medical care. At any rate, they were not the only ones to breathe a sigh of relief on 5 March 1953, when Joseph Vissarionovich Stalin went to his final reward.

Stalin dies amid signs that he was planning a new purge

Stalin's passing seemed to open the door for an easing of Cold War tensions. Although his death did not destabilize the USSR, as some of its foes had hoped, a more moderate and flexible leadership emerged. Malenkov at first took over as head of both the Communist party and the Soviet government, but within a few weeks, as his comrades sought to preclude a return to one-man rule, he was compelled to relinquish the former post to Nikita S. Khrushchev. For the next two years, the USSR was governed by a "collective leadership," with Premier Malenkov as the main spokesperson, while he and Khrushchev maneuvered behind the scenes for power.

Malenkov, an intelligent and sophisticated man who felt that policies of confrontation were straining his country's resources without adding to its security, moved quickly to defuse Cold War tensions so the regime could focus more fully on domestic concerns. He abandoned claims that Stalin had made upon territory in northeast Turkey, and he sought to repair Soviet relations with Iran, Israel, Greece, and Yugoslavia. Internally, he strove to deemphasize heavy industry, increase production of consumer goods, and improve living standards. And, while calling for the peaceful resolution of international disputes, he moved away from the Stalinist line that conflict between Communism and capitalism was inevitable. This change helped pave the way for an armistice in Korea.

New Soviet leaders adopt more moderate approach

THE ARMISTICE AGREEMENT

By early 1953, both sides were looking for a way out of the Korean quagmire. Eisenhower, who had promised in his campaign to end the war and had visited Korea before taking office, tried to break the stalemate in January by hinting that he might "unleash" Jiang Jieshi and the Nationalists on Taiwan to invade mainland China. This threat heightened anxieties but produced no immediate breakthrough. After Stalin's death in March, however, the new Soviet leadership launched a "peace offensive," with Malenkov announcing that there were no disputes between the United States and the USSR that could not be resolved by peaceful means. A few weeks later, in a similar spirit, Chinese premier Zhou Enlai offered a major concession on the prisoner exchange issue, suggesting that those prisoners who did not wish to return to their previous country might be turned over to a neutral nation.

Communists enhance peace offers after Stalin's death

The peace talks, which had temporarily been suspended, reconvened in April amid expressions of hope. But the new U.S. administration, inherently distrustful of any Communist initiative, found the details of the Chinese offer unacceptable. An alternative plan, under which the prisoner exchange would be handled by a commission made up of personnel from various neutral nations, was more to its liking.

Several months of difficult negotiations ensued. In May, during a visit to India, Secretary of State Dulles implied that the United States might widen the war—and perhaps even use nuclear weapons—if no agreement were reached. In June, in an effort to sabotage the peace talks and preclude any prisoner exchange, South Korean leader Syngman Rhee purposely allowed over 27,000 prisoners of war to "escape." In July, determined to achieve a more favorable cease-fire line, the Communists launched a major military offensive.

Panmunjom talks produce truce in July 1953

But the talks proceeded all the while. The new American leaders, hoping to reduce their defense expenses and pressed by their NATO allies for an end to Asian fighting, disavowed Rhee's actions and labored to bring him in line. The new Soviet leaders, engaged in an internal power struggle and compelled in June to help East German authorities put down widespread demonstrations against their heavy-handed rule, sought an easing of Cold War tensions to stabilize their situation. Their Chinese allies took heed, and on 27 July 1953, in an atmosphere of silence and resignation, the armistice was signed at Panmunjom (Document 22C).

The agreement ended the fighting, but it was a cease-fire, not a treaty of peace. An international peace conference convened at Geneva in 1954 to negotiate such a treaty, but its efforts in this regard came to naught, and it wound up focusing mostly on Indochina (Chapter 11). Formal talks at Panmunjom continued for decades, but these too accomplished little. The two Koreas remained bitter foes, heavily armed and hostile, for the rest of the Cold War era.

War costs millions of Korean lives, but Korea remains divided

For Korea, the war was an appalling disaster. Three years of constant combat had resulted in wholesale slaughter. At least four million people, most of them Koreans, were killed in what was elsewhere called a "limited" war. Yet neither side could claim victory, as the final cease-fire line was not far from the original division on the 38th parallel. In the long run, the South Koreans fared better: Buoyed by a mutual defense pact with America and massive U.S. aid, they gained substantial prosperity, although full freedom and democracy eluded them for decades. North Koreans got neither prosperity nor freedom, as Kim Il-sung's dictatorial regime persisted in emphasizing military strength and internal repression throughout the Cold War and beyond.

Neither Americans nor Communists gain from Korean War

Few nations, in fact, could take much satisfaction in the war's outcome. The United States could claim to have saved South Korea, but it had failed to win the war and had suffered some embarrassing setbacks. Furthermore, it had vastly extended its commitments, expanding its containment policy into a global anti-Communist crusade. It had frightened its traditional allies, who were increasingly alarmed at the growing militarization of U.S. foreign policy. It had driven its major adversaries, the Soviet and Chinese Communists, into each other's arms. And by rescuing Syngman Rhee and propping up Jiang Jieshi, it had seemed to show that it would aid any regime, no matter how brutal or undemocratic, that faced a Communist threat.

The Communist powers likewise had little to celebrate. The People's Republic of China had gained substantial military credibility by holding its own against the mighty Americans. But it also found itself more dependent than ever on Soviet assistance and, thanks to implacable U.S. hostility, shut out of both the UN and Taiwan. The Soviet Union, by remaining officially neutral, had seemed to have it both ways: It had tested Western resolve and diverted American resources without risking its own forces in the process. But the results were hardly to Moscow's liking: The Korean War had triggered an American backlash that seemed to threaten the security of the USSR itself. As the United States poured vast sums into rebuilding, rearming, and defending West Germany and Japan, the Soviets once again found themselves surrounded by armed and hostile powers. They thus felt compelled to maintain a massive military force at an enormous cost and to engage in a long, debilitating arms race with the much wealthier Americans.

Oddly enough, the chief beneficiaries of the Korean War were Germany, Japan, and Nationalist China, the three great losers of the conflicts that closely preceded it. The outbreak of hostilities in Korea gave added impetus to U.S. efforts, already under way, to transform Japan and West Germany into trusted friends and partners in the anti-Communist cause. During the course of 1950, the United States overcame the fears of its reluctant European allies and got them to agree to the rearming of West Germany—a prospect that was unthinkable only a few years earlier. Japan, meanwhile, had become a staging ground for U.S. operations in Korea and a silent partner in the UN war effort there. On 8 September 1951, the Japanese reaped the benefits of the changing world scene when the United States signed a security treaty committing itself to their defense and, by the Treaty of San Francisco the following year, ended its occupation.

West Germany, Japan, and Taiwan benefit from Korean War

The Nationalist Chinese, largely written off by the West early in 1950, gained a new lease on life as a result of the Korean War. The Americans poured in military and economic aid to support the Taiwan regime. They abandoned any thoughts of recognizing Communist China, at least for the time being, and contrived to have the Nationalists retain the UN seat representing all of China. In 1954, the United States even concluded a mutual defense treaty with Jiang Jieshi's Nationalist government. But American aid had its limits: For all its support of Jiang, the United States consistently refused to help him launch a war to retake the Chinese mainland.

Indeed, although the Korean conflict represented a widening of the Cold War, it also helped establish the boundaries of that contest. The Soviets had encouraged adventurism on the part of their clients, but they were unwilling to commit their own forces or to rescue protégés whose adventures went awry. The Chinese had shown that they were capable of protecting their own borders, but unwilling to extend themselves too far beyond and wary of risking a nuclear attack upon their territory. The Americans had demonstrated that they could effectively project their power to protect anti-Communist regimes. But they would engage only in limited wars fought by limited means and would accept tactical setbacks rather than chance all-out conflict. Their nuclear arms might prove useful as deterrents but not as weapons to be used in actual combat. The memories of Korea, and the terrifying specter of a nuclear conflict, would supply both sides with a healthy restraint during future Cold War confrontations.

Korean conflict widens Cold War but also keeps it limited

8

New Leaders and New Realities, 1953–1957

The Cold War environment changed significantly between 1953 and 1957. In part the change resulted from new leadership in Washington and Moscow, and in part it was induced by some new global realities. One was the crumbling of Europe's colonial empires, promoted by anti-Western liberation movements susceptible to Soviet support. Another was the emergence of nonaligned nations that sought to side with neither East nor West. A third was the development of horrific new weapons that made an all-out superpower war a threat to both sides' existence. The new leaders, whatever their preconceptions, had to deal with the new realities.

THE "NEW LOOK" IN U.S. FOREIGN POLICY

In the United States, Dwight Eisenhower took office in 1953 committed both to meeting the Soviet threat and to balancing the federal budget—objectives that proved hard to reconcile. Secretary of State John Foster Dulles, determined to combat Communism the world over, chafed at fiscal restraints he feared might jeopardize U.S. security. But Treasury Secretary George M. Humphrey, asserting that America's main advantage was its powerful economy, argued that excessive defense spending could undermine that economic edge. While agreeing with Dulles that U.S. security was paramount, the president saw the Cold War as a long-term struggle and insisted that the costs of countering the current threat must not subvert America's future security by weakening its economy and bankrupting its treasury. He and his team thus worked hard to cut expenses and trim the vast military establishment inherited from President Truman.

Eisenhower aims both to cut costs and maintain security

One result was increased reliance on atomic weapons instead of conventional force. From a political perspective, nuclear armaments had two big advantages: They were relatively inexpensive, compared to the high costs of equipping and maintaining vast standing armies, and they enabled democratic governments to avoid unpopular efforts to increase the number of troops, especially by military conscription. Voters were far less likely to balk at new weapons than at attempts

Focus on nuclear retaliation helps to cut U.S. military costs to raise their taxes and to draft their sons. Dulles himself alluded to these considerations in 1954 (Document 23), explaining a policy called "massive retaliation":

> The total cost of our security efforts . . . could not be continued long without grave budgetary, economic and social consequences . . . [T]he basic decision was to depend primarily on greater capacity to retaliate instantly by means and at places of our own choosing. As a result it is now possible to get . . . more basic security at less cost.

Defense Secretary Charles E. Wilson put it much more succinctly: Nuclear arms provided a "bigger bang for the buck."

Eisenhower's efforts, known as the "New Look" in American policy, did bring sizable cuts in military costs. Within a few years, the U.S. defense budget decreased by almost a third, while the country doubled its supply of nuclear weapons and began producing large numbers of giant B-52 jet bombers capable of delivering these weapons to targets in the USSR.

But "massive retaliation" had its limits. The threat of nuclear response might be credible in some areas, such as in defending Western Europe, where vital U.S.

The B-52 Bomber.

In the 1950s, B-52 bombers, with their eight jet engines and long-range in-flight refueling capability, became the mainstay of America's "massive retaliation" strategic deterrent, which relied on their ability to deliver nuclear strikes against the USSR. Note that some were eventually equipped with long-range air-to-surface missiles, as shown here, enabling them to hit Soviet targets without entering Soviet air space.

interests were at stake. But as the Soviets developed their own nuclear strike capacity, it hardly seemed likely that America would risk an atomic war in situations where its own security was not directly threatened. In June 1953, for example, when anti-Communist demonstrations and a general strike broke out in Soviet-occupied East Germany, the Americans openly encouraged the strikers but did not intervene when the Soviets used soldiers and tanks to crush the strikes. And in Korea the next month America settled for an armistice, having earlier chosen not to widen that war by attacking Communist China or resorting to nuclear force.

The Eisenhower team thus sought creative ways to counter the Communists in situations where a nuclear response was neither appropriate nor credible. One approach involved "covert operations" by the Central Intelligence Agency (CIA). Under the direction of Allen Dulles, the secretary of state's brother, the CIA subverted a nationalist regime in Iran (1953) and a democratically-elected left wing government in Guatemala (1954). A second tactic used military advisors to aid anti-Communist forces. As the French left Indochina following their 1954 defeat by Communist-led forces (Chapter 11), the Americans began sending personnel to help organize and train the army of non-Communist South Vietnam, hoping this would be an indirect and inexpensive way to counter Communism.

CIA uses covert operations, and America aids anti-Communist forces

A third device was formation of alliances aimed at blocking Communist advances in certain vulnerable areas. If NATO could serve as an effective vehicle for the defense of Western Europe, reasoned John Foster Dulles, similar alliances might prove useful in "trouble spots" such as Southeast Asia and the Middle East. In 1954, seeking to assure Southeast Asian nations of U.S. support following France's withdrawal from Indochina (Chapter 11), he helped found the Southeast Asia Treaty Organization (SEATO), made up of the United States, Britain, France, Australia, New Zealand, Thailand, Pakistan, and the Philippines (Document 25). But unlike NATO, it provided no military guarantees, calling only for mutual consultation in the event of aggression. Furthermore, its title belied its composition: Key nations of Southeast Asia were not SEATO members, and most of its members were not in Southeast Asia. In 1955, the Americans went along with Britain in forming the Baghdad Pact, which incorporated Turkey, Iraq, Iran, and Pakistan into a new alliance, later called the Central Treaty Organization (CENTO) after Iraq withdrew. But this alliance proved counterproductive, alienating Egyptians and other Arab nationalists, and thus opening the way for increased Soviet influence in the Middle East.

America forms regional alliances to help contain Communism

These new U.S. policies were all designed more to stop Communist expansion than to liberate "captive nations." They amounted, in effect, to an extension and institutionalization of Truman's containment policy, which Republicans had vilified in the 1952 campaign. Intent on cutting costs and preparing for a long Cold War, Eisenhower accepted the realities of an ambiguous world order. As a result, his "New Look" in U.S, foreign policy turned out to be mainly a better-organized and more cost-effective version of the old.

Eisenhower's "New Look" sustains and enhances Truman's containment policy

KHRUSHCHEV AND THE WEST

Meanwhile, Soviet Cold War policy was also changing shape. Premier Georgi Malenkov, who in 1953 introduced a "new course" designed to spur the domestic economy and improve relations with the West, came under increasing fire from

Kremlin hard-liners. Military leaders and champions of heavy industry, fearful that their resources would be diverted to the consumer economy, made common cause with Malenkov's chief rival, Communist party boss Nikita Khrushchev. In February 1955, Malenkov was forced to resign and was replaced as premier by Defense Minister Nikolai Bulganin. The chief beneficiary of this change was Khrushchev, who had already emerged as the dominant force in the Kremlin.

Nikita S. Khrushchev, a hard-bitten Communist who had risen from obscure poverty to become one of the world's most powerful leaders, soon proved a flexible and creative innovator who was not afraid to challenge traditional assumptions. Crude, uncouth, and lacking in social graces, he nonetheless blended crafty wit, clever spontaneity, formidable ambition, and energetic opportunism in a mixture baffling to both colleagues and foes. Before long he turned against the hard-liners and, adopting many of Malenkov's policies, began to devise a new course based on "peaceful coexistence" with the capitalist world and efforts to court nonaligned nations.

Khrushchev emerges as crude but clever Soviet leader

May 1955 witnessed a flurry of diplomatic activity, as Khrushchev began putting his stamp on Soviet foreign policy. Early in the month, the USSR put forth an arms control proposal with some serious innovations. It foresaw the creation of a permanent monitoring system, with foreign inspectors stationed at key airports and seaports and along major highways and railways in each of the superpowers. By calling for a ban on nuclear testing and the gradual reduction of nuclear stockpiles, it put the Eisenhower administration in an awkward spot. Faced with a Soviet preponderance in conventional forces, and committed to countering it with "massive retaliation," the Americans had little interest in reducing their nuclear arsenal. With the ambiguities of their position thus exposed, they scrambled to find an effective response to Moscow's initiative.

Later that month, following NATO's decision to admit West Germany, the foreign ministers of Soviet bloc nations met in Warsaw at Khrushchev's initiative to chart a collective response. The result was the formation of a military alliance consisting of Poland, Hungary, Czechoslovakia, Bulgaria, Romania, the USSR, and eventually East Germany. This agreement, known as the "Warsaw Pact" (Document 27), would act as a counterweight to NATO and would place over six million soldiers under Soviet command in Eastern Europe (See Map 3, Page 65). But it also served an additional purpose: It provided a pretext for continued presence of Soviet troops in Eastern Europe, thereby keeping this region firmly under Moscow's control. It thus proved an odd alliance: During its whole history, it would use its forces only against its own members.

Soviets form Warsaw Pact to counter NATO, control Eastern Europe

That same month, Khrushchev and his comrades helped ease international tensions by agreeing to a peace treaty with Austria, which had been part of Germany from 1938 to 1945 and, like Germany, had since been divided into British, French, American, and Soviet occupation zones. Austria initially was to be included in an overall settlement with Germany, but since such a settlement was beyond reach in 1955, the "Austrian State Treaty" was negotiated as a separate pact. By its terms all occupying powers agreed to remove their forces, and Austria became a neutral, independent country. This was a major concession for the Soviets, for it meant giving up territory that had been under their control. But it did give them some advantages. It compelled the Western powers also to remove their forces from

Soviet compromise with West creates unified, neutral Austria

Austria, thus eliminating NATO's land contact with Hungary and decreasing it with Yugoslavia. And it showed that Moscow could be reasonable, thus undermining the Western hard-liners and paving the way for direct talks between Soviet and Western leaders. Shortly thereafter, Khrushchev and Bulganin made a state visit to Yugoslavia, where they initiated a limited rapprochement with the troublesome Tito regime.

Geneva hosts first Cold War summit conference

One result of all this activity was the Cold War's first summit conference, held at Geneva in July 1955. The British and French had pushed for such a meeting and Eisenhower, overriding Dulles's reservations, agreed to go along. He was joined by Khrushchev and Bulganin from the USSR, Premier Edgar Faure of France, and British prime minister Anthony Eden.

Khrushchev rejects the U.S. "open skies" plan as a spying gimmick

The meeting's most dramatic event was Eisenhower's unexpected "open skies" proposal, designed to steal the spotlight from Moscow's recent arms control initiatives. Speaking directly to Khrushchev and Bulganin, Eisenhower put forth a scheme by which the superpowers would exchange blueprints of their military force dispositions and allow each to make regular flights over the other's territory. It was a bold diplomatic stroke, but, as Eisenhower himself later admitted, there was little likelihood that the USSR would accept. For one thing, since the location and nature of most U.S. installations were already public knowledge, Moscow stood to gain much less than Washington from the information exchange. For another thing, since the Americans had a big lead in atomic weapons and long-range bombers, the Kremlin was disinclined to expose its relative weakness. Unwilling to forgo the secrecy that helped offset this weakness by keeping his foes guessing, Khrushchev derided the plan as a "very transparent espionage device" and refused to give it serious consideration.

"Spirit of Geneva" seems to bolster "peaceful coexistence"

Not much of substance was accomplished at Geneva. An impasse was reached over Germany, with Moscow refusing to consider reunification until West Germany had been disarmed, and little real progress was made in other areas. Psychologically, however, the summit was a success: The talks were cordial, the leaders got along well, and cultural and economic ties between East and West were improved. Later that year, as the USSR decreased the size of its army, returned a naval base to Finland, and extended diplomatic recognition to West Germany, the "spirit of Geneva" appeared to be working well. And in November, when the peripatetic Khrushchev announced in India that "the socialists and the capitalists have to live side by side," an age of "peaceful coexistence" seemed to be at hand.

Difficulties nonetheless remained. At a foreign ministers' conference in the fall of 1955, Foreign Minister Molotov and Secretary of State Dulles found they could agree on nothing in the absence of their more congenial bosses. Tensions in Africa and Asia, where Moscow was gaining influence, also cast some shadows on the after-summit glow. The legacy of distrust, it soon became clear, could not be entirely dispelled by meetings among leaders.

MOSCOW AND THE NONALIGNED NATIONS

Khrushchev possessed both a deep belief in the superiority of the Soviet system and a profound horror of nuclear war. Like Malenkov, he rejected the Marxist tenet that war was inevitable while capitalism existed and instead concluded that all-out war must by all means be avoided. At the same time, however, he was determined to work for the eventual destruction of capitalism and triumph of world Communism. His approach thus in some ways mirrored the West's containment policy: In time, he reckoned, the inherent conflicts within capitalism would cause it to self-destruct, and people the world over would pursue a socialist future.

Since direct conflict with the West would place the USSR and the world in dire peril, Khrushchev opted instead for indirect confrontation in what was coming to be called the Third World—Asian, African, and Latin American countries that were part of neither the capitalist West nor the Communist bloc. As Asians and Africans gained independence from Western control, Moscow sought to win their friendship and support, providing arms, advisors, and financial aid to various national liberation movements and to liberated nonaligned nations. Taking his cue from Leninist theory linking capitalism and imperialism, Khrushchev treated these movements and nations as Communism's natural allies in the global struggle with the West, and later even championed and supported "national liberation wars" (Document 37). In so doing, he deftly depicted the United States, a nation born of anti-colonial revolution and an advocate of national self-determination, as the leader of the imperialist camp and opponent of revolutionary nationalism.

Khrushchev woos Asians and Africans with anti-imperialism

Khrushchev's approach was especially relevant to Asia, where Moscow sought to exploit anti-Western sentiments in former European colonies such as India and Indonesia. In these new nations, as elsewhere in the Third World, the nationalist movements predated the Cold War and thus were not fully part of it, but their struggles and issues often were affected by it.

India, once the British Empire's "crown jewel," had gained independence in 1947 after years of nonviolent struggle led by Mohandas ("Mahatma") Gandhi. But fear and distrust between Hindus and Muslims had resulted in the former colony's division into two new nations: the Hindu-dominated Republic of India and Muslim Pakistan. For reasons unrelated to the Cold War, they were mortal enemies.

Jawaharlal Nehru, who had been Gandhi's close associate, was the Republic of India's prime minister from 1950 until 1964. Brooding yet lively, morbid yet energetic, he strove to create a more stable world free from the danger of nuclear war. Only in such a world could impoverished nations like India, to say nothing of those still trapped in colonial bondage, develop their resources to build better lives. To that end, he championed nonalignment, avoiding Cold War commitments and siding with neither superpower (Document 26B).

India's Nehru advocates nonalignment with East or West

Pakistan would have none of this. Its foreign policy was largely determined by its rivalry with India. While India carved out a centrist course, Pakistan linked its fortunes to the United States, from which it derived significant military and economic aid. Seeing this situation as a chance to gain India's friendship, Khrushchev and his comrades provided it with similar support. Ironically, then, the Soviets aided India, the world's largest democracy, and the Americans backed Pakistan, an authoritarian dictatorship. Such was the logic of the Cold War.

Americans aid repressive Pakistan so Soviets aid democratic India

Indonesia, formerly the Dutch East Indies, had gained independence in 1949, following a four-year struggle against the Dutch. A chain of islands nearly 3,400 miles long, it had a mostly Islamic population approaching 100 million, making it the world's largest Muslim nation. Its president, a former civil engineer and nationalist firebrand who called himself Sukarno, like Nehru, embraced nonalignment. In 1955 at Bandung, Indonesia, Sukarno hosted a conference of 29 Asian and African

Indonesia's Sukarno hosts Bandung conference creating nonaligned movement

nations (Documents 26A and 26C), resulting in a "nonaligned movement" aiming for an independent course not beholden to East or West. In addition to Sukarno, India's Nehru, Yugoslavia's Tito, and Egypt's Gamal Abdel Nasser all sought a leading role.

The Bandung Conference stamped Sukarno as a nonaligned leader aspiring to global stature. But unlike Nehru, Sukarno was not motivated by visions of stability and peace. He was a thoroughly romantic revolutionary who dreamed of nations on fire with the fervor of forceful change, a man enthralled by the spiritual purification derived from righteous action. The Americans, who distrusted Nehru and disapproved of Nasser, regarded Sukarno with the horrified fascination of a jungle traveler confronting a cobra. But the Soviets, anxious to woo the nonaligned nations and undermine the West, established close ties with him. Indonesia became a Soviet client and remained so until the 1960s, when an unsuccessful war with Malaysia and a failed military coup led to the eclipse of Sukarno and a murderous campaign of suppression against the Indonesian Communists. By 1967 Sukarno was removed, and General Suharto, whose anti-Communist crusade killed over 100,000 people and filled Indonesia's rivers with headless corpses, emerged as military strongman and led Indonesia into the Western camp.

Soviets back Sukarno until he's ousted by pro-Western Suharto

Nasser, Nehru, and Tito.

Egypt's Nasser, India's Nehru, and Yugoslavia's Tito—three key leaders of the "nonaligned movement"—were all smiles as they met in Yugoslavia in summer of 1956. Note, however, that the need of weaker and poorer countries to get arms and aid from one superpower or the other made it difficult for any of them to remain truly nonaligned in the Cold War era.

The Indonesia story illustrates the limits of nonalignment. It was fine for Indonesia and India to advocate a third option, but making this option effective was a different story. Indonesia was a client state, first of the East and later of the West, and client states cannot truly be nonaligned. In seeking economic and military aid from the superpowers, emerging nations in Africa and Asia often compromised not only their alignment but also their very independence.

Indonesian debacle shows limits of nonalignment and risks for Soviets in wooing nonaligned nations

These events also showed how treacherous it was for Moscow to go fishing in the troubled waters of nonaligned nations. Even where the Kremlin did make inroads, as in Indonesia, there was no guarantee its leverage would last. Once Sukarno was removed, Moscow's influence was gone, and a sizable Soviet investment was washed down the drain.

Still, in the mid-1950s, Soviet attempts to gain influence among nonaligned nations appeared to be bearing fruit, as Moscow acquired important friends in India, Indonesia, and elsewhere. As the Kremlin extended economic and military aid to new nations in Africa and Asia, Soviet stature in the Third World seemed to be on the rise.

KHRUSHCHEV AND STALIN'S LEGACY

In 1956, his standing enhanced by impressive performance on the international stage, Khrushchev turned his attention to the Soviet Communist Party's Twentieth Congress, which met in Moscow in February. There, in a highly publicized opening speech (Document 28), he trumpeted his call for "peaceful coexistence." The highlight of the gathering, however, was his dramatic "secret speech." Late in the evening of 24 February, delegates were summoned back to the hall for a special closed session to which no outsiders were admitted. Beginning around midnight, Khrushchev delivered an astonishing address (Document 29) that methodically exposed and denounced the crimes of Joseph Stalin. He accused the late dictator of creating a "cult of the individual," ordering the torture and murder of numerous loyal Communists, and imprisoning legions of innocent people. He also blamed Stalin for disastrous mistakes, such as leaving his country badly unprepared for war against Germany and causing the Soviet break with socialist Yugoslavia. The delegates, many of whom (like Khrushchev) had been loyal supporters of Stalin, were stunned by the candor and content of this address.

Khrushchev denounces Stalin in 1956 "secret speech"

The speech did not stay secret for long. Copies were distributed among party members, to be read at private meetings throughout the USSR, and by June the CIA had obtained, translated, and published it in the West. Khrushchev no doubt intended the address as a break with the past and a move against internal Stalinist rivals. But this speech and his other pronouncements also had a wider significance: By disassociating the Soviet system from the violent abuses of its Stalinist past, Khrushchev aimed to make it a more attractive model for developing nations.

At first it appeared that the congress might lead to a further easing of anxieties. In April, the Cominform, created in 1947 to help Moscow maintain its influence over other Communist parties, was formally dissolved. That same month Khrushchev made a state visit to Britain—his first to a major Western power. In June, the Stalinist Molotov stepped down as foreign minister, although he, Malenkov, and other Khrushchev rivals would remain members of the Party Presidium (the main leadership group of the Soviet Communist Party) until the follow-

Khrushchev seeks to ease tensions with Tito and with West

ing year. That same month Tito, the Yugoslav Communist leader who had defied Stalin, was welcomed with open arms in Moscow. These developments, along with Khrushchev's call for "separate roads to socialism" and renunciation of Stalinist terror, seemed to show that the Soviets were eager to improve their image, relax tensions with the West, and perhaps even ease their grip on Eastern Europe.

Despite the Kremlin's softer line, however, the Warsaw Pact nations were still dominated largely by disciples of Stalin. In denouncing their mentor, Khrushchev implicitly disparaged them, thus setting the stage for dramatic developments in Poland and Hungary.

In July 1956, in the Polish city of Poznán, a bloody clash occurred between rioting workers and city police. As the crisis threatened to escalate into a nationwide liberation movement, the Polish government began replacing hard-line officials with moderates not directly linked to Soviet control. On 19 October, Wladislaw Gomulka, who had been purged by Stalin as a "Titoist" and only released from prison in 1955, was selected as first secretary of the Polish United Workers' (Communist) Party. Alarmed, Khrushchev flew to Warsaw and threatened to use Soviet troops to keep the Polish leaders in line. Gomulka, with broad support among Polish workers, held his own by warning of massive popular resistance to any such attack. Rather than face a possible war in Poland, the Kremlin leader backed down and, reassured that Gomulka would not take Poland out of the Soviet bloc, agreed to work with the new Polish leader.

Riots in Poland bring moderate Communist Gomulka to power

In Hungary, things did not work out so well. Encouraged by the Polish success, on 22 and 23 October students in Budapest began rioting for the return of Imre Nagy, a reformist premier forced from office the previous year. The Soviets sent planes and tanks to help put down the riots, but this action merely stoked the fires of revolt, as Hungarian "freedom fighters" clashed in the streets with Soviet soldiers. Nagy returned as premier and, with Moscow's consent, on 27 October formed a new government that included non-Communists. The next day the Soviets began withdrawing their forces (Document 30A). Khrushchev seemed once again willing to compromise and allow an East European nation to pursue its own road to socialism.

Riots in Hungary bring reformist Nagy to power

But the Hungarians, unlike the Poles, would not settle for partial autonomy. The riots continued, amid demands for further reforms and independence from Soviet control. Bowing to this pressure, on 1 November Nagy announced that he would form a multiparty government, declare Hungary's neutrality, and withdraw it from the Warsaw Pact. His statement engendered euphoria in Hungary and the West, but the joy was short lived. On the morning of 4 November, Soviet tanks rolled into Budapest, and Soviet soldiers were soon battling with thousands of Hungarian resisters (Document 30B). János Kádár, head of the Hungarian Communist Party, announced the formation of a new government (Document 30C) and appealed to Moscow for military aid to "smash the dark forces of reaction." Within a week the resistance was crushed, thousands of Hungarians lay dead, and Kádár was in firm control. Nagy sought asylum in the Yugoslav embassy, but he was eventually talked into leaving and executed for treason.

Hungarians defy Soviets, who send troops and tanks to crush revolt

The West was caught flatfooted by the brutal suppression of the Hungarian revolt. The United States and Britain, deeply at odds over the simultaneous Suez crisis (discussed in the following section), were incapable of a joint response. John

Foster Dulles, who had cancer surgery on the eve of the Soviet invasion, was physically incapacitated. The imminence of U.S. presidential elections on 6 November complicated things further. But even without these distractions, there was little chance that the Americans or their allies would actually intervene. Western speeches and radio broadcasts had encouraged the Hungarian rioters and led some to think that U.S. help might be forthcoming. But the logistics of providing such aid were so complex, the dangers so great, and the chances of success so slim, that it was never seriously considered. When push came to shove, as these events made clear, the West was unprepared to interfere directly in the Communist bloc.

West does not interfere with Soviet repression in Eastern bloc

Nevertheless, the tragic events in Hungary had a devastating impact on international relations, destroying the climate of hope that had been created by Khrushchev's initiatives. The UN formally denounced the Soviet invasion, while Western leaders expressed shock and outrage at the bloody affair. Several hundred thousand Hungarians fled their homeland to take up residence in the West. And as the Communist world retrenched, a harsher attitude toward the West reemerged. Both Tito and Gomulka gave tacit support to the Soviet move against Hungary, and Khrushchev himself publicly adopted a tough, unapologetic stance. "When it is a question of fighting against imperialism," he announced on the last day of 1956, "we can state with conviction that we are all Stalinists."

Soviet brutality in Hungary reinforces East–West hostility

The Hungarian revolt.

During their 1956 uprising against Soviet rule, Hungarians staged large anti-Soviet demonstrations, including one in which a sculpted head of Stalin, the late Soviet dictator, was knocked off its statue onto a street in Budapest. Note, however, that Moscow soon sent forces to brutally crush the rebellion and bring the wayward satellite back in line.

THE SUEZ CRISIS, 1956

In late October 1956, while Moscow was preoccupied with the Hungarian revolt and America with its upcoming elections, a major crisis erupted in the Middle East. Its immediate cause was an Israeli invasion of Egypt and rapid intervention by Britain and France on the Israeli side. But the factors that engendered these events, and made the region a tinderbox throughout the Cold War and beyond, were the West's dependence on Mideast oil, the rise of Arab nationalism, and the formation of a Jewish state in the midst of the Muslim world.

Oil, Israel, and Arab nationalism foster Middle East tensions

It just so happened that the world's most extensive oil reserves were in the Middle East. The vast petroleum deposits of Saudi Arabia, Iraq, and other Persian Gulf lands were crucial to the industrial economies of Western Europe and Japan. In World War II, the Japanese had attacked America largely because of their need for oil, and Germany's inability to supply its armored units and airplanes with gasoline had helped ensure its defeat. Notwithstanding the large domestic petroleum resources of both the United States and the USSR, victory in the Cold War might well depend on access to Middle Eastern oil.

The rise of Arab nationalism was linked with the formation of Israel in 1948 and Arab humiliation at Israeli hands in the war that followed (Chapter 5). For decades, the Arab world had been torn by dynastic rivalries pitting the Hashemite monarchs of Jordan and Iraq against the ruling dynasties of Egypt and Saudi Arabia. But in the wake of the military debacle of 1948–1949, new Arab forces had arisen to oppose these regimes, hoping to overcome divisions among Arabs by creating secular governments devoted to Israel's destruction. Ironically, since Israel was supported at first by both the United States and the USSR, and since Marxism, with its denial of religious values, remained an alien philosophy among the Muslims of the Middle East, these new forces were at first both anti-Western and anti-Soviet.

The most notable changes occurred in Egypt, largely as a result of its army's defeat by Israel in 1948–1949 and Britain's continuing control of the Suez Canal. In July 1952, Egypt's King Farouk was overthrown by a group of military officers, one of whom, Colonel Gamal Abdel Nasser, eventually emerged as Egypt's dictator. It soon became obvious that he aspired to use anti-Zionist feelings to unite the Arab peoples and gain leadership of the Muslim world. In 1955, he attended the Bandung Conference, and soon thereafter he sought to establish himself as a leader of the nonaligned movement. Both Washington and Moscow watched uneasily.

Nasser emerges as Egypt's leader, aims to unite Arab world

Concerned that Nasser might turn to the Soviets for assistance, America offered Egypt substantial aid and tried to get Britain to accommodate Nasser's demands for full sovereignty over the Suez Canal. The Americans hoped that Nasser would align Egypt with the West and join the Baghdad Pact, but long-standing regional rivalries prevented this affiliation. In September 1955, Nasser tried to outflank Washington by agreeing to sell cotton to the USSR in exchange for Czech weapons. Moscow then opportunistically advanced itself as the champion of Arab nationalism against U.S. and British imperialism.

Soviets woo Arabs by supporting Arab nationalism

Washington and London, hoping to keep Nasser out of the Soviet camp, agreed in 1955 to help fund an immense Egyptian power and irrigation project called the Aswan High Dam. But in July 1956, suspecting that Nasser was smuggling arms to Algerian rebels fighting against France, and upset by his decision to recognize Red China (in protest against a U.S. decision to let France sell Israel arms initially intended for NATO), the Americans withdrew their funding from the dam project (Document 31A). Nasser then dramatically nationalized the Suez Canal (Document 31B), taking full control of that waterway and intending to use its lucrative toll revenues to build the dam. Seeing a chance to gain influence, Moscow quickly agreed to supply financial and technical aid. Britain and France now saw Nasser as an unstable demagogue, ready to hold hostage the oil and other products passing through the canal whenever he—or Moscow—considered such action useful.

Nasser nationalizes Suez Canal after America cuts aid

Nasser, who was not at all unstable, became the hero of the Arab world, and Syria and Jordan drew closer to Egypt. But Arab nationalism now threatened European prosperity, and Israel feared for its existence should Nasser manage to unite the Arabs. In the fall of 1956—fearful that Nasser was planning to cut off Europe's oil supplies (which was unlikely, given his need for the canal tolls) and then attack Israel—Britain, France, and Israel conspired to start a preventive war against Egypt. They concealed their plans from Washington, largely because U.S. courtship of Nasser had irritated and frightened London and Paris. The conspirators assumed that the Soviets, distracted by the crises in Poland and Hungary, would not intervene on Egypt's side.

Britain, France, and Israel secretly plot war against Egypt

The Israelis invaded Egypt on 29 October. As planned, the British and French then intervened to "restore order," though their true purpose was to retake the canal and remove Egypt as a threat to Israel's existence. But they failed to capture the canal in heavy fighting by airborne and amphibious forces. The Americans, whose aerial espionage had detected Israeli preparations two weeks earlier, were annoyed. Fearing that the real winners in a prolonged war would be the USSR and its Arab nationalist allies, they condemned the attack and sought UN resolutions calling for withdrawal of all invading troops (Document 31C). Moscow, fearing an Egyptian defeat and happy to embarrass Britain, urged joint U.S.-Soviet intervention to end the crisis. Faced with U.S. opposition and fearful of Soviet intervention, London and Paris were forced to accept a cease-fire in November and a pullout in ensuing months.

Americans and Soviets condemn attack, forcing Middle East truce

The crisis passed, but its impact was profound. Eisenhower was chagrined at having had to disavow his allies while siding with Nasser and Khrushchev, and British prime minister Eden resigned in disgrace. France and Britain were mortified by their failure to seize the canal, and their impotence foreshadowed not only the decline of their Middle East influence but also the end of their empires.

No one came out of the Suez crisis untarnished. Moscow won points with the Arabs by backing Egypt, but its military weakness in the Middle East had been striking. Nasser enhanced his standing as an Arab hero, but he depended on the Soviets for assistance, a prospect that hardly enthused him. This marriage of convenience would last until the mid-1970s, when abrogation of the Soviet–Egyptian friendship would end a relationship with which neither side had been fully comfortable. The Soviets would remain outsiders in the region, unable to match Washington's potential influence. And Moscow's hypocrisy in condemning the aggression was exposed by the simultaneous Soviet suppression of the Hungarian revolt.

Soviets and Nasser maintain an uneasy "friendship"

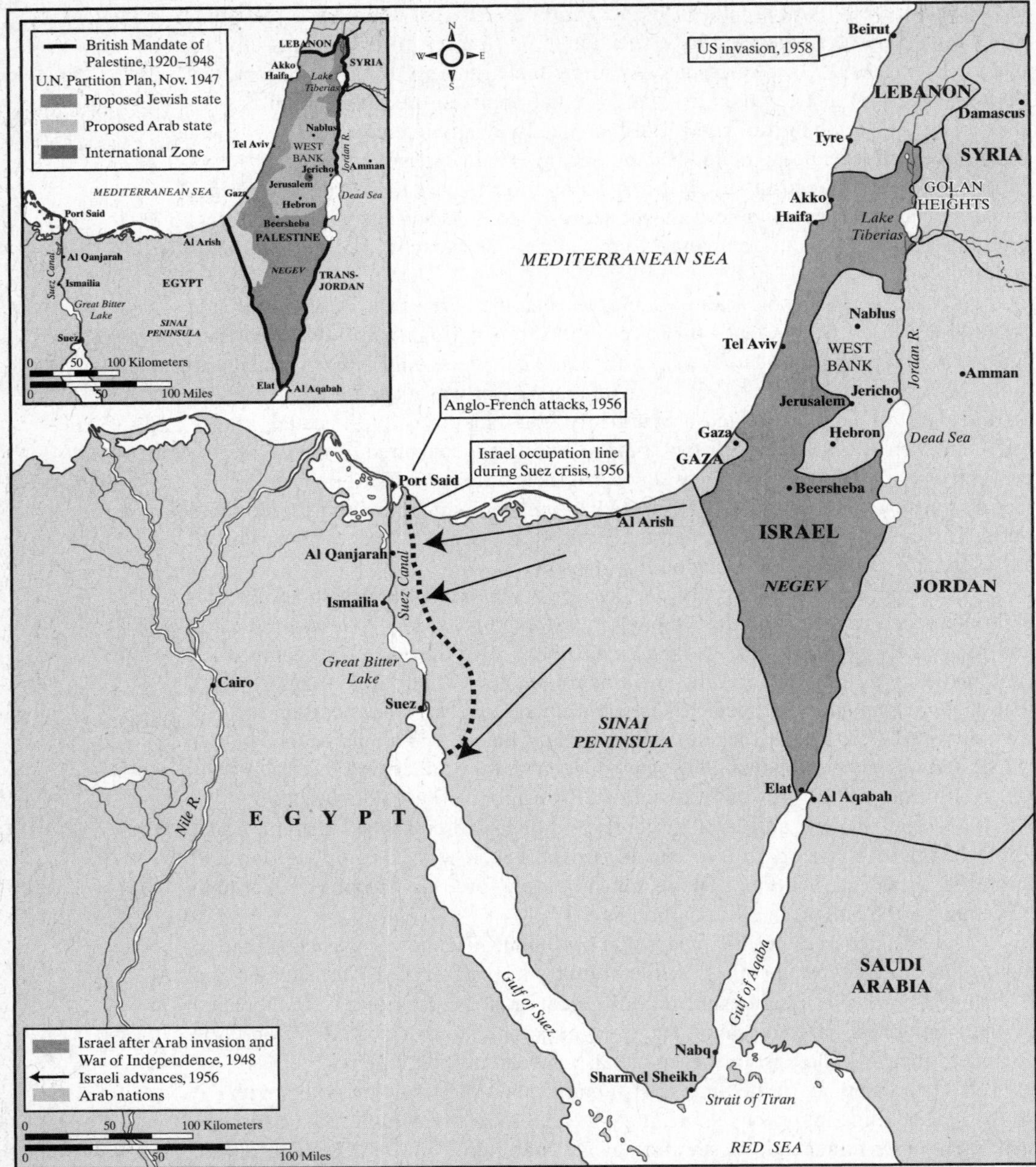

MAP 6 Arab-Israeli Conflicts, 1945–1960.

Although the UN voted in 1947 to partition Britain's Palestine mandate into Jewish and Arab states (inset map), Israel's creation in 1948 triggered a war with neighboring Arab nations, which Israel won handily. A new war broke out in 1956 when Britain and France plotted with Israel to retake the Suez Canal, recently nationalized by Egypt. Note, however, that (in a Cold War rarity) the United States and the USSR both condemned the attack, leading to a ceasefire and eventual Israeli withdrawal.

Washington's hypocrisy was shown by its subsequent intervention in the Middle East. In 1957, the Eisenhower Doctrine (Documents 32A and 32B), an extension of the Truman Doctrine, offered military and economic aid to any Middle Eastern nation facing Communist subversion. It was invoked in July 1958 when General Abdel Karim Kassem, backed by Iraqi Communists and Arab nationalists, overthrew the Hashemite monarchy in Iraq. Eisenhower responded by landing Marines in Lebanon to protect that country and Jordan from similar coups. The superpowers clearly were willing to use force when their own interests were at stake.

As coup in Iraq boosts Soviet influence, U.S. Marines land in Lebanon

THE ARMS RACE AND THE SPACE RACE

Not only did the crises of 1956 derail the movement toward East–West détente, they also nearly cost Khrushchev his job. Incensed at his denunciation of Stalin and disturbed by the Hungarian debacle, hard-liners like Molotov made common cause with Malenkov and others whose influence had waned. In June 1957, while Khrushchev was in Finland, his foes decided to strike. A majority of the Party Presidium, including Malenkov and Molotov, voted to oust him from his position as first secretary. Returning quickly, the besieged Soviet leader fought back, insisting that he could be removed only by the Party's Central Committee, which had elected him. With the help of Defense Minister Georgi Zhukov, who dispatched aircraft to bring its members quickly to Moscow, Khrushchev convened the Central Committee and it reaffirmed his position. He then had his chief rivals demoted to obscure posts: Malenkov became manager of a power station in Kazakhstan, and Molotov was made ambassador to Mongolia.

Khrushchev derails bid by rivals to oust him

Khrushchev's victory over the "Anti-Party Group," as he called it, did not give him unfettered power. Even after he assumed the office of premier in March 1958, thus becoming head of the Soviet government as well as the Communist party, he still had to maintain the support of various elements and factions. His foreign policy reflected his ambivalent position. On one hand, he sought to restore momentum to improvement of East–West relations, which had been interrupted by the events of 1956. On the other hand, to mollify Soviet hard-liners and enhance his own power status, he often resorted to belligerent speeches and displays of military muscle. He thus undermined his efforts at détente and helped accelerate the arms race.

Khrushchev tries both to ease East–West tensions and boost Soviet power

In the 1950s, both the Soviets and Americans developed new nuclear weapons that were far more powerful than the atomic bombs that had obliterated Hiroshima and Nagasaki. Those original devices were based on nuclear *fission*—splitting uranium or plutonium atoms to release the energy in their nuclei, creating a chain reaction of tremendous force. But after the Soviets developed such a weapon in 1949, President Truman had authorized work on a new U.S. bomb based on nuclear *fusion*, releasing far more energy by fusing together the atoms of hydrogen isotopes. In November 1952, using an atomic fission bomb to produce the million-degree heat needed for such fusion, American scientists achieved the first "thermonuclear" explosion. Its force was equivalent to over three million tons (megatons) of TNT—hundreds of times greater than earlier atomic weapons. The age of the hydrogen bomb had arrived.

The next year the Soviets tested their own H-bomb, showing that they were closing the gap in developing destructive technologies. But in their ability to mass-produce nuclear weapons and deliver them to distant targets, they remained well behind the United States. In 1953, the Americans possessed over a thousand atomic bombs—at least ten times as many as the Soviets—and were building a fleet of B-52 bombers capable of reaching the USSR. Under Eisenhower's "massive retaliation" strategy their lead continued to grow, and they also began building "tactical" nuclear weapons for battlefield use.

Americans and Soviets both build H-bombs, but Americans maintain big lead

Khrushchev's response was to try to deceive the West by creating the impression that the Soviets had far more weapons than they actually possessed, hoping to enhance his nation's clout by exaggerating its strength. In June 1955, for example, the Soviets impressed observers with the large number of new long-range bombers flown over Moscow on Aviation Day. In fact, they had only a small number of such bombers, but created an impression of having many more by flying the same planes several times over the city.

This deception only added to the arms race. In America, as Eisenhower's critics raised fears of a "bomber gap" favoring the USSR, he ordered the deployment of a new aircraft to get a better sense of Soviet capabilities. The U-2 spy plane, designed to elude interception by flying long distances at very high altitudes, began photographing Soviet installations in 1956. Its secret flights found no evidence of a large fleet of Soviet bombers, suggesting instead that America still had far more long-range bombers. But the administration, to avoid compromising U-2 secrecy, did not reveal its findings. Besides, the fact that the Soviets had *any* such bombers left Americans feeling vulnerable. Programs of civil defense, complete with construction of shelters intended to protect survivors of a nuclear attack from deadly radioactive fallout, were started across the land. Never again would U.S. citizens feel fully secure.

Americans fear "bomber gap," but secret U-2 spy flights reveal Soviet weakness

For all their destructive capacity, however, jet bombers were no ultimate weapon. They were piloted by humans, took many hours to reach their targets, and were to some extent susceptible to enemy defense. Much more fearsome were new unmanned rockets, capable of delivering nuclear payloads from one continent to another. These intercontinental ballistics missiles (ICBMs) would soon become the very essence of the nuclear arms race.

On 26 August 1957, the USSR announced it had successfully tested the world's first ICBM. This was a stunning achievement: For the first time, the Soviets had beaten the Americans in developing a major weapons system. But even more shocking news came six weeks later. On 4 October 1957, Soviet scientists launched into orbit an artificial earth satellite called Sputnik I, from a Russian word for "fellow traveler." The space race was on, and the USSR had the lead!

Soviet long-range missile and earth satellite stun West

This news was devastating for Americans. It undermined their faith in their own science and their educational system, with critics soon claiming that U.S. schools lagged woefully behind the Soviets in science and mathematics. In the developing nations, the news added greatly to Soviet prestige, showing that great progress could be made by following the socialist path.

The U.S. space program, embarrassed by its apparent lag, sped up efforts to launch its own earth satellite. But in December 1957, one of America's new

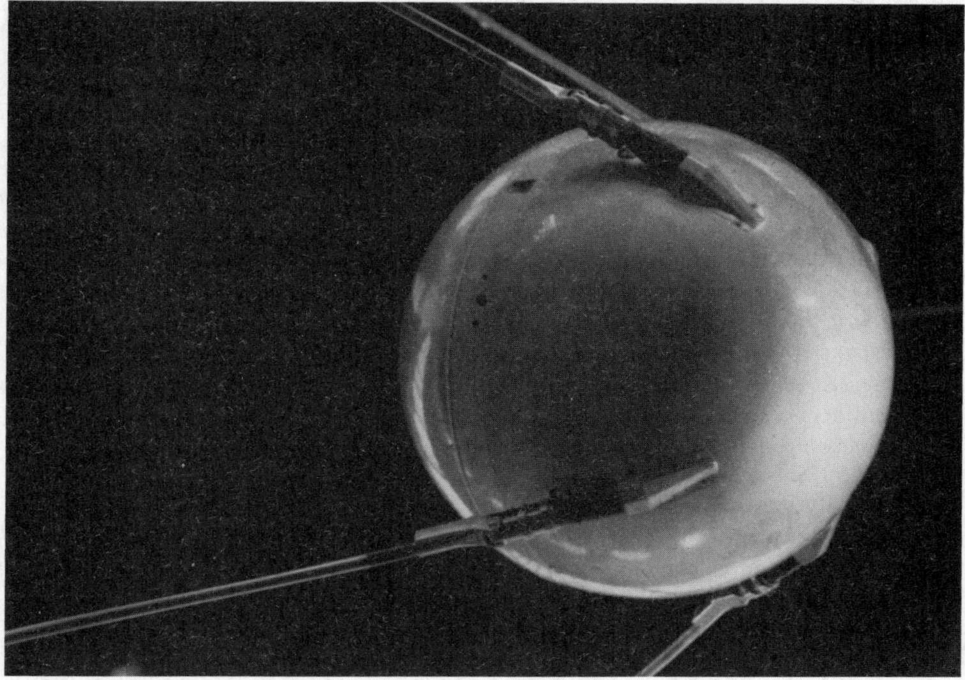

Sputnik I.

As the first object ever launched by humans into outer space, Sputnik I gained global acclaim as a momentous feat for Soviet science. As shown in this mockup display, it was an aluminum sphere almost two feet in diameter with four antennae and a radio transmitter that emitted a persistent beep. Its launch shocked Americans, who had presumed that their country was ahead in space technology, and triggered a Soviet–American space race that became a highly visible feature of the Cold War.

Vanguard missiles blew up on its launching pad, further compounding the national sense of humiliation and frustration. Only in January 1958 did the Americans finally join the Soviets in space, when scientists led by Wernher von Braun, a missile expert who had helped develop German rockets during World War II, successfully propelled a small satellite into orbit.

America races to regain lead in rocketry and space

By then, however, American self-confidence was shattered. In November 1957, the Soviets launched Sputnik II, a much larger satellite carrying a dog on board. The USSR clearly had far more powerful rockets than America did. Dire warnings of a "missile gap" were issued throughout the land, as critics of the administration warned of imminent danger. In fact, no such "gap" existed: The Soviets, deciding to await further technological advances before investing heavily in ICBMs, built only a small number of their primitive early missiles. But Americans did not know this, and Khrushchev skillfully exploited their fears by trumpeting his country's nonexistent lead.

Ironically, Khrushchev's deceptions and saber-rattling speeches gave an unintended boost to the U.S. military industry. Eager to gain increased funding for new

Khrushchev exploits Western fears, provoking U.S. arms buildup

weapons, Pentagon planners buttressed their case by pointing to the "missile gap." Aware from the secret U-2 flights that this "gap" was nonexistent, and resistant to the growing influence of America's "military-industrial complex" (Document 38), President Eisenhower refused to panic. But U.S. nuclear forces did grow substantially in the next few years.

More important than their numbers, however, was the impact of Soviet missiles on the perceived strategic balance. If the USSR had rockets that could launch a dog into space, it clearly had the capacity to deliver nuclear warheads against the United States, and to do so much more quickly than long-range bombers could. Not only did this capacity destroy what was left of the American sense of security, it also called into question NATO's reliance on the threat of a U.S. nuclear response to deter a Soviet conventional attack. American presidents could no longer threaten to use atomic weapons with impunity, and their allies could no longer be confident of U.S. nuclear support in the event of a Soviet invasion. Crossing the nuclear threshold was now riskier than ever, since it could lead to vast devastation in the United States itself.

By late 1950s, Cold War has become entrenched

By the late 1950s, then, the Cold War was becoming a permanent state of affairs. On one hand, hobbled by historic hostility and divided by deep distrust, the two sides were unable to resolve their differences and arrive at an accommodation. On the other hand, faced with the terrifying consequences of a nuclear confrontation, neither could seriously contemplate an attack upon the other. They thus maneuvered for advantage in a complex and volatile environment, while striving to manage their rivalry so it did not destroy them both.

9

The Perpetuation of the Cold War, 1957–1961

By 1957, it was clear that, despite the openings presented by Stalin's death and the hopes generated by Khrushchev's secret speech, the Cold War was not going away. During the next few years, both sides sought to defuse the conflict, sometimes by bluster and sometimes by accommodation. For a while it appeared that real progress was being made, but the legacy of distrust, combined with superpower meddling in Africa and the disastrous U-2 incident of 1960, precluded any real détente and extended the Cold War.

THE QUESTION OF GERMAN NEUTRALITY

For a time in the mid-1950s, while the world was absorbed with Khrushchev's attack on Stalin, the rebellions in Poland and Hungary, and the Suez Crisis, the German Question seemed to fade into the background. But it did not stay there long. In October 1957, just a few days after the Soviet Union launched "Sputnik," the world's first artificial satellite, Polish foreign minister Adam Rapacki proposed the establishment of a "denuclearized zone in Central Europe," consisting of Poland, Czechoslovakia, and both parts of Germany.

The Rapacki Plan was a response to NATO's decision to rearm West Germany. In 1956, Chancellor Adenauer had asked the West to provide his nation with bombers, artillery, and missiles that could give it a nuclear capability if properly configured and armed. The missiles would not be delivered until 1980, but the bombers and artillery were deployed at once, and European leaders began to think twice about the possibility of German neutrality. In the United States, George Kennan suggested that the West press for neutralization of all of Central and Eastern Europe, using as a bargaining chip the possible "nuclearization" of West Germany. Former secretary of state Dean Acheson retorted that this would be very dangerous, since a neutralized Germany would float between East and West, raising the specter of renewed German efforts to dominate Europe. In addition, the

The Rapacki Plan seeks to settle the German Question

withdrawal of U.S. troops might make it possible for the USSR to communize Central Europe through internal subversion.

Whatever advantage Americans might hope to derive from it, the prospect of West Germany becoming a nuclear power worried Moscow and prompted some serious thinking in the Communist bloc about ways to head off this horror. The Rapacki Plan provided a thoughtful alternative to the remilitarization of Germany and a possible first step toward resolving the German Question.

In 1958, however, the United States formally rejected the Rapacki Plan on the premise that Western troops in Germany, unless equipped with nuclear weapons, would be at the mercy of the vast Soviet conventional forces in Central and Eastern Europe. Washington also pointed out that the plan would require the West to give up something it might wish to do (arming West Germany) while requiring the Soviets to refrain from doing something they had no intention of doing (arming Poland, Czechoslovakia, and East Germany). In reality, as Michael Beschloss pointed out, the West had little to lose, since it was *not* planning to give nuclear weapons to Bonn, while a nuclear-free zone in Central Europe involving some sort of international monitoring might have weakened Soviet control over Poland, Czechoslovakia, and East Germany. At any rate, Moscow gained a propaganda advantage from the proposal, but since the attention of the world was largely diverted by Sputnik, even that advantage was limited.

The United States rejects the Rapacki Plan

Still, the West's decision to rearm West Germany, and its rejection of the Rapacki Plan, pointed up an uncomfortable anomaly in its approach to Central Europe. Whatever Western leaders might say in public about the tragedy of a divided Germany, in private they were just as happy to keep it that way, and they were by no means enthralled with any notion of unification that would entail German neutrality.

Konrad Adenauer, who served as West German chancellor from 1949 until 1963, consistently opposed Soviet offers to reunify and neutralize Germany. His motives were complex. He was convinced that any reunited Germany must be firmly tied to the West if it hoped to avoid a repetition of the Nazi nightmare, given what he considered the Germans' ingrained tendency to behave so terribly as to unite the world against them. As a Rhenish Catholic, he despised the East German *Saupreussen* ("sow Prussians"), considering them Eastern European militarists with marginal ties to the West. He also feared that, since most East Germans were Protestant and socialist, his Catholic and capitalist Christian Democratic Union would probably be voted out of office in a reunified nation. His reluctance to surrender West German gains presented Moscow with an imposing roadblock, but even had he been more forthcoming, other Western leaders would have been difficult to convince.

Adenauer opposes Soviet efforts to reunify Germany

The United States, led by Dwight Eisenhower, wanted to tie any reunited Germany to NATO and the European Economic Community (EEC). (The EEC was a "Common Market" formed in 1957 to further integrate the economies of the countries in the European Coal and Steel Community: Italy, France, West Germany, Belgium, Luxembourg, and the Netherlands; Document 33). Failing that, the Americans preferred to keep Germany divided. In 1954, when Moscow offered a united Germany from which all foreign troops would be withdrawn, under some sort of system which would perpetuate East Germany's socialist accomplishments, the United States was not interested. France, preoccupied with its collapsing empire, wanted closer economic ties with West Germany but remained troubled by the prospect of a reunified,

Konrad Adenauer meets with Charles de Gaulle, 1959.
West German chancellor Adenauer (83) and French president de Gaulle (69) had lived through both world wars of the twentieth century. A principal cause of those wars had been Franco-German animosity, and these two statesmen were determined to reconcile their nations in order to prevent future wars.

rearmed, economically powerful Germany dominating Central Europe—even if that nation was firmly allied to NATO. Once Charles de Gaulle came to power in 1958, French opposition became more pronounced; Gaullists were skeptical of NATO's usefulness under the doctrine of massive retaliation, which posited an all-out nuclear response to any conventional Soviet attack on Western Europe. Most Frenchmen found it hard to believe that any U.S. government would risk the incineration of America to defend Paris against Communism. De Gaulle accordingly sought closer ties with West Germany through the EEC and the Franco-German Friendship Treaty of 1963. Nor would Britain be any more likely to embrace Soviet initiatives: Twice already, in 1917 and 1941, the intervention of the New World had saved the Old from German domination. London would follow America's lead on the German Question, regardless of whether a Conservative or a Labour government sat in Whitehall.

France doubts U.S. resolve to defend Europe with nuclear weapons

KHRUSHCHEV'S BERLIN ULTIMATUM, 1958–1959

By mid-1958, then, German reunification and neutralization lay dead in the water, and the Rapacki Plan floated motionless alongside. Khrushchev spent the early months of that year consolidating his power: In March, he ousted Premier Bulganin and assumed that office himself, ending any pretense of collective leadership. That autumn he once again addressed the German Question. On 10 November, he declared his intent to sign a peace treaty with East Germany that would force the Western powers to negotiate access rights to West Berlin directly with the East German government. Washington, London, and Paris quickly replied that their rights in West Berlin were guaranteed by the 1945 Yalta agreements, which predated the creation of East Germany. On 27 November, Khrushchev promised no alteration in Berlin's status for a period of six months, during which negotiations should lead to the withdrawal of all foreign troops and UN recognition of Berlin as a free city. Eisenhower was willing to consider this, as long as both East and West Berlin were included and all access routes were patrolled by the UN; but Khrushchev wanted to turn East Berlin over to East Germany. His lengthy note abandoned previous Soviet insistence on reunification and neutralization: The unfortunate existence of two Germanies could be accepted, but the anomalous occupation of Berlin must end. The note carried the tone of an ultimatum: six months and out, or else.

Khrushchev issues an ultimatum on Berlin

Khrushchev hoped to use this threat as a negotiating tool to prevent West Germany from deploying nuclear weapons. If West Germany were to withdraw from NATO and East Germany from the Warsaw Pact, Germany would be effectively neutralized even if it were not reunified. But Khrushchev had bluffed too often, having threatened to use rockets during the Suez and Lebanon crises. Eisenhower, who knew the real limitations of the Soviet nuclear arsenal from U-2 espionage data, did not believe Moscow would go to war over Berlin. The six-month deadline baffled him, since he was unaware of Khrushchev's fear that the Sino-Soviet split was widening and would soon become public. For the time being, Beijing endorsed the 10 November note, being favorably inclined toward anything that would worsen relations between Moscow and Washington; but Khrushchev wanted results quickly, while he could still derive some leverage from the eroding Chinese alliance.

In the spring of 1959, a mild war scare afflicted the United States as the 27 May deadline approached. Eisenhower handled the situation skillfully, denying the existence of any real crisis, secure in the knowledge that the Soviet nuclear capability was exaggerated, and consistently demonstrating both his willingness to negotiate and his refusal to panic. He did, of course, have contingency plans: If the deadline passed and East Germany tried to cut off access to West Berlin, he was prepared to initiate a new airlift and sever relations with Moscow. But he doubted this would be necessary, and his doubts were well placed. London and Paris pushed for a summit meeting to settle the issue; Eisenhower and Secretary of State Dulles (then dying of cancer), wishing to avoid a meeting with Khrushchev unless there were guaranteed results, countered with the offer of a conference of foreign ministers in Geneva. It convened on 11 May, after Khrushchev hinted that his Berlin deadline would not expire as long as the meeting was proceeding satisfactorily. Simultaneously, he invited Eisenhower to visit the USSR, and the tension began to lift.

Eisenhower realizes that Khrushchev is bluffing

Eisenhower decided in July that if the foreign ministers' conference showed progress, he would invite Khrushchev to America for a few days in September. He asked Robert Murphy, his special representative, to convey the suggestion to Soviet first deputy premier Frol Kozlov. Unfortunately, Murphy was unaware of the linkage between the offer of the visit and the progress of the conference. He delivered an unconditional invitation, which Khrushchev accepted on 22 July. The Soviet leader announced that he would come in September for *ten* days and tour the entire country. Eisenhower, who had not bargained for this, was exasperated

Eisenhower invites Khrushchev to visit America

Soviet premier Khrushchev and U.S. vice president Nixon debate in Moscow, 1959.

On 7 July 1959, Khrushchev and Nixon paid an official visit to the American pavilion at an exhibition in Moscow. Moments after this photograph was taken, the two men engaged in an impromptu debate in a replica of a modern American kitchen. This "kitchen debate" showcased each man's conviction that his system of government was the best in the world, and gave Nixon the reputation of being a forceful leader who could stand up to Khrushchev.

and complained that the mix-up would not have occurred had Dulles been alive. Khrushchev, however, was exhilarated: A face-to-face sojourn with Eisenhower on U.S. soil would underline for the entire world the equality of status between the United States and the USSR, which he had sought to confirm through bluster and bluff since 1953.

U.S. vice president Richard Nixon arrived in Moscow the day after Khrushchev's acceptance to open an exhibition of American art and technology. Under the circumstances, his journey took on significance well beyond its original purpose. As Nixon and Khrushchev toured the kitchen of a "typical American home" exhibit, they needled each other, traded thinly veiled insults, and extolled the virtues of their respective systems. The "Kitchen Debate," captured on film, did wonders for Nixon's image in the United States and both stimulated and amused Khrushchev, who enjoyed the rare occasions on which adversaries stood up to him in blunt, earthy terms. For his part, Nixon recalled years later that of all the statesmen he had known, none had a "more devastating sense of humor, agile intelligence, tenacious sense of purpose and brutal will to power" than Khrushchev. This peculiar combination of crude Russian peasant and shrewd politician would shortly become the first Russian head of state to visit the United States.

Nixon and Khrushchev confront one another in Moscow

KHRUSHCHEV'S TRIP TO AMERICA

On 15 September 1959, Premier and Mrs. Khrushchev arrived in Washington for a twelve-day visit that fascinated the world. The Soviet leader spent his first ten days meeting U.S. politicians and film stars, touring New York, Los Angeles, San Francisco, and Pittsburgh, discussing hybrid corn with Iowa farmer Roswell Garst, and publicly bemoaning his inability to visit Disneyland (security forces could not guarantee his safety among large crowds). Dislike for the Soviet Union was of course widespread, so not everyone was friendly. Conservative columnist William F. Buckley suggested dyeing the Hudson River red so that Khrushchev could sail into New York harbor on a sea of blood, but no one implemented this novel suggestion.

At the end of the visit, Khrushchev and Eisenhower spent two days in private talks at Camp David, the presidential retreat in Maryland's Catoctin Mountains. As might have been expected, the boisterous, earthy Ukrainian and the businesslike, impatient Kansan did not become close friends. Khrushchev's indirect effort to raise the subject of U.S. relations with China has intrigued historians ever since; apparently, he was laying the groundwork for a future attempt to barter Soviet help in scuttling China's nuclear program for a Western pledge to deny such weapons to West Germany and Japan. Although Eisenhower was aware of the deepening Sino-Soviet rift, he did not accept the gambit. But he did raise the German Question on the second day, persuading Khrushchev to cancel his Berlin ultimatum in exchange for a presidential promise to seek a fair solution in the near future and to endorse a summit meeting of the four great powers. Khrushchev, delighted, invited the entire Eisenhower family to visit Russia in June 1960 and flew back to a hero's welcome in Moscow.

Eisenhower and Khrushchev make headway at Camp David

On the face of it, the trip produced modest results, but on a less tangible level its effects were significant. Khrushchev had demonstrated his equality with

Dwight D. Eisenhower and Nikita S. Khrushchev at Camp David, Maryland, 25 September 1959.

Khrushchev's visit to the United States fascinated the world. Part of his twelve-day trip was a summit meeting with President Eisenhower at the presidential retreat at Camp David, Maryland. There the two leaders agreed that Khrushchev would cancel his Berlin ultimatum, Eisenhower would endorse a four-power summit conference, and Eisenhower would visit the Soviet Union in June 1960. The Cold War grew decidedly less frigid, at least for a time.

Eisenhower and had defended Soviet interests with vigor and skill; his stature in his own government was enhanced considerably. Eisenhower, entering the final year of his presidency, now believed that Khrushchev was a man with whom he might work for a truly lasting peace that would constitute his final legacy to his country and the world. The Soviet people, proud of their leader's achievement, hoped for a restoration of the wartime friendship with America that many remembered wistfully. The Americans, getting a close look at the first Communist leader ever to visit their shores, sensed with some surprise that Khrushchev was not a monster but a man, and not an entirely unpleasant man at that. The visit helped to stabilize U.S.–Soviet relations and furnished a benchmark against which later trips would be judged. What did it matter that the German Question had not been settled? No one had thought it would be, and at least it had been rendered less explosive. Further progress could be expected at the summit in 1960.

The Cold War thaws as a result of Khrushchev's visit

THE NUCLEAR TEST BAN ISSUE

One of the key issues to be discussed at the summit was the banning of nuclear tests. During the 1950s, as both superpowers tried out their nuclear bombs, scientists grew increasingly concerned about the deadly fallout these explosions caused. World attention had been drawn to the problem in 1954, when a huge U.S. H-bomb test in the western Pacific rained radioactive fragments onto a boat full of Japanese fishermen, poisoning them with radiation sickness. Before long, scientists and luminaries like Albert Einstein and Albert Schweitzer were calling for an end to nuclear tests. The Soviet arms proposal of 10 May 1955 advocated a ban on nuclear blasts, and, in the U.S. presidential campaign of 1956, candidate Adlai Stevenson proposed a joint moratorium on the testing of hydrogen bombs. Unfortunately for Stevenson, Moscow compromised him by endorsing his proposal. And the Eisenhower administration, which was using its tests to develop a new generation of weapons, remained opposed to any moratorium.

Concerns over fallout spur efforts to ban nuclear testing

By the following year, however, the international clamor had become so strident—and so damaging to the U.S. image—that the administration began to rethink its position. Even Secretary of State Dulles, who had little use for arms control, gradually changed his tune as it became clear that U.S. opposition to a test ban was giving Moscow an edge in the court of world opinion. The Soviets, meanwhile, were scoring public relations points by periodically offering to suspend their nuclear tests for two or three years, provided the United States would follow suit.

At first the Americans, who were working on a "clean" bomb that was relatively fallout-free, tried to finesse the issue by floating a counterproposal hedged with provisions unacceptable to Moscow. But on 31 March 1958, the Soviets, having just finished a series of nuclear tests, announced the voluntary suspension of their own testing program and invited the United States to join them. Their timing was superb. The Americans, on the verge of beginning their own series of tests, refused to go along and thus offended world opinion. To save face, Eisenhower called for a conference of technical experts from East and West to devise an inspection and detection system. After some hesitation, Khrushchev agreed, and in the summer of 1958, technicians from the United States, Britain, and the USSR met at Geneva and designed a workable approach. Eisenhower, sensing a chance to restore his nation's

Moscow and Washington temporarily suspend testing

lost prestige, invited the Soviets to meet and negotiate a comprehensive test ban treaty, beginning on 31 October. For good measure, he announced that the United States (which was completing its own test series) would cease testing for a year beginning on that date. The British soon followed suit. The Soviets finally agreed to the talks, and, after a few quick tests in early November, they announced their own moratorium. Hopes were raised throughout the world that a test ban was within reach.

But difficulties remained. It was true that the nuclear powers had decided to stop contaminating the planet with fallout, at least for the time being, and this was cause for hope. And indeed, for almost three years no atomic tests by either side were detected. Moreover, in a key concession made early in 1959, the United States and Britain agreed to decouple the test ban from other arms issues. But the talks, held in Geneva, soon ran into a stumbling block. The United States announced that the detection system worked out by the experts was deficient in one key respect: It could not identify small nuclear tests conducted underground. This flaw did not prove fatal, but it did delay things for almost a year as negotiators looked for a way around the problem. Finally, early in 1960, the United States and Britain suggested that the ban apply only to aboveground tests and underground blasts large enough to be detected with existing seismic equipment. Joint research could then seek technical advances to pick up smaller explosions. In March the Soviets agreed, provided that both sides declare a moratorium on underground tests while the detection research was proceeding. In principle, the Western powers were willing to accept this, and there was reason to believe that remaining issues could be resolved at the Paris summit, scheduled to begin in May.

THE U-2 AFFAIR

Both Eisenhower and Khrushchev had wanted a summit earlier in the year, but French president Charles de Gaulle managed to delay it until after an atomic test in February 1960 made France the fourth member of the nuclear club, so he could host the meeting in Paris as an equal of the other three. Standing six feet five in a nation whose average man was a foot shorter, de Gaulle dominated France both physically and politically. Having resurrected French honor from the disgrace of collaboration with Nazi Germany in the 1940s, he returned from retirement in 1958 to rescue French democracy and eventually to extricate his country from a debilitating war in Algeria (see the following section). In the process, he implemented a new constitution and presided over the rapid modernization of one of Europe's most traditional societies.

To the Germans, de Gaulle was a formidable adversary turned potential ally; to the Soviets, a bemusing combination of farsighted statesman and strutting peacock; but to the British and Americans, he was an arrogant and ungrateful ally whose tenacious defense of French grandeur was neither understood nor appreciated. Frosty, suspicious, and eloquent, he stood not only for French dignity and sovereignty but also for a Europe positioned between Washington and Moscow, a Europe of independent nations and integrated economies, a Europe in which the United States and Britain possessed neither permanent interests nor a permanent place. He remembered Eisenhower fondly as an American general who had treated him and his country with respect, and he made it clear that if push came to shove, France would side with the

De Gaulle seeks a larger global role for France

West. But he insisted on an equal say in U.S. strategic decisions, being unimpressed with Soviet bluffs and suspecting that if the Cold War ever turned hot, it would be through American miscalculation rather than Russian aggression. In 1966, he would take France out of the NATO military command, asserting French sovereignty while remaining America's ally from (as he saw it) a position of equality. In 1960, holding the atomic bomb, he could play his hand to the limit and infuriate both sides with his penchant for independent action.

So de Gaulle had his way. The summit would convene in Paris on 16 May. Meanwhile there was work to be done. Khrushchev had hoped for a summit before the end of 1959 because he intended to announce a Soviet Army troop reduction of 1.2 million men in January 1960. This move, undertaken to cut costs, would deprive him of elbow room for concessions at Paris and would put him under pressure from Kremlin hard-liners to stand firm against the West. Given de Gaulle's intransigence, he was forced to make this disclosure well before the summit. Ironically, this attracted Eisenhower's attention and helped convince him that Khrushchev was ready to make serious moves in the direction of arms control. With real progress being made on the nuclear test ban issue, it appeared that the summit would furnish the occasion for Eisenhower to end his long career with a meaningful arms control measure and for Khrushchev to cap the arms race so that the Soviet economy could redirect its emphasis to consumer goods.

Khrushchev reduces the size of the Soviet army

Inspections posed the most challenging remaining obstacle, since the U.S. Senate would be reluctant to ratify any treaty if it looked like the Russians could cheat. Since 1956, however, Eisenhower had received high-quality, top-secret photographic intelligence as to the nature and extent of the USSR's ballistic missile deployment. These photographs were provided by the CIA's U-2 reconnaissance planes, which could be expected to afford superb monitoring capability between the signing of a test ban and the anticipated deployment of a U.S. spy satellite in the early 1960s.

The U-2 was designed to cruise at 70,000 feet, far higher than any other aircraft and well above the 45,000-foot maximum range of the best Soviet surface-to-air missile. It carried huge cameras equipped with telescopic lenses that permitted continuous photography of a strip of land 750 miles wide. Taking off from bases in Japan, Pakistan, Turkey, West Germany, and Norway, it could traverse the USSR from any direction with a range of 4,750 miles. Beginning with its first mission on 4 July 1956, the U-2 flew only on the explicit orders of the president, who assisted the CIA and Department of Defense in target selection. The plane was so secret that America's own National Security Agency tracked its initial flights over Russia without knowing what it was. Its photographs convinced Eisenhower that as late as January 1960 Moscow had not a single operational ICBM, and the knowledge that the USSR was engaged neither in planning a nuclear attack nor in accelerating its weapons production helped the president to resist post-Sputnik demands for a vast missile buildup.

The U-2 spy plane enables the United States to photograph Soviet territory

Eisenhower could not, of course, disclose the source of his information, any more than Moscow could tell the world about the U-2. Khrushchev was outraged by the flights, but to publicize them would be to admit that Soviet antiaircraft weapons could not defend the world's largest nation against repeated violations of its airspace. He lodged a generalized protest after the 1956 flights but remained silent thereafter. As a retired military officer, Eisenhower knew that it was only a matter of time before the Soviets developed a weapon that could bring the U-2 down, and when Khrushchev accepted his invitation to come to America, he suspended all flights over Russia for an indefinite period. Had that prohibition continued a few more months, the course of the Cold War might have been changed radically.

CIA director Allen Dulles asked in the spring for resumption of the U-2 missions, and Eisenhower, anxious for all possible insight into Soviet deployments prior to the summit, reluctantly agreed. Two presummit runs were authorized; the first, on 9 April, proceeded without incident. But the second, on 1 May, was reported missing. Soon the USSR announced that a U.S. plane had crashed in Soviet territory. Assuming that the pilot, a CIA operative named Francis Gary Powers, had either been killed in the crash or committed suicide per instructions, the United States put out a cover story that the plane was a weather flight that had strayed off course (Documents 34A and 34B).

Eisenhower resumes U-2 flights just before the Paris summit

In Moscow, Khrushchev faced a crisis. Holding off hard-liners who wanted to use the incident as a pretext for canceling the summit, he decided to expose the wrecked aircraft as a spy plane (Document 34C). After further U.S. denials, he revealed that the pilot had been captured alive (for Powers had parachuted to safety and declined to take his own life). He hoped thus to put Eisenhower on the defensive and force him to apologize for intelligence services which had exceeded his orders—a standard defense mechanism used by politicians for ages. Khrushchev could then accept the apology and proceed to the summit in triumph, while Eisenhower would fly to Paris with egg on his face.

It was a promising scenario, and it unfurled flawlessly for a few days. The difficulty was that Khrushchev's solution to his dilemma placed Eisenhower in one of his own. If he denied authorizing U-2 flights, it would appear to the world that the U.S. president had so little control that his subordinates could trigger a major crisis without his knowledge. And Khrushchev might have more surprises up his sleeve: Who knew what Powers had said under interrogation? If Eisenhower lied, Khrushchev might be able to throw the lie back in his face. On the other hand, if he told the truth, he would become the first U.S. president to admit that his nation practiced peacetime espionage. It was difficult to imagine how Khrushchev could sit down with him in Paris and welcome him to Russia after such a disclosure, particularly since the Soviet leader had repeatedly assured his colleagues and people that Eisenhower was a man who could be trusted.

The U-2 crash creates problems for Khrushchev and Eisenhower

Either way, it was a gamble. Eisenhower chose the option for which his entire career as a military officer had conditioned him. He put out a statement to the effect that the U-2 flights had been carried out under his general orders and might continue until the USSR agreed to reciprocal inspection of bases and installations. With that revelation, the U-2 affair took on a different dimension, putting an end to the recent thaw in the Cold War and rupturing personal relations between Khrushchev and Eisenhower.

Eisenhower admits to peacetime espionage

THE COLLAPSE OF THE PARIS SUMMIT

Khrushchev was beside himself. Eisenhower's decision to resume U-2 flights had placed him in a tough position. The crash of the 1 May flight and the pilot's survival presented him with an enticing opportunity; now the president's astonishing decision to accept personal responsibility for acts of espionage held him up to ridicule and left him few options. He responded with an emotional tirade that left little doubt that the Paris summit was in danger. Had he known that Eisenhower had instructed that the presidential plane, Air Force One, be equipped with high-resolution cameras for use during the president's travels within the USSR, his reaction might have been even stronger.

Still, something might be salvageable in Paris. The Soviet Presidium authorized Khrushchev to get there early; if he could obtain a public apology from Eisenhower, the summit and the president's trip to Russia might yet go forward. On 14 May, he arrived in Paris and conferred the next day with de Gaulle, who told him flatly that he could not expect a head of state to apologize for routine espionage, and with British prime minister Harold Macmillan, who was no more helpful. Macmillan was more eager than Eisenhower or de Gaulle to settle the German Question, but he had worked with both men during World War II and had no intent of letting Britain be used as a cat's paw for Khrushchev. Meanwhile, Eisenhower's famous temper was beginning to flare. He was convinced that Khrushchev was using the U-2 incident as a pretext to wreck the summit and even considered calling it off himself. By the evening of 15 May, the summit seemed stillborn.

De Gaulle and Macmillan take Eisenhower's side

The next day the roof fell in. As de Gaulle opened the conference, Khrushchev demanded the floor and read a lengthy statement denouncing the United States, withdrawing his invitation to Eisenhower, and suggesting that the summit be postponed for six to eight months—until a new American president was inaugurated! Eisenhower replied that the flights would not resume while he was in office, and de Gaulle defended the United States by calling attention to a Soviet satellite that flew over France eighteen times a day. Khrushchev insisted on an apology for the sake of his country's honor and his own internal political situation (an embarrassing admission that startled the U.S. delegation). Macmillan made an emotional plea that all the intense effort of the past two years should not be cast aside, but the meeting broke up in turmoil. Khrushchev refused to meet again without some expression of U.S. regret, and by the next evening, it was clear that the summit was ruined (Documents 34D and 34E).

The U-2 affair destroys the Paris summit

The results were devastating. Khrushchev, both genuinely angry and under great pressure at home, wrote Eisenhower off; he would postpone further attempts to solve the German Question and slow the arms race until a new man sat in the White House. Years later he would claim that he never enjoyed full control of his government after the U-2 affair. The episode, and especially Eisenhower's admission of responsibility, undercut Khrushchev's authority by playing into the hands of Soviet hard-liners and "metal-eaters" (who pushed for a massive military buildup). It intensified tensions between Moscow and Beijing, and contributed to pressures on Khrushchev to strengthen the Soviet global posture, thus helping to lay the groundwork for the Berlin and Cuban crises of 1961 and 1962.

Khrushchev's authority is reduced by the U-2 affair

For his part, Eisenhower was enraged and frustrated, feeling that Khrushchev was wrecking his hopes for a peaceful world on the shoals of an impossible demand. He may also have privately regretted his own decision to let the U-2 fly so close to the summit. He was, however, heartened by de Gaulle's unequivocal support. The French president, a fatalist who had expected little from the conference anyway, was incensed

Khrushchev denounces the United States at the abortive Paris summit conference in May 1960. Flanked by Defense Minister Marshal Rodion Malinovsky (to his left) and Foreign Minister Andrei Gromyko (to his right), Nikita Khrushchev expresses his outrage against the United States at a press conference in Paris. The shooting down of an American U-2 spy plane on 1 May 1960, followed by Eisenhower's decisions first to lie about the nature of the flight and then to admit it, left Khrushchev vulnerable to criticism from Kremlin hard-liners who complained that he had been too trusting of Eisenhower. Under pressure at home and furious with Eisenhower, Khrushchev flew to Paris and destroyed the summit conference.

at Khrushchev's conduct. He returned to the Elysée Palace to continue wrestling with the Algerian snarl and make plans for closer ties with West Germany. Finally, Harold Macmillan's devastation at the summit's collapse was unfeigned. Less than four years after the Suez debacle, London was liquidating its African and Middle Eastern empires and was openly yearning for a Soviet–American rapprochement. Britain was reduced to a supporting role in Cold War drama, a fact that would be underscored in 1962–1963, when Skybolt, EEC, John Profumo, and Kim Philby (Chapter 10) would drive further nails into the coffin of British world leadership.

The summit's collapse calls attention to Britain's weakness

THE COLD WAR COMES TO AFRICA

As the superpowers focused their attention on Europe, a vast sea change was taking place on the continent to the south. The great colonial empires of Britain, France, Spain, Belgium, and Portugal were beginning to disappear as the African nations one-by-one achieved independence. Neither superpower had previously shown much interest in Africa. But the newly independent nations would provide tempting Cold War targets, with some prized for mineral wealth, others for strategic location, and all for their votes in the UN General Assembly, where the Soviet bloc was grossly outnumbered. Decolonization offered Moscow the opportunity to alter the balance, and Khrushchev was not one to let such a chance go by.

In 1959, Khrushchev's government established an Africa Institute and hired distinguished historian I. I. Potekhin to direct it. By then it was obvious that many African nationalists, resentful toward Europe after decades of domination, were skeptical of the West and inclined toward socialism. These considerations, along with Khrushchev's strategy of weakening the West by wooing the Third World, led the USSR to establish the People's Friendship University in Moscow in 1960 and to present itself as the natural ally of liberation movements.

Moscow takes an interest in emerging African nations

Washington looked askance at the potential expansion of Soviet influence, but it had few vital interests in Africa. U.S. policy toward Africa was therefore ambivalent. There was some support for nationalism, such as Eisenhower's rebuke of the Suez invasion in 1956 and Senator John Kennedy's 1957 speech urging the French to leave Algeria. But neither Eisenhower nor Kennedy articulated any consistent policy toward African liberation. The decolonization of Africa coincided with the most intense phase of the U.S. civil rights movement (1955–1965), and no U.S. government could move more forcefully to promote rights for Africans than it was moving to promote them for African Americans.

The Cold War's impact on Africa, therefore, was localized in a handful of emerging nations. Wherever Moscow decided to push, Washington, with its containment mentality, would usually push back. The Americans were opposed to colonialism and were glad to see the empires fall, but they were also closely tied to European nations whose empires were crumbling, and they were reluctant to see the Communists gain a foothold anywhere.

The ambiguities of the U.S. approach were nowhere more evident than in Algeria, the largest of France's North African colonies. In 1954, a number of radical nationalist groups, composed of disenchanted urban professionals and veterans of the French army, had merged to form the *FLN* (National Liberation Front), which then launched an All Saints' Day uprising in 45 Algerian cities on 1 November 1954. The French, having recently been embarrassed in Indochina (Chapter 11), were in no mood to capitulate again or to surrender their most desirable overseas possession. France thus sent 750,000 troops to Algeria in a war that lasted more than seven years. That level of commitment required the conscription of large numbers of men who had little sympathy for colonialism. Marked by widespread atrocities on both sides, the conflict was labeled *la sale guerre*, "the dirty war."

The Algerian War creates a dilemma for France

At first the FLN disdained Communist aid and turned for help to other Islamic countries: Tunisia, Morocco, and Nasser's Egypt. Moscow backed the FLN out of a desire to embarrass France, and the French Communist Party followed suit, but prospects for communizing an independent Algeria were never strong. Marxism's materialistic philosophy proved no more attractive in Islamic Algeria than it had in Islamic Egypt, and the Algerian Communist Party remained the orphan stepchild of the Algerian war.

MAP 7 Decolonization and Cold War Clashes in Africa and the Middle East, 1945–1990.
Soviet efforts to gain influence among emerging nations victimized by Western imperialism, and U.S. resistance to these efforts, intertwined the Cold War with African and Asian anticolonial struggles. Observe that by the 1970s almost all colonial and mandate areas in Africa and the Middle East had gained independence from European rule, and that some of these areas had become Cold War battlegrounds.

In Washington, the war was viewed with concern—not because of potential Communist inroads, but because of its destabilizing effects on France, a key U.S. ally. Senator Kennedy's 1957 speech asking France to quit Algeria argued that this would be in the best interests of France itself. The Eisenhower administration backed the French halfheartedly. When de Gaulle assumed power in 1958, it appeared that the situation might stabilize. De Gaulle studied the issue, temporized, waffled, and earned the title "prince of ambiguity" for his indiscernible posture. After an abortive coup in Algiers in January 1960, he tilted against independence, provoking the *FLN* to turn to Moscow and Beijing for aid. This in turn prodded de Gaulle to negotiate with the rebels, and the war finally ended with Algerian independence in 1962.

Washington tepidly supports the French in Algeria

In supporting the Algerian rebels, the Soviets managed to embarrass France, but they did not gain much else. Throughout the Cold War years, Algeria would remain friendly to Moscow but would never become in any sense a member of the "Communist bloc" and would vote as it pleased in the UN. With Tunisia following a similar course, and Morocco drawing closer to the United States, the independence of North Africa would carry with it no distinct Cold War advantages for the USSR.

Algeria gains independence, but Soviets gain little

Neither, for that matter, would the concurrent rebellion in the Congo, Belgium's only colony, which had not been prepared for self-government. In 1957, a British decision to give independence to Ghana (formerly the Gold Coast) galvanized African aspirations for self-rule. One year later de Gaulle visited the French Congo, which bordered the Belgian colony, to campaign for votes in favor of autonomy and further association with France in an upcoming referendum. His wartime prestige had been strong in central Africa, and his visit inspired a Congolese cultural association known as ABAKO to transform itself into a political party.

De Gaulle's visit to Africa stirs interest in the Belgian Congo

ABAKO was led by Joseph Kasavubu, deputy of the Congolese prophet Simon Kimbangu, who had died in a Belgian prison in 1951 after 30 years of captivity and who was rumored to be advising Kasavubu from beyond the grave. More terrestrial leadership came from Patrice Lumumba, a young postal worker who attended an All-African Peoples' Conference in Ghana in December 1958 and returned preaching pan-African solidarity in the struggle against imperialism. Lumumba assumed leadership of the Congolese National Movement, which stood for centralization after independence, in opposition to federalist regional leaders like Kasavubu and the wealthy Moïse Tshombe of mineral-rich Katanga province. On 4 January 1959, the prohibition of an ABAKO meeting in the colonial capital of Léopoldville triggered widespread riots in an area plagued by increasing African unemployment. More than a hundred Congolese were killed, and the Belgian government panicked.

Belgians suddenly saw the possibility of an Algerian-style colonial war and began to notice the Congo's drain on the Belgian economy. King Baudouin promised the Congo independence following a period of constitutional reform, but when a meeting was held in Brussels in January 1960 to plan the transition, the Belgians were shocked to hear all Congolese representatives ask for immediate independence. The Congolese in turn were astonished when Belgium granted the request, setting 30 June 1960 as Independence Day. Lumumba was Belgium's favorite Congolese politician, and when his movement won a plurality of seats in the Congo's first national election, he was installed as prime minister with Kasavubu as president. The Belgians appear to have hoped that the new government would remain dependent on Brussels and that white Belgians would continue to exercise broad authority in the Congo. The Congolese appear to have hoped for independence and modernization under stable leadership.

Belgium suddenly grants independence to the Congo

None of these hopes were realized. Five days after independence, Congolese troops mutinied against their Belgian commanders. This crippled the new government and terrified European residents, who appealed to Brussels to return and protect them. The resulting reintroduction of Belgian troops muddied the waters even further. On 11 July 1960, Tshombe pulled Katanga out of the Congo; its foreign business community wanted no part of a centralized Congolese regime and was willing to bet the wealthy province could make it on its own. Belgium supported Tshombe with military units under a Belgian commander. South Kasai province, where the Belgian diamond company *Forminière* was influential, seceded in turn on 8 August.

The Congo Crisis involves both superpowers and the UN

Facing the double danger of a disintegrating nation and the resumption of Belgian control, Lumumba asked for help from the UN, the United States, and the USSR. The sudden power vacuum in a country with huge strategic mineral resources threatened to make tropical Africa a theater of the Cold War. To keep the superpowers at arm's length, the United Nations sent in a peacekeeping force. UN secretary general Dag Hammarskjöld, a man who combined traits normally associated with corporate executives, backroom political vote mechanics, devout Lutherans, and introspective Scandinavian mystics, would labor mightily to stabilize the Congo from then until he died in a highly suspect plane crash in September 1961.

Lumumba feared that Hammarskjöld's approach would solidify the Congo's partition, since Katanga and South Kasai were likely to be reliant on Belgium and the United States if they became independent. Short on options, he turned to Moscow for assistance, but this discredited him in Western eyes and led to the collapse of his fragile coalition (Documents 35A–C). This action, coupled with his affection for pan-Africanism, led to the widespread belief in the West that he was a closet Communist. On 5 September, he was dismissed by Kasavubu and replaced by Joseph-Désiré Mobutu (later Mobutu Sese Seko), the pro-Western head of the Congolese armed forces. The Congolese parliament supported Lumumba, but the UN forces denied him transportation and communication facilities, thereby confirming Kasavubu's action.

Lumumba's dismissal complicates the Congo situation

For months there was no effective central government in the Congo. Lumumba's deputy, Antoine Gizenga, established a pro-Soviet government at Stanleyville in October 1960. Lumumba was on his way there on 25 November when he was arrested by Congolese troops, turned over to his enemies in Katanga, and murdered in February 1961. The Soviets quickly made him a pan-African Marxist martyr, renaming Moscow's People's Friendship University in his honor. But Lumumba was a nationalist and a centralizer rather than an ideologue, and in this way he was similar to Ghana's Kwame Nkrumah, Tanzania's Julius Nyerere, Zambia's Kenneth Kaunda, and Kenya's Jomo Kenyatta. All these men emerged from African elites to lead their lands to independence, and all were far more interested in self-rule than Cold War ideology.

At any rate, Soviet efforts to gain a foothold in the Congo were doomed. With Lumumba gone, Moscow placed its dwindling hopes on Gizenga, but the latter would be defeated and arrested in 1962, ending the Stanleyville regime. Russians were as European as Belgians, and just as unwelcome in the Congo. When a small Soviet expeditionary force arrived in Stanleyville and began to persecute anti-Lumumba elements, it aroused nearly universal hostility and had to be

Soviet efforts in the Congo fail

escorted out of the Congo by UN forces. Within a few years, Katanga would rejoin the Congo, and the Western-oriented Mobutu would take control of the country, rename it Zaïre, and rule it for more than a generation.

Zaïre's tragic birth pangs proved that imperial withdrawal could actually lead to increased foreign intervention. They also showed that the UN, although it never lived up to its original expectations, could play a positive role in a very difficult situation. It managed to prevent the Belgians from reoccupying the Congo, escort the Soviets out, keep the Congolese economy from collapsing, and obstruct Katanga's secessionist efforts, while avoiding direct European or American intervention. The Congo also showed that Africa was not immune from the conflicts of the Cold War. Although the USSR suffered a setback in the Congo, it nonetheless stepped up its involvement elsewhere in Africa and continued to court the emerging nations.

THE U.S. PRESIDENTIAL CAMPAIGN OF 1960

As the dream of détente deteriorated and the Congo dissolved into disarray, the United States geared up for its 1960 elections. With the economy in recession and Richard Nixon the likely Republican nominee, the fight for the Democratic nomination drew a surplus of senators: Kennedy, Johnson, Humphrey, and Symington, all much younger than Eisenhower and all eager to blame him for the collapse of the Paris summit and the perpetuation of the Cold War. One must, of course, avoid going *too* far, as Kennedy discovered when he accused Eisenhower of irresponsibility in refusing to apologize to Khrushchev. The blunder brought avalanches of irate letters cascading onto Kennedy's desk, and as the other contenders hastened to vilify Khrushchev, the Massachusetts senator trimmed his sails to the wind. Handsome, intelligent, and articulate, he was the front-runner throughout the campaign and won the nomination on the first ballot in Los Angeles in July. The Republicans duly nominated Nixon the following month.

Kennedy and Nixon seek the U.S. presidency

Slowly the limelight began to shift away from Eisenhower, which, given the continuing decline in his fortunes, was probably a good thing. After the cancellation of his Russian visit, the president decided to tour several Pacific nations, including Japan. The announcement of his visit coincided with a parliamentary debate over the renewal of the Japanese-American Security Treaty, and this, combined with the unpopularity of Japanese prime minister Nobosuke Kishi and the disclosure of the presence of U-2 aircraft in Japan, led to massive anti-American demonstrations. It became necessary to cancel Eisenhower's visit, and, as he sailed for Taiwan, the People's Republic of China thoughtfully began shelling the offshore islands of Jinmen and Mazu. A grim and exasperated president, looking every one of his 70 years, returned to Washington on 25 June. One week later, the Soviets shot down another American spy plane.

This was not a U-2 but a modified B-47 bomber, called the RB-47. On 1 July, it vanished along the north coast of the USSR; Khrushchev soon announced that it had violated Soviet airspace and had been destroyed. Two survivors were in Soviet custody. In fact, the plane had been 30 miles *outside* Soviet airspace, but this could not be revealed without compromising American monitoring installations. As the UN Security Council debated the matter, an American C-47 got lost in the Pacific and strayed over the Kurile Islands. The Russians failed to bring it down, but Eisenhower might well have been tempted to cross the Wright Brothers off his list of American heroes.

Cold War tensions affect the American presidential campaign

Ironically, the escalating tension played into the hand of Nixon, who trumpeted his modest foreign policy experience as vice president for eight years. At 47, he was only four years older than Kennedy, but the American people might decide that the world situation required the election of the more experienced candidate. Khrushchev, fearing that release of Powers and the two RB-47 airmen might aid in the election of Nixon, whose politics he despised, kept them under lock and key until after the election.

Khrushchev's second visit to the United States causes controversy

That September, Khrushchev again visited the United States, this time not as Eisenhower's guest but as a head of state on his way to address the UN General Assembly on its fifteenth anniversary. His sojourn bore out Marx's assertion that history repeats itself as farce. Because of threats against his life, Khrushchev was restricted to Manhattan (a curious refuge for someone in danger), but he made the most of it, embracing Fidel Castro at Harlem's Hotel Theresa, entertaining the press with a variety of quips and crudities, and vilifying Eisenhower, who spoke at the assembly's opening session and left quickly. When Prime Minister Macmillan addressed the assembly and mentioned Khrushchev's behavior in Paris, the Soviet leader, seated with the USSR's delegation, heckled the speaker repeatedly and finally took off his shoe and pounded it on the desk. The assembly president broke his gavel trying to regain order, whereupon Khrushchev and Foreign Minister Gromyko began to pound their fists on their desks in a consistent rhythm. By this time, America's image of the Soviet leadership had changed dramatically: The reasonable Khrushchev of September 1959 had been superseded by the uncouth buffoon of September 1960.

The 1960 election was very close. That the Democrats could win in such a volatile international climate may be attributed to several factors, including the persistent recession and Kennedy's offer of support to the jailed civil rights leader Dr. Martin Luther King, Jr., which helped attract many African American voters. But Kennedy was also able to turn the global situation to his advantage by alleging the existence of a "missile gap" between the USSR and the United States. He charged Eisenhower and Nixon with having designed a defense budget so penurious that it starved the American missile program. Meanwhile, he claimed, the Soviets were turning out ICBMs in large numbers.

Kennedy narrowly wins the U.S. general election

There was no "missile gap," but Kennedy didn't know that and Eisenhower didn't think he could tell him. To prove that the Soviet missile program was actually *behind* that of the United States would require the publication of U-2 photographs and other highly sensitive intelligence information, some of it from sources behind the iron curtain. Rather than compromise such sources, Eisenhower kept silent. Nixon was narrowly defeated in November (which didn't totally displease Eisenhower, who never thought much of Nixon), and Kennedy found out for himself upon taking office in 1961 that the "missile gap" was imaginary.

By then Khrushchev was ready to extend an olive branch to the new president. He offered to release the two RB-47 fliers if Kennedy promised not to exploit them for propaganda purposes and not to authorize any more flights over Soviet territory. The president agreed and was able to announce the release at his first news conference. (Powers was exchanged for Soviet agent Rudolf Abel in 1962.) Kennedy hoped that, despite their obvious differences, he would be able to find some common ground on which he and the Soviets could begin to dismantle the more dangerous structures of the Cold War. If espionage flights had been the chief issue, he would have been halfway home. But two far more serious problems awaited him: a new Communist regime in Cuba and the omnipresent German Question. Together they would intensify the Cold War and imperil not only the political futures of Kennedy and Khrushchev, but the very existence of life on earth.

Khrushchev releases U.S. airmen as a gesture to Kennedy

10

Crisis and Coexistence, 1961–1964

The Cold War's most dangerous phase coincided roughly with the presidency of John Kennedy, who began his term in 1961 with a ringing inaugural address (Document 39). "In the long history of the world, only a few generations have been granted the role of defending freedom in its hour of maximum danger," he exulted. "I do not shrink from this responsibility—I welcome it." During the next few years, as he became locked in a deadly war of nerves with Moscow, and as his European allies began to edge out of the U.S. orbit, Kennedy would have ample opportunity to regret those words.

Kennedy begins his term as a combative Cold Warrior

Later, the tragic circumstances of his death led first to a romanticization of his life and legacy and later to a reaction focusing mainly on his incessant pursuit of women. Both do violence to historical fact. Kennedy kept his public and personal lives separate at a time when journalistic restraint made it possible to do so; he occasionally crossed the separation line, but no more so than other public figures had done. As for the myth of Camelot, it was a frothy confection that no one in the White House took seriously. Kennedy was no crusading liberal: He was a pragmatic politician who disdained ideology and openly sought the middle way. His foreign policy was that of a staunch Cold Warrior who loathed Communism, feared nuclear war, and was anxious to alleviate Third World discontents so that Moscow could not capitalize on them. He was convinced that Russia had started the Cold War—and determined that America would finish it!

THE BAY OF PIGS FIASCO

Castro's 26th of July Revolution ousts Batista in Cuba

Kennedy inherited from Eisenhower a major problem in Cuba, where a revolutionary regime came to power in 1959. Since the Spanish-American War, the United States had treated the island nation as part of its sphere of influence and maintained close ties with various Cuban leaders. In the 1950s, however, the dictatorship of Fulgencio Batista encouraged large-scale investment by organized crime and turned Cuba into a playground for wealthy "Yanquis" (a Latin American term for

U.S. residents). This was resented by many Cubans, who held Washington responsible for their misery. On 26 July 1953, Fidel Castro, a Jesuit-educated, upper-class *pistolero* with a law degree from the University of Havana, launched a seemingly quixotic revolution with an attack on an army barracks. Castro stood for land reform and the purification of Cuban society from Yanqui influence and corruption. His puritanical revolution caught the Cubans' fancy, and Castro's forces slowly gained ground. Batista's army suffered morale problems and melted away after several demoralizing defeats at the hands of Castro's forces. On New Year's Eve, 1958, Batista fled to Miami. The 26th of July Movement took power eight days later.

By July 1960, a split between the United States and Cuba was evident (Document 36). Castro's forthright anti-Yanquiism and leftist reforms, coupled with the presence in his entourage of Marxists like his brother Raúl and Ernesto "Che" Guevara, led the Eisenhower administration to cut off sugar imports from Cuba. Diplomatic ties were severed in January 1961. Moscow indicated its willingness to buy large quantities of Cuban sugar (a commodity which Russians consume in huge quantities), and Cuba tilted toward the Soviet camp.

Castro splits with Washington and embraces Moscow

Moscow thus gained an ally 90 miles south of the Florida Keys, and an "unsinkable aircraft carrier" in the Caribbean, while the United States acquired a persistent headache. Communist Third World expansion had come to America's backyard! However, thousands of anti-Castro Cubans fled the island in 1959–1960, giving the United States a pool from which to form a counterrevolutionary invasion force. Eisenhower gave preliminary assent to a Central Intelligence Agency plan to depose Castro, sketched on lines similar to the overthrow of a leftist regime in Guatemala in 1954, when a small-scale insurgency composed of Guatemalan dissidents, CIA pilots, and a ramshackle radio transmitter had frightened President Jacobo Arbenz into surrendering power. Shortly after taking office in 1961, Kennedy gave final approval to what would become known as the Bay of Pigs invasion.

Eisenhower plans to overthrow the Castro regime

Kennedy had no qualms about trying to oust Castro, provided he could get away with it. His advisors were divided concerning Moscow's probable reaction. Some believed that if it could be done swiftly, Khrushchev would be unlikely to move; America had clear military superiority in the Caribbean, and Latin America was an area of peripheral interest to the USSR. Others feared Moscow *would* move, not in the Caribbean but in Central Europe, around Berlin, where the Soviets had a huge military advantage.

Despite the German Question's propensity for turning up everywhere (like the proverbial bad penny), few in Washington doubted that the invasion scheme was feasible. But it wasn't, and the failure to examine it critically led to total failure. The CIA assumed that anti-Castro feeling in Cuba was so strong that a successful landing would trigger massive riots and defections from the Cuban army. Under such conditions, a brigade of fewer than 3,000 Cuban exiles could provide the spark to ignite revolution. U.S. involvement would be limited to two preinvasion air strikes to disable the Cuban air force; the pilots would be CIA agents posing as Cuban defectors, flying planes painted to look as if they were stolen from the Cuban air force. If things went wrong, the brigade could melt into the mountains and begin guerrilla warfare. Castro himself had done this in December 1956 with sixteen associates; two years later, in January 1959, they had toppled the regime.

Invasion plans are based on CIA assumptions

Fidel and Raúl Castro review troops in Havana.
Fidel Castro's 26th of July Revolution moved quickly from anti-Americanism to Communism between 1959 and 1961, ably assisted by Fidel's younger brother Raúl, commander of the Cuban armed forces and a classical Marxist. The U.S.-backed Bay of Pigs invasion in 1961 failed to overthrow the Castro regime, but both Castros and Soviet leader Khrushchev worried that U.S. president Kennedy would try again. This reasoning helped lead to the Cuban Missile Crisis of 1962.

What was wrong with this plan? Nearly everything. There was no reliable evidence of widespread anti-Castro feeling in Cuba; indeed, most of Castro's foes were either in exile or in prison. The island was so large that a quick *fait accompli* with a small invasion force was implausible, yet such an outcome was needed to forestall a Soviet response. If the initial air strikes failed to destroy the Cuban air force, the invasion force could be cut to pieces—but there was no backup plan to cover this contingency. Finally, although the original landing (Operation TRINIDAD) was to occur at a site from which the brigade could take refuge in the mountains, the revised plan (Operation ZAPATA) would bring it ashore at Playa Girón (the Bay of Pigs), from which the mountains were inaccessible. The implications of this change were never made clear to Kennedy or other key officials. Still, basic military analysis would have shown the plan's absurdity, and the failure to demand such analysis was Kennedy's fault.

Absence of rigorous military analysis obscures the plan's weaknesses

On 12 April 1961, three days before the air strikes were to begin, Soviet cosmonaut Yuri Gagarin became the first person to orbit the earth. This Russian

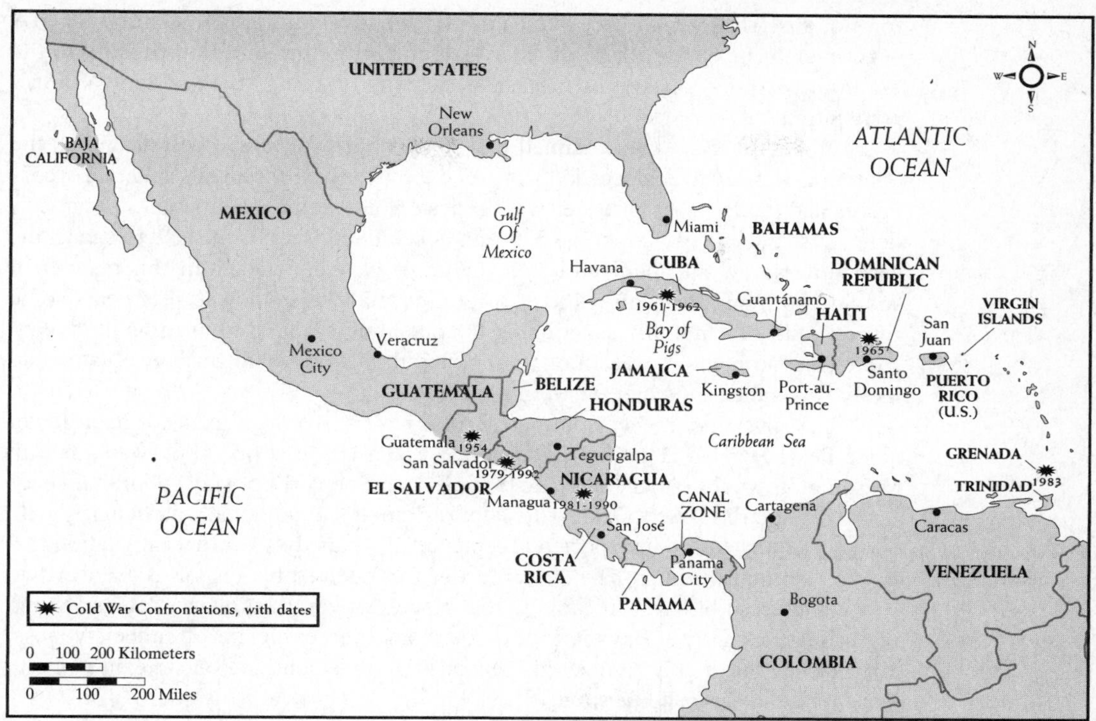

MAP 8 Cold War Clashes in Central America and the Caribbean, 1945–1990.
Fearful of Communist expansion in their own "back yard," Americans forcibly resisted efforts to establish leftist regimes in the countries of Central America and the Caribbean Sea. Notice the large number of Cold War confrontations that occurred in this region.

space triumph made Washington despondent. If successful, the landing in Cuba would turn the tables on Moscow, but ZAPATA was, in the words of one witness, "a perfect failure." The first air strike, on 15 April, saw six B-26 bombers with Cuban air force insignia destroy less than half of Castro's fighter planes. Kennedy, who had reduced the number of bombers from sixteen to six, then canceled the second strike. The CIA objected and was told to call the president, but, perhaps fearful that he would scrub the entire operation, they waited until the morning of 17 April and then asked him to have the U.S. aircraft carrier *Essex* provide air cover for the landing. No such request had previously been broached; indeed, Kennedy had recently received a cable from a U.S. Marine officer confirming that the invaders expected no U.S. military support. Kennedy denied the request for air cover, and the invaders were routed: 114 were killed, 1,189 were captured, and the rest escaped by sea.

The Bay of Pigs invasion fails

By 19 April it was over, and recriminations began. Kennedy was furious at the CIA, which he felt had misled him, but he squelched any public head-hunting by assuming full blame as "the responsible officer of the government." He then replaced Allen Dulles as CIA head and ordered a housecleaning of the agency. In turn, many at the CIA blamed Kennedy

Controversy swirls around the failed invasion

for not ordering U.S. forces to support the invasion. Some dismissed CIA personnel surfaced eleven years later as members of the unit that broke into the Watergate Hotel, setting in motion the events leading to President Nixon's resignation.

CIA apologists later claimed that, had proper air cover been provided, the operation would have succeeded. This is dubious, given the plan's inherent weaknesses and the fact that air cover was requested only at the last moment. Kennedy's defenders saw him as blameless, but even he admitted it was a mistake to cancel the second air strike. Had he lived longer, he might have concluded that his main error was in approving the plan without a rigorous study. Eisenhower, too, bears some responsibility for initially sanctioning the plan, but it is hard to imagine the organizer of the Normandy invasion of 1944 giving final approval to a scheme that would likely have failed even had everything worked.

U.S. prestige, to say nothing of America's self-image, had not been lower since Pearl Harbor. Between Gagarin and Playa Girón, April 1961 was a month Washington would rather forget. Astronaut Alan Shepard's 5 May suborbital space flight did little to revive the administration's good humor, particularly with Khrushchev's unexpected acceptance of Kennedy's February invitation to a summit meeting. The Soviet leader had delayed his response for over two months, but now, reckoning that Kennedy would be on the defensive, and regarding Kennedy's Bay of Pigs performance as evidence of indecisiveness, Khrushchev was ready to meet his second U.S. president and once again come to grips with the German Question.

Khrushchev sees an opportunity to exploit Kennedy's failure

THE VIENNA SUMMIT, JUNE 1961

Of all the Cold War summits, the Vienna meeting of 3–4 June 1961 was the most unfortunate. The participants got along badly, and misperceptions growing out of their talks led to two major crises: a serious one over Berlin in 1961 and a potentially catastrophic one in Cuba in 1962. In the two years following this meeting, war between the superpowers was a real possibility.

Kennedy and Khrushchev found they spoke different languages: not only Russian and English, but also different political languages. Kennedy was a pragmatist who considered ideologically motivated people impractical. Having watched Khrushchev maneuver on the world stage, he judged that the Soviet leader was pragmatic as well. But Khrushchev, while recognizing politics as a "merciless business" at which he could be quite ruthless, had an idealistic faith in Marxism which verged on the romantic. It had, after all, lifted him out of poverty and allowed him to rise to the top position in the USSR. It was also, in his view, the "wave of the future" which would triumph over capitalism because it was more just and equitable. Kennedy's first error was in thinking that Khrushchev was just as skeptical of grand designs as he was. Then, when he realized this was not the case, he thought he could argue ideology with the Soviet leader. The result was a series of talks that were tense, grinding, and often curt.

Kennedy and Khrushchev are divided by both style and issues

Beyond the two leaders' communication problems lay the grave issues dividing them. Some were less vexing than expected. Kennedy was clearly in an awkward spot concerning Cuba, thanks to the Bay of Pigs, but Khrushchev took a

Kennedy and Khrushchev meet at the Vienna Summit, 3–4 June 1961. This photograph captures the first handshake between the two leaders at the beginning of the conference. Kennedy misjudged Khrushchev going in, believing that the Soviet leader was just as coolly rational and nonideological as he himself was. The result was a divisive and unpleasant confrontation in which neither side conceded anything. Khrushchev then misjudged Kennedy coming out: He grew contemptuous of the young American president, whom he considered a spoiled playboy. He tested Kennedy's resolve over Berlin that summer and found to his surprise that Kennedy was a good deal stronger than he had seemed at Vienna.

fairly detached view: Castro was not a true Marxist, no matter what he said, and Cuba was no more a threat to the United States than Turkey was to the USSR. Laos (Chapter 11) was at the forefront of Kennedy's mind, but the Soviet leader showed little interest in the subject. When the talks turned to Berlin, however, the centrality of the German Question was evident once more.

At Vienna, Khrushchev attempts to force a Berlin settlement

By 1958, Khrushchev had given up the idea of a reunited and neutralized Germany, opting instead for a peace treaty with East Germany as a lever to remove the Western Allies from Berlin. He had repeatedly postponed his own deadlines and allowed Kennedy several months to formulate a new U.S. position. Now he faced a great opportunity to intimidate the young president, fresh from disaster in Cuba, and force a settlement on Berlin. He was under pressure from Kremlin hard-liners, the Chinese, and his own political instincts. He had not reached the pinnacle of Soviet power by flinching from pressing home an advantage.

Kennedy insists on the legality of U.S. presence in Berlin

Kennedy, startled by the vehemence of Khrushchev's demands on Berlin, countered with a consistent argument: America was in West Berlin not by force but by agreement. Moscow's desire to alter the balance of power was disturbing and dangerous. Khrushchev proposed a limited compromise in the form of an interim accord, by which the superpowers would indicate their intent to turn the problem over to the Germans. But Kennedy declined, sensing that it could undermine U.S. credibility to accept such a bargain in the wake of the Bay of Pigs debacle.

The Vienna summit concludes in chilly disagreement

The conversation then turned ugly. Khrushchev stated that he wanted peace, but it seemed Kennedy wanted war (a word rarely used in diplomatic discourse). Kennedy, taken aback, replied that the responsibility for forcing change rested with Moscow. Noting that "the calamities of war will be shared equally," the Soviet premier vowed to sign a treaty with East Germany by December 1961 unless Washington accepted an interim agreement. Grimly, Kennedy rejoined that "if that is true, it's going to be a cold winter." Never before in the Cold War had such words been spoken between the superpower leaders; even Truman's April 1945 dressing down of Molotov, if it actually occurred, cannot compare with Vienna.

The lessons of Vienna were ominous. Kennedy, dismayed by his inability to persuade Khrushchev of U.S. resolve, was sobered. He knew that, after the Bay of Pigs and Vienna, the United States must respond firmly to any challenge over Berlin, but he didn't know how much firmness would produce an acceptable result. Khrushchev returned from Vienna certain that Kennedy was no match for him. He saw at the summit a callow, unseasoned young man, born to wealth and accustomed to deference; there was no category of person with whom Khrushchev would be less sympathetic. Yet he also saw in Kennedy a belligerence he had not sensed in Eisenhower, and the mixture of immaturity and pugnacity concerned him. That combination had gotten Kennedy into trouble at the Bay of Pigs, and it might get him into trouble again over Berlin. The dangerous difference was that, while Cuba was not worth a nuclear conflict, Germany might be. With the American feeling cornered and the Soviet sensing an opportunity, Central Europe became a very uneasy place in the wake of the Vienna summit.

THE BERLIN WALL, AUGUST 1961

Vienna leads to confrontation in Central Europe

The perilous game of superpower chess continued after Vienna. On 8 July, Khrushchev rescinded the 1.2-million-man cut in Soviet army strength he had announced in January 1960. Kennedy countered with his own version of Truman's 1947 "all-out speech" on Greece and Turkey. In a televised address on 25 July, he asked Congress for authority to call up U.S. reserves and disclosed plans for a large military buildup, including preparations for an encore of the Berlin airlift (Document 40A). The most arresting parts of the speech dealt with measures to provide fallout shelters in the event of a nuclear war. Kennedy's intent was to persuade the Kremlin that America, if pushed, would go to war rather than retreat from Berlin.

Refugees pour out of East Germany through Berlin

With a showdown looming, both sides examined their options. It had occurred to Washington as early as March 1961 that East Germany might move to close the border between East and West Berlin in order to staunch the steady hemorrhage of refugees. Ever since the end of the blockade, people could go from one part of Berlin to the other simply by walking through the Brandenburg Gate; 40,000 East Berliners crossed every day to and from jobs in West Berlin. It was a hole in the iron curtain, through which passed many of the most talented people in East Germany. More than 2,500,000 had used this escape hatch since 1949. The deepening crisis of July 1961 accelerated this movement.

Two key U.S. senators, Mike Mansfield and J. William Fulbright, speculated openly during summer 1961 that the border could easily be closed. Fulbright opined that the Soviets could do so without breaking any written agreement with the United States. Presidential historian Michael Beschloss later raised the possibility that Kennedy may have planted such comments to alert Khrushchev to a viable solution. In early August, when asked at a press conference about Fulbright's statement, the president declined to warn the USSR against a border cutoff, using language that indicated little interest in the refugees but deep interest in the status of West Berlin. At least one secret channel was available by which Kennedy could have issued the same sort of caveat he had sent during the Bay of Pigs invasion, when he had warned Moscow against exploiting the opportunity to move against Berlin. No such warning came from the White House that August.

Speculation grows that the border in Berlin may be closed

On the other side of the iron curtain, Walter Ulbricht, head of East Germany's ruling Socialist Unity Party, had been lobbying Khrushchev for months to let him close the border. On 31 July, he suggested that the air corridors from Berlin to West Germany should be cut in order to keep refugees from leaving. Khrushchev rejected this, fearing it might lead to war, but agreed finally to let Ulbricht seal the border with barbed wire; if the West did not try to break through, a wall could replace the wire.

Construction began shortly past midnight on 13 August. The first news reached Washington six hours later—a graphic display of how rudimentary communication was in 1961. The U.S. response was thunderous silence. The State Department, having long feared that the Soviets might renew their 1948 blockade, had not prepared for the possibility that West Berlin would be isolated from *East* rather than West Germany. Kennedy's advisors urged restraint, and National Security Advisor McGeorge Bundy pointed out the obvious propaganda advantages Ulbricht had handed the United States. The president himself made no comment on the subject for a week. His critics complained that he should have ordered American forces to destroy the barrier before it hardened into a wall, as began to happen three days after the wire was strung. His defenders replied that such action would have led to war. Neither seemed to consider that, if the wire was cut, the East Germans could simply restring it the next night further *inside* their border, so that the Americans would have to invade in order to cut it! It is hard to conceive of a U.S. response that would have prevented the completion of the Berlin Wall, short of withdrawing from West Berlin. And there is no reason to believe that this was contemplated at the time.

East Germany seals the border and builds the Berlin Wall

The sealing of the border nonetheless touched off a major Cold War crisis (Documents 40A and 40B). The next weekend, Kennedy dispatched to Berlin retired General Lucius Clay, a hard-line anti-Communist who had commanded U.S. forces in Europe at the time of the 1948 Berlin Blockade, and Vice President Lyndon Johnson. And, in a move that Clay had suggested but Truman had rejected as too dangerous in 1948, Kennedy ordered an armored convoy of U.S. troops and vehicles sent from West Germany through East German territory to West Berlin. Fortunately, the Soviets did not try to stop it, but increased American forces in West Berlin heightened

Construction of the Berlin Wall, 1961.
The 1961 superpower confrontation over Berlin culminated with the East German decision to construct a wall between the two halves of the divided city. The Berlin Wall, reinforced with concrete, topped with barbed wire, and patrolled by armed guards, came to symbolize the Cold War division between capitalism and Communism. It ended the "brain drain" of East German refugees fleeing westward and benefited both superpowers by cooling off the German Question.

tensions considerably, as did Kennedy's decision to call up a number of military reserve and National Guard units. At one point, in October, a U.S. diplomat's attempt to cross from West to East Berlin to attend an opera triggered a terrifying standoff, with American and Soviet tanks facing each other at a checkpoint along the divide.

Eventually tensions subsided, and it became clear that the Berlin Wall conferred real benefits on both sides. Although it did not solve the German Question, it certainly defused it. Khrushchev was able to stem the flow of East German refugees and defang the critics who had long pressured him to deal resolutely with Berlin. At the same time, the West got a propaganda windfall from this highly visible symbol of Communism's repugnance. And Kennedy could breathe easier, sensing that Khrushchev had noted the U.S. resolve not to leave Berlin and had shown the dexterity to effect a workable compromise. If Kennedy did not urge Fulbright to signal that a border cutoff was acceptable to Washington, he probably should have. Berliners, of course, drew little comfort from the wall that divided their city. And the accelerating nuclear arms race would continue to make the world a very dangerous place.

The Berlin Wall benefits both sides in the Cold War

THE U.S. ARMS BUILDUP AND THE SOVIET RESPONSE

When Kennedy took office in 1961, the United States had a huge lead in deliverable nuclear weapons, with many times more operational ICBMs and long-range bombers than the USSR. Kennedy, however, had promised during his campaign to reinvigorate American leadership, regain the Cold War initiative, and close the "missile gap" that allegedly favored Moscow. Therefore, even though that "gap" was soon shown to be nonexistent, his administration accelerated the weapons-building programs begun under his predecessor, increasing the numbers of missiles far beyond those that Eisenhower had considered more than adequate. The decision was made to build and deploy 1,000 of the new solid-fuel Minuteman ICBMs and as many as forty-one nuclear submarines, each carrying sixteen Polaris missiles capable of reaching the USSR. When added to the fleet of over a thousand strategic bombers, these would give the United States by the mid-1960s an overpowering "triad" (land-based missiles, submarine-launched missiles, and bombers) of awesome destructive power, far beyond anything the USSR could hope to have operational by then.

Kennedy launches a U.S. nuclear buildup

Kennedy's secretary of defense was Robert S. McNamara, a man with dazzling managerial skills, an unrelenting attention to detail, and a ruthless bent for efficiency and rationality. McNamara seized control over the sprawling military bureaucracy, antagonizing the Pentagon brass as he rode roughshod over their most beloved traditions and cherished weapons systems. Undaunted by precedent or sentiment, and possessing the full support of his president, he imposed a sweeping new strategic vision, even as he presided over a nuclear arms buildup of staggering proportions.

Like many European statesmen and U.S. defense experts, McNamara felt that the Dulles doctrine of "massive retaliation"—calling for a full-scale American nuclear response in the event of Soviet aggression—had lost its credibility. Its rigidity also seemed to tie the hands of U.S. presidents by forcing them to choose in a crisis between nuclear Armageddon and surrender. He thus promoted a policy of "flexible response," designed to provide decision makers with options for gradual escalation of hostilities in the event of a conventional attack by Soviet forces in Central Europe. In 1962, he also announced a new nuclear strategy known as "counterforce," implying that U.S. weapons would be launched not against Soviet cities but only against military targets. Since a counterforce attack would not kill tens of millions of people (and thus ensure a massive response), it seemed to be more plausible that a president might actually employ it.

"Flexible Response" replaces "Massive Retaliation"

From a Soviet perspective, however, the combination of the U.S. nuclear buildup and counterforce retargeting seemed to indicate that the Americans were moving toward a "first-strike capacity." This meant that the United States, with a well-coordinated attack upon Soviet military targets, might be able to destroy Moscow's ability to retaliate and render the USSR defenseless. Whether or not the Americans were actually seeking this capability, the Soviets saw little choice but to defend against it.

For financial reasons, Moscow had decided not to invest in large numbers of first-generation ICBMs, preferring to wait until more sophisticated weapons could be produced. Khrushchev instead relied on bluster and deception to exaggerate Soviet strength, thus contributing inadvertently to

Khrushchev's deception helps provoke Kennedy's overreaction

America's massive overreaction. With an economic base much smaller than that of the United States, the Kremlin leader could not hope to match the U.S. buildup without sacrificing his prized programs to improve Soviet agriculture and consumer goods production.

In October 1961, to reassure his NATO allies of U.S. resolve in the wake of the Berlin Wall crisis, Kennedy authorized Deputy Secretary of Defense Roswell Gilpatric to reveal to the world the extent of U.S. superiority. In February, McNamara had exposed the "missile gap" as a sham but had made no specific comparisons. Gilpatric now delineated in brutal terms the precise correlation of forces: The U.S. nuclear arsenal consisted of 5,000 warheads, while the Soviets possessed 300, and the USSR deployed only 6 ICBMs capable of reaching the United States (although it also had submarine-based missiles that could do so).

Gilpatric's speech discloses U.S. nuclear superiority

Gilpatric's speech not only conveyed Kennedy's message, as Soviet pressure on West Berlin eased noticeably. It also disarmed and humiliated Khrushchev. No longer could he rattle rockets and intimidate anyone who threatened Soviet interests. To make matters worse, Kennedy himself observed in a March 1962 magazine interview that under certain conditions, the United States might launch a nuclear first strike against the USSR. Khrushchev, sobered, looked for an area of the world that annoyed Kennedy as much as Berlin annoyed him. He found Cuba.

THE CUBAN MISSILE CRISIS

Kennedy admitted in Vienna that he had made a mistake at the Bay of Pigs, but he didn't promise not to try again. Perhaps his talk about a mistake simply meant that next time he would not fail. Given Washington's obvious hatred for Castro, and a failed CIA attempt to overthrow or kill him called Operation MONGOOSE (of which Moscow was aware), an American invasion of Cuba seemed plausible to the Soviets. Thus, Kennedy's arms buildup, Gilpatric's speech, and the Cuban situation all led Khrushchev to conclude by spring 1962 that the USSR should station nuclear missiles in Cuba. He had two immediate aims: to defend Cuba against a U.S. invasion and to redress the strategic balance by locating Soviet missiles close to America. He had in mind medium-range SS-4s, with a range of 1,200 miles, and intermediate-range SS-5s, which could travel about 2,500 miles; neither could reach the United States from the USSR but both could do so from Cuba.

Khrushchev decides to place missiles in Cuba

In spring of 1962, the Soviets offered, and Castro accepted, up to 40 missile launchers, each equipped with two missiles and one nuclear warhead. Delivery and installation would occur between August and November. Secrecy was essential, since Kennedy could not be expected to accept an altered strategic balance, especially with congressional elections approaching on November 6. Once the missiles were fully installed and the elections were over, Khrushchev could then travel to America, reveal the missiles' presence, and press in a major UN speech for Western withdrawal from Berlin. It was a daring and dangerous plan, based on the assumption that the missiles could be installed in Cuba without American detection. And this assumption proved false.

For his part, Kennedy did not consider the impact on Moscow of the Gilpatric speech and other American rhetoric. He discounted Khrushchev's fear of an invasion of Cuba, since he knew he did not plan to invade. He never suspected

Moscow might place missiles in Cuba, so he did not convey the sort of precise warning he had issued over Berlin. When CIA director John McCone reported in August that Cuba was receiving from Russia large shipments that probably included missiles, neither Kennedy nor McNamara believed it. Nor did CIA analysts, who processed over 2,000 reports of missiles arriving in Cuba but dismissed them because many such reports proved phony. Even accounts from CIA agents in Cuba were not considered credible—until they reported 80-foot cylinders being carried on trucks that couldn't make turns without slicing off mailboxes! This got Kennedy's attention and led him to issue warnings to Moscow on 4 and 13 September, but it was too late for Khrushchev to stop an operation already more than half completed. And neither Kennedy nor his advisors ever considered what to do if the Soviets ignored the warnings.

Kennedy and his advisors discount warnings of Soviet missile deployment

The U.S. congressional election campaign was under way, and Republican senator Kenneth Keating charged Kennedy with covering up evidence of Soviet missiles in Cuba. Administration officials denied the charges since their evidence, like Keating's, was anecdotal, and since they did not believe Khrushchev would take the risk. Then, on 14 October 1962, the U-2 again flew into the midst of the Cold War. A flight over Cuba by Major Rudolph Anderson brought back clear photographic evidence of missile launcher construction. McGeorge Bundy informed Kennedy on the morning of 16 October. The Cuban Missile Crisis was on.

U-2 photographs reveal Soviet missile launchers in Cuba

The U.S. response was prepared by the "ExComm" (Executive Committee of the National Security Council), a group of key officials and advisors meeting in utmost secrecy. For the first few days, the president was a sporadic participant in their daylong meetings, keeping to his announced schedule of appointments and appearances; he began to meet regularly with them only on Saturday, 20 October. The group proposed and the president agreed that the U.S. objective should be the removal of the *missiles*, not the Castro regime. Three options were identified. The first, which Kennedy dismissed as unworkable, was to negotiate removal of the missiles: What could he offer to induce Moscow to withdraw? The second was a conventional air strike to destroy the missiles, and the third was a naval blockade or "quarantine" to prevent warheads and other weapons from reaching the island. Accepting the presence of the missiles was not even considered. According to Bundy, the reasons were not strategic: The missiles did not alter the global balance, and America had been vulnerable to nuclear attack for years. Rather, they were political: Soviet missiles in the Western Hemisphere, 90 miles from the United States, would be intolerable to the American people. Nothing short of decisive action would be acceptable.

Washington considers how to obtain removal of the missiles

Kennedy decided on Sunday for the third option, against the advice of many, if not most, of the ExComm. The deciding argument was that an air strike could not guarantee removal of more than 60 percent of the missiles. It would have to be followed by additional strikes and probably an invasion. By contrast, the quarantine offered a first step that could always be escalated if it proved ineffective. Kennedy himself, despite (or because of) his naval background, had little confidence in naval interdiction, but he chose this option because it seemed the lesser of two evils. He disclosed the presence of the missiles and the imposition of the quarantine in an address to the nation and the world at 7:00 P.M. EDT on Monday, 22 October (Document 41A).

Kennedy decides on a naval quarantine of Cuba

Concurrently, the United States began a massive military buildup in south Florida. Nothing was done to conceal it, both because it would have been futile to try and because it was important that Moscow see what was going on. Khrushchev, startled by Kennedy's reaction, stalled for time. For two days, Soviet spokesmen were authorized to answer inquiries with nothing more than standard public relations responses. Kennedy's address had made much of Soviet secrecy and duplicity and of Foreign Minister Gromyko's failure to disclose the missiles when he had met with the president a few days earlier. This approach assured Washington the unanimous backing of NATO and the Organization of American States, as well as several African nations, which denied landing and refueling rights to Cuba-bound Soviet aircraft.

Naval confrontation ends when the Soviets back off

On Tuesday, 23 October, Khrushchev warned that Soviet submarines would sink the U.S. blockaders, and the world watched in spellbound terror as Cuba-bound Soviet vessels approached American ships. The next day, however, the crisis eased, when the Soviet ships stopped and turned back rather than run the blockade. Khrushchev had been bluffing! Afraid that his ships would be boarded and searched, and thus reveal Soviet military secrets,

U.S. aircraft carriers off Guantánamo Bay, Cuba, during the 1962 Cuban Missile Crisis. Khrushchev's decision to place nuclear missiles in Cuba in 1962 proved a disastrous miscalculation. The Cuban Missile Crisis that followed brought the world to the brink of nuclear war. Ultimately U.S. naval power in the Caribbean proved too much for the Soviets to overcome, as this photograph of American aircraft carriers off Guantánamo Bay illustrates.

he decided to avoid confrontation. His refusal to challenge U.S. naval superiority meant that the game was up. By nightfall it was clear the missiles would be removed, and the rest of the crisis was spent working out the conditions.

But plenty of tension and danger remained. A long letter from Khrushchev arrived at the U.S. embassy in Moscow at 5:00 P.M. (10:00 A.M. EDT) on Friday, 26 October (Document 41B). Transmitted through Soviet channels, it did not reach Washington for eight hours. As in the Berlin crisis of 1961, slow communications led to irksome delays, compounded by the fact that Khrushchev's lengthy letter had to be cabled in sections. Had it arrived more quickly, much of the next day's tension and aggravation might have been avoided. In any case, it was remarkably forthright. Khrushchev claimed the missiles were deployed for defensive purposes only, but admitted he could not convince Kennedy of this. He stated flatly that nuclear war was out of the question and proposed that he would send no more weapons to Cuba in return for a U.S. promise not to invade the island. The letter (released in 1973) ended with a now-famous passage that encapsulated Khrushchev's emotions and fears:

Khrushchev's 26 October letter offers a settlement

> If you have not lost your self-control and sensibly conceive what this might lead to, Mr. President, we and you ought not now to pull on the ends of the rope in which you have tied the knot of war, because the more the two of us pull, the tighter that knot will be tied. And a moment may come when that knot will be tied so tight that even he who tied it will not have the strength to untie it . . . Let us not only relax the forces pulling on the ends of the rope. Let us take measures to untie the knot.

The letter clarified several things. Khrushchev knew that the quarantine was effective. He knew that America's massive superiority in the Caribbean precluded him from using force to break it. He knew from Kennedy's prior warnings that bringing pressure on West Berlin could lead to nuclear war. He knew that he could not fire his Cuban missiles without *ensuring* nuclear war, and he knew that nuclear war was unacceptable. In such circumstances, he could only haggle over terms. The conditions he offered were clearly insufficient for Washington, since they did not assure the withdrawal of the missiles. But they did form the basis for an eventual understanding.

The letter's full implications were not immediately grasped at the White House, where tired men wrestled with their own worst fears. Saturday, 27 October, proved the most trying day of the crisis. As the ExComm convened at 9:00 A.M. EDT, Radio Moscow broadcast a second letter from Khrushchev (Document 41C). This one upped the ante, offering for the first time to remove the missiles from Cuba but demanding in return both a no-invasion pledge and the removal of fifteen U.S. Jupiter-C missiles from Turkey. The obsolete Jupiters were scheduled to be withdrawn once Polaris submarines were deployed in the eastern Mediterranean, but Kennedy did not want to remove them under the gun. Unfortunately, he realized, the request would look reasonable to the rest of the world, which would not understand his willingness to risk total war over such a trivial item. Indeed, Kennedy would not have run the risk and would have accepted the bargain had he been unable to find a way around it.

Khrushchev's 27 October letter deepens the crisis

What did the second letter imply? Was Khrushchev still in charge in the Kremlin? Apparently Khrushchev was afraid on Friday that an invasion of Cuba was imminent, so that day's letter sought a quick solution. On Saturday, the situation appeared less menacing, and the Turkish missile demand was added. But no one in Washington knew this at the time. While the ExComm was puzzling over the letters, a U-2 on a routine Pacific mission accidentally strayed into Soviet airspace. The Soviet Air Force scrambled but allowed the plane to return; a U.S. first strike was unlikely to occur in such a remote area. Kennedy, who had ordered such missions canceled at the outset of the crisis, remarked, "There is always some son of a bitch who doesn't get the word." His sense of humor was notably absent that afternoon when word arrived that another U-2, this one on an authorized overflight of Cuba, had been detected—and this one had been shot down!

Washington, needing to know the operational status of the Cuban missiles, was sending U-2s over Cuba several times a day. This one was piloted by Major Anderson, the man who had brought back the photos showing the first solid evidence of missile deployment. General Stepan Grechko, commander of Soviet air defenses on Cuba, tried to reach General Issa Pliyev, commander of all Soviet forces there, for authorization to bring down the U-2. Unable to reach Pliyev, he gave the order on his own; the plane was shot down and the pilot killed. Soviet defense minister Rodion Malinovsky wired a rebuke to Grechko, but the damage was done. Khrushchev was staggered by the incident, and while Kennedy overruled previously agreed-upon procedures that called for air strikes on Cuba should a U.S. plane be attacked, he began to wonder how long he could wait before ordering military action. He assumed the incident was a deliberate provocation and became suspicious of Khrushchev's intentions. Those intentions, it turned out, were pacific: A cable from Castro begging Moscow to launch a nuclear strike against the United States arrived that afternoon and was ignored.

A U-2 plane is shot down over Cuba

At this point, Washington turned creative. McGeorge Bundy, backed by Attorney General Robert Kennedy, proposed that the first letter be accepted as a basis for agreement. If the missiles were withdrawn, the United States would pledge not to invade Cuba. The second letter would simply be ignored. Concurrently, ABC reporter John Scali was sent to meet with Alexander Fomin, a Soviet embassy official who was also a KGB (Soviet state security) agent. The two had already served as an unofficial channel between Kennedy and Khrushchev earlier in the crisis; now Scali, briefed on Saturday's events, read Fomin the riot act. He told him to inform Khrushchev that the United States was resolved to remove the missiles and that an invasion of Cuba was near. Robert Kennedy delivered a similar warning to Soviet ambassador Anatoly Dobrynin, coupled with a private assurance that, once the crisis was resolved, the Jupiters would be removed from Turkey (Document 41D). This could not, however, be part of the bargain: The understanding must be secret.

The United States pledges not to invade Cuba if missiles are removed

The strategy worked. At 9:00 A.M. EST Sunday, 28 October, Radio Moscow broadcast another letter from Khrushchev. Accepting the U.S. assurance that Cuba would not be invaded, he would have the missiles dismantled and returned to the USSR. No mention was made of missiles in Turkey. The Cuban Missile Crisis was over, and the Cold War was changed irrevocably.

Moscow and Washington reach agreement

Although both Kennedy and Khrushchev acted prudently during the crisis, determined to prevent nuclear war, the danger was nonetheless real. Unknown to Washington, the Soviets already had thirty-six operational nuclear missiles and nine short-range tactical nuclear weapons in Cuba. Had Kennedy launched an air strike, at least some of these would have survived, and a U.S. invasion would have been needed to finish the job. Since there were 43,000 Soviet troops in Cuba (and not 10,000, as the CIA thought), a U.S. landing would doubtless have led to bitter fighting and mass casualties. And, given the presence of Soviet tactical "nukes" and the difficulties of maintaining contact between Cuba and Moscow, it could well have escalated into all-out war between the superpowers.

The Missile Crisis brings few benefits to the superpowers

The Cuban Missile Crisis frightened the world and brought few tangible gains for either side. Khrushchev, although defeated, could claim publicly that he had saved Cuba from invasion and privately that he had gotten U.S. missiles out of Turkey. But to risk nuclear war over such small stakes was reckless. Kennedy gained domestic popularity and international respect, although all he had accomplished was to restore the status quo. His no-invasion pledge was honored by later presidents despite its lack of binding force: It was predicated upon

Kennedy and Khrushchev argue on the brink of nuclear destruction during the Cuban Missile Crisis. This political cartoon shows the dangers of nuclear "brinkmanship" as Kennedy and Khrushchev decide that negotiating on a bench would be a safer course. The American triumph during the Missile Crisis sobered the leaders of the superpowers, while the rest of the world worried that during the next crisis, they might not step back from the brink in time. One result of the Crisis was agreement to install a "Hot Line," or a direct line of communication between Washington and Moscow, in order to prevent future misunderstandings.

international inspection of Cuba, which Kennedy knew that Castro would never grant. Binding or not, the pledge proved a godsend to Castro, whose regime outlasted both the Cold War and the USSR!

The crisis also carried several key lessons for Moscow. For one thing, U.S. naval power, not nuclear weapons, had proven decisive, making the quarantine effective and leaving the Soviets short of options. If they wanted to remain competitive in future crises, they would have to build a navy to match. For another, Khrushchev's attempt to close the missile gap cheaply and quickly had failed, since the United States would not abide nuclear rockets on its doorstep. If the Soviets wished to achieve nuclear parity, they would have to follow the arduous and expensive path of building their own vast fleet of ICBMs.

STRESSES AND STRAINS IN THE WESTERN ALLIANCE

During the missile crisis, America's European allies gave it strong public support but privately were disturbed by U.S. failure to consult them on key decisions. This was especially true of France's de Gaulle, who had long advocated an independent course. Against U.S. wishes, he had made France a nuclear power, shrugging off gibes at the size of his *force de frappe* by noting that nuclear powers were Great Powers, no matter how small their arsenals. Convinced of the need for Franco-German cooperation, he continued French participation in the EEC, despite his dislike for its structure. Under his influence, a prosperous Western Europe was pondering the limits of NATO and considering a possible role as a third force between Washington and Moscow.

De Gaulle's fixation on national sovereignty was viewed as anachronistic by the White House, which saw Britain, France, and West Germany as junior partners in a U.S-dominated alliance. But America's view of his ideas as antiquated relics of old world chauvinism begged the question posed by nationalism's persistent appeal. Collective security organizations like NATO and the UN might be of limited value in specific situations, but they could never, in de Gaulle's view, earn the affection and dedication of Europeans accustomed for centuries to celebrate their differences, not as defects but as sources of strength.

France challenges Washington's view of U.S.–Europe relations

To de Gaulle, nationalism and sovereignty were not limiting factors. Any organization that respected national identities and gave a leading role to *all* Great Powers could claim his support. He sought not the equality of all nations but the rightful participation of powerful states like France, Britain, and West Germany in all decisions affecting the future of Europe. After all, the United States could not garrison Europe forever, and its insistence on defending Europe by threatening a nuclear strike on the USSR simply meant that Moscow, if it wanted to move west (which de Gaulle doubted), would do so only under conditions designed to preclude U.S. retaliation. It therefore behooved Europe to maintain friendly ties with the United States while seeking its own identity as a third force.

London, like Washington, at first underestimated de Gaulle. But by 1962 it was clear that the Algerian albatross no longer adorned the neck of France. With a nuclear capability, a thriving economy, and effective, farsighted leadership, Paris seemed ready to make its own way in the Cold War. Harold Macmillan's British government accordingly sought to join the EEC, an option consistent with Kennedy's hope of more closely uniting Europe and America in economic as well as political affairs. But while Britain saw its decision as an effort to draw closer to a dynamic France, de Gaulle interpreted it differently.

In the first place, he didn't want England *too* close to France. It was one thing for London to participate in decisions affecting Europe, but quite another for it to dilute French domination of the EEC. In the second place, the British demanded special arrangements to protect their own agriculture and the economies of their Commonwealth associates. De Gaulle and other European leaders justifiably believed that, if special privileges were granted every member, the EEC would never work. In the third place, he interpreted Britain's decision to seek entry as evidence of its intention to act as a stalking horse for the United States. He had long resented the Anglo-American treatment of his Free French movement in World War II, and now he saw the British desire to join the EEC as one more manifestation of the English-speaking powers' arrogant ambition to dominate the world.

De Gaulle opposes British entry into the EEC

Negotiations progressed throughout 1962, culminating in a devastating turn-of-the-year for British prime minister Macmillan. At a conference with Kennedy in Bermuda just before Christmas, he learned that the United States was pulling out of its joint effort with Britain to develop the Skybolt missile. Kennedy preferred to use the cheaper American-built Polaris, and since the United States controlled the nuclear material used in Polaris warheads, the decision reduced Britain to a dependent nuclear power. This blow to British pride was followed on 14 January 1963 by de Gaulle's blunt, cruelly disappointing announcement that France would veto British entry into the EEC.

As if these disasters were insufficient, two scandals titillated Britain in summer 1963. First, Kim Philby, a top official of the British espionage service (MI-6), defected to the USSR. Then it was alleged that Secretary of State for War John Profumo had shared state secrets with call girls Christine Keeler and Mandy Rice-Davies, who in turn had passed them on to their Soviet clients. Macmillan, besieged, resigned in October 1963, and Harold Wilson's Labour party came to power the following year.

Macmillan resigns after setbacks and scandals

Konrad Adenauer, at 87, preceded Macmillan into retirement by three days. *Der Alte* narrowly won the 1961 election and then hung on for two more years, long enough to sign a Franco-German Friendship Treaty early in 1963. The United States also changed leaders that year, owing to Kennedy's murder in Dallas, but de Gaulle soldiered on, pursuing his vision of a "Europe from the Atlantic to the Urals" that would include a less belligerent Russia. But this concept, which was far ahead of its time, made little impact on Moscow or Washington by the time de Gaulle retired in 1969.

THE LIMITED TEST BAN TREATY OF 1963

Meanwhile, in the wake of the Cuban crisis, both Washington and Moscow had begun to contemplate changes that could prevent a repetition of the 1962 brush with eternity. Renewed talk of a nuclear test ban circulated through both capitals, but issues like on-site inspections continued to defy easy solution. To improve communication channels, so sadly primitive during the missile crisis,

A "hot line" connects Washington and Moscow

a "hot line" was installed to link the White House and the Kremlin. The brainchild of nuclear scientist Leo Szilard, it was not a telephone but a circuit composed of telegraph lines and printers that ran through London and Scandinavia. It was appallingly slow by modern standards and did not allow for voice contact, but it was a big improvement over 1962 conditions.

Perhaps the greatest change took place in John F. Kennedy. Pampered and privileged in his youth, he had long since learned that life is not always happy. Back surgery in 1954 nearly killed him and left him in constant pain; his wife miscarried a girl in 1956, and seven years later their second son lived for scarcely a day. Now the harrowing October of 1962 left him questioning Cold War dogmas, while his skyrocketing popularity gave him room to maneuver. On 10 June 1963, he gave the finest speech of his life at American University in Washington (Document 42).

Eloquent, resonant, and in parts poetic, the "Peace Speech" (as Kennedy called it) articulated a peaceful man's abhorrence of war and proposed that a reexamination of Cold War attitudes was imperative if humanity hoped to avoid annihilation. The speech promised that America would not conduct atmospheric nuclear tests as long as other nations refrained from doing so. It sought to develop broad public backing for a test ban treaty and to impress Khrushchev with Kennedy's commitment to détente with the USSR. Coming from a master of Cold War oratory, the speech startled and inspired many, both within the United States and abroad.

Kennedy's "Peace Speech" brings hopes for détente

Then, a few weeks later, the president visited Berlin. Arriving on 26 June to commemorate the fifteenth anniversary of the 1948 airlift, Kennedy was greeted by over a million people, gathered at a plaza within sight of the Wall. Reverting to Cold War rhetoric, he delivered a bitterly anti-Communist valedictory (Document 43), toying with the crowd and ending with the words: "Today, all free men, wherever they may live, are citizens of Berlin. And therefore, as a free man, I take pride in the words, 'Ich bin ein Berliner.' " He thus became a hero to the Germans and a source of somber reflection to Konrad Adenauer, who speculated that despite fifteen years of democratic rule, Germany might someday give its devotion to another charismatic speaker like Hitler.

In Berlin, Kennedy returns to Cold War rhetoric

Fortunately this lapse into Cold War rhetoric did not derail the test ban talks. Khrushchev was as concerned as Kennedy about atomic fallout and was eager to conclude a treaty that would put his country on an equal footing with America. After the United States dropped its demand for on-site inspections, Moscow agreed to what would become the Limited Test Ban Treaty, signed on 5 August 1963 (Document 44). It forbade atmospheric tests by its signatories (the United States, the USSR, and Britain—but not France) but allowed underground blasts, since these were hard to detect without inspections. It did not halt, or even slow, the arms race, since both sides could still develop new weapons through underground testing. But it did deal effectively with the fallout problem, and it showed that it was possible for the superpowers to work out an arms agreement.

The United States and the USSR sign a Limited Nuclear Test Ban Treaty

EXIT KENNEDY, EXIT KHRUSHCHEV

The Test Ban Treaty, although limited, did provide a sense that superpower relations were improving. That impression deepened in the next few months, partly due to U.S. Senate ratification of the treaty in September and partly because the German

Question lay dormant. South Vietnam now took center stage, with Buddhist demonstrations, a military coup (Chapter 11), and Kennedy's gnawing fear that the United States was being drawn into a highly dubious venture. But he also believed, recalling Khrushchev's 1961 diffidence over Laos, that Southeast Asia was too peripheral to superpower interests to intensify the Cold War.

In November, the president turned to domestic politics. To patch up a quarrel between Texas Democrats, he traveled to San Antonio and Dallas on 22 November and ran into an ambush. He died within minutes of being shot in the head, and the presidency passed to Lyndon B. Johnson.

Kennedy is murdered in Texas on 22 November 1963

In domestic affairs, Johnson was a superb political operator, a man of both close-range and long-distance vision, a tough yet compassionate figure who blended skeptical pragmatism with a strong stream of idealism. But his experience in foreign affairs was limited, and he lacked Kennedy's mental flexibility and willingness to grapple with unconventional solutions. Fiercely anti-Communist, he would instinctively deepen U.S. involvement in Vietnam and would prove less willing to continue along the path of cooperation initiated by the test ban.

Johnson becomes president with limited foreign policy experience

Khrushchev was devastated by the events in Dallas. He broke down when Gromyko told him the news and wept the next day while paying his respects at the U.S. embassy. He feared for the future of détente and lamented the premature death of an adversary with whom he had shared more than one serious crisis and whom he felt he had begun to understand. No doubt, as his seventieth birthday approached, he was also reminded of his own mortality. He did not know that his own career would soon end.

In the final year of his rule, Khrushchev kept a low profile in world affairs. In the interests of superpower relations, he quietly tried to restrain the Vietnamese Communists, but failing this, he again showed little concern for Southeast Asia. In March 1964, a rumor spread in the United States that he had either been removed from office or died of heart failure, but it proved premature. During the American presidential campaign, the Soviet leader kept silent, hoping to do nothing that might help the right-wing Republican nominee, Barry Goldwater. But by election time, Khrushchev himself was gone, forcibly retired on 14 October by a Presidium conspiracy led by Soviet president Leonid Brezhnev. Although Khrushchev's failures in foreign affairs, particularly in Cuba and Berlin, were cited as reasons for his fall, a more proximate cause was his plan to restructure the Soviet Communist Party—a threat to the standing and careers of many party functionaries.

The Soviet Presidium forces Khrushchev into retirement

Khrushchev's fall, and his replacement by Brezhnev as party first secretary and by Alexei Kosygin as Soviet premier, gave a huge boost to the Soviet military establishment. For all his bluster, Khrushchev had been reluctant to commit vast resources to a massive military buildup, for fear this might derail his plans to improve the consumer economy. Brezhnev and Kosygin, having no such qualms, presided over a sustained weapons buildup of epic proportions. This enabled the USSR to surpass the United States in numbers of strategic missiles, but it also exacted a frightful toll on the overall Soviet economy.

Moscow's new leadership intensifies the arms race

Brezhnev, a Khrushchev protégé who had risen through the ranks by maintaining an image of quiet competence while building a powerful base, lacked his predecessor's flair for the dramatic. Colorless and unimaginative, yet determined and effective, he imbued the Soviet leadership with an aura of stability, prudence, and pragmatism. A skilled machine politician, he managed by patronage and consensus, satisfying the various elements of his coalition while consolidating his power and undermining his rivals. In domestic affairs, he clamped down on dissent and jettisoned the more extreme initiatives of Khrushchev (including the anti-Stalin campaign and the party restructuring), while continuing his predecessor's general political thrust. In foreign policy, as relations with Communist China deteriorated, he eventually sought to improve relations with the West, pursuing his version of détente while continuing a relentless arms buildup.

Brezhnev proves less dramatic than Khrushchev

So within a single year, from October of 1963 to October of 1964, West Germany, Britain, the United States, and the USSR all changed leaders. Meanwhile, the focus of the Cold War was beginning to shift—away from Europe and toward Southeast Asia.

11

Southeast Asia and the Cold War, 1945–1970

When Lyndon Johnson became president of the United States, Southeast Asia was one of his lowest priorities. His ambitious domestic agenda included civil rights laws, a war on poverty, and a wide range of measures designed to remake America into a "Great Society." Soviet leader Brezhnev, preoccupied with consolidating his power and building his nation's strength, also had little interest in the region. Soon, however, the struggle for Southeast Asia, in progress since World War II, became the focal point of the Cold War.

THE STRUGGLE FOR SOUTHEAST ASIA

Southeast Asian independence movements become part of the Cold War

From the Japanese conquest of Southeast Asia through the final defeat of Japan, World War II created the context for a series of indigenous revolts in Western colonies like Malaya, the Philippines, and Indochina. These movements predated the Cold War and existed independently of superpower rivalry, but they were exploited by participants in the Cold War and eventually were absorbed into it. Since these movements were anti-Western in nature, and since Communists usually played leading roles, they often received support from Moscow and opposition from the United States.

Britain defeats a Maoist insurgency in Malaya

In the British colony of Malaya, apparently on instructions from Moscow, the Malayan Communist Party launched an anti-British rebellion in 1948. But because of the Maoist orientation of the Malayan Communists, the USSR eventually lost interest and left the rebels on their own. Faced with a manhunt conducted by 40,000 British regulars, the revolutionaries (who never numbered more than 5,000) resorted to hit-and-run attacks. These caused extensive damage but failed to cripple the economy. By late 1953, the rebellion was confined to isolated jungle areas, and in 1956, the British granted independence to the colony without incident. The revolt disbanded in 1960.

Communists fared no better in the Philippines, which had been a Spanish colony before 1898 and a U.S. possession from then until 1946. During World War II, when the islands were occupied by Japan, the People's Anti-Japanese Army, or *Hukbong Bayan Laban sa Hapon*, was formed. After liberation (1944) and independence (1946), President Manuel Roxas drove these "Huks" underground, where they morphed into the *Hukbong Mapagplayang Bayan* (People's Liberation Army). The Philippine Communist Party joined the Huk revolt in 1948, but Moscow remained aloof, reluctant to challenge the United States in an area where the latter maintained major military bases. Nonetheless, the Huks developed into a strong military force by 1950, largely due to governmental ineptitude and the attraction of their ideas for the peasantry. The tide turned when the CIA threw its support to populist defense secretary Ramón Magsaysay. By the mid-1950s, thanks to Magsaysay's popularity with the peasants and middle class, massive U.S. aid, and lack of Soviet or Chinese help, the Huks were defeated. Magsaysay, at five feet eleven inches a giant among the small-statured Filipinos, became a folk hero and is still revered in many parts of the Philippines, remaining a staunch U.S. ally until his death in a plane crash in 1957.

The CIA helps defeat the Huks in the Philippines

French Indochina, a large colony that included the lands of Laos, Cambodia, and Vietnam, presented a unique case. Of all the outbreaks of the Cold War in Southeast Asia, by far the most serious occurred in French Indochina, where a shared border with China and a lack of effective governmental resistance foreshadowed results very different from those in Malaya and the Philippines. France had ruled Indochina since the nineteenth century but never suppressed the region's ancient cultures. Demands for liberation were voiced as early as 1919, when a young Vietnamese Communist named Nguyen Tat Thanh, later called Ho Chi Minh ("he who brings enlightenment"), tried to gain accreditation at Versailles as a spokesman for Indochinese independence. A former merchant seaman and an expert pastry chef, Ho was a quiet, resourceful Communist who led by example, not pontification. Two decades later, he and a small group of associates, including Pham Van Dong and Vo Nguyen Giap, created the Vietnam Doc Lap Dong Minh (League for Vietnamese Independence), or "Vietminh," at the May 1941 plenum of the Indochinese Communist Party.

Ho Chi Minh helps create and lead the Vietminh

During World War II, Vietminh fought on the Allied side, receiving arms and aid from the Americans, who saw it as a useful underground resistance movement against the Japanese occupiers. In December 1944, Vietminh guerrilla units were formed under the command of Giap, a young French-educated high school history teacher with a law degree from the University of Hanoi. Giap hated the French, who guillotined his sister-in-law and allowed his wife and child to die in a French prison in 1943. Many of those who joined his units were non-Communists, who rallied to Vietminh because it was the only effective agency aiming at liberation and independence.

Although the Japanese were annoyed by Vietminh's guerrilla tactics, their forces in Indochina were never defeated. Rather than turn over their weapons to the French, these troops surrendered in 1945 to Vietminh, which was composed of Asians like themselves. Thus, on 2 September 1945, the tiny, frail figure of Ho Chi Minh addressed a rally of 400,000 people in Hanoi, proclaiming Vietnamese independence in an address deliberately modeled on the U.S. Declaration of Independence.

Ho Chi Minh proclaims Vietnam's independence in 1945

But real independence proved elusive. Ho anticipated support from America, the first colony to defeat a colonial power, but Truman's anti-Communism and desire to back France undermined that hope. Indochina was divided into two occupation zones, under Britain in the south and Nationalist China in the north. The British, against their better judgment, allowed France to move back into the south, while the civil war in China soon forced Chiang Kai-shek to call his troops home.

Vietminh now hoped that France would make a deal rather than wage a costly and lengthy colonial war. Ho believed that if Paris were offered economic concessions and the preservation of French property in Indochina, it might recognize Vietnamese independence. This was not a totally naive position, given the attitude of Jean Sainteny, chief of French intelligence in south China, who saw military reimposition of French colonial control as problematic at best. Two months of talks resulted in the Ho–Sainteny Accords of 6 March 1946, under which France would recognize Vietnam as a "free state with its own government, parliament, army, and finances." Vietnam would become part of the French Union, and France would station 25,000 troops in the north until the end of 1952. In return, Vietminh would end its guerrilla war in the south. But the Ho–Sainteny Accords were doomed from the start. The only reason Paris let Sainteny sign them was to gain unopposed entry of French troops into the north, so that France could eventually destroy Vietnamese independence. Similarly, the reason Ho agreed to the accords was to buy time in which to consolidate his hold by destroying all opposition, giving Giap time to prepare his forces for battle.

The Ho–Sainteny Accords fail to achieve a peaceful settlement

By fall 1946, the accords' inadequacy was clear. Incidents between Vietminh and French troops multiplied, and on 23 November, a French warship shelled the Vietnamese quarter of the port of Haiphong, killing at least 6,000 and perhaps as many as 20,000 people. On 19 December, Vietminh soldiers in Hanoi killed 37 Frenchmen, in response to which French forces attacked and took the city. Ho, seriously ill throughout the previous week, escaped out a back window as the French came in the front door. The First Indochina War was under way.

The First Indochina War begins

Ho Chi Minh, waging a struggle for independence and self-determination, expected at least a modicum of international support. But Cold War politics quickly dashed his hopes. The United States encouraged Paris to persevere in its anti-Communist course, and London, though favorably disposed toward Vietnamese independence, followed suit. Stalin, true to his spheres-of-influence concept, ignored the conflict in Indochina, and the Chinese Communists were too busy with their own civil war to be of any help.

Despite the solitary nature of its struggle, Vietminh gave the French more than they could handle. By 1952, the territory under French control was smaller than in 1947. Vietminh greatly increased its military strength and began to conduct large-scale offensive operations. Giap and Ho refused to use their main forces in open encounters, preferring to focus on building up an army and fearful of direct conventional battles against the French. Meanwhile, following the Communist victory in China in 1949, the Chinese sent substantial aid to Vietminh, so that by 1952 Giap had a well-equipped regular army of 300,000 men with which to oppose 150,000 French and 300,000 colonial troops.

Vietminh builds up a large, well-equipped army

By late 1952, after six years of fruitless attempts to defeat Hanoi, the French people had good reason to question the high cost in money and lives of their leaders' chosen course. That policy had cost 90,000 casualties and 1.6 trillion francs, twice the amount of Marshall Plan aid to France. Maintaining a force of 150,000 men in Asia also kept France weak in Europe. Add to this the fact that French economic recovery was lagging behind that of Germany, and it is easy to see why even devoted patriots began to question the war.

France begins to question the value of the Indochina War

By early 1953, both Giap and French general Henri Navarre sought to break the deadlock. Giap launched a drive toward Laos in hopes of enticing the French to defend it and, in so doing, overextend their supply lines. Navarre decided to block Vietminh's advance by garrisoning a dismal little village called Dienbienphu, which sat astride a major road linking Vietnam and Laos. Nothing could have pleased Giap more. By March 1954, he surrounded it with 40,000

Giap exploits French errors at Dienbienphu

North Vietnamese leaders plan the Dienbienphu campaign, 1953.

Here we see the leadership of the Politburo of the Lao Dong Party. From left to right: an unidentified man; Pham Van Dong, under secretary for economic affairs, soon to be appointed chief Vietminh negotiator at the 1954 Geneva Conference; Ho Chi Minh, president, prime minister, and minister of foreign affairs, the "soul of the revolution"; Truong Chinh, general secretary of the party and the "architect of the revolution"; and Vo Nguyen Giap, minister of national defense and commander of the Vietminh armed forces. They met in a remote area of North Vietnam to plan strategy for driving French forces out of the fortified village of Dienbienphu. The strategy was successful, and the defeat at Dienbienphu forced the French to end the First Indochina War.

regulars, armed with large numbers of antiaircraft guns and howitzers concealed in caves beneath dense foliage. The French had fewer than 20,000 men in their garrison. They didn't know that the concealed artillery could put Dienbienphu's airstrip out of operation. Nor did they realize that Vietminh porters could supply enough ammunition to sustain continuous artillery fire and massive infantry attacks. Giap attacked on 13 March 1954 and assured himself of victory in five days by taking all three French strongpoints in the northern hills. From 18 March to 7 May, the French held out, but their fate was sealed.

Meanwhile, Paris had decided to seek a settlement that would remove France from Indochina. In February, Britain, France, the United States, and the USSR agreed to a conference at Geneva starting on 26 April, presumably to discuss Berlin but really to focus on Indochina. Some French officials, unreconciled to the loss of their colony, asked the United States to intervene to save Dienbienphu. Their allies in Washington, including Secretary of State Dulles and Vice President Nixon, suggested various actions, including massive air strikes, infantry landings, and the use of tactical nuclear weapons. But President Eisenhower, who feared a land war in Asia and possessed that sense of proportion common to the greatest generals, refused to consider this lunacy. He responded to the suggestion of nuclear strikes with a characteristic outburst: "My God, you boys must be crazy. We can't use those terrible things on Asians twice in ten years!" Instead he endorsed Dulles's call for a political and military effort to destroy Communism in Southeast Asia, knowing that neither the British nor the U.S. Congress would go along. Dienbienphu fell to Vietminh on 7 May 1954.

The United States refuses to intervene in the Indochina War

Now the French military position was hopeless. On 17 June, socialist Pierre Mendès-France took over as premier, threatening to resign if a peace settlement were not concluded by 20 July. In Geneva, he, Soviet foreign minister Molotov, and Chinese foreign minister Zhou Enlai worked out a plan to divide Indochina into four states: North Vietnam, South Vietnam, Laos, and Cambodia. North Vietnam would be ruled by Vietminh, while South Vietnam would be led by the anti-Communist politician Ngo Dinh Diem. The two would be divided at the 17th parallel, as suggested by Molotov; elections to reunify Vietnam under one government would be held in 1956. Laos and Cambodia would become independent and neutral nations under coalition governments. Vietminh foreign minister Pham Van Dong, faced with the loss of Chinese support, reluctantly came on board. The United States placed no obstacle in the way of a settlement, but did not sign the final agreement and took a strong interest in South Vietnam. On 20 July 1954, as Mendès-France's deadline ran out, the First Indochina War ended with the signing of the Geneva Accords (Document 24).

The Geneva Accords end the First Indochina War

Mendès-France won at Geneva a far more favorable pact than the French had any right to expect, yet this could not ease the effects of defeat on the French Empire. Conversely, Ho Chi Minh felt betrayed by the USSR and China, who settled for much less than Giap won on the battlefield. Zhou Enlai was the real winner: he got a divided Vietnam, which was much more to China's liking than a united and potentially troublesome southern neighbor. He would have preferred to leave France in full control of Indochina, since this would prevent the United States from intervening there and threatening China, as it recently had in Korea. But Zhou, one of the most skillful diplomats in modern history, was not inclined to chase chimeras.

China emerges as the real winner at Geneva

Cosmopolitan, suave, and ruthless, resolute yet amazingly flexible, he would defend the interests of his nation for more than a generation, and he would take what he could get. If in the process he outmaneuvered Moscow, played false with Vietminh, and played ball with Mendès-France, that was all to be expected in the Cold War, a complex struggle in which neither ideology, nor nationalism, nor the balance of power could fully explain the behavior of a diplomat or a nation. Zhou's machinations guaranteed that, while Vietminh succeeded in expelling the French, it failed to unify Vietnam. That would have to come later, if it came at all.

THE COLD WAR IN VIETNAM AND LAOS

Ho Chi Minh's initial effort to unify Vietnam had failed, but the verdict was not yet final. Vietminh earned enormous respect by liberating Vietnam from the French. In the south, to overcome this, Ngo Dinh Diem would have to build a regime that could, by its behavior, demonstrate that the country was better off in its hands. Diem's nationalist credentials were impeccable, but he did not appreciate the need for drastic social reforms to destroy the vestiges of French colonialism. Even if he had, his government lacked support among the masses, the police, and the army and thus was not equipped to execute reforms that would harm the interests of entrenched social and political groups.

After Geneva, Ho waited with scant optimism for the 1956 elections, which he assumed would never be held. Diem had denounced the Geneva Accords while the ink remained moist; both he and his U.S. sponsors knew that an election so soon would be won by Vietminh. Their joint opposition ensured that it would not take place. Diem's rule in the south, therefore, evolved through three stages: 1954–1955, during which he managed, against all expectations, to maintain himself in office; 1955–1957, during which his government created a strong belief in its capability for constructive action; and 1957–1963, during which disenchantment with Diem grew, resulting in a consistent erosion of his support.

The United States and South Vietnam refuse to permit free elections

Ngo Dinh Diem was an enigma. His modern authoritarian ideas, emotional fondness for medieval monarchic concepts, and professed belief in democracy created a complex outlook defying simple labels. A devout Catholic in a Buddhist land, a lifelong bachelor with monastic tendencies, and an honest man whose family and advisors were hopelessly corrupt, Diem was one of the century's most unusual leaders. Hating both Communism and colonialism, he erred in believing that once both were expelled, his new nation would be free. Yet his reluctance to alter the old colonial structures discredited him in the eyes of the poor, while his democratic principles alienated the army and worried the Catholic Church. Ho Chi Minh too was hated and mistrusted by many, but he enjoyed an extensive base of support allowing him to enact broad social and economic reforms. Diem never built that base.

Ngo Dinh Diem attempts to build an anti-Communist state

In 1957, Moscow suggested a permanent partition and the admission of both Vietnams to the UN. Washington, reluctant to recognize a Communist regime in the north, rejected the offer. That decision proved to be a calamity for South Vietnam, which subsequently suffered through fifteen years of war, only to lose in the end. Had Eisenhower accepted the deal, Ho would have been frantic with despair over yet another sellout by his "friends." In hindsight, of course, the

The United States rejects a Soviet offer to recognize both Vietnams

United States should have agreed. But in the context of the Cold War, both Moscow's offer (in hopes of holding on to what it had) and the U.S. rejection (in hopes of rolling back the Geneva Accords) are understandable. Superpower interests took precedence over those of both Vietnams.

For several years, Ho discouraged armed attacks against the Diem regime, considering the situation unripe for insurrection. However, following Mao Zedong's famous "East Wind over West Wind" speech in Moscow in 1957, calling for Communist insurgencies, and following Ho's partial retirement in 1958 at age 68, the Party's new leadership began to change its policy. General Secretary Le Duan and Premier Pham Van Dong eventually concluded that armed revolt was the only way to reunify Vietnam. In 1959, they authorized the formation of "Viet Cong" (VC) guerrilla units in the south, and in 1960, they created the National Liberation Front (NLF), in a ploy reminiscent of the 1941 formation of Vietminh. The United States supported Diem against the VC, even though he was a dictator, because he was anti-Communist. In reality, *both* Vietnams were one-party states, with a few opposition parties as window dressing. Both had secret police, rigged elections, ubiquitous propaganda, and political reeducation camps. They differed in their economic and social systems, and in South Vietnam's openness to religious diversity—which, ironically, would pose an enormous problem for Diem.

North Vietnam decides to unify Vietnam by force

North Vietnam's eventual decision to launch a revolt in the south had a profound impact on neighboring Laos. A mountainous, sparsely populated, destitute country whose capital city of Vientiane had only two traffic lights in 1963, Laos controlled a network of roads, fords, and pathways called the Ho Chi Minh trail—the only route by which North Vietnam could send supplies and personnel to the south. The Geneva Accords had stipulated that Laos remain neutral, but this was easier said than done.

Laos enters the Cold War

Since the early 1950s, Laos had been effectively divided. Most of the country was under the nominal control of a neutral coalition government led by Prince Souvanna Phouma, whose outwardly placid demeanor was well suited to the complex balancing act required of Laotian leaders. His half brother, Prince Souvanouvong, a Communist, led a Vietminh-style army called the Pathet Lao, which controlled two northern provinces. The United States backed two other factions, one standing for pro-Western neutrality and another, headed by CIA protégé Phoumi Nosavan, standing for militant anti-Communism and destruction of the Pathet Lao. Hanoi, needing extensive use of the Ho Chi Minh Trail to conduct its insurrection in the south, tried to maintain a low profile and work through the Pathet Lao.

Souvanna Phouma did his best to construct a government of national unity. In December 1960, however, Washington's favorite, Phoumi Nosavan, broke a U.S.-sponsored cease-fire and captured Vientiane, pushing Souvanna Phouma into the arms of the Pathet Lao. A Communist counterstroke in March 1961 routed Phoumi's forces and opened all of Laos to attack. John Kennedy, the new U.S. president, now faced the prospect that Laos might fall to the Communists, enabling North Vietnam to outflank South Vietnam. He considered military intervention, but the Joint Chiefs of Staff, traumatized by the Korean experience, insisted that commanders of any U.S. troops in Asia must be authorized to use nuclear weapons. Recoiling from that, Kennedy sent Averell Harriman, former ambassador to London and Moscow, to seek a compromise in Laos.

Pathet Lao advances encourage Kennedy to seek neuutralization

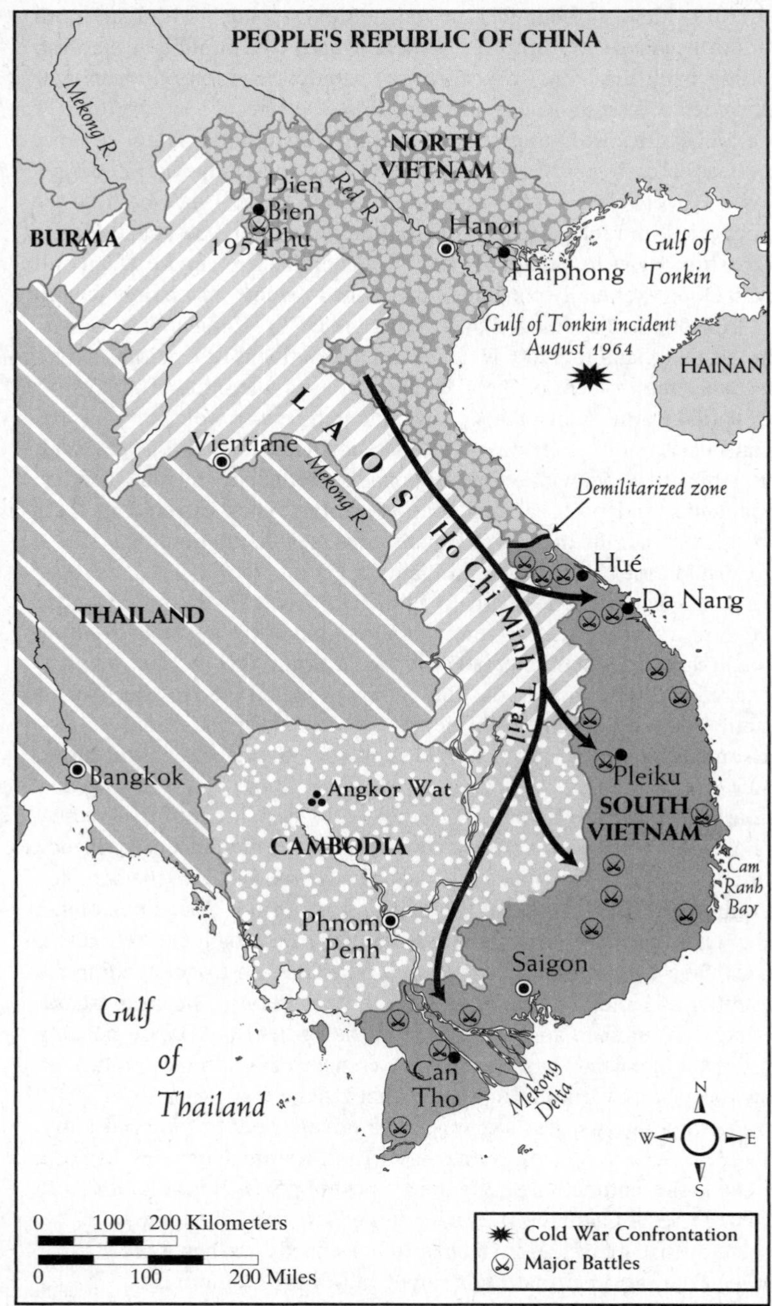

MAP 9 Vietnam, Laos, and Cambodia, 1954–1975.

After Vietminh defeated France in the First Indochina War (1946–1954), the Geneva Conference divided Indochina into North Vietnam, South Vietnam, Laos, and Cambodia. But note that North Vietnam, sustaining its forces by the Ho Chi Minh Trail through neutral Laos and Cambodia, defeated America and South Vietnam in the Second Indochina War (1964–1975), enabling Communists also to take over Laos and Cambodia.

Harriman, nicknamed "Crocodile" for his tendency to snap at those guilty of fuzzy thinking, had decades of experience in dealing with Communists. Seventy years old and increasingly deaf, he could still work eighteen-hour days for weeks on end without suffering any loss of efficiency. He quickly reached several conclusions. The neutralist course was the only one that might enable the United States to avoid war in Laos. Khrushchev did not want war in Laos, both because he thought it would fall to Communism anyway and because issues such as Berlin were far more important. Zhou Enlai did not want to provoke a Korean-style U.S. intervention but was willing to run risks in Laos in the belief that Washington would not intervene. Ho Chi Minh wanted a Communist Laos, but not at the cost of provoking American or Chinese intervention. There was room for maneuver, and Harriman made sure that Kennedy saw it.

Harriman untangles the situation in Laos

Now Laos became even more entangled with the Cold War. The Bay of Pigs debacle in April 1961 convinced Kennedy that he could not afford another humiliation at Communist hands. He decided to back Souvanna Phouma's neutralist approach in hopes of achieving a negotiated settlement. When he met Khrushchev at Vienna in June, their standoff over Berlin was tempered by their agreement that Laos was not worth a conflict and that a neutralist solution was acceptable to both. The issue dragged on for the rest of 1961, with endless negotiations at Geneva leading even the impassive Andrei Gromyko to complain to Harriman that "One cannot sit indefinitely on the shores of Lake Geneva, counting swans." A breakthrough came in May 1962, when Pathet Lao pressure led Kennedy to send the Seventh Fleet to the Gulf of Thailand and U.S. ground forces to Thailand. Simultaneously, Souvanna Phouma initiated direct talks, setting a 15 June deadline for success (as Mendès-France had done in 1954).

Moscow, Beijing, and Hanoi now concluded that a settlement was less risky than continued military pressure. They decided to put Laos on the back burner, apparently reasoning that if Vietnam were united under Communist control, Laos would become Communist anyway. On 11 June, Souvanna Phouma announced the formation of a government of national unity. Agreements were signed in Geneva on 23 July, reaffirming Laotian neutrality and setting a schedule for removal of all foreign forces. The neutral regime continued to wink at Hanoi's use of the Ho Chi Minh Trail, but in all other respects the arrangement held until 1975, when Hanoi's victory in Vietnam brought the Pathet Lao to power in Laos.

The superpowers agree on Laotian neutrality

Meanwhile, U.S. aid to South Vietnam was increasing rapidly. Kennedy's administration kept elevating the number of American military advisors, from 300 in January 1961 to 16,000 by the summer of 1963. Various U.S. military initiatives, like the 1962 Strategic Hamlet Program, had little effect on the insurgency. Then Diem ran afoul of the Buddhist majority (70 percent of the population). For years, he had funneled government posts, land, and power to the Catholic minority. In summer 1963, the militant United Buddhist Church, led by a nationalist monk named Thich Tri Quang, took advantage of government repression to stage provocations aimed at uniting South Vietnamese nationalists to overthrow Diem and return to traditional Vietnamese values by expelling the United States.

Buddhist hunger strikes in May led the regime to declare martial law in several places. Then, on 11 June 1963, a Buddhist monk knelt on a Saigon street, had himself drenched with gasoline, and committed suicide by lighting a match. He was followed over the next few weeks by a number of emulators, and images of burning monks shocked the world. Diem's sister-in-law callously offered to furnish fuel for what she termed "the next barbecue." Appalled, Kennedy insisted that Diem compromise, but even had he been willing, caving in to U.S. pressure would have destroyed his credibility and played into the hand of the Buddhists. As government atrocities mushroomed, Diem on 20 August imposed martial law nationwide and suspended all civil liberties.

Buddhist protests imperil the Diem regime in Saigon

Kennedy was no happier with the war than he was with Diem. The Strategic Hamlet Program was a failure, and Viet Cong strength in the south was growing. Kennedy began talking about installing a government in Saigon that would ask the United States to pull out. On 11 October, he issued a secret directive that 1,000 U.S. advisors be withdrawn by December. Simultaneously, American ambassador Henry Cabot Lodge and CIA operative Lucien Conein conveyed Washington's wishes to certain key military leaders. Diem got wind of this and devised a counterplot, involving a phony revolt that would result in the murders of Lodge, Conein, and the military plotters. Unfortunately for Diem, his closest military advisor, who was supposed to put this plan into effect, was part of the plot against him. On 1 November 1963, the government was overthrown. Diem and his brother, assured safe conduct by the rebels, were arrested and murdered (according to General Duong Van Minh, they committed "accidental suicide"). A military dictatorship now ruled in Saigon.

Kennedy secretly begins withdrawal and authorizes a coup

Three weeks after the coup, John Kennedy followed the Ngo brothers to the grave. His replacement, Lyndon Johnson, was not interested in a government that would ask the Americans to leave. He wanted instead to "nail the coonskin to the wall," to inflict a decisive defeat on the Communist side in the Cold War. If the response had been up to Nikita Khrushchev or Zhou Enlai, some sort of compromise might have been reached. Russia and China, after all, had sold out their comrades before. But the response was in the hands of Hanoi, and it was not long in coming.

THE AMERICAN INVOLVEMENT IN VIETNAM

Lyndon Johnson's main concerns after taking office were getting elected in 1964 and achieving his domestic agenda. In Vietnam, his position was awkward. He reversed Kennedy's 11 October withdrawal directive, hoping that the revolt could be put down swiftly and Communism contained. If the war went badly and he tried to get out, conservative lawmakers would hold up his social programs until he gave the Pentagon what it wanted. But if he escalated the conflict, he would alienate key senators like Mike Mansfield, J. William Fulbright, and Richard Russell. He also needed *them* for his social legislation, and they wanted America out of Indochina.

Johnson seeks victory in Vietnam

Hanoi's position was also delicate. Annoyed by Khrushchev's disinterest in their struggle and resentful of his efforts to get them to abandon it, the Lao Dong Party (North Vietnamese Communists) tilted toward Beijing late in 1963. But China was Vietnam's age-old enemy, and Mao Zedong had his own agenda. He urged Ho to fight a war of attrition, reasoning that it would tie both North Vietnam and the United States to a long, expensive conflict. This gave Mao a way to fight America without risking a repetition of Korea, where U.S. technology had claimed a million Chinese lives. Hanoi distrusted Mao's advice and was

The Lao Dong Party sends the NVA south

reluctant to alienate Moscow by increasing its support for the VC against Khrushchev's wishes. But to let the VC wither and die was to give up hope for reunification and to tolerate an indefinite U.S. presence in Indochina. Finally, on 28 March 1964, the Lao Dong Party opted to fully support revolution in the south by sending in regular units of the North Vietnamese Army (NVA). For this, it needed the arms Mao could supply, and its tilt toward Beijing continued.

The first NVA units reached the south in August. At the same time, Washington concluded that U.S. forces would have to bomb North Vietnam and mine its harbors to cut off its support for the Viet Cong. Congressional approval was obtained through passage of the Gulf of Tonkin Resolution, following an alleged attack by North Vietnamese patrol boats on U.S. surveillance ships in that body of water (Document 46). Seizing this opportunity, the Johnson administration asked Congress for extensive authority to use military force in Southeast Asia. The resulting resolution, passed by voice vote in the House of Representatives and by 98-2 in the Senate, authorized the president to "take all necessary steps, including the use of armed force, to assist any member . . . of the Southeast Asia Collective Defense Treaty requesting assistance in defense of its freedom." It was a blank check for U.S. military action.

The Gulf of Tonkin Resolution authorizes U.S. combat intervention in Vietnam

Direct American involvement in the Vietnam War posed a dilemma for Beijing. The Chinese Communists split between those who thought China should draw closer to Moscow and prepare for war against the United States, and those who feared that such action would only delay the revolutionizing of Chinese society. Mao backed the latter faction, depicting American weapons as "paper tigers" and holding that China, which could not really compete with the industrial West, must rely on its own revolutionary spirit for survival. Lin Biao, head of the Chinese People's Liberation Army and a close ally of Mao, endorsed this line in his 1965 article, "Long Live the Victory of People's War". In late 1965, China detached itself from Vietnam and other external affairs, concentrating on an internal upheaval known as the Great Proletarian Cultural Revolution (Chapter 12). Beijing continued to supply Hanoi with arms and encouragement, but nothing else. North Vietnam was on its own.

China supplies North Vietnam but avoids military action

After Johnson's victory in the 1964 election, most of his advisors favored mass bombing of North Vietnam. Many Americans, including some of the president's main critics, were certain that Southeast Asia was vital to U.S. interests. Secretary of State Dean Rusk went so far as to link it to the German Question, contending that the U.S. guarantee of West Berlin would lose its credibility should South Vietnam fall. Still, the president walked a cautious path until February 1965, when a VC raid on U.S. military advisors at Pleiku convinced him to initiate bombing. By mid-February, the United States was engaged in Operation ROLLING THUNDER (whose name came from the Christian hymn "How Great Thou Art"), a systematic bombing campaign that continued until 1968.

The United States begins systematic bombing of North Vietnam

The bombing, far from sapping Hanoi's morale, inspired it to greater effort. The first shipments of Soviet and Chinese arms to the Viet Cong down the Ho Chi Minh Trail took place in late 1964. Early the next year, CIA reports indicated that VC strength was increasing exponentially and that a Communist victory could not be ruled out. The rebel threat to the U.S. air base at Danang led Johnson to grant the request of General William Westmoreland, commander

The United States commits combat troops to Vietnam

American soldiers advance on Viet Cong positions near Vo Dot, South Vietnam, in 1965. Soldiers from the U.S. 173rd airborne brigade move on Viet Cong positions at the tree line in the distance. President Johnson's decision to commit combat troops to Vietnam in March 1965 placed the United States squarely in the middle of the Second Indochina War, reversing the twelve-year-old American resolve to avoid involvement in a land war in Asia. The "Vietnam War" (as it was called in the United States) was controversial from the beginning and tormented American society for years beyond its unsatisfactory conclusion in 1973.

of American forces in Vietnam, for two battalions of marines, despite the opposition of the U.S. ambassador, General Maxwell Taylor. Once American troops were committed, Johnson would find it impossible to resist further requests (Document 48A). By the end of 1965, troop levels reached 184,300, with another 200,000 on the way. In pursuing this course of action, the president committed the United States to a land war in Asia while misleading the American public as to the scope of the commitment. The sense of betrayal fostered by this duplicity would contribute greatly to the antiwar protests of the late 1960s.

In making this extensive troop commitment, Johnson had no reason to fear a Korea-style Chinese intervention. China by 1966 was knee-deep in the Cultural Revolution, and Moscow's postwar record indicated that Soviet military action was unlikely. But the limited war in Vietnam carried all the liabilities of limited war in Korea: significant U.S. casualties, a stalemate with no prospects for quick victory, and the sense that the military was being unduly restricted by civilian politicians. Democracies find it easier to fight total war than limited war, as Truman's experience demonstrated.

As in Korea, a lack of clear war aims plagued the U.S. command. Westmoreland tried to win a war with no well-defined goals and no consensus on what would constitute victory, short of the total destruction of Communism in Vietnam. He fought a conventional war against a guerrilla insurgency, hoping that he could kill enough of the enemy to drive North Vietnam to negotiate. But he had no way of knowing how many deaths that would take and no awareness of the level of Ho Chi Minh's commitment to the war. U.S. forces killed Vietnamese by the thousands, and total Communist deaths between 1961 and 1975 surely exceeded a million. But the Lao Dong Party believed it could raise at least 250,000 new recruits *each year* and that America simply couldn't kill that many. The U.S. goal was fuzzy and probably unattainable.

U.S. objectives in Vietnam lack clarity

As for negotiations, it was difficult to envisage a plausible bargaining scenario. Vietminh had come to Geneva in 1954 sure that its Dienbienphu victory would bring it a unified nation, only to have Moscow and Beijing sell it out and divide Vietnam. But the Lao Dong Party would not make the same mistake twice. North Vietnam consciously adopted a long, painful process to conquer the south. Hanoi had no expectation of quick victory, and the war from its perspective was not a stalemate but an endless chain of small encounters designed to weaken America's will. This strategy slowly succeeded, a fact implicitly recognized in Lyndon Johnson's rueful comment: "If I were Ho Chi Minh, I'd never negotiate."

ESCALATION WITHOUT VICTORY, 1965–1967

Hanoi's ability to resist the U.S. onslaught derived from a number of factors. First was the simplicity of its goal: to reunify Vietnam by expelling the Americans and conquering the south. The Lao Dong Party focused the nation's energies on an understandable and attractive objective. Great sacrifice would be required, but the end was concrete in nature and easily imaginable: No one believed that the Americans would stay forever, and no one thought South Vietnam could long survive their departure. Inspired by this goal, the Communists persevered for years despite terrible hardship.

Three factors assist Hanoi in preventing a U.S. victory

Second, North Vietnam's economy could not be destroyed by bombing. An agrarian nation with few industrial areas, it could hardly be "bombed back to the Stone Age," as General Curtis LeMay suggested. Compared with America, it was already there. Hanoi's weapons were furnished by its allies: trucks and AK-47 rifles from China; tanks, planes, and surface-to-air missiles from Russia. They were produced at facilities in those nations, well beyond the reach of U.S. bombing.

Third, the NVA followed the same strategy it had used against France: Employ guerrilla tactics against a superior foe until you can entice that foe into a situation where you have the advantage. NVA commander Vo Nguyen Giap knew how to fight set-piece battles and knew that he would lose them unless he could select the proper time, place, and conditions. Time was on his side, and his skills far surpassed those of U.S. generals reluctant to part with methods honed on European plains in the 1940s and Korean hills in the 1950s. The Communists' ability to live off the land and mix with the local people made it impossible for the United States to force them to fight a conventional war until it was in their interest to do so.

So when the U.S. government sent American marines ashore at Danang on 8 March 1965, it was confronting an adversary much better prepared and much more focused on attainable objectives than Washington realized. As if this were not dangerous enough, almost at once an antiwar movement began in the United States. On 24 March, the University of Michigan was the site of a "Teach-In" against the war, as classes throughout the day were devoted to the situation in Vietnam. Johnson's decision two weeks later to let U.S. combat troops engage in offensive operations was met with an antiwar rally in Washington organized by a radical group called "Students for a Democratic Society," or SDS. On 15 May, a National Teach-In took place on campuses in all 50 states, and that October, antiwar protests were conducted simultaneously in 40 American cities. The war was becoming the defining feature of Johnson's administration, imperiling the consensus needed for his Great Society reforms. Yet thus far the reaction was out of proportion to the American involvement. By year's end, U.S. troop strength in Vietnam stood at 184,300, and only 636 American soldiers had been killed. Later increases in casualties and draft calls would turn the antiwar movement into the most extensive grassroots protest in American history.

An antiwar movement forms in the United States

In November, a small U.S. detachment moving through the Ia Drang Valley was ambushed by an NVA regiment. After a three-day battle, 240 American soldiers had been killed, a total which shocked Defense Secretary McNamara and angered Johnson; but the NVA counted 1,800 dead and a like number seriously wounded. This decided an internal dispute between Giap and General Nguyen Chi Thanh, who felt the United States could be defeated by conventional means: Casualties on that scale were unacceptable to Hanoi. From then on, the NVA would avoid large battles in favor of Giap's hit-and-run tactics. Westmoreland failed to make a similar adjustment, and American military fortunes began a barely perceptible decline.

North Vietnam decides to employ guerrilla tactics

On Christmas Day, 1965, Johnson suspended Operation ROLLING THUNDER to give Hanoi a chance to seek a negotiated settlement. He received no response and resumed the bombing on 31 January 1966. The next few months proved difficult. The Senate Foreign Relations Committee opened televised hearings on the war four days after the bombing resumed; Secretary Rusk doggedly defended the U.S. position against skeptical witnesses and suspicious senators. Two months later National Security Advisor McGeorge Bundy, disturbed over the rapid increase in U.S. troop commitment, resigned. He was replaced by Walt Whitman Rostow, an inflexible Cold Warrior and a true believer in the virtues of strategic bombing. Meanwhile, Senator Wayne Morse tried to get the Senate to repeal the Gulf of Tonkin Resolution but failed by a vote of 92–5. Most senators still felt the war was winnable, and those who didn't were reluctant to withdraw authority from a president in the midst of a conflict.

The mood of the country was both more and less warlike than that of the Congress. U.S. casualties were still fairly low, and most people, if they thought about the conflict at all, considered it an unpleasant necessity akin to the Korean War. The "Baby Boom" generation, however, had different ideas. They were beneficiaries of the new housing, schools, and roads of the postwar era; the GI Bill had given their parents access to better education and jobs; they had responded to Kennedy's youth and vigor and had joined the Peace Corps, Johnson's War on Poverty, and the Civil Rights Movement. Their parents found their sexual mores and rock music disturbing. This generation now had to answer draft calls for the Vietnam War, and they were convinced neither of its value nor its morality.

No single response to the war came from the Baby Boomers. Some enlisted eagerly, some were drafted reluctantly, some sought escape in student deferments or conscientious objector status, some (given Johnson's odd decision not to call up the reserves) enlisted in the reserve forces to avoid combat, and a few fled to foreign lands. Many took part in antiwar protests, which grew in size and frequency throughout the 1960s. For Lyndon Johnson's generation, the sight of thousands of Americans demonstrating in the streets against U.S. policy was deeply disturbing. Totalitarian regimes could repress such protests, but a democratic society had to respond in some way to popular pressure. In April 1966, Johnson called on Ho Chi Minh to make peace in return for $5 billion in aid and a huge development program. Hanoi responded with silence. On 1 May, the United States bombed VC camps in Cambodia for the first time, and the antiwar demonstrations at home continued.

Resistance to the war grows in the United States

By early 1967, American troop levels in Vietnam had risen to 385,300. Six thousand U.S. soldiers died there in 1966, bringing the war's total to 6,644. General Westmoreland continued to seek a military victory but could not find a strategy to cope with Giap's guerrilla warfare. Defense Secretary McNamara, horrified at the growing death toll and suspicious of the accuracy of the U.S. military's "body counts," advised Johnson to deescalate the conflict and seek a negotiated settlement. He was eased out of office late in 1967. That September, Johnson offered the San Antonio Formula: The bombing of North Vietnam would stop as soon as talks began. Hanoi had other plans, and the war went on.

Bombing of the north intensified, as did aerial defoliation of the south: Huge quantities of potent herbicides, including the carcinogenic Agent Orange, were sprayed over jungles across South Vietnam to deprive the enemy of cover. Antipersonnel raids by B-52 bombers produced areas of destruction similar to that of an atomic blast. Body counts showed colossal casualty rates among Communist forces. None of it seemed to make a difference. Johnson, desperate for a way out, met Soviet premier Kosygin in a strange one-day summit in Glassboro, New Jersey, in summer 1967 (Chapter 12). But nothing came of the talks, because neither Russia nor China had as much influence over Hanoi in 1967 as they had exercised in 1954. The Lao Dong Party was resolved to fight until the United States withdrew and then to continue its subversion of the south.

Johnson searches in vain for a negotiated settlement

Meanwhile, American support for the war eroded rapidly. In April, an antiwar protest in New York drew over 100,000 people, and six months later 50,000 marched on the Pentagon. The antiwar movement, though growing larger by the day, was never united, save in seeking to end U.S. involvement in Vietnam. Liberals who saw the war as a mistake, radicals who opposed capitalism, and pacifists who hated violence all came together to try to force Johnson to end the war.

Johnson responded by questioning his critics' patriotism and trying to prove that the war was being won. But U.S. troop levels at the end of 1967 were 485,600, and the death toll for that year was 9,377, bringing the total for the war to 16,021. Intelligence showed that, despite this huge effort, North Vietnamese and VC control continued to grow in the south. As 1967 ended, the validity of American strategy and public support for the war hung by slender threads. North Vietnam would cut them in 1968.

THE TET OFFENSIVE

In Vietnam, the Lunar New Year, or "Tet," was the year's main holiday. For several years, a truce had been observed so that both sides might celebrate in peace. The Americans expected a low level of hostilities during this period. Had they known more Vietnamese history, they might have recalled that an earlier ruler had routed invading Chinese troops who were observing Tet festivities in 1789. On 21 January 1968, nine days before Tet, the NVA baited its trap, laying siege to a remote U.S. outpost at Khe Sanh. This was done to draw American forces away from South Vietnamese cities, exposing them to Viet Cong attack.

It was not a terribly clever ploy, but Westmoreland fell for it. He redeployed U.S. forces toward Khe Sanh, presuming the cities would be safe during Tet. It would have been just as logical to assume that Khe Sanh would be safe, but Westmoreland's logic stopped short of that conclusion. On 30 January, the first day of Tet, the VC invaded thirteen provincial capitals, captured the ancient imperial capital of Hué, and used nineteen commandos to attack and briefly occupy parts of the U.S. embassy in Saigon (see map on page 164). The attacks came without warning, and in the subsequent judgment of a West Point textbook on military history, the Tet Offensive was an American intelligence disaster equivalent to Pearl Harbor.

The Tet Offensive surprises U.S. forces in Vietnam

By late February, order was restored. Westmoreland portrayed Tet as a VC defeat, and in a military sense it was. The VC lost their best people, and the North Vietnamese who replaced them turned what had been a largely indigenous southern movement into a subsidiary of the NVA. The VC's casualties were horrendous, and they failed to hold any of the cities they attacked. Hanoi's real objective, however, was not a military one. Giap said later that he had hoped to spark uprisings throughout South Vietnam by showing that the Americans could not protect its people. Clearly, that goal was not attained. Ironically, Hanoi *did* succeed in influencing U.S. public opinion, which it had not set out to do!

The Viet Cong lose militarily but win politically

Tet proved to be Johnson's political death knell, not because it turned most Americans against the war (public opinion polls showed the contrary), but because it confirmed two key groups in their convictions. The antiwar movement had always seen the war as unjustified, immoral, and unwise. But others felt that Johnson was not waging the war effectively and that American troops were being asked to fight with one hand behind their backs. Tet verified this belief and turned this group against continued U.S. involvement. Deprived of this support, with his domestic agenda in ruins, Johnson faced a challenge for the Democratic presidential nomination from Senator Eugene McCarthy, whose entry into the primary races in November 1967 had been greeted with polite disdain. Tet turned him into a viable candidate, as those who were upset with Johnson now saw a vote for McCarthy as a way to send the White House a message.

On 27 February, Westmoreland made public a request for 206,000 more troops. The shock to the nation was even deeper than the trauma of Tet. After years of duplicity in its portrayal of the situation in Vietnam, the Johnson administration seemed ethically bankrupt. Even worse, Americans began to realize that, despite what they had been promised, a victorious end to the war was nowhere in sight. CBS news anchorman Walter Cronkite observed that the war was likely to end in a stalemate, and a few days later, he broadcast a secret CIA estimate that, at present levels, the war could last a century. Johnson had been fatally wounded at "Credibility Gap," and on 12 March, McCarthy nearly buried him, losing the New Hampshire primary by fewer than 300 votes out of 50,000 cast (and winning it weeks later, after absentee ballots were counted). Four days later Senator Robert Kennedy, brother of the slain president, entered the Democratic race, splitting the antiwar vote but providing the peace movement with a candidate far more formidable than McCarthy. That same day, a U.S. platoon massacred nearly 500 women and children in a remote village called My Lai. The news was hidden for twenty months.

Tet and Westmoreland's troop demands shock the U.S. public

On 26 March, Johnson assembled the Senior Advisory Group on Vietnam, a panel of statesmen and experts whom he consulted often. As recently as November 1967, they had advised him to stand firm. Now, headed by presidential troubleshooter Philip Habib and Dean Acheson, who as Truman's secretary of state had helped lead the nation into the Korean War, they overwhelmingly recommended disengagement. Johnson was stunned and bitter. Five days later, on 31 March, he addressed the nation and announced that he would not seek another term (Document 48B). Vice President Hubert Humphrey entered the race as Johnson's heir, despite his own misgivings about the war.

Johnson decides not to seek reelection

NIXON TAKES COMMAND

In April 1968, it seemed the war might soon be over, but more than half of U.S. combat deaths in Vietnam still lay ahead. The year itself turned into an unimaginable horror. Peace talks opened in Paris on 12 May, but no real progress was made. Robert Kennedy was murdered on 5 June, moments after defeating Humphrey and McCarthy in the California presidential primary. In events unrelated to Vietnam, American civil rights leader Martin Luther King was gunned down on 4 April; student and working-class riots in May nearly toppled de Gaulle's regime in France; the USSR invaded Czechoslovakia in August to destroy Alexander Dubcek's reformist government; and in Mexico City in October, President Gustavo Díaz Ordaz's troops opened fire on a crowd of demonstrators and killed more than 300, two weeks before the start of the Olympic games.

Chaos convulses the world in 1968

A dazed world turned its eyes to U.S. presidential politics. Former vice president Richard Nixon won the Republican nomination in July, narrowly defeating California governor Ronald Reagan. Humphrey prevailed over McCarthy to become the Democratic nominee, but not before antiwar protests during the party's convention in Chicago turned brutal. Scenes of police clubbing protesters and rioters looting stores were telecast throughout the world, seriously weakening the moral credibility of both the antiwar movement and the Chicago police and damaging the Democrats so badly it was hard to see how Humphrey could win.

Amazingly, he nearly did. Torn between loyalty to Johnson and his own conscience, he missed a splendid chance at the convention to reconcile with the Kennedy forces by denouncing the war, an act which would have isolated McCarthy and reunified the party. Not until late September did Humphrey voice a willingness to seek a quick end to the war. Johnson loyally supported the Democratic cause by halting Operation ROLLING THUNDER on Halloween

Nixon defeats Humphrey in the U.S. presidential election

night, sparking a surge to Humphrey five days before the election. He then quietly voted for Richard Nixon. Assisted by George Wallace of Alabama, who ran as a third-party candidate and split the prowar vote with Nixon, Humphrey closed to within a percentage point; but Nixon held on and narrowly won the election. As 1968 mercifully ended, U.S. troop levels in Vietnam stood at 536,000. Deaths that year totaled 14,589, the highest single year total of the war.

By 30 April 1969, American troop strength peaked at 543,300. Nixon, despite his militaristic campaign rhetoric, had no intention of escalating the conflict or of seeking a quick pullout. Resolved not to become the first U.S. president to lose a war, he wanted to remove troops gradually while strengthening South Vietnam with a flood of military equipment. That material would be used by local forces rather than by Americans, a concept enshrined as a worldwide principle in the "Nixon Doctrine" of July 1969 (Documents 54A and 54B). At the same time, the CIA's "Phoenix" program employed infiltration techniques to cripple the VC's operations through the unmasking and (in many cases) killing of approximately 60,000 VC agents in the south.

The Nixon Doctrine constitutes a new American approach

Nixon's phased withdrawal began with the removal of 25,000 troops in June and was soon incorporated in the Pentagon budgets by Defense Secretary Melvin Laird. This annoyed National Security Advisor Henry Kissinger, who felt that scheduled troop pullouts deprived him of negotiating leverage with Hanoi. Laird also coined the term "Vietnamization" to describe the execution of the Nixon Doctrine in Southeast Asia. Despite Johnson's 1964 campaign pledge that "We don't want American boys to do the fighting for Asian boys," South Vietnam had not begun drafting eighteen-year-olds until Nixon took office, while Americans of that age had been fighting in Vietnam since 1965. Vietnamization, of course, had its enemies, including the U.S. antiwar movement (which saw it as a delaying tactic) and South Vietnamese president Nguyen Van Thieu (who considered it a betrayal of America's commitment). Thieu undermined the Paris peace talks so well that Nixon lost interest in them and dispatched Kissinger to meet secretly in February 1970 with Hanoi's special emissary, Le Duc Tho. It took nearly three years for those secret talks to pay off.

Clearly Nixon's strategy would take time, and America was growing impatient. Ho Chi Minh's death in September 1969 had no impact on North Vietnam's bargaining posture; on his deathbed, the world's most famous pastry chef enjoined his successors to avoid another Geneva conference in which Moscow and Beijing could once more sell the Lao Dong Party down the Mekong River. The antiwar movement continued, sponsoring nationwide "moratorium" demonstrations on 15 October, followed by a huge march on Washington on 15 November. A day later, the *New York Times* published the first accounts of the March 1968 My Lai massacre. As 1970 began, U.S. troop levels were down to 475,200, but total American dead now exceeded 40,000. Nixon wanted a break in the stalemate, and he wanted it quickly.

The antiwar movement peaks in the United States

Nixon's impatience mirrored that of the American people, and it led to a widening of the war. Throughout the 1960s, North Vietnam made skillful use of the Ho Chi Minh Trail, which ran through neutral Laos and Cambodia. NVA and VC units often took refuge in camps just across the border to avoid pursuit by U.S. forces. In March 1970, a military coup deposed Cambodia's neutralist Prince

Sihanouk, replacing him with pro-American general Lon Nol. The United States at once pressured Lon Nol to expel the NVA and VC forces, and on 30 April, Nixon announced an American invasion of Cambodia to close down the camps and supply routes. The Vietnam War now became the Second Indochina War, and U.S. campuses erupted in protest. The Ohio National Guard fired on one such demonstration at Kent State University, killing four students and sending ripples of revulsion across the nation. Several more students were killed at Jackson State University in Mississippi that same week. Many colleges canceled classes and exams, either in protest against the war or as a sign of helplessness in the face of angry students.

Nixon's Cambodian incursion widens the Vietnam War

American operations in Cambodia ended on 30 June. Six months later, Congress prohibited the use of U.S. combat troops in Laos and Cambodia. But the Ho Chi Minh Trail was still open, and American forces were still mired in South Vietnam. Desperate to find a way out, Nixon and Kissinger increasingly placed their hopes on détente with China and Russia, hoping that Beijing and Moscow could help them end the war.

Vietnamese children flee for their lives as American napalm attacks set their village aflame, 1972. Phan Thi Kim Phuc runs naked with three other frantic children as their village, Trang Bang, burns in the distance. This Pulitzer Prize–winning photograph symbolized for many the agony of rural Vietnam during the Second Indochina War.

12

China, SALT, and the Superpowers, 1967–1972

By the late 1960s, the world strategic balance seemed to be shifting in Moscow's favor. As a result of a massive weapons buildup, the Soviet Union was rapidly closing the gap between itself and the United States, at least in terms of land-based strategic missiles. Meanwhile, the United States was sinking ever more deeply into the morass of Vietnam, expending its resources and credibility in a war whose increasing unpopularity was fraying the fabric of American society. As the war dragged on with no end in sight, the sense of American superiority seemed to be sinking into the swamps of war-torn Southeast Asia.

Despite the U.S. setbacks, however, the appearance of Soviet gain was both illusory and deceptive. The USSR's economy continued to falter, as the Brezhnev–Kosygin efforts to modernize production and increase consumer goods supply proved ineffective and inadequate. The Soviets might be gaining strategically, but they were falling behind economically. And even their strategic gains were offset by the emergence of a formidable new foe: the People's Republic of China (PRC), a fellow Communist state and former Soviet ally.

THE SINO-SOVIET SPLIT

The antagonism between the Soviets and Chinese had both historical and ideological roots. In the nineteenth century, the imperial Russian government took advantage of weakness and turmoil in China to impose unequal treaties, helping itself to territory previously claimed by the Chinese. Although the Soviet government renounced such treaties after it came to power, it returned no land, and large areas remained in dispute along the 4,000-mile border between the two countries. Then, during the long struggle between Chinese Communists and Nationalists, the Soviets often seemed to side with the Nationalists, urging the Communists to collaborate with Jiang Jieshi even as he sought to destroy them. During the Civil War of 1946–1949, Mao Zedong and his comrades received only limited support from Stalin. And Mao's brand of Communism, based on

Chinese–Russian relations rooted in historic hostilities

mobilization of the peasant masses, was at odds with the more traditional model of a Marxist-Leninist proletarian vanguard espoused by the USSR.

At first, in the fervor following the Chinese Communist victory in 1949, such differences mattered little. Mao needed massive aid to build his new society, and the obvious place to turn was to the USSR. He thus initiated a policy of "leaning to one side," aligning the PRC with the USSR and traveling to Moscow in December 1949 to negotiate with Soviet leaders. Stalin was rude and drove a hard bargain, but in the "Treaty of Friendship and Alliance" of February 1950 (Document 18), the Soviets agreed to provide equipment for Chinese construction projects and about $300 million worth of credits to assist Chinese development. Although this aid was only a fraction of what Mao thought he needed, he welcomed it as a first step.

The USSR and the PRC form alliance in 1950

In the 1950s, the USSR supplied significant assistance to the PRC. During the Korean War, although they avoided sending combat troops, the Soviets gave the Chinese technological support and sold them military hardware, including several submarines and a number of MiG fighter aircraft. The USSR quickly became China's main trading partner, accounting for roughly half of all Chinese foreign commerce. The Soviets sent thousands of advisors and technicians to China, trained thousands of Chinese in Russia, provided industrial plans and expertise, and helped construct several hundred industrial projects in China. At least until 1958, the Chinese borrowed heavily from Soviet experience and sought to emulate the Soviet model—even adopting a Soviet-style "Five-Year Plan" for rapid industrialization.

In 1950s, the USSR aids and supports the PRC

But by then the sheen of socialist solidarity was fading. As long as Stalin was alive, Mao had accepted a secondary role as junior partner to the Soviet dictator. But after Stalin's death in 1953, seeing himself now as the senior socialist leader and judging that China had earned full partner status by fighting off the West in Korea, he accorded Stalin's successors no such esteem. In 1955, at the Bandung Conference of Asian and African nations (Chapter 8), to which the Soviets were not invited, the Chinese pursued an independent course and sought to assert themselves as leaders of the nonaligned movement. That year also brought the purge and suicide of Gao Gang, the Chinese Communist Party boss in Manchuria, accused of carving out his own kingdom there and resented by Mao for his close ties with Moscow. In 1956, when Soviet leader Khrushchev attacked Stalin's legacy in his "secret speech" (Document 29), Mao was irate that he was not consulted and fearful that Khrushchev's attack on Stalin would weaken and divide the socialist world. And having recently fought a war in Korea against the United States, which continued to recognize the Nationalists on Taiwan as China's legitimate rulers, Mao saw Khrushchev's call for peaceful coexistence with the West as a sellout of socialist standards.

Outwardly the Communist giants presented a united front, with the Chinese supporting Moscow's 1956 crackdown in Hungary and Khrushchev promising in 1957 to provide China with an atomic bomb. But tensions grew behind the scenes. In 1958, without consulting Moscow, Mao abandoned the Soviet model and launched the "Great Leap Forward," a campaign of mass mobilization designed to rapidly remake China into a society based on huge peasant communes that ran both farming and industry. Along with it came a cult of Mao reminiscent of the Stalin cult that Khrushchev had condemned. The Soviets were critical of Mao's experiment,

Tensions mount between Mao's PRC and Khrushchev's USSR

upset that he rebuffed a bid to integrate Chinese and Soviet forces, and angered when he sparked a crisis with America by shelling the Nationalist-controlled islands of Jinmen and Mazu (Quemoy and Matsu) close to the Chinese coast.

Although Moscow and Beijing did conclude a new economic agreement early in 1959, Sino-Soviet relations continued to deteriorate. In July, after Beijing signaled it would not consent to Soviet control of atomic warheads in China, Khrushchev canceled his earlier offer to furnish the Chinese with a nuclear bomb. In September, when border clashes broke out between China and India, the Soviets sided diplomatically with India, a neutral democracy whose friendship Moscow was trying to cultivate. That same month, the Chinese watched in dismay as Khrushchev visited the United States and held cordial talks with Eisenhower. A follow-up visit by the Soviet leader to Beijing failed to placate the Chinese, still mortified at seeing their supposed socialist ally openly court their most powerful imperialist enemy.

In 1960, Sino-Soviet tensions result in open rift

In 1960, the split became an open rupture. By then, the Great Leap Forward was a catastrophic failure, and China's economy was in desperate straits. Having seen their advice rejected and experience ignored, the Soviets showed scant sympathy. Khrushchev traveled to India early in the year to sign a treaty granting economic aid to China's Asian rival. That spring, he began withdrawing Soviet technicians from China, signaling the end of Sino-Soviet cooperation. Beijing indirectly attacked the USSR by disparaging Yugoslavia, with which Soviet relations had recently improved, and criticizing "peaceful coexistence" in a publication called "Long Live Leninism" (Document 45A). Moscow responded with verbal assaults against Albania, which was openly aligning itself with China (Document 45B).

Cuban crisis and Sino-Indian border war widen Sino-Soviet rift

In the early 1960s, as the Great Leap Forward's failure for a time discredited Mao's radical approach, the ascendancy in China of moderates led by Liu Shaoqi led to a brief easing of tensions between Beijing and Moscow. Rejecting the Great Leap's most radical features, the Chinese moderates reinstated Soviet-style economic practices. But the atmosphere was soon soured by Khrushchev's renewed campaign against Stalinism, begun in Moscow at the Twenty-second Soviet Communist Party Congress in October 1961. Zhou Enlai, who attended as head of the Chinese delegation, expressed Beijing's displeasure by departing early after publicly placing a wreath on Stalin's grave. In 1962, during an acrimonious border dispute between China and the USSR, Soviet officials encouraged Muslims in northwest China to depart for Soviet territory. In October of that year, Chinese disgust over Soviet capitulation in the Cuban Missile Crisis, coupled with Moscow's sympathy for India in a Sino-Indian border war that began that month, destroyed any hopes for Sino-Soviet rapprochement. By 1963, the two sides were publicly attacking each other (Document 45C), and not just Yugoslavia and Albania, while border clashes became increasingly frequent.

During the middle 1960s, the two Communist titans squared off against one another as competitors for leadership of the world Communist movement. The ideological war of words heated up, with each side accusing the other of heresies and the Chinese even calling the Soviets fascists and imperialists. Mao weighed in with a bitter diatribe entitled "On Khrushchev's Phony Communism and Its Historical Lessons for the World." In various places throughout the Third World, Communist parties split into pro-Soviet and pro-Chinese factions. The fall of Khrushchev in October of 1964, which coincided with the successful testing of China's first atomic bomb, was welcomed by Chinese leaders and helped foster a temporary thaw in Sino-Soviet relations. The new Soviet premier, Aleksei Kosygin, traveled to Beijing early in 1965 but failed to achieve any lasting reconciliation. Before long, the two nations were again at odds, and the USSR was building up its military forces along its border with China.

In 1966, determined to keep China from following the path of bureaucratic elitism he perceived in the USSR, Mao emerged from semi-retirement to launch the "Great Proletarian Cultural Revolution," another mass mobilization campaign to transform the consciousness of the Chinese people. For the next few years, the Chinese virtually withdrew from international affairs, as their energies focused inward. Universities were shut down, industrial enterprises were closed, and legions of youthful "Red Guards," waving copies of the "Little Red Book" of *Quotations from Chairman Mao* (Document 49), were employed to force bureaucrats and professionals to work in the fields. The Soviet system was vilified, and the Soviet embassy in Beijing was besieged by rampaging Red Guards early in 1967.

Mao's Cultural Revolution vilifies Soviets and isolates China

MUTUAL ASSURED DESTRUCTION AND MISSILE DEFENSE SYSTEMS

Sino-Soviet bitterness did not slow the Soviet–American nuclear arms race. In 1967, the United States completed the ICBM buildup begun under Kennedy, deploying the last of its 1,000 Minuteman missiles. The U.S. lead, however, was evaporating. Between 1965 and 1968 the Soviets, producing new ICBMs at an unprecedented rate, more than tripled their operational long-range missiles, achieving a total of 950 by early 1969. Although surprised by the rapidity of the Soviet buildup, which far exceeded U.S. intelligence predictions, American officials did not at first see it as a threat to U.S. security. Defense Secretary McNamara had come to believe that international peace was best secured by a situation of "mutual assured destruction," in which each side could obliterate the other in response to any attack. This condition, known by the apt acronym of "MAD," would theoretically prevent either superpower from launching an attack by making such an action suicidal. It might also help slow the arms race, since a numerical lead in such a situation offered little real advantage. And, as McNamara and his colleagues were aware, the development of MIRVs (multiple independently-targeted reentry vehicles) would soon enable each missile to carry a number of nuclear warheads and thus destroy multiple targets.

Soviet missile buildup brings MAD balance of terror

Of greater concern to Washington was the rapid Soviet development of an antiballistic missile (ABM) system that would use nuclear-armed rockets to intercept incoming ICBMs. Such a system, if extensive enough, could potentially destroy the MAD balance of terror by giving one side the hope of surviving a nuclear counterattack. Once a nation had an effective ABM system, it could conceivably launch a surprise strike on its foe without fear of obliteration in response. Furthermore, the deployment of such a system could accelerate the arms race, encouraging each side to deploy massive numbers of rockets and warheads to potentially overwhelm its adversary's missile defense.

ABM systems threaten MAD balance of terror

Washington was appalled, then, in 1966, when U.S. intelligence discovered that the Soviets were constructing an ABM system around Moscow. As pressures mounted for America to build its own ABMs, Johnson and McNamara instead tried a different tack. They began working to convince the Soviets that it would be far cheaper and safer to negotiate upper limits on their nuclear stockpiles than to engage in a costly and dangerous race to develop ABMs.

In June 1967, following a brief visit to the United Nations in New York, Soviet premier Kosygin met with President Johnson and his aides in Glassboro, New Jersey (selected because it was precisely halfway between the UN and the White House).

Washington presses Moscow to pursue arms control talks instead of ABMs

Although the Glassboro summit achieved no breakthroughs regarding the Vietnam War (Chapter 11), it did help set the stage for important future developments in arms control. At the meeting, Defense Secretary McNamara made an impassioned plea to the Soviets to restrict their ABM development, arguing that it was bound to trigger a massive and expensive new arms race that would undermine each side's security and sap its resources still further. Although Kosygin was unmoved, contending angrily that defensive systems were "moral" and offensive ones were not, the logic nonetheless had an impact on Soviet planners, paving the way for serious efforts at strategic arms limitation.

Gradually, the two superpowers began feeling their way toward arms control. In 1967, they signed an accord banning nuclear weapons from outer space. That same year, although he reluctantly approved development of a U.S. ABM system, McNamara decried the "mad momentum" by which each side's weapons programs encouraged and incited the other. In 1968, a Nuclear Non-Proliferation Treaty (Document 50), designed to prevent additional nations from joining the nuclear club, was signed by the United States, the USSR, Britain, and numerous other countries (although not by France and China). Soviet foreign minister Gromyko then announced that Moscow was ready to engage in preliminary discussions about restricting strategic weapons. By August, private plans were being made for President Johnson to visit the USSR in order to help initiate the opening round of arms limitation talks.

But the visit never came. Instead, a series of developments took place that eventually changed the nature of the Cold War and dramatically altered relations between the superpowers.

THE INVASION OF CZECHOSLOVAKIA AND THE BREZHNEV DOCTRINE

The first of these events was the Soviet invasion of Czechoslovakia in August 1968. Early that year Antonin Novotny, a heavy-handed dictator who had ruled his nation since 1953, was compelled to step down as leader of the Czechoslovak Communist Party. He was replaced by Alexander Dubček, a reform-minded Slovak who initiated measures designed to institute a form of "democratic socialism." These reforms expanded civil rights, allowed freedom of the press, and began democratizing the political system. This "Prague Spring," as it was called, inspired much excitement in the West, but engendered deep consternation among Soviet leaders, who feared that the reforming zeal might spread and loosen their hold on Eastern Europe.

Reforms in Czechoslovakia threaten Soviet hold on Eastern Europe

Moscow sought to halt this trend and reassert its control. A face-to-face conference in late July between Soviet and Czechoslovak leaders, followed by an early August meeting of Eastern European party bosses, seemed to ease the crisis but did not bring a solution that was fully acceptable to Moscow. Hopes for peaceful settlement were then cruelly dashed on 20 August, when the Kremlin launched a military invasion of Czechoslovakia. Once again, as in Hungary in 1956, the world witnessed the brutal spectacle of Soviet troops and tanks invading a socialist neighbor and ally (Documents 51A and 51B). The Soviets crushed all resistance, forced Dubček and his colleagues to rescind their reforms, and then gradually removed the reformers from all positions of power. The following April, Dubček was replaced by Moscow-loyalist Gustáv Husák, who brought the wayward Soviet ally firmly back into line.

Soviets invade Czechoslovakia and crush reform movement

This invasion had far-reaching effects. In the long run, by enabling the USSR to maintain and consolidate control over Eastern Europe, it may have helped give Moscow the security it needed to improve relations with the West. But in the short run, it cast a pall over international relations and seriously damaged the USSR's public stature. In the resulting climate of anti-Soviet outrage, Lyndon Johnson—his presidency already ruined by the Vietnam War—had

Invasion of Czechoslovakia sets back U.S.–Soviet arms control efforts

Soviet invasion of Czechoslovakia, 1968.

As Soviet tanks rolled into Prague in August 1968 to crush a liberal reform movement launched earlier that year, defiant youths waved a Czechoslovak flag at the intruders. The USSR's invasion of its Communist ally crushed the Czech reform movement, but it also heightened anti-Soviet feelings in China, which feared that this attack might set a precedent for Soviet intervention in other Communist countries.

to cancel his trip to Russia and leave arms control to his successors. Meanwhile, in an ominous coincidence, both superpowers successfully tested new multiple-warhead missiles that threatened to accelerate the arms race by allowing each side to increase its destructive capacity quickly and cheaply.

Even among Communists, the Soviet invasion of Czechoslovakia evoked considerable hostility. Western European Communist parties joined the chorus condemning Moscow for its brutal intervention. Among socialist nations, Romania and Yugoslavia openly expressed displeasure, while others reluctantly voiced support for the Soviets. Most concerned were the Chinese, whose relations with Moscow had been deteriorating steadily. Alarmed by the Soviet use of force against a socialist neighbor, and fearful that China might be next, they openly and vehemently condemned the Soviet invasion.

Brezhnev Doctrine asserts Soviet right to intervene in other socialist countries

Sino-Soviet relations were further damaged by the subsequent promulgation of the "Brezhnev Doctrine." In late September, an article in *Pravda*, the official Soviet Communist Party newspaper, stressed that decisions by leaders in Communist countries "must damage neither socialism in their own country nor the fundamental interests of the other socialist countries" (Document 52A). In November, speaking in Poland, Soviet Party boss Brezhnev added that "when . . . forces hostile to socialism seek to reverse the development of any socialist country," this becomes "a common problem and concern of all socialist countries" (Document 52B). Although Brezhnev later denied the existence of any "doctrine," there was little doubt, in Beijing or elsewhere, that Moscow was asserting the right to intervene in other Communist countries whenever it felt that Soviet interests were threatened.

Invasion of Czechoslovakia and Brezhnev Doctrine upset the PRC

The Soviet invasion of Czechoslovakia had ominous implications for Sino-Soviet relations, for it illustrated Moscow's willingness to use military forces to suppress other socialist nations that acted independently. The Brezhnev Doctrine further exacerbated Chinese fears by providing a rationale for such intervention, which from Beijing's perspective was naked Soviet imperialism. Soon these tensions and fears would erupt into direct military confrontation.

THE SINO-SOVIET BORDER WAR OF 1969

From 1966 through 1968, in the throes of its Great Proletarian Cultural Revolution, the PRC largely ignored the outside world. By 1969, however, with that revolution's fury spent and the army restoring order, Chinese leaders were again forced to focus on foreign affairs. In the tense atmosphere resulting from the Soviet invasion of Czechoslovakia, Sino-Soviet territorial disputes degenerated into armed conflict.

Border war erupts in 1969 between the PRC and the USSR

On 2 March 1969, fighting erupted between Soviet and Chinese forces on Damanskii (Zhen Bao) Island, in the Ussuri River along the Russian–Manchurian border. This was more than just another frontier incident: At least thirty-one Soviet soldiers were killed. Within weeks, the Soviets struck back with overpowering force, as each side blamed the other for starting hostilities (Documents 53A and 53B). The next month further fighting broke out on China's northwest border, along the disputed boundary with Soviet Central Asia. Soon both sides were rapidly increasing their border forces. In August, the Soviets hinted that they would use nuclear weapons in a Sino-Soviet conflict, and the Chinese began building shelters and girding for war.

But neither side stood to benefit from war. The Chinese, even with their vast population, could scarcely hope to win an all-out conflict with a nuclear superpower. And the Soviets, even if they won, could hardly hope to occupy and control a defeated and embittered China. In September, therefore, Premier Kosygin traveled to Beijing to meet with his counterpart Zhou Enlai and defuse the volatile situation. Negotiations began in October, and the two sides pulled back from the brink of armed conflict.

The specter of war, however, made a lasting impact on both countries. For the Soviets, who found themselves compelled to keep vast military forces on the Chinese border, it deepened their desire to normalize the situation in Europe and stabilize relations with the West. For the Chinese, it underscored the extent of their isolation and the danger of their situation. Now, as their troubles with Moscow increased, China's leaders started to consider a notion that had previously been unthinkable. They began to contemplate rapprochement with the long-despised leader of the imperialist camp, the United States of America.

Fear of Soviets prompts the PRC to seek rapprochement with America

THE ROOTS OF DÉTENTE

Early in 1969, while Soviet–Chinese antagonisms were intensifying, a new administration took over in Washington. Richard Nixon came to the White House with a well-earned reputation as a devout anti-Communist and a militant Cold Warrior. Inherently suspicious and insecure, he had reached the pinnacle of U.S. politics through hard-nosed ambition and opportunism. Ironically, although these attributes later brought his presidency to an unhappy early end, they served him well in relations with the Communist world.

Nixon was assisted in foreign policy by Henry Kissinger, his national security advisor and future secretary of state. A Harvard scholar and student of great power politics, Kissinger felt that the superpower rivalry could be managed to protect both sides' interests and that peace could be maintained by a balance of power based on mutual self-interest. Brilliant, secretive, and clever, he was hampered little by scruples about ideology or human rights and thus well-disposed to work with Nixon in moving U.S. policy toward détente with Russia and China.

Nixon and Kissinger pursue détente with the USSR and the PRC

East–West détente was hardly a new idea. In the 1950s, touting "peaceful coexistence," Soviet leader Khrushchev took limited steps toward reducing tensions between Moscow and Washington. In 1966, as Western Europe moved out of the U.S. shadow, French president de Gaulle visited Moscow, established closer ties with Eastern Europe, and withdrew French forces from the unified NATO command. That same year, a new West German coalition government, led by Chancellor Kurt Kiesinger and Foreign Minister Willy Brandt, cautiously began a new *Ostpolitik* (Eastern Policy) based on improved relations with the Soviet bloc. Sensing a chance to drive a wedge between Western Europe and America, Moscow encouraged such initiatives, with Brezhnev calling for a European security arrangement based on international recognition of the conditions and borders existing since World War II. Meanwhile both NATO and the Warsaw Pact sought ways to stabilize the military situation in Central Europe, while Moscow and Washington warily started inching toward arms control negotiations. But the Soviet invasion of Czechoslovakia in August 1968 undermined

European efforts at détente produce only modest progress

these efforts, scuttling a planned summit meeting between Johnson and Kosygin and postponing the onset of arms limitation talks.

Thus by the time Nixon came to office, little headway had been made. But the new president, convinced that progress was possible, spoke in his inaugural address of "a new era of negotiation" in which nations would "cooperate to reduce the burden of arms, to strengthen the structure of peace." He and Kissinger would go beyond previous initiatives and pursue a new policy of détente to deal with new global realities.

Soviet arms buildup prompts Nixon to seek arms control

One such reality was the USSR's arms buildup, bringing it to the verge of strategic parity with America. In his campaign, Nixon had advocated U.S. strategic superiority, but once in office he lowered his sights and toned down his rhetoric. The vast Soviet weapons buildup, combined with the huge costs of arms production and destabilizing potential of new technologies, convinced him and Kissinger that it was preferable to limit Soviet arms through negotiation rather than to expend enormous resources to maintain a U.S. lead.

Another new reality was the relative decline in American power and prestige resulting from the debacle in Vietnam. Having promised to extricate his nation from this conflict, Nixon initiated a gradual withdrawal of American forces from Southeast Asia and a reduction of U.S. military commitments around the world. In 1969, he enunciated the Nixon Doctrine (Documents 54A and 54B), calling for American friends and clients (such as Japan and Iran) to rely less on the United States and assume the main role in their region's defense. By encouraging Moscow to moderate its behavior and restrain its Third World clients, détente could help maintain stability during and after the U.S. disengagement.

Economic woes and conflict with China push Soviets toward détente with the Americans

The Soviets had their own reasons for seeking détente. First, like the Americans (and everyone else on the planet), they had a stake in preventing nuclear war and slowing the arms race. Second, their growing conflict with China compelled them to seek to stabilize their relations with the West. Third, as their economy continued to stagnate, they recognized that progress in this area would require increased trade and access to Western technology.

Soviets seek equal status with Americans in pursuing détente

Concern for recognition and equality also affected Moscow's thinking. For both security and status, the Soviets were eager to have their hard-won World War II gains, including Eastern Europe's revised boundaries and Germany's division, win international recognition. Likewise, as their massive weapons buildup moved them toward parity with the United States, they wanted this new status locked in by international agreement. Otherwise the Americans, with their vast resources and advanced technologies, could launch a new arms buildup that would leave the USSR behind. And finally, there was national pride. Equality with the West had been a Russian goal for centuries: To be treated as an equal, with its equal status recognized in international agreements, would be no small triumph for the Brezhnev regime.

There was a major difference, however, between the Nixon and Brezhnev approaches to détente, and this involved the issue of "linkage." Nixon and Kissinger expected that, in return for trade and arms control concessions, Moscow would alter its conduct, restrain its expansionism, and rein in belligerent clients. They especially wanted Moscow to pressure North Vietnam to accept a negotiated settlement in Vietnam. But the Soviets resisted U.S. efforts at linkage, assuming and expecting that the superpowers would continue to confront each other where their interests clashed, even as they negotiated issues (such as arms control) where their concerns coincided. They saw no reason to reduce their aid to North Vietnam, or modify their behavior in Africa and the Middle East, to accommodate Washington's concerns. Besides, to remain leaders of world Communism in the face of China's challenge, they had to continue their support for Third World Communist parties and national liberation movements.

Soviets resist U.S. effort to link détente to Third World conduct

Hence despite strong support for détente in both Moscow and the West, progress was rather slow. Early in 1969, the Soviets informed the new administration that they were ready to negotiate on a broad range of issues, including arms control and ABMs, but they also made it clear that they opposed linkage. The Nixon team, for its part, wanted to shore up relations with Western Europe and review its own military policy before sitting down to talk. To bolster its bargaining position, it also pressed for congressional approval of a U.S. ABM system, known as "Safeguard," which squeaked through the Senate in August after a long and heated public debate. Its passage gave the Soviets pause, so arms control talks did not begin until November 1969.

The Strategic Arms Limitation Talks (SALT) nonetheless soon became the centerpiece of Soviet–American détente. There were seven sessions, each lasting several months, which met alternately in Helsinki and Vienna over the next two and a half years. The official Soviet delegation was headed by Deputy Foreign Minister Vladimir S. Semenov, while the American team was led by Gerald C. Smith, director of the U.S. Arms Control and Development Agency. At various points, however, the "real" negotiations were conducted behind the scenes through a private White House channel involving Henry Kissinger and Soviet ambassador Dobrynin.

U.S.–Soviet arms control talks (SALT) begin in 1969

Four major obstacles had to be addressed before real progress could be made. First was the issue of linkage, which Moscow eventually finessed by compromising in practice but remaining firm on principle. Second was the presence in Europe of U.S. nuclear missiles which, since they could reach the USSR, the Soviets wanted to count as part of the American strategic arsenal. In the interest of progress, however, Moscow finally agreed to defer this discussion to future talks. Third was the development of MIRVs, or multiple-warhead missiles. Although both sides wanted to restrict or ban their deployment, negotiations foundered on the issue of verification—the traditional bugaboo of U.S.–Soviet arms control talks. In the end, no accord on MIRVs would be reached, leaving a major lacuna in the eventual SALT I accords. Finally, the two sides clashed over the connection between defensive and offensive weapons. Anxious to forestall a new arms race in missile defense systems, Moscow proposed that negotiators should first conclude a separate ABM agreement, while the United States preferred an integrated and comprehensive treaty that would cover both ABMs and ICBMs. In a compromise arrangement announced on 20 May 1971, they ultimately decided to work toward a separate ABM treaty while negotiating a simultaneous accord restricting offensive arms.

Linkage, MIRV, and ABM issues hamper SALT progress

Even then, some difficult issues remained. One involved how many ABM sites would be permitted each side. Another was the issue of whether to include submarine-launched ballistic missiles (SLBMs) in the treaty limiting offensive arms. Talks thus continued for another year, and final decisions were not reached until May 1972. By then, two dramatic developments had altered the international situation: détente in Europe between West Germany and the USSR and rapprochement in Asia between the United States and China.

WILLY BRANDT AND *OSTPOLITIK*

In October 1969, as Washington and Moscow prepared for strategic arms talks, the Federal Republic of Germany got a new leader. As longtime mayor of West Berlin, Willy Brandt had become a symbol of freedom to Germans East and West. As head of West Germany's Social Democratic Party (SPD) since 1958, he had also become a symbol of change and reform. As foreign minister in Kurt Kiesinger's coalition government from 1966 to 1969, he had cautiously sought to improve West German relations with the Soviet bloc. Now, as chancellor, he began boldly pushing his precedent-shattering "eastern policy," or *Ostpolitik.*

Brandt's *Ostpolitik* seeks to normalize West German relations with Soviet bloc

The thrust of this policy was to forsake as unrealistic the goal of German reunification, futilely proclaimed for two decades by his Christian-Democratic predecessors, and to work for greater cooperation with the East. This meant accepting Europe's political realities, including Communist control of East Germany, no matter how unpleasant they might seem. As West Berlin's mayor in 1961, Brandt had watched in frustration as the Berlin Wall went up without effective opposition from Washington. Now, with his U.S. allies bogged down in Vietnam and with Soviet rule in Eastern Europe reinforced by the Brezhnev Doctrine, Brandt concluded he had little to gain by clinging to causes long since lost. So he proposed to make concessions to the Soviets and East Germans in return for stability and normalization in Central Europe.

Brandt's *Ostpolitik* accepts reality of Germany's division

His first step was to adopt the notion of "two states in one nation," accepting the reality of Germany's political division. His next step was to have his government sign the Nuclear Non-Proliferation Treaty, forswearing any West German effort to acquire its own nuclear weapons and thereby easing Soviet fears of a rearmed and hostile Germany. Since his own Western allies were opposed to a nuclear-equipped Federal Republic, Brandt's concession made good diplomatic sense, and it opened the door to improved relations with Moscow.

Brandt's next move was to seek accommodation with some Eastern bloc countries. He offered to negotiate treaties with Poland and the USSR that would accept the loss of German lands to them at the end of World War II, and he proposed a trade pact with Czechoslovakia. He even offered to negotiate a nonaggression pact with East Germany, but the latter refused to consider this bid unless the West German government granted it full diplomatic recognition. Nevertheless, in March 1970, at the invitation of East German prime minister Willi Stoph, Brandt visited the German Democratic Republic and was greeted by large, friendly crowds. His talks with Stoph made little progress, but the fact that they occurred was itself an achievement.

Soviets see Ostpolitik as a chance to solidify World War II gains

Brandt's initiatives presented Moscow with a historic opportunity. For years, the Soviets had sought international acceptance of political and territorial adjustments resulting from World War II. These included the USSR's annexation of lands along its western frontier, the transfer to Poland of part of prewar Germany, Moscow's sphere of influence over Eastern Europe, and the division of Germany into two states. Now that this goal seemed within his grasp, Brezhnev was willing to do business with West Germany and pressure his East German allies to go along.

The Soviets thus accepted Brandt's offer to negotiate, and the two sides moved quickly toward a nonaggression pact. The Treaty of Moscow, signed on 12 August 1970, did more than simply renounce war between the two nations. It recognized as permanent the existing German boundaries, thereby affirming the loss of German territory east of the Oder-Neisse Line. It also acknowledged the existence of two separate German states, and it opened new trade channels between the USSR and the Federal Republic. Twenty-five years after World War II, the Soviets and Germans finally reached an accord. The treaty was a triumph for both Brezhnev and Brandt, and a significant step toward resolving the German Question.

Soviet–West German treaty affirms existing borders and spurs trade

Parallel talks between West Germany and Poland resulted in a similar pact in December 1970. Brandt traveled to Warsaw to sign this treaty, which also confirmed Polish territorial gains east of the Oder-Neisse Line. The trip's most poignant moment was his visit to the Warsaw ghetto memorial, where he humbly paid homage to the victims of Hitler's Third Reich. The Germans had come a long way.

Polish–West German treaty affirms existing border

But the Berlin problem remained. West Germans wanted West Berlin to be part of their Federal Republic, despite its physical separation, while East Germans considered East Berlin their capital. Divided into Soviet, British, French and U.S. occupation zones since World War II, Berlin had long been central to the Cold War. Resolving its situation would not be easy.

In March 1970, following Brandt's East German visit, Berlin's four occupying powers began discussions on its status. These "quadripartite" talks at first made little headway, in part because East Germans refused to cooperate unless their government received full diplomatic recognition. But in May 1971, when Erich Honecker replaced Walter Ulbricht as head of the East German Communists, real progress became possible. Honecker was less intransigent than Ulbricht and more willing to follow the wishes of Moscow, which by then had decided that its interests in détente outweighed East Germany's desire for recognition. The USSR was anxious for ratification of the Treaty of Moscow, which was held up in West Germany's parliament pending an agreement on Berlin. And it needed a Berlin settlement to help realize a Soviet dream: an all-European security conference that would legitimize the status quo in Europe.

The resulting Berlin Accords, signed on 3 September 1971, were a compromise that fully satisfied neither side (Document 55). West Germans obtained a Soviet guarantee of free access to West Berlin and recognition of their economic and cultural ties with the city. They even gained the right to negotiate on the city's behalf. But their desire for full political integration of West Berlin into the Federal Republic was rebuffed. The East Germans, forced to defer their hopes for diplomatic recognition, gained little more than Moscow's gratitude for a relaxation of tensions. Still, the pact was a milestone for both Germans and Soviets, opening the way for the Basic Treaty of 1972 between East and West Germany and for a multinational European security conference that would open at Helsinki in 1973

Berlin Accords leave city divided but ease East–West tensions

(Chapter 13). And it moved the issue of Berlin, which had long bedeviled East–West relations, off the center stage of the Cold War.

THE SINO-AMERICAN RAPPROCHEMENT

Even more remarkable than the easing of tensions in Central Europe was the improvement of relations between Beijing and Washington. Since the Chinese Revolution and Korean War (Chapters 6–7), the United States and Communist China had been bitter foes. During the 1950s, Washington had viewed "Red China" as a dangerous Soviet satellite, while Beijing saw the Americans as imperialist warmongers who sustained the Nationalist regime on Taiwan. Chinese troops fought American soldiers in the Korean conflict, and the two nations almost came to blows in 1954 and 1958 over Beijing's shelling of Nationalist-controlled offshore islands. Even in the 1960s, when the rift between Moscow and Beijing became increasingly apparent, there was no thaw in relations between China and America. The United States continued to deny recognition to the People's Republic, to block its entrance into the UN, and to prop up the Nationalists on Taiwan as the rightful rulers of China. American involvement in the Vietnam War, coupled with Chinese aid to Hanoi, effectively precluded any rapprochement, while the excesses of the Cultural Revolution seemed to confirm U.S. fears about the nature of Mao's rule.

Events of 1960s leave China isolated from both the USSR and the United States

By 1970, however, the world scene was changing. America's gradual withdrawl from Vietnam, and the corresponding decline of U.S. power in Asia, had major implications for both countries. For Beijing, it meant that the Americans were no longer as serious a threat, and it raised concerns that the vacuum created by U.S. withdrawal would be filled by the USSR. For Washington, it opened up the prospect that China might serve as a counterweight to prevent Soviet expansion as the American presence declined. Beijing's hostility to Moscow, combined with increasing signs of U.S.–Soviet détente, left the Chinese isolated and vulnerable—and even fearful that the two superpowers might conspire against them. And Washington, eager to gain greater leverage in its relationship with Moscow, was looking for ways to exploit the Sino-Soviet split.

U.S. withdrawal from Vietnam opens way for U.S.–China rapprochement

The result was "triangular diplomacy," a U.S. effort to exploit the rift between China and Russia and improve relations with both. Slowly and cautiously, Washington and Beijing began to signal each other that they wanted to make contact and improve relations. In November 1968, shortly after Nixon's election, Chinese premier Zhou Enlai called for new diplomatic talks with the United States, to begin in Warsaw in February 1969. Nixon quickly agreed. He was a staunch Cold Warrior who had earned a reputation for strident hostility toward Communism. But he was also a pragmatic opportunist who was willing to change course when he saw an advantage in doing so, and he now perceived that improved relations with China could work to America's benefit. His strong anti-Communist credentials were in fact a blessing, for they shielded him from charges of being "soft on Communism" as he moved toward dialogue with Beijing.

Washington pursues "triangular diplomacy" with Moscow and Beijing

As it turned out, a few days before the Warsaw talks were set to begin, the Chinese abruptly backed out. This action appeared to be a protest against the recent defection to the United States of a Chinese official, but it also may have reflected the ongoing power struggle in Beijing between Premier Zhou Enlai, who favored Sino-American rapprochement, and Chairman Mao's heir apparent Lin Biao, who opposed it. At any rate, it proved only a temporary setback, as the violent border clashes and intensification of Sino-Soviet hostilities during 1969 gave Beijing added reason to approach the United States. Nixon, meanwhile, was discreetly asking Presidents de Gaulle of France, Ceausescu of Romania, and Yahya Khan of Pakistan to convey to the Chinese his desire for better relations. He also took some economic and diplomatic steps to signal his interest in an easing of tensions. As a result, in January 1970, discussions finally began in Warsaw between Chinese and American diplomats.

But the road to rapprochement was rocky. On 1 May 1970, the United States expanded the Vietnam War, invading Cambodia in an effort to destroy Communist bases and supply lines. The Chinese again canceled the Warsaw talks, as Mao sharply condemned the U.S. "aggressors." In the next few months, public relations between the two countries degenerated even further. Nixon nonetheless persisted in his quest. In October, he told *Time* magazine that he wanted to visit China before he died. Later that month, in Washington, he asked

The U.S. invasion of Cambodia aborts U.S.–Chinese talks, but Nixon persists

Nixon and Mao.

For two decades following the Communist takeover of China in 1949, Communist China and capitalist America were bitter foes. But by 1970, China's growing fear of the USSR was prompting it to end its isolation from the West, while U.S. president Nixon was quietly seeking to open a dialogue with China. By protecting him from changes of being soft on Communism, Nixon's reputation as a strident Cold Warrior enabled him to make a dramatic trip to China where he met with legendary Communist leader Mao Zedong in February 1972.

Yahya Khan, who was about to visit Beijing, to transmit his willingness to send a key official to meet with Chinese leaders. The next day, at a reception for Romanian president Ceausescu, he made public reference to the "People's Republic of China." This was an important signal, for previous U.S. presidents had avoided using the official name of the country Americans knew as "Red" or "Mainland" China. The Chinese got the message. In December, the Pakistanis informed Nixon that Zhou Enlai was willing to meet with the president's personal representative, and Mao Zedong advised American writer Edgar Snow that he would welcome a visit from Nixon himself. In January 1971, the Romanians conveyed to Washington a similar message from Zhou.

The real breakthrough in Sino-American relations came in 1971. In March, the Nixon administration removed restrictions on travel to China, and in April, it further eased restraints on trade. That same month, in a highly publicized goodwill gesture, the Chinese invited the U.S. table tennis team to the world championship matches in Beijing. Zhou Enlai himself met with the American players, spoke of a new relationship between China and the United States, and consented to a reciprocal visit to America by the Chinese team. This "ping-pong diplomacy" helped set the stage for further dramatic developments.

"Ping-pong diplomacy" paves way for U.S.–Chinese rapprochement

On 15 July 1971, in a televised address, Nixon made the stunning announcement that he had accepted an invitation to visit China within the next ten months. It turned out that, during a visit to Pakistan the previous week, Henry Kissinger had slipped away from reporters and made a clandestine trip to Beijing, where he held lengthy talks with Zhou Enlai and even met Chairman Mao. While there, he discussed items of U.S.–Chinese interest, smoothed over disputes related to Taiwan, and laid the groundwork for Nixon's visit.

The president's announcement created great excitement in the West, but it had serious repercussions in the East. Obsessed with secrecy and fearful of leaks, Nixon and Kissinger had concealed the latter's trip from the USSR, American friends, and even the U.S. State Department. The Chinese Nationalists in Taiwan felt betrayed, as did their American supporters. Japan, the main U.S. ally in Asia, was shocked and dismayed that it was not consulted and began to reconsider its heavy reliance on Washington.

Nixon announces he will visit the PRC, upsetting Japan and Taiwan

The Soviets, fearful that their two main foes might collude against them, began moving more briskly toward détente with the West. By September, they had reached agreement in the talks on Berlin and were making progress in SALT. Negotiations toward a Nixon–Brezhnev summit meeting were accelerated, and in October it was announced that the U.S. president would visit Moscow in the spring of 1972.

Meanwhile several remaining obstacles to Sino-American rapprochement were cleared away. In September 1971, Lin Biao, the main Chinese opponent of improved relations with Washington, was killed in a plane crash attempting to escape to the USSR after an abortive coup attempt. In October, Kissinger made another visit to Beijing to hold further talks with Zhou and prepare for Nixon's visit. And despite a U.S. "two Chinas" effort to secure UN seats for both the Nationalists and Communists, the United Nations voted to expel the Taiwan government and replace it with the People's Republic.

Lin Biao's demise and UN seat for PRC clear way for U.S.–Chinese détente

Nixon's official state visit to China, which riveted the world's attention in February 1972, was important more for its symbolism than for its diplomatic achievements. Accompanied by television cameras and myriad reporters, Nixon flew to the People's Republic, met with officials, attended the ballet, and visited the Great Wall. In private talks with Chinese leaders, however, he made little progress toward resolving the Taiwan issue, the one great stumbling block to normal relations. The United States did acknowledge the view, held by both the Communists and Nationalists, that there should be only one China and that it should include Taiwan. The Americans also agreed that they would eventually remove their military forces from Taiwan, as tensions in the area subsided. But they were not yet ready to withdraw formal recognition from the Nationalist regime. The Chinese for their part made it clear that full diplomatic relations, and expanded trade agreements, could not be established until this recognition was withdrawn. This impasse would delay normalized relations for almost seven years.

Nixon's China visit brings global hope but modest diplomatic progress

Still, whatever its diplomatic value, the symbolic significance of Nixon's trip was immense. The "Shanghai Communiqué" (Document 56), issued upon the president's departure, committed each side to work toward normalizing relations and easing tensions in Asia. The euphoria was palpable, as longtime bitter foes agreed to work together to keep the peace and resolve issues of mutual concern. This trip, and Nixon's upcoming visit to Moscow that May, seemed to signify the end of the age of confrontation and the dawn of the era of détente.

Zhou Enlai and Nixon in Shanghai, 1972.

At the end of his historic visit to China in February 1972, President Nixon met with Chinese premier Zhou Enlai in Shanghai. Although it did not resolve the key issues between the two countries, Nixon's China visit signaled a new stage in the Cold War, when "triangular diplomacy" enabled Americans to exploit the rift between China and the USSR, while moving toward détente with both the Communist giants.

PART III THE SEARCH FOR A SOLUTION

13

The Heyday of Détente, 1972–1975

During 1972 and the first half of 1973, the Cold War appeared to be ending. President Nixon's visit to China in February 1972 was only the first in a series of hopeful developments. In May, Nixon traveled to Moscow, where he and Soviet leader Brezhnev signed some historic agreements, including major arms control treaties. In December, East and West Germany concluded a "Basic Treaty." Early in 1973, U.S. military involvement in Vietnam ended. That summer Brezhnev and Nixon met again, this time in Washington, and a multinational European security conference began in Helsinki. All the basic elements of the Cold War—the German Question, the status of Eastern Europe, the contest for Asia, and the nuclear arms race—seemed headed toward resolution.

Soon, however, it became clear that détente had promised more than it could deliver. The Middle East crisis of fall 1973 again brought the superpowers to the brink of armed conflict. U.S. meddling in Chile, and renewed fighting between North and South Vietnam, made it obvious that East–West rapprochement did not extend to the Third World. Difficulties and delays in the arms control talks, along with public clashes over trade and human rights, also soured the goodwill. Still, détente's basic framework remained in place throughout the 1970s.

THE FOUNDATIONS OF DÉTENTE, 1972–1973

1972 Moscow summit opens détente era

Even before Nixon's trip to China, preparations had begun for a U.S.–Soviet summit conference in Moscow in May 1972. It proved to be one of the most productive summits of the Cold War era. As the first visit by an American president to the USSR since World War II, and the first such peacetime visit ever, it also had great symbolic significance. More than any other event, it signified the dawn of the age of détente.

Getting to the summit, however, was no easy task, for some major hurdles blocked the way. One was the fact that, as the Moscow meeting approached, several key issues remained unresolved in the strategic arms limitation talks (SALT). Since the SALT treaty signings were to be the summit's centerpiece, this was no small nuisance. The other problem was the ongoing Vietnam War, which escalated in spring of 1972, threatening to scuttle the summit.

The unsettled questions in the arms control talks involved the number and nature of ABM sites to be permitted each side and the issue of whether the SALT treaty should encompass submarine-launched ballistics missiles (SLBMs) as well as land-based ICBMs. Having backed away from an earlier proposal to limit ABM sites to one for each national capital, the Americans were pushing for a pact that would permit ABM sites (such as the one they were building) to defend land-based missiles. They were also pressing to include SLBMs in the offensive arms control agreement, in part because the Pentagon wanted to restrain the rapid Soviet submarine missile buildup. Having been surpassed by the Soviets in numbers of ICBMs, the U.S. military was anxious not to fall behind in SLBMs. But Moscow, upset that the Americans raised new demands in the final stages of negotiation, was cool to these U.S. initiatives.

Superpowers work to solve ABM and SLBM issues before summit

As the summit approached and pressure for agreement mounted, Henry Kissinger met with Soviet officials in Moscow and Soviet Ambassador Dobrynin in Washington in a bid to break the logjam. In Helsinki, SALT negotiators redoubled their efforts, continuing to meet even after the summit began. The ABM issue was largely resolved in April, but the final decision on SLBMs was reached only at the summit with the participation of Nixon and Brezhnev.

The escalation of the Vietnam War also posed a serious challenge. The North Vietnamese launched a major offensive that spring, and the United States responded with massive bombing of North Vietnam and mining of Haiphong harbor, damaging several Soviet ships and causing a number of casualties. When Nixon announced the escalation, two weeks before his scheduled Moscow trip, there was broad expectation that the summit might be canceled. But the Soviet leaders, although they publicly condemned the American bombing, proceeded with the conference. Détente was too important to them to be jeopardized by other issues.

Vietnam War escalation fails to derail summit

The Nixon–Brezhnev summit thus took place as scheduled in Moscow from 22 to 30 May 1972. It was rich in both imagery and achievements. The leaders signed agreements on the basic principles of U.S.–Soviet relations, measures to prevent the accidental outbreak of nuclear war, an upgrade of the Washington–Moscow "hot line," and scientific and cultural connections. They laid the groundwork for a major U.S.–Soviet Trade Agreement, to be concluded later that year. But the most important measures they signed were the Treaty on the Limitation of Anti-Ballistic Missile Systems (the "ABM treaty") and the Interim Agreement on the Limitation of Strategic Offensive Arms ("SALT I").

The ABM treaty (Document 57A) limited each side to two defensive missile sites: one to guard its capital, the other to protect ICBMs. Since the Soviets had already built one to shield Moscow, and the Americans were constructing one to defend missiles in North Dakota, the treaty gave each the opportunity to duplicate the other's system. In fact neither side sought to do this, so in 1974 they added a protocol restricting each to one ABM site.

ABM treaty allows each side two sites, later reduced to one

SALT I (Document 57B) was a temporary measure, designed to constrain each side from building ICBMs beyond 1972 levels for five years, during which a permanent pact was to be negotiated. At U.S. insistence, it limited the numbers of submarine-launched missiles, but it also allowed completion of those under construction and replacement of older land-based missiles by SLBMs. The Soviets could thus accept SLBM limits without sacrificing their current building program.

SALT I freezes ICBMs at 1972 levels for five years

The final pact left the USSR with a preponderance of 1,618–1,054 in ICBMs and a 950-to-710 edge in SLBMs. This apparent Soviet advantage caused great consternation among U.S. "hawks," thus posing problems when the treaty went to the U.S. Senate for ratification. Senate approval finally came in September 1972, but only after Senator Henry Jackson added an amendment that future arms control treaties must not leave the USSR with a numerical lead. This lead was in fact illusory, since SALT I did not include long-range bombers, U.S. missiles in Europe, the missiles of America's NATO allies, or multiple-warhead missiles (MIRVs)—all areas where the West had a big advantage. Distrusting both Nixon and the Soviets, however, Jackson and his supporters wanted to ensure that their concerns were honored during future talks.

SALT I sustains Soviet long-range missile lead, upsetting U.S. hawks

The Moscow summit was also intended to facilitate progress elsewhere. Nixon and Kissinger hoped that, in combination with the U.S.–Chinese rapprochement, it might encourage North Vietnam to compromise and thus help extricate America from Southeast Asia. Shortly after the summit, a key Soviet official named Nikolai Podgorny (who held the largely honorary title of Soviet president) visited North Vietnam, conveying new U.S. proposals to its leaders and urging them to work toward a negotiated settlement. But Podgorny was coolly received in Hanoi, where Soviet détente with the West was seen as betrayal.

The summit did have some success at boosting détente in Europe. In Moscow, the two sides agreed to work toward both a Conference on Security and Cooperation in Europe (CSCE) and mutual and balanced force reductions (MBFR) between NATO and the Warsaw Pact.

The CSCE was a longtime Soviet goal, first proposed by Molotov in 1954, and a key element of Brezhnev's foreign policy. Although existing borders in Eastern and Central Europe, and by implication Soviet control there, had recently been recognized in bilateral treaties, Moscow was eager to have them sanctioned by a multinational agreement. The Soviets wanted a CSCE to solidify their supremacy in Eastern Europe, bring Communist East Germany into the family of nations, provide formal Western recognition of the political and territorial gains made by the USSR in the 1940s, and serve as the international peace conference that had not yet occurred after World War II. For obvious reasons, the United States was less excited about such a conference, but Nixon agreed to go along in the interests of détente and on the understanding that MBFR talks would also take place. Preliminary discussions began in August 1972 and laid the groundwork for the Helsinki Conference that opened the next summer.

Summit paves way for CSCE in Helsinki

Unlike the CSCE, MBFR was a NATO initiative, based on Western Europe's security concerns. Since the mid-1960s, U.S. senator Mike Mansfield had been championing a resolution advocating unilateral withdrawal of most U.S. forces from Europe. Fearful it might someday pass, NATO leaders in the late 1960s had begun to push for talks with the Warsaw Pact to reduce both sides' forces. The Soviets at first resisted, seeing the initiative as designed mainly to prolong U.S. presence in Europe, but in 1972, they agreed to parallel CSCE and MBFR talks. Preparations for the latter began in January 1973, and the talks opened in Vienna in October. They would drag on inconclusively for years.

Meanwhile real progress came in Central Europe. On 3 June 1972, the nonaggression pacts that West German chancellor Willy Brandt had earlier negotiated with Poland and the USSR went into force, and the final protocol of the Berlin Accords was signed. Although these agreements had been worked out earlier, their activation added to the momentum created by the Moscow summit, setting the stage for direct talks between East and West Germany.

In August 1972, as preparatory talks began for the CSCE in Helsinki, East and West German officials started meeting in Berlin to work on a treaty between them. The resulting "Basic Treaty," concluded that December, did not meet East Germany's goal of full mutual recognition and normalized relations, but it did provide for an exchange of "permanent missions" between the Federal and Democratic Republics. It expanded commercial and cultural ties, committed each side to respect the other's boundaries, and cleared the path for both to apply for UN membership. It also paved the way for treaties between West Germany and a number of Eastern European states, and for formal recognition of East Germany by most Western nations, during the next few years.

Basic Treaty expands contacts between East and West Germany

THE AMERICAN WITHDRAWAL FROM VIETNAM

Across the Atlantic, Nixon was still searching for a way out of the Vietnam quagmire. His Vietnamization policy had worked no better than Americanization had, and the Ho Chi Minh Trail was still open, despite South Vietnam's efforts to close it by invading Laos and Cambodia in 1971. At home, support for the war was evaporating. Americans were shocked by revelations at the trial of Lieutenant William Calley for atrocities in My Lai, where a 1968 operation designed to kill Viet Cong agents had instead massacred nearly 500 civilians. And they were offended by the "Pentagon Papers," a secret study of the war commissioned in 1967 by Robert McNamara and published by *The New York Times* in 1971. These documents, illegally photocopied and leaked by Defense Department analyst Daniel Ellsberg, painted a devastating portrait of U.S. government efforts to deceive the American people about the situation in Vietnam.

Nixon seeks way out of Vietnam as Americans turn against war

Nixon's visits to Beijing and Moscow had reflected his hope that they could pressure Hanoi to negotiate. But Podgorny's visit to Hanoi had accomplished little, and there were few signs that North Vietnam was in a receptive mood. This war was between the United States and North Vietnam, and, if a settlement was to be reached, it would be due to their own actions and reactions.

As the 1972 presidential election approached, Nixon and Kissinger adopted a two-track strategy to bring peace before election day. One track consisted of intensified secret talks with North Vietnamese emissary Le Duc Tho, mostly held in the Paris apartment of Jean Sainteny, the persistent diplomat who had helped arrange the abortive Ho-Sainteny Accords of 1946 (Chapter 11). The other track involved heightened military pressure. On 15 April 1972, American B-52s pounded Hanoi, prompting mass antiwar protests in the United States. One month later the U.S. Navy laid mines in Haiphong harbor and other North Vietnamese ports.

Nixon uses peace talks and bombs in a bid to end Vietnam War

In October, the two-track approach appeared to pay off. Le Duc Tho, eager for an end to the bombing and resigned to Nixon's reelection, abandoned Hanoi's demand that South Vietnam's president Thieu resign and a coalition government be set up in Saigon. He would take the best terms he could get (which, prior to the election, might be very good) in exchange for a respite during which Hanoi could prepare a final assault. Kissinger offered total U.S. withdrawal, while North Vietnamese forces remained in place in the south. This was a major but unavoidable concession since, as American historians James Olson and Randy Roberts later noted, "Ten years of war and the greatest expenditure of firepower in history had not dislodged them." Thieu objected strenuously, sensing a U.S. sellout and threatening not to sign the treaty unless major changes were made. With the election a few days off, Kissinger stated publicly that "peace is at hand," but Nixon's landslide reelection came and went with no peace agreement.

Washington and Hanoi near agreement in October 1972

Nixon tried to bring Thieu around by secret promises of U.S. support in case the treaty was violated, but his public support for Thieu's demands angered Hanoi and led to suspension of the peace talks on 13 December. Nixon then issued an ultimatum, telling North Vietnamese premier Pham Van Dong to "resume serious negotiations within 72 hours or suffer the consequences." On 18 December, the United States began the eleven-day "Christmas Bombing," a massive aerial assault on North Vietnam. Moscow publicly condemned the bombing, but worked privately to end the impasse, urging Hanoi to resume negotiations in return for an end to the bombing.

The talks resumed and quickly reached an agreement. On 23 January 1973, Nixon announced that they had achieved "peace with honor" (Document 58A); four days later, the Paris Peace Accords (Document 58B) formally ended U.S. involvement in the Second Indochina War. Washington agreed to stop bombing the north and remove its forces from the south, while Hanoi promised not to renew its attack on the south and to return all American prisoners of war. In the end, the United States kept its bargain, but North Vietnam did not.

1973 Paris Peace Accords end U.S. role in Vietnam

THE WASHINGTON SUMMIT, CSCE, AND CHILEAN COUP

The summer of 1973 was the high-water mark of détente. With the German Question apparently settled, and with U.S. involvement in Vietnam finally ended, the stage was set for continued East–West rapprochement.

In June Brezhnev traveled to Washington for his second summit conference with Nixon. Although not as dramatic or productive as the previous year's Moscow extravaganza, it was nonetheless a major event. Discussions encompassed issues ranging from arms control to China and the Middle East. Several agreements were signed, including one on peaceful uses of atomic energy and another calling for prompt conclusion of a permanent arms control pact (SALT II) to replace the temporary SALT I accord. Especially heartening was the "Agreement on the Prevention of Nuclear War," by which the two sides pledged to hold "urgent consultations" should a conflict between other countries threaten to draw them into an atomic showdown.

1973 Washington summit continues spirit of détente

The mood, as indicated by the joint communiqué at the end of the conference and by officials on both sides, was one of cooperation and goodwill. It was Brezhnev's first visit to the United States, and he took the opportunity to meet

Brezhnev and Nixon in Washington.
In June 1973, Soviet Communist Party leader Brezhnev traveled to America for his second summit meeting with President Nixon. Although not as historic as their 1972 Moscow summit, where they signed the SALT I and ABM treaties, it reinforced détente and was marked by the signing of several accords. One of them, an "Agreement on the Prevention of Nuclear War," whereby both sides pledged to hold urgent consultations in the event of a major confrontation, would prove helpful in defusing a frightening Middle East Crisis that arose later that year.

Nixon, not just in Washington and at Camp David, but also at the president's home in California. Mutual respect and harmony were the watchwords of the day, and even the spreading Watergate scandal failed to dampen the enthusiasm, since the Senate hearings recessed during Brezhnev's visit.

On 3 July 1973, shortly after the summit, the long-awaited CSCE opened in Helsinki. Thirty-five nations were represented, including the United States, Canada, and all the European countries save Albania. Even though it would take a few years to conclude the final accords, the fact that the meetings had begun enhanced the climate of collaboration. Further momentum was added that September, when the UN admitted both East and West Germany.

35-nation CSCE opens in Helsinki

Soon, however, disturbing developments began to dim the glow. In the fall of 1973, a crisis in Chile and conflict in the Middle East made it clear that détente had limits and that superpower collaboration did not include the Third World.

In 1970, a Marxist economics professor, Salvador Allende, was elected president of Chile. The existence of a freely elected Marxist leader in the Western Hemisphere (or anywhere else) was anathema to Washington. The CIA had managed to prevent his election in 1964 by pouring money into Chilean politics, and it had sought in vain to do so again in 1970 with massive aid to his opponents and bribes to Chilean legislators. Even after his election, Washington continued to subvert him, cutting off Chile's foreign credit and recalling outstanding loans. The resulting cash shortfall led to serious inflation, amplified by Allende's efforts to stimulate consumer goods production through massive pay increases for the poor.

CIA works to subvert Chile's Marxist president Allende

By 1973, Chile's economy was in shambles. Inflation hit 566 percent, impoverishing the middle class. The price of copper fell steadily on the world market, further undermining Allende. Moscow furnished much fraternal rhetoric but minimal financial assistance; Brezhnev was already underwriting one weak Latin American economy in Cuba, and he had learned the lessons of the Cuban Missile Crisis. Chile was even further from the Kremlin than Cuba and far harder to defend. During that year, a series of strikes by engineers, physicians, and truckers impaired Allende's ability to govern, and finally the Chilean military stepped in. A junta seized power on 11 September 1973, following a siege during which Allende committed suicide. U.S. leaders were delighted with the coup, while the Soviets, who understood that "peaceful coexistence" had its limits, were nonetheless dismayed to lose a potential client in the Americas. But Moscow was distracted by preparations for the next month's Yom Kippur/ Ramadan War, which marked the culmination of years of tension and conflict in the Middle East.

Chilean coup destroys Allende, showing limits of détente

THE CRISIS IN THE MIDDLE EAST

From the 1950s onward, the Middle East was increasingly an area of Cold War contention. Israel emerged as a modern, Westernized republic in the midst of an underdeveloped region. Its highly trained and motivated population, the vast financial aid given it by Western governments, the state of siege against it by the Arabs, and the vivid memory of the Holocaust blended to create an advanced, militaristic society at once self-confident and fearful. Arab guerrilla raids across its frontiers sharpened its siege mentality. Meanwhile, Egyptian president Nasser's fear of Israel caused him to make Egypt a police state and give his military vast sums that he might rather have used to improve his people's welfare. It also led him to cooperate with Moscow, which sent him large amounts of military aid and thousands of technicians. As Nasser modernized Egypt's military with substantial Soviet aid, the West supplied Israel with weapons, creating a local arms race—and a very dangerous situation.

Cold War combines with Arab–Israeli strife to inflame Middle East

More dangerous still was a new Soviet Middle East strategy. The overthrow of Soviet client Abdel Karim Kassem in Iraq in 1963 convinced Moscow that regional and familial rivalries could negate its political gains. The Kremlin therefore adopted a coalition strategy designed to minimize the damage from inter-Arab squabbles by portraying Zionism as the common enemy of all Arabs, with U.S. imperialism cast in the role of its banker. This new propaganda offensive poisoned the debate with overtones of anti-Semitism and nudged Washington closer to Israel. More significantly, the new Soviet stance made the Middle East a central theater of the Cold War and laid the foundations for a severe international crisis in the event of a new war between Israel and Egypt. The stage was set for a superpower showdown.

Soviets promote anti-Zionism to unite Arabs against West

This Soviet strategy contained both a danger and an incongruity. The danger was that it increased the likelihood of war; the incongruity was that Moscow was backing the side most likely to lose. Perhaps the Soviets did not accurately assess the situation, or perhaps they reasoned that even an Arab defeat might serve their interests by creating anti-American hostility in the oil-rich Arab countries. At any rate, the Soviet line encouraged Arab states to take a firmer stance toward Israel, in hopes that the USSR would intervene militarily if war broke out. Moscow intensified its anti-Zionist propaganda and seemed to be inviting the Arabs to act.

Repeated border incidents between Israel and Syria led to a crisis in May 1967. On 13 May, Moscow informed Nasser that Israeli troops were massing on the Syrian border. Although this report proved false, Nasser decided to use the occasion to enhance his prestige in the Arab world. He may not have envisioned all-out war, but that is what he got. In the ensuing days, he committed Egyptian forces to the Sinai Peninsula and demanded removal of its UN peace-keeping force. On 22 May, Egypt blockaded the Gulf of Aqaba. Israeli prime minister Levi Eshkol's government reaffirmed its peaceful intentions, and Washington urged caution on all parties. These responses intrigued both Moscow and Cairo. On 28 May, Soviet premier Kosygin apparently assured Nasser that if war came, Moscow would keep Washington distracted. He did not specify how this would be done.

Soviet support for Egypt helps to stoke 1967 war plans

Nasser evidently thought the Arabs could hold their own against Israel, as long as the United States was neutralized. He therefore escalated the crisis, signing a mutual defense pact with Jordan on 30 May and strongly denouncing Israel's lack of action on the Palestinian refugee problem. Iraq and Kuwait joined the developing alliance on 4 June. But Israel was not about to sit back and let the Arabs attack. In a predawn preemptive strike on 5 June, Israeli jets destroyed Egypt's air force on the ground.

The Israeli first strike made Tel Aviv look aggressive, and the Egyptian army had been prepared to ride out the initial wave. Presumably, Israel's obvious aggression would disconcert the Americans, who would in some way be restrained by the USSR. But Israel's predawn strike deprived Nasser of the Arab world's only truly modern military force, and since the Arabs were forced to operate without air cover, the "Six-Day War" was one-sided from the start. The Israelis took the entire Sinai Peninsula and the eastern bank of the Suez Canal, while quickly expelling Syria from the Golan Heights (Map 10). They offered Jordan's King Hussein an informal separate peace, which he knew he could not accept if he wished to remain in power. The price he paid for refusing this offer was Israeli occupation of the most valuable part of his kingdom, the West Bank of the Jordan River.

Israel's preemptive strike devastates Arabs in 1967 "Six-Day War"

By the time the UN Security Council arranged a cease-fire on 11 June, the Arab states had lost huge territories, much of their productive capacity, and their political self-respect. Arabs would bear the scars of 1967 for decades, with Israel occupying the Sinai until 1979 and the West Bank and Golan Heights long thereafter. The Arab defeat also gave great impetus to the Palestinian guerrilla movement, as militants took over the Palestine Liberation Organization or PLO (created in 1964). And it led Nasser to conclude that his only chance for future victory lay in drawing Moscow into the fighting—a prospect from which Brezhnev understandably shrank.

Israel occupies Sinai, West Bank, Golan Heights

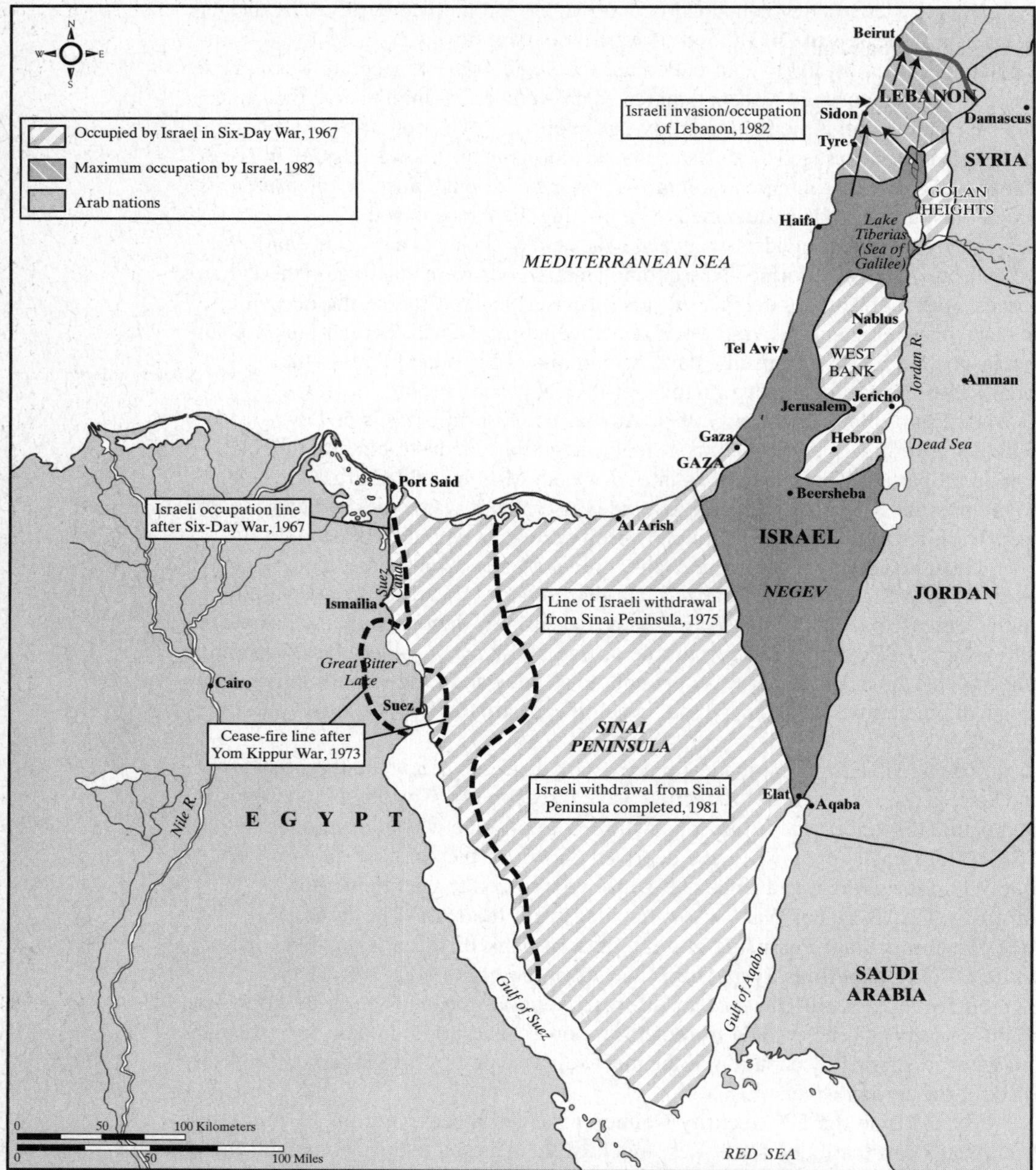

MAP 10 Arab–Israeli Conflicts, 1960s–1980s.
Moscow's bid to gain Middle East influence by backing anti-Israel Arab nationalists contributed to several major crises. Observe that, in the Six-Day War of 1967, Israel occupied the Sinai Peninsula, Gaza, the West Bank, and the Golan Heights, but Egypt regained control of the Sinai following the 1973 Yom Kippur War and the 1979 peace treaty between Egypt and Israel.

Exhilarated by its swift victory, Israel enjoyed a new leverage over the Arabs: If they wanted their lands back, they would have to recognize Israel's right to exist. King Hussein was willing to negotiate on this basis, but the PLO, annoyed at Jordan's conservatism and fearful of a breach in the united Arab front against Israel, tried to assassinate him in June 1970. Then, on 6–9 September, Palestinians hijacked four commercial jets and flew them to northern Jordan, hoping to sabotage negotiations with Israel by blowing them up.

PLO and Syria battle Jordan; Americans, Soviets, and Egypt help end 1970 crisis

Hussein resolved to expel the Palestinians from Jordan and turned his army loose on them in what the PLO would call "Black September." In response, on 19 September, Syria invaded Jordan in defense of the PLO. America then came to Jordan's aid: Nixon issued a warning to Moscow and put the U.S. military on a partial alert. But Syria pressed on, and a desperate Hussein asked Washington to help arrange Israeli air support, which would doubtless have destroyed Hussein's moral authority in his kingdom and would have led to Egyptian and perhaps Soviet intervention. Unwilling to run such a risk, Nixon on 21 September declared that the United States would help Jordan if it could not halt Syria alone and would keep both Moscow and Cairo out of the fighting. In fact, Moscow was already trying to curb the Syrians, whose forces began withdrawing from Jordan the next day. Nasser, who acceded to Soviet demands to begin talks with Israel through the UN, mediated a settlement between Jordan and the PLO a few hours before he died of a heart attack on 28 September 1970.

Nasser was succeeded by his longtime friend and vice president, Anwar Sadat, who had filled the role of heir apparent mainly because he seemed to pose no threat to his chief. To the general public, he seemed a rather indolent, good-natured fellow whose most striking attributes were his dark skin and deep voice. But Sadat's apparent lack of ambition concealed a shrewd, calculating military officer who had earned his rank as a demolitions specialist in World War II and had never lost his taste for danger. He would indulge that taste consistently between his accession to power in 1970 and his assassination by Islamic fundamentalists in 1981.

Sadat soon determined that Egypt could not afford a permanent state of war with Israel. A compromise was needed, and only Washington had sufficient leverage to bring Israel to the bargaining table. Sadat laid the groundwork by ousting Soviet advisors in 1972 and adopting a more equivocal stance between the United States and the USSR. But even then the Americans seemed unwilling to press Tel Aviv, so he continued to accept Soviet weapons, as did Syria. Obviously, something more was needed to get Nixon's attention.

Sadat succeeds Nasser in 1970 and ousts Soviet advisors

By the end of June 1973, Sadat and Syrian president Hafez Assad had formulated a rough plan of attack against Israel; they brought Hussein on board in September and obtained Saudi support for an oil embargo against any nation supporting Israel. Sadat warned that war was imminent in a 28 September speech, but its outbreak inexplicably surprised Israeli intelligence. War began on both fronts on 6 October—for Jews, Yom Kippur (the Day of Atonement), and for Muslims, the tenth of Ramadan, the anniversary of Muhammad's conquest of Mecca.

Backed by other Arab states, Egypt and Syria attack Israel in 1973

At first, Egypt and Syria achieved remarkable success, but it was later reversed by massive U.S. arms shipments to Israel. The Americans opted for this course after Israeli prime minister Golda Meir warned Nixon that Israel would win, no matter what it took to do so. Fearful that Israel might possess and use an atomic bomb, the United States provided conventional weapons in large quantities in hopes they would prove sufficient. This decision, combined with Egyptian and Syrian hesitation (possibly because they had not expected to achieve such stunning success and were unsure about how to proceed), enabled Israel to push back the invaders, eventually surrounding Egypt's Third Army on the west bank of the Suez Canal.

Israel rebounds with aid of U.S. arms

Nixon, seeing his opportunity, quietly informed Sadat that Washington would seek a negotiated settlement and would not let the Third Army be destroyed. The United States and USSR worked together in the Security Council to obtain approval of a resolution calling for a cease-fire and peace talks (Document 59A). Israel and Egypt formally agreed (Documents 59B and 59C), but fighting nonetheless continued.

The situation then grew ominous. Placing their airborne forces on full alert, the Soviets dispatched a message to Nixon, calling for joint U.S.–Soviet action to enforce the cease-fire, but stating a willingness to act on their own if America would not join them. Receiving this message late in the evening of 24 October, Kissinger and the National Security Council took it as a threat of unilateral Soviet intervention. Without awakening Nixon, they ordered a global alert of all U.S. conventional and nuclear forces. The resulting crisis, though it ended quickly and did not receive the dramatic publicity of the Cuban Missile Crisis, was in some respects more dangerous. In 1962, the U.S. alert was restricted to conventional forces; in 1973, the move to DEF CON 3 (Defense Condition 3) included nuclear forces. In 1962, Kennedy and Khrushchev were the ones calling the shots, while in 1973 Nixon was not involved in placing U.S. forces on alert, and Washington and Moscow were to some extent at the mercy of Sadat and Meir. And these two were hardly controllable: One had just begun an unprovoked war (ignoring Soviet counsels of caution); the other had hinted that she might end it by resorting to nuclear force!

Soviet proposal to intervene leads to U.S. global alert

In any event, the crisis subsided in less than 48 hours. Baffled and alarmed by the American alert, Moscow cautiously opted not to respond militarily. The Soviets supported U.S. proposals for a UN peacekeeping force, and Washington pressured Israel to accept the cease-fire. On 28 October, Egypt and Israel negotiated directly for the first time since 1956. The resulting truce would permit the reopening of the Suez Canal in 1975.

The Yom Kippur War was the first true test of the value of détente in a major East–West crisis. The results were mixed. On one hand, improved relations and bilateral conventions did not avert the crisis or prevent it from escalating dramatically. Although the Soviets knew in advance of the Arab attack, they could not restrain their Arab friends and did not consult the Americans. Détente did not deter either superpower from providing vast supplies of weapons to its clients; nor did it keep Nixon's aides from resorting on their own to nuclear brinkmanship. On the other hand, as Moscow and Washington both avowed in the wake of the crisis, the enhanced understanding and communications between them helped bring the war to an expeditious end and kept it from becoming a far more catastrophic conflict.

Détente does not prevent crisis but helps contain it

PROGRESS AND PROBLEMS IN EAST–WEST RELATIONS, 1974–1975

The Middle East crisis of October 1973 cast a chill over the warm glow of détente. It also led to a cold winter in many countries, as the Organization of Petroleum Exporting Countries (OPEC), led by oil-rich Arab lands irate over Western support for Israel in the Yom Kippur War, imposed an embargo on oil shipments to Israel's friends. Fuel shortages, sharp price increases, and lowered thermostats followed, accompanied by a cooling of the international climate.

By June 1974, when Nixon and Brezhnev met in Moscow for their third summit conference, the early enthusiasm for détente had faded. A deadlock in the ongoing arms control talks had dashed early hopes that a SALT II treaty might be concluded at this meeting. The mood was subdued and somber. Some minor agreements were signed, but they were overshadowed by domestic developments in both the United States and the USSR. In the midst of the conference, Soviet dissident and world-renowned physicist Andrei Sakharov announced that he was starting a hunger strike, calling world attention to human rights abuses in the USSR. By clumsily cutting off U.S. network efforts to telecast stories on Sakharov, Soviet authorities merely added to their reputation for heavy-handedness.

1974 Moscow summit eclipsed by Sakharov and Watergate

More detrimental to détente was the worsening Watergate mess. During the presidential campaign of 1972, some Nixon minions had been caught breaking into the Democratic National Committee headquarters in Washington's Watergate office complex to repair implanted bugging devices. To prevent political damage, Nixon and his associates sought to cover up the scandal and in so doing worked to obstruct the U.S. justice system. By summer 1974, the House Judiciary Committee was holding hearings that led to a recommendation for impeachment of the president. The Watergate affair emboldened Nixon's foes and undermined his foreign policy effectiveness; during the Moscow summit, he seemed agitated and distressed. On 9 August, five weeks after his return from Moscow, he resigned his office rather than face impeachment proceedings. The Brezhnev regime, with limited appreciation for American political and legal sensitivities, could only surmise that anti-Soviet forces in America had destroyed the architect of détente.

Watergate forces Nixon to resign, disconcerting Soviet leaders

Nixon's replacement, Gerald Ford, having limited foreign affairs experience, retained the services of Kissinger, who in 1973 had become secretary of state as well as national security advisor. Together they sought to sustain détente by arranging with Brezhnev a new summit meeting in November 1974 near the Russian Pacific port of Vladivostok.

Somewhat unexpectedly, the Vladivostok summit breathed new life into détente's sagging spirit. To the pleasant surprise of Ford and Kissinger, the Soviets were eager to negotiate seriously with the new administration. In the months before the summit they made concessions to overcome the SALT II impasse, finally agreeing to trade their edge in strategic missiles for limits on strategic bombers and MIRVs. At Vladivostok, the two leaders agreed in principle to an overall "ceiling" of 2,400 on the total number of "launchers" (a term encompassing both long-range missiles and bombers) permitted each side and a sublimit of

Ford and Brezhnev in Vladivostok achieve arms control breakthrough

1,320 on the number of these that could have multiple warheads (Documents 61A and 61B). This was a major breakthrough, for it seemed to remove the key obstacle to an arms control agreement and to set the stage for a speedy conclusion of the arms talks in Geneva. Brezhnev and Ford began making plans for another summit the next spring, at which they expected to sign a SALT II treaty.

No such conference occurred. Early in 1975, superpower relations again turned sour. Partly this change was due to unexpected snags in SALT, as negotiators bickered about whether U.S. cruise missiles (low-flying medium-range missiles that could be launched from planes, ships, or bases into Soviet territory) and Soviet "Backfire" bombers (medium-range aircraft that could be modified to reach the United States) should be included in the overall limit on strategic weapons. But the climate was also affected by a rupture in trade negotiations between Moscow and Washington and by unsettling developments in Southeast Asia.

Disputes over arms and trade delay SALT II progress

By 1975, the prospect of increased trade with the USSR had lost its appeal to many Americans. One reason was the "great grain robbery" of 1972. Taking advantage of the spirit of détente and the Nixon administration's desire to sell off U.S. grain surpluses, the Soviets cut a deal to buy vast amounts of American grain at prices well below market level over the next three years, assisted by extremely generous credit terms. By decreasing the supply of American grain, this deal in turn helped to drive up U.S. domestic prices, and embarrassed American officials had to admit that they had been outsmarted.

A more serious snag resulted from efforts by opponents of détente in the U.S. Congress to force the Soviets to improve their human rights performance in return for economic concessions. During 1973 and 1974, as Congress considered trade reform measures that would grant most favored nation (MFN) status to the USSR, Senator Henry Jackson and Representative Charles Vanik put forth a proposal to refuse the Soviets such status until they agreed to ease restrictions on the emigration of Jews. The MFN arrangement, which would have given the USSR the same commercial rights as America's most privileged trading partners, was a central feature of the U.S.–Soviet Trade Agreement negotiated in 1972 after the Moscow summit.

U.S. hawks block U.S.–Soviet trade pact by tying it to Jewish emigration

The "Jackson-Vanik Amendment," cleverly designed to attract the support of American Jews, human rights advocates, and foes of détente, became a major international issue. Moscow protested vehemently that it amounted to intrusion in its internal affairs, as well as a breach of the trade agreement. Throughout 1974, as the bill made its way through the U.S. Senate, the Nixon and Ford administrations sought to work out a compromise acceptable to congressional and Soviet leaders. In the end, however, their efforts came to naught. The Soviets were willing to make quiet concessions in order to get the troublesome amendment removed, but they did not want to give the impression of caving in to U.S. demands. When a related bill was amended to put severe limits on the amount of credit the USSR could receive, Moscow apparently decided that MFN status was no longer worth the price and repudiated the U.S.–Soviet Trade Agreement in January 1975. A severe blow was dealt to détente, and Soviet Jews gained nothing.

Events in Southeast Asia likewise undermined détente. The Vietnam settlement, which had seemed so promising in 1973, had started to come undone in 1974. In violation of the agreement, North Vietnam began infiltrating large numbers of soldiers into the south. The Americans appealed to Moscow but to no avail: The

Soviets were both unwilling and unable to restrain Hanoi. Détente had done little to extricate the United States from Vietnam, and now it did nothing to stop the Communists from continuing the war. Weakened by the Watergate scandal, Nixon was further constrained when Congress overrode his veto in November 1973 to pass the War Powers Act, restricting a president's ability to commit troops to combat without asking Congress for a declaration of war. His successor, Gerald Ford, had no intention of honoring Nixon's pledge to Thieu to intervene militarily if Hanoi violated the Paris Accords.

After two years of preparation, North Vietnam in early 1975 launched a major offensive in the central highlands. It was a huge conventional operation against a South Vietnamese army riddled with corruption and skeptical of its ability to resist. Strategic targets throughout the south fell in March, while Communist forces in Laos (the Pathet Lao) and Cambodia (the Khmer Rouge) made significant gains. Phnom Penh fell to the Khmer Rouge on 17 April, and on 30 April, the North Vietnamese captured Saigon, which they renamed Ho Chi Minh City. Ho's dream of a unified Vietnam finally came true. North Vietnamese units then entered Laos to assist the Pathet Lao in its final campaign, which ended successfully in October 1975, concluding the Second Indochina War.

Communists win in Vietnam, Cambodia, and Laos

Americans waited for other dominoes to fall, but they did not. The fall of Southeast Asia to Communism had only a modest effect on the Cold War. Moscow and Beijing transferred their seemingly endless quarrel to Vietnam, which became a Soviet client, and Cambodia, which was backed by China. The ultramodern U.S. naval base at Cam Ranh Bay was turned over to the Soviets, who made little use of it. Clearly, it was too simplistic to view events in this region purely in Cold War terms. Superpower rivalry continued in Southeast Asia, but it was only one of the factors affecting that area and not necessarily the most important.

Still, the fall of Saigon in April 1975, coming on top of the renunciation of the U.S.–Soviet Trade Agreement in January, helped derail hopes for another Ford-Brezhnev summit. It was followed in May by the Khmer Rouge seizure of a U.S. merchant ship called the Mayaguez. The resulting American raid created a short-lived crisis, placing a further strain on East–West relations. The time was hardly ripe for a U.S. visit by the Soviet leader.

A summit meeting of sorts did occur in July 1975, when both Ford and Brezhnev traveled to Finland to sign the Helsinki Accords. Accompanied by Secretary of State Kissinger and Foreign Minister Gromyko, the two leaders used the occasion to hold bilateral discussions. They agreed to continue the process of détente and pursuit of a SALT II accord. Their meeting was preceded closely by a dramatic "Apollo-Soyuz" coupling in outer space between orbiting U.S. astronauts and Soviet cosmonauts, adding to the overall impression of international goodwill.

Ford and Brezhnev meet in Helsinki at Final Act signing

The gathering's main significance, however, was the Helsinki Final Act (Document 62). After two years of work, CSCE participants had reached agreement on issues ranging from the inviolability of international borders to improved trade among European nations to freedom of expression and emigration for all European peoples. On 1 August 1975, leading officials from 35 countries assembled to sign the Final Act. It was truly a historic event, marking the success of détente efforts in Europe and, in many respects, the final

Helsinki Final Act crowns work on détente and CSCE

European peace settlement of World War II. It also marked the fruition of West Germany's *Ostpolitik*, although ironically its architect, Willy Brandt, had the previous year been forced by scandal to resign as German chancellor.

In some respects, the Helsinki Final Act was a crowning achievement for Soviet foreign policy, for with it Moscow achieved its long-sought goal of broad international recognition for the new boundaries and territorial adjustments that resulted from World War II. In other respects, however, it worked to the Soviets' disadvantage, for in order to get an agreement they consented to language on human rights and individual freedoms (included in "Basket Three" of the Final Act) that would be used against them by internal dissidents and external foes.

Helsinki accords solidify Soviet gains but highlight human rights problems

Meanwhile détente, which had begun like an express train, had come to resemble a roller coaster. Each vital achievement seemed to entail a slow, painstaking, uphill climb, while major setbacks often came at breakneck downhill speed. The superpowers had found ways to collaborate in areas of mutual concern. But the Cold War was far from over.

14

The Decline of Détente, 1975–1979

In the latter half of the 1970s, the bonds of East–West rapprochement unraveled. The continuing development of weapons technologies, along with superpower clashes in the Third World and confrontations over human rights, reversed the momentum established earlier in the decade. By 1976, President Ford and Secretary of State Kissinger studiously avoided the use of the word "détente," and the Carter administration, which took office the following year, did likewise. Progress continued in areas such as U.S.–Chinese relations and strategic arms negotiations, at least until 1979. But by the decade's close, a series of crises and revolts, culminating in the Soviet invasion of Afghanistan in December 1979, combined to end the era of détente.

EUROCOMMUNISM, ANGOLA, AND THE DECLINE OF DÉTENTE

The Helsinki Accords, despite their historic significance, did not end East–West tensions in Europe. Indeed, these tensions intensified in the mid-1970s because of a phenomenon known as "Eurocommunism." Communist parties in several Western European states, particularly Italy and France, began making electoral gains, in part by asserting their independence and visibly distancing themselves from Moscow. This worried the Americans, who feared that the Western alliance would be compromised if Communists achieved high positions in NATO countries. At first, it cheered the Soviets, but soon they became wary of maverick Communist movements that might sabotage détente without bringing any meaningful extension of the USSR's influence. Moscow's experience had shown time and again that it was often easier to deal with capitalists than with Communists it could not control.

Eurocommunism worries both Washington and Moscow

The most serious challenges arose in Portugal. In 1974, following the "Revolution of Flowers," which overthrew the fascist dictatorship of Marcelo Caetano, a military coup brought to power Vascos dos Santos Gonçalves, a leftist military officer who soon brought Communists into his

Revolution in Portugal disturbs NATO

government and established close ties with Moscow. By 1975, amid rumors that this NATO nation might soon let the Soviet navy use its seaports, Washington became increasingly nervous. Ford and Kissinger both warned Moscow to stay out of Portuguese affairs, and the Soviets, who helped finance the Portuguese Communists, apparently got the message. Rather than jeopardize détente and risk confrontation in an American sphere of influence, Moscow stood by as Gonçalves was deposed in August and a Communist-led uprising in November was suppressed.

The Soviets were less cautious, however, in dealing with the Portuguese West African colony of Angola (see map on page 130). In 1975, as Gonçalves's government moved to liberate its African colonies, Moscow stepped up its aid to the Popular Movement for the Liberation of Angola (MPLA), a Marxist group engaged in a civil war against various forces backed by Americans, South Africans, and others. Eventually, it even helped airlift 160,000 Cuban troops into the region, enabling the MPLA to gain the upper hand by early 1976. The U.S. Congress, unwilling to risk "another Vietnam," refused to let Ford send American troops to help the anti-Communist forces. So the Angolan civil war dragged on, lasting until 1990, when the Cubans and South Africans finally withdrew as the Cold War neared its end.

Communist intervention in Angola concerns Washington

The Angolan debacle caused great concern in Washington, not because U.S. security was threatened, but because American policymakers thought they detected a major new Soviet Third World offensive. Hitherto, they reasoned, the USSR had actively intervened primarily in areas along its periphery and had been very reluctant to try to extend its power to distant regions. Now, under the cover of détente, it seemed to be acting much more boldly. From Moscow's perspective, however, the Angolan initiative was merely a continuation of its traditional practice of aiding national liberation movements throughout the world, providing them with Soviet arms and assistance and letting the soldiers of client states bear the brunt of the battle. It was in no way inconsistent, the Soviets assured their American critics, with the spirit of détente.

Be that as it may, the Angolan affair was a setback for superpower relations. In the United States, former California governor Ronald Reagan mounted a serious bid for the Republican presidential nomination, accusing Ford and Kissinger of allowing the USSR to surpass America as the world's number one power and gaining broad support from conservative and anti-Communist quarters. In March 1976, in an effort to shore up his right flank, Ford announced that he would no longer use the word "détente," and Kissinger began using tough talk about stopping Soviet expansionism. Efforts to make progress in the SALT negotiations were virtually placed on hold, as relations with Moscow were sacrificed in favor of domestic politics.

Ford survived the Reagan challenge, but he did not fare as well in the general election. Tarnished by the Watergate legacy and his subsequent pardon of Richard Nixon, and weakened by conservative attacks on his foreign policy during the primaries, the president began the race with a huge deficit in the polls that he never quite made up. In defending détente during a televised debate, he mistakenly denied that Poland was under Soviet domination, forfeiting his presumed edge over his rival in foreign policy expertise. In November of 1976, the Democratic nominee, Jimmy Carter, was elected president by a narrow margin.

Carter narrowly defeats Ford in 1976 U.S. presidential election

HUMAN RIGHTS AND THE DECLINE OF DÉTENTE

Although Jimmy Carter was probably the least "hawkish" of Cold War presidents, at least in the early years of his term, his election caused consternation in Moscow. The Soviets had learned that, despite the prevalent perception that Democrats were "softer" on Communism, it was easier to work with pragmatic and realistic Republicans who were willing, like themselves, to put national interest before ideology in dealing with world problems. They did not know what to make of Carter, a born-again Christian peanut farmer who seemed poised to push American policy in a different and destabilizing direction. And they were scarcely reassured when he chose as his national security advisor Zbigniew Brzezinski, a Polish émigré and hard-line anti-Soviet scholar.

Carter's election upsets Moscow

The new president was an enigma, not only to the Kremlin but also to many in his own country. Raised in the rural South, he had earned an engineering degree from the U.S. Naval Academy and later served as governor of Georgia. He had a deep and abiding Baptist faith, which profoundly affected his outlook, and a prodigious capacity for processing information. In running for president, he turned his inexperience into an advantage by depicting himself as an outsider, contrasting his own integrity with the devious ways of Washington. But once he was in office, his halo of moral righteousness hampered his relations with both the Kremlin and the Congress, neither of which was used to a president who put principle ahead of pragmatism.

U.S.–Soviet relations in the early stages of the Carter administration were dominated and damaged by two major issues: arms control and human rights. Although Carter was deeply dedicated to each of these concerns, he wanted to treat them as separate entities. In practice, however, they became intertwined, often to the detriment of both.

On arms control, the new administration pushed quickly for reductions and limits far beyond those agreed to at Vladivostok. Cyrus Vance, the new secretary of state, went to Moscow in March 1977 to put forth some new U.S. proposals. They called for extensive cuts in strategic weapons and MIRVs, drastic reductions in "modern" ICBMs (like the USSR's mammoth new SS-18), and curtailment of plans for new types of ICBM (such as the projected American MX). The United States was particularly concerned about Soviet SS-18 missiles, which were large enough to carry many warheads and potentially accurate enough to destroy American ICBMs in their underground silos.

Washington and Moscow disagree over arms reductions

The Soviets, who had put years of effort into negotiating a SALT II treaty that now seemed within reach, were dismayed that the Carter team wanted to scrap much of this and start over with a sweeping new proposal. Brezhnev, who had overcome stiff opposition from his own military to the "equal ceilings" agreement at Vladivostok, was in no mood or position to make further concessions. He rejected the new U.S. approach and insisted that continued discussions must be based on the tentative accords already reached in the SALT II negotiations. The result was a setback for the arms talks, deterioration in East–West relations, and an impression in Moscow that the new U.S. administration was both unsophisticated and insincere.

This impression was further enhanced by Carter's approach to human rights (Document 63). Internal dissent, which had been simmering in the USSR for years, got a major boost from the human rights provisions of the

Carter's human rights policy antagonizes the USSR

Helsinki Final Act of 1975. Prominent Soviet dissidents formed self-styled "monitoring groups" and issued open letters, publicly accusing their government of violating the accords. The Brezhnev regime responded by exiling several dissenters and by trying to clamp down on contacts between those who remained and the Western press.

Carter, who was both genuinely concerned for human rights and anxious to maintain the support of hard-line Democrats like Senator Jackson, calculated that he could launch a major initiative in this area without damaging U.S.–Soviet relations. He was wrong. His administration made public statements critical of Soviet and Eastern European authorities, put increasing stress on human rights in U.S. radio broadcasts beamed to the Communist bloc, and sent letters of support to leading Soviet dissenters. The Kremlin responded by evicting or harassing several Western journalists and arresting several dissenters for alleged collaboration with the CIA. At one point, in reply, Carter felt compelled to issue a personal statement denying that detained dissident Anatoly Shcharansky had ever been associated with U.S. intelligence. But this did not help Shcharansky, who was convicted of treason and sentenced to hard labor. Nor did it satisfy the Soviets, who protested American interference in their internal affairs and warned Washington that continued U.S. support for anti-Soviet "sedition" would undermine détente.

Carter nonetheless persisted in his policies, insisting that his concern for human rights was a matter of global principle and not directed specifically against the USSR. He did, in fact, cut aid to several U.S. clients for human rights violations. But Brezhnev had little understanding of or appreciation for Carter's Christian idealism. From his perspective, the American human rights campaign was little more than an attempt to embarrass the Soviet government and weaken its hold on Eastern Europe.

The human rights imbroglio intensified in fall 1977 when a new round of CSCE meetings, designed in part to evaluate the success of the Helsinki Final Act, opened in Belgrade. Moscow hoped to use this occasion to rejuvenate and consolidate détente, but the United States wanted to focus on how nations were complying with the document's humanitarian provisions. Prior to the conference, Washington issued a report, deeply resented in Moscow, which graded the USSR and other Communist bloc nations on their human rights performance, giving them poor marks. The conference was dominated by rancorous debates on this issue. Despite Soviet objections and the private concerns of several U.S. allies, the Americans managed to establish as a legitimate international concern the internal human rights practices of nations that had signed the Helsinki Accords.

CONFRONTATION AND CONFUSION IN EAST AFRICA

Carter's human rights crusade did not always work to U.S. advantage. This was especially true in the Horn of Africa, where Ethiopia was an American friend and neighboring Somalia a Soviet client (see map on page 130). The Somalis, who were culturally and ethnically similar to the Ethiopians, gained their independence in 1960. But part of Somalia, the Ogaden, had been given to Ethiopia during previous colonial partitions. The Somalis wanted it back. They were courted by Moscow, which coveted the access to the Indian Ocean provided by air and naval bases in Somalia.

Soviet aid to Somalia began in 1963 and intensified after a military coup brought Colonel Mohammed Siad Barre to power in 1969. The USSR built an air base inland and a major naval facility at the port of Berbera. By the mid-1970s, more than 2,000 Soviet technicians were stationed in Somalia. This balanced the U.S. ties with Ethiopia and Saudi Arabia, which between them controlled much of the Red Sea coast. But in 1974, a military coup overthrew Ethiopian emperor Haile Selassie and power passed to a Marxist colonel named Mengistu Haile Mariam. The United States, already in the process of transferring its naval and telecommunications facilities to a newly acquired base on the Indian Ocean island of Diego Garcia, had no desire to subsidize a Marxist regime. So in February 1977, America denounced the Mariam government for human rights violations and cut off all aid. Moscow thus gained a splendid opportunity to construct a network of clients in Ethiopia, Somalia, and South Yemen (which became Marxist in 1967 as a result of civil war in Yemen), ringing the southern entrance to the Red Sea.

The Soviets sense an opportunity in the Horn of Africa

If ideology were the dominant factor in international relations, this alliance could have been fashioned overnight. But if the history of the late twentieth century points to anything, it is the remarkably enduring attraction of nationalistic and ethnic rivalries. Somalia, seeing an opportunity to regain the Ogaden, broke its alliance with Moscow and invaded Ethiopia. Soviet forces were expelled from Berbera and replaced by American advisors, but Carter's scruples were offended by the invasion, and for reasons of both principle and public relations, the United States refused to ship arms to the Somali aggressors. The USSR supplied Ethiopia with huge quantities of weapons, while Cuba sent troops to repel the Somali assault. This unprecedented direct Soviet intervention in Africa led to an uneasy stalemate, as Moscow refused to permit a counterassault by Ethiopia, which was having its own problems with an uprising in its province of Eritrea.

Soviets and Cubans intervene in African ethnic wars

The conflicts in the Horn of Africa would eventually lead to a monstrous human tragedy. By the late 1980s, both Ethiopia and Somalia would be in desperate straits, with their economies in shambles, their social fabrics weakened by years of combat and hardship, and famine stalking their lands. As the Cold War came to an end in 1991, Ethiopia overthrew its Marxist government, and Somalia ousted the military dictatorship of Siad Barre. Superpower interest in the area was dictated by its proximity to the Indian Ocean (for Moscow) and the Red Sea (for Washington). The wild card in the deal was Jimmy Carter's absorption in issues of human rights, which led the Americans to offend both sides and bewilder their friends in the region.

Carter's human rights policy proves counterproductive in Africa

PEACE BETWEEN EGYPT AND ISRAEL

Although it was making inroads in Africa, the Kremlin could take little comfort from concurrent events in the Middle East. At first Carter, reversing the Nixon–Ford policy, sought to include the USSR as a partner in resolving the Arab–Israeli conflict. In October 1977, the two superpowers even issued a joint statement calling for renewed peace talks in Geneva. But the following month, Egyptian president Anwar

Sadat stunned the world by traveling to Jerusalem, setting in motion a process that would lead to peace between Egypt and Israel, an enhanced U.S. role, and a steep decline in Soviet influence in the Middle East.

Sadat's initial victories in the Yom Kippur/Ramadan War of 1973 (Chapter 13), despite his later reverses, won him immense acclaim in Egypt. This position of strength enabled him to embark on a dramatic new course. He concluded that peace with Israel was an economic necessity and that a new war might well reveal whether rumors that Israel had a nuclear device were accurate. Disinclined to obtain this information in such a direct manner, he set out to work for peace.

Sadat stuns the world by offering peace with Israel

Thus, on 20 November 1977, Sadat flabbergasted the world by making a surprise flight to Jerusalem and a speech (Document 64A) to the Israeli parliament (Knesset). In Menachem Begin, Israel's recently elected prime minister, he found both a tenacious adversary and a prudent statesman. Begin, whose ancestry was Polish, had headed a Jewish terrorist organization in the 1940s and had masterminded the bombing of Jerusalem's King David Hotel in an effort to force British withdrawal. Worse still in Arab eyes, he had planned and executed a 1948 massacre of Arab villagers at Deir Yasin. Courtly and devout, passionately protective of Israeli independence, and incorrigibly realistic regarding means to attain that end, his patriotic credentials were impeccable. Just as Nixon was one of the few U.S. politicians who could open the door to China, Begin was one of the few Israelis with the moral leverage to negotiate with an Egyptian. Their November meeting, although marked by strong disagreements, was highly promising.

Carter brokers preliminary accords at Camp David

Begin flew to Egypt on 25 December for further discussions. Israel was ready to trade occupied land for peace with Egypt, since destruction of the common anti-Israeli front would give Tel Aviv unprecedented security. The talks that followed underscored the bankruptcy of Soviet Middle East strategy and the success of U.S. efforts to exclude Moscow from any influence in the region. Begin and Sadat agreed from the outset that any permanent settlement would have to be facilitated and guaranteed by the United States. With Carter acting as mediator, the two leaders held a twelve-day marathon meeting at Camp David in September 1978. They agreed on a framework for a peace treaty and established a three-month deadline for its conclusion (Document 64B).

Carter's shuttle diplomacy finalizes Israeli–Egyptian peace

The Israeli Knesset grudgingly authorized a military pullback from Sinai, but peace talks stalled over Egypt's efforts to tie the full resumption of diplomatic relations to Israel's willingness to relax its control over Palestinians in Gaza and the West Bank. The deadline passed without a treaty. Jews in Israel did not care to admit that Palestinians wanted freedom as much as they did, while Egyptians and other Arabs did not realize how much Israel's security concerns stemmed from the experience of Nazi genocide and the long-standing Arab–Israeli tension. Finally, Carter himself flew to Cairo and Jerusalem to negotiate final arrangements between Sadat and Begin. The Egyptian–Israeli treaty was signed in Washington on 26 March 1979 (Document 64C). Through it all, the USSR had been little more than a bystander, eliminated from any substantive role in the peace process.

The Signing of the Peace Treaty between Egypt and Israel, 26 March 1979.
U.S. president Jimmy Carter, whose role in the negotiations was crucial, looks on approvingly as Egyptian president Anwar Sadat (on Carter's right) and Israeli prime minister Menachem Begin (on Carter's left) sign the treaty of peace. The removal of Egypt from the Arab coalition against Israel made further Arab–Israeli conventional wars useless and ushered in both an era of hope in the region and an era of increasing Palestinian reliance on terrorism.

THE CHINA CARD, THE AMERICA CARD, AND THE VIENNA SUMMIT

Superpower relations, meanwhile, were severely complicated by a split in the U.S. government between Secretary of State Vance and National Security Advisor Brzezinski. With the apparent blessing of their president, the two men pursued contradictory policies while struggling for preeminence within the administration. Vance and his colleagues stressed cooperation with the USSR and worked to preserve détente. Having failed in their early attempt to get Moscow to accept deep cuts in strategic arms, they fell back to the Vladivostok approach and worked toward a SALT II treaty based on the Brezhnev–Ford agreement. Brzezinski, however, disliked and distrusted the Soviets and felt that Vance and arms negotiator Paul Warnke were too soft and accommodating. He favored confrontation with Moscow and to this end pushed for an accelerated U.S. arms buildup and further rapprochement with China.

The U.S. government splits over policies toward the USSR

At first the secretary of state seemed to gain the upper hand. Carter, who saw himself as a man of peace and was determined to end the arms race, decided not to

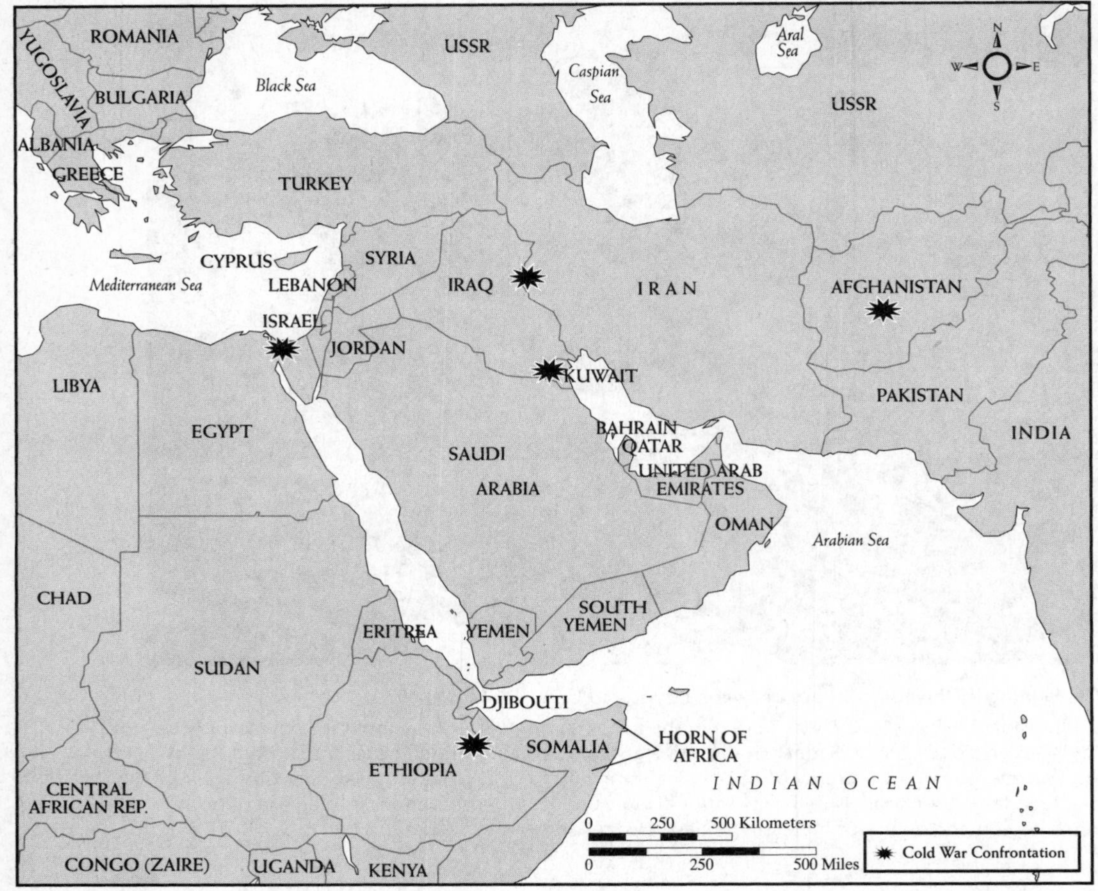

MAP 11 The Middle East, 1945–1991.

U.S. support for Israel, and Soviet support for Marxists and Arab Nationalists, helped make the Middle East a Cold War battleground. In the late 1970's United States National Security Advisor Brzezinski believed that an "arc of crisis" marked by regional conflicts curved from Ethiopia through the Middle East to Afghanistan.

link progress on SALT with Soviet behavior in Ethiopia or elsewhere. Siding with Vance, he concluded that arms control was too important for U.S. interests to be used as a reward or punishment. The negotiations continued throughout 1978 despite the gradual worsening of superpower relations, and made enough progress so that by the end of the year agreement was close at hand.

Washington recognizes the People's Republic of China

The president decided, however, that he must also respond to the Soviet geopolitical challenge, and here he turned to Brzezinski. In an undisguised effort to "play the China card," the national security advisor went to Beijing in May 1978. There he met with Chinese leaders, joined them in criticizing the USSR, and renewed efforts to improve economic and diplomatic ties between Washington and Beijing. In December, the dramatic announcement was made that the two countries would establish full diplomatic relations, effective 1 January 1979 (Documents

65A and 65B). The United States simultaneously agreed to sever its formal ties with the Nationalist government on Taiwan, though a number of informal connections remained.

The normalization of U.S.–Chinese relations was followed closely by a highly publicized visit to America by Chinese vice premier Deng Xiaoping. The diminutive and astute Deng, a veteran of the Long March and survivor of three separate purges, emerged as China's effective leader in the wake of the 1976 deaths of Zhou Enlai and Mao Zedong. In a noteworthy address to the United Nations in 1974, he had adroitly identified China not with the American and Soviet superpowers, but with the emerging "Third World" (Document 60), thereby characterizing China as a fully independent power with interests that transcended the Cold War. Once in power, he overcame the opposition of the radical left and launched China on a course of modernization, experimentation with free market incentives, and further accommodation with the West. Arriving in Washington in late January 1979, he charmed almost everyone, delighting conservatives by denouncing the Soviet "hegemonists." Then, soon after his return home, China launched a sudden invasion of Vietnam, its Communist neighbor to the south.

Deng Xiaoping visits the United States

Although China aided Hanoi during its long war against the United States, relations between the two deteriorated sharply after 1975. Vietnam drew closer to Moscow, while China aligned with Communist Cambodia. Matters finally came to a head late in 1978, following the conclusion of a formal alliance between Moscow and Hanoi in November. In December, Vietnam invaded Cambodia, driving from power the murderous regime of Pol Pot and the Khmer Rouge, which since 1975 had killed over a million people with its radical deurbanization campaign. In January 1979, the Vietnamese installed a moderate Communist government in Phnom Penh. But the fighting was far from over. In February, the Chinese invaded northern Vietnam, intending to "punish" Hanoi for its aggression and help the beleaguered Khmer Rouge. Deftly playing the "America card," Deng Xiaoping had informed his U.S. hosts of his intentions and then timed the Chinese attack to follow close on the heels of his visit, thereby giving the impression that he had Washington's support. Although the Americans privately tried to dissuade Deng from his plans, in public they did not condemn the Chinese invasion unequivocally, opting instead for an "evenhanded" approach to the conflict. Furthermore, in a move that made a mockery of Carter's human rights crusade, they continued to recognize and send arms to the genocidal Khmer Rouge.

China invades Vietnam, and the United States backs the Khmer Rouge

Predictably, these events affected Soviet–American relations. The December announcement of mutual U.S.–Chinese recognition came at a time when arms negotiators seemed close to an agreement, and plans were being discussed for a January summit in Washington to sign the SALT II accords. But the events of early 1979 chilled the international climate, and although both Carter and Brezhnev wanted a summit, the time was just not right. Furthermore, the remaining arms control issues proved more troublesome than expected. It was not until May, following tedious work by negotiators in Geneva, augmented by private correspondence between Brezhnev and Carter and numerous meetings between Vance and Dobrynin, that a final accord was reached.

The long-delayed summit finally took place in June of 1979. Although it had originally been planned for Washington, in deference to the declining

SALT II is signed at the Vienna summit

health of the aging Soviet dictator, the meeting was held in Vienna. Both leaders attached great importance to the event. At their initial encounter, in fact, the atheistic Brezhnev declared to the deeply religious Carter that "God will not forgive us if we fail." And at the signing ceremonies for SALT II, the leader of the free world warmly embraced the head of the Communist bloc.

The SALT II treaty was, of course, the heart of the Vienna summit (Document 66). Coming almost five years after preliminary agreement had been reached at Vladivostok, it nonetheless followed the general understandings that had been achieved at that meeting. A ceiling of 2,400 was placed on the aggregate number of strategic launchers permitted to either side, with a reduction to 2,250 after 1981. The number of these that could be equipped with MIRVs was set at 1,320. Long-range bombers fitted with cruise missiles were to be counted as multiple-warhead vehicles and limited to 28 cruise missiles each. For verification purposes, each side agreed that it would not interfere with the other's technological efforts (such as the use of spy satellites) to monitor compliance.

The conclusion of the SALT II accords marked the culmination of a decade of negotiations that had begun in November 1969 with the original arms control talks in Helsinki. The process was far from perfect, and in some cases, it may have actually created pressures to develop and build new weapons, either as bargaining chips or as conciliatory gestures to hard-liners and military brass. The results, too, were less than conclusive: Each side was left with a vast nuclear arsenal of awesome destructive capability, far in excess of what might be needed for legitimate defensive purposes. Each weapons system continued to possess its own momentum, its own logic, and its own avid supporters. The arms control treaty was a finite and limited device, designed primarily to prevent future escalation of the arms race rather than to reduce or eliminate existing stockpiles. Still, the agreement did seem to show that, despite their conflicting interests and their often dangerous global competition, the two superpowers were capable of reaching agreement on overriding issues of mutual concern.

The Vienna summit and the SALT II treaty also marked the pinnacle of Brezhnev's career. In internal affairs, he had increasingly consolidated his power, methodically removing his opponents inside the government and repressing dissidents outside. In 1977, he had assumed the position of Soviet president while maintaining his post as general secretary of the Communist party. This made him the official head of state as well as the effective ruler. That same year he had implemented a new constitution, updating and replacing the old "Stalin Constitution" of 1936. In foreign affairs, he had staked his reputation on the simultaneous pursuit of defense and détente, and he had apparently won. By virtue of its relentless arms buildup and its tenacious negotiations, the USSR gained a recognized position of diplomatic and strategic equality with the United States. The Soviet Union's territorial gains in World War II, and its domination of Eastern Europe, were now widely recognized and accepted in international accords. Brezhnev himself met, and negotiated as an equal, with three American presidents. Under him, the USSR became not just a military giant that was feared the world over but also a respected and accepted member of the world family of nations, symbolized by the fact that the 1980 Olympic Summer Games were scheduled for Moscow.

Brezhnev's career passes its zenith

Ironically, these achievements proved illusory. By the time Carter and Brezhnev met in Vienna, forces were already in motion that would undermine SALT, the spirit of détente, and even the USSR itself. The SALT II treaty was never to be ratified, and détente was doomed by the end of the year.

THE "ARC OF CRISIS" AND THE "WINDOW OF VULNERABILITY"

Even before Carter and Brezhnev signed the SALT II accords, détente was in serious trouble. The main reason for this was a growing American perception that Moscow was using it to gain the advantage, both in Third World influence and in strategic weapons capability.

The previous four years witnessed a string of Communist triumphs. In 1975, Communists took power in South Vietnam, Laos, and Cambodia. In 1976, the Soviet-backed MPLA, assisted by Cuban forces, gained the upper hand in Angola. In 1977, the Kremlin acquired an important new client in Ethiopia. In 1978, in a development that attracted scant notice at the time, a Marxist regime came to power in Afghanistan. Early in 1979, a non-Communist but anti-Western revolution toppled the shah of Iran, and a simultaneous crisis between South and North Yemen led to increased Soviet influence in both. Proponents of détente argued that these were mainly localized rivalries, that they mostly involved forces that were not under Kremlin control, that the antagonists were more interested in getting Moscow's weapons than in joining the Soviet bloc, and that these ventures were doing more to drain the USSR's resources than to increase its influence. But to worried hard-liners like Brzezinski, there was an "arc of crisis" stretching from Afghanistan, through the Persian Gulf, and down into eastern Africa. In this area, as well as in Southeast Asia and central Africa, many believed that Communism was on the march.

Successive Communist victories imperil détente

Of even greater concern to American officials was the continuing Soviet arms buildup. Partly because of his own proclivities, and partly to ensure Soviet military support for his pursuit of détente, Brezhnev spent vast sums on weaponry, and by the late 1970s, the USSR actually surpassed the United States in several important categories. Most worrisome of all was the mammoth new SS-18 missile, a far more potent weapon than any previous Soviet ICBM. In terms of throw weight, or weapons carrying capacity, the SS-18 could carry larger and more numerous warheads than any U.S. missile, and it was accurate enough to destroy or incapacitate a hardened underground missile silo. This made it potentially a first-strike weapon. Although the SALT II treaty would limit SS-18s to ten warheads each, it also allowed the USSR to retain 308 of these missiles. Theoretically, by launching just 211 of them in a surprise first-strike attack, the Soviets could deliver 2,110 nuclear warheads, or two against *each* of America's 1,000 Minuteman and 54 Atlas ICBMs, thus destroying virtually the entire U.S. fleet.

Soviet SS-18 deployment raises fears of a first strike capability

For several years, an unofficial "Committee on the Present Danger," composed of leading U.S. hard-liners and opponents of détente, had been warning publicly of just such a scenario. They feared that by demolishing American ICBMs, the Kremlin could deprive the United States of the ability to retaliate against the USSR's remaining strategic missiles, leaving American leaders in a terrible predicament. They could still use their nuclear submarines and bombers to

The Committee on the Present Danger detects a "Window of Vulnerability" retaliate against Soviet cities, but this would only invite a counterattack against U.S. population centers. If, however, they chose not to retaliate, they would in effect be giving Moscow a free hand to use its vast conventional military forces to launch unstoppable offensives in Europe, Asia, or the Middle East. The danger would decrease in the mid-1980s, it was assumed, when America's accurate new MX ICBMs and D-5 SLBMs came on line. Until that time, however, there would purportedly exist a "window of vulnerability," during which the U.S. land-based nuclear deterrent was very much at risk.

The "window of vulnerability," like the missile gap of the late 1950s, had far more political than strategic significance. It was a classic "worst-case" scenario, ascribing to the Soviet weapons much greater reliability than they usually had and overlooking the enormous technical difficulties of launching and coordinating a mammoth first strike. Critics of this concept further noted that, while ICBMs accounted for the vast preponderance of the USSR's nuclear capability, they made up a much smaller portion of the U.S. strategic force. This meant that a preemptive Soviet attack, even if it managed to wipe out most of the U.S. ICBMs, would still leave the Americans with an overall edge in deliverable nuclear warheads. It also meant that, since land-based missiles were much more vulnerable than those launched by submarine or aircraft, the Soviets were potentially far more susceptible to a first strike than were their U.S. adversaries. Still, to American hard-liners, these arguments missed the point: It was the *perception* of U.S. vulnerability, rather than the reality, that might well embolden the Soviets and immobilize the Americans during a major crisis.

All of these concerns came to the fore in summer 1979, when Jimmy Carter returned from Vienna and submitted the freshly signed SALT II treaty to the U.S. Senate for ratification. Nobody expected an easy fight. Carter was an enigmatic president, disliked by many in his own party, with little popular support or personal loyalty to draw upon. His standing in the polls was low, thanks to a shaky economy and double-digit inflation. Earlier he had offended military hawks by canceling plans to build the B-1, a sophisticated new U.S. bomber, without even trying to use it as a bargaining chip in the arms control talks. His "inaction" in the face of Soviet Third World gains, his conclusion of a treaty giving up control over the Panama Canal, and his "abandonment" of Taiwan in order to normalize relations with China had earned him many enemies on the right. And on the eve of the Vienna summit, Senator Henry Jackson, the influential Democrat who had bedeviled Nixon's efforts at détente, scorned the SALT II treaty and accused the administration of "appeasement."

SALT II encounters resistance in the U.S. Senate

Additional problems arose during the ratification process, which eventually lasted six months. In September, a major flap developed over the "discovery" of a Soviet "combat brigade" in Cuba, during which Senate hearings on SALT II were temporarily suspended. The "crisis" lasted until 1 October, when President Carter declared that he had received Soviet pledges not to enlarge the brigade, which apparently had been there for years.

Meanwhile, developments in Europe were placing an added strain on U.S.–Soviet relations. NATO leaders who had generally supported détente were nonetheless concerned that the SALT treaties might undermine the security of Western Europe. West German chancellor Helmut Schmidt in particular had expressed the fear that, by neutralizing the superpowers' strategic arsenals,

Schmidt fears that SALT II will undermine Western security

SALT II would amplify the Warsaw Pact's military preeminence in Europe. In effect, the less danger there was of a global nuclear conflict, the more temptation there might be for the Soviet bloc to use its superior forces to attack Western Europe. To Schmidt, this meant that NATO must either upgrade and modernize its forces to provide a more credible deterrent or else convince the Soviets to downgrade and weaken theirs.

NATO was particularly concerned about the ongoing Soviet deployment of an accurate new triple-warhead intermediate-range ballistic missile (IRBM) called the SS-20. Unlike its unreliable predecessors, the SS-20 was *mobile*, making it less vulnerable to a Western strike in the event of a European war. The Carter administration was not too worried at first, but with the signing of the SALT II treaty, it wanted to reassure both its NATO allies and domestic critics that it could be tough in dealing with Moscow. So in August of that year, it decided to modernize its NATO forces in Europe by replacing older weapons systems with 108 Pershing II IRBMs and 464 Tomahawk ground-launched cruise missiles.

The reaction in Moscow was swift and vehement. On 6 October, Brezhnev gave a major speech, vigorously denouncing this decision as destabilizing and destructive while warning that it would undermine détente (Document 67A). From a Soviet perspective, the new weapons were potentially strategic in nature, since they carried nuclear warheads and were capable of reaching the USSR. In some respects, they were even more dangerous than ICBMs, since Pershing IIs reportedly could reach their targets in fewer than ten minutes, and the slower cruise missiles flew too low to be detected by radar. Brezhnev therefore offered to reduce the number of Soviet IRBMs capable of reaching Western Europe if NATO would agree not to deploy the new U.S. weapons.

NATO force modernization provokes opposition in Moscow

NATO responded in December with a "dual-track" approach, resolving to proceed with negotiations to reduce intermediate-range nuclear forces (INF) while simultaneously preparing to install the new missiles in 1983 (Document 67B). The deployment would be canceled, the Soviets were assured, if agreement could be reached by then in the INF talks. For Western politicians, this approach served two important purposes: It gave the Kremlin an incentive to bargain in good faith, and it helped allay the fears of the jittery populations in the nations where the new missiles were slated to be deployed. But it could hardly be expected to win points in Moscow.

THE CRISIS IN IRAN

In November 1979, while the U.S. Senate was still considering the SALT II treaty, and while NATO leaders were pondering their response to Brezhnev's IRBM offer, the focus of world attention suddenly shifted to Iran. On 4 November, an Iranian mob stormed the U.S. embassy in Tehran and seized a large number of American hostages, setting in motion a crisis that would undermine détente and destroy the Carter presidency.

The crisis in Iran was the culmination of a long series of developments that transformed that nation from a friend to a foe of the United States. From 1953 until 1979, Shah Mohammed Reza Pahlavi ruled Iran in accordance with Washington's interests, and the country became a U.S. surrogate in the Persian Gulf. The exploitation

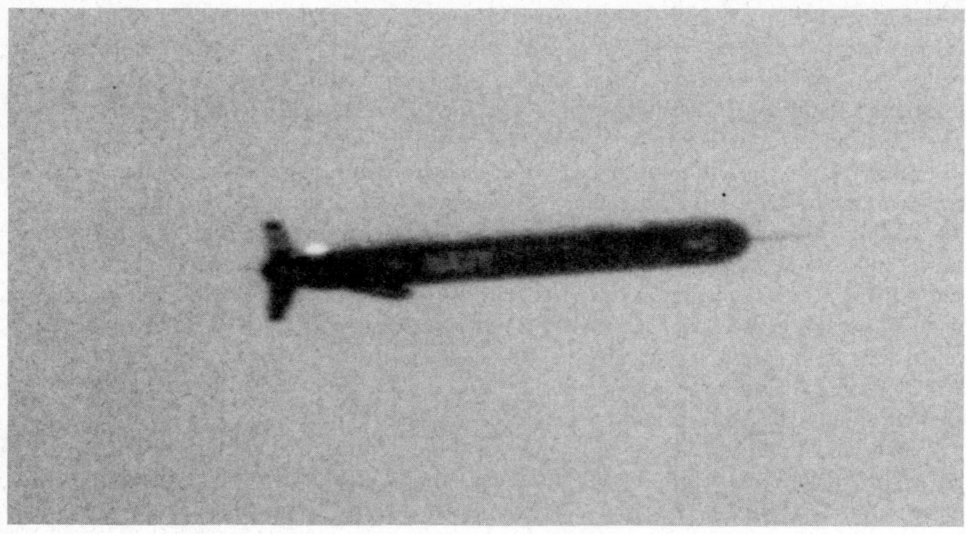

A U.S. Tomahawk Cruise Missile shoots across the sky during a demonstration in 1979. President Carter's decision to deploy these missiles in Europe gave the United States a strategic advantage over the Soviets, since cruise missiles flew too low to be detected by Soviet radar. Soviet leader Leonid Brezhnev promptly denounced the decision as destructive of détente, and the Cold War quickly grew colder.

of Iran's oil deposits brought the nation vast wealth and equally vast problems. Oil revenues grew from $34 million in 1953 to $20 *billion* in 1978. The government spent huge sums on economic and social projects that the shah called the "White Revolution," but industrial advances and access to education and medical care were offset by the strains and stresses of rapid modernization. By the late 1970s, Tehran and other cities were swollen with internal migrants seeking industrial employment. Health care and sanitation systems could not keep pace with this influx, and nearly half of urban families lived in a single room. Meanwhile, traditional Muslim values eroded as materialism challenged religious beliefs. Drug abuse and premarital sex ravaged a whole generation of young people. In response, a conservative religious opposition emerged, headed by Muslim clerics like the Ayatollah Ruhollah Khomeini, who was exiled to Iraq in 1963.

Ayatollah Khomeini leads religious opposition to the Shah

Several events combined in 1978 to doom the shah's regime. In response to newspaper columns attacking Khomeini, widespread rioting erupted in the holy city of Qum, and the political and clerical oppositions joined forces. Simultaneously, the country was flooded with Khomeini's writings and taped cassettes of his sermons smuggled in from Iraq. When the shah protested, the Iraqis expelled Khomeini, who moved to Paris and issued directions to the revolution by radio via the British Broadcasting Corporation. He preached that Zionism, Christianity, and Marxism were all in league against Islam and that Muslims must adopt a theocratic state in order to defeat them. Carter's brokering of the Egyptian–Israeli accords lent credibility to these words. In the context of the Cold War, this ironically placed Moscow and Washington on the same side, in opposition to a revolution antagonistic to both. It would, of course, hurt the United States more, since Iran was a U.S. satellite.

In a few months, everything fell apart in Iran. The suspicious destruction of a packed movie house, bloody riots in Tehran that killed hundreds, and a deadly earthquake that took nearly 20,000 lives all undermined the regime. Khomeini became the symbol of a united opposition, keeping the character of his movement vague and ill defined, so that all antigovernment forces could support it. Unable to govern, the shah left the country for cancer treatment on 6 January 1979. On 1 February, Khomeini returned to Iran. A few days later, a temporary anti-shah coalition including air force technicians, Marxist guerrillas, and Islamic fundamentalists took power in Tehran. Khomeini quickly installed an Islamic Republic and continued his vehement denunciations of the United States. The stage was set for crisis.

An Islamic Republic is proclaimed in Iran

On 22 October 1979, anti-American sentiments in Iran were inflamed when the former shah, by this time dying of cancer, was admitted to a U.S. hospital. This led to mass demonstrations, and eventually to the storming of the U.S. embassy in Tehran and the seizure of American hostages on 4 November. Some hostages were soon released, but most were held captive for the next fifteen months, producing a drawn-out, debilitating crisis. From November 1979 until the liberation of the remaining hostages in January 1981, America appeared to the world as an impotent giant, unable to win the release of the hostages yet unwilling to ignore them and move on to other issues. This added to the impression of Carter's weakness and eroded his support further. And the loss of U.S. intelligence facilities in Iran, by hampering American capacity for monitoring Soviet compliance with SALT II, further undermined the treaty's chances within the U.S. Senate. Not only had the shah's government served as an American surrogate in maintaining the flow of Persian Gulf oil; it had also provided the CIA with electronic listening posts from which Soviet troop movements, rocket launchings, and nuclear tests could be monitored. In the absence of such facilities, key senators proved unwilling to ratify the SALT II treaty. The crisis in Iran thus had an enormous impact upon East–West relations, weakening détente and providing the setting for a full-scale resumption of the Cold War.

The Iranian hostage crisis weakens Carter and results in Iran–Iraq War

The crisis also brought severe problems for Iran. Carter froze all Iranian assets in the United States, and, since Khomeini lacked the political experience needed to create an effective government, the country careened toward chaos. Emboldened by such developments, neighboring Iraq declared war on Iran in 1980, beginning a crippling conflict that cost the lives of millions. Despite the fact that Khomeini's regime was as violently anti-Communist as it was anti-American, Moscow sought to gain influence in Tehran by blaming the United States and selling arms to Iran. But by this time, the Kremlin, led by the aging and sickly Brezhnev, was seriously distracted by a major crisis of its own.

THE SOVIET INVASION OF AFGHANISTAN

By December 1979, it was already clear that East–West relations were in very serious trouble and that the SALT II treaty was floundering in the U.S. Senate. Détente lay bruised and battered, its survival doubtful. Then, at the end of the month, came the final *coup de grâce:* The USSR launched a massive invasion of the neighboring state of Afghanistan.

The Soviet invasion of Afghanistan came in response to a series of events that threatened Moscow's recently gained hegemony in that country. In April of 1978, a Communist coup overthrew the Western-oriented regime of Muhammad Daoud and brought to power a leftist dictatorship headed by Nur Muhammad Taraki. At first, the Kremlin was delighted to gain a new client in a neighboring country, but before long, it watched in dismay as an extremist faction led by Hafizullah Amin tried to force radical socialism down the throats of the fiercely independent and devoutly Muslim Afghan people, alienating almost everyone. Moderate Communists led by Babrak Karmal were quickly forced out of government. Before long the entire country was in revolt, and by August 1979, the Soviets were quietly urging Taraki to slow the pace of reform and get rid of Amin. His attempt to do so backfired, however, and Amin wound up ousting Taraki and taking full power himself. This merely served to intensify the revolt as Afghanistan disintegrated into chaos.

A Communist government in Afghanistan proves inept

Initially, Washington displayed little concern over events in Afghanistan, a barren, landlocked country with minute strategic significance. But in late 1979, as the Soviets increased their involvement and began to assemble troops near the Afghan border, the Carter administration became increasingly disturbed. It tried to warn the Kremlin not to get further involved, but this was to no avail.

The Soviet Union invades Afghanistan

On 24 December 1979, Soviet troops began crossing into Afghanistan; three days later Soviet paratroopers stormed the government headquarters and carried out a bloody coup. Amin was killed, and the moderate pro-Soviet Babrak Karmal was installed at the head of a new regime. By January of 1980, Moscow had 85,000 troops helping to stabilize the situation, bolster the new government, and crush the Afghan revolt.

The Kremlin's actions were mainly designed to salvage its recent gains in Afghanistan and make the best of a bad situation. Amin's brutal rule had discredited Communism among Afghans while igniting a massive rebellion. By replacing him with the more prudent Karmal, and by applying overwhelming force, Moscow hoped to be able to disarm the opposition and quickly defeat the rebels. The intervention might well bring an international outcry, as had the earlier Soviet invasions of Hungary and Czechoslovakia, but this seemed preferable to watching its Afghan clients be overthrown and replaced by hostile forces. Besides, experience indicated that the clamor would eventually die down.

Of all the miscalculations of the Brezhnev regime, this was the most calamitous. The Afghanistan invasion turned out to be a disaster of the first magnitude for the USSR. Karmal, though less radical, proved no more popular than Amin, and the vast influx of Soviet forces served only to unite all rebel factions against him. The Kremlin's reputation for heavy-handed brutality was greatly enhanced, and its credibility in the Third World was seriously strained—especially when it clumsily tried to claim that it had been "invited" to intervene by the Afghans and that Amin had been conspiring with the Muslims and the CIA. As time went on, even its military prestige was diminished by its inability to bring the war to a successful conclusion. For the next decade, Soviet troops would be tied down in a bloody, dispiriting, hopeless war against Afghan guerrillas armed with zealous Muslim faith and Western-supplied weapons. As the Soviet economy staggered, valuable resources were siphoned off by the long, debilitating conflict. And the USSR, which looked to be the essence of indomitable power and control, would last only a dozen more years.

The Soviet miscalculation proves disastrous

15

The Return of the Cold War, 1980–1985

The Cold War, having thawed a bit in the 1970s, returned with full frigidity in the early 1980s. In 1980, the United States responded to the Soviet war in Afghanistan by cutting off grain and technology sales to the USSR, boycotting the Moscow Olympics, and substantially boosting its military spending. That same year, Americans elected a new president who was a committed Cold Warrior, vigorously opposed to détente and inherently distrustful of what he called the "evil empire." Relations degenerated as each side sought to enhance its military capabilities, discredit the other's reputation, and gain the upper hand in the Third World. Not until 1985, when a new generation of leaders came to power in Moscow, would there again be significant progress in East–West relations.

THE DEMISE OF DÉTENTE

The Soviet invasion of Afghanistan in late 1979 cut the ground from under U.S. backers of détente and drove a final nail into its coffin. President Jimmy Carter, who had earlier worked to improve relations with Moscow, denounced the invasion (Document 68A) and said it had made "a more dramatic change in my opinion of what the Soviets' ultimate goals are than anything they've done in the previous time I've been in office" (Document 68B). It also prompted a drastic change in his policies. On 3 January 1980, he asked the Senate to defer consideration of the SALT II treaty, effectively shelving the cornerstone of détente. The following day he declared that he was imposing sanctions against sales of grain and electronic technology to the USSR, restricting Soviet fishing rights in American waters, and taking other punitive steps. Later he organized a 60-nation boycott of the 1980 Olympic Summer Games in Moscow.

Carter reacts vehemently to Soviet invasion of Afghanistan

Carter's actions were fueled not only by indignation but also by concerns that the attack on Afghanistan was part of a larger Soviet strategy designed to gain access to the Indian Ocean and the Persian Gulf, which he feared would enable Moscow to disrupt the Western world's oil shipments.

Carter Doctrine declares Persian Gulf a vital U.S. interest

Thus, in his State of the Union message on 23 January 1980, he announced what came to be called the Carter Doctrine (Document 69). Henceforth, he declared, "an attempt by any outside force to gain control of the Persian Gulf will be regarded as an assault on the vital interests of the United States of America, and . . . will be repelled by any means necessary, including military force." He also took steps to increase U.S. military preparedness, including a renewal of draft registration and substantial increases in defense spending. He promised military and economic aid to Pakistan, Afghanistan's neighbor, through which America would secretly funnel aid to the anti-Soviet Afghan rebels. And in July, following a lengthy review of U.S. global strategy, he signed a presidential directive (PD-59) that seemed to shift U.S. emphasis from deterring nuclear war to planning to fight and win one. Although PD-59 was classified, its basic thrust was leaked to the press as a signal to Moscow and others of Carter's tough new approach.

The president also hoped that taking such strong measures would shore up his political position. In April, he authorized an attempt to rescue the American hostages in Tehran, but the White House aborted it after eight U.S. soldiers were killed in a helicopter-airplane accident in the Iranian desert. That summer, Carter overcame a serious challenge from Senator Edward Kennedy and won renomination as the Democratic candidate for president, while Ronald Reagan emerged as his Republican opponent. Foreign policy concerns, including a growing perception of Soviet belligerence and U.S. impotence, promised to play a huge role in the upcoming campaign.

Foreign policy plays key role in 1980 U.S. elections

Then, as the campaign began, Iran and Iraq went to war. The conflict grew out of an Iraqi dream of unifying the Arab world under Baghdad's leadership, along with concerns about Iran's Islamic fundamentalism, which threatened Iraqi president Saddam Hussein's secular regime. In September 1980, Saddam accused Iran of violating a 1975 treaty that guaranteed Iraq access to the Persian Gulf through the Shatt al-Arab waterway. Using this issue as a pretext for war, he hoped for quick victory over a nation at odds with its longtime American protector: With its U.S. assets frozen, he figured, Iran would be unable to get spare parts for its American-made jets and tanks. For his part, Iran's new leader, the Ayatollah Khomeini, hoped to weaken Iraq by appealing to its Islamic fundamentalists. Both would be disappointed.

Iraq attacks Iran in 1980, starting a deadly eight-year war

The war lasted eight years and cost the lives of over a million Iraqis and perhaps two million Iranians, as each side wreaked havoc on the other's oil pipelines and refineries. Jordan, Saudi Arabia, Egypt, and Kuwait supported Iraq, while Libya and Syria backed Iran. Islamic fundamentalism, seen as a threat by Iraq and its backers, was also a factor in the 1981 assassination of Egypt's Sadat. Moscow opportunistically sold arms to both sides but eventually veered toward Iran. Israel weighed in by sending warplanes to destroy an Iraqi nuclear reactor in 1981. In an effort to balance the scales, the United States supplied Iraq with weapons and intelligence data, but otherwise played both ends against the middle throughout the long war, which ended in 1988 with a modest Iraqi victory.

Superpowers each seek to exploit Iran–Iraq War

The wars in Afghanistan, Iran, and Iraq left East–West relations in shambles. Brezhnev's long search for international respect and economic stability, as well as his efforts to end the Cold War, had been sacrificed to the Kremlin's compulsion for solving its problems with force, especially in Afghanistan. By failing to show restraint, either in its strategic buildup or in its Third World ventures, Moscow had persistently embarrassed its Western friends and played into the hands of its foes. Nowhere was this dynamic more apparent than in the case of Jimmy Carter, who initially had wanted to work with the Kremlin to create a more peaceful world.

Carter's forceful response to the Soviets was not enough to save his presidency. Faced with a faltering economy and a leader who seemed powerless either to get the Soviets out of Afghanistan or to end the hostage crisis, Americans rejected Carter's reelection bid in November 1980. Instead they elected an unabashed hard-liner who believed that détente was a major mistake and was determined to stand up forcefully to the Soviet regime.

THE REAGAN REVOLUTION

Reagan's strident anti-Communism heralds new U.S. era

When he came to the White House in January 1981, Ronald Reagan brought a sunny disposition, an abiding faith in the goodness of America, a visceral dislike of Communism, and an aggressive approach to world affairs. A former movie actor, he often tended to blur the lines between fiction and reality and to simplify complex issues into contests between right and wrong. At the same time, he possessed a remarkable knack for lifting people's spirits and projecting an image of optimism and confidence, qualities that would make him one of the Cold War's most popular and effective politicians.

Reagan and His Aides.

Ronald Reagan, who began his term in 1981 as the most stridently anti-Communist Cold War president, is seen here conversing in the White House with key aides later in his term. After rejecting détente and pursuing a renewed arms race with the USSR in an effort to secure U.S. superiority and bankrupt the Soviet system, Reagan later moved from confrontation to cooperation with Moscow.

The Brezhnev regime, frustrated by the vacillations and inconsistencies of U.S. policy in the Carter years, was guardedly hopeful that Reagan would prove a tough-minded yet pragmatic Republican in the Nixon mold. It was in for a big disappointment. Reagan quickly jettisoned Carter's human rights approach, which the Kremlin found so annoying, but he replaced it with a fervent and impassioned anti-Communism that tended to reduce superpower relations to a global struggle between good and evil. In a press conference nine days after he took office, he depicted the Soviet leaders as dishonorable rogues bent on world domination who would "reserve unto themselves the right to commit any crime, to lie, to cheat, in order to attain their goal" (Document 70A). Two years later, in the most widely quoted speech of his presidency, he called the USSR an "evil empire" and said it was "the focus of evil in the modern world" (Document 70B).

The new administration thus differed sharply from the previous three. Rather than trying to control the arms race, Reagan's advisors wanted to intensify it. Some, including Secretary of Defense Caspar Weinberger and Assistant Secretary Richard Perle, saw arms pacts with Moscow as inherently detrimental to U.S. interests. They felt that such treaties lulled the West into complacency, legitimized Soviet behavior, and limited the United States more than the USSR, since Moscow would invariably cheat. A renewed arms race, they contended, might further strain the Kremlin's resources, weaken the Soviet economy, and undermine the Soviet system. In their view, whatever helped the USSR was bad for America, and whatever hurt it was good. To them détente bordered on unilateral disarmament, and the time had come to rearm.

Reagan denounces détente and renews arms race

So Reagan's first priority was to expand the U.S. arsenal. Defense spending, substantially raised during Carter's last year, was boosted further by Reagan, and Weinberger firmly resisted any effort to trim it. They reintroduced weapons, such as the B-1 bomber, shelved by the Carter administration, and intensified existing arms programs. Over the next five years, the Pentagon went on a spending spree, investing billions in programs such as "Stealth" aircraft (supposedly "invisible" to enemy radar), air- and ground-launched cruise missiles, the Trident submarine and its D-5 missiles, the Pershing II intermediate-range missile, and the MX ICBM.

Among these weapons, the MX (which Reagan called the "Peacekeeper") raised some peculiar problems. In a bid to win military support for SALT II, Carter had reluctantly approved this highly accurate and powerful ICBM that could carry ten nuclear warheads. However, since fixed land-based missiles were theoretically susceptible to a Soviet first strike, there was much debate about where and how to deploy it. Various elaborate schemes were advanced to make MX missiles less vulnerable, including plans for making them mobile by placing them on railway trains, but none proved practical or cost effective. Finally, after several years, the Reagan administration decided simply to base the new missiles in converted Minuteman silos, tacitly admitting that the "window of vulnerability" (Chapter 14) was not a serious concern.

A second priority was to counteract Soviet Third World inroads by providing support for anti-Communist regimes, whatever their human rights record, and covert sponsorship of revolts against Soviet client states. The Reagan approach involved overlooking abuses and atrocities by U.S. friends and patrons in Chile, El Salvador, Pakistan, South Africa, the Philippines, and elsewhere, as long as the regimes

The MX "Peacekeeper" Missile. Capable of carrying ten nuclear warheads that could each hit a separate Soviet target, the MX (for "Missile Experimental") was a key component of Reagan's massive arms buildup. Initially intended to be mobile, so it could potentially be moved to survive a Soviet strike, it was eventually deployed in stationary underground silos, after various mobile basing schemes proved controversial and impractical.

Reagan team aids anti-Communist regimes and revolts

remained rigidly anti-Soviet. Meanwhile, the CIA supplied arms and money to insurgent "freedom fighters" in places such as Afghanistan, Angola, Ethiopia, and Nicaragua—and even to Cambodian rebels, despite the fact that their forces included the murderous Khmer Rouge. Such policies did help counter Soviet influence, but they also undercut the U.S. image as a champion of democracy, legality, and human rights.

This approach was most evident in Central America, where a leftist insurgency in El Salvador and the socialist Sandinista movement in Nicaragua raised fears of new Soviet inroads. Carter had tried to save the Nicaraguan dictatorship of Anastasio Somoza, but continued sending U.S. aid to that country after the Sandinistas overthrew him in 1979. When Reagan took over, he claimed that Central America was the major target of Soviet Cold War expansionism. There was no definitive evidence to support this claim, but Moscow clearly did send military aid to leftists in El Salvador and Nicaragua. The Reagan administration responded by organizing and equipping the Contra rebels, a Honduras-based military force bent on ousting the Sandinistas. The resulting civil war ruined the Nicaraguan economy, eventually leading to the Sandinistas' defeat in a free election in 1990. Under Reagan, the United States also gave substantive aid to El Salvador, disregarding grave human rights abuses by that country's armed forces.

Reagan calls for arms reduction, not just limitation

Despite his confrontational attitude, however, Reagan could be pragmatic in dealing with the USSR. He lifted Carter's grain embargo, largely in deference to domestic political and economic concerns. He adhered to the general terms of the unratified SALT II treaty, despite his disdain for that pact, since the Pentagon feared that its renunciation might lead to an unrestrained Soviet arms buildup. And, although he toughened the U.S. stance, Reagan continued arms control talks with Moscow. In the INF discussions, he put forth a "zero-option" plan calling for elimination of all Soviet intermediate-range missiles (especially the mobile SS-20s) in return for cancellation of NATO's planned deployment of cruise missiles and Pershing IIs (Document 71). In strategic weapons talks, he transformed SALT into START (Strategic Arms *Reduction* Talks) and advocated sweeping cuts in the number of missile warheads permitted each side. Critics charged, with some justification, that these were propaganda ploys rather than serious proposals, since they were heavily weighted against the USSR. And the Soviets indeed treated them as such. But Reagan, to the dismay of some of his advisors, had a genuine desire for drastic arms reduction. Several years later, in a much different climate, these proposals would serve as the basis for fruitful and productive negotiations.

Reagan warns of Soviet power but predicts Communist demise

There was, in fact, a dichotomy in Reagan's approach. On one hand, to justify his arms buildup and aggressive Third World policies, he portrayed the USSR as a fearsome colossus that was steadily increasing its military might and influence in the Third World. On the other hand, he doubted the Soviet system's viability and did not believe it could successfully compete with the West. Indeed, in March 1983, he prophetically dismissed Communism as a "sad, bizarre chapter in history whose last pages are even now being written" (Document 70B).

THE END OF THE BREZHNEV ERA

Brezhnev's last years hurt by Afghan War and economic stagnation

The latter depiction proved closer to the truth. By the early 1980s, the USSR had become a bumbling giant ruled by a gerontocracy of aging and infirm leaders who had increasingly lost confidence in their system. Brezhnev, who could barely stand without support, continued to preside over a grossly inefficient economy and a vast bureaucracy rife with cronyism and corruption. Bogged down in Afghanistan and locked into a crippling new contest with the Americans, the Soviet Union drifted into the deadening "period of stagnation" that characterized the last few years of the Brezhnev era.

Solidarity union emerges in Poland but is banned by martial law

The Soviets maintained control in Eastern Europe, but not without difficulty. In summer 1980, during an economic crisis, a genuine workers' movement arose in Poland, creating an independent trade union called Solidarity. Over the next year, it grew increasingly popular and bold, organizing strikes and demonstrations and pressing for democratic reforms as well as economic concessions. As the situation deteriorated and Poland drifted into disarray, Moscow got increasingly alarmed. Fearful that the Polish Communists were losing their grip and that the unrest might spread throughout Eastern Europe, the Soviets held military exercises along the Polish border and hinted they might intervene. NATO warned Moscow to stay out, and by fall of 1981, a potential crisis loomed. But the Kremlin, with uncharacteristic sophistication, got the Polish authorities to resolve the problem themselves. In December 1981, Poland's Communist leader, General Wojciech Jaruzelski, declared martial law and cracked down on Solidarity, arresting its leaders and later outlawing the union (Documents 72A and 72B). In the West, a frustrated Reagan could do little more than impose economic sanctions on Poland and the USSR, while asking Americans to put candles in their windows as a sign of support for the Poles.

MAP 12 Cold War Confrontations in Latin America, 1950s–1980s.
Although Marxist thinking made inroads throughout Latin America, and various Cold War clashes affected Central America and the Caribbean, Soviet influence in South America was small. An elected Marxist regime ruled Chile from 1970 to1973, and Argentina fought Britain for the Falkland Islands in 1982, but these places were too remote from Moscow for it to have any real impact.

Martial law in Poland helped Moscow escape from an awkward situation, but it did not solve the underlying problem. Throughout 1982, the Polish economy deteriorated further, and U.S. sanctions only made matters worse. The USSR, already strapped by its own feeble economy and its ongoing war in Afghanistan, was compelled to drain its own scarce resources to prop up the staggering Poles. Whatever its political and strategic benefits, the maintenance of such client regimes was a serious economic liability for the USSR.

Meanwhile, its incursions in the Third World were beginning to look more like defensive operations to sustain its sagging influence, or opportunistic efforts to exploit local rivalries, than elements of a coordinated quest for world domination. The USSR realized few lasting gains from the Iran–Iraq War, despite its attempts to meddle, and it prudently chose not to intervene in the short Falklands War between Britain and Argentina in 1982 (Map 12, page 229). In the latter conflict, the ruling Argentine military junta, having been led by American UN ambassador Jeane Kirkpatrick to believe that Washington would back its claims to the British-held Falkland Islands (which Argentina called the Malvinas), invaded those islands in April. When the Reagan administration instead supported Britain's counterattack with all aid short of war, the junta asked Moscow for help, holding out promises of favorable credit terms for sales of Argentine wheat to the USSR. But the concept of Soviet troops landing on remote south Atlantic islands to fight the British would have been ludicrous even had the Soviet army not been bogged down in the deepening Afghan quagmire. Britain won the war, the Argentine junta fell, and the Kremlin remained aloof.

Soviets stay out of Falklands War as Britain defeats Argentina

Moscow also suffered a serious loss of face in the Middle East that year, when it failed to aid the PLO during an Israeli invasion of Lebanon designed to eradicate the Palestinian presence there (Map 10,page 200). Worse still, its reputation as a weapons provider was badly tarnished when Israeli pilots in American-made planes easily destroyed numerous aircraft, tanks, and weapons supplied by the Soviets to Arab friends. Thus, although Israel was soon compelled to withdraw, and although 239 U.S. soldiers sent to Lebanon to keep the peace were killed the next year by a terrorist bomb, Moscow could draw little comfort from the Lebanese conflict.

Israeli invasion of Lebanon shows Soviet Mideast weakness

THE ANDROPOV OFFENSIVE

On 7 November 1982, the 65th anniversary of the Bolshevik Revolution, Brezhnev stood as usual atop the Lenin Mausoleum, reviewing the endless military parades in the cold, damp Moscow weather. Three days later he was dead. The last year of his life had been marred by a serious scandal affecting members of his family, by a minor stroke that left him increasingly feeble, and by a backstage power struggle among those who hoped to succeed him.

The winner of that struggle was Yuri Andropov. As longtime head of the Committee on State Security (KGB), the Soviet police apparatus, Andropov had earned a reputation as an effective, innovative, and sophisticated administrator. Flexible, intelligent, and direct, he might have made a very effective general secretary had he come to power sooner. But by the time he reached the top, he was 68 years old and in poor health. In domestic affairs, he sought to instill more

Brezhnev's funeral, November 1982. The death of Leonid Brezhnev, who had served as the main Soviet leader since 1964, set the stage for significant changes in Soviet leadership and policies. His pallbearers included his two immediate successors, Yuri Andropov and Konstantin Chernenko, pictured with his casket on the right side of this photo.

discipline and efficiency into the Soviet system, cracking down on the corruption and absenteeism that had plagued the Brezhnev economy, and granting more autonomy to local industrial managers. He was blocked, however, by the inertia and stagnation of the immense Soviet bureaucracy and by his own kidney failure. He lasted only fifteen months in office.

Andropov succeeds Brezhnev, seeks to reform Soviet system

On the international scene, Andropov at first sought to improve relations with both China and the West. In neither case did he achieve much success. Adopting a conciliatory tone toward China, he reopened low-level talks with Beijing early in 1983, following through on an initiative begun under Brezhnev. These talks made some progress in expanding trade but brought little improvement in the political climate between the two countries. The Chinese refused to improve relations with Moscow as long as there were still Soviet troops in Afghanistan, Vietnamese forces in Cambodia, and a massive Soviet military presence along China's border.

Andropov tries but fails to improve relations with China

Toward the West, Andropov launched a "peace offensive," hoping to revive the stalled arms talks and head off the scheduled deployment of new U.S. missiles in Europe. Fearful that Reagan was actually out to destroy the USSR, Andropov sought to impede him by exploiting a growing peace movement in Western Europe and America. Here he was inadvertently aided by Reagan and his advisors, whose rapid arms buildup and aggressive rhetoric not only terrified Andropov, but also led many in the West to regard them as reckless, trigger-happy cowboys.

Andropov's peace offensive exploits peace movement in the West

In the early 1980s, as détente disappeared and the arms buildup accelerated, fears of a nuclear holocaust returned with full force. Films such as *The Day After*, depicting nuclear war and its impact, heightened U.S. public anxiety. A grassroots "nuclear freeze" campaign, calling for an end to all new nuclear weapons, arose

Films and freeze movement fuel Western fears of nuclear war

across America, gaining broad support. In May 1983, the U.S. House of Representatives passed a "freeze" resolution (Document 75), and American Catholic bishops published a pastoral letter calling nuclear arms immoral. In Western Europe, protests challenged the planned deployment of U.S. Pershing II and cruise missiles, slated for the end of 1983. The "Greens," a political party that intensely opposed this deployment, garnered support in Germany, buttressed by antinuclear demonstrations in numerous places.

Andropov's peace initiative sought to exploit such sentiments. In late 1982, he advanced new arms control proposals, seeming to show new flexibility in Moscow's position (Document 73). In START negotiations, he called on both sides to cut strategic missiles by 25 percent and to reduce significantly the number of nuclear warheads. In INF talks, he offered to decrease the number of Soviet intermediate-range missiles to equal the combined total of French and British missiles, in return for cancelation of the planned U.S. deployment. Like Reagan's "zero option," these offers aimed to influence public opinion while maintaining the proposer's overall advantage. Still, they showed a Soviet willingness to discuss *reductions* rather than limitations.

Andropov's public relations campaign welcomes U.S. girl in Moscow

Andropov followed these proposals with a public relations campaign, designed to portray the Reagan team as warmongers and win sympathy for Moscow in the Western peace movement. Speaking at Prague in January 1983, he adroitly identified with the "forces of peace" and called for a new East–West nonaggression pact by which both sides would forswear first use of nuclear or conventional weapons. In February, letters to Andropov from concerned U.S. citizens began appearing in the Soviet press. In April, Samantha Smith, an American girl who had written one of these letters, was invited to visit the USSR, and in July her Soviet hosts warmly and publicly received her.

Western leaders rebuff Andropov's efforts, support INF deployment

Andropov's peace offensive nonetheless came to naught, as Western leaders resisted peace movement pressures. In March, despite ill-concealed Soviet efforts to sway the election against him, conservative Christian Democrat Helmut Kohl was reaffirmed as West German chancellor. In May, the heads of the seven leading industrial democracies (Britain, France, Germany, Italy, Japan, Canada, and the United States) met at Williamsburg, Virginia, and endorsed NATO's decision to deploy U.S. Pershing II and cruise missiles. In June, Prime Minister Margaret Thatcher's Conservatives won a clear majority in the British House of Commons. Indeed, by raising the specter of outside influence, Soviet efforts to exploit the peace movement may actually have helped the hardliners. At any rate, whatever their private misgivings about Reagan, NATO leaders refused to let internal and external pressures disrupt alliance solidarity.

THE STRATEGIC DEFENSE INITIATIVE

Another reason for the peace offensive's failure was Ronald Reagan's unique dream. In March 1983, he suddenly announced, to the surprise of many of his advisors, a project to create an elaborate space-based weapons system designed to intercept enemy ICBMs. "What if free people," he asked in a televised address, "could rest secure in the knowledge . . . that we could intercept and destroy strategic ballistic missiles before they reached our own soil or that of our allies?" (Document 74).

Keying in to the fears that had spawned the nuclear freeze movement, he challenged U.S. scientists to develop new technologies to make nuclear weapons "impotent and obsolete." Although Reagan called this project his "Strategic Defense Initiative," it soon became known as "Star Wars," after a popular American movie series in which the forces of good used futuristic space technology to combat an evil empire.

Reagan proposes space-based SDI to end ICBM threat

The Strategic Defense Initiative, or SDI, raised some serious problems. There was no guarantee such a system would work, at least as the president envisioned it. Using advanced technologies, scientists might design weapons that could shoot down missiles, but there was no way to make them foolproof, and the few hostile missiles that would get through could still do incalculable damage. And there was nothing to stop a sophisticated adversary from inventing weapons to frustrate or destroy SDI components. For such reasons, knowledgeable supporters of SDI saw it not as an impenetrable shield for the entire country but rather as a more limited system for defending land-based missiles against a surprise attack.

Another problem with SDI was that it violated the spirit, if not the letter, of the ABM treaty. For more than a decade, that 1972 agreement had been a cornerstone of arms control and a bulwark of mutual deterrence. Now, by reopening the question of missile defense, Reagan called into question the whole basis of East–West discussions. And the president's offer to "share" this technology, while apparently sincere, was so widely at variance with traditional U.S. behavior that Moscow did not take it seriously. For the next five years, Reagan's "shield" would hang like a sword over the arms control process.

From the Soviets' perspective, the biggest fear was that SDI could negate their strategic deterrent. A U.S. president, armed with such a system, might be tempted to launch a preemptive strike against Soviet ICBMs, knowing that SDI could protect America against a counterattack by Moscow if some of its missiles survived the U.S. strike. And America would not need to attack in order to gain the edge: When two gunslingers face each other, even if neither intends to shoot, the one with an effective shield has a big psychological advantage. Besides, although Soviet scientists discounted the possibility of a foolproof missile defense, SDI renewed Moscow's fears about U.S. technology. Time and again, from A-bomb to MIRV to cruise missile, the Soviets had seen their monumental efforts to gain parity and security frustrated by Western technological advances. If Star Wars could be made to work, they would again be vulnerable.

Soviets fear SDI will leave them vulnerable to U.S. attack

From Reagan's perspective, however, SDI supplied several key benefits. By promising to end the threat of nuclear war, it disarmed his critics in the peace movement. It helped him answer Andropov's peace offensive without making major concessions on either strategic arms or INF deployment. It replaced his "reckless cowboy" image with that of a visionary, albeit one who would rely on technology to resolve human relations problems. And it gave him a pathway to peace that America could pursue on its own, without relying on cooperation with Communists, whom he deeply distrusted.

SDI disarms Reagan's critics by positioning him as peace advocate

The Kremlin's response to SDI was as harsh as it was predictable. Andropov blasted it as a U.S. bid to "disarm the Soviet Union," and then he launched a new campaign to discredit it. He enlisted Soviet scientists, who published an appeal to their colleagues everywhere to oppose SDI. He advocated intensified arms control efforts, hoping to preclude both SDI research and INF deployment. And, meeting with a U.S. delegation in August 1983, he called for total demilitarization of outer space, including a ban on all space-based weapons.

THE KAL INCIDENT AND THE GRENADA INVASION

Andropov's efforts were soon undercut by portentous developments. One was his own illness: By fall 1983, he disappeared from public view, a victim of the kidney disease that later took his life. Another was a tragic incident in the skies near the Soviet island of Sakhalin, just north of Japan. A third was the U.S. invasion of a tiny Caribbean island.

On 1 September 1983, a South Korean airliner, KAL flight 007, veered off course during a scheduled flight between America and South Korea (Document 76). It flew through Soviet airspace, passing over a sensitive missile and submarine base, until it was shot down by a Soviet pilot who evidently thought it was a spy plane. All 269 persons aboard were killed. The downing of the passenger aircraft and killing of innocent civilians brought a wave of international outrage against the USSR. Reagan accused the Kremlin of an act of "barbarism" and used the incident as a further justification for his weapons buildup. Moscow refused to accept the blame and, when it finally admitted responsibility, accused the United States of precipitating the incident by using a civilian plane for an espionage mission. Each side blasted the other, and Andropov finally issued a statement saying that all illusions about Reagan's policy were dispelled "once and for all."

Soviets shoot down South Korean airliner flying through their space

The next month, U.S. invasion of the Caribbean island nation of Grenada (Map 8) further poisoned international relations. It came in response to the overthrow of the Marxist New Jewel Movement by an even more radical Marxist group. Cuban engineers and construction workers were building an immense airfield on the island, and Washington distrusted their intentions. In October 1983, the Reagan administration sent U.S. Marines and Rangers to Grenada, defeating a small force of Cuban troops and installing a provisional government. The attack, which was carried out quickly, deposed the Marxist regime with only verbal protests from Moscow, similar to the protests Washington raised whenever the Soviets moved against Eastern Europe.

The United States invades Grenada to oust Marxist regime

These developments ended hopes for progress in arms control talks, at least in the short run. In November, the deployment of U.S. cruise and Pershing II missiles began as scheduled in Britain and Germany. The Soviets responded, as promised, by breaking off the INF talks in Geneva, and shortly thereafter the START negotiations recessed indefinitely. By the end of 1983, superpower relations seemed to have reached a new low.

Americans begin INF deployment; Soviets break off arms talks

THE ENCORE OF THE SOVIET OLD GUARD

Toward the end of 1983, as his health declined, Andropov began making personnel changes to ensure his legacy, promoting younger, reform-minded officials to positions of increased responsibility. In the process, he evidently sought to secure the succession of his dynamic young protégé, Mikhail Gorbachev, as the main Soviet leader. But Andropov did not live long enough to achieve his goal: On 9 February 1984, he succumbed to his illness. Four days later an old Brezhnev crony, Konstantin Chernenko, became general secretary of the Soviet Communist Party. In an apparent compromise between the old guard and the younger generation, Gorbachev acquired the position of second secretary, making him second in command.

Chernenko was the oldest and least capable of the Soviet Cold War leaders. A man of modest ability and limited vision, he had risen in the party ranks through hard work and dogged loyalty to Brezhnev, his longtime patron and friend. During Brezhnev's last years, Chernenko had played a major role, propping up the infirm leader in public and conducting business for him behind the scenes. Now, at age 72, Chernenko had reached the pinnacle of his career, but he had neither the energy nor ambition to revitalize the Soviet system. Caution and prudence were the keywords of his watch. To some extent, then, his accession brought a return to the stagnation and drift of the last Brezhnev years and a short-lived resurgence of the old guard. Still, he did not seek to undo all of Andropov's reforms, merely to slow the pace.

Chernenko succeeds Andropov in encore of Brezhnev's old guard

For most of Chernenko's brief tenure as party boss, the Soviet approach toward world affairs remained rigid and unimaginative. The war in Afghanistan continued with no end in sight, and Moscow reinforced its commitment to the Jaruzelski regime in Poland with a fifteen-year economic pact. Despite occasional glimmers of flexibility, intransigence reigned in dealings with the West, and relations with China did not improve. Unlike Andropov, who sought to enhance Soviet ties with the world's most populous Communist country, Chernenko was cool toward China, especially as the climate warmed between Washington and Beijing.

Initially U.S.–Chinese relations suffered under Reagan, due to his sympathy for Taiwan and antipathy toward Communists. But as U.S. relations with the USSR worsened, Reagan and his aides began to see Beijing as a counterpoise against Moscow. In 1982, they took a step toward reconciliation by agreeing to gradually reduce arms sales to Taiwan, a major bone of contention between Washington and Beijing. During 1983, a number of key U.S. officials went to China, and the atmosphere began to improve. But the most dramatic developments came in 1984, when Chinese premier Zhao Ziyang made a state visit to Washington in January, and President Reagan responded with a trip to Beijing in April. These visits brought no major accords, but they did restore the momentum of U.S.–Chinese rapprochement. And they also made great theater, giving Reagan a statesmanlike aura and enhancing his status in the upcoming presidential campaign.

U.S.–Chinese relations improved by Reagan and Zhao Ziyang

Although Chinese officials politely but firmly rebuffed the president's bid to enlist their support against Moscow, the Kremlin was clearly displeased by the Reagan visit. In May, shortly after the president left Beijing, Moscow issued a statement denouncing China for its role in a border clash with Vietnam while he was there. A few days later, the Soviets disclosed that an impending trip to China by First Deputy Prime Minister Ivan Arkhipov had been postponed.

Meanwhile, Soviet–American relations further deteriorated. Hoping that Reagan might lose the upcoming U.S. elections, the Kremlin tried to avoid doing anything that might improve international relations and thus boost his reelection bid. START and INF talks remained suspended, as the Soviets resisted efforts by their

U.S.–Soviet relations decline; Soviets boycott 1984 Olympics

unruly ally, Romania's Nicolae Ceausescu, to get them to moderate their stance. Unless the Americans removed their new missiles from Western Europe, insisted Moscow, no negotiations were possible. In May, the "deep freeze" in East–West relations was intensified by the announcement that Soviet and Eastern European athletes would not attend the Olympic Summer Games in Los Angeles. Although Moscow attributed this decision to concerns for the athletes' safety, few doubted that it was a retaliation against Reagan's anti-Soviet policies and Carter's boycott of the 1980 Moscow games.

In August, a bizarre incident added to the strain between Moscow and Washington. Playfully testing his sound equipment before a radio broadcast, Reagan announced that he had "just signed legislation which outlaws Russia forever," adding that "the bombing begins in five minutes." Journalists overheard this odd statement and reported it widely. Moscow replied by blasting the president's irresponsible conduct and blatant hostility toward the USSR. The episode had few lasting repercussions, but it did highlight Reagan's "recklessness," the Kremlin's sensitivity, and the deplorable state of U.S.–Soviet relations.

Reagan's reelection in 1984 seems to signal continued Cold War

If the Soviets believed that such incidents, combined with heightened world tensions, would damage the president's reelection chances, their hopes were in vain. Reagan's standing in the polls remained high, and he recovered from a lackluster performance in his first televised debate by seeming strong and self-assured in his second. In November, he was returned to office by a wide margin. On the surface, the prospects for easing anxieties seemed dim.

Behind the scenes, however, things were starting to change. Alarmed, perhaps, by the KAL 007 affair and by Pentagon preparations for nuclear war, in 1984 Reagan began altering his approach. Distressed that peace rested mainly on fears of mutual assured destruction, fearful that Moscow might mistake his motives as aggressive, and concerned that a misunderstanding between superpowers could lead to catastrophe, he toned down his anti-Soviet rhetoric and became more open to negotiations and meetings with Soviet leaders.

Led by Gorbachev, younger leaders rise in the USSR

Meanwhile, in the Kremlin, as aging Soviet leaders grew increasingly feeble, younger and more flexible ones became more assertive and visible. In December 1984, Mikhail Gorbachev made a highly publicized visit to Britain, where he spoke with apparent authority. It was he, not Chernenko, who that month announced the death of Soviet defense minister Dmitri Ustinov, and it was Gorbachev who led mourners at the burial rites. A few months later, the young second secretary made another trip abroad, this time to West Germany. Chernenko, whose health was rapidly failing, largely disappeared from public view.

A perceptible change in Moscow's foreign policy accompanied Gorbachev's growing visibility. Once they saw that Reagan would be reelected, the Soviets moderated their tone and tried to make the best of things. Late in 1984, they launched a new peace offensive, designed to mend fences with both China and the West. In December, First Deputy Prime Minister Arkhipov made his long-delayed trip to Beijing, becoming the highest Soviet official to visit China in more than fifteen years. That same month, in Britain, Gorbachev cleverly reminded his listeners that he and they shared a "common European home," suggesting that their relations should not depend on what happened in Washington. He expanded this theme on his subsequent German trip.

In January 1985, after a year of posturing and probing, the Soviets consented to resume the arms control talks. Bowing to reality, they dropped their insistence that Washington first remove its newly installed missiles from Europe. The two sides agreed also to discuss space-based weapons, along with intermediate-range missiles and strategic arms, and to begin the new talks on 12 March 1985. The day before they opened, word came from Moscow that Konstantin Chernenko had died the previous evening.

Soviets launch new peace offensive, resume arms control talks

Chernenko's death marked the passing of the generation of Soviet leaders who rose in the ranks under Stalin, shaped by the searing experiences of industrialization, collectivization, and World War II. Obsessed with security and control, they had built the USSR into a military colossus of awesome power and strength, while maintaining tight constraints over domestic society. In so doing they had relied on a vast, stultifying bureaucracy that both secured their power and stifled creativity. Waiting in the wings was a new generation, unencumbered by the presentiments of their predecessors and prepared to change the way Moscow did business. A new day was dawning in the Kremlin, and in the Cold War.

Chernenko's death ends era, new generation takes charge

16

The Thaw in the Cold War, 1985–1988

The selection of Mikhail Gorbachev as general secretary of the Soviet Communist Party in March 1985 marked a turning point in the Cold War. Representing a new generation of Soviet leaders, Gorbachev soon showed that he was ready to reform the Soviet system, reduce military forces, ease international tensions, and hold talks with U.S. leaders about serious arms reductions. His goals coincided in many ways with those of Ronald Reagan, who by then had toned down his earlier anti-Soviet rhetoric and was eager to reduce the risk of nuclear war. In the next few years the Americans and Soviets, led by these two very different men, took major steps toward reversing the arms race and ending the Cold War.

THE DAWN OF THE GORBACHEV ERA

On 11 March 1985, only hours after the announcement that Konstantin Chernenko had died, the Soviet news agency reported the selection of Mikhail Gorbachev as the next general secretary. Longtime foreign minister Andrei Gromyko gave a strong nominating speech praising Gorbachev's intelligence, vigor, organizational skill, and strength. "This man has a nice smile," Gromyko allegedly remarked, "but he has iron teeth."

Reform-minded Gorbachev becomes Soviet leader

Gorbachev was 54 years old when he became general secretary, making him the youngest Soviet leader since Malenkov. Born in a farming village in south central Russia, as a youth he had experienced both the rigors of physical labor and the trauma of the Nazi invasion. A gifted student, he attended law school at Moscow State University in the early 1950s and then returned to his native province, where he began working his way up through the ranks of the Communist Youth League and the Communist Party. Talented, energetic, and articulate, he possessed supreme self-confidence and mental agility that made him a standout among local party officials. A devoted Leninist, he was nonetheless offended by the police state brutality of the Stalin years and thus sympathetic to the reform-minded, humanizing policies of Khrushchev.

Although Gorbachev had less use for the Brezhnev regime, he was circumspect enough to play along with the system in order to advance his career. In the 1970s, he attracted the attention of several high officials, including future party boss Andropov, and in 1978 he was summoned to Moscow to serve as party secretary in charge of agriculture. Two years later he joined the Politburo, the party's main policy-making body, and in 1982 he supported Andropov's bid to become general secretary. He was groomed as Andropov's successor, but his patron's early death delayed his succession, and he was obliged to bide his time during Chernenko's brief rule. Now Gorbachev's turn had come, and he was ready to move.

The situation he inherited was critical. Over the preceding two decades, as military costs ate up a huge share of the Soviet budget, the economic growth rate had declined. The industrial equipment and transportation system had grown increasingly outmoded. Productivity was low, consumer goods were in short supply, their quality was shoddy, and living standards were more like those of a Third World country than a modern superpower. In the workplace, drunkenness and absenteeism were endemic, and the government bureaucracy was riddled with corruption and cynicism. Agricultural output was inadequate, and the USSR regularly had to import huge amounts of grain. Public health, too, was in sorry shape, with infant mortality rising and average life-span shrinking. And, despite their awesome military might, the Soviets were falling so far behind in computer and electronics technology that they no longer could be sure of maintaining their superpower status in the foreseeable future.

Gorbachev faces social and economic crises in the USSR

A key element of Gorbachev's approach was the spirit of openness, or *glasnost*, that he sought to impart to the political and cultural environment. The USSR, he reasoned, could not deal successfully with its problems if it continued to pretend they did not exist. What was needed, in his opinion, was a full and frank discussion of the situation, which would hopefully unlock the energy and creativity that had been stifled by the moribund system. Although *glasnost* did not amount to full freedom of speech, it did allow citizens a greater opportunity to speak their minds than before, and it enabled academics to begin to write the truth about Soviet society and the Soviet past. Eventually, it also unleashed a torrent of pent up nationalist strivings and ethnic hostilities that undermined the very foundations of the USSR.

Gorbachev pushes *glasnost:* openness in facing Soviet problems

In domestic affairs, the new party boss launched a sustained effort at *perestroika*, or restructuring of the Soviet system. At first it was fairly mild, largely mirroring the policies of earlier reformers such as Khrushchev and Andropov, and involving campaigns to combat alcoholism and absenteeism, root out corruption, and improve the productivity of Soviet workers. Eventually, however, Gorbachev went far beyond his predecessors and introduced changes designed to decentralize the economy, grant more autonomy to farmers and factory managers, introduce profit incentives and a limited market economy, permit the establishment of privately owned businesses, and encourage foreign corporations to participate in enterprises within the USSR. To the end, however, he resisted the onset of full free market capitalism: His mission was to save socialism, not replace it.

Gorbachev pursues *perestroika:* restructuring of Soviet system

To some extent, Gorbachev's approach mirrored that of Franklin Roosevelt, the U.S. president who had likewise taken over in an economic crisis. Aleksandr Yakovlev, a close Gorbachev aide who became the Politburo member in charge of ideology, had done research on Roosevelt while at Columbia University and had been impressed with that president's pragmatic flexibility. Just as Roosevelt had "saved" capitalism by introducing elements of socialism into the U.S. economy, Gorbachev sought to rescue socialism by fostering capitalist incentives in the USSR. Just as Roosevelt had initiated numerous new programs in an effort to find something that worked, Gorbachev launched numerous initiatives with no clear pattern or scheme. Just as Roosevelt had launched a New Deal, Gorbachev promoted New Thinking.

In Gorbachev's New Thinking (Document 80), foreign and domestic policies were deeply intertwined. If the USSR was to maintain its superpower status, it had to create an economy capable of fostering technological innovation and vastly increased production of services and goods. To do so, it must end the enormous drain caused by military expenses and support of foreign clients. The arms buildup gave the Soviets vast destructive power, but it did not bring security; instead it frightened the West into remaining united and developing weapons capable of destroying the USSR. Domination of Eastern Europe, and sponsorship of client regimes in places like Cuba and Afghanistan, whatever the political benefits, placed a huge burden on the weak Soviet economy. Moscow needed to draw down its vast military forces, slash its defense budget, and greatly reduce the amount it spent propping up client states. And it could not accomplish these things without a more relaxed international climate and better relations with the West.

Gorbachev's New Thinking involves cutting arms costs to aid Soviet economy

In his early months in office, pursuing the "common European home" theme he had sounded in the waning months of Chernenko's regime, Gorbachev sought to improve relations with Western European nations, hoping to encourage them to be more independent of their American allies. Just as Soviet belligerence had helped forge the Atlantic alliance and keep it bound together, Soviet accommodation, he hoped, might erode the cohesion of that alliance by removing its raison d'être.

These efforts were unwittingly assisted by the U.S. president, whose early strident rhetoric and rapid arms buildup had upset many Europeans. In May 1985, Reagan was scheduled to visit a military cemetery at Bitburg, West Germany, as part of a trip to Europe to commemorate the fortieth anniversary of the end of World War II. It turned out, however, that a number of Nazi SS troops were buried there, so Reagan was urged to cancel the engagement. Under pressure from West German leaders, however, he went ahead with his cemetery speech, after a clumsy attempt to defend the SS members as "victims" of Nazism. He then sought to repair the damage with a hastily arranged trip to a Nazi concentration camp to honor its victims, but by then Reagan had managed to offend veterans' groups, Jews, and many others in both Europe and America.

The president's Strategic Defense Initiative also strained U.S.–European relations. The fact that SDI was intended to protect against intercontinental missiles that endangered the United States and the USSR, but not necessarily against medium- and short-range weapons that threatened Western and Central Europe, was not lost on America's NATO allies. European leaders worried that the Star Wars system, combined with probable Soviet development of a missile defense system in response, might increase the likelihood of war in Europe by lessening its dangers for the superpowers. Their worries were probably unfounded, since even with SDI in place, a war in Europe would still bring

Reagan's SDI strains relations between America and Europe

unacceptable risks for both Washington and Moscow. But Reagan's apparent SDI obsession troubled Europeans and conjured up old anxieties about the reliability of their American ally.

Aided by Foreign Minister Gromyko, Gorbachev initially tried to exploit these divisions. He denounced the SDI and warned that, if the United States continued to pursue this venture, it would undermine the arms talks that had recently resumed in Geneva. He even implied that the Soviets might again walk out of these talks unless progress was made on banning space-based weapons. On the positive side, in April 1985 he declared that Moscow would unilaterally halt its nuclear testing and cease deploying new intermediate-range nuclear missiles aimed at Western Europe. The next month he announced that the USSR was eager to improve relations with the European Economic Community and that Soviet bloc countries would be permitted for the first time to negotiate bilateral agreements with the EEC. This was an obvious attempt to encourage Western Europe's economic independence from America, but it could also supply a more subtle assistance to the Soviets: If the nations of Eastern Europe could forge closer economic ties with the West, they might become less of a drain on Moscow's strained resources.

Soviets seek to exploit divisions between America and Europe

For all his focus on Europe, however, and despite some simultaneous efforts to improve relations with China, Gorbachev knew that no easing of world tensions could occur without direct talks between the USSR and the United States. He thus began to move in that direction. Acting on an earlier agreement, in July 1985, he engineered the promotion of Andrei Gromyko, known in the West as *Mr. Nyet* ("Mr. No") for his stubborn intransigence, from foreign minister to the largely ceremonial post of Soviet president (chairman of the Soviet presidium). The new foreign minister, Eduard Shevardnadze, an urbane, articulate Georgian and close friend of Gorbachev, soon became a symbol of Moscow's new realism and flexibility. In the next few years he worked closely with George Shultz, Reagan's taciturn and pragmatic secretary of state, to improve Soviet–American relations.

Gorbachev and Shevardnadze seek better relations with the United States

In their efforts to improve the international climate, Gorbachev and Shevardnadze met with a surprisingly ready response from Ronald Reagan, widely seen as a hard-line anti-Soviet Cold Warrior. For all his belligerent talk, Reagan was a dreamer who had long harbored hopes of ending the nuclear threat and shaping a more peaceful world. He abhorred the notions of nuclear deterrence and mutual assured destruction, and was partial to schemes, like SDI, that might end the balance of terror. During 1984, increasingly anxious to meet with Soviet leaders to reduce the nuclear threat, he had moderated his anti-Soviet rhetoric, talked of his plans to form a constructive relationship with Moscow, and complained that aging Soviet leaders kept dying before he could meet them. In 1985, with his last campaign behind him and his place in history ever more on his mind, he further pursued such a summit. In March, when Vice President George H. W. Bush went to Moscow for Chernenko's funeral, he brought with him a letter from Reagan inviting Gorbachev to visit America. Although eager to meet the president, the new Soviet leader was reluctant to have their first encounter occur on Reagan's turf. The two leaders finally agreed to meet in November at Geneva, the site of the ongoing arms control talks.

Reagan seeks dialog with Soviets and end to nuclear threat

SUMMITRY, START, AND STAR WARS

The two world leaders prepared for their first meeting—the first superpower summit in more than six years—in very different ways. Reagan, whose attitude toward the USSR had been shaped more by anti-Communist impressions than by a grasp of Soviet historical and cultural complexities, took a simple, straightforward approach. To help him bone up for the historic encounter, his aides provided him with briefing papers and a tutor on Russian culture; one aide even played Gorbachev in a mock debate with the president, speaking Russian to help him get used to conversing through an interpreter. But Reagan was not the sort to immerse himself deeply in details: His preference was person-to-person politics, and his main goal was to get to know the man with whom he shared the awesome task of preserving the planet's future.

Gorbachev and Reagan prepare to meet in Geneva

Gorbachev, at his typical frenetic pace, moved simultaneously on several fronts, using his public relations skills to pressure the Americans into a more accommodating position. In August he gave an interview to *Time* magazine, noting with approval Reagan's expressed view that nuclear war was unwinnable and suggesting that this could become the basis for future agreement between the two powers. In October, he flew to Paris, met with French president François Mitterrand, stressed the importance of Soviet relations with Western Europe, and declared that the USSR would pursue its agenda by "force of example" rather than "force of arms." He also offered to negotiate a 50 percent cut in strategic nuclear forces, provided that the United States drop its Star Wars program, and to work toward an agreement on intermediate-range missiles without waiting for progress on strategic and space-based weapons.

Gorbachev calls for serious arms cuts prior to Geneva summit

The formal meetings in Geneva (Documents 77A, 77B, and 77C) produced no dramatic breakthroughs. Exchanges at times got testy, especially regarding SDI, which Reagan portrayed as the key to arms reduction and Gorbachev denounced as a major roadblock to the same. At one point, to cut the tension, Reagan suggested that the two leaders go for a walk without their aides. Then, by a fireplace in a boathouse on lovely Lake Geneva, with only their interpreters present, the two men talked for well over an hour. Though continuing to spar over SDI, they agreed in principle to work toward a 50 percent cut in nuclear arms, and on the way back they agreed to meet again in America the next year and Moscow the year after that. At the end of the summit, they issued a joint statement calling for an interim agreement on intermediate-range nuclear forces (INF) and the creation of "nuclear risk reduction centers" in Washington and Moscow. But no progress was made on SDI, an issue on which neither man was willing to budge.

Gorbachev and Reagan develop a working relationship at Geneva

Still, the summit was far from inconsequential. The world's two most powerful leaders had met, taken each other's measure, and established a personal chemistry that would serve them well in the tough years ahead. Although frustrated by the president's apparent SDI obsession, Gorbachev was pleased to find that Reagan was not afraid to discuss sweeping changes in the nuclear status quo. The president, for his part, saw in Gorbachev a warmth and candor that other Soviet leaders had lacked, and this perception had an important impact. Ronald Reagan had met with the new leader of the evil empire—and decided that he could work with the guy!

Reagan and Gorbachev in Geneva, 1985.

In their first summit meeting at Geneva in November 1985, President Reagan and new Soviet leader Gorbachev began a relationship that would soon produce major changes in the international climate. Although the Geneva meeting achieved no major breakthrough, it set the stage for a series of subsequent summits that would help to end the Cold War and reverse the nuclear arms race.

In the aftermath of Geneva, Gorbachev moved quickly to maintain the momentum and to jump-start the Strategic Arms Reduction Talks (START), which had made little progress since their resumption in March 1985. In a highly touted January 1986 speech, he put forth a stunning proposal to abolish all nuclear weapons in three stages by the year 2000, while also cutting conventional weapons to a level precluding either side from launching a sustained attack. In the INF arena, he announced that for the first time Moscow was ready to negotiate removal of all U.S. and Soviet intermediate-range missiles from Europe, without reference to French and British nuclear missiles, thus seemingly endorsing Reagan's "zero-option" proposal of 1981. And he professed his willingness to accept comprehensive verification measures, including on-site inspections, to ensure that both sides complied. This was no small concession: For four decades, Soviet resistance to such procedures had been a major obstacle to arms control.

These proposals were meant partly to call Reagan's bluff and partly to subvert his SDI. Like his predecessors, Gorbachev worried about U.S. technology; he feared that a workable Star Wars system could upset the balance of terror and give the United States a huge political and psychological advantage. Worse yet, from his perspective, U.S. progress on SDI could initiate a new arms race, forcing Moscow to follow suit with a costly missile defense of its own.

Gorbachev advocates sweeping arms cuts, hoping to derail SDI

This, in turn, would further strain Soviet resources and severely endanger his domestic economic agenda. In this context, Gorbachev's audacious proposal to eliminate nuclear weapons provided a much cheaper and more secure way to accomplish what SDI was supposedly intended to achieve. If Reagan was serious in his call for major cuts in both sides' nuclear arsenals, then perhaps he would agree to limits on SDI in return for real arms reduction. If not, Gorbachev could at least say that he was serious about ending the arms race and Reagan apparently was not.

The Soviet proposals did occasion some dissension in Western ranks. Certain Reagan advisors, including arms negotiator Paul Nitze, wanted to take up Gorbachev's challenge and work out a "grand compromise" whereby deep cuts in nuclear weaponry would be accompanied by U.S. agreement to confine Star Wars research to the laboratory. The president, however, was too deeply wedded to SDI to go along with that proposal. At the same time, many European leaders had serious reservations about cutting arms too sharply. Having invested considerable political capital in getting their nations to accept the presence of new U.S. intermediate-range missiles, they were in no rush to see these missiles removed. And, having depended for decades on nuclear deterrence to maintain the peace in Europe, they were a bit wary of the prospect that talk of a "nuclear-free world" might someday become a reality.

SDI concerns some Reagan aides and U.S. allies

Events soon proved they had reason for concern. Throughout spring and summer of 1986, Gorbachev continued to press Reagan on SDI and to put forth creative arms control proposals. He called for a total ban on nuclear testing, including underground blasts, knowing that such a prohibition could hamper SDI research. He suggested that both sides pledge to abide by the ABM treaty, which forbade deployment of space-based missile defenses, for at least 15 years. But Reagan, who saw SDI as the key to freeing the world from the threat of nuclear war, argued through his aides that the ABM treaty, which allowed development of defenses based on "other physical principles," did not prohibit SDI. He pushed for a second summit, which he hoped could resolve such issues. But Gorbachev, who in Geneva had accepted Reagan's invitation to visit the United States, now refused to do so until progress was made in the arms reduction talks.

Reagan, wedded to SDI, pushes for another summit

In August a serious international incident brought a chilling reminder that the Cold War was not over. In New York, the FBI arrested a Soviet UN official, Gennadi Zakharov, on charges of spying. A week later in Moscow, the Soviets seized an American reporter named Nicholas Daniloff on similar charges. The negotiating climate worsened, as both sides saw that no summit could occur until the Zakharov–Daniloff affair was resolved. After difficult negotiations, they agreed that both men would be freed and sent home, and that Reagan and Gorbachev would meet that fall for preliminary talks at a neutral site: Reykjavik, the capital of Iceland.

The Reykjavik meeting of 11–12 October 1986 proved anything but preliminary. Instead it was the Cold War's most bizarre and astonishing summit conference. In the barren and surreal atmosphere of Hofdi House, not far from the Icelandic capital, the two leaders and their aides conducted extraordinary discussions and almost concluded some breathtaking agreements.

Reagan and Gorbachev meet at Reykjavik in Iceland

Gorbachev came prepared to talk about far more than INF and preparations for a U.S. trip. Early on the first day of the two-day conference, he put forth a package proposal calling on both sides to reduce all strategic weapons by 50 percent, eliminate intermediate-range missiles in Europe, work out a comprehensive nuclear test ban treaty, and commit to adhere to the ABM treaty for at least ten years. Reagan expressed interest, but also wanted to remove Soviet intermediate-range missiles from Asia and replace the ABM treaty with a new agreement that would let both sides research and test strategic defenses. Later, when the president repeated his pledge to share SDI technology, Gorbachev refused to take it seriously, citing U.S. unwillingness to share with the Soviets such harmless technologies as oil well equipment "or even milking machines."

A long night and day of tough negotiations ensued. The Americans proposed to eliminate all ballistics missiles in ten years, after which each side could deploy defensive systems against the remaining strategic weapons (long-range bombers and cruise missiles). But Gorbachev upped the ante. Why not abolish *all* nuclear weapons, he suggested, not just ballistics missiles, over the next ten years? Reagan, faced with a chance to fulfill his dream of ending the nuclear threat, gave a rather positive response—somewhat to his aides' chagrin. Amid growing tension and excitement, the two sides tentatively agreed to cut their nuclear arsenals in half by 1991 and to eliminate them entirely by 1996! A momentous agreement seemed within reach.

Reagan and Gorbachev seem to agree to eliminate nuclear weapons

But then it all unraveled. Gorbachev insisted that SDI research must be confined to the laboratory during the ten-year period; seeing this as a bid to kill SDI, Reagan resolutely refused. Each man found the other's obstinacy infuriating: Gorbachev could see no reason for Reagan to develop a defense against weapons that would be eliminated, and Reagan could similarly see no reason for Gorbachev to oppose it. In the end, they reached no accord and parted on bitter terms (Document 78).

Discord over SDI scuttles Reykjavik agreement

In the aftermath of Reykjavik, as each side blamed the other for the unhappy outcome, East–West relations seemed to have suffered a serious setback. Western European leaders, still facing Soviet supremacy in conventional forces, reacted in horror to the news that Reagan had almost agreed without consulting them to abolish nuclear arms—and thus dismantle NATO's main deterrent—in ten years. Reagan's aides even said he had not meant to do so, but his diaries, published much later, show that indeed he had. In Geneva, the arms control talks reverted to total deadlock, with each side retreating to earlier stances and resorting to recriminations against the other. For the time being, the prospects for nuclear disarmament, and for a Gorbachev visit to Washington, appeared very dim.

Resentments and recriminations follow Reykjavik summit

In retrospect, however, Reykjavik was not the disaster it then seemed. The reactions from Western Europe, and from many in Washington, make it clear that an agreement to abolish nuclear weapons would have faced fierce opposition and months or years of wrangling if ever it was to be approved. And once their tempers cooled, Gorbachev and Reagan both realized that, for all their frustrations over SDI, Reykjavik had shown them that they shared a common dream of an end to the Cold War and a world without nuclear weapons.

TRIALS AND TRIBULATIONS IN MOSCOW AND WASHINGTON

The declining fortunes of both Gorbachev and Reagan reinforced the climate of gloom that followed Reykjavik. In the USSR, a series of setbacks dampened the enthusiasm of Soviet citizens for both Gorbachev and *perestroika.* In the United States, a serious scandal shook the Reagan administration, eroding the president's public support and destroying the myth that he was a "Teflon president" to whom no criticism stuck.

Even before Reykjavik, Gorbachev's reform efforts had met numerous frustrations. His anti-alcohol campaign, designed to improve both public health and worker productivity, made modest headway but created a shortage of sugar, as resourceful Soviet drinkers bought huge amounts of it to distill illicit spirits. Systematic foot-dragging by Soviet bureaucrats, resistant to changing their ways, hampered his political and economic reforms. And as he struggled to combat corruption and remove Brezhnev holdovers from official positions, his own supporters publicly questioned the pace and tenor of his reforms. On one hand, impatient radicals such as Boris Yeltsin, the city of Moscow's new Communist Party boss, railed at the slow progress of *perestroika* and the continued existence of a privileged class of time-serving careerists in the bloated bureaucracy. On the other hand, cautious conservatives such as Egor Ligachev, the Politburo member widely seen as Gorbachev's second in command, voiced concern that reform might get out of hand and that the party might lose control of the Soviet system.

Gorbachev's reforms trigger problems and dissent in the USSR

External and internal disasters likewise contributed to Gorbachev's woes. In Afghanistan, which he aptly depicted as a "bleeding wound," the death toll mounted and the prospects of Soviet victory faded. In 1986, armed with U.S.-supplied Stinger antiaircraft missiles, the Afghan rebels began to turn the tide by shooting down Soviet helicopters. In the USSR, a catastrophic accident occurred in April of that year at the Chernobyl nuclear power station located north of Kiev. A reactor exploded, killing dozens of people and releasing a huge cloud of radiation that contaminated thousands of square miles and endangered the health of millions. Reverting to traditional behavior, Moscow first tried to cover up the disaster, but Gorbachev eventually had to face the problem squarely and even ask Western help. It was nonetheless a damaging blow to the Soviet nuclear industry, an embarrassment for Gorbachev, and a setback for his efforts to bolster his nation's prestige and improve its economy.

Afghan War and Chernobyl nuclear accident hamper Gorbachev

Ronald Reagan had problems of a different sort. In November 1986 elections, less than a month after Reykjavik, the president's Republican Party lost control of the U.S. Senate, leaving both houses of Congress in the hands of his Democratic foes. Meanwhile, reports emerged that members of his administration had taken part in an elaborate scheme to sell U.S. weapons to Iran in return for Iranian assistance in freeing American hostages being held in Lebanon. Further reports revealed that, in violation of U.S. laws, profits from these sales had been used to support and equip the Contra rebels fighting Nicaragua's Sandinista regime. Thus began to unravel the most damaging scandal of the Reagan years.

The Iran–Contra scandal had its roots in two separate circumstances. One was the Reagan administration's effort to undermine the Soviet-supported Sandinistas by backing the Contras, an assortment of rebel "freedom fighters" and former military officers that was organized and assisted by the CIA. When Congress, alarmed by reports that the CIA was mining Nicaraguan harbors and violating international law, voted in 1984 to forbid further aid to the Contras, the administration sought to circumvent this ban by funding the rebels through private aid from wealthy U.S. citizens and foreign governments. The other circumstance was the captivity of seven U.S. hostages, held in Lebanon by pro-Iranian elements, and

Reagan backs arms-for-hostages deal with Iran

Reagan's sympathy for them and their families. Despite his public commitment not to make concessions to hostage-takers, and over the strong objections of his secretaries of state and defense, the president in 1985 authorized the sale of U.S. antitank and antiaircraft missiles to Iran in return for Iranian efforts to get the hostages released.

These separate situations were connected by the activities of Lieutenant Colonel Oliver North, a Marine Corps officer attached to the staff of the National Security Council (NSC). North, a decorated Vietnam veteran and self-proclaimed superpatriot who had been tasked with raising money for the Contras, increasingly got involved in the arms-for-hostages dealings. Enthralled by the prospect of having the anti-American regime of Ayatollah Khomeini in Iran inadvertently assist the "freedom fighters" in Nicaragua, North arranged to divert to the Contras some of the profits from the Iranian arms purchases. But this diversion was illegal, since the monies used were not private funds but proceeds from the sale of U.S. property.

NSC aide North diverts profits from arms sale to fund Nicaraguan rebels

The scandal broke in fall 1986. In October, the Sandinistas gunned down a U.S. plane bringing weapons to the Contras, and a captured crew member named Eugene Hasenfus soon admitted that he was part of a CIA operation. In early November, a Lebanese magazine blew the whistle on the arms-for-hostage deals. As U.S. media pieced together the story, administration officials sought to cover up the truth, and the president himself made inaccurate statements. But on 25 November, following an in-house investigation, Attorney General Edwin Meese disclosed that arms sale proceeds had indeed been funneled to the Contras. Although Reagan quickly fired Oliver North and denied all knowledge of the diversion, his credibility was damaged and his popularity plummeted. Americans concluded that their president was either lying about what he knew or hopelessly out of touch with what went on in his administration. Even his ardent supporters, who could justify the Contra funding in the name of national security, were horrified that Reagan had let his minions sell weapons to Iran.

For over a year the scandal slowly unfolded, with three separate investigations looking into it. The first, a Reagan-appointed commission led by former senator John Tower, absolved the president of illicit behavior in its February 1987 report, but it disparaged his lackadaisical management and poor control over subordinates. The second, a joint House-Senate probe, held televised hearings in the summer and fall of 1987, thus keeping the issue in the public eye. The third, an independent inquiry led by Special Prosecutor Lawrence Walsh, eventually brought charges against North and others, but it did not indict Reagan himself.

Iran–Contra scandal damages Reagan's reputation

The scandal embarrassed Reagan and hurt his reputation but did not destroy his presidency. One reason for this was that, despite his aides' testimony that they had kept him informed, he denied that he had fully understood what was happening, and his confused accounts of the affair made his denials plausible. Another reason was that, despite his subordinates' wrongdoing, the public on the whole still liked him and excused his failure to keep his charges in line. A third reason was that even his foes in Congress were hesitant to put the country through another wrenching disruption only thirteen years after Watergate had forced Richard Nixon to resign.

The main reason for Reagan's rebound, however, was that world events intervened and captured center stage, allowing the old Cold Warrior

U.S. concerns and world events help Reagan survive scandal

to assume the role of peacemaker. And here he got a major assist from his hard-pressed Soviet counterpart, who was likewise eager to restore his flagging fortunes by working toward world peace.

THE REVIVAL OF DÉTENTE

Gorbachev faced two painful realities early in 1987. One was that *perestroika* was not working and that economic progress would require more time, more reforms, and more serious cuts in defense spending. The other was that Reagan was unwilling to budge on SDI. Moscow could thus either bide its time until Reagan left office, assuming his successor would be less wedded to the Star Wars dream, or it could separate out SDI and negotiate other issues where real headway was possible.

In February 1987, Gorbachev chose the latter approach, "unpacking the package" he had proposed in Iceland. The domestic economic news was so bad that he did not have the luxury of waiting two years for progress on the international front. Besides, he already had a relationship with Reagan, and some idea of what he could expect, whereas a new U.S. president would be an unknown quantity. And the very fact that Reagan had been weakened by the Iran–Contra scandal, combined with the president's natural desire to score a diplomatic triumph before he left office, might make it easier to work with him than any potential successor.

Gorbachev decouples INF issues from SDI and START

At any rate, on 28 February 1987, the Soviet leader announced that Moscow was now prepared to negotiate an end to all intermediate-range missiles in Europe, whether or not agreement could be reached on strategic or space-based weapons. The INF talks could now be "decoupled" from the SDI issue. This dramatic concession removed the main obstacle to a comprehensive INF treaty based on the "zero option" that Reagan had proposed in 1981.

Washington insists that INF ban must be global, not just in Europe

It nonetheless put the United States in an awkward spot. The zero option had originally been more propaganda ploy than serious bargaining position, since few in Washington expected that the Kremlin might go along. Now that the improbable had occurred, many in the West had second thoughts: The elimination of all intermediate-range missiles from Europe would leave the USSR with a large conventional advantage there, as well as with a number of intermediate-range missiles in Asia. Still, the Americans could hardly abandon a proposal they had themselves initiated and advocated for six years. Thus in spring and summer of 1987, Washington simultaneously pressed its NATO allies to accept an INF accord and urged the Kremlin to give up *all* its remaining intermediate-range missiles, not just those in Europe.

In INF treaty, Americans and Soviets agree to destroy all intermediate-range missiles

The result, after concessions by both the Soviets and West Germans, was what came to be known as "global zero-zero." In September, the United States and the USSR announced that they had agreed in principle to destroy *all* missiles that had ranges of 500–5,500 kilometers (roughly 300–3,400 miles), with full on-site inspection and verification. For the first time in history, an agreement had been reached to abolish a whole category of weapons!

This understanding finally cleared the way for Gorbachev's visit to Washington. And what a visit it was! The mediagenic Soviet leader took the U.S. capital by storm, bantering with politicians, hosting a party for celebrities, and even getting out of his limousine to work the crowds like a U.S. politician.

At the White House, on 8 December, he and Reagan signed the INF treaty (Document 81), amid self-congratulatory remarks about its unprecedented nature. The two leaders basked in the glow of their historic achievement and newly enhanced popularity.

But not all was sweetness and light. The INF treaty, even when fully implemented, would only eliminate about 4 percent of the superpowers' nuclear warheads. Serious discussions were needed if there was to be any real progress on reduction of strategic weapons or on resolving the Star Wars issue. Behind the scenes, Gorbachev chafed at Reagan's indifference to details and his propensity for providing unsolicited advice on democracy and human rights. The two sides made some progress on several START issues, but no breakthrough on SDI. Instead, they papered over their discord by instructing their Geneva delegates to work out an agreement by which both sides would pledge to uphold the 1972 ABM treaty for "a specified period of time." Research and testing of space-based systems would be permitted to the extent authorized by that treaty, but the two sides continued to differ on what the treaty meant.

SDI recedes as an issue despite continuing discord

Ironically, by this time both sides realized that SDI would be more difficult to develop than Reagan had at first foreseen and that even a scaled-down version was unlikely before the end of the century. Moreover, the growing U.S. deficit and Democratic control of Congress made it unlikely that funding would continue at the levels Reagan desired. As a result, SDI was losing its importance as an issue and, for the United States, its potential as a bargaining chip. As it faded, other developments dominated East–West relations.

Soviets ebb in Afghanistan as Americans arm rebels

The most encouraging of these developments was the Kremlin's decision to pull out of the Afghan War. Unlike his predecessors, Gorbachev saw little value in investing scarce Soviet resources in Third World regional conflicts. Almost from the outset he had sought a face-saving way to disengage Soviet forces from Afghanistan. His first instinct was to send more troops, hoping to overpower the resistance and quickly end the war. But this approach merely increased casualties and prompted a massive flight of Afghans from their homeland. In 1986, therefore, Gorbachev changed course and began seeking a negotiated settlement. Moscow engineered the ouster of Babrak Karmal, the widely despised Soviet-backed Afghan ruler, and replaced him with the moderate and accommodating security chief Najibullah. In June, Gorbachev called for "national reconciliation" of all Afghan forces, a signal that Moscow was ready to bargain with anti-Soviet insurgents to form a coalition government. Shortly thereafter, however, the United States began supplying the rebels with Stinger antiaircraft missiles, thus boosting their fortunes and relieving the pressure on them to compromise with Najibullah. In the long run, America would pay a steep price for thus arming the Afghan rebel forces, which included radical Islamists who later formed violent anti-Western groups called al Qaeda and the Taliban. In the short run the conflict continued, and progress toward peace was stalled.

Gorbachev decides to withdraw Soviet troops from Afghanistan

Finally, in February 1988, fresh from his triumphal trip to Washington, Gorbachev moved to cut his losses. In yet another of his trademark stunning announcements, he declared that the USSR was willing to withdraw its troops from Afghanistan over a ten-month period, beginning on 15 May (Document 82). Difficult talks remained, for the United States insisted on the right to provide continuing aid to the rebels, "symmetrical" to any assistance Moscow gave Najibullah. Finally, the Kremlin accepted this arrangement, and the troop evacuation began on schedule in May. The following year, after it was completed, Foreign Minister Shevardnadze formally apologized to the international community for the Soviet role in Afghanistan.

Reagan's visit to Moscow demonstrates easing of East–West tensions

Meanwhile, a few weeks after the withdrawal commenced, Ronald Reagan arrived in Moscow for his fourth summit conference with Gorbachev. Officially the meeting's purpose was to sign the instruments of the ratified INF accords, but this was largely a formality. Unofficially it was to maintain the momentum of the new détente and to help Gorbachev shore up his sagging support at home. Although short on substance, it was rich in imagery, with the two leaders strolling together through Red Square and embracing at Lenin's tomb. In a trip laden with ironies, the most vocally anti-Soviet of all U.S. presidents spoke in front of a statue of Lenin and stood at the Bolshoi Ballet while the U.S. national anthem was played. When asked in Red Square if he still saw the USSR as an evil empire, he simply said, "No. That was another time, another era." Reagan and the Soviets had each come a very long way.

Reagan and Gorbachev in Moscow, 1988. In May 1988, Reagan went to Moscow for his fourth summit meeting with Gorbachev. The trip produced no major results but provided some striking sights, including that of the two leaders conversing in Red Square with Saint Basil's cathedral behind them. Note that Reagan's presidency and the Cold War were by this time both coming to an end.

The Moscow summit of 1988 was the climax and high point of the Gorbachev–Reagan relationship. The two men would meet once again as leaders, in December of that year, when Gorbachev visited the UN to make another groundbreaking speech. But by then Reagan's term was ending, and the old Cold War cowboy was preparing to ride off into the sunset.

Reagan's legacy was laden with irony. His unsophisticated grasp of Cold War realities, frustrating at times to both his friends and foes, had enabled him to envision a world without a Cold War and nuclear weapons. His staunch anti-Communism had freed him to cut deals with the Communists by covering his right flank at home. And his personal approach to world affairs had helped him see in Gorbachev a Communist leader who shared his own fondest dreams.

Hence, improbable as it had seemed a few years earlier, the aging anti-Communist president and the dynamic young Soviet leader had together embarked on a new form of détente that was far more promising than the old. Nixon and Brezhnev had worked to curtail the arms race, but with each side maintaining vast nuclear forces and with continued conflict over regional issues and Third World struggles. Reagan and Gorbachev, on the other hand, worked not just to end weapons-building programs but also to eliminate existing weapons systems. And, for the first time, Moscow seemed ready to cut its losses and forgo its costly support for client regimes and insurgencies. As the Reagan era neared its conclusion, there was better reason than ever before to hope that the Cold War was ending. But the epic events of the next few years would astonish even the most hopeful observers of 1988.

Reagan and Gorbachev's new form of détente paves way for the end of Cold War

17

The End of the Cold War, 1988–1991

Between 1988 and 1991, a series of remarkable developments shattered the Soviet bloc, transformed international relations, and ended the Cold War. As Gorbachev's reforms foundered, he pushed for further changes in the Soviet system, in turn releasing centrifugal forces that pulled that system apart. The nations of Eastern Europe gained independence, ousting Communist rulers and liberating themselves from Soviet control. Within the USSR, as *perestroika* failed and Gorbachev's popularity plummeted, the various national republics began asserting independence. In 1991, after a failed bid by Communist hard-liners to seize control and restore central Soviet power, the USSR disintegrated and ultimately ceased to exist.

GORBACHEV AND BUSH

The last few months of 1988 brought leadership changes in both superpowers. On 1 October, Mikhail Gorbachev was selected as Soviet president after forcing the aged Andrei Gromyko into retirement. Although this position was largely honorary, it did make Gorbachev official head of state, and soon he would enhance its powers. His selection marked the culmination of a series of bold political strokes that saw him remove or demote his main opponents, win endorsement of *perestroika* by party and state officials, and gain a freer hand in pursuing reforms. On 8 November, following a rather nasty campaign, Americans elected Vice President George H. W. Bush to replace Ronald Reagan as president. Since Bush had broad international experience and had participated in many of Reagan's policy decisions, his election suggested continuity in U.S. foreign policy. Still, although publicly loyal to Reagan, Bush was less enamored of Gorbachev—and less enthralled with the SDI—than the outgoing president.

At the UN, Gorbachev pledges troop cuts and renounces force

In some respects, the omens for continued improvement in East–West relations looked promising. In December 1988, Gorbachev made his second visit to America, this time to address the UN General Assembly in New York. In his speech (Document 83), which proved yet another blockbuster, he proclaimed a

Bush, Reagan, and Gorbachev in New York. In December 1988, Gorbachev traveled to New York to speak at the United Nations, where he promised large cuts in his military forces and called for greater freedom for all nations. While there, he met with George H. W. Bush, recently elected to succeed Ronald Reagan as president the next month, and posed with both men in front of the Statue of Liberty. By this time, however, serious problems in the USSR and the failure of Gorbachev's economic reforms were undermining his stature as Soviet leader.

momentous shift in Soviet foreign policy. Advocating "freedom of choice" for all nations, he declared that ideology had no place in international affairs and that strong nations must "renounce the use of force" in dealing with other countries. To show that these were not empty words, he pledged that his nation would unilaterally reduce its overall military forces by 500,000 troops and 10,000 tanks, and its presence in Eastern Europe by 50,000 troops and 5,000 tanks. While in New York he also met jointly with Reagan and Bush and turned his patented charm on everyone in sight.

Economic woes and earthquake disaster plague the USSR

In other respects, the signs were less auspicious. Even as he won battles within the Soviet leadership, Gorbachev lost the support of the Soviet people, as their living standards continued to decline and his reforms failed to take hold. A calamitous harvest in 1988 added to the discontent. Meanwhile, long-submerged ethnic rivalries and nationalist aspirations began to tear the fabric of enforced social discipline that held the USSR together. To make things even worse, a devastating earthquake hit Soviet Armenia while Gorbachev was in New York. Soviet efforts to deal with the disaster proved inadequate and incompetent, forcing Gorbachev to cut short his U.S. visit, fly to the stricken region, and accept international aid in coping with the catastrophe.

Furthermore, when the new U.S. president took office in January 1989, it soon became evident that he and the Soviet president were operating on different wavelengths and at different speeds. Gorbachev was in a hurry: Indeed, the failure of his domestic policies seemed both to show that he was running out of time and to make him even bolder in his foreign policy. Bush, on the other hand, was determined to take his time and not to be rushed into tumultuous new departures on the international scene. Thus, one leader sought to force the pace of change, while the other tried to slow it down.

George Herbert Walker Bush, whose father had been a U.S. senator and whose son would be a future president, was something of an American aristocrat. Raised in comfort and privilege, he had become a model of *noblesse oblige*, performing heroically as a U.S. Navy pilot during World War II and later serving effectively in a wide range of government posts. Lacking strong political convictions, and admittedly deficient in what he called "the vision thing," Bush was the epitome of caution, prudence, and pragmatism. Yet his presidency coincided with the most far-reaching changes in international affairs since the era of Harry Truman.

As seasoned Cold Warriors, Bush and his aides were suspicious of Gorbachev, seeing him as a more capable foe than his aged and ailing predecessors. Gorbachev, it was true, had pushed through some liberal reforms, but he was still a devout Marxist whose ultimate goal was to strengthen his country by cutting its excessive expenditures on arms and aid to client states. His promised force reductions, when seen in this light, seemed like little more than efforts to make the Soviet military more efficient while throwing the West off guard and inducing it to disarm. Gorbachev might be a sincere proponent of peace, but he might also be a slick-talking salesman using charm and concessions to soften the NATO alliance and weaken Western vigilance. And Bush was not about to let his vigilance be weakened.

Cautious and pragmatic Bush initially distrusts Gorbachev

He thus began his term with a lengthy review of U.S. foreign policy. For several months, all initiatives were placed on hold, as dozens of bureaucrats spent hundreds of hours appraising American strategies on numerous regions and issues. Determined to avoid the sort of early administration pressures that had led Kennedy into the Bay of Pigs fiasco and the ill-starred Vienna summit (Chapter 10) and Carter into his ill-fated arms control initiative (Chapter 14), Bush kept a relatively low international profile. He resisted efforts to arrange an early meeting with Gorbachev and responded tepidly to the Soviet leader's force reduction proposals.

Bush begins term with extensive foreign policy review

But Gorbachev was not to be denied. Increasingly impatient with Bush, and fearful that in Washington "the hawks were again on the move," the Soviet leader followed his UN speech with a series of bold actions and proposals. In January 1989, he revealed details of his force reduction plan, which would cut the size of the Soviet military by about one eighth, and assured Western skeptics that the tanks removed from Eastern Europe would be modern and not outdated ones. That same month his Warsaw Pact allies also announced cutbacks in their combat force levels. In February, the USSR reported

Gorbachev pushes major force cuts in Europe

that it had completed its withdrawal from Afghanistan on schedule. In March, Foreign Minister Shevardnadze unveiled conciliatory new Soviet proposals at new talks in Vienna on Conventional Forces in Europe (CFE), replacing the long-stalled mutual and balanced force reduction (MBFR) talks (Chapter 13). In April, Gorbachev flew to London, complained to Prime Minister Thatcher about Bush's foot dragging, and solicited her help in getting the Americans to be more responsive. In May, during a controversy in West Germany over U.S. plans to modernize its European-based tactical nuclear weapons (those with a range of less than 300 miles), he declared that Moscow would unilaterally cut 500 such weapons from its Eastern European stockpiles. He also offered to further reduce the number of tanks and artillery pieces deployed by the Warsaw Pact. And, in a private letter to the U.S. president, he disclosed that Moscow had stopped supplying arms to its Central American clients.

All this activity put Bush on the spot. As he prepared to attend a fortieth anniversary NATO summit in late May, his aides and allies pressed him to come up with an effective response to Gorbachev's challenge, in order to shore up both alliance solidarity and his sagging public image. Bush responded by agreeing to negotiate with the Soviets on tactical nuclear weapons and then by using the NATO meeting in Brussels to propose his own plan for sweeping military cuts. According to his proposal, both superpowers would reduce the number of troops they deployed in Europe (outside the USSR) to 275,000 and the number of combat aircraft to 15 percent below the current NATO level. The plan's image of equality was deceptive, since it would require the USSR to cut ten times more troops, and considerably more aircraft, than the United States. Both the NATO allies and the Kremlin nonetheless welcomed it as a positive step. Seeking to regain the public relations initiative, Bush also challenged Moscow to relax its grip on Eastern Europe, noting that people who lived in a "common European home" should be "free to move from room to room."

Bush responds with his own force cut proposal

Meanwhile, in mid-May, while NATO leaders were preparing for their Brussels summit, the peripatetic Soviet president once again went on the road. This time his travels took him to Beijing for a "socialist summit" with Deng Xiaoping and other Chinese leaders. It was a tumultuous visit. Chinese students, emboldened in part by Gorbachev's reforms, were staging a massive prodemocracy protest in Beijng's Tienanmen Square when he arrived. Although his visit was designed to improve relations, Gorbachev did not hesitate to call openly for more democracy in China, while urging a peaceful resolution of the student demonstrations.

Gorbachev in China calls for greater democracy

His words were of little help. On 4 June 1989, two weeks after Gorbachev left Beijing and shortly after Bush left Brussels, Chinese soldiers ruthlessly crushed the protests with appalling brutality and bloodshed. The Tienanmen Square Massacre (Documents 84A and 84B) provided graphic evidence that China's Communist rulers would use wanton force if necessary to maintain their unfettered power. But that same day, elsewhere in the Communist world, a far different picture emerged. In Poland, peaceful and free elections resulted in an overwhelming defeat for that country's Communist rulers and helped set in motion a chain of events that would bring down Communist rulers throughout the Soviet bloc.

Chinese troops massacre Tienanmen Square protesters

THE REVOLUTIONS OF EASTERN EUROPE

In his historic UN address of December 1988 (Document 83), Gorbachev implied that the USSR would forsake the use of force in pursuing its foreign policy. To the peoples of Eastern Europe, the full implications of this new approach at first were not entirely clear. Was Moscow repudiating the Brezhnev Doctrine, by which it had long claimed the right to intervene in the affairs of socialist countries? In March 1989, Gennadii Gerasimov, the Kremlin's most forthright spokesperson, seemed to answer this question affirmatively when he said that each Eastern European nation had the right to decide its own fate. In June, other Soviet officials made similar statements, and Gorbachev explicitly disowned the Brezhnev Doctrine during a visit to France.

Soviet leaders renounce Brezhnev Doctrine

These statements, of course, were just words. It remained to be seen how Soviet leaders would react to challenges in Eastern Europe. Hungary and Poland, where major political changes were already under way, supplied the first true tests of the Kremlin's intent.

In Hungary, the changes began in 1988, when János Kádár, who had ruled that nation since 1956, stepped down as general secretary. His successor, Károly Grósz, sought to emulate Gorbachev by launching his own version of *glasnost.* With Moscow's blessings, Grósz opened up Hungarian society, brought reformers into power, and instituted democratic procedures. In February 1989, his regime announced constitutional changes designed to transform Hungary into a multiparty state and then scheduled free elections for the coming year. The leaders then sought to shed their repressive image, hoping to make a favorable impression on voters. In May, after earlier checking with Gorbachev, they opened their borders to the West by ripping down the barbed wire fences that separated Hungary from Austria. The USSR did not obstruct this action, which tore a vast hole in the "iron curtain." Before long, thousands of East Germans entered Hungary, seeking to use that country as an escape route to the free and prosperous West.

Hungary opens "iron curtain" border with Austria

In Poland, the road to reform was more tortuous and contentious. Since 1981, the country had been led by Wojciech Jaruzelski, the general who had declared martial law and banned the Solidarity trade union. But Jaruzelski, one of the most enigmatic Cold War leaders, was both a pragmatist and a patriot, and he eventually realized that the outlawed labor union had far more support among the Polish people than he did. In 1987, he initiated a *perestroika*-type reform of the anemic Polish economy but gained little support due to strong opposition from the outlawed Solidarity movement. Lech Wałęsa, a shipyard electrician who had risen from obscurity in 1980 to become Solidarity's leader and a Nobel Peace Prize winner, once again emerged as the effective head of the Polish opposition. In 1988, during a televised debate viewed by millions of Poles, he scored a clear triumph over the party's selected spokesperson.

Early in 1989, as the deadlock continued and the economy deteriorated, Jaruzelski agreed to roundtable discussions between government and union representatives. These talks led, in April, not only to legalization of Solidarity but also to sweeping changes in the political system. A new legislative body, the Senate, was created alongside the old *Sejm*, and elections were scheduled for 4 June. All seats in the Senate, and 35 percent of those in the *Sejm*, were placed up for grabs, with the Polish people at long last given a chance to make a real choice. The result was a humiliating defeat for the government, which lost all the contested seats in the *Sejm* and all but one seat in the Senate, and an overwhelming victory for Solidarity. Under pressure from Gorbachev, the Polish Communists agreed to accept a coalition government, with Solidarity's Tadeusz Mazowiecki serving as prime minister and Jaruzelski as president.

Reformers rout Communists in Polish elections

The impact of events in Hungary and Poland was profound. In two key Soviet satellites, under very different circumstances, Communist leaders agreed to democratic reforms. And far from blocking these developments, Moscow actually encouraged them. In October, in an effort to illustrate this new approach, the irrepressible Gerasimov announced in Helsinki that the Brezhnev Doctrine was dead and that Kremlin policy was now in tune with a famous American singer. "You know the Frank Sinatra song *My Way*?" he asked his astonished listeners. "Hungary and Poland are doing it *their* way. We now have the *Sinatra* doctrine."

The developments in Hungary and Poland soon produced a chain reaction that led, by the end of 1989, to revolutionary changes throughout Eastern Europe. The glue that cemented the Soviet bloc had been provided by the Soviet army, which Moscow had used to suppress democratic reforms in Hungary in 1956 and Czechoslovakia in 1968, and to frighten Poland into declaring martial law and banning Solidarity into 1981. Once it was clear that Gorbachev did not intend to repeat these performances, the people of Eastern Europe began to challenge their Communist rulers with growing audacity.

Events came to a head in the fall of 1989 in eastern Germany, often the focal point of Cold War confrontation. Despite living standards that were relatively high for a Communist country, the people of East Germany were impoverished compared to their West German counterparts. As Gorbachev's reforms brought a measure of democracy to the USSR, East Germans had grown increasingly resentful of the oppressive regime of party boss Erich Honecker.

Many decided that the time had come to leave. Throughout the summer, East Germans poured into Hungary, bent on traveling to the West through the newly opened border with Austria. Hungarian authorities at first refused to let them go, honoring an earlier agreement with the East German regime. But in September, as the numbers mounted, the Hungarians changed their mind and, with Gorbachev's approval, let thousands of East Germans make their way to the West. When East Germany responded by prohibiting travel to Hungary, those who wished to leave simply went to Czechoslovakia and jammed into the compound of the West German embassy in Prague. Finally, in early October, following awkward negotiations between Prague and East Berlin, they were allowed to travel to West Germany in special trains.

East Germans escape to West through Hungary and Czechoslovakia

Others chose to stay and fight. In late September, a group called "New Forum" began sponsoring antigovernment rallies in Leipzig, calling for democratic reforms. Soon similar protests were held in other cities. In October, the Leipzig demonstrations became a weekly event, with the crowds increasing as the month progressed. As events spun out of control, the East German government began to contemplate using massive force to quell the disturbances, much as Chinese authorities had done four months earlier at Tienanmen Square.

East Germans demonstrate weekly for reform

Into this dangerous situation strode Gorbachev, who showed up in East Berlin in early October to help celebrate the fortieth anniversary of the German Democratic Republic. In a bizarre ceremony that seemed totally out of touch with reality, he joined Honecker and other officials in extolling the achievements of a state that was under siege. Large crowds gathered to greet the Soviet president, chanting "Gorby! Gorby!" and calling loudly for his help in bringing them their freedom. In public, Gorbachev referred to an earlier appeal by Ronald Reagan to tear down the Berlin Wall (Document 79) and predicted that all walls separating Europeans must eventually fall. In private, he urged his hosts to consider reforms, noting that "life punishes those who come late" and warning them not to expect Soviet help in trying to quell the protests.

Gorbachev urges East German rulers to reform

Soon after Gorbachev left, the regime faced another massive demonstration scheduled for 9 October in Leipzig. To avoid bloodshed, local civic leaders convinced the police to let it proceed unhindered. The next week, over 100,000 persons took part in yet another protest. A few days later, the ailing Honecker was replaced as party leader by Egon Krenz, long his designated heir. But Krenz assumed command of a ship that was sinking, with thousands seeking to leave it on any lifeboat available. On 1 November, as the protests continued to grow, he went to Moscow to meet with Gorbachev, who urged him to move toward a more pluralistic society. Returning,

The opening of the Berlin Wall.

On 9 November 1989, in a desperate bid to stem a mass outflow of people to the West, East German officials opened up the border crossings, hoping that their citizens would stop leaving if they knew they could freely travel back and forth. As word quickly spread through Berlin that the wall was now open, thousands of Berliners gathered at the wall to celebrate, dancing on it and later dismantling it. The fall of the Berlin Wall sparked a series of revolutions that ended Communist rule in Eastern Europe.

Krenz tried to seize the moment by reforming the party and government, jettisoning unpopular officials and calling for free elections. But the crowds in the streets kept growing, and the flood of refugees heading to the West became a virtual torrent.

Faced with an impossible situation, Krenz and his comrades then took a desperate gamble. Perhaps, they reasoned, if East Germans knew they could legally travel back and forth to the West, they would be less likely to permanently leave their homes. So on 9 November 1989, they decided to ease restrictions on such travel. Their spokesman, perhaps misunderstanding, instead announced that almost all such restrictions were lifted at once (Document 85).

East German rulers open borders, and Berlin Wall falls

The results were far more sweeping than the East German leaders had intended. As rumors quickly spread that the Berlin Wall was open, hundreds of thousands of Berliners gathered there to celebrate with unrestrained euphoria. Before long they started to dismantle brick-by-brick the Cold War's most powerful symbol!

Although the fall of the Berlin Wall did help stem the flood of East German refugees, it did not save the East German regime. Instead it unleashed in both Germanies a tidal wave of support for the country's reunification. In December, Krenz and his comrades were forced to step down, as the country prepared for democratic elections scheduled for March 1990.

Meanwhile, the historic events in Germany were followed in quick succession by sweeping revolutionary developments throughout Eastern Europe. One by one the remaining Communist leaders, no longer protected by the threat of Soviet force, were toppled from their posts. In the last two months of 1989, events moved at a dizzying pace.

In Bulgaria, a revolution took place at the same time East German authorities were opening the wall. Todor Zhivkov, who had ruled his country as dictator since 1954, had become an embarrassment to his supporters, especially as he maneuvered to secure his incompetent son's advancement. On 9 November, in a carefully conceived palace coup, Foreign Minister Petur Mladenov replaced Zhivkov as general secretary. The next day Gorbachev was among the first to congratulate Bulgaria's new leader. In the face of rising protests, Mladenov then moved quickly to reform his country and party, in preparation for free elections to be held the following June.

Bulgarian reformers oust dictator and schedule free elections

A revolution in Czechoslovakia followed hard on the heels of those in East Germany and Bulgaria. In late October, police broke up large demonstrations in Prague marking the 71st anniversary of the country's founding. But on 17 November, another Prague demonstration turned into a vast rally in favor of democratic reforms. The Communist regime, led by President Gustáv Husák and party boss Milos Jakes (who had succeeded Husák as general secretary in 1987), responded with brutal force, sending antiterrorist troops and riot police to beat the assembled crowd. Far from intimidating the protesters, however, this action seemed to spur them on. A few days later, they formed an opposition group called "Civic Forum," which organized more and bigger protests. Each day, thousands gathered at Prague's Wenceslas Square to sing, chant for freedom, and listen to speeches by prominent figures like dissident playwright Václav Havel and former party boss Alexander Dubček, the man who had led the reform efforts of 1968 (Chapter 12). As it had done elsewhere, Moscow made clear that it would not support the use of force to maintain the beleaguered regime. On 24 November, as the

Czechoslovakia's "velvet revolution" ends Communist rule

situation deteriorated, Jakes and other party leaders resigned; Husák followed them into retirement on 10 December. By year's end a new government, made up mostly of non-Communists, was formed, with Havel as president and Dubček as head of the national assembly. With minimal violence and bloodshed, Czechoslovakia's "velvet revolution" thus ended four decades of Communist rule.

The Romanians were not so lucky. Their efforts to oust the regime of Nicolae Ceausescu met with harsh repression, and their revolution proved by far the bloodiest of those in Eastern Europe. Ceausescu had ruled his nation ruthlessly since 1965, reserving the top posts for himself and his family and creating a Stalin-style personality cult. In a typical Cold War irony, this most brutal of all Eastern European tyrants was regularly courted by U.S. leaders, since he pursued an independent course in foreign affairs. More recently, he had resisted Gorbachev's efforts to get him to institute reforms and had thus incurred the exasperation of the Soviet chief. Still, as his fellow Communist dictators fell all about him in 1989, Ceausescu fiercely clung to power.

Bloody Romanian revolt ends brutal Ceausescu regime

In mid-December, however, riots broke out in the city of Timisoara over government attempts to evict a popular Hungarian pastor and human rights activist. Police efforts to crush the riots resulted in wanton bloodshed, and within days there were protest rallies in other Romanian cities. Crowds in Bucharest shouted down Ceausescu when he tried to speak on 21 December. The next day, as rioters stormed government offices, the regime called out troops to disperse them by force. But the soldiers refused to fire, defying the orders of their longtime leader, and instead joined the revolt. Ceausescu and his wife tried to flee, but they soon were captured, given a quick trial, and sentenced to death. On 25 December, a firing squad pumped several hundred bullets into their bodies, putting a bloody end to the Romanian nightmare.

GERMAN UNIFICATION AND SUPERPOWER COLLABORATION

Bush and Gorbachev at Malta agree to expedite arms talks

By late 1989, events in Eastern Europe had finally convinced George Bush, and most remaining skeptics, that the Gorbachev revolution was genuine. On 2–3 December, in the midst of the epic events shaking the Soviet bloc, the two leaders held their first summit, a relatively informal meeting on a Soviet ship in the surging seas off the Mediterranean island of Malta. Gorbachev, fresh from a visit to Rome where he had conferred with the pope about human rights and religious freedom in the USSR, was looking for help from America. He confided to Bush that his economic reforms were not going well and that his success hinged on improving Soviet living standards. The U.S. president, admitting that he was caught off guard by the changes in Eastern Europe, now sought to support the Soviet leader's position, suggesting a host of arms control proposals and initiatives to help the Soviet economy. The two men agreed to accelerate the START and CFE talks, expressing hope that agreements could be completed and signed during the coming year. Superpower cooperation was suddenly the order of the day!

This cooperation did not mean that all problems were solved. Only few weeks later, superpower relations suffered a temporary setback due to a U.S. invasion of Panama, in which Bush used military action to topple the regime of Manuel Noriega, who had defied American efforts to halt drug traffic through his country. Washington clearly had not bought Gorbachev's claim that great powers must renounce force in dealing with other countries. And both sides knew that tough talks lay ahead on the questions of German unification and arms control.

During 1990, the nations of Eastern Europe followed up their revolutions by transitioning to democratic rule. In Hungary, when the long-awaited elections were finally held in March, voters rejected their former Communist leaders in favor of candidates from "Democratic Forum" and other centrist groups. Arpád Goncz, a prominent writer and dissident, soon became the new head of state. In Romania, where elections in May were marred by charges of fraud, a "National Salvation Front" composed mostly of former Communists was the overall winner, with one of them, Ion Iliescu, affirmed as president by a large majority. In Czechoslovakia, in free elections held in June, "Civic Forum" and its candidates largely carried the day and then reaffirmed Václav Havel as president. In Bulgaria that same month, the former Communists actually outpolled their democratic opposition, but by October the democrats had gained control of both the presidency and legislature. Zhelyu Zhelev, detained for years by the Zhivkov regime, became the country's leader. In Poland, President Jaruzelski agreed to step down in September, and in voting held a few months later, Solidarity leader Wełęsa eventually emerged victorious. Moscow and Washington mostly stayed out of these events, content to watch history take its course.

Democracy comes to Eastern Europe

In Germany, however, the situation was more complex. Its future depended not just on East and West German voters but also on its neighbors and the countries that kept it divided. Late in 1989, when West German chancellor Helmut Kohl put forth a plan for unification, the Soviets declared the division of Germany essential to Europe's security, and the Poles voiced concern that a united Germany might demand restoration of the lands ceded to Poland in 1945. Even Western politicians, who for years had paid lip service to the goal of German unity, secure in their belief that Moscow would never allow it, now had some misgivings. The ever cautious Bush administration, concerned that events were moving the German Question back onto center stage, called for a gradual approach supervised by the original occupying powers (the United States, Britain, France, and the USSR). This led to a "two plus four" framework (two Germanies plus four supervising powers), worked out at the Ottawa foreign ministers' meeting of February 1990.

But the Germans were not to be denied, and their long-sought unity was not to be delayed. In March 1990 elections, East Germans voted overwhelmingly for candidates who favored a unified Germany, with surprise victory going to a conservative coalition linked with West German chancellor Kohl. In May, the two Germanies agreed to integrate their economic and monetary systems, effective 1 July. West Germany's economy absorbed that of the East, and the West German deutsche mark became the currency of both.

East Germans vote for unity with West

Despite the rapid progress, a major obstacle loomed on the road to German unity. To allay the fears of his NATO partners, who had nightmares about recreating an uncontrollable *Reich*, Kohl promised that a united Germany would stay in the Western alliance. But Moscow, still allied with East Germany in the increasingly inconsequential Warsaw Pact, clung to its traditional stance favoring a neutral, demilitarized Germany. The West Germans eventually solved the problem by buying off the Soviets, making major economic concessions in return

West Germans buy Soviet consent to German unity

for Moscow's acquiescence. They agreed to fulfill all of East Germany's financial obligations toward the USSR and to grant the Soviets an enormous bank credit of five billion deutsche marks. They also agreed to cut the size of their army and eventually to help pay the cost of removing Soviet troops from East Germany.

Finally, on a visit to the USSR in July, Kohl elicited Gorbachev's assurance that Moscow would not block unification and that the Germans could remain in NATO if they wished (Documents 87A and 87B). This cleared away the last major hurdle. In September, the "two plus four" treaty was signed, ending the occupying powers' rights and giving Germany the green light to unite. On 3 October 1990, in a development that would have been almost unthinkable a few years earlier, the East German regime (the German Democratic Republic) was disbanded, and the West German government (the Federal Republic of Germany) took charge of the whole country. The German Question, so central to the Cold War, was at last resolved with a united Germany.

Germany reunites as West takes over East

Meanwhile, with the Cold War winding down, relations between the superpower leaders continued to improve. In late May, Gorbachev flew to Washington for his second meeting with Bush. He arrived in a somber mood, acutely aware that the Soviet economy was getting worse and that nationalist pressures in the Soviet republics were tearing the USSR apart. But the Western air seemed to rejuvenate him: At home he was a pariah, disparaged by his own people, but in America he was a popular hero. Huge, friendly crowds greeted him everywhere he went. President Bush, by now a big Gorbachev booster, took him to Camp David, where the two men played horseshoes, walked in the woods, and discussed matters of global concern. The Soviet leader then traveled to Minneapolis and San Francisco, where he appealed to U.S. business leaders to launch new enterprises in the USSR. The symbolism could not have been more poignant: The head of the Communist world was seeking aid from the titans of American capitalism.

Gorbachev, hailed in America, seeks economic support

The two leaders had hoped to sign a major arms control treaty during the Washington summit, but slow progress in the START negotiations precluded this possibility. Still, they did sign statements outlining the framework for a comprehensive accord and advocating even greater cuts in the arsenals of both sides. They also signed a treaty calling for the cessation of chemical weapons production and reduction of existing stockpiles. Finally, in a testament to the growing emphasis on economic cooperation, they endorsed a new commercial agreement by which the United States at last granted most-favored nation trading status to the USSR. Gorbachev returned to Moscow in early June, refreshed and reinvigorated for the challenges ahead. A month later, on 6 July 1990, NATO issued a sweeping statement called the London Declaration (Document 86), effectively proclaiming that the Cold War was over and that Europe had entered a "new, promising era."

U.S.–Soviet accords and NATO declaration mark end of Cold War

Then, in August 1990, the spirit of superpower collaboration was tested by Iraq's sudden invasion of Kuwait (Map 11, page 214). Baghdad, saddled with an $80 billion debt from its 1980–1988 war with Iran, was unable to repay it because a glut of oil on the world market had lowered prices to about $10 a barrel. Iraq owed much of this money to Kuwait, which opposed efforts in OPEC to lower production and raise prices. In summer 1990, pressed by Iraqi leader Saddam Hussein to revise its position, Kuwait agreed to cut production, support higher prices, and make small territorial concessions to Iraq.

Saddam then miscalculated tragically. With the Cold War apparently over, with Moscow distracted by unrest among its non-Russian nationalities, and with Washington having given him weapons during his war with Iran, he decided that the time was ripe for a bold stroke that would begin the unification of the Arab world. On 2 August 1990, he invaded Kuwait without warning and conquered it in less than a day. That action gave Iraq control of 21 percent of the world's oil supply and shocked Washington. President Bush ordered a massive U.S. military buildup to defend Saudi Arabia against an Iraqi invasion, although there was no conclusive evidence that one was being planned. He moved in the UN to isolate Iraq and impose economic sanctions to force it out of Kuwait. Moscow supported these measures, and the next month Gorbachev and Bush held a quick meeting in Helsinki to discuss the crisis, agreeing to work together to secure Iraqi withdrawal. For the first time since the Suez affair of 1956, the United States and the USSR appeared to be on the same side during an international crisis. For a world used to fearing that any local conflict could spark a superpower confrontation, this was a very welcome change.

Iraq overruns Kuwait, sparking Persian Gulf crisis

Following U.S. congressional elections on 6 November, Bush became more aggressive. He doubled the number of U.S. troops in the Persian Gulf to 500,000 and converted the force into an offensive one. He assembled a military coalition of 32 countries from six continents, including even Syria, which had long been unfriendly to America, and got the UN to pass a resolution calling for Iraqi withdrawal from Kuwait by 15 January 1991. Negotiations to achieve this withdrawal proved fruitless. Moscow tried to mediate the dispute, but with the Soviet economy crumbling and the Communist Party losing its grip on power, Gorbachev lacked the political leverage to bring the parties together.

The U.S.-led coalition struck on 16 January 1991, beginning the first Persian Gulf War. When it ended on 27 February, Kuwait was liberated and much of Iraq destroyed. The war altered the power balance in the Middle East, and Washington at once moved toward peace negotiations between the Arab states and Israel, which had prudently stayed out of the conflict despite Iraqi missile attacks on its territory. Soviet influence in the Persian Gulf virtually vanished, due partly to Moscow's preoccupation with internal unrest, partly to the poor performance of the military hardware it had earlier given Iraq, and partly to Washington's preeminence.

Soviets stay out as U.S.-led coalition defeats Iraq in Persian Gulf War

Meanwhile, further progress in East–West rapprochement came in November 1990, when members of NATO and the Warsaw Pact signed an agreement to reduce their conventional forces in Europe. The CFE treaty, which committed both sides to substantial cuts in the numbers of troops, tanks, and aircraft deployed in Europe, marked the culmination of many months of difficult negotiations and the realization of a dream that had begun in 1973 with the original MBFR talks. Its ratification was delayed in early 1991 by a dispute over the status of several Soviet divisions, which Moscow claimed to be naval forces rather than ground combat units. But even as this issue was resolved, it was overtaken by events. On 1 July 1991, the Warsaw Pact, the embodiment of Communist military might in Europe, was formally dissolved.

CFE treaty cuts forces in Europe as Warsaw Pact dissolves

By this time the United States and the USSR had finally reached a START accord (Document 88), agreeing on the terms of a comprehensive treaty to reduce strategic arms and reverse the nuclear arms race. Bush traveled to Moscow for yet another summit with Gorbachev, and, on 31 July, the two presidents signed the landmark treaty, taking a major step toward the extensive arms cuts envisioned at Reykjavik in 1986. Within seven years, the USSR agreed to cut its deliverable nuclear warheads by half, and the United States agreed to reduce its own by more than a third.

START treaty decrees vast cuts in nuclear arms

The START treaty was in many ways an epic achievement. After more than four decades of competing for strategic supremacy, and more than two decades of difficult negotiations, the superpowers finally agreed to vastly reduce their immense atomic inventories. Within months, both sides would put forth proposals for still more drastic cuts. The nuclear arms race, the most frightening aspect of the Cold War, at long last came to an end.

By summer 1991, in fact, few could doubt that the Cold War itself was over. All its major components—the Soviet occupation of Eastern Europe, the German Question, the superpower contest for Third World influence, and the arms race—had been either eliminated or resolved. Still, as people tried to appreciate the enormity of these events and adjust to a new world order, the internal decay of the USSR was paving the way for still more startling developments.

By 1991 all key Cold War issues resolved

THE COLLAPSE OF THE SOVIET STATE

Ironically, the USSR's disintegration was aided by Gorbachev's reforms, which helped to eliminate the pervasive fear that had governed the Soviet peoples since Stalin's time. That fear turned out to be part of the cement that held the Soviet Union together. Once it was gone, rather than working collectively to solve the nation's problems, many Soviet citizens showed little loyalty to either the Communist Party or Soviet state.

This was especially true of the non-Russian peoples who comprised fully half of the Soviet population and the various union republics that made up the USSR. Since 1988, some had been acting with increasing defiance of the central government in Moscow. Early that year, a violent clash erupted between Armenians and Azerbaijanis over Nagorno-Karabakh, a predominantly Armenian enclave in the midst of Azerbaijan. Gorbachev's efforts to resolve the dispute only made matters worse, and by 1989, the Kremlin was faced with two constituent nationalities effectively at war with one another. Meanwhile, the Baltic republics of Estonia, Latvia, and Lithuania, which had been annexed forcibly at the start of World War II, were testing Moscow's resolve to keep them in the union. In summer 1988, Lithuanians held nationalist demonstrations; later that year Estonia declared its right to repudiate Soviet laws.

Non-Russian nationalists in the USSR push for autonomy

The revolutions in Eastern Europe during 1989 gave a huge boost to nationalist hopes within the USSR. As Soviet bloc nations broke free of Moscow's rule, Soviet republics sought to follow suit. Lithuania took the lead by proclaiming its sovereignty, declaring invalid its 1940 annexation by the USSR and ending the Communist Party's monopoly of power in the republic. Estonia and Latvia followed closely behind. In Georgia, after Soviet forces brutally suppressed a large nationalist rally in April, separatist sentiments spread quickly. In Ukraine, Nationalists founded an organization called "Rukh" ("the movement") to agitate for independence.

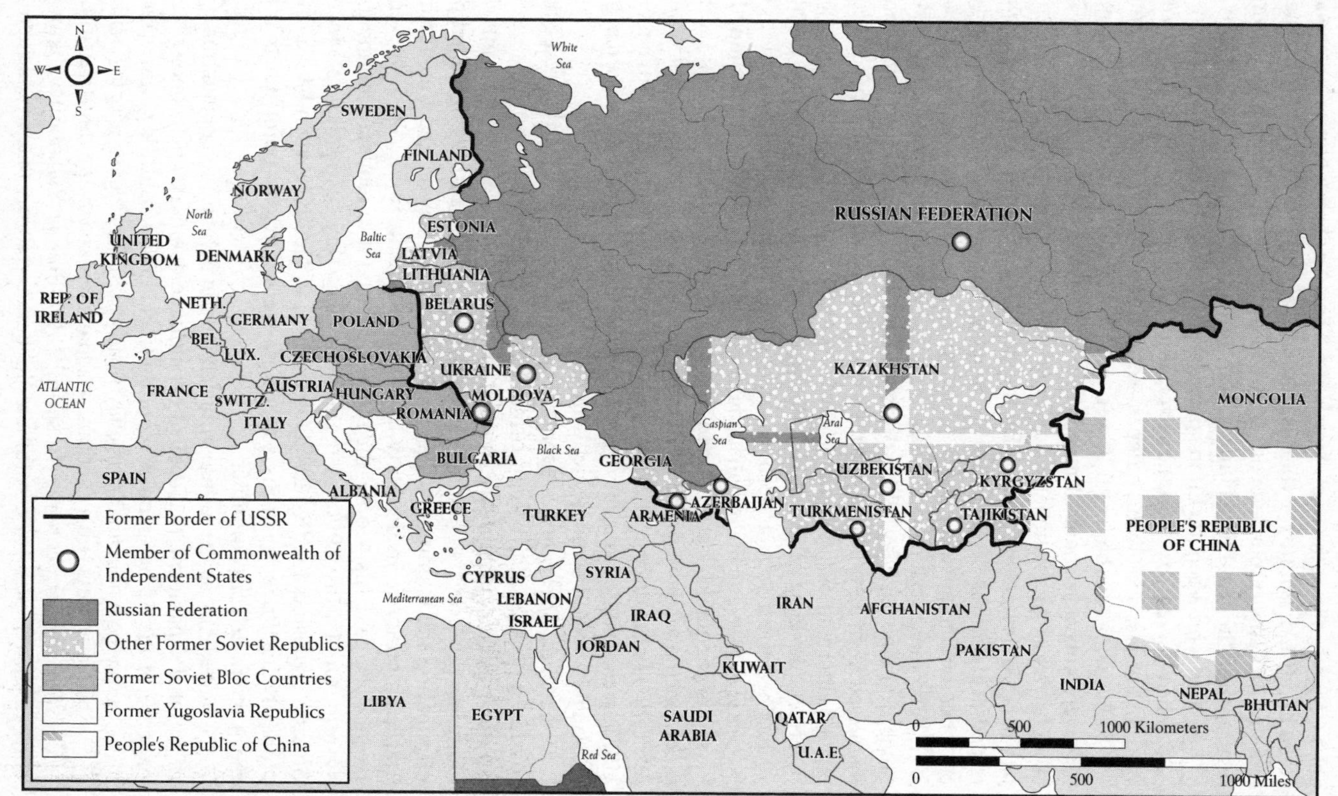

MAP 13 Disintegration of the Communist Bloc, 1989–1992.

The revolutions of 1989 not only ended Communist rule in Eastern Europe but also inspired many Soviet republics to assert their autonomy. Observe that, despite Gorbachev's efforts to preserve the USSR, in 1991 it disintegrated into 15 separate countries, many of which formed a loose-knit Commonwealth of Independent States.

By 1990, Moscow was losing control. In January, Gorbachev went to Lithuania to urge its rebellious people to behave with more restraint. His visit had little impact: On 11 March, the Lithuanian legislature issued a declaration of independence and elected anti-Communist Vytautus Landsbergis as president. During the next few months, Moscow responded with shows of military force, seizing government buildings, sealing the republic's borders, and cutting off its oil and gas. In May, the crisis eased a bit when the Lithuanians agreed to delay implementing their independence decree. By then, however, both Estonia and Latvia had declared their intent to move toward independence. Armenia, still locked in intermittent conflict with Azerbaijan, followed suit in August. In June, Moldavia proclaimed its sovereignty and changed its name to Moldova. In October, elections in Georgia brought victory to a nationalist coalition, which soon announced its determination to pursue an independent course. By the year's end, all the remaining republics had issued declarations of sovereignty, stopping short of asserting complete independence but moving toward greater autonomy.

Many Soviet republics assert sovereignty

The most serious challenge arose in Russia, the largest and most populous Soviet republic. In May 1990, Boris Yeltsin, an outspoken reformer who had been dismissed from party leadership after openly criticizing the slow pace of reform, was elected chairman of the Supreme Soviet of the Russian Republic. This made him, in effect, president of Russia. Flamboyant, confrontational, and charismatic, Yeltsin had become a popular hero by virtue of his courageous denunciations of bureaucratic elitism and his populist democratic style. Under his leadership, the Russian republic quickly proclaimed its sovereignty, declared that its laws took precedence over those of the Soviet regime, and asserted greater control over its own territory and resources. These actions struck at the heart of the Soviet system: The USSR presumably could survive without the Baltic States and Armenia, but without Russia there could be no Soviet Union.

Russian republic asserts sovereignty under Yeltsin

At first Gorbachev responded to the challenges creatively, seeking always to stay a step ahead of his critics. Since 1988, he had moved to democratize Soviet politics, permitting contested elections, creating a popularly elected Congress of People's Deputies, instituting a revised and strengthened presidency, eliminating the Communist Party's monopoly of power, and transferring considerable authority from the party to the government. Ironically, however, the more freedom he gave his people, the more they used it to repudiate him and the Soviet system. On 1 May 1990, at the annual May Day festivities in Moscow's Red Square, protesters loudly jeered Gorbachev. In October, when he was awarded the Nobel Peace Prize, even his supporters were quick to point out that he did not merit the prize for economics.

Indeed, it was the failure of his economic policies, in conjunction with the rise of national separatism, that spelled his ultimate doom. As the economy declined, the patience of the Soviet peoples wore thin, and enthusiasm for *perestroika* yielded to growing cynicism. Gorbachev's early confidence gave way to vacillation, as he wavered between a cautious, gradualist approach and rapid transformation to a free market economy. In spring 1990, Premier Nikolai Ryzhkov put forth a comprehensive plan for careful and deliberate reforms that would increase wages, prices, and market incentives within the context of continued central planning. Yeltsin soon countered by backing a bold and drastic 500-day plan to achieve a market

Yeltsin pushes bold economic plan, while Gorbachev wavers

economy by privatizing state properties and giving the republics control of natural resources, taxation, and economic policy. Not surprisingly, the republics preferred Yeltsin's approach. Gorbachev temporized and hedged, at one point seeming to come to terms with Yeltsin, but later adopting a "compromise" plan that retained most economic power in the hands of the central state. He then pressed for and received emergency powers to dictate economic policies and maintain internal control.

These moves seemed to show that Gorbachev was turning to the right, siding with Soviet hard-liners. On paper, at least, the changes enhanced his authority to deal with the growing crisis. But they also cost him the allegiance of reformers, who had been his main base of support. Many of his economic advisors went over to Yeltsin, who defiantly declared his intent to implement the 500-day plan within the Russian Republic. In December, Foreign Minister Shevardnadze rocked the Soviet government by warning of a coming dictatorship and abruptly resigning his post. The apparent reassertion of central control caused dismay throughout the republics.

The dismay turned to anger in January 1991. Within the Kremlin, hard-liners like Defense Minister Dmitrii Yazov and Interior Minister Boris Pugo pressed for strong action to keep the republics in line. The crackdown began on 2 January, when the Ministry of Defense sent paratroopers to seven troublesome republics to root out military deserters and draft dodgers. On 11–13 January, with the world's attention focused on the looming Persian Gulf War, Soviet troops and tanks, aided by the Ministry of Interior's "Black Beret" special forces, seized control of Lithuanian press and broadcast facilities in a bloody show of force. A week later, a similar incident occurred in Latvia, with Soviet forces attacking the offices of the Latvian Ministry of Interior. Although Gorbachev denied that he had ordered these assaults, neither did he condemn them, and he tried to blame the nationalists for causing the disorders.

The Kremlin cracks down on dissident Baltic republics

Meanwhile, however, in a desperate bid to keep the USSR together, Gorbachev promoted a new "union treaty" designed to give republics a semblance of sovereignty while preserving central authority. According to this arrangement, the Soviet government would maintain control over finances, resources, transportation, communications, and military forces, but the republics would be able to determine their own social and economic systems and exercise some internal autonomy. The USSR would become the "Union of Sovereign Soviet Republics," with "Sovereign" replacing "Socialist" in the official name.

In a bid to save union, Gorbachev backs treaty boosting republics' rights

In March, after several months of discussions on the proposed union treaty, Gorbachev held a national referendum on whether to preserve the Soviet Union "as a renewed federation of equal sovereign republics in which human rights and the freedoms of all nationalities will be fully guaranteed." The result was an apparent victory for Gorbachev, with 76 percent of voters supporting the resolution. It was marred, however, by the fact that six of the 15 republics (the Baltic States, Armenia, Georgia, and Moldova) refused to take part. The Soviet leader nonetheless went ahead with his plans, negotiating the final details of the agreement with the nine participating republics at a special conference in April. In June and July, the legislatures of eight of these republics ratified the accord, with only Ukraine electing to delay. The formal signing of the new union treaty was set to take place on 20 August 1991. Now, as the central government prepared to sign away some of its powers, it was the hard-liners' turn to be dismayed.

Voters support union treaty, but six republics opt out

During all these maneuvers, George Bush maintained an attitude of caution. Even as the Soviet people turned their backs on Gorbachev, the U.S. president refused to abandon his newfound collaborator. Although he found the crackdown in the Baltics "disturbing," he avoided direct criticism of Gorbachev and continued his efforts to enhance cooperation between Washington and Moscow. As he had shown two years earlier when he maintained ties with China following the Tienanmen Square Massacre, George Bush preferred to deal with a known quantity rather than risk international turmoil. So he happily traveled to Moscow at the end of July to bolster the Soviet president and sign the START treaty.

Hard-liner coup ousts Gorbachev on the eve of union treaty signing

Within three weeks of Bush's departure, the hard-liners made their move. On the evening of Sunday, 18 August—two day's before the union treaty was scheduled to be signed—a group of them detained Gorbachev at his dacha (vacation home) in the Crimea. The next morning, 19 August, the Soviet press agency announced that he was released from his presidential duties "for health reasons" (Document 89A). Declaring a state of emergency, an

Yeltsin waves to supporters after foiling coup.

In August 1991, after Soviet hard-liners detained Gorbachev in a poorly led coup, huge crowds assembled in Moscow to support Boris Yeltsin, the Russian president who had called on Russians to resist the coup. The coup fell apart when military forces called off an attack on Yeltsin's headquarters ordered by the coup leaders, but with Yeltsin and other republic leaders now acting with full independence, Gorbachev proved unable to reassert authority and hold the Soviet Union together.

eight-man "emergency committee" took control. Ostensibly led by Vice President Gennadii Yanaev, it was dominated by conservatives like Yazov and Pugo. This was, in fact, a coup: Tanks and troops were moved into Moscow and other major cities, the Baltic republics were blockaded, and attempts were made to seize control of the media.

Quickly, however, the coup ran into problems. Yanaev proved ineffective: In a televised press conference, with shaking hands betraying his fear, he appeared to be fortified with vodka. Meanwhile Russian president Yeltsin galvanized public opposition. He avoided arrest and made it to the Russian Parliament building in Moscow, where he declared the coup unconstitutional and called on Russians to obey his government instead of the emergency committee. Then, in a dramatic gesture that contrasted sharply with Yanaev's pitiful performance, he climbed atop a tank and issued an appeal for Russians to resist the coup (Document 89B). Before long, tens of thousands of people surrounded the parliament building, where they spent the next few days erecting barricades, taunting soldiers, and listening to defiant speeches. Huge crowds assembled in Leningrad and other cities, as resisters everywhere responded to Yeltsin's plea.

Coup leaders bumble as Yeltsin defiantly rouses opposition

Meanwhile, ensconced in his surrounded headquarters, Yeltsin kept in touch by phone with the outside world, taking several supportive calls from George Bush. Despite his inclination to condemn the coup, the U.S. president had initially taken a "wait and see" approach. Now, inspired by Yeltsin's courage, Bush rallied to his support (Document 89C).

Then, on 20 August, the moment of truth approached. As the coup leaders ordered more troops into Moscow, soldiers who had gone over to Yeltsin's side prepared to defend the parliament building against the anticipated attack. But the onslaught never came: Faced with mass popular opposition and resistance from their troops to an attack, the commanders delayed it and finally called it off early on 21 August. Later that day, as troops and tanks withdrew from Moscow and some coup members flew to the Crimea to negotiate with Gorbachev, it was clear that the August coup, derisively dubbed the "vodka putsch," had failed (Document 89D).

Coup leaders call off attack on resisters after troops balk

Gorbachev snubbed the coup members and flew back to Moscow on 22 August to resume his duties, only to find that power had shifted to Yeltsin, whose Russian government soon banned the Communist Party and took over most of the functions and offices hitherto controlled by the USSR. With little left to stop them, various republics renewed their independence claims. Negotiating with Yeltsin, Gorbachev tried to revise the union treaty to create a "Union of Sovereign States" that would preserve some central authority. But when Ukraine and other republics balked, this effort came to naught.

Gorbachev tries to resume his role, but power has shifted to Yeltsin

Finally, abandoning Gorbachev entirely, the presidents of Russia, Ukraine, and Belarus met near Minsk and on 8 December agreed to a new course. Asserting that the USSR had effectively ceased to exist, they invited the former Soviet republics to join them in a loose confederation called the "Commonwealth of Independent States" (CIS). More of a coordinating committee than a government, the CIS had no central authority and placed no serious restraints on the sovereignty of its members. Within a few weeks, all former republics except the Baltic States and Georgia agreed to participate.

Yeltsin and other republic leaders form Commonwealth of Independent States

Gorbachev resigns as the USSR ceases to exist

Gorbachev was disconsolate, but there was little he could do. Only a few years earlier he had been a giant, the world's most prominent and popular political figure, but now he seemed pitifully dwarfed. Bowing to reality, on 25 December 1991, he resigned as president of the USSR, a realm that no longer existed. His remarks on the occasion were short and subdued (Document 90), but he cited the momentous changes that had occurred since he took power. "We are now living in a new world," he declared. "An end has been put to the Cold War."

18

A Hard and Bitter Peace

Gorbachev's resignation and the subsequent hauling down of the Soviet flag from atop the Kremlin closed the final chapter of the Cold War. The division of the world into two armed camps, the terrifying and expensive nuclear arms race, the bloody conflicts in places like Korea and Vietnam, and the tensions and hatreds that washed over the globe for nearly half a century had been relegated to the history books. Few were sorry to see the long twilight struggle end, but its demise, perhaps appropriately, occasioned little of the wild rejoicing that followed the end of World War II. The sound heard round the world as the Cold War ended was a collective sigh of relief from a weary, somewhat cynical, but somewhat hopeful human race.

GENERAL CONCLUSIONS

For over four decades, the Cold War dominated international relations, profoundly influenced the global economy, and to some extent affected the life of almost everyone on the planet. Arising out of the ashes of wartime cooperation between the Soviet Union and the Western Allies, it rapidly degenerated into what John F. Kennedy called "a hard and bitter peace," full of confrontation, conflict, deception, and intrigue. As the superpowers and their allies strove mightily to gain the advantage, expending massive resources in the process, less powerful nations struggled merely to survive, or perhaps to derive some benefit from playing upon the global rivalry. The Cold War was a long and complex process that defies easy explanations or facile judgments. Nevertheless, there are a number of general conclusions that we can draw about it.

First: Although the Cold War was not inevitable, conflict between the Soviet Union and the Western democracies after Hitler's defeat was much more likely than was friendship, given the incompatibility of their ideologies and goals. Capitalist democracy, the prevailing ideology of the West, favored free markets and free elections, with people free to choose their own livelihoods and leaders. It supplied millions of people with comfortable living standards, but it also brought vast inequalities in privilege and wealth and spawned huge global empires in which non-Western peoples felt exploited and oppressed. Marxist-Leninist Communism, the central Soviet ideology, promoted violent revolutions to destroy the capitalist system, expropriate capitalist wealth, create classless societies based on equal sharing of resources, and free oppressed and exploited peoples from Western imperial rule. It provided full employment and extensive social services for its people, but it also created single-party dictatorships that stifled human rights, allowed little freedom, and furnished little wealth.

From 1917 to 1941, the Soviets depicted the West as a society in the final, decadent stages of capitalist greed and exploitation, a rotten society fit only for consignment to the dustbin of history. They denounced the democracies of Britain, France, and the United States in the same terminology they used against the fascist dictatorships of Germany and Italy and made repeated efforts to subvert all these political systems in order to establish Communist rule. The West, for its part, portrayed the USSR as a remorseless police state bent on the destruction not only of its political and economic rivals but also of organized religion, family values, and human decency itself. It backed up these judgments with military intervention against the Bolsheviks in 1918 and consistent verbal hostility thereafter.

Then Germany invaded Russia in June 1941, and Winston Churchill, in one of the most imaginative left-handed compliments ever recorded, declared his new-found friendship for Moscow by asserting that "If Hitler invaded Hell, I would at least make a favorable reference to the Devil in the House of Commons." For his part, Joseph Stalin treated his unlikely allies with sarcasm, contempt, and suspicion whenever they differed with him on military judgments. The West suspected that he had ordered the massacre of tens of thousands of Polish military officers in the Katyn Forest in 1940 and watched as he refused Allied planes permission to land on Soviet airstrips after flights to aid the anti-Nazi uprising in Warsaw in 1944. Franklin Roosevelt at first believed that he could do business with Stalin, whom he tried to flatter and treat as a confidant, but by the end of his life in 1945, he came to believe that Stalin was more interested in Soviet aggrandizement than in friendship with the West. Once Hitler was gone, and the common threat of German domination was removed, there was little to hold the Soviets and the Western Allies together and a great deal to push them apart.

Second: The Cold War began in Germany because Europe was the fulcrum of the global balance of power in 1945, and Germany was the fulcrum of Europe. No other region of the world was so valuable to the superpowers. Despite the terrible devastation caused by the war, Germany's tremendous industrial potential and its highly educated and ambitious population could not be discounted. Germany was also, because of the territorial settlements reached at Tehran and ratified at Yalta, the one region in which Soviet and Western troops stood toe to toe. The border between West and East Germany, and particularly the divided city of Berlin, logically became the central focal points of the developing Cold War.

Additionally, Germany was the one area in which all-out war between the superpowers seemed not only possible but likely. Soviet fears of resurgent German militarism were profound: No one in the Kremlin, or in the country as a whole, wanted to live through (or die in) a third German invasion in the same century. The stakes in other areas of the world, including the oil fields of the Middle East, were simply not as high. After the construction of the Berlin Wall in 1961 and the energy crisis of the mid-1970s, this perception would change dramatically, but although history can be read backward, it must be lived forward. In the late 1940s, Germany was the great bone of contention, with Soviet desires for massive reparations from a weakened, incapacitated Germany clashing directly with Western hopes for a free and prosperous Germany that could serve both as a bulwark against Communist expansion and as the main engine of Europe's economic recovery.

Third: The availability of nuclear weapons was to a significant degree responsible for the unusual nature of the Cold War. The horrifying possibility of nuclear holocaust led the superpowers to be cautious about confronting one another directly, and this absence of direct confrontation may well have prevented a conventional third world war. Instead, the Soviets and Americans pursued each other by proxy, competing for the affections of newly emerging nations, threatening each other's surrogates, and occasionally (as in Korea, Vietnam, and Afghanistan) fighting conventional wars in regions where the other's vital interests were not directly threatened. From time to time, each side feared that its opponent might react to a crisis elsewhere by forcing a showdown in Europe, but this never occurred, in part because both sides realized that a European conflict might lead to nuclear war.

This "positive" influence of nuclear weapons was more than offset by negative ones. The nuclear arms race quickly became self-fulfilling, prolonging the Cold War and giving military establishments on both sides a vested interest in continued tension. As a result, each side ended up with the capacity to destroy the entire world dozens of times over, at a cost of colossal sums of money, huge commitments of productive capacity, and devastating psychological consequences. Hundreds of millions of people lived and died in fear that a nuclear war might break out either by design or by accident. The grinding frustration of money wasted and dreams deferred, juxtaposed with a permanent, subliminal balance of terror, helped account for the bitter edge so characteristic of the Cold War.

Fourth: The Cold War era's two dominant developments, the East–West conflict and "Third World" decolonization, were inextricably interwoven. Western Europe's devastation during World War II, and the subsequent demise of its great global empires, not only left the Soviets and Americans as the main global powers but also facilitated the Cold War's globalization. As Africans and Asians fought to free themselves from Europe's colonial control, and as some Latin Americans sought to escape U.S. economic domination, the Soviets supported "national liberation movements" as a way to weaken the West and advance Communist interests. The United States, caught between its commitments to its European allies and its support for national self-determination, sought to counter Soviet advances by backing anti-Communist elements in the emerging nations. Despite the efforts of some of these new nations to form a nonaligned movement, their desperate needs and conflicting ideologies eventually forced most of them to seek support from one superpower or the other, fostering regional conflicts and turning Third World nations into Cold War battlegrounds.

Fifth: The Cold War evolved through a number of phases, three of which were crucial to its development.

a. The Critical Period of 1948–1949, which included the Truman Doctrine and Marshall Plan, the founding of the Cominform, the Berlin Blockade, the formation of NATO, and the Chinese Revolution. The Truman Doctrine and Marshall Plan committed America to devote its vast resources to containment of Communism, and the Soviet response—including opposition to Marshall

Plan aid and creation of the Cominform—further transformed the victorious Grand Alliance into two hostile camps. The Berlin Blockade sparked the Cold War's first major crisis, but it also showed both sides that postwar crises could be contained and that the costs of war might well outweigh the prizes to be gained by winning. After the blockade, policymakers talked less about the inevitability of a third world war and more about the necessity of avoiding one. NATO provided a framework for the Cold War and the nuclear arms race. It led eventually to the creation of the Warsaw Pact and the division of Europe into heavily armed alliances, and it committed the West to vigorous efforts to maintain its atomic advantage, in order to offset the preponderance of Soviet conventional forces in that divided continent. The Communist takeover in China intensified the burgeoning "Red Scare" in the United States and resulted in a massive U.S. global effort to counter the spread of Communism. By the end of this period, the structures and beliefs that dominated the Cold War were pretty much in place.

b. **The Critical Period of 1961–1962,** including the construction of the Berlin Wall and the Cuban Missile Crisis. The wall defused the chronic Berlin crises of 1948–1961 and reduced tensions in Germany considerably. The Soviets now had a way to staunch the hemorrhage of skilled workers fleeing from East to West, while Washington possessed a propaganda club with which to bludgeon Moscow. It was a situation that neither side especially liked, but it was one that both could live with. The missile crisis took the superpowers to the brink of nuclear war and convinced them not only that they must prevent such a catastrophe but also that each had an overriding interest in avoiding nuclear brinkmanship and lessening global tensions. At the same time, it helped persuade Soviet leaders to embark on a massive and sustained buildup of their naval and nuclear forces. The Cold War thus entered a new phase, as each side sought to minimize direct confrontation and maneuver for advantage through weapons buildup, arms negotiations, and struggles in the Third World.

c. **The Critical Period of 1985–1986,** which included Reagan's efforts to end the strategic standoff, the passing of the World War II generation of Soviet leaders and accession of Gorbachev, the American introduction of advanced technological weaponry into the Afghanistan conflict, the reversal of the arms race, and the revolutions of Eastern Europe. Ironically, many Western experts in the 1970s and 1980s dreaded the demise of the older generation of Communists, fearing that younger Soviet leaders who had not experienced firsthand the terrible suffering of World War II would be more likely to risk war. But Reagan, whose vision of a nuclear-free world was seen as naïve by both his hard-line aides and his critics, welcomed the emergence of Gorbachev, who brought to power a new group of leaders less shackled by fear of Germany and more willing to seek accommodation with the West. The failure of Gorbachev's economic reforms, and the devastating impact of sophisticated U.S. technology on Soviet forces in Afghanistan, helped convince Gorbachev that the Soviets, in order to compete economically and technologically with the West, must drastically cut their costly commitments to military force and support for satellite regimes. These developments broke the logjam that had existed for decades and set in motion events that led to global arms reduction, the destruction of the Berlin Wall, the liberation of Eastern Europe, and the end of the Cold War.

Sixth: Ironically, many of the things that the USSR did to strengthen itself during the Cold War provoked reactions in the West that actually weakened Soviet security. Moscow's efforts to bolster its position in Central Europe, for example, helped first to provoke the creation of NATO and then to reinforce its cohesion. And more often than not, whenever the Kremlin moved to upgrade its weaponry, redress the strategic balance (as in Cuba in 1962), or enhance its political leverage over a nonaligned nation, its actions provoked an American response that ensured Washington's relative supremacy. In the end, the Soviets could not overcome the economic and technological advantages enjoyed by the United States, no matter how hard they worked to do so.

Seventh: The Soviet system proved more rigid than those of the Western democracies and, therefore, less adaptable to changing circumstances and technological progress. Gorbachev, recognizing this lack of adaptability, decided to seek both economic and political democratization simultaneously in order to reform the system from its roots to its branches.

Unfortunately for him, his efforts at political democratization undercut his economic program, depriving the central authorities of the means to impose strict discipline and loosening the bonds of fear that held the whole system together. Gorbachev's attempt to do too much too quickly, coupled with his underestimation of the potency of the appeal of nationalism, split the Communist party and wrecked the Soviet Union.

THE LEGACY OF THE COLD WAR

The end of the Cold War and the collapse of the Soviet state brought on a worldwide surge of hopefulness and relief. Nations that had existed for years under occupation and oppression now found themselves independent and free. People who had lived most or all of their lives with the fear of a nuclear holocaust now could face the future with fresh confidence and security. In Russia and the United States, military budgets were slashed, force levels were cut, and nuclear arsenals were reduced. A new age of peace and freedom seemed to be dawning, as nations prepared to work toward what George H. W. Bush called a "new world order."

Yet even as Eastern peoples celebrated their new freedom and Western nations congratulated themselves on their "victory" in the Cold War, it was painfully obvious that the new world order was not necessarily less perilous nor more stable than the old. The Cold War may have ended, but it had left behind a legacy of economic woes and political antagonisms, as well as hatreds, resentments, and fears, that would not soon disappear.

In Soviet successor states and former Soviet satellites, the heady flush of exultation soon gave way to the bitter realities of economic crisis and political chaos. The transition from central state planning to free market economy proved far more lengthy and painful than most imagined, while nationalist rivalries and antagonisms, long suppressed by Soviet force, quickly reemerged. In Russia itself, the transition was marked by political and economic instability until the early twenty-first century, when global demand for its oil and gas brought a measure of prosperity, and a new regime reimposed central state controls reminiscent of the Soviet era.

The West for a time in the wake of the Cold War enjoyed prosperity and stability, but even there, grave challenges emerged. Europe moved toward greater integration, as former nations of the Soviet bloc joined NATO and the European Union, an enhanced and enlarged successor to the EEC. But the breakup of Yugoslavia into smaller ethnic republics led to bloody wars and "ethnic cleansings" in the 1990s. America reigned as the sole surviving superpower, enjoying unmatched wealth and influence. But its global dominance and continuing Middle East presence inspired the growth of shadowy Islamist terrorist networks that were violently anti-Western. Their attacks on America and its allies led the United States into wars in Iraq (2003), where it deposed the Saddam Hussein regime but then struggled to restore stability, and Afghanistan (2001), where ironically it faced some of the same forces it had armed to fight the Soviets in the 1980s.

In retrospect, it seemed, there were some advantages to the Cold War. For over four decades, a large measure of international stability was maintained by the worldwide balance of terror. Ethnic hostilities in the USSR and Eastern Europe were held in check by the overwhelming reality of Soviet power, while civil and social strife in the socialist world were similarly suppressed. The military-industrial complexes on both sides of the iron curtain provided secure employment to many and impressive wealth to a few. Prosperity reigned in the capitalist world, fueled in part by international tension, and technological spin-offs from military research and space exploration helped bring the "good life" to the masses. Even in the socialist world, where goods were scarce and life was comparatively drab, there was full employment, job security, and a broad panoply of state-supplied basic services ranging from health care to housing. And the international scene seemed simpler and more stable: In a bipolar world, alliances remained rather steady, and it was relatively easy to distinguish one's friends from one's foes.

Still, the Cold War was hardly a golden age of tranquility and stability. Although no third world war broke out, millions continued to perish in regional conflicts. Indeed, during most of the Cold War years, there was almost always a "hot" war going on somewhere, whether in China, Korea, Vietnam, Cambodia, Angola, Afghanistan, or elsewhere. At least fifteen million died in such conflicts, as well as in the countless insurrections, civil wars, and persecutions that arose. The world lurched from crisis to crisis, any one of which could have led to a devastating local conflict or an all-out nuclear war. And although there is no way to measure adequately the psychological impact of decades of life under the nuclear sword, there is no reason to suppose that it was beneficial to humanity.

The fact is, however, that the world survived the Cold War. Bitter adversaries, facing the possibility of mutual annihilation, somehow found ways to contain their conflict in the interest of self-preservation. Despite their rhetoric, leaders on both sides learned to live with the ambiguity inherent in a continual state of international confrontation and to adjust to a world in which nuclear weapons had radically altered the calculus of war and peace. In the aftermath of the Cold War, as the nations of the world sailed into uncharted waters, they could take comfort in the fact that they had already made their way through very stormy seas and had managed to endure a hard and bitter peace.

Cold War Documents

1. The Yalta Conference, February 1945

During World War II, despite mutual distrust, the Soviet Union and the Western powers cooperated in a Grand Alliance to defeat Nazi Germany. From 1941 to 1944, the Soviets bore the brunt of this struggle, reversing the German onslaught, while the British and Americans, who were also fighting Japan without Soviet help, delayed opening a second front in the west—much to Moscow's dismay. Not until June of 1944 did they finally launch their "D-day" invasion of Nazi-occupied France.

In February of 1945, the "Big Three" leaders—U.S. president Franklin Roosevelt, British prime minister Winston Churchill, and Soviet premier Joseph Stalin—convened at Yalta in the Soviet Crimea. By then the Anglo-American forces had driven the Germans from France, the Soviets had occupied Poland, and German defeat was in sight. The war against Japan, however, seemed far from over. Anxious to secure Soviet cooperation in this conflict, Roosevelt was willing to concede Russian dominance in Poland, which was already occupied by the Red Army and administered by a Soviet-sponsored provisional government. He and Churchill tried to get the best bargain they could, but the final agreement on Poland, regardless of its language, would be implemented by the occupying Soviets. Later, as the Communists assumed full control, the Western leaders would be accused of having sold out the Poles.

The Yalta agreements on Poland and Japan are reproduced in the following section. The statement on Poland was released at the end of the conference, but the secret agreement on Japan was not made public until several years later.

A. Declaration on Poland

A new situation has been created in Poland as a result of her complete liberation by the Red Army. This calls for the establishment of a Polish Provisional Government which can be more broadly based than was possible before the recent liberation of the Western part of Poland. The Provisional Government which is now functioning in Poland should therefore be reorganized on a broader democratic basis with the inclusion of democratic leaders from Poland itself and from Poles abroad. This new government should then be called the Polish Provisional Government of National Unity.

M. Molotov, Mr. Harriman, and Sir A. Clark Kerr are authorized as a mission to consult . . . with members of the present Provisional Government and with other Polish democratic leaders from within Poland and from abroad, with a view to the reorganization of the present Government along the above lines. This Polish Provisional Government of National Unity shall be pledged to the holding of free and unfettered elections as soon as possible on the basis of universal suffrage and secret ballot. In these elections all democratic and anti-Nazi parties shall have the right to take part and to put forward candidates.

When a Polish Provisional Government of National Unity has been properly formed in conformity with the above, the Government of the USSR, which now maintains diplomatic relations with the present Provisional Government of Poland, and the Government of the United Kingdom and the Government of the USA will establish diplomatic relations with the new Polish Provisional Government of National Unity, and will exchange Ambassadors by whose reports the respective Governments will be kept informed about the situation in Poland.

The three Heads of Government consider that the Eastern frontier of Poland should follow the Curzon Line with digressions from it in some regions of five to eight kilometers in favor of Poland. They recognize that Poland must receive substantial accessions of territory in the north and west. They feel that the opinion of the new Polish Provisional Government of National Unity should be sought in due course on the extent of these accessions and that the final delimitation of the Western frontier of Poland should thereafter await the peace conference.

B. Agreement Regarding Soviet Entry into the War Against Japan

The leaders of the three great powers—the Soviet Union, the United States of America, and Great Britain—have agreed that in two or three months after Germany has surrendered and the war in Europe has terminated the Soviet Union shall enter into the war against Japan on the side of the Allies on condition that:

1. The status quo in Outer Mongolia (The Mongolian People's Republic) shall be preserved,
2. The former rights of Russia violated by the treacherous attack of Japan in 1904 shall be restored, viz.:
   - **(A)** the southern part of Sakhalin, as well as all the islands adjacent to it, shall be returned to the Soviet Union,
   - **(B)** the commercial port of Dairen shall be internationalized, the pre-eminent interests of the Soviet Union in this port being safeguarded and the lease of Port Arthur as a naval base of the USSR restored,
   - **(C)** the Chinese-Eastern Railroad and the South-Manchurian Railroad which provides an outlet to Dairen shall be jointly operated by the establishment of a joint Soviet-Chinese Company, it being understood that the pre-eminent interests of the Soviet Union shall be safeguarded and that China shall retain full sovereignty in Manchuria;
3. The Kurile islands shall be handed over to the Soviet Union. . . .

The heads of the three great powers have agreed that these claims of the Soviet Union shall be unquestionably fulfilled after Japan has been defeated.

For its part the Soviet Union expresses its readiness to conclude with the National Government of China a pact of friendship and alliance between the USSR and China in order to render assistance to China with its armed forces for the purpose of liberating China from the Japanese yoke.

DISCUSSION QUESTIONS

1. Why did Roosevelt and Churchill agree to allow the Soviet-sponsored Provisional Government to continue in power in Poland?
2. Why did they want it reorganized to include democratic leaders and committed to "free and unfettered" elections?

3. What factors would make it possible for the Soviets to establish Communist control in Poland, despite these provisions?
4. Why did the agreement on Japan promise the Soviet Union so much territory in East Asia?
5. To what extent were Roosevelt and Churchill guilty of having "sold out" Poland at Yalta? What other choice did they have?

2. The Potsdam Conference, July–August 1945

Germany's surrender in May 1945 was followed by its division into zones of occupation, with the Soviets in the east and the other Allies in the west, and by another major conference of Allied leaders. From 17 July through 2 August 1945, at the city of Potsdam near the German capital of Berlin, Stalin met again with Western leaders—but they were not the same ones he had dealt with at Yalta. Roosevelt's death in April meant that a new president, Harry Truman, would represent the United States. Churchill was present at the start of the Potsdam conference, but he and his cabinet were soon turned out of power as the result of recent elections, and he was replaced at Potsdam by a new prime minister, Clement Attlee.

The conference saw growing contention between the Soviets and the West but resulted in what seemed a reasonable compromise. The Soviet Union would take the $10 billion in reparations it demanded from Germany from its occupation zone alone, rather than from the entire country. In return, the Americans and British would agree to the new Polish–German borders favored by Moscow and would grant the Soviets a percentage of capital equipment from the western-occupied zones. As the conference closed on 2 August, it was clear that the Grand Alliance was functioning less smoothly now that Germany had been defeated, but at this stage no government was yet talking about Cold War.

Excerpts from the Berlin (Potsdam) Conference Report, 2 August 1945

III. Germany

The Political and Economic Principles to Govern the Treatment of Germany in the Initial Control Period

A. POLITICAL PRINCIPLES

1. In accordance with the Agreement on Control Machinery in Germany, supreme authority in Germany is exercised, on instructions from their respective Governments, by the Commanders-in-Chief of the armed forces of the United States of America, the United Kingdom, the Union of Soviet Socialist Republics, and the French Republic, each in his own zone of occupation, and also jointly, in matters affecting Germany as a whole, in their capacity as members of the Control Council. . . .

B. ECONOMIC PRINCIPLES 11. In order to eliminate Germany's war potential, the production of arms, ammunitions and implements of war as well as all types of aircraft and sea-going ships shall be prohibited and prevented. Production of metals, chemicals, machinery and other items that are directly necessary to a war economy shall be rigidly controlled and restricted. . . .

IV. Reparations From Germany

1. Reparation claims of the USSR shall be met by removals from the zone of Germany occupied by the USSR, and from appropriate German external assets.
2. The USSR undertakes to settle the reparation claims of Poland from its own share of reparations.
3. The reparation claims of the United States, the United Kingdom and other countries

entitled to reparations shall be met from the Western Zones and from appropriate German external assets.

4. In addition to the reparations to be taken by the USSR from its own zone of occupation, the USSR shall receive additionally from the Western zones:

(a) 15 percent of such usable and complete industrial capital equipment from the metallurgical, chemical and machine manufacturing industries as is unnecessary for the German peace economy and should be removed from the Western Zones of Germany, in exchange for an equivalent value of food, coal, potash, zinc, timber, clay products, petroleum products, and such other commodities as may be agreed upon.

(b) 10 percent of such industrial capital equipment as is unnecessary for the German peace economy and should be removed from the Western Zones, to be transferred to the Soviet Government on reparations account without payment or exchange of any kind in return. . . .

8. The Soviet Government renounces all claims in respect of reparations to shares of German enterprises which are located in the Western Zones of occupation in Germany as well as to German foreign assets in all countries except those specified in paragraph 9 below.

9. The Governments of the UK and USA renounce their claims in respect of reparations to shares of German enterprises which are located in the Eastern Zone of occupation in Germany, as well as to German foreign assets in Bulgaria, Finland, Hungary, Rumania and Eastern Austria. . . .

IX. Poland

A. We have taken note with pleasure of the agreement reached among representative Poles from Poland and abroad which has made possible the formation, in accordance with the decisions reached at the Crimea Conference, of a Polish Provisional Government of National Unity recognized by the Three Powers. The establishment by the British and the United States Governments of diplomatic relations with the Polish Provisional Government of National Unity has resulted in the withdrawal of their recognition from the former Polish Government in London, which no longer exists. . . .

The Three Powers note that the Polish Provisional Government of National Unity, in accordance with the decisions of the Crimea Conference, has agreed to the holding of free and unfettered elections as soon as possible on the basis of universal suffrage and secret ballot in which all democratic and anti-Nazi parties shall have the right to take part and to put forward candidates, and that the representatives of the Allied press shall enjoy full freedom to report to the world upon developments in Poland before and during the elections.

B. The following agreement was reached on the western frontier of Poland:

In conformity with the agreement on Poland reached at the Crimea Conference the Three Heads of Government have sought the opinion of the Polish Provisional Government of National Unity in regard to the accession of territory in the north and west which Poland should receive. . . .

The Three Heads of Government agree that, pending the final determination of Poland's western frontier, the former German territories east of a line running from the Baltic Sea immediately west of Swinamunde, and thence along the Oder River to the confluence of the western Neisse River and along the western Neisse to the Czechoslovak frontier . . . shall be under the administration of the Polish State and for such purposes should not be considered as part of the Soviet zone of occupation in Germany. . . .

XIII. Orderly Transfer of German Populations

The Three Governments . . . recognize that the transfer to Germany of German populations, or elements thereof, remaining in Poland, Czechoslovakia, and Hungary, will have to be undertaken. They agree that any transfers that take place should be effected in an orderly and humane manner . . .

DISCUSSION QUESTIONS

1. Why did the members of the Grand Alliance continue working together at Potsdam despite their differences?
2. Who was assigned supreme authority in occupied Germany? Why was this done?
3. Why were the Soviets determined to receive industrial reparations from defeated Germany?
4. Why did the Western leaders agree to the new Polish–German borders favored by Moscow?
5. In what ways did the Potsdam agreements set the stage for the future division of Europe into Eastern and Western Blocs?

3. The Atomic Bombing of Hiroshima, August 1945

On 6 August 1945, the United States dropped an atomic bomb on the city of Hiroshima in Japan, obliterating that city and inaugurating the atomic age. This bomb, and the one dropped on Nagasaki three days later, helped bring the Pacific War to an expeditious end, without the need for an Allied invasion of Japan. It also thus prevented the Soviets, who on August 8 declared war on Japan in accordance with their Yalta commitment, from invading and occupying part of Japan. And it left them scrambling to catch up with the Americans in atomic weaponry.

The impact of Hiroshima and Nagasaki on Soviet–American relations was profound. The Truman administration, delighted with its new weapon, became less willing to compromise with Moscow. Stalin promptly diverted massive Soviet resources, desperately needed to repair the devastation caused by the German invasion, to an all-out program designed to build a comparable bomb as quickly as possible. After the Soviet bomb was tested successfully in 1949, Truman made the decision to begin development of a much more powerful hydrogen-fusion (or thermonuclear) bomb; the Soviets followed suit, and the nuclear arms race was on.

Statement by President Truman, 6 August 1945

Sixteen hours ago an American airplane dropped one bomb on Hiroshima, an important Japanese Army base. That bomb had more power than 20,000 tons of T.N.T. It had more than two thousand times the blast power of the British "Grand Slam," which is the largest bomb ever yet used in the history of warfare.

The Japanese began the war from the air at Pearl Harbor. They have been repaid many fold. And the end is not yet. With this bomb we have now added a new and revolutionary increase in destruction to supplement the growing power of our armed forces. In their present forms these bombs are now in production and even more powerful forms are in development.

It is an atomic bomb. It is a harnessing of the basic power of the universe. The force from which the sun draws its power has been loosed against those who brought war to the Far East.

Before 1939, it was the accepted belief of scientists that it was theoretically possible to release atomic energy. But no one knew any practical method of doing it. By 1942, however, we knew that the Germans were working feverishly to find a way to add atomic energy to the other engines of war with which they hoped to enslave the world. But they failed. We may be grateful to Providence that the Germans got the V–1's and the V–2's late and in limited quantities and even more grateful that they did not get the atomic bomb at all.

The battle of the laboratories held fateful risks for us as well as the battles of the air, land, and sea, and we have now won the battle of the laboratories as we have won the other battles. . . . We have spent two billion dollars on the greatest scientific gamble in history—and won.

But the greatest marvel is not the size of this enterprise, its secrecy, nor its cost, but the achievement of scientific brains in putting together infinitely complex pieces of knowledge held by many men in different fields of science into a workable plan. And hardly less marvelous has been the capacity of industry to design, and of labor to operate, the machines and methods to do things never done before so that the brain child of many minds came forth in physical shape and performed as it was supposed to do. . . . What has been done is the greatest achievement of organized science in history. It was done under high pressure and without failure.

We are now prepared to obliterate more rapidly and completely every productive enterprise the Japanese have above ground in any city. We shall destroy their docks, their factories, and their communications. Let there be no mistakes; we shall completely destroy Japan's power to make war.

It was to spare the Japanese people from utter destruction that the ultimatum of July 26 was issued at Potsdam. Their leaders promptly rejected that ultimatum. If they do not now accept our terms, they may expect a rain of ruin from the air, the like of which has never been seen on this earth. Behind this air attack will follow sea and land forces in such numbers and power as they have not yet seen and with the fighting skill of which they are already well aware. . . .

The fact that we can release atomic energy ushers in a new era in man's understanding of nature's forces. Atomic energy may in the future supplement the power that now comes from coal, oil, and falling water, but at present it cannot be produced on a basis to compete with them commercially. Before that comes, there must be a long period of intensive research.

It has never been the habit of the scientists of this country or the policy of this Government to withhold from the world scientific knowledge. Normally, therefore, everything about the work with atomic energy would be made public.

But under present circumstances it is not intended to divulge the technical processes of production or all the military applications, pending further examination of possible methods of protecting us and the rest of the world from the danger of sudden destruction.

I shall recommend that the Congress of the United States consider promptly the establishment of an appropriate commission to control the production and use of atomic power within the United States. I shall give further consideration and make further recommendations to the Congress as to how atomic power can become a powerful and forceful influence towards the maintenance of world peace.

DISCUSSION QUESTIONS

1. Why was Truman so pleased with the development and use of the atomic bomb? What benefits did he expect from it?
2. How did Truman justify the use of atomic weapons? Why did he call Hiroshima a "Japanese Army base"? Why did he mention Pearl Harbor and Germany's effort to build an atomic bomb?
3. Did Truman assume that the dropping of the bomb on Hiroshima would make an invasion of Japan unnecessary? How do you know?
4. What impact was the atomic bomb likely to have on Soviet–American relations? Why might Stalin be less than pleased that his American allies had developed such a powerful weapon?

4. Stalin's Election Speech, February 1946

On 9 February 1946, Joseph Stalin delivered an "election" speech to an assembly of voters in Moscow. In the USSR, elections were not designed to give voters a choice between competing candidates or programs. There was only one candidate for each position, and that candidate always endorsed the Communist Party's positions. Election speeches were therefore used to inform citizens of those positions, to defend and justify them, and to identify the candidate as a person worthy of trust and responsibility. When one of the party leaders spoke, everyone listened attentively, for the speech might contain hints as to the future actions of the Soviet government.

On this occasion, Stalin reasserted the validity of Marxist-Leninist thought, blamed World War II on conflicts among capitalists, and painted the contrast between capitalism and Communism in vivid colors not used in official Soviet pronouncements since 1941. Although it was intended largely to rally the Soviet peoples for continued sacrifices in rebuilding their war-torn country, his speech was viewed by many in the West as a declaration of Cold War against the capitalist world.

Highlights of Stalin's Election Speech, 9 February 1946

Comrades! Eight years have elapsed since the last elections. This is a period rich in events of a decisive character. The first four years passed in strenuous work of the Soviet people in the fulfillment of the Third Five–Year Plan. During the past four years the events of the struggle against the German and Japanese aggressors developed—the events of the Second World War. Doubtless the war was the main event of that period.

It would be incorrect to think that the war arose accidentally or as the result of the fault of some of the statesmen. Although these faults did exist, the war arose in reality as the inevitable result of the development of the world economic and political forces on the basis of monopoly capitalism.

Our Marxists declare that the capitalist system of world economy conceals elements of crisis and war, that the development of world capitalism does not follow a steady and even course forward, but proceeds through crises and catastrophes. The uneven development of the capitalist countries leads in time to sharp disturbances in their relations, and the group of countries which consider themselves inadequately provided with raw materials and export markets try usually to change this situation and to change the position in their favor by means of armed force. As a result of these factors, the capitalist world is sent into two hostile camps and war follows.

Perhaps the catastrophe of war could have been avoided if the possibility of periodic redistribution of raw materials and markets between the countries existed in accordance with their economic needs, in the way of coordinated and peaceful decisions. But this is impossible under the present capitalist development of world economy.

Thus, as a result of the first crisis in the development of the capitalist world economy, the First World War arose. The Second World War arose as a result of the second crisis. . . .

What about the origin and character of the Second World War? In my opinion, everybody now recognizes that the war against fascism was not, nor could it be, an accident in the life of the people; that the war turned into a war of the peoples for their existence; that precisely for this reason it could not be a speedy war, a "lightning war."

As far as our country is concerned, this war was the most cruel and hard of all wars ever experienced in the history of our motherland. But the war has not only been a curse; it was at the same time a hard school of trial and a testing of all the people's forces. . . .

And so, what is the balance of the war; what are our conclusions? . . .

Now victory means, first of all, that our Soviet social system has won, that the Soviet social system has successfully stood the test in the fire of war and has proved its complete vitality. . . .

The war has shown that the Soviet multinational state system has successfully stood the test, has grown still stronger during the war and has proved a completely vital state system. . . .

Third, our victory implies that it was the Soviet armed forces that won. Our Red Army had won. The Red Army heroically withstood all the adversities of the war, routed completely the armies of our enemies and emerged victoriously from the war. . . .

Now a few words on the plans for the work of the Communist Party in the near future. . . . The fundamental task of the new Five-Year Plan consists in restoring the areas of the country which have suffered, restoring the pre-war level in industry and agriculture, and then exceeding this level by more or less considerable amounts. . . .

DISCUSSION QUESTIONS

1. How did Stalin explain the outbreak of World War II?
2. How can you tell that Stalin's explanation is based on Marxist principles?
3. Why did Stalin emphasize so strongly that the Soviet social and state systems had triumphed, in addition to the obvious victory of the Red Army?
4. Why was this speech viewed with alarm in Washington and London?
5. If an American or British politician had been making a similar speech, how would his or her reasoning and explanations have differed from those of Stalin?

5. Churchill's Iron Curtain Speech, March 1946

In February 1946, several weeks after Stalin's election speech, former British prime minister Winston Churchill visited the United States. Increasingly concerned over Soviet behavior, he confided his fears in President Truman. The two men decided that Churchill should deliver a major address in Fulton, Missouri, to alert the world to the Soviet threat. That candid speech, in which Churchill used the term "iron curtain" to describe the barrier Moscow had placed between the West and the Communist-dominated nations of Eastern Europe, startled many Americans and infuriated Stalin. Churchill issued a ringing call for the continuation of Anglo-American wartime cooperation, this time against a Soviet Union he viewed as bent on world domination. Although he was no longer prime minister, his dramatic and quotable speech made headlines throughout the world and came to be considered a declaration of Cold War.

Stalin's reaction to the "iron curtain" speech was vigorous and direct. In a subsequent interview in the Soviet newspaper *Pravda*, he characterized Churchill as a man bent on war against the Soviet Union. He defended Soviet actions in Eastern Europe, pointing out the importance of that region for Soviet security and insisting that the governments there were democratic. Considering it unlikely that Truman would have appeared on the platform with Churchill had he disagreed with the latter's remarks, Stalin also asserted that the Americans and British were banding together against their wartime Soviet allies.

A. Highlights of Churchill's "Iron Curtain" Speech, 5 March 1946

The United States stands at this time at the pinnacle of world power. It is a solemn moment for the American democracy. For with this primacy in power is also joined an awe-inspiring accountability to the future. . . . Opportunity is here now, clear and shining, for both our countries. To reject it or ignore it or fritter it away will bring upon us all the long reproaches of the after-time. It is necessary that constancy of mind, persistency of purpose, and the grand simplicity of decision shall guide and rule the conduct of the English-speaking peoples in peace as they did in war. We must and I believe we shall prove ourselves equal to this severe requirement. . . .

A shadow has fallen upon the scenes so lately lighted by the Allied victory. Nobody knows what Soviet Russia and its Communist international organization intends to do in the immediate future, or what are the limits, if any, to their expansive and proselytizing tendencies. I have a strong admiration and regard for the valiant Russian people and for my wartime comrade, Marshal Stalin. There is sympathy and good-will in Britain—and I doubt not here also—toward the peoples of all the Russias and a resolve to persevere through many differences and rebuffs in establishing lasting friendships.

We understand the Russian need to be secure on her western frontiers . . . by the removal of all possibility of German aggression. We welcome Russia to her rightful place among the leading nations of the world. . . . It is my duty, however . . . to place before you certain facts about the present position in Europe.

From Stettin in the Baltic to Trieste in the Adriatic, an iron curtain has descended across the Continent. Behind that line lie all the capitals of the ancient states of central and eastern Europe. Warsaw, Berlin, Prague, Vienna, Budapest, Belgrade, Bucharest, and Sofia, all these famous cities and the populations around them lie in what I might call the Soviet sphere, and all are subject, in one form or another, not only to Soviet influence but to a very high and increasing measure of control from Moscow. . . .

The Russian-dominated Polish Government has been encouraged to make enormous and wrongful inroads upon Germany, and mass expulsions of millions of Germans on a scale grievous and undreamed of are now taking place. The Communist parties, which were very small in all these eastern states of Europe, have been raised to preeminence and power far beyond their numbers and are seeking everywhere to obtain totalitarian control. Police governments are prevailing in nearly every case, and so far, except in Czechoslovakia, there is no true democracy. Turkey and Persia are both profoundly alarmed and disturbed at the claims which are made upon them and at the pressure being exerted by the Moscow government.

An attempt is being made by the Russians in Berlin to build up a quasi-Communist party in their zone of occupied Germany by showing special favors to groups of left-wing German leaders. . . .

Whatever conclusions may be drawn from these facts—and facts they are—this is certainly not the liberated Europe we fought to build up. Nor is it one which contains the essentials of permanent peace. . . .

In front of the iron curtain which lies across Europe are other causes for anxiety. In Italy the Communist Party is seriously hampered by having to support the Communist-trained Marshal Tito's claims to former Italian territory at the head of the Adriatic. Nevertheless, the future of Italy hangs in the balance. Again, one cannot imagine a regenerated Europe without a strong France. . . .

However, in a great number of countries, far from the Russian frontiers and throughout the world, Communist fifth columns are established and work in complete unity and absolute obedience to the directions they received from the Communist center. Except in the British Commonwealth, and in the United States, where Communism is in its infancy, the Communist parties or fifth columns constitute a growing challenge and peril to Christian civilization. . . .

The outlook is also anxious in the Far East, and especially in Manchuria. The agreement which was made at Yalta, to which I was a party, was extremely favorable to Soviet Russia, but it was made at a time when no one could say that the German war might not extend all through the summer and autumn of 1945 and when the Japanese war was expected to last for a further eighteen months from the end of the German war. In this country you are so well informed about the Far East, and such devoted friends of China, that I do not need to expatiate on the situation there. . . .

On the other hand . . . I repulse the idea that a new war is inevitable; still more that it is imminent.

It is because I am sure that our fortunes are still in our hands, in our own hands, and that we hold the power to save the future, that I feel the duty to speak out now that I have an occasion to do so.

I do not believe that Soviet Russia desires war. What they desire is the fruits of war and the indefinite expansion of their power and doctrines.

But what we have to consider here today while time remains, is the permanent prevention of war and the establishment of conditions of freedom and democracy as rapidly as possible in all countries. Our difficulties and dangers will not be removed by closing our eyes to them; they will not be removed by more waiting to see what happens; nor will they be relieved by a policy of appeasement. What is needed is a settlement, and the longer this is delayed, the more difficult it will be and the greater our dangers will become.

From what I have seen of our Russian friends and allies during the war, I am convinced that there is nothing they admire so much as strength, and there is nothing for which they have less respect than for military weakness. For that . . . reason the old doctrine of a balance of power is unsound. We cannot afford, if we can help it, to work on narrow margins, offering temptations to a trial of strength. If the western democracies stand together in strict adherence to the principles of the United Nations Charter, their influence for furthering these principles will be immense and no one is likely to molest them. If, however, they become divided or falter in their duty, and if these all-important years are allowed to slip away, then indeed catastrophe may overwhelm us all.

Last time I saw it all coming, and cried aloud to my own fellow countrymen and to the world, but no one paid any attention. Up till the year 1933 or even 1935, Germany might have been saved from the awful fate which has overtaken her and we might all have been spared the miseries Hitler let loose upon mankind. There never was a war in all history easier to prevent by timely action than the one which has just desolated such great areas of the globe. It could have been prevented without the firing of a single shot, and Germany might be powerful, prosperous, and honored today, but no one would listen and one by one we were all sucked into the awful whirlpool.

We surely must not let that happen again. This can only be achieved by reaching now, in 1946 . . . a good understanding on all points with Russia under the general authority of the United Nations . . . , supported by the whole strength of the English-speaking world and all its connections. . . .

If the population of the English-speaking Commonwealth be added to that of the United States, with all such cooperation implies in the air, on the seas all over the globe, and in science and in industry, and in moral force, there will be no quivering, precarious balance of power to offer its temptation to ambition or adventure. On the contrary there will be an overwhelming assurance of security. If we adhere faithfully to the Charter of the United Nations and walk forward in sedate and sober strength, seeking no one's land or treasure, seeking to lay no arbitrary control upon the thoughts of men, if all British moral and material forces and convictions are joined with your own in fraternal association, the high roads of the future will be clear, not only for us but for all, not only for our time but for a century to come.

B. Excerpts from *Pravda*'s Interview with Stalin, March 1946

Q. How do you assess the last speech of Mr. Churchill which was made in the United States?

A. I assess it as a dangerous act calculated to sow the seed of discord among the Allied governments and hamper their cooperation.

Q. Can one consider that the speech of Mr. Churchill is damaging to the cause of peace and security?

A. Undoubtedly, yes. In substance, Mr. Churchill now stands in the position of a firebrand of war. And Mr. Churchill is not alone here. He has friends not only in England but also in the United States of America.

In this respect, one is reminded remarkably of Hitler and his friends. Hitler began to set war loose by announcing his racial theory, declaring that only people speaking the German language represent a fully valuable nation. Mr. Churchill begins to set war loose also by a racial theory, maintaining that only nations speaking the English language are fully valuable nations, called upon to decide the destinies of the entire world.

The German racial theory brought Hitler and his friends to the conclusion that the Germans, as the only fully valuable nation, must rule over other nations. The English racial theory brings Mr. Churchill and his friends to the conclusion that nations speaking the English language, being the only fully valuable nations, should rule over the remaining nations of the world. . . .

But the nations have shed their blood during five years of cruel war for the sake of liberty and the independence of their countries, and not for the sake of exchanging the lordship of Hitler for the lordship of Churchill . . .

There is no doubt that the set-up of Mr. Churchill is a set-up for war, a call to war with the Soviet Union. . . .

Q. How do you assess that part of Mr. Churchill's speech in which he attacks the democratic regime of the European countries which are our neighbors and in which he criticizes the good neighborly relations established between these countries and the Soviet Union?

A. This part of Mr. Churchill's speech is a mixture of the elements of the libel with the elements of rudeness and lack of tact. Mr. Churchill maintains that Warsaw, Berlin, Prague, Vienna, Budapest, Belgrade, Bucharest, and Sofia, all these famous cities and the population of those areas, are within the Soviet sphere and are all subjected to Soviet influence and to the increasing control of Moscow.

Mr. Churchill qualifies this as the "boundless expansionist tendencies of the Soviet Union." It requires no special effort to show that Mr. Churchill rudely and shamelessly libels not only Moscow but also the above-mentioned States neighborly to the USSR.

To begin with, it is quite absurd to speak of the exclusive control of the USSR in Vienna and Berlin, where there are Allied control councils with representatives of four States, where the USSR has only one fourth of the voices. . . .

Secondly, one cannot forget the following fact: the Germans carried out an invasion of the USSR through Finland, Poland, Rumania, Bulgaria and Hungary. The Germans were able to carry out the invasion through these countries by reason of the fact that these countries had governments inimical to the Soviet Union.

As a result of the German invasion, the Soviet Union has irrevocably lost in battles with the Germans, and also during the German occupation and through the expulsion of Soviet citizens to German slave labor camps, about 7,000,000 people. In other words, the Soviet Union has lost in men several times more than Britain and the United States together.

It may be that some quarters are trying to push into oblivion these sacrifices of the Soviet people which insured the liberation of Europe from the Hitlerite yoke. But the Soviet Union cannot forget them. One can ask, therefore, what can be surprising in the fact that the Soviet Union, in a desire to ensure its security for the future, tries to achieve that these countries should have governments whose relations to the Soviet Union are loyal? How can one, without having lost one's reason, qualify these peaceful aspirations of the Soviet Union as "expansionist tendencies" of our Government?

. . . As for Mr. Churchill's attack on the Soviet Union in connection with the extending of the western boundaries of Poland, as compensation for the territories seized by the Germans in the past, there it seems to me that he quite blatantly distorts the facts. As is known, the western frontiers of Poland were decided upon at the Berlin conference of the three powers, on the basis of Poland's demands. The Soviet Union repeatedly declared that it considered Poland's demands just and correct. It may well be that Mr. Churchill is not pleased with this decision. But why does Mr. Churchill, not sparing his darts against the Russians in the matter, conceal from his readers the fact that the decision was taken at the Berlin conference unanimously, that not only the Russians voted for this decision but also the British and Americans?

. . . Mr. Churchill further maintains that the Communist parties were very insignificant in all these Eastern European countries but reached exceptional strength, exceeding their numbers by far, and are attempting to establish totalitarian control everywhere; that police-government prevailed in almost all these countries, even up to now, with the exception of Czechoslovakia, and that there exists in them no real democracy. . . .

The growth of the influence of Communism cannot be considered accidental. It is a normal function. The influence of the Communists grew because during the hard years of the mastery of fascism in Europe, Communists showed themselves to be reliable, daring and self-sacrificing fighters against fascist regimes for the liberty of peoples. . . .

DISCUSSION QUESTIONS

1. What evidence did Churchill give of Soviet expansionism? What developments made him so insistent that Anglo-American cooperation must be preserved after World War II?
2. If Churchill recognized "the Russian need to be secure on her western frontiers," why did he object so strongly to what the Russians were doing in Eastern Europe?
3. Why did Churchill assert that "the old doctrine of the balance of power is unsound"? With what did he propose to replace it?
4. Was Stalin justified in his accusation that Churchill's speech reflected Anglo-American racism? Why or why not?
5. How did Stalin justify the extension of Soviet influence into many Eastern European countries? How did he explain the growth of Communist parties in those countries?

6. The Baruch and Gromyko Plans for Control of Atomic Weapons, 1946

In 1946, the United States enjoyed a monopoly on the production of atomic weapons, but no one believed it would last forever. Conscious that sooner or later the Soviet Union would develop its own nuclear capability, Washington sought to devise a policy that would simultaneously internationalize atomic energy, forestall Soviet acquisition of atomic weapons, and prevent a nuclear arms race. Bernard Baruch, a well-known consultant and advisor to American presidents, was selected by President Truman to present the American plan to the United Nations Atomic Energy Commission on 14 June 1946.

On its face, the Baruch Plan appeared to be a generous proposal, with its unprecedented willingness to place an American technology under international control. The Russians, however, saw it as a carefully conceived ploy to maintain the U.S. nuclear monopoly and open secret Soviet facilities to international inspection. But they could not simply reject it without damaging their standing in the eyes of world opinion. So on 19 June 1946, Soviet delegate Andrei Gromyko presented a draft treaty designed to prohibit the manufacture and deployment of atomic weapons. All such weapons would be destroyed three months after the conclusion of the convention; punishment for violators would be fixed by mutual agreement three months after that. Inspection of plants and stockpiles was not mentioned at all. As a result of the fundamental differences between the American and Soviet approaches, neither plan was approved, and efforts to prevent a nuclear arms race proved futile.

A. Speech by Bernard Baruch to the UN Atomic Energy Commission, 14 June 1946

My fellow-members of the United Nations Atomic Energy Commission, and my fellow-citizens of the world:

We are here to make a choice between the quick and the dead. That is our business.

Behind the black portent of the new atomic age lies a hope which, seized upon with faith, can work our salvation. If we fail, then we have damned every man to be the slave of fear. Let us not deceive ourselves: We must elect world peace or world destruction.

Science has torn from nature a secret so vast in its potentialities that our minds cower from the terror it creates. Yet terror is not enough to inhibit the use of the atomic bomb. The terror created by weapons has never stopped man from employing them. . . .

Science, which gave us this dread power, shows that it can be made a giant help to humanity, but science does not show us how to prevent its baleful use. So we have been appointed to obviate that peril by finding a meeting of the minds and the hearts of our peoples. Only in the will of mankind lies the answer.

It is to express this will and make it effective that we have been assembled. We must provide the mechanism to assure that atomic energy is used for peaceful purposes and preclude its use in war. To that end, we must provide immediate, swift, and sure punishment of those who violate the agreements that are reached by the nations. Penalization is essential if peace is to be more than a feverish interlude between wars. . . .

The United States proposes the creation of an International Atomic Development Authority, to which should be entrusted all phases of the development and use of atomic energy, starting with the raw material and including—

(1) Managerial control or ownership of all atomic-energy activities potentially dangerous to world security.

(2) Power to control, inspect, and license all other atomic activities.

(3) The duty of fostering the beneficial uses of atomic energy.

(4) Research and development responsibilities of an affirmative character intended to put the Authority in the forefront of atomic knowledge and thus to enable it to comprehend, and therefore to detect, misuse of atomic energy. . . .

I offer this as a basis for beginning our discussion.

But I think the peoples we serve would not believe . . . that a treaty, merely outlawing possession or use of the atomic bomb, constitutes effective fulfillment of the instructions of this Commission. Previous failures have been recorded in trying the method of simple renunciation, unsupported by effective guaranties of security and armament limitation. No one would have faith in that approach alone. . . . If I read the signs aright, the peoples want a program not composed merely of pious thoughts but of enforceable sanctions—an international law with teeth in it.

We of this nation, desirous of helping to bring peace to the world and realizing the heavy obligations upon us, arising from our possession of the means for producing the bomb and from the fact that it is part of our armament, are prepared to make our full contribution toward effective control of atomic energy.

When an adequate system for control of atomic energy, including the renunciation of the bomb as a weapon, has been agreed upon and put into effective operation and condign punishments set up for violations of the rules of control which are to be stigmatized as international crimes, we propose that:

(1) Manufacture of atomic bombs shall stop;

(2) Existing bombs shall be disposed of pursuant to the terms of the treaty, and

(3) The Authority shall be in possession of full information as to the know-how for the production of atomic energy. . . .

Now as to violations: in the agreement, penalties of as serious a nature as the nations may wish and as immediate and certain in their execution as possible, should be fixed for:

(1) Illegal possession or use of an atomic bomb;
(2) Illegal possession, or separation, of atomic material suitable for use in an atomic bomb;
(3) Seizure of any plant or other property belonging to or licensed by the Authority;
(4) Willful interference with the activities of the Authority;
(5) Creation or operation of dangerous projects in a manner contrary to, or in the absence of, a license granted by the international control body.

It would be a deception, to which I am unwilling to lend myself, were I not to say to you and to our peoples, that the matter of punishment lies at the very heart of our present security system. It might as well be admitted, here and now, that the subject goes straight to the veto power contained in the Charter of the United Nations so far as it relates to the field of atomic energy. The Charter permits penalization only by concurrence of each of the five great powers—Union of Soviet Socialist Republics, the United Kingdom, China, France and the United States. I want to make very plain that I am concerned here with the veto power only as it affects this particular problem. There must be no veto to protect those who violate their solemn agreements not to develop or use atomic energy for destructive purposes. . . .

And now I end. I have submitted an outline for present discussion. Our consideration will be broadened by the criticism of the United States proposals and by the plans of the other nations, which, it is to be hoped, will be submitted at their early convenience. . . .

B. Draft International Agreement to Forbid the Production and Use of Atomic Weapons, Proposed by Andrei Gromyko on 19 June 1946

Article I

The high contracting parties solemnly declare that they will forbid the production and use of a weapon based upon the use of atomic energy, and with this in view take upon themselves the following obligations:

(a) Not to use, in any circumstance, an atomic weapon;
(b) To forbid the production and keeping of a weapon based upon the use of atomic energy;
(c) To destroy within a period of three months from the entry into force of this agreement all stocks of atomic energy weapons, whether in a finished or semi-finished condition.

Article 2

The high contracting parties declare that any violation of Article 1 of this agreement shall constitute a serious crime against humanity.

Article 3

The high contracting parties, within six months of the entry into force of the present agreement, shall pass legislation providing severe punishment for the violation of the terms of this agreement.

Article 4

The present agreement shall be of indefinite duration.

Article 5

The present agreement is open for signature to all states, whether or not they are members of the United Nations. . . .

Article 7

After the entry into force of the present agreement, it shall be an obligation upon all states, whether members or not of the United Nations. . . .

DISCUSSION QUESTIONS

1. What were the main differences between the American and Soviet approaches to control of nuclear weapons?
2. Why did Baruch insist that the veto rights enjoyed by great powers in the UN Security Council must not protect violators of nuclear

control agreements? Why might the Soviets disagree?

3. Why would the Americans be willing to permit international inspection of their facilities? Why would the Soviet Union object to such inspections of its facilities?
4. Why did the Gromyko Plan recommend outright prohibition and destruction of atomic weapons rather than international control of nuclear materials?
5. Do you accept Baruch's assertion that "The terror created by weapons has never stopped man from employing them"? Why or why not?

7. The Truman Doctrine, 1947

America's declaration of Cold War was issued on 12 March 1947. Ever since the end of World War II, Britain had supported the government of Greece in its attempts to suppress a Communist insurgency. That internal uprising was soon supported by Yugoslavia, and by February 1947 the British found themselves unable to bear the financial and military burdens involved in aiding the Greeks. The U.S. State Department, led by George Marshall and Dean Acheson, worked with President Truman to formulate a policy that would assist not only Greece but also its similarly endangered neighbor, Turkey. Advised by congressional leaders to take his case to the public, Truman did precisely that, addressing a joint session of Congress and a nationwide radio audience on 12 March. Truman asked Congress for legislation to permit the administration to step into the protector's position being vacated by Great Britain. Following the suggestion of Senator Vandenberg, he identified the Communist threat as a global one, applicable not only to Greece and Turkey but to Western Europe and Asia as well. This policy, which came to be called the "Truman Doctrine," set the stage for U.S. aid to regimes that were threatened by Communist insurgencies throughout the Cold War era.

President Truman's Speech to the Nation, 12 March 1947

Mr. President, Mr. Speaker, Members of the Congress of the United States:

The gravity of the situation which confronts the world today necessitates my appearance before a joint session of the Congress. The foreign policy and the national security of this country are involved.

One aspect of the present situation, which I wish to present to you at this time for your consideration and decision, concerns Greece and Turkey. . . .

The very existence of the Greek state is today threatened by the terrorist activities of several thousand armed men, led by Communists, who defy the Government's authority at a number of points, particularly along the northern boundaries. . . .

Greece's neighbor, Turkey, also deserves our attention. . . . Since the war Turkey has sought additional financial assistance from Great Britain and the United States for the purpose of effecting that modernization necessary for the maintenance of its national integrity. That integrity is essential to the preservation of order in the Middle East. . . .

One of the primary objectives of the foreign policy of the United States is the creation of conditions in which we and other nations will be able to work out a way of life free from coercion. This was a fundamental issue in the war with Germany and Japan. Our victory was won over countries which sought to impose their will, and their way of life, upon other nations. . . .

At the present moment in world history nearly every nation must choose between alternative ways of life. The choice is too often not a free one.

One way of life is based upon the will of the majority, and is distinguished by free institutions, representative government, free elections, guarantees of individual liberty, freedom of speech and religion, and freedom from political oppression.

The second way of life is based upon the will of a minority forcibly imposed upon the majority. It relies upon terror and oppression, a controlled press and radio, fixed elections, and the suppression of personal freedoms.

I believe that it must be the policy of the United States to support free peoples who are resisting attempted subjugation by armed minorities or by outside pressures. I believe that we must assist free peoples to work out their own destinies in their own way. I believe that our help should be primarily through economic and financial aid which is essential to economic stability and orderly political processes.

The world is not static, and the *status quo* is not sacred. But we cannot allow changes in the *status quo* in violation of the Charter of the United Nations by such methods as coercion, or by such subterfuges as political infiltration. In helping free and independent nations to maintain their freedom, the United States will be giving effect to the principles of the Charter of the United Nations.

It is necessary only to glance at a map to realize that the survival and integrity of the Greek nation are of grave importance in a much wider situation. If Greece should fall under the control of an armed minority, the effect upon its neighbor, Turkey, would be immediate and serious. Confusion and disorder might well spread throughout the entire Middle East. . . .

I therefore ask the Congress to provide authority for assistance to Greece and Turkey in the amount of $400,000,000 for the period ending June 30, 1948. . . .

In addition to funds, I ask the Congress to authorize the detail of American civilian and military personnel to Greece and Turkey, at the request of those countries, to assist in the tasks of reconstruction, and for the purpose of supervising the use of such financial and material assistance as may be furnished. I recommend that authority also be provided for the instruction and training of selected Greek and Turkish personnel.

Finally, I ask that the Congress provide authority which will permit the speediest and most effective use, in terms of needed commodities, supplies, and equipment, of such funds as may be authorized.

If further funds, or further authority, should be needed for purposes indicated in this message, I shall not hesitate to bring the situation before the Congress. On this subject the executive and legislative branches of the Government must work together. This is a serious course upon which we embark. I would not recommend it except that the alternative is much more serious . . .

The seeds of totalitarian regimes are nurtured by misery and want. They spread and grow in the evil soil of poverty and strife. They reach their full growth when the hope of a people for a better life has died. We must keep that hope alive. The free peoples of the world look to us for support in maintaining their freedoms. If we falter in our leadership, we may endanger the peace of the world—and we shall surely endanger the welfare of this nation. . . .

DISCUSSION QUESTIONS

1. How did Truman underscore the gravity of the situation in Greece and Turkey?
2. What reasoning did Truman use to convince his listeners that economic aid would help to prevent the spread of Communism?
3. This speech has been characterized as America's "declaration of Cold War." Do you consider this an accurate description? Why or why not?
4. How might Stalin have reacted to Truman's speech? Why?
5. What aspects of this speech suggest that the Truman Doctrine could become part of a global strategy, with implications going far beyond Greece and Turkey?

8. The Marshall Plan, 1947

Shortly after the proclamation of the Truman Doctrine, U.S. secretary of state George Marshall traveled to Moscow to attend a conference of foreign ministers. There he spoke extensively with Stalin and learned that the Soviet leader was convinced that European capitalism was in its death throes. War-torn Europe had never recovered from the devastation of World War II, and in France and Italy, it appeared that widespread economic misery would enable Communists to win the 1948 elections. Returning to Washington, Marshall informed Truman of his concerns and set the State Department to work on measures designed to promote European economic recovery.

On 5 June 1947 Marshall embodied the final version of these measures in a commencement address at Harvard University. Although the proposal was officially called the European Recovery Program, it became widely known as the Marshall Plan, in hopes that Marshall's immense popularity would help win congressional approval for the large expenses involved. As matters developed, approval came easily, both because of widespread fear of Communism and because of the Plan's preference for grants of credits to purchase American goods rather than for outright gifts of money. The purchases stimulated the prosperous U.S. economy even further, and the Marshall Plan fueled spectacular economic recovery in Western Europe during the following decade.

Marshall's Commencement Address at Harvard University, 5 June 1947

I need not tell you gentlemen that the world situation is very serious. That must be apparent to all intelligent people. I think one difficulty is that the problem is one of such enormous complexity that the very mass of facts presented to the public by press and radio make it exceedingly difficult for the man in the street to reach a clear appraisement of the situation. Furthermore, the people of this country are distant from the troubled areas of the earth and it is hard for them to comprehend the plight and consequent reactions of the long-suffering peoples, and the effect of those reactions on their governments in connection with our efforts to promote peace in the world.

In considering the requirements for the rehabilitation of Europe, the physical loss of life, the visible destruction of cities, factories, mines, and railroads was correctly estimated, but it has become obvious during recent months that this visible destruction was probably less serious than the dislocation of the entire fabric of European economy. For the past ten years conditions have been highly abnormal. The feverish preparation for war and the more feverish maintenance of the war effort engulfed all aspects of national economies. Machinery has fallen into disrepair or is entirely obsolete. Under the arbitrary and destructive Nazi rule, virtually every possible enterprise was geared into the German War machine. Long-standing commercial ties, private institutions, banks, insurance companies, and shipping companies disappeared, through loss of capital, absorption through nationalization, or by simple destruction.

In many countries, confidence in the local currency has been severely shaken. The breakdown of the business structure of Europe during the war was complete. Recovery has been seriously retarded by the fact that two years after the close of hostilities a peace settlement with Germany and Austria has not been agreed upon. But even given a more prompt solution of these difficult problems, the rehabilitation of the economic structure of Europe quite evidently will require a much longer time and greater effort than had been foreseen. . . .

Aside from the demoralizing effect on the world at large and the possibilities of disturbances arising as a result of the desperation of the people concerned, the consequences to the economy of the United States should be apparent to all. It is logical that the United States should do whatever it is able to do to assist in the return of normal economic health in the world, without which there can be no political stability, and no assured peace.

Our policy is directed not against any country or doctrine but against hunger, poverty, desperation, and chaos. Its purpose should be the revival of a working economy in the world so as to permit the emergence of political and social conditions in which free institutions can exist. Such assistance, I am convinced, must not be on a piecemeal basis as various crises develop. Any assistance that this Government may render in the future should provide a cure rather than a mere palliative. Any government that is willing to assist in the task of recovery will find full cooperation, I am sure, on the part of the United States Government. Any government which maneuvers to block the recovery of other countries cannot expect help from us. Furthermore, governments, political parties, or groups which seek to perpetuate human misery in order to profit therefrom politically or otherwise will encounter the opposition of the United States.

It is already evident that, before the United States Government can proceed much further in its efforts to alleviate the situation and help start the European world on its way to recovery, there must be some agreement among the countries of Europe as to the requirements of the situation and the part those countries themselves will take in order to give proper effect to whatever action might be undertaken by this Government. It would be neither fitting nor efficacious for this Government to undertake to draw up unilaterally a program designed to place Europe on its feet economically. This is the business of the Europeans. The initiative, I think, must come from Europe. The role of this country should consist of friendly aid in the drafting of a European program and of later support of such a program so far as it may be practical for us to do so. The program should be a joint one, agreed to by a number, if not all, of European nations.

An essential part of any successful action on the part of the United States is an understanding on the part of the people of America of the character of the problem and the remedies to be applied. Political passion and prejudice should have no part. With foresight, and a willingness on the part of our people to face up to the vast responsibility which history has clearly placed upon our country, the difficulties I have outlined can and will be overcome.

DISCUSSION QUESTIONS

1. Why was Marshall so concerned about the economic situation in Europe? Why did he think that American aid was essential?
2. Why was it likely that destitute Europeans might turn to Communism if nothing was done to alleviate their poverty?
3. What arguments might have been advanced in 1947 by Americans opposed to helping Europe recover?
4. Why did Marshall insist that Europeans take a principal role in the plan's implementation? Why did the plan favor grants to purchase U.S. goods rather than outright gifts of money?

9. George F. Kennan, "The Sources of Soviet Conduct," 1947

George Frost Kennan was a career foreign service officer in the U.S. Department of State and a highly regarded student of Russian and Soviet affairs. Early in 1946, while serving at the American embassy in Moscow, he sent a lengthy message to Washington providing an expert analysis of Soviet behavior. Placing Soviet expansionism squarely within the context of traditional Russian suspicion and insecurity, he argued that the USSR could not be fully trusted or reasoned with by the West, and must instead be treated with firm resistance and strength. This "Long Telegram" made a deep impression on Kennan's superiors and helped shape their thinking about U.S. foreign policy.

Returning to Washington later that year, Kennan wrote a paper entitled "Psychological Background of Soviet Foreign Policy." Early in 1947, following an impressive public lecture, he was asked to submit an article for publication in the journal *Foreign Affairs.* The State Department authorized him to do so, as long as he did not use his own name. So he took the paper he had written, signed it with an "X," and sent it to the journal.

Kennan was now becoming a very influential man. That spring, he was placed at the head of the State Department's Policy Planning Staff, which was instrumental in developing the Marshall Plan. In July his article, now titled "The Sources of Soviet Conduct," appeared in *Foreign Affairs.* The "X-article," as it came to be known (despite the fact that its writer's identity was soon disclosed in *The New York Times*), is excerpted below. It provided a conceptual basis for the new U.S. foreign policy embodied in the Truman Doctrine and Marshall Plan. Describing Soviet expansion as "a fluid stream which moves constantly, wherever it is permitted to move," Kennan called for "a policy of firm containment, designed to confront the Russians with unalterable counter-force at every point where they show signs of encroaching upon the interests of a peaceful and stable world. . . . " This "containment" policy would serve as a foundation of American Cold War behavior for the next four decades.

The Sources of Soviet Conduct*

The political personality of Soviet power as we know it today is the product of ideology and circumstances: ideology inherited by the present Soviet leaders from the movement in which they had their political origin, and circumstances of the power which they now have exercised for nearly three decades in Russia. There can be few tasks of psychological analysis more difficult than to try to trace the interaction of these two forces and the relative role of each in the determination of official Soviet conduct. Yet the attempt must be made if that conduct is to be understood and effectively countered.

It is difficult to summarize the set of ideological concepts with which the Soviet leaders came into power. Marxian ideology, in its Russian-Communist projection, has always been in process of subtle evolution. The materials on which it bases itself are extensive and complex. But the outstanding features of Communist thought as it existed in 1916 may perhaps be summarized as follows: (a) that the central factor in the life of man, the fact which determines the character of public life and the "physiognomy of society," is the system by which material goods are produced and exchanged; (b) that the capitalist system of production is a nefarious one which inevitably leads to the exploitation of the working class by the capital-owning class and is incapable of developing adequately the economic resources of society or of distributing fairly the material goods produced by human labor; (c) that capitalism contains the seeds of its own destruction and must, in view of the inability of the capital-owning class to adjust itself to economic change, result eventually and inescapably in a revolutionary transfer of power to the working class; and (d) that imperialism, the final phase of capitalism, leads directly to war and revolution.

The rest may be outlined in Lenin's own words: "Unevenness of economic and political development is the inflexible law of capitalism. It follows from this that the victory of Socialism may come originally in a few capitalist countries or even in a single capitalist country. The victorious proletariat of that country, having expropriated the capitalists and having organized Socialist production at home, would rise against

---

* George F. Kennan, "The Sources of Soviet Conduct," *Foreign Affairs* 25 (July 1947) 566–582. Reprinted by permission of *Foreign Affairs*. Copyright 1947 by the Council on Foreign Relations, Inc.

the remaining capitalist world, drawing to itself in the process the oppressed classes of other countries." It must be noted that there was no assumption that capitalism would perish without proletarian revolution. A final push was needed from a revolutionary proletariat movement in order to tip over the tottering structure. But it was regarded as inevitable that sooner or later that push be given. . . .

The circumstances of the immediate post-Revolution period—the existence in Russia of civil war and foreign intervention, together with the obvious fact that the Communists represented only a tiny minority of the Russian people—made the establishment of dictatorial power a necessity. . . .

Lenin, had he lived, might have proved a great enough man to reconcile these conflicting forces to the ultimate benefit of Russian society, though this is questionable. But be that as it may, Stalin, and those whom he led in the struggle for succession to Lenin's position of leadership, were not the men to tolerate rival political forces in the sphere of power which they coveted. Their sense of insecurity was too great. Their particular brand of fanaticism, unmodified by any of the Anglo-Saxon traditions of compromise, was too fierce and too jealous to envisage any permanent sharing of power. From the Russian-Asiatic world out of which they had emerged they carried with them a skepticism as to the possibilities of permanent and peaceful coexistence of rival forces. Easily persuaded of their own doctrinaire "rightness," they insisted on the submission or destruction of all competing power. . . .

Let it be stressed again that subjectively these men probably did not seek absolutism for its own sake. They doubtless believed—and found it easy to believe—that they alone knew what was good for society and that they would accomplish that good once their power was secure and unchallengeable. But in seeking that security of their own rule they were prepared to recognize no restrictions, either of God or man, on the character of their methods. And until such time as that security might be achieved, they placed far down on their scale of operational priorities the comforts and happiness of the peoples entrusted to their care.

Now the outstanding circumstance concerning the Soviet regime is that down to the present day this process of political consolidation has never been completed and the men in the Kremlin have continued to be predominantly absorbed with the struggle to secure and make absolute the power which they seized in November 1917. They have endeavored to secure it primarily against forces at home, within Soviet society itself. But they have also endeavored to secure it against the outside world. For ideology, as we have seen, taught them that the outside world was hostile and that it was their duty eventually to overthrow the political forces beyond their borders. . . .

Now it lies in the nature of the mental world of the Soviet leaders, as well as in the character of their ideology, that no opposition to them can be officially recognized as having any merit or justification whatsoever. Such opposition can flow, in theory, only from the hostile and incorrigible forces of dying capitalism. As long as remnants of capitalism were officially recognized as existing in Russia, it was possible to place on them . . . part of the blame for the maintenance of a dictatorial form of society. But as these remnants were liquidated, little by little, this justification fell away. . . . And this fact created one of the most basic of the compulsions which came to act upon the Soviet regime: since capitalism no longer existed in Russia and since it could not be admitted that there could be serious or widespread opposition to the Kremlin springing spontaneously from the liberated masses under its authority, it became necessary to justify the retention of the dictatorship by stressing the menace of capitalism abroad.

This began at an early date. In 1924, Stalin specifically defended the retention of the "organs of suppression," meaning, among others, the army and the secret police, on the ground that "as long as there is a capitalist encirclement there will be danger of intervention with all the consequences that flow from that danger." In accordance with that theory, and from that time on, all internal opposition forces in Russia have consistently been portrayed as the agents of foreign forces of reaction antagonistic to Soviet power.

By the same token, tremendous emphasis has been placed on the original Communist thesis of a basic antagonism between the capitalist and Socialist worlds. It is clear, from many indications, that this emphasis is not founded in reality. The real facts concerning it have been confused by the existence abroad of genuine resentment provoked by Soviet philosophy and tactics and occasionally by the existence of great centers of military power, notably the Nazi regime in Germany and the Japanese government of the late 1930s, which did indeed have aggressive designs against the Soviet Union. But there is ample evidence that the stress laid in Moscow on the menace confronting Soviet society from the world outside its borders is founded not in the realities of foreign antagonism but in the necessity of explaining away the maintenance of dictatorial authority at home. . . .

II. So much for the historical background. What does it spell in terms of the political personality of Soviet power as we know it today?

Of the original ideology, nothing has been officially junked. Belief is maintained in the basic badness of capitalism, in the inevitability of its destruction, in the obligation of the proletariat to assist in that destruction and to take power into its own hands. But stress has come to be laid primarily on those concepts which relate most specifically to the Soviet regime itself: to its position as the sole truly Socialist regime in a dark and misguided world, and to the relationship of power within it.

The first of these concepts is that of the innate antagonism between capitalism and Socialism. We have seen how deeply that concept has become imbedded in foundations of Soviet power. It has profound implications for Russia's conduct as a member of international society. It means that there can never be on Moscow's side any sincere assumption of a community of aims between the Soviet Union and powers which are regarded as capitalist. It must invariably be assumed in Moscow that the aims of the capitalist world are antagonistic to the Soviet regime and, therefore, to the interests of the peoples it controls. If the Soviet government occasionally sets its signature to documents which would indicate the contrary, this is to be regarded as a tactical maneuver permissible in dealing with the enemy (who is without honor) and should be taken in the spirit of *caveat emptor.* Basically, the antagonism remains. . . . And from it flow many of the phenomena which we find disturbing in the Kremlin's conduct of foreign policy: the secretiveness, the lack of frankness, the duplicity, the war suspiciousness, and the basic unfriendliness of purpose. These phenomena are there to stay, for the foreseeable future. There can be variations of degree and of emphasis. When there is something the Russians want from us, one or the other of these features of their policy may be thrust temporarily into the background; and when that happens there will always be Americans who will leap forward with gleeful announcements that "the Russians have changed," and some will even try to take credit for having brought about those "changes." But we should not be misled by tactical maneuvers. These characteristics of Soviet policy . . . are basic to the internal nature of Soviet power, and will be with us, whether in the foreground or the background, until the internal nature of Soviet power is changed.

This means that we are going to continue for a long time to find the Russians difficult to deal with. It does not mean that they should be considered as embarked upon a do-or-die program to overthrow our society by a given date. The theory of the inevitability of the eventual fall of capitalism has the fortunate connotation that there is no hurry about it. The forces of progress can take their time in preparing the final *coup de grace.* Meanwhile, what is vital is that the "Socialist fatherland"—that oasis of power which has been already won for Socialism in the person of the Soviet Union—should be cherished and defended by all good Communists at home and abroad, its fortunes promoted, its enemies badgered and confronted. The promotion of premature, "adventuristic" revolutionary projects abroad which might embarrass Soviet power in any way would be an inexcusable, even a counter-revolutionary act. The cause of Socialism is the support and promotion of Soviet power, as defined in Moscow.

This brings us to the second of the concepts important to contemporary Soviet outlook. That is the infallibility of the Kremlin. The Soviet concept of power, which permits no focal points of organization outside the Party itself, requires that the Party leadership remain in theory the sole repository of truth. For if truth were to be found elsewhere, there would be justification for its expression in organized activity. But it is precisely that which the Kremlin cannot and will not permit.

The leadership of the Communist Party is therefore always right, and has been always right ever since in 1929 Stalin formalized his personal power by announcing that decisions of the Politburo were being taken unanimously.

On the principle of infallibility there rests the iron discipline of the Communist Party. In fact, the two concepts are mutually self- supporting. Perfect discipline requires recognition of infallibility. Infallibility requires the observance of discipline. And the two together go far to determine the behaviorism of the entire Soviet apparatus of power. But their effect cannot be understood unless a third factor be taken into account: namely, the fact that the leadership is at liberty to put forward for tactical purposes any particular thesis which it finds useful to the cause at any particular moment and to require the faithful and unquestioning acceptance of that thesis by the members of the movement as a whole. This means that truth is not a constant but is actually created, for all intents and purposes, by the Soviet leaders themselves. It may vary from week to week, from month to month. It is nothing absolute and immutable—nothing which flows from objective reality. It is only the most recent manifestation of the wisdom of those in whom the ultimate wisdom is supposed to reside, because they represent the logic of history. The accumulative effect of these factors is to give to the whole subordinate apparatus of Soviet power an unshakable stubbornness and steadfastness in its orientation. This orientation can be changed at will by the Kremlin but by no other power. Once a given party line has been laid down on a given issue of current policy, the whole Soviet governmental machine, including the mechanism of diplomacy, moves inexorably along the prescribed path, like a persistent toy automobile wound up and headed in a given direction, stopping only when it meets some unanswerable force. The individuals who are the components of this machine are unamenable to argument or reason which comes to them from outside sources. Their whole training has taught them to mistrust and discount the glib persuasiveness of the outside world. . . .

But we have seen that the Kremlin is under no ideological compulsion to accomplish its purposes in a hurry. Like the Church, it is dealing in ideological concepts which are of long-term validity, and it can afford to be patient. . . . Again, these precepts are fortified by the lessons of Russian history: of centuries of obscure battles between nomadic forces over the stretches of a vast unfortified plain. Here caution, circumspection, flexibility and deception are the valuable qualities. . . . Thus the Kremlin has no compunction about retreating in the face of superior force. And being under the compulsion of no timetable, it does not get panicky under the necessity for such retreat. Its political action is a fluid stream which moves constantly, wherever it is permitted to move, toward a given goal. Its main concern is to make sure that it has filled every nook and cranny available to it in the basin of world power. But if it finds unassailable barriers in its path, it accepts these philosophically and accommodates itself to them. The main thing is that there should always be pressure, increasing constant pressure, toward the desired goal. There is no trace of any feeling in Soviet psychology that that goal must be reached at any given time.

These considerations make Soviet diplomacy at once easier and more difficult to deal with than the diplomacy of individual aggressive leaders like Napoleon and Hitler. On the one hand it is more sensitive to contrary force, more ready to yield on individual sectors of the diplomatic front when that force is felt to be too strong, and thus more rational in the logic and rhetoric of power. On the other hand it cannot be easily defeated or discouraged by a single victory on the part of its opponents. And the patient persistence by which it is animated means that it can be effectively countered not by sporadic acts which represent the momentary whims of democratic opinion but only by intelligent long-range policies on the part of Russia's adversaries—policies no less steady in their purpose, and no less variegated and resourceful in their application, than those of the Soviet Union itself.

In these circumstances it is clear that the main element of any United States' policy toward the Soviet Union must be that of a long-term, patient but firm and vigilant containment of Russian expansive tendencies. It is important to note, however, that such a policy has nothing to do with outward histrionics: with threats or blustering or superfluous gestures of outward "toughness." While the Kremlin is basically flexible in its reaction to political realities, it is by no means unamenable to considerations of prestige. Like almost any other government, it can be placed by tactless and threatening gestures in a position where it cannot afford to yield even though this might be dictated by its sense of realism. The Russian leaders are keen judges of human psychology, and as such they are highly conscious that loss of temper and of self-control is never a source of strength in political affairs. They are quick to exploit such evidences of weakness. For these reasons, it is a *sine qua non* of successful dealing with Russia that the foreign government in question should remain at all times cool and collected and that its demands on Russian policy should be put forward in such a manner as to leave the way open for a compliance not too detrimental to Russian prestige.

III. In the light of the above, it will be clearly seen that the Soviet pressure against the free institutions of the Western world is something that can be contained by the adroit and vigilant application of counter-force at a series of constantly shifting geographical and political points, corresponding to the shifts and maneuvers of Soviet policy, but which cannot be charmed or talked out of existence. The Russians look forward to a duel of infinite duration, and they see that already they have scored great successes. It must be borne in mind that there was a time when the Communist Party represented far more of a minority in the sphere of Russian national life than Soviet power today represents in the world community.

But if ideology convinces the rulers of Russia that truth is on their side and that they can afford to wait, those of us on whom that ideology has no claim are free to examine objectively the validity of that premise. The Soviet thesis not only implies complete lack of control by the west over its own economic destiny, it likewise assumes Russian unity, discipline and patience over an indefinite period. Let us . . . suppose that the western world finds the strength and resourcefulness to contain Soviet power over a period of ten to fifteen years. What does that spell for Russia itself?

The Soviet leaders, taking advantage of the contributions of modern technique to the arts of despotism, have solved the question of obedience within the confines of their power. Few challenge their authority; and even those who do are unable to make that challenge valid against the organs of suppression of the state. The Kremlin also proved able to accomplish its purpose of building up in Russia, regardless of the interests of the inhabitants, an industrial foundation of heavy metallurgy, which is . . . continuing to grow and is approaching those of the other major industrial countries. All of this, however, both the maintenance of internal political security and the building of heavy industry, has been carried out at a terrible cost of human life and in human hopes and energies. It has necessitated the use of forced labor on a scale unprecedented in modern times under conditions of peace. It has involved the neglect or abuse of other phases of Soviet economic life, particularly agriculture, consumers' goods production, housing and transportation.

To all that, the war has added its tremendous toll of destruction, death and human exhaustion.

In consequence of this, we have in Russia today a population which is physically and spiritually tired. The mass of the people are disillusioned, skeptical, and no longer as accessible as they once were to the magical attraction which Soviet power still radiates to its followers abroad. The avidity with which people seized upon the slight respite accorded to the Church for tactical reasons during the war was eloquent testimony to the fact that their capacity for faith and devotion found little expression in the purposes of the regime.

In these circumstances, there are limits to the physical and nervous strength of the people themselves. These limits are absolute ones, and are binding even for the cruelest dictatorship, because beyond them people cannot be driven. The forced labor camps and the other agencies of constraint provide temporary means of compelling people to work longer hours than their own volition or mere economic pressure would dictate; but if people survive them at all they become old before their time and must be considered as human casualties to the demands of dictatorship. In either case their best powers are no longer available to society and can no longer be enlisted in the service of the state. . . .

In addition to this . . . Soviet economic development . . . has been precariously spotty and uneven. Russian Communists who speak of the "uneven development of capitalism" should blush at the contemplation of their own national economy. Here is a nation striving to become in a short period one of the great industrial nations of the world while it still has no highway network worthy of the name and only a relatively primitive network of railways. Much has been done to increase efficiency of labor and to teach primitive peasants something about the operation of machines. But maintenance is still a crying deficiency of all Soviet economy. Construction is hasty and poor in quality. . . . And in vast sectors of economic life it has not yet been possible to instill into labor anything like that general culture of production and technical self-respect which characterizes the skilled worker of the west.

It is difficult to see how these deficiencies can be corrected at an early date by a tired and dispirited population working largely under the shadow of fear and compulsion. And as long as they are not overcome, Russia will remain economically a vulnerable, and in a certain sense an impotent, nation, capable of exporting its enthusiasm and radiating the strange charm of its primitive political vitality but unable to back up those articles of export by the real evidences of material power and prosperity.

Meanwhile, a great uncertainty hangs over the political life of the Soviet Union. That is the uncertainty involved in the transfer of power from one individual or group of individuals to others.

This is, of course, outstandingly the problem of the personal position of Stalin. We must remember that his succession to Lenin's pinnacle of pre-eminence in the Communist movement was the only such transfer of individual authority which the Soviet Union has experienced. That transfer took 12 years to consolidate. It cost the lives of millions of people and shook the state to its foundations. The attendant tremors were felt all through the international revolutionary movement, to the disadvantage of the Kremlin itself.

It is always possible that another transfer of pre-eminent power may take place quietly and inconspicuously, with no repercussions anywhere. But again, it is possible that the questions involved may unleash, to use some of Lenin's words, one of those "incredibly swift transitions" from "delicate deceit" to "wild violence" which characterize Russian history, and may shake Soviet power to its foundations. . . .

Thus the future of Soviet power may not be by any means as secure as Russian capacity for self-delusion would make it appear to the men in the Kremlin. That they can keep power themselves, they have demonstrated. That they can quietly and easily turn it over to others remains to be proved. Meanwhile, the hardships of their rule and vicissitudes of international life have taken a heavy toll of the strength and hopes of the great people on whom their power rests. It is curious to note that the ideological power of Soviet authority is strongest today in areas beyond the frontiers of Russia, beyond the reach of its police power. . . . And who can say with assurance that the strong light still cast by the Kremlin on the dissatisfied peoples of the western world is not the powerful afterglow of a constellation which is in actuality on the wane? This cannot be proved. And it cannot be disproved. But the possibility remains . . . that Soviet power, like the capitalist world of its conception, bears within it the seeds of its own decay, and that the sprouting of these seeds is well advanced.

IV. It is clear that the United States cannot expect in the foreseeable future to enjoy political intimacy with the Soviet regime. It must continue to regard the Soviet Union as a rival, not a partner, in the political arena. It must continue to expect that Soviet policies will reflect no abstract love of peace and stability, no real faith in the possibility of a permanent happy coexistence of the Socialist and capitalist worlds, but rather a cautious, persistent pressure toward the disruption and weakening of all rival influence and rival power.

Balanced against this are the facts that Russia, as opposed to the Western world in general, is still by far the weaker party, that Soviet policy is highly flexible, and that Soviet society may well contain deficiencies which will eventually weaken its own total potential. This would of itself warrant the United States entering with reasonable confidence upon a policy of firm containment, designed to confront the Russians with unalterable counter-force at every point where they show signs of encroaching upon the interests of a peaceful and stable world.

But in actuality the possibilities for American power are by no means limited to holding the line and hoping for the best. It is entirely possible for the United States to influence by its actions the internal developments, both within Russia and throughout the international Communist movement, by which Russian policy is largely determined. This is not only a question of the modest measure of informational activity which this government can conduct in the Soviet Union and elsewhere. . . . . It is rather a question of the degree to which the United States can create among the peoples of the world generally the impression of a country which knows what it wants, which is coping successfully with the problems of its internal life and with the responsibilities of a world power, and which has a spiritual vitality capable of holding its own among the major ideological currents of the time. To the extent that such an impression can be created and maintained, the aims of Russian Communism must appear sterile and quixotic, the hopes and enthusiasm of Moscow's supporters must wane, and added strain must be imposed on the Kremlin's foreign policies. For the palsied decrepitude of the capitalist world is the keystone of Communist philosophy. Even the failure of the United States to experience the early economic depression which the ravens of Red Square have been predicting . . . since hostilities ceased would have deep and important repercussions throughout the Communist world.

By the same token, exhibitions of indecision, disunity and internal disintegration within this country have an exhilarating effect on the whole Communist movement. At each evidence of these tendencies, a thrill of hope and excitement goes through the Communist world; . . . new groups of foreign supporters climb onto what they can only view as the bandwagon of international politics; and Russian pressure increases all along the line in international affairs.

It would be an exaggeration to say that American behavior unassisted and alone could exercise a power of life and death over the Communist movement and bring about the early fall of Soviet power in Russia. But the United States has it in its power to increase enormously the strains under which Soviet policy must operate, to force upon the Kremlin a far greater degree of moderation and circumspection than it has had to observe in recent years, and in this way to promote tendencies which must eventually find their outlet in either the breakup or the gradual mellowing of Soviet power. For no mystical, Messianic movement—and particularly not that of the Kremlin—can face frustration indefinitely without eventually adjusting itself in one way or another to the logic of that state of affairs.

Thus the decision will really fall in large measure in this country itself. The issue of Soviet-American relations is in essence a test of the over-all worth of the United States as a nation among nations. To avoid destruction the United

States need only measure up to its own best traditions and prove itself worthy of preservation as a great nation.

Surely there was never a fairer test of national quality than this. In the light of these circumstances, the thoughtful observer of Russian-American relations will find no cause for complaint in the Kremlin's challenge to American society. He will rather experience a certain gratitude to a Providence which, by providing the American people with this implacable challenge, has made their entire security as a nation dependent on their pulling themselves together and accepting the responsibilities of moral and political leadership that history plainly intended them to bear.

DISCUSSION QUESTIONS

1. What did Kennan consider to be the main principles of Communist ideology?
2. What did Kennan see as the main reasons for Soviet hostility toward the West?
3. Why did Kennan believe that Soviet leaders could never be fully trusted by the West?
4. What did Kennan think the West should do to counter Soviet expansionism? Why did he caution Western leaders to avoid gestures of outward "toughness" toward the USSR?
5. Why did Kennan's ideas have such an important influence on U.S. policymakers?

10. The Founding of the Cominform, 1947

By fall of 1947, the division of Europe into two opposing camps was virtually complete. In Eastern Europe, anxious to create a buffer zone between themselves and Germany—and to gain access to materials needed to rebuild the USSR—the Soviets had installed "friendly" governments dominated by Communists. In Western Europe, anxious to impede the spread of Communism and secure their own foreign markets, the Americans had initiated the Marshall Plan, designed to foster economic recovery and stability.

In part because of its emphasis on rebuilding the economy of Germany, which had recently devastated the USSR, the Marshall Plan was seen in Moscow as a serious threat. In order to respond to this, and to encourage closer coordination among the European Communist parties, the Soviets called representatives of these parties to a special meeting in Poland in September of 1947. There Andrei Zhdanov, the chief Soviet spokesperson, called for the formation of a new international organization to advance the interests of Communism. The result was the establishment of the Communist Information Bureau, or Cominform, with its headquarters in Belgrade, Yugoslavia.

The new organization, which would last until 1956, was in some ways a throwback to the old Communist International, or Comintern, a worldwide association of Communist parties which had been disbanded during World War II. Like the Comintern, the Cominform could be used not only to secure socialist solidarity, but to prod Communists elsewhere to follow Moscow's lead. Among other things, the Cominform would engineer a wave of strikes in France and Italy in fall of 1947, and make a futile bid to force the wayward Yugoslav Communists back into line the following spring.

A. Manifesto Proclaiming the Cominform, 5 October 1947

In the international situation brought about by the Second World War and in the period that followed fundamental changes took place. The characteristic aspect of these changes is a new balance of political forces interplaying in the world arena, a shift in the relationship between states which were the victors in the Second World War, and their reevaluation.

As long as the war lasted the Allied states fighting against Germany and Japan marched in step and were one. Nevertheless, in the Allies' camp already during the war there existed differences regarding the aims of the war as well as the objectives of the post-war and world organization. The Soviet Union and the democratic countries believed that the main objective of the war was the rebuilding and strengthening of democracy in Europe, the liquidation of fascism and the prevention of a possible aggression on behalf of Germany, and that its further aim was an achievement of an all-around and lasting cooperation between the nations of Europe.

The United States of America and with them England placed as their war aim a different goal—the elimination of competition on the world market (Germany and Japan) and the consolidation of their dominant position. This difference in the definition of war aims and post-war objectives has begun to deepen in the post-war period.

Two opposite political lines have crystallized. On one extreme the USSR and the democratic countries aim at whittling down imperialism and the strengthening of democracy. On the other hand the United States of America and England aim at the strengthening of imperialism and choking democracy. . . .

In this way there arose two camps—the camp of imperialism and anti-democratic forces, whose chief aim is an establishment of a world-wide American imperialists' hegemony and the crushing of democracy; and an anti-imperialist democratic camp whose chief aim is the elimination of imperialism, the strengthening of democracy, and the liquidation of the remnants of fascism. . . .

In these conditions the anti-imperialist democratic camp has to close its ranks and draw up and agree on a common platform to work out its tactics against the chief forces of the imperialist camp, against American imperialism, against its English and French allies, against the Right-Wing Socialists above all in England and France. To frustrate those imperialistic plans of aggression we need the efforts of all democratic and anti-imperialist forces in Europe. . . .

B. Resolution of Conference of Communist Parties on Establishing the Cominform, 5 October 1947

The Conference states that the absence of connections between Communist parties who have taken part in this conference is in the present situation a serious shortcoming. Experience has shown that such division between Communist parties is incorrect and harmful. The requirement for an exchange of experience and voluntary coordination of actions of the separate parties has become particularly necessary now in conditions of the complicated post-war international situation and when the disunity of Communist parties may lead to damage for the working class. Because of this, members of the conference agreed upon the following:

First, to set up an Information Bureau of representatives of the Communist Party of Yugoslavia, the Bulgarian Workers Party (of Communists), the Communist Party of Rumania, the Hungarian Communist Party, the Polish Workers Party, the Communist Party of the Soviet Union (Bolshevik), the Communist Party of France, the Communist Party of Czechoslovakia, and the Communist Party of Italy.

Second, the task given to the Information Bureau is to organize and exchange experience and, in case of necessity, coordinate the activity of Communist parties on foundations of mutual agreement.

Third, the Information Bureau will have in it representatives of the Central Committees—two from each Central Committee. Delegations of the Central Committee must be appointed and replaced by the Central Committees.

Fourth, the Information Bureau is to have a printed organ—a fortnightly and later on weekly. The organ is to be published in French and Russian and, if possible, in other languages.

Fifth, the Information Bureau is to be in Belgrade.

DISCUSSION QUESTIONS

1. How did the authors of this manifesto and resolution justify the formation of the Cominform?
2. What reasons did they give for the breakdown of the wartime alliance and division of Europe into two hostile camps?
3. Why did they refer to their own camp as "democratic" and the Western camp as "imperialist"? What did they see as the main goals of the Western "imperialist" powers?
4. How did they think the Cominform could help Communists respond to the Western threat?
5. What concerns might have affected their decision to place Cominform headquarters in Belgrade, Yugoslavia?

11. THE COMMUNIST *Coup* IN CZECHOSLOVAKIA, FEBRUARY 1948

Of all the nations of Eastern Europe, Czechoslovakia had the strongest industrial base, the most successful experience with democracy and, thanks to its abandonment by England and France in the face of Nazi demands in 1938, the biggest beef against the West. There was general goodwill toward the USSR and much popular support for the Czechoslovak Communists. Stalin had reason to expect that Communism might triumph there in free elections, and the Czechs had reason to expect that they could maintain their democratic traditions and still be friendly to Moscow.

For several years after World War II, this seemed to be a real possibility. As the rest of Eastern Europe fell under Communist control, Czechoslovakia remained democratic. President Edvard Benes, who had signed an alliance with Stalin in 1943, worked to preserve his nation as a bridge between East and West. Free elections in 1946 gave the Communists a plurality in the National Assembly, but Klement Gottwald, the new Communist premier, led a coalition government called the National Front, which included non-Communist parties and maintained close ties with the West.

All this began to change with the coming of the Marshall Plan in 1947. The Czechoslovak leaders, anxious to improve their economy, unanimously agreed to accept American aid. But Stalin, fearful that this might promote U.S. economic hegemony in Eastern Europe, forced them to withdraw their application and instead to join a Soviet-sponsored "Molotov Plan" for aid to Communist countries.

The situation quickly deteriorated. The Czechoslovak Communists began to browbeat and tyrannize the other members of the National Front, who responded in February 1948 by resigning their positions, hoping the government would fall. This was a disastrous miscalculation. Aided by their socialist allies, the Communists remained in office and carried out a coup. As the following correspondence makes clear, President Benes strove to maintain a modicum of democracy and independence, but the Communists refused to cooperate. As a result, Czechoslovakia became part of the Soviet Bloc, and Moscow consolidated its control over all of Eastern Europe.

A. Letter from President Benes to the Czechoslovak Communist Party Presidium, 24 February 1948

You sent me a letter on February 21 in which you express your attitude on a solution of the crisis and ask me to agree with it. Allow me to formulate my own attitude.

I feel fully the great responsibility of this fateful hour on our national and state life. From the beginning of this crisis I have been thinking about the situation as it was forming itself, putting these affairs of ours in connection with world affairs.

I am trying to see clearly not only the present situation but also the causes that led to it and the results that a decision can have. I am aware of the powerful forces through which the situation is being formed.

In a calm, matter of fact, impassionate and objective judgment of the situation I feel, through the common will of various groups of our citizens which turn their attention to me, that the will is expressed to maintain the peace and order and discipline voluntarily accepted to achieve a progressive and really socialist life.

How to achieve this goal? You know my sincerely democratic creed. I cannot but stay faithful to that creed even at this moment because democracy, according to my belief, is the only reliable and durable basis for a decent and dignified human life.

I insist on parliamentary democracy and parliamentary government as it limits democracy. I state I know very well it is necessary to social and economic content. I built my political work on these principles and cannot—without betraying myself—act otherwise.

The present crisis of democracy here too cannot be overcome but through democratic and parliamentary means. I thus do not overlook your demands. I regard parties associated in the National Front as bearers of political responsibility. We all accepted the principle of the National Front and this proved successful up to the recent time when the crisis began.

This crisis, however, in my opinion, does not deny the principle in itself. I am convinced that on this principle, even in the future, the necessary cooperation of all can be achieved. All disputes can be solved for the benefit of the national and common state of the Czechs and the Slovaks.

I therefore have been in negotiation with five political parties. I have listened to their views and some of them also have been put in writing. These are grave matters and I cannot ignore them.

Therefore, I again have to appeal to all to find a peaceful solution and new successful cooperation through parliamentary means and through the National Front.

That much for the formal side. As far as the personal side is concerned, it is clear to me, as I have said already, that the Prime Minister will be the chairman of the strongest party element, Gottwald.

Finally, on the factual side of this matter it is clear to me that socialism is a way of life desired by an overwhelming part of our nation. At the same time I believe that with socialism a certain measure of freedom and unity is possible and that these are vital principles to all in our national life.

Our nation has struggled for freedom almost throughout its history. History also has shown us where discord can lead.

I beg of you therefore to relive these facts and make them the starting point for our negotiations. Let us all together begin negotiations again for further durable cooperation and let us not allow prolongation of the split of the nation into two quarreling parts.

I believe that a reasonable agreement is possible because it is indispensable.

B. Reply by the Czechoslovak Communist Party Presidium to the Letter of President Benes, 25 February 1948

The Presidium of the Central Committee of the Communist Party acknowledges your letter dated February 24, and states that it cannot enter into negotiations with the present leadership of the National Socialist, People's, and Slovak Democratic Parties because this would not conform to the interests of the unity of the people nor with the interests of further peaceful development of the republic.

Recent events indisputably proved that these three parties no longer represent the interests of the working people of the cities and countryside, that their leaders have betrayed the fundamental ideas of the people's democracy and National Front . . . , and that they assumed the position of undermining the opposition.

This was shown again and again in the government, in the Constitutional National Assembly, in the press of these parties, and in actions that, with menacing levity, were organized by their central secretariats against the interests of the working people, against the security of the state, against the alliances of the republic, against state finance, against nationalized industry, against urgent agricultural reforms—in one word, against the whole constructive efforts of our people and against the very foundations, internal and external, of the security of the country.

These parties even got in touch with foreign circles hostile to our people's democratic order and our alliances, and in collaboration with these hostile foreign elements they attempted disruption of the present development of the republic.

This constantly increasing activity was crowned by an attempt to break up the government, an attempt that, as it was proved, should have been accompanied by actions aiming at a putsch.

Massive people's manifestations during the last few days clearly have shown that our working people denounce, with complete unity and with indignation, the policy of these parties and ask the creation of a government in which all honest progressive patriots devoted to the republic and the people are represented. . . .

In conformity with this powerfully expressed will of the people, the Presidium of the Central Committee of the Communist Party approved the proposals of Premier Klement Gottwald according to which the government will be filled in with prominent representatives of all parties and also big nationwide organizations.

We stress that a government filled in this way will present itself, with full agreement with the principles of parliamentary democracy, before the Constitutional National Assembly with its program and ask for its approval.

Being convinced that only such a highly constitutional and parliamentary process can guarantee the peaceful development of the republic, and at the same time that it corresponds to the ideas of a complete majority of the working people, the Presidium of the Central Committee hopes firmly after careful consideration that you will recognize the correctness of its conclusions and will agree with its proposals.

DISCUSSION QUESTIONS

1. What reasons did President Benes advance for preserving democracy in Czechoslovakia?
2. Why did he think it was important to restore the National Front?
3. What concessions was he willing to make to the Communists?
4. What reasons did the Communists give for rejecting his pleas? What charges did they make against the non-Communist parties which resigned from the National Front?

12. The Treaty of Brussels, 1948

The Communist takeover of Czechoslovakia in February 1948 helped expedite the creation of an anti-Soviet military alliance in Western Europe. On 17 March, five nations—Belgium, the Netherlands, Luxembourg, Britain, and France—met at Brussels to sign a treaty committing them to mutual consultation and cooperation in the event of aggression against any one of them. In the spirit of the Marshall Plan, the Treaty of Brussels pledged its signatories to close economic cooperation; it was designed to remain in force for fifty years.

Although the only potential enemy mentioned in the treaty was Germany, it was clear to everyone that the Soviet Union was the real target. The Marshall Plan had begun the economic reintegration of western Germany into Western Europe, and the Americans, British, and French were moving toward creation of a single currency for their three occupation zones in Germany. No one believed that a fragmented, occupied Germany posed any credible threat to the peace of Europe in 1948. The events of February 1948 in Prague, on the other hand, confirmed the Western conviction that Soviet objectives included the extension of Communist political and economic systems throughout the world. The Treaty of Brussels and the consultative council it created would serve as the embryo for the North Atlantic Treaty Organization (Document 15).

Excerpts from the Treaty of Brussels, 17 March 1948

Article I

Convinced of the close community of their interests and of the necessity of uniting in order to promote the economic recovery of Europe, the high contracting parties will so organize and coordinate their economic activities as to produce the best possible results, by the elimination of conflict in their economic policies, coordination of production and development of commercial exchanges. . . .

Article II

The high contracting parties will make every effort . . . to promote the attainment of a higher standard of living by their peoples. . . .

Article IV

If any of the high contracting parties should be the object of an armed attack in Europe, the other high contracting parties will, in accordance with the provisions of Article 51 of the Charter of the United Nations, afford the party so attacked all military and other aid and assistance in their power.

Article V

All measures taken as a result of the preceding article shall be immediately reported to the Security Council. They shall be terminated as soon as the Security Council has taken the measures necessary to maintain or restore international peace and security. . . .

Article VI

. . . None of the high contracting parties will conclude any alliance or participate in any coalition directed against any other of the high contracting parties.

Article VII

For the purpose of consulting together on all questions dealt with in the present treaty, the high contracting parties will create a consultative council which shall be so organized as to be able to exercise its functions continuously. The Council shall meet at such times as it shall deem fit. At the request of any of the high contracting parties, the Council shall be immediately convened in order to permit the high contracting parties to consult with regard to any situation which may constitute a threat to peace, in whatever area this threat should arise, with regard to the attitude to be adopted and the steps to be taken in the case of a renewal by Germany of an aggressive policy, or with regard to any situation constituting a danger to economic stability. . . .

DISCUSSION QUESTIONS

1. Why did the Brussels treaty mention Germany but not the USSR? How can you tell that the USSR was the treaty's real target?
2. Why did the treaty assure its readers that any military measures taken by its signatories would immediately terminate once the UN Security Council took action?
3. Why did the treaty consider economic cooperation as important as military cooperation?
4. What was the purpose of the consultative council created by the treaty?

13. The Expulsion of Tito from the Communist Bloc, 1948

In spring 1948, not long after the Communist coup in Czechoslovakia, a crisis arose between the USSR and Communist Yugoslavia. Relations between the two socialist states had been strained for some time. As a national hero who led his country's wartime anti-Nazi resistance, Marshal Tito, the postwar Yugoslav leader, enjoyed broad popular support. Unlike other East European Communists, he did not owe his position to Moscow and thus felt free to pursue his own course. Determined to strengthen his nation's industry, he refused to let Stalin exploit its natural resources to rebuild the USSR. Bent on enhancing Yugoslav power, he demanded territory from Italy, intervened in the Greek civil war, and talked grandly of forming a federation of Balkan Communist countries. Stalin, who had little use for any Communist he could not control, grew increasingly annoyed and frustrated with Tito's independence.

Finally, in June 1948, the Soviet dictator made his move. He cut off aid to Yugoslavia, withdrew all Soviet advisors, and arranged an economic boycott by the entire Soviet Bloc. At his insistence, the recently founded Cominform issued a denunciation of the Yugoslav leaders, expelled them from its membership, and called on the "healthy elements" of the Yugoslav Communist Party to throw them out. Its formal resolution, excerpted below, accused them of various harmful, arrogant, anti-Soviet behaviors.

Unfortunately for Stalin, his efforts failed. Tito moved quickly to oust the Stalinists in his own entourage, and the United States, anxious to exploit any division within the Communist ranks, provided trade and economic assistance to help him overcome the boycott. Stalin, whose Red Army forces had withdrawn from Yugoslavia after brutally liberating it in 1944, and whose attention in June 1948 was focused increasingly on the developing Berlin Blockade crisis, apparently decided that getting rid of Tito was not worth the price of invasion. At any rate, the Yugoslav leader survived and went on to guide his nation on a separate road to socialism, independent of Moscow's control.

Cominform Resolution on the Situation in Yugoslavia, 28 June 1948

1. The Cominform asserts that the leadership of the Yugoslav Communist Party has lately undertaken an entirely wrong policy on the principal questions of foreign and internal politics, which means a retreat from Marxism-Leninism. . . .
2. The Cominform finds that the leadership of the Yugoslav Communist Party created a hateful policy in relation to the Soviet Union and to the All-Communist Union of Bolsheviks. In Yugoslavia an undignified policy of underestimating Soviet military specialists was allowed. Also, members of the Soviet Army were discredited. . . . All these facts prove that the leading persons in the Communist Party of Yugoslavia took a stand unworthy of Communists, on the line of which they began to identify the foreign policy of the Soviet Union with that of the imperialist powers, and they treat the Soviet Union in the same manner as they treat the bourgeois states. . . .
3. In their policy inside the country the leaders of the Communist Party of Yugoslavia are retreating from positions of the working class and departing from the Marxist theory of classes and class struggle. . . . Leading Yugoslav politicians are carrying out a wrong policy in the villages, ignoring the class differences in the villages . . . despite the well-known Lenin precept that a small individual economy inexorably gives birth to capitalism and the bourgeoisie. . . .
4. The Cominform is sure that the leadership of the Yugoslav Communist Party is revising the Marxist-Leninist theory about the Party. . . .
5. The Information Bureau maintains that the bureaucratic regime inside the party is pernicious to the life and the progress of the Yugoslav Communist Party. There is no intra-party democracy in the party, the electoral principle is not realized, there is no criticism and self criticism.
6. The Information Bureau maintains that the criticism of the Central Committee of the Communist Party of Yugoslavia that was made by the Central Committee of the [Communist Party of the Soviet Union] and by the Central Committees of the other Communist parties as a brotherly help to the Yugoslav Communist Party creates for its leadership all the conditions necessary for the correction of the faults committed. But the leaders of the Communist Party of Yugoslavia, affected by exaggerated ambition, megalomania and conceit, instead of

honestly accepting this criticism and taking the path of Bolshevik correction of these mistakes, received the criticism with dislike, took a hostile standpoint toward it, and in an anti-party spirit categorically and generally denied their faults. . . .

7. With regard to the situation created in the Communist Party of Yugoslavia . . . the Central Committee of the [Communist Party of the Soviet Union] and other Central Committees of the other brotherly parties, decided to discuss the situation . . . at a meeting of the Information Bureau. . . . But . . . the Yugoslav leaders answered with a refusal. . . .

The Information Bureau finds that, as a result of all this, the Central Committee of the Communist Party of Yugoslavia puts itself and the Yugoslav Communist Party outside the family of brotherly Communist parties, outside the united Communist front, and therefore outside the ranks of the Information Bureau.

The Information Bureau maintains that the basis of all these faults of the leadership of the Communist Party of Yugoslavia is the incontestable fact that in its leadership in the last five to six months openly nationalistic elements prevailed that were formerly masked. . . .

The Information Bureau does not doubt that in the core of the Communist Party of Yugoslavia there are enough sound elements that are truly faithful to Marxism- Leninism, faithful to the internationalistic traditions of the Yugoslav Communist Party, and faithful to the united Socialist front. The aim of these sound elements of the Communist Party of Yugoslavia is to force their present party leaders to confess openly and honestly their faults and correct them; to part from nationalism; to return to internationalism and in every way to fix the united Socialist front against imperialism, or if the present leaders of the Communist Party of Yugoslavia prove unable to do this task, to change them and raise from below a new internationalistic leadership of the Communist Party of Yugoslavia. . . .

DISCUSSION QUESTIONS

1. What reasons did the Cominform give for the split between Yugoslavia and the rest of the Communist Bloc? What charges did it make against the Yugoslav leaders?
2. According to the Cominform, how did Yugoslav Marxism differ from orthodox Marxism?
3. What did the Cominform want Yugoslav Communists to do in order to resolve the situation?
4. Why did Stalin want to get rid of Tito? Why was Tito able to survive Stalin's efforts to get rid of him?

14. The Berlin Blockade, 1948–1949

The first major military crisis of the Cold War began in June 1948. The Western allies had responded to the Communist coup in Czechoslovakia with the Treaty of Brussels and a decision to create an independent West German state. This threatened the Soviet objective of a permanently crippled Germany, and when the West announced the creation of a common West German currency called the deutsche mark, Moscow moved to seal off West Berlin and force the Western Powers to remove their troops from the divided city.

Like Germany as a whole, Berlin had been divided into occupation zones at the end of World War II, with the Soviets in the East and the Americans, British, and French in the West. Since the city sat in the midst of Soviet-occupied East Germany, Stalin assumed that he could drive the others out simply by cutting off the roads and railways that linked it with the West. Since few believed that the West could remain in Berlin if the Soviets moved against it, Stalin surely thought his actions involved minimal risk.

The American response, however, caught him by surprise. President Truman announced that the United States would stay in Berlin, and he ordered a military airlift to supply West Berliners with food, fuel, and supplies. Secretary of State Marshall subsequently sent a protest note to the Soviet government, demanding that the blockade be lifted and categorically asserting U.S. rights, responsibilities, and determination to remain in Berlin. The Berlin Blockade lasted eleven months, but the airlift proved effective, and the crisis ended in May 1949 when the Soviets quietly lifted their blockade.

Note from Secretary of State Marshall to the Soviet Ambassador, 6 July 1948

EXCELLENCY: The United States Government wishes to call to the attention of the Soviet Government the extremely serious international situation which has been brought about by the actions of the Soviet Government in imposing restrictive measures on transport which amount now to a blockade against the sectors in Berlin occupied by the United States, United Kingdom and France. The United States Government regards these measures of blockade as a clear violation of existing agreements concerning the administration of Berlin by the four occupying powers.

The rights of the United States as a joint occupying power in Berlin derive from the total defeat and unconditional surrender of Germany. The international agreements undertaken in connection therewith by the Governments of the United States, United Kingdom, France and the Soviet Union defined the zones in Germany and the sectors in Berlin which are occupied by these powers. They established the quadripartite control of Berlin on a basis of friendly cooperation which the Government of the United States earnestly desires to continue to pursue.

These agreements implied the right of free access to Berlin. This right has long been confirmed by usage. It was directly specified in a message sent by President Truman to Premier Stalin on June 14, 1945, which agreed to the withdrawal of United States forces to the zonal boundaries provided satisfactory arrangements could be entered into between the military commanders, which would give access by rail, road and air to United States forces in Berlin. Premier Stalin replied on June 16 suggesting a change in date but no other alteration in the plan proposed by the President. Premier Stalin then gave assurances that all necessary measures would be taken in accordance with the plan. Correspondence in a similar sense took place between Premier Stalin and Mr. Churchill. In accordance with this understanding, the United States, whose armies had penetrated deep into Saxony and Thuringia, parts of the Soviet zone, withdrew its forces to its own area of occupation in Germany and took up its position in its own sector in Berlin. Thereupon the agreements in regard to the occupation of Germany and Berlin went into effect. The United States would not have so withdrawn its troops from a large area now occupied by the Soviet Union had there been any doubt whatsoever about the observance of its agreed right of free access to its sector of Berlin. The right of the United States to its position in Berlin thus stems from precisely the same source as the right of the Soviet Union. It is impossible to assert the latter and deny the former.

It clearly results from these undertakings that Berlin is not a part of the Soviet zone, but is an international zone of occupation. Commitments entered into in good faith by the zone commanders, and subsequently confirmed by the Allied Control Authority, as well as practices sanctioned by usage, guarantee the United States together with other powers, free access to Berlin for the purpose of fulfilling its responsibilities as an occupying power. The facts are plain. Their meaning is clear. Any other interpretation would offend all the rules of comity and reason.

In order that there should be no misunderstanding whatsoever on this point, the United States Government categorically asserts that it is in occupation of its sector in Berlin with free access thereto as a matter of established right deriving from the defeat and surrender of Germany and confirmed by formal agreements among the principal Allies. It further declares that it will not be induced by threats, pressures or other actions to abandon these rights. It is hoped that the Soviet Government entertains no doubts whatsoever on this point.

This Government now shares with the Governments of France and the United Kingdom the responsibility initially undertaken at Soviet request on July 7, 1945, for the physical well-being of 2,400,000 persons in the western sectors of Berlin. Restrictions recently imposed by the Soviet authorities in Berlin have operated to prevent this Government and the Governments of the United Kingdom and of France from fulfilling that responsibility in an adequate manner.

The responsibility which this Government bears for the physical well-being and the safety of the German population in its sector of Berlin is outstandingly humanitarian in character. This population includes hundreds of thousands of women and children, whose health and safety are dependent on the continued use of adequate facilities for moving food, medical supplies and other items indispensable to the maintenance of human life in the western sectors of Berlin. The most elemental of these human rights which both our Governments are solemnly pledged to protect are thus placed in jeopardy by these restrictions. It is intolerable that any one of the occupying authorities should attempt to impose a blockade upon the people of Berlin.

The United States Government is therefore obliged to insist that in accordance with existing agreements the arrangements for the movement of freight and passenger traffic between the western zones and Berlin be fully restored. There can be no question of delay in the restoration of these essential services, since the needs of the civilian population in the Berlin area are imperative. . . .

DISCUSSION QUESTIONS

1. What might Stalin have hoped to accomplish by cutting off Western access to Berlin?
2. Why did the Americans decide to stay in Berlin, despite the Soviet blockade? What were the advantages and disadvantages of an airlift as a means of supplying the city?
3. According to Marshall, what were the legal and moral foundations of the American presence in West Berlin?
4. On what basis did Marshall insist that the Soviets had no right to restrict Western access to the city?
5. What were the implications of Marshall's assertion that the United States would "not be induced by threats, pressures or other actions" to abandon Berlin?

15. The NATO Alliance, 1949

Throughout its existence, the United States had been reluctant to commit itself to "entangling alliances" with other nations in peacetime. One of the principal reasons for its struggle for independence from Great Britain had been the desire to keep clear of Europe's quarrels. But Soviet actions in Czechoslovakia and Berlin in 1948 convinced Washington to modify its position and conclude a military alliance with eleven other nations in Europe and North America. This alliance, known as NATO (the North Atlantic Treaty Organization), testified to America's assumption that the Cold War would last indefinitely.

The NATO alliance was constructed upon the foundations laid by the Treaty of Brussels. The consultative council created at Brussels had organized a standing military committee, which spent much of 1948 discussing the potential threat of a Soviet invasion of Western Europe. The Berlin blockade helped convince skeptics that this was a real danger. In such an environment, nations that only four years earlier had been allied with the Soviet Union in a war against

Nazi Germany now gave notice that they considered their former ally a greater threat than their former foe. This was underscored by NATO's inclusion of Italy, which had fought on Germany's side in World War II, and Portugal, whose fascist government had remained neutral. Neither had been part of the Treaty of Brussels, but the Berlin Blockade frightened the signatories of that accord, as well as the United States, into including them in the new alliance.

The Treaty of Washington (North Atlantic Treaty), 4 April 1949

The Parties to this Treaty reaffirm their faith in the purposes and principles of the Charter of the United Nations and their desire to live in peace with all peoples and all governments.

They are determined to safeguard the freedom, common heritage, and civilization of their peoples, founded on the principles of democracy, individual liberty, and the rule of law.

They seek to promote stability and well-being in the North Atlantic area.

They are resolved to unite their efforts for collective defense and for preservation of peace and security.

They therefore agree to this North Atlantic Treaty:

Article I

The Parties undertake, as set forth in the Charter of the United Nations, to settle any international disputes in which they may be involved by peaceful means in such a manner that international peace and security, and justice, are not endangered, and to refrain in their international relations from the threat or use of force in any manner inconsistent with the purposes of the United Nations.

Article 2

The Parties will contribute toward the further development of peaceful and friendly international relations by strengthening their free institutions, by bringing about a better understanding of the principles upon which these institutions are founded, and by promoting conditions of stability and well-being. They will seek to eliminate conflict in their international economic policies and will encourage economic collaboration between any or all of them.

Article 3

In order more effectively to achieve the objectives of this Treaty, the Parties, separately and jointly, by means of continuous and effective self-help and mutual aid, will maintain and develop their individual and collective capacity to resist armed attack.

Article 4

The Parties will consult together whenever, in the opinion of any of them, the territorial integrity, political independence or security of any of the Parties is threatened.

Article 5

The Parties agree that an armed attack against one or more of them in Europe or North America shall be considered an attack against them all; and consequently they agree that, if such an armed attack occurs, each of them, in exercise of the right of individual or collective self-defense recognized by Article 51 of the Charter of the United Nations, will assist the Party or Parties so attacked by taking forthwith, individually and in concert with the other Parties, such action as it deems necessary, including the use of armed force, to restore and maintain the security of the North Atlantic area.

Any such armed attack and all measures taken as a result thereof shall immediately be reported to the Security Council. Such measures shall be terminated when the Security Council has taken the measures necessary to restore and maintain international peace and security.

Article 6

For the purpose of Article 5 an armed attack on one or more of the Parties is deemed to include an armed attack on the territory of any of the Parties in Europe or North America, on the Algerian dependents of France, on the occupation forces of any Party in Europe, on the islands under the jurisdiction of any Party in the North Atlantic area north of the Tropic of Cancer or on the vessels or aircraft in this area of any of the Parties.

Article 7

This Treaty does not affect, and shall not be interpreted as affecting, in any way the rights and obligations under the Charter of the Parties which are members of the United Nations, or the primary responsibility of the Security Council for the maintenance of international peace and security.

Article 8

Each Party declares that none of the international engagements now in force between it and any other of the Parties or any third state is in conflict with the provisions of this Treaty, and undertakes not to enter into any international engagement in conflict with this Treaty.

Article 9

The Parties hereby establish a council, on which each of them shall be represented, to consider matters concerning the implementation of this Treaty. The council shall be so organized as to be able to meet promptly at any time. The council shall set up such subsidiary bodies as may be necessary; in particular it shall establish a defense committee which shall recommend measures for the implementation of Articles 3 and 5.

Article 10

The Parties may, by unanimous agreement, invite any other European state in a position to further the principles of this Treaty and to contribute to the security of the North Atlantic area to accede to this Treaty. Any state so invited may become a party to the Treaty by depositing its instrument of accession with the Government of the United States of America. . . .

Signed by representatives of:

Kingdom of Belgium	Grand Duchy of Luxembourg
Canada	Kingdom of the Netherlands
Kingdom of Denmark	Kingdom of Norway
France	Portugal
Iceland	United Kingdom
Italy	United States

DISCUSSION QUESTIONS

1. Which provisions of the Treaty of Brussels are reflected in the North Atlantic Treaty?
2. What were the differences between this document and the Treaty of Brussels? What might account for these differences?
3. Article 5 states that an attack upon one of the parties shall be considered an attack upon them all. Given the inclusion of the United States, and its possession of nuclear weapons, what were the main implications of this article?
4. Why did the treaty contain a provision for adding new members to the alliance? Which nations might have been considered potential members, and why?
5. How can you tell that the USSR was the main target of the treaty, even though it was not mentioned by name?

16. Acheson on the Communist Triumph in China, 1949

By 1949, it was clear that the Communists were winning the Chinese civil war and that only a massive U.S. military intervention could save the Nationalist regime of the Guomindang (Kuomintang). Facing a dangerous Soviet challenge in the West, however, including the Berlin Blockade, American officials decided that protecting Europe was their main priority and that they must thus not get diverted into an Asian war.

Dean Acheson, who became secretary of state in January 1949, was deeply committed to Europe's defense, having previously been involved in implementing the Truman Doctrine and Marshall Plan. Ironically, his tenure in office was dominated by

Asian events. In his first year China fell to the Communists, and a political firestorm broke out in Washington about the U.S. role. In this letter of transmittal for a State Department "White Paper" on China, Acheson sought to explain events in China and justify the actions of the Truman administration.

Secretary of State Acheson's Letter of Transmittal for U.S. State Department "White Paper" on China, 30 July 1949

Two factors have played a major role in shaping the destiny of modern China.

The population of China during the eighteenth and nineteenth centuries doubled, thereby creating an unbearable pressure upon the land. The first problem which every Chinese Government has had to face is that of feeding this population. So far none has succeeded. The Kuomintang attempted to solve it by putting many land-reform laws on the statute books. Some of these laws have failed, others have been ignored. In no small measure, the predicament in which the National Government finds itself today is due to its failure to provide China with enough to eat. A large part of the Chinese Communists' propaganda consists of promises that they will solve the land problem.

The second major factor which has shaped the pattern of contemporary China is the impact of the West and of Western ideas. For more than three thousand years the Chinese developed their own high culture and civilization, largely untouched by outside influences. . . . Then in the middle of the nineteenth century the heretofore impervious wall of Chinese isolation was breached by the West. These outsiders brought with them aggressiveness, the unparalleled development of Western technology, and a high order of culture which had not accompanied previous foreign incursions into China. Partly because of these qualities and partly because of the decay of Manchu rule, the Westerners, instead of being absorbed by the Chinese, introduced new ideas which played an important part in stimulating ferment and unrest.

By the beginning of the twentieth century, the combined force of overpopulation and new ideas set in motion that chain of events which can be called the Chinese revolution. It is one of the most imposing revolutions in recorded history and its outcome and consequences are yet to be foreseen. Out of this revolutionary whirlpool emerged the Kuomintang, first under . . . Dr. Sun Yat-sen and later Generalissimo Chiang Kai-shek, to assume the direction of the revolution. The leadership of the Kuomintang was not challenged until 1927 by the Chinese Communist party which had been organized in the early twenties under the ideological impetus of the Russian revolution. . . . To a large extent the history of the period between 1927 and 1937 can be written in terms of the struggle for power between the Kuomintang and the Chinese Communists. . . .

Perhaps largely because of the progress being made in China, the Japanese chose 1937 as the departure point for the conquest of China proper, and the goal of the Chinese people became the expulsion of a brutal and hated invader. . . .

In contrast . . . to the unity of the people of China in the war against Japan were the divided interests of the Kuomintang and the Chinese Communists . . . Once the United States became a participant in the war, the Kuomintang was apparently convinced of the ultimate defeat of Japan and saw an opportunity to improve its position for a show-down struggle with the Communists. The Communists, for their part, seemed to see in the chaos of China an opportunity to obtain . . . full power in China. This struggle for power in the latter years of the war contributed largely to the partial paralysis of China's ability to resist. . . .

When peace came the United States was confronted with three possible alternatives in China: (1) it could have pulled out lock, stock and barrel; (2) it could have intervened militarily on a major scale to assist the Nationalists to destroy the Communists; (3) it could, while assisting the Nationalists to assert their authority over as much of China as possible, endeavor to avoid a civil war by working for a compromise between the two sides.

The first alternative would . . . have represented an abandonment of our international responsibilities and our traditional policy of friendship with China. . . . The second alternative policy, while it may look attractive theoretically and in retrospect, was wholly impracticable. . . .

It is obvious that the American people would not have sanctioned such a colossal commitment of our armies in 1945 or later. We therefore came to the third alternative policy whereunder we . . . attempted to assist in working out a *modus vivendi* which would avert civil war but nevertheless preserve and even increase the influence of the National Government . . .

. . . [O]ur policy at that time was inspired by the two objectives of bringing peace to China under conditions which would permit stable government and progress along democratic lines, and of assisting the National Government to establish its authority over as wide areas of China as possible. As the event proved, the first objective was unrealizable because neither side desired it to succeed: the Communists because they refused to accept conditions which would weaken their freedom to proceed with . . . the communization of all China; the Nationalists because they cherished the illusion, in spite of repeated advice to the contrary from our military representatives, that they could destroy the Communists by force of arms.

The second objective of assisting the National Government, however, we pursued vigorously from 1945 to 1949. The National Government was the recognized government of a friendly power. Our friendship, and our right under international law alike, called for aid to the Government instead of to the Communists who were seeking to subvert and overthrow it. . . .

The reasons for the failures of the Chinese National Government appear in some detail in the attached record. They do not stem from any inadequacy of American aid. Our military observers on the spot have reported that the Nationalist armies did not lose a single battle during the crucial year of 1948 through lack of arms or ammunition. The fact was that the decay which our observers had detected . . . early in the war had fatally sapped the powers of resistance of the Kuomintang. Its leaders had proved incapable of meeting the crisis confronting them, its troops had lost the will to fight, and its Government had lost popular support. The Communists, on the other hand, through a ruthless discipline and fanatical zeal, attempted to sell themselves as guardians and liberators of the people. The Nationalist armies did not have to be defeated; they disintegrated. History has proved time and again that a regime without faith in itself and an army without morale cannot survive the test of battle . . .

It has been urged that relatively small amounts of additional aid—military and economic—to the National Government would have enabled it to destroy Communism in China. The most trustworthy military, economic, and political information available to our Government does not bear out this view.

A realistic appraisal of conditions in China, past and present, leads to the conclusion that the only alternative open to the United States was full-scale intervention in behalf of a Government which had lost the confidence of its own troops and its own people. . . .

The unfortunate but inescapable fact is that the ominous result of the civil war in China was beyond the control of the government of the United States. Nothing that this country did or could have done within the reasonable limits of its capabilities could have changed that result; nothing that was left undone by this country contributed to it. It was the product of internal Chinese forces, forces which this country tried to influence but could not. A decision was arrived at within China, if only a decision by default. . . .

DISCUSSION QUESTIONS

1. Which two factors, in Acheson's view, played a key role in shaping modern China's destiny? Which did he considered more important? Why?
2. According to Acheson, why did the Nationalists fail to win the support of the Chinese people?
3. What were the two main objectives of U.S. policy in China after World War II? To what extent were they incompatible? How do you account for U.S. failure to achieve these objectives?
4. What did Acheson see as the main reasons for the Communist victory and Nationalist defeat? How did he justify the U.S. decision not to intervene to save the Nationalists?

17. Mao Proclaims the People's Republic of China, 1 October 1949

By fall of 1949, with Communists controlling most of mainland China, their victory in the Chinese civil war was assured. It was not a total triumph: Further fighting would go on for months, and the Nationalists would flee to Taiwan and continue to function there for decades. But this did not diminish the reality that half a billion Chinese people, one-fifth of all humanity, had come under Communist rule. Even before their victory was complete, the Chinese Communists moved to declare their new regime. On 1 October 1949, Mao Zedong (Mao Tse-tung), Communist Party leader and head of the new government, issued the following proclamation.

Mao's Statement Proclaiming the People's Republic of China, 1 October 1949

People all over China have been plunged into bitter suffering and tribulation since Chiang Kai-shek's Kuomintang reactionary government betrayed the fatherland, conspired with the imperialists and launched a counter-revolutionary war. However, the People's Liberation Army, supported by the people all over the country, fighting heroically and selflessly to . . . protect the people's lives and property and relieve the people's suffering and struggle for their rights has . . . overthrown the reactionary rule of the National Government. Now the people's liberation war has been fundamentally won and a majority of the people has been liberated.

On this foundation the first session of the Chinese People's Political Consultative Conference, composed of delegates of all democratic parties, groups, people's organizations, the People's Liberation Army in various regions, overseas Chinese and patriotic democratic elements of the whole country, has been convened. Representing the will of the people, this session of Chinese peoples:

- Enacted the organic law of the Central People's Government of the peoples of the Republic of China;
- Elected Mao Tse-tung [Mao Zedong] chairman of the Central People's Government. . . .
- Proclaimed the founding of the People's Republic of China, and
- Decided Peking [Beijing] should be the capital of the People's Republic of China.

The Central People's Government Council of the People's Republic of China took office today in this capital and unanimously made the following decisions:

- Proclamation for the formation of the Central People's Government, People's Republic of China.
- Adoption of a common program for the Chinese People's Political Consultative Conference as a policy of the Government. . . .
- Appointment of:
- Chou En-lai [Zhou Enlai] as Premier of the State Administration Council and concurrently minister of the Ministry of Foreign Affairs,
- Mao Tse-tung [Mao Zedong] as Chairman of the People's Revolutionary Military Council of the Central People's Government,
- Chu Teh [Zhu De] as commander-in-chief of the People's Liberation Army . . .

At the same time the Central People's Government Council decided to declare to the governments of all other countries that this is the sole legal Government representing all the people of the People's Republic of China. This Government is willing to establish diplomatic relations with any foreign government that is willing to observe the principles of equality, mutual benefit, mutual respect of territorial integrity and sovereignty.

DISCUSSION QUESTIONS

1. Why did the Communists proclaim a new government, even while fighting was still going on?
2. How did Mao justify the overthrow of the Nationalist government and the formation of the People's Republic?
3. Why did the proclamation declare the new regime the "sole legal government" of China?
4. Why did it declare that the new regime was "willing to establish diplomatic relations with any foreign government"?

18. The Soviet–Chinese Friendship Treaty, February 1950

Although the Communist victory in China seemed to be a huge gain for the Soviets, Stalin was not so sure. He had signed an advantageous treaty with the Nationalists in 1945 and had maintained ties with them until their defeat was assured. And China's new leaders, despite their outward loyalty to Moscow, were not Soviet puppets like those in Eastern Europe. Fresh from his ill-fated clash with Tito, Stalin was wary of Communist leaders he could not control.

Thus when Mao came to Moscow in December 1949 seeking a new agreement, it took two months of tough negotiations to hammer out a new treaty, and the Chinese Communists got less than they had wanted. Still, the Soviet–Chinese Friendship Treaty was a conspicuous achievement, and a tribute to the negotiating skills of Chinese premier Zhou Enlai (Chou En-lai). In addition to entering a thirty-year alliance with the new Chinese government, the Soviets agreed to provide it with economic credits and industrial equipment and to turn over to it the railways and seaports that the Nationalists had let them control.

A. Communique Announcing the Soviet–Chinese Treaty, 14 February 1950

In the course of a recent period, negotiations have taken place in Moscow between J. V. Stalin, Chairman of the Council of Ministers of the USSR, and A. Y. Vishinsky, USSR Minister of Foreign Affairs, on the one hand, and Mr. Mao Tse-tung, Chairman of the Central Government of the Chinese People's Republic and Mr. Chou Enlai, Premier of the State Administrative Council and Foreign Minister of the People's Republic, on the other hand, during which important political and economic problems on relations between the Soviet Union and the Chinese People's Republic were discussed.

The negotiations, which took place in an atmosphere of cordiality and friendly mutual understanding, confirmed the striving of both sides to strengthen in every way and to develop relations of friendship and cooperation between them as well as their desire to cooperate for the purpose of guaranteeing general peace and the security of the nations. The negotiations were ended by the signing in the Kremlin February 14 of:

1. A Treaty of Friendship, Alliance and Mutual Aid between the Soviet Union and the Chinese People's Republic.

2. Agreements on the Chinese Changchun railway, Port Arthur and Dalny (Dairen), under which, after the signing of the peace treaty with Japan, the Chinese Changchun railway will pass into complete ownership of the Chinese People's Republic, while Soviet troops will be withdrawn from Port Arthur.

3. Agreements by which the Government of the USSR will give to the Government of the Chinese People's Republic a long term economic credit for payment of deliveries of industrial and railway equipment from the USSR.

The above-mentioned treaty and agreements were signed on the part of the USSR by Mr. A. Y. Vishinsky and on the part of the Chinese People's Republic by Mr. Chou En-lai.

In connection with the signing of the Treaty of Friendship, Alliance and Mutual Aid and agreement on the Chinese Changchun railway, Port Arthur and Dalny, Mr. Chou En-lai and A. Y. Vishinsky exchanged notes to the effect that a corresponding treaty and agreements concluded Aug. 14, 1945 between China and the Soviet Union have become invalid and that both governments affirm complete guarantee of the independent status of the Mongolian People's Republic as a result of the referendum of 1945 and the establishment with her of diplomatic relations by the Chinese People's Republic.

Simultaneously, Mr. Chou En-lai and A. Y. Vishinsky also exchanged notes regarding a decision of the Soviet Government to hand over without compensation to the Government of the Chinese People's Republic property acquired by Soviet economic organizations from Japanese owners in Manchuria, as well as on a decision of the Soviet Government to hand over without compensation to the Government of the Chinese People's Republic all buildings of the former military settlement in Peking (Peiping).

B. Treaty of Friendship, Alliance and Mutual Aid Between the USSR and the Chinese People's Republic

. . . The high contracting parties undertake that they will undertake jointly all necessary measures at their disposal to prevent any repetition of aggression and violation of peace on the part of Japan or any other state which directly or indirectly would unite with Japan in acts of aggression. In the event of one of the agreeing parties being subjected to attack by Japan or any state allied with her, thus finding itself in a state of war, the other high contracting party will immediately render military or other aid with all means at its disposal.

The high contracting parties likewise declare their readiness, in the spirit of sincere cooperation, to take part in all international actions which have as their object to ensure peace and security throughout the entire world and will completely devote their energies to the speediest realization of these objects.

The high contracting parties undertake in the way of mutual agreement to work for the conclusion in the shortest possible space of time, jointly with other powers allied during the second World War, of a peace treaty with Japan.

The high contracting parties will not conclude any alliance directed against the other high contracting party, nor will they participate in any coalition, or in actions or measures directed against the other party.

The high contracting parties will cooperate with each other in all important international questions touching on the mutual interests of the Soviet Union and China, being guided by the interest of strengthening peace and universal security.

The high contracting parties undertake, in the spirit of friendship and cooperation and in accordance with the principles of equality, . . . with joint respect for state sovereignty and territorial integrity and non-intervention in the internal affairs of the other country to develop and strengthen economic and cultural ties between the Soviet Union and China, and to render each other every possible economic aid, and realize the necessary economic cooperation. . . .

The present agreement is to remain in force for thirty years, and unless one of the high contracting parties one year previous to the expiring of the agreement declares its desire to denounce the agreement, it will remain in force for a further period of five years. . . .

DISCUSSION QUESTIONS

1. Why was the treaty such an important accomplishment for the Chinese Communists? Why were the negotiations so long and difficult?
2. Why did the communique insist that the Soviet–Chinese agreements of 1945 were no longer valid?
3. Why was the alliance directed mainly against Japan and its potential allies?
4. Why did the Soviets agree to hand over to China property and railways located in Manchuria? Why did they agree to grant long-term credits to China?

19. McCarthy on "Communists" in the U.S. Government, 1950

The Communist victory in China, combined with news that the Soviets had developed an atomic bomb, had a devastating impact on American morale. Some Americans, searching for culprits, sought to blame these setbacks on disloyalty within the U.S. government. Foremost among them was Joseph R. McCarthy (1909–1957), Republican senator from Wisconsin, who in February 1950 gave a speech in West Virginia charging that these reverses resulted from Communist influence among high U.S. officials. Later that month he repeated the speech in the U.S. Senate, displaying tactics later labeled "McCarthyism." His accusations, along with the disclosure of some genuine instances of espionage and betrayal, led to a Red Scare that swept the nation during the next few years. The loyalty of many innocent officials, academics, writers, and performers was publicly questioned. McCarthy continued to make such charges until 1954, when he was discredited and ultimately censured by the U.S. Senate.

Excerpts from Speech by Senator McCarthy to the U.S. Senate, 20 February 1950

. . . Today we are engaged in a final, all-out battle between communistic atheism and Christianity. The modern champions of communism have selected this as the time. And, ladies and gentlemen, the chips are down—they truly are down. . . .

Six years ago . . . there was within the Soviet orbit 180,000,000 people. . . . Today, only six years later, there are 800,000,000 people under the absolute domination of Soviet Russia—an increase of over 400 percent. . . . This indicates the swiftness of the tempo of Communist victories and American defeats in the cold war. As one of our outstanding historical figures once said, "When a great democracy is destroyed, it will not be because of enemies from without, but rather because of enemies from within." The truth of this statement is becoming terrifyingly clear as we see this country each day losing on every front.

At war's end we were physically the strongest nation on earth and, at least potentially, the most powerful intellectually and morally. Ours could have been the honor of being a beacon in the desert of destruction, a shining living proof that civilization was not yet ready to destroy itself. Unfortunately, we have failed miserably and tragically to arise to the opportunity.

The reason why we find ourselves in a position of impotency is not because our only powerful potential enemy has sent men to invade our shores, but rather because of the traitorous actions of those who have been treated so well by this Nation. It has not been the less fortunate or members of minority groups who have been selling this Nation out, but rather those who have had all the benefits that the wealthiest nation on earth has had to offer—the finest homes, the finest college education, and the finest jobs in Government we can give.

This is glaringly true in the State Department. There the bright young men who are born with silver spoons in their mouths are the ones who have been worst. . . . I would like to cite one rather unusual case—the case of a man who has done much to shape our foreign policy.

When Chiang Kai-shek was fighting our war, the State Department had in China a young man named John S. Service. His task, obviously, was not to work for the communization of China. Strangely, however, he sent official reports back to the State Department urging that we torpedo our ally Chiang Kai-shek and stating, in effect, that communism was the best hope of China.

Later, this man—John Service—was picked up by the Federal Bureau of Investigation for turning over to the Communists secret State Department information. Strangely, however, he was never prosecuted. However, Joseph Grew, Under Secretary of State, who insisted on his prosecution, was forced to resign. Two days after Grew's successor, Dean Acheson, took over as Under Secretary of State, this man—John Service—who had been picked up by the FBI and who had previously urged that communism was the best hope of China, was not only reinstated . . . but promoted. And finally, under Acheson, placed in charge of all placements and promotions.

Today, ladies and gentlemen, this man Service is on his way to represent the State Department and Acheson in Calcutta—by far and away the most important listening post in the Far East.

Now, let's see what happens when individuals with Communist connections are forced out of the State Department. Gustave Duran, who was labeled as (I quote) "a notorious international Communist," was made assistant to the Assistant Secretary of State in charge of Latin American affairs. He was taken into the State Department from his job as a lieutenant colonel in the Communist International Brigade. Finally, after intense congressional pressure and criticism, he resigned in 1946 from the State Department—and, ladies and gentlemen, where do you think he is now? He took over a high-salaried job as Chief of Cultural Activities Section in the office of the Assistant Secretary General of the United Nations. . . .

This, ladies and gentlemen, gives you somewhat of a picture of the type of individuals who have been helping to shape our foreign policy. In my opinion the State Department, which is one of the most important government departments, is thoroughly infested with Communists.

I have in my hand 57 cases of individuals who would appear to be either card carrying members or certainly loyal to the Communist Party, but who nevertheless are still helping to shape our foreign policy.

One thing to remember in discussing the Communists in our Government is that we are not dealing with spies who get 30 pieces of silver to steal the blueprints of a new weapon. We are dealing with a far more sinister type of activity because it permits the enemy to guide and shape our policy. . . .

DISCUSSION QUESTIONS

1. What reasons did McCarthy give for recent setbacks in U.S. policy? What insinuations did he use to cast doubt on the loyalty of certain U.S. officials?
2. What evidence did he provide to support his charges? What tactics did he use to gain support and sympathy?
3. Why were many Americans willing to believe his accusations?
4. What other explanation than McCarthy's might account for the actions of John Service?

20. Acheson on the American Defense Perimeter in Asia, 1950

By 1949, Korea, partitioned after World War II into Soviet and U.S. occupation zones, was home to two hostile states, with Communist North Korea supported by the Soviets and South Korea backed by the Americans. That year, responding to the Communist triumph in China, the United States began to reassess the situation in East Asia. In January 1950, Secretary of State Dean Acheson delivered a major speech before the National Press Club in which he identified a U.S. "defense perimeter" stretching from Japan to the Philippines. His omission of South Korea led to the impression that America would not defend it if it were attacked. Five months later North Korea invaded the south, beginning the Korean War.

Excerpts from Acheson's Speech to the National Press Club, 12 January 1950

This afternoon I should like to discuss with you the relations between the peoples of the United States and the peoples of Asia . . .

What is the situation in regard to the military security of the Pacific area, and what is our policy in regard to it?

In the first place, the defeat and the disarmament of Japan has placed upon the United States the necessity of assuming the military defense of Japan . . . , both in the interest of our security and in the interests of the security of the entire Pacific area. . . . We have American—and there are Australian— troops in Japan. I am not in a position to speak for the Australians, but I can assure you that there is no intention of any sort of abandoning or weakening the defenses of Japan, and that whatever arrangements are to be made, either through permanent settlement or otherwise, that defense must and shall be maintained.

This defensive perimeter runs along the Aleutians to Japan and then goes to the Ryukyus. We hold important defense positions in the Ryukyu Islands, and those we will continue to hold. In the interest of the population of the Ryukyu Islands, we will at an appropriate time offer to hold these islands under trusteeship of the United Nations. But they are essential parts of the defensive perimeter of the Pacific, and they must and will be held.

The defensive perimeter runs from Ryukyus to the Philippine Islands. Our . . . defensive relations with the Philippines are contained in agreements between us. Those agreements are being loyally carried out and will be loyally carried out. Both peoples have learned by bitter experience the vital connections between our mutual defense requirements.

So far as the military security of other areas in the Pacific is concerned, it must be clear that no person can guarantee these areas against military attack. But it must also be clear that such a guarantee is hardly sensible or necessary within the realm of practical relationship. Should such an attack occur . . . the initial reliance must be on the people attacked to resist it and then upon the commitments of the entire civilized world under the Charter of the United Nations, which so far has not proved a weak reed to lean on by any people who are determined to protect their independence against outside aggression. But it is a mistake, I think, in considering Pacific and Far Eastern problems to become obsessed with military considerations. Important as they are, there are other problems that press, and these other problems are not capable of solution through military means. These other problems arise out of the susceptibility of . . . many countries in the Pacific area, to subversion and penetration. That cannot be stopped by military means. . . .

. . . [W]hat we conclude, I believe, is that there is a new day which has dawned in Asia. It is a day in which the Asian peoples are on their own, and know it, and intend to continue on their own. It is a day in which the old relationships between east and west are gone, relationships which at their worst were exploitation and at their best were paternalism. That relationship is over, and the relationship of east and west must now be in the Far East one of mutual respect and mutual helpfulness. We are their friends. Others are their friends. We and those others are willing to help, but we can help only where we are wanted and only where conditions of help are really sensible and possible. So what we can see is that this new day in Asia, this new day which is dawning, may go on to a glorious noon or it may darken and it may drizzle out. But that decision lies within the countries of Asia and within the power of the Asian people. It is not a decision which a friend or even an enemy from the outside can make for them.

DISCUSSION QUESTIONS

1. Why did Acheson reaffirm the U.S. commitment to the military defense of Japan?
2. Why did he not include South Korea in the U.S. defense perimeter?
3. What did he think nations outside the perimeter should do if they were attacked? What role did he envision for the United Nations?
4. What did he see as the future role of the United States in East Asia?

21. NSC–68: American Cold War Strategy, 1950

Early in 1950, responding to concerns that the Communists were winning the Cold War, a group of U.S. officials drafted a secret document called NSC (National Security Council) 68. President Truman reviewed it in April and approved it later that year. Asserting that America faced a period of maximum danger, it called for vast military expenditures and substantial sacrifices, arguing there was no other choice for the nation to maintain its freedom. Although NSC–68 was top secret, its substance soon became widely known, but it was not declassified until 1975.

Excerpts from NSC–68 (Report to the President, 7 April 1950)

Within the past thirty-five years the world has experienced two global wars of tremendous violence. It has witnessed two revolutions—the Russian and the Chinese—of extreme scope and intensity. It has also seen the collapse of five empires—the Ottoman, the Austro-Hungarian, the German, Italian, and Japanese—and the drastic decline of two major imperial systems, the British and the French. During the span of one generation, the international distribution of power has been fundamentally altered . . .

Two complex sets of factors have . . . altered [the] historical distribution of power. First, the defeat of Germany and Japan and the decline of the British and French Empires have interacted with the development of the United States and the Soviet Union in such a way that power has increasingly gravitated to these two centers. Second, the Soviet Union, unlike previous aspirants to hegemony, is animated by a new fanatic faith, antithetical to our own, and seeks to impose its absolute authority over the rest of the world. Conflict has therefore become endemic and is waged, on the part of the Soviet Union, by violent or non-violent methods in accordance with the dictates of expediency. With the development of increasingly terrifying weapons of mass destruction, every individual faces the ever-present possibility of annihilation should the conflict enter the phase of total war.

On the one hand, the people of the world yearn for relief from the anxiety arising from the risk of atomic war. On the other hand, any substantial further extension of the area under the domination of the Kremlin would raise the possibility that no coalition adequate to confront the Kremlin with greater strength could be assembled. It is in this context that this Republic and its citizens in the ascendancy of their strength stand in their deepest peril.

The issues that face us are momentous, involving the fulfillment or destruction not only of this Republic but of civilization itself. . . . With conscience and resolution this Government and the people it represents must now take new and fateful decisions.

The fundamental purpose of the United States is . . . to assure the integrity and vitality of our free society, which is founded upon the dignity and worth of the individual. . . .

The fundamental design of those who control the Soviet Union and the international communist movement is to retain and solidify their absolute power, first in the Soviet Union and second in the areas now under their control. In the minds of the Soviet leaders, however, achievement of this design requires the dynamic extension of their authority and the ultimate elimination of any effective opposition to their authority. . . .

The Soviet Union is developing the military capacity to support its design for world domination. The Soviet Union actually possesses armed forces far in excess of those necessary to defend its national territory. . . . This excessive strength, coupled now with an atomic capability, provides the Soviet Union with great coercive power for use in time of peace in furtherance of its objectives and serves as a deterrent to the victims of its aggression from taking any action in opposition to its tactics which would risk war. . . .

We do not know accurately what the Soviet atomic capability is but the Central Intelligence Agency . . . estimates, concurred in by State, Army, Navy, Air Force, and Atomic Energy Commission, assign to the Soviet Union a production capability giving it a fission bomb stockpile within the following ranges:

By mid–1950 10–20

By mid–1951 25–40

By mid–1952 45–90

By mid–1953 70–135

By mid–1954 200 . . .

The Soviet Union now has aircraft able to deliver atomic bombs. Our intelligence estimates assign to the Soviet Union an atomic bomber capability already in excess of that needed to deliver all available bombs. We have at present no evaluated estimate regarding the Soviet accuracy of delivery on target. It is believed that the Soviets cannot deliver their bombs on target with a degree of accuracy comparable to ours, but a planning estimate might well place it at 40–60 percent. . . . For planning purposes, therefore, the date the Soviets possess an atomic stockpile of 200 bombs would be a critical date for the United States, for the delivery of 100 atomic bombs on targets in the United States would seriously damage this country. . . .

Several conclusions seem to emerge. First, the Soviet Union is widening the gap between its preparedness for war and the unpreparedness of the free world. . . . Second, the Communist success in China, taken with the politico-economic situation in the rest of South and South-East Asia, provides a springboard for further incursion in this troubled area. . . . Third, the Soviet Union holds positions in Europe which, if it maneuvers skillfully, could be used to do great damage to the Western European economy and to the maintenance of the Western orientation of certain countries, particularly Germany and Austria. . . .

In short, as we look into the future, the programs now planned will not meet the requirements of the free nations. . . .

It is estimated that, within the next four years, the USSR will attain the capability of seriously damaging vital centers of the United States, provided it strikes a surprise blow and provided further that the blow is opposed by no more effective force than we now have programmed. . . .

Four possible courses of action by the United States in the present situation can be distinguished. They are:

- **a.** Continuation of current policies, with current and currently projected programs for carrying out these policies;
- **b.** Isolation;
- **c.** War; and

d. A more rapid building up of the political, economic and military strength of the free world than provided under *a*, with the purpose of reaching . . . a tolerable state of order among nations without war and of preparing to defend ourselves in the event that the free world is attacked. . . .

A more rapid build-up of political, economic, and military strength and thereby of confidence in the free world than is now contemplated is the only course which is consistent with progress toward achieving our fundamental purpose. The frustration of the Kremlin design requires the free world to develop a successfully functioning political and economic system and a vigorous political offensive against the Soviet Union. These, in turn, require an adequate military shield under which they can develop. It is necessary to have the military power to deter, if possible, Soviet expansion, and to defeat, if necessary, aggressive Soviet or Soviet-directed actions of a limited or total character. The potential strength of the free world is great; its ability to develop these military capabilities and its will to resist Soviet expansion will be determined by the wisdom and will with which it undertakes to meet its political and economic problems. . . .

At any rate, it is clear that a substantial and rapid building up of strength in the free world is necessary to support a firm policy intended to check and roll back the Kremlin's drive for world domination. . . .

A program for rapidly building up strength and improving political and economic conditions will place heavy demands on our courage and intelligence; it will be costly; it will be dangerous. But half-measures will be more costly and more dangerous, for they will be inadequate to prevent and may actually invite war. Budgetary considerations will need to be subordinated to the stark fact that our very independence as a nation may be at stake.

A comprehensive and decisive program to win the peace and frustrate the Kremlin design should be so designed that it can be sustained for as long as necessary to achieve our national objectives. It would probably involve:

(1) The development of an adequate political and economic framework for the achievement of our long-range objectives.
(2) A substantial increase in expenditures for military purposes. . . .
(3) A substantial increase in military assistance programs. . . .
(4) Some increase in economic assistance programs and recognition of the need to continue these programs until their purposes have been accomplished.
(5) A concerted attack on the problem of the United States balance of payments. . . .
(6) Development of programs designed to build and maintain confidence among other peoples in our strength and resolution, and to wage overt psychological warfare designed to encourage mass defections from Soviet allegiance and to frustrate the Kremlin design in other ways.
(7) Intensification of affirmative and timely measures and operations by covert means in the fields of economic warfare and political and psychological warfare with a view to fomenting and supporting unrest and revolt in selected strategic satellite countries.
(8) Development of internal security and civilian defense programs.
(9) Improvement and intensification of intelligence activities.
(10) Reduction of Federal expenditures for purposes other than defense and foreign assistance, if necessary by the deferment of certain desirable programs.
(11) Increased taxes. . . .

In summary, we must, by means of a rapid and sustained build-up of the political, economic and military strength of the free world, and by means of an affirmative program intended to wrest the initiative from the Soviet Union, confront it with convincing evidence of the determination and ability of the free world to frustrate the Kremlin design of a world dominated by its will. Such evidence is the only means short of war which eventually may force the Kremlin to abandon its present course of action and to negotiate acceptable agreements on issues of major importance. . . .

DISCUSSION QUESTIONS

1. In what ways did NSC–68's analysis differ from that of George Kennan (Document 9)?
2. Why did NSC–68 call for a sustained military buildup? What other steps did it recommend?
3. What conditions in 1950 prompted the drafting and approval of NSC–68?
4. Why did it consider 1954 a crucial year? What assumptions about Soviet intentions were implicit in this calculation?

22. The Korean War, 1950–1953

On 25 June 1950, Communist North Korea invaded South Korea and quickly overran its border forces. The Truman administration, reeling from the recent Communist victory in China, quickly got the UN Security Council to call for the immediate withdrawal of invading forces. On 27 June, Truman announced a series of measures to deal with the crisis, and the Security Council passed a new resolution calling on UN members to help repel the Communist assault. Led by the United States, a multinational UN force won a series of early victories, but the war later bogged down in a stalemate after Chinese Communist troops joined the North Korean side. The fighting finally ended in 1953 with an armistice negotiated in Panmunjom, Korea.

A. Statement by President Truman, 27 June 1950

In Korea, the Government forces, which were armed to prevent border raids and to preserve internal security, were attacked by invading forces from North Korea. The Security Council of the United Nations called upon the invading troops to cease hostilities and to withdraw to the 38th Parallel. This they have not done but, on the contrary, have pressed the attack. The Security Council called upon all members of the United Nations to render every assistance to the United Nations in the execution of this resolution. In these circumstances, I have ordered United States air and sea forces to give the Korean Government troops cover and support.

The attack upon Korea makes it plain beyond all doubt that communism has passed beyond the use of subversion to conquer independent nations and will now use armed invasion and war. It has defied the orders of the Security Council of the United Nations issued to preserve international peace and security. In these circumstances, the occupation of Formosa [Taiwan] by Communist forces would be a direct threat to the security of the Pacific area and to United States forces performing their lawful and necessary functions in that area.

Accordingly, I have ordered the Seventh Fleet to prevent any attack upon Formosa. As a corollary of this action, I am calling upon the Chinese Government on Formosa to cease all air and sea operations against the mainland. The Seventh Fleet will see that this is done. The determination of the future status of Formosa must await the restoration of security in the Pacific, a peace settlement with Japan, or consideration by the United Nations.

I have also directed that United States forces in the Philippines be strengthened and that military assistance to the Philippine Government be accelerated.

I have similarly directed acceleration in the furnishing of military assistance to the forces of France and the Associated States in Indochina and the dispatch of a military mission to provide close working relations with those forces.

I know that all members of the United Nations will consider carefully the consequences of this latest aggression in Korea in defiance of the Charter of the United Nations. A return to the rule of force in international affairs would have far-reaching effects. The United States will continue to uphold the rule of law. . . .

B. Resolution of the United Nations Security Council, 27 June 1950

The Security Council

Having determined that the armed attack upon the Republic of Korea by forces from North Korea constitutes a breach of the peace;

Having called for an immediate cessation of hostilities; and

Having called upon the authorities of North Korea to withdraw forthwith their armed forces to the 38th parallel; and

Having noted from the report of the United Nations Commission for Korea that the authorities in North Korea have neither ceased hostilities nor withdrawn their armed forces to the 38th parallel, and that urgent military measures are required to restore international peace and security; and

Having noted the appeal from the Republic of Korea to the United Nations for immediate and effective steps to secure peace and security,

Recommends that the Members of the United Nations furnish such assistance to the Republic of Korea as may be necessary to repel the armed attack and to restore international peace and security in the area.

C. Excerpts from the Panmunjom Armistice Agreement, 27 July 1953

Preamble

The undersigned, the Commander in Chief, United Nations Command, on the one hand, and the Supreme Commander of the Korean People's Army and the Commander of the Chinese People's Volunteers, on the other hand, in the interest of stopping the Korean conflict, with its great toll of suffering and bloodshed on both sides, and with the objective of establishing an armistice which will insure a complete cessation of hostilities and of all acts of armed force in Korea until a final peaceful settlement is achieved, do individually, collectively and mutually agree to accept and to be bound and governed by the conditions and terms of armistice set forth in the following articles and paragraphs. . . .

Article I. Military Demarcation Line and Demilitarized Zone

1. A military demarcation line shall be fixed and both sides shall withdraw two kilometers from this line so as to establish a demilitarized zone between the opposing forces. A demilitarized zone shall be established as a buffer zone to prevent the occurrence of incidents which might lead to a resumption of hostilities. . . .

6. Neither side shall execute any hostile act within, from, or against the demilitarized zone.

7. No person, military or civilian, shall be permitted to cross the military demarcation line unless specifically authorized to do so by the Military Armistice Commission. . . .

9. No person, military or civilian, shall be permitted to enter the demilitarized zone except persons concerned with the conduct of civil administration and relief and persons specifically authorized to enter by the Military Armistice Commission. . . .

Article II. Arrangements for Cease-Fire and Armistice

12. The commanders of the opposing sides shall order and enforce a complete cessation of all hostilities in Korea by all armed forces under their control, . . . effective twelve (12) hours after this armistice agreement is signed. . . .

13. In order to insure the stability of the military armistice so as to facilitate the attainment of a peaceful settlement through the holding by both sides of a political conference . . . , the commanders of the opposing sides shall:

(a) Within seventy-two hours after this agreement becomes effective, withdraw all of their military forces, supplies and equipment from the demilitarized zone. . . .

(b) Within ten (10) days after this agreement becomes effective, withdraw all of their military forces, supplies and equipment from the rear and the coastal islands and waters of Korea of the other side. . . .

Article III. Arrangements Relating to Prisoners of War

51. The release and repatriation of all prisoners of war held in the custody of each side at the time this armistice agreement becomes effective shall be effected in conformity with the following provisions. . . .

(a) Within sixty (60) days after this armistice agreement becomes effective each side shall, without offering any hindrance, directly repatriate and hand over in groups all those prisoners of war in its custody who insist on repatriation to the side to which they belonged at the time of capture. . . .

(b) Each side shall release all those remaining prisoners of war, who are not directly repatriated, from its military control and from its custody and hand them over to the Neutral Nations Repatriation Commission. . . .

Article IV. Recommendations to the Governments

60. In order to insure the peaceful settlement of the Korean question, the military commanders of both sides hereby recommend to the Governments of the countries concerned on both sides that, within three (3) months after the armistice agreement is signed and becomes effective, a political conference of a higher level of both sides be held by the representatives appointed respectively to settle through negotiation the questions of the withdrawal of all foreign forces from Korea, the peaceful settlement of the Korean question, etc. . . . .

Annex. Terms of Reference for Neutral Nations Repatriation Commission

1. In order to insure that all prisoners of war have the opportunity to exercise their right to be repatriated following an armistice, Sweden, Switzerland, Poland, Czechoslovakia and India shall each be requested by both sides to appoint a member to a Neutral Nations Repatriation Commission which shall be established to take custody in Korea of those prisoners of war who, while in the custody of the detaining powers, have not exercised their right to be repatriated. . . .

3. No force or threat of force shall be used against the prisoners of war specified in paragraph 1 above to prevent or effect their repatriation. . . .

4. All prisoners of war who have not exercised their right of repatriation following the effective date of the armistice agreement shall be released from the military control and from the custody of the detaining side . . . within 60 days . . . to the Neutral Nations Repatriation Commission. . . .

11. At the expiration of ninety (90) days after the transfer of custody of the prisoners of war to the Neutral Nations Repatriation Commission . . . the question of disposition of the prisoners of war who have not exercised their right to be repatriated shall be submitted to the political conference recommended . . . in article 60, . . . which shall endeavor to settle this question within thirty (30) days. . . . The Neutral Nations Repatriation Commission shall declare the relief from the prisoner of war status to civilian status of any prisoners of war who have not exercised their right to be repatriated and for whom no other disposition has been agreed to by the political conference within one hundred twenty (120) days after the Neutral Nations Repatriation Commission has assumed their custody. Thereafter, according to the application of each individual, those who choose to go to neutral nations shall be assisted by the Neutral Nations Repatriation Commission and the Red Cross Society of India. The operation shall be completed within thirty (30) days, and upon its completion, the Neutral Nations Repatriation Commission shall immediately cease to function and declare its dissolution. . . .

DISCUSSION QUESTIONS

1. Why did Truman respond so forcefully to the North Korean invasion? Why did he send forces to defend South Korea when he had not done so to defend Nationalist China?
2. Why did he work through the United Nations rather than aiding South Korea on his own?
3. Why did the Chinese Communists intervene in Korea? Why did they send "volunteers," rather than openly declaring war?
4. Why did the Panmunjom armistice set up a "demilitarized zone"? How did the armistice finesse the issue of repatriating captured North Korean soldiers?

23. Dulles on "Massive Retaliation," 1954

In 1953, determined both to cut military costs and bolster U.S. defense, President Eisenhower authorized a thorough reappraisal of American Cold War strategy. The resulting new strategy shifted U.S. emphasis from conventional military forces to deterrence by nuclear weapons, which could deliver "a bigger bang for the buck." In a major speech in early 1954, Secretary of State John Foster Dulles explained the new strategy of "massive retaliation."

Highlights of Dulles's Speech to the Council on Foreign Relations, 12 January 1954

. . . The Soviet Communists are planning for what they call "an entire historical era," and we should do the same. They seek through many types of maneuvers gradually to divide and weaken the free nations by overextending them in efforts which, as Lenin put it, are "beyond their strength, so that they come to practical bankruptcy." Then, said Lenin, "our victory is assured." Then, said Stalin, will be "the moment for the decisive blow."

In the face of this strategy, measures cannot be judged adequate merely because they ward off an immediate danger. It is essential to do this, but it is also essential to do so without exhausting ourselves. And when the Eisenhower administration applied this test, we felt that some transformations were needed.

It is not sound military strategy permanently to commit US land forces to Asia to a degree that leaves us no strategic reserves.

It is not sound economics to support permanently other countries; nor is it good foreign policy, for in the long run, that creates as much ill will as good will.

Also, it is not sound to become permanently committed to military expenditures so vast that they lead to what Lenin called "practical bankruptcy." . . .

Take first the matter of national security. We need allies and we need collective security. And our purpose is to have them, but to have them on a basis which is more effective and . . . less costly. . . . The way to do this is to place more reliance on community deterrent power, and less dependence on local defensive power. . . . We want for ourselves and for others a maximum deterrent at a bearable cost.

Local defense will always be important. But there is no local defense which alone will contain the mighty land power of the Communist world. Local defenses must be reinforced by the further deterrent of massive retaliatory power.

A potential aggressor must know that he cannot always prescribe battle conditions that suit him. Otherwise, for example, a potential aggressor who is glutted with manpower might be tempted to attack in confidence that resistance would be confined to manpower. He might be tempted to attack in places where his superiority was decisive.

The way to deter aggression is for the free community to be willing and able to respond vigorously at places and with means of its own choosing.

Now, so long as our basic policy concepts were unclear, our military leaders could not be selective in building our military power. If the enemy could pick his time and his place and his method of warfare—and if our policy was to remain the traditional one of meeting aggression by direct and local opposition—then we had to be ready to fight in the Arctic and in the tropics; in Asia, the Near East, and in Europe; by sea, by land, and by air; by old weapons and by new weapons.

The total cost of our security efforts . . . was over $50,000,000,000 per annum, and involved, for 1953, a projected budgetary deficit of $9,000,000,000; and for 1954 a projected deficit of $11,000,000,000. This was on top of taxes comparable to wartime taxes and the dollar was depreciating in its effective value. And our allies were similarly weighed down. This could not be continued for long without grave budgetary, economic, and social consequences.

But before military planning could be changed the President and his advisers . . . had to make some basic policy decisions. This has been done. And the basic decision was . . . to depend primarily upon a great capacity to retaliate instantly by means and at places of our choosing. And now the Department of Defense and the Joint Chiefs of Staff can shape our military establishment to fit what is our policy, instead of having to try to be ready to meet the enemy's many choices. . . . And as a result it is now possible to get . . . more basic security at less cost. . . .

DISCUSSION QUESTIONS

1. In what ways did Dulles think it was harmful to permanently commit U.S. ground forces to defending other countries overseas?
2. How would "massive retaliation" deter the Soviet Union from invading Western Europe?
3. Why would the Soviet Union believe that the United States would use nuclear weapons to oppose a conventional military attack?
4. What were some potential drawbacks of "massive retaliation" for America and its allies?

24. The Geneva Conference, 1954

French efforts to reimpose a colonial regime on Indochina in 1946 were opposed by the League for Vietnamese Independence (Vietminh), a nationalist coalition led by a Communist named Ho Chi Minh. Since Washington wanted to stabilize its French ally, the United States provided France with financial support in the long and bloody First Indochina War (1946–1954). This support, however, did not save France from decisive defeat at the battle of Dienbienphu in spring 1954.

In April of that year, while the battle was going on, the French met at Geneva with representatives of Britain, the United States, the People's Republic of China, the USSR, and various Indochinese factions. Following the loss of Dienbienphu, a new French premier, Pierre Mendès-France, negotiated an agreement to end the war. It confirmed the division of Indochina into four states—Laos, Cambodia, North Vietnam, and South Vietnam—and called for elections to unify Vietnam in July 1956. The United States and South Vietnam refused to sign the Geneva accords, partly out of fear that the Communists, who controlled North

Vietnam, would dominate the elections to unify Vietnam. The elections were thus never held. The North Vietnamese then decided to infiltrate the South with guerrilla units known as Viet Cong, leading eventually to the Second Indochina (or Vietnam) War.

Final Declaration of the Geneva Conference, 21 July 1954

FINAL DECLARATION, dated the 21st of July, 1954, of the Geneva Conference on the problem of restoring peace in Indo-China, in which the representatives of Cambodia, the Democratic Republic of Viet-Nam, France, Laos, the People's Republic of China, the State of Viet-Nam, the Union of Soviet Socialist Republics, the United Kingdom, and the United States of America took part.

1. The Conference takes note of the agreements ending hostilities in Cambodia, Laos and Viet-Nam and organizing international control and the supervision of the execution of the provisions of these agreements.

2. The Conference . . . expresses its conviction that the execution of the provisions set out in the present declaration and in the agreements on the cessation of hostilities will permit Cambodia, Laos and Viet-Nam henceforth to play their part, in full independence and sovereignty, in the peaceful community of nations. . . .

4. The Conference takes note of the clauses in the agreement on the cessation of hostilities in Viet-Nam prohibiting the introduction into Viet-Nam of foreign troops and military personnel as well as of all kinds of arms and munitions. The Conference also takes note of the declarations made by the Governments of Cambodia and Laos of their resolution not to request foreign aid, whether in war material, in personnel or in instructors except for the purpose of the effective defense of their territory. . . .

5. The Conference takes note of the clauses in the agreement on the cessation of hostilities in Viet-Nam to the effect that no military base under the control of a foreign State may be established in the regrouping zones of the two parties, the latter having the obligation to see that the zones allotted to them shall not constitute part of any military alliance and shall not be utilized for the resumption of hostilities or in the service of an aggressive policy. The Conference also takes note of the declarations of the Governments of Cambodia and Laos to the effect that they will not enjoin in any agreement with other States if this agreement includes the obligation to participate in a military alliance not in conformity with the principles of the Charter of the United Nations or, . . . so long as their security is not threatened, the obligation to establish bases on Cambodian or Laotian territory for the military forces of foreign Powers.

6. The Conference recognizes that the essential purpose of the agreement relating to Viet-Nam is to settle military questions with a view to ending hostilities and that the military demarcation line is provisional and should not in any way be interpreted as constituting a political or territorial boundary. The Conference expresses its conviction that the execution of the provisions set out in the present declaration and in the agreement on the cessation of hostilities creates the necessary basis for the achievement in the near future of a political settlement in Viet-Nam.

7. The Conference declares that, so far as Viet-Nam is concerned, the settlement of political problems, effected on the basis of respect for the principles of independence, unity and territorial integrity, shall permit the Viet-Namese people to enjoy the fundamental freedoms, guaranteed by democratic institutions established as a result of free general elections by secret ballot. In order to ensure that sufficient progress in the restoration of peace has been made, and that all the necessary conditions obtain for free expression of the national will, general elections shall be held in July 1956, under the supervision of an international commission composed of representatives of the Member States of the International Supervisory Commission [comprised of Canada, India, and Poland] referred to in the agreement on the cessation of hostilities. . . .

8. The provisions of the agreements on the cessation of hostilities intended to ensure the protection of individuals and of property must be most strictly applied and must, in particular, allow everyone in Viet-Nam to decide freely in which zone he wishes to live.

9. The competent representative authorities of the Northern and Southern zones of Viet-Nam, as well as the authorities of Laos and Cambodia, must not permit any individual or collective reprisals against persons who have collaborated in any way with one of the parties during the war, or against members of such persons' families.

10. The Conference takes note of the declaration of the Government of the French Republic to the effect that it is ready to withdraw its troops from the territory of Cambodia, Laos and Viet-Nam, at the request of the governments concerned and within periods which shall be fixed by agreement between the parties. . . .

12. In their relations with Cambodia, Laos and Viet-Nam, each member of the Geneva Conference undertakes to respect the sovereignty, the independence, the unity and the territorial integrity of the above mentioned states, and to refrain from any interference in their internal affairs. . . .

DISCUSSION QUESTIONS

1. Why did the Geneva Conference decide on a temporary division of Vietnam between North and South, with elections to unify the country after two years?
2. If Vietnam's division was not meant to be permanent, why did it last more than twenty years?
3. Why did the declaration strive to preclude the military presence of outside powers in Vietnam, Laos, and Cambodia?
4. Why were the United States and South Vietnam dissatisfied with the Geneva agreement? Why were they hesitant to support the elections called for in paragraph 7?
5. Why would Ho Chi Minh and the North Vietnamese also have been dissatisfied with the Geneva accords? What more might they have expected, given their victory over France?

25. The SEATO Alliance, 1954

After France's defeat in Indochina, hoping to keep Communism from spreading through the whole region, U.S. secretary of state Dulles negotiated an alliance called the Southeast Asia Treaty Organization (SEATO). A poor imitation of NATO, its guarantees were weak, and the area it covered was vast and hard to defend. Key nations needing SEATO protection—such as Burma, South Vietnam, Laos, and Cambodia—were not in the alliance, and most SEATO members were not in Southeast Asia. Dulles recognized these limitations, but hoped American involvement in SEATO would deter Communist aggression.

Highlights of the Southeast Asia Collective Defense Treaty, 8 September 1954

Article I

The Parties undertake, as set forth in the Charter of the United Nations, to settle any international disputes in which they may be involved by peaceful means in such a manner that international peace and security and justice are not endangered, and to refrain in their international relations from the threat or use of force in any manner inconsistent with the purposes of the United Nations.

Article II

In order more effectively to achieve the objectives of this Treaty, the Parties, separately and jointly, by means of continuous and effective self-help and mutual aid will maintain and develop their individual and collective capacity to resist armed attack and to prevent and counter subversive activities directed from without against their territorial integrity and political stability.

Article III

The Parties undertake to strengthen their free institutions and to cooperate with one another in the further development of economic measures, including technical assistance, designed both to promote economic progress and social well-being and to further the individual and collective efforts of governments toward these ends.

Article IV

1. Each Party recognizes that aggression by means of armed attack in the treaty area against any of the Parties or against any State or territory which the Parties by unanimous agreement may hereafter designate, would endanger its own peace and safety, and agrees that it will in that event act to meet the common danger in accordance with its constitutional processes. Measures taken under this paragraph shall be immediately reported to the Security Council of the United Nations.
2. If, in the opinion of any of the Parties, the inviolability or the integrity of the territory or the sovereignty or political independence of any Party in the treaty area, or of any other state or territory to which the provisions of paragraph 1 of this Article from time to time apply, is threatened in any way other than by armed attack or . . . by any fact or situation which might endanger the peace of the area, the Parties shall consult immediately in order to agree on the measures which should be taken for the common defense.
3. It is understood that no action on the territory of any State designated by unanimous agreement under paragraph 1 of this Article or on any territory so designated shall be taken except at the invitation or with the consent of the government concerned.

Article V

The Parties hereby establish a Council, on which each of them shall be represented, to consider matters concerning the implementation of this Treaty. The Council shall provide for consultation with regard to military and any other planning as the situation obtaining in the treaty area may from time to time require. The council shall be so organized as to be able to meet at any time. . . .

Article VII

Any other State in a position to further the objectives of this Treaty and to contribute to the security of the area may, by unanimous agreement of the Parties, be invited to accede to this Treaty. . . .

Article VIII

As used in this Treaty, the "treaty area" is the general area of Southeast Asia, including also the entire territories of the Asian Parties, and the general area of the Southwest Pacific not including the Pacific area north of 21 degrees 30 minutes north latitude. The Parties may, by unanimous agreement, amend this Article to include within the treaty area the territory of any State acceding to this Treaty in accordance with Article VII or otherwise to change the treaty area. . . .

Article X

This Treaty shall remain in force indefinitely, but any Party may cease to be a Party one year after its notice of denunciation has been given to the Government of the Republic of the Philippines. . . .

Understanding of the United States of America

The United States of America in executing the present Treaty does so with the understanding that its recognition of the effect of aggression and armed attack and its agreement with reference thereto in Article IV, paragraph 1, apply only to communist aggression but affirms that in the event of other aggression or armed attack it will consult under the provisions of Article IV, paragraph 2. . .

Done at Manila, this eighth day of September, 1954.

United States	New Zealand
Great Britain	Philippine Republic
France	Thailand
Australia	Pakistan

DISCUSSION QUESTIONS

1. What were the similarities and differences between NATO (Document 14) and SEATO? What factors accounted for the differences?
2. What were the main limitations of SEATO? Why did Dulles move ahead with it anyway?
3. How would a U.S. policymaker assess the SEATO treaty in 1954? How would a Soviet official assess it?
4. What features of SEATO indicate its intent to protect some nations not in the alliance?

26. The Bandung Conference and the Nonaligned Movement, 1955

In April 1955, representatives of 24 African and Asian nations met at Bandung in Indonesia. That country's president, Sukarno, opened the meeting with a stirring speech urging Asians and Africans to unite in ending all vestiges of colonialism and working for world peace. Later in the conference, India's prime minister Nehru asserted that Asians and Africans could best exercise moral and political influence by refusing to align with either power bloc. Among its resolutions, the conference then adopted a "Declaration on the Promotion of World Peace and Cooperation," whose principles included "Abstention from the use of arrangements of collective defence to serve the particular interests of any of the big powers." Nehru and Sukarno, along with Nasser of Egypt, Nkrumah of Ghana, and Tito of Yugoslavia, went on to found the Nonaligned Movement, a group of nations that sought to avoid affiliation with the major power blocs.

A. Excerpts from Speech by Indonesian President Sukarno at the Opening of the Asian-African Conference in Bandung, 18 April 1955*

Your Excellencies, Ladies and Gentlemen, Sisters and Brothers. It is my great honour and privilege on this historic day to bid you welcome to Indonesia. . . .

It is a new departure in the history of the world that leaders of Asian and African peoples can meet together in their own countries to discuss and deliberate upon matters of common concern. . . Our nations and countries are colonies no more. Now we are free, sovereign and independent. . . .

* Reprinted from George McTurnan Kahin, THE ASIAN-AFRICAN CONFERENCE: BANDUNG, INDONESIA, APRIL, 1955 (Ithaca, NY: Cornell University Press, 1956), pp. 39–51.

We are of many different nations, we are of many different social backgrounds and cultural patterns. Our ways of life are different. Our national characters . . . are different. Our racial stock is different, and even the colour of our skin is different. But what does that matter?

. . . All of us, I am certain, are united by more important things than those which superficially divide us. We are united, for instance, by a common detestation of colonialism in whatever form it appears. We are united by a common detestation of racialism. And we are united by a common determination to preserve and stabilise peace in the world. . . .

For us, colonialism is not something far and distant. We have known it in all its ruthlessness. We have seen the immense human wastage it causes, the poverty it causes, and the heritage it leaves behind. . . .

I say to you, colonialism is not yet dead. How can we say it is dead, so long as vast areas of Asia and Africa are unfree?

. . . The battle against colonialism has been a long one; and do you know that today is a famous anniversary in that battle? On the eighteenth day of April, one thousand seven hundred and seventy five, just one hundred and eighty years ago, Paul Revere rode at midnight through the New England countryside, warning of the approach of British troops and of the opening of the American War of Independence, the first successful anti-colonial war in history . . .

But remember, that battle which began 180 years ago is not yet completely won, and it will not have been completely won until we can survey this our own world, and can say that colonialism is dead . . .

No task is more urgent than that of preserving peace. Without peace our independence means little. The rehabilitation and upbuilding of our countries will have little meaning. Our revolutions will not be allowed to run their course.

What can we do? The peoples of Asia and Africa wield little physical power. Even their economic strength is dispersed and slight. We cannot indulge in power politics . . .

What can we do? We can do much! We can inject the voice of reason into world affairs. We can mobilise all the spiritual, all the moral, all the political strength of Asia and Africa on the side of peace. Yes, we! We, the peoples of Asia and Africa, 1,400,000,000 strong, far more than half the human population of the world, we can mobilise what I have called the Moral Violence of Nations in favour of peace. We can demonstrate to the minority of the world which lives on the other continents that we, the majority, are for peace, not for war, and that whatever strength we have will always be thrown on to the side of peace.

However, we cannot, we dare not, confine our interests to the affairs of our own continents. The States of the world today depend one upon the other and no nation can be an island into itself. . . . The affairs of all the world are our affairs, and our future depends upon the solutions found to all international problems, however far or distant they may seem . . .

If this Conference succeeds in making the peoples of the East whose representatives are gathered here understand each other a little more, . . . then this Conference . . . will have been worthwhile. . . . But I hope that this Conference will give more than understanding only. . . . I hope that this Conference will give guidance to mankind, will point out to mankind the way which it must take to attain safety and peace. I hope that it will give evidence that Asia and Africa have been reborn, nay, that New Asia and a New Africa have been born!

. . . Let us not be bitter about the past, but let us keep our eyes firmly on the future. Let us remember that no blessing of God is so sweet as life and liberty. Let us remember that the stature of all mankind is diminished so long as nations or parts of nations are still unfree. Let us remember that the highest purpose of man is the liberation of man from his bonds of fear, his bonds of human degradation, his bonds of poverty—the liberation of man from the physical, spiritual and intellectual bonds which have for too long stunted the development of humanity's majority . . .

B. Excerpts from Speech by India's Prime Minister Nehru to the Bandung Conference Political Committee, April 1955*

We have just had the advantage of listening to the distinguished leader of the Turkish Delegation who . . . gave us an able statement . . . representing the views of one of the major blocs. . . . I have no doubt that an equally able disposition could be made on the part of the other bloc. I belong to neither and I propose to belong to neither whatever happens in the world . . .

We do not agree with the communist teachings, we do not agree with the anti-communist teachings, because they are both based on wrong principles. I never challenged the right of my country to defend itself; it has to. We will defend ourselves with whatever arms and strength we have . . . I am dead certain that no country can conquer India. Even the two great power blocs together cannot conquer India; not even the atom or the hydrogen bomb. I know what my people are. But I know also that if we rely on others, whatever great powers they might be, if we look to them for sustenance, then we are weak indeed . . .

. . . I speak with the greatest respect of these Great Powers because they are not only great in military might but in development, in culture, in civilization. But I do submit that greatness sometimes brings quite false values. . . . When they begin to think in terms of military strength—whether it be the United Kingdom, the Soviet Union or the USA—then they are going away from the right track and the result of that will be that the overwhelming might of one country will conquer the world. Thus far the world has succeeded in preventing that; I cannot speak for the future . . .

. . . So far as I am concerned, it does not matter what war takes place; we will not take part in it unless we have to defend ourselves. If I join any of these big groups I lose my identity . . . If all the world were to be divided up between these two big blocs what would be the result? The inevitable result would be war. Therefore every step that takes place in reducing that area in the world which may be called the unaligned area is a dangerous step and leads to war. It reduces that objective, that balance, that outlook which other countries without military might can perhaps exercise.

. . . I submit that moral force counts and the moral force of Asia and Africa must, in spite of the atomic and hydrogen bombs of Russia, the USA or another country, count . . .

. . . I am a positive person, not an 'anti' person. I want positive good for my country and the world. Therefore, are we, the countries of Asia and Africa, devoid of any positive position except being pro-communist or anti-communist? Has it come to this, that the leaders of thought who have given religions and all kinds of things to the world have to tag on to this kind of group or that and be hangers-on of this party or the other carrying out their wishes and occasionally giving an idea? It is most degrading and humiliating to any self-respecting people or nation. It is an intolerable thought to me that the great countries of Asia and Africa should come out of bondage into freedom only to degrade themselves or humiliate themselves in this way . . .

I submit to you, every pact has brought insecurity and not security to the countries which have entered into them. They have brought the danger of atomic bombs and the rest of it nearer to them than would have been the case otherwise. They have not added to the strength of any country, I submit, which it had singly. It may have produced some idea of security, but it is a false security. It is a bad thing for any country thus to be lulled into security . . .

---

* Reprinted from George McTurnan Kahin, THE ASIAN-AFRICAN CONFERENCE: BANDUNG, INDONESIA, APRIL, 1955 (Ithaca, NY: Cornell University Press, 1956), pp. 64–72.

C. Principles of the Bandung Conference's "Declaration on the Promotion of World Peace and Cooperation," 24 April 1955*

Free from mistrust and fear, and with confidence and goodwill towards each other, nations should practise tolerance and live together in peace . . . and develop friendly cooperation on the basis of the following principles:

1. Respect for fundamental human rights and for the purposes and principles of the Charter of the United Nations.
2. Respect for the sovereignty and territorial integrity of all nations.
3. Recognition of the equality of all races and of the equality of all nations large and small.
4. Abstention from intervention or interference in the internal affairs of another country.
5. Respect for the right of each nation to defend itself singly or collectively, in conformity with the Charter of the United Nations.
6. (a) Abstention from the use of arrangements of collective defence to serve the particular interests of any of the big powers.
   (b) Abstention by any country from exerting pressures on other countries.
7. Refraining from acts or threats of aggression or the use of force against the territorial integrity or political independence of any country.
8. Settlement of all international disputes by peaceful means, such as negotiation, conciliation, arbitration or judicial settlement . . .
9. Promotion of mutual interests and cooperation.
10. Respect for justice and international obligations.

DISCUSSION QUESTIONS

1. What were Sukarno's goals for the Bandung Conference? How did he think Asian and African nations, lacking wealth and power, could advance the cause of world peace?
2. Why did Sukarno emphasize the struggle of Asians and Africans against colonialism? Why did he note that it was the 180th anniversary of the start of the American Revolution?
3. Why did Nehru see it as weakness for Asian or African nations to align with one of the big power blocs? Why did he claim that such power blocs would lead eventually to war?
4. What were the advantages and disadvantages of nonalignment for Asians and Africans?

27. The Warsaw Pact, 1955

In May of 1955, following a Western decision to let West Germany rearm and join NATO, officials from the USSR and Eastern Europe met in Poland to form a new treaty system called the Warsaw Pact. Ostensibly intended to counter NATO and defend Eastern Europe, it also provided a pretext for continued Soviet troop presence there, and a convenient way for Moscow to keep its satellites in line. Originally designed for twenty years, it would last until 1991.

---

* Reprinted from George McTurnan Kahin, THE ASIAN-AFRICAN CONFERENCE: BANDUNG, INDONESIA, APRIL, 1955 (Ithaca, NY: Cornell University Press, 1956), pp. 84–85.

The Warsaw Security Pact, 14 May 1955

The Contracting Parties, reaffirming their desire for the establishment of a system of European collective security based on the participation of all European states irrespective of their social and political systems, which would make it possible to unite their efforts on safeguarding the peace of Europe; mindful . . . of the situation created in Europe by the ratification of the Paris agreements, which envisage the formation of a new military alignment in the shape of "Western European Union," with the participation of a remilitarized Western Germany and the integration of the latter in the North-Atlantic bloc, which increased the danger of another war and constitutes a threat to the national security of the peaceable states; being persuaded that in these circumstances the peaceable European states must take the necessary measures to safeguard their security and in the interests of preserving peace in Europe; guided by the objects and principles of the Charter of the United Nations Organization; being desirous of further promoting and developing friendship, cooperation and mutual assistance in accordance with the principles of respect for the independence and sovereignty of states and of non-interference in their internal affairs, have decided to conclude the present Treaty of Friendship, Cooperation and Mutual Assistance. . . .

Article 1

The Contracting Parties undertake, in accordance with the Charter of the United Nations Organization, to refrain in their international relations from the threat or use of force, and to settle their international disputes peacefully and in such manner as will not jeopardize international peace and security.

Article 2

The Contracting Parties declare their readiness to participate in a spirit of sincere cooperation in all international actions designed to safeguard international peace and security. . . . The Contracting Parties will furthermore strive for the adoption, in agreement with other states which may desire to cooperate in this, of effective measures for universal reduction of armaments and prohibition of atomic, hydrogen and other weapons of mass destruction.

Article 3

The Contracting Parties shall consult with one another on all important international issues affecting their common interests, guided by the desire to strengthen international peace and security. They shall immediately consult with one another whenever, in the opinion of any one of them, a threat of armed attack on one or more of the Parties to the Treaty has arisen, in order to ensure joint defence and the maintenance of peace and security.

Article 4

In the event of armed attack in Europe on one or more of the Parties to the Treaty by any state or group of states, each of the Parties to the Treaty, in the exercise of its right to individual or collective self-defence in accordance with Article 51 of the Charter of the United Nations Organization, shall immediately, either individually or in agreement with other Parties to the Treaty, come to the assistance of the state or states attacked with all such means as it deems necessary, including armed force. The Parties to the Treaty shall immediately consult concerning the necessary measures to be taken by them jointly in order to restore and maintain international peace and security.

Measures taken on the basis of this Article shall be reported to the Security Council in conformity with the Provisions of the Charter of the United Nations Organization. These measures shall be discontinued immediately [when] the Security Council adopts the necessary measures to restore and maintain international peace and security.

Article 5

The Contracting Parties have agreed to establish a Joint Command of the armed forces . . . , which shall function on the basis of jointly established principles. They shall likewise adopt other agreed measures necessary to strengthen their defensive power, in order to protect the peaceful labours of their peoples, guarantee the inviolability of their frontiers and territories, and provide defence against possible aggression.

Article 6

For the purpose of the consultations among the Parties envisaged in the present Treaty, and also for the purpose of examining questions which may arise in the operation of the Treaty, a Political Consultative Committee shall be set up, in which each of the Parties to the Treaty shall be represented by a member of its Government or by another specifically appointed representative. . . .

Article 7

The Contracting Parties undertake not to participate in any coalitions or alliances and not to conclude any agreements whose objects conflict with the objects of the present Treaty. . . .

Article 8

The Contracting Parties declare that they will act in a spirit of friendship and cooperation with a view to further developing and fostering economic and cultural intercourse with one another, each adhering to the principle of respect for the independence and sovereignty of the others and non-interference in their internal affairs.

Article 9

The present Treaty is open to the accession of other states, irrespective of their social and political systems, which express their readiness by participation in the present Treaty to assist in uniting the efforts of the peaceable states in safeguarding the peace and security of the peoples. . . .

Article 11

The present Treaty shall remain in force for twenty years. . . .

DISCUSSION QUESTIONS

1. Why were the Soviets so upset about West Germany's admission to NATO?
2. What were the stated and unstated purposes of the Warsaw Pact?
3. In what ways was it similar to NATO (Document 15), and in what ways did it differ?
4. What did the USSR gain by having a joint military command with its Warsaw Pact allies?

28. Khrushchev on Peaceful Coexistence, 1956

Emerging as Soviet leader, Nikita Khrushchev made "peaceful coexistence" a central theme of his approach to world affairs. In February 1956, in a major address to the Twentieth Congress of the Soviet Communist Party, he called for peaceful competition between Communism and capitalism, contended that Communism would inevitably prevail because it was a fairer system, and declared it both possible and necessary to avoid another world war. This was a significant reinterpretation of the Marxist premise that war was inevitable as long as capitalism survived.

Excerpts from Khrushchev's Report to the 20th Party Congress, 14 February 1956

. . . For the strengthening of world peace, it would be of tremendous importance to establish firm, friendly relations between the two biggest powers of the world, the Soviet Union and the United States. . . .

We want to be friends with and to cooperate with the United States in the effort for peace and security of the peoples as well as in the economic and cultural fields. We pursue this with good intentions, without holding a stone behind our back. . . .

If good relations are not established between the Soviet Union and the United States, and mutual distrust exists, this will lead to an arms race on a still greater scale and to a still more dangerous growth of the forces on both sides. . . .

The Leninist principle of the peaceful coexistence of states with different social systems was and remains the general line of our country's foreign policy.

It is alleged that the Soviet Union advocates the principle of peaceful coexistence exclusively from tactical considerations of the moment. However it is well known that we have advocated peaceful coexistence . . . from the very inception of Soviet power. Hence, it is not a tactical stratagem but a fundamental principle of Soviet foreign policy. . . .

When we say that in the competition between the two systems of capitalism and socialism, socialism will triumph, this by no means implies that victory will be reached by armed intervention. . . . We believe that after seeing for themselves the advantages that communism holds out, all working men and women on earth will sooner or later take to the road of the struggle to build a socialist society.

We have always asserted and continue to assert that the establishment of a new social order in any country is the internal affair of its people. Such are our positions, based on the great teachings of Marxism-Leninism.

The principle of peaceful coexistence is gaining increasingly wider international recognition. And this is logical, since there is no other way out of the present situation. Indeed, there are only two ways: either peaceful coexistence or the most devastating war in history. There is no third alternative.

We presume that countries with differing social systems cannot just simply exist side by side. There must be progress to better relations, to stronger confidence among them, to cooperation.

As will be recalled, there is a Marxist-Leninist premise which says that while imperialism exists wars are inevitable. While capitalism remains on earth the reactionary forces representing the interests of the capitalist monopolies will continue to strive for war gambles and aggression, and may try to let loose war.

But there is no fatal inevitability of war. Now there are powerful social and political forces, commanding serious means capable of preventing . . . war by the imperialists and—should they try to start it—of delivering a smashing rebuff to the aggressors and thwarting their adventuristic plans.

To this end it is necessary for all the forces opposing war to be vigilant and mobilized. It is necessary for them to act as a united front and not to slacken their efforts in the fight to preserve peace. . . .

DISCUSSION QUESTIONS

1. What did Khrushchev mean by "peaceful coexistence," and how did he expect it to work?
2. Why did he assert that Marxists no longer considered war inevitable? What changes did he note on the world scene that made this assertion possible?
3. How did he think Communists should behave toward the capitalist world during peaceful coexistence? Why did he believe Communism would win a peaceful struggle with capitalism?
4. What benefits might he have hoped to derive for himself and his country from this speech?

29. Khrushchev's Secret Speech on Stalin and His Crimes, 1956

The most significant development of the Twentieth Party Congress occurred during its last night, when delegates were summoned back to the conference hall to hear a confidential speech by Nikita Khrushchev. In a lengthy, rambling, methodical speech, he systematically exposed and condemned the crimes of the Stalin era. To the astonishment of assembled party loyalists, he denounced the late dictator for creating a personality cult, blamed him for the torture and murder of numerous party members, accused him of imprisoning multitudes of innocent people, and charged him with disastrous mistakes that damaged his country and cost millions of lives.

Khrushchev's "secret speech" did not stay secret for long. Summaries were distributed and read at private meetings throughout the USSR, and by summer of 1956, the U.S. government had obtained a copy, which it translated and published.

Highlights of Khrushchev's Secret Speech to the 20th Party Congress, 25 February 1956

Comrades, in the report of the Central Committee of the Party at the 20th Congress, . . . a lot has been said about the cult of the individual and its harmful consequences.

After Stalin's death the Central Committee of the Party began explaining concisely and consistently that it is . . . foreign to the spirit of Marxism-Leninism to elevate one person, and to transform him into a superman possessing supernatural characteristics akin to those of a god. Such a man supposedly knows everything, sees everything, thinks for everyone, can do anything, and is infallible. . . . .

Such a belief about a man, and specifically about Stalin, was cultivated among us for many years. . . .

Stalin originated the concept of enemy of the people. This term . . . made possible . . . the most cruel repression, violating all norms of revolutionary legality, against anyone who in any way disagreed with Stalin. . . . This led to glaring violations of revolutionary legality, and to the fact that many entirely innocent persons, who in the past had defended the party line, became victims.

. . . It became apparent that many party, Soviet and economic activists, who were branded in 1937–1938 as enemies, were actually never enemies, spies, wreckers, etc., but were always honest Communists; they were only so stigmatized, and often no longer able to bear barbaric tortures they charged themselves (at the order of the investigative judges-falsifiers) with all sorts of grave and unlikely crimes. . . . It was determined that of the 139 members and candidates of the party's Central Committee who were elected at the 17th Congress, 98 persons, i.e., seventy percent, were arrested and shot (mostly in 1937–1938). . . .

Even more widely was the falsification of cases practiced in the provinces. . . . Many thousands of honest and innocent Communists have died as a result of this monstrous falsification of "cases," as a result of the fact that all kinds of slanderous "confessions" were accepted, and as a result of the practice of forcing accusations against oneself and others. . . .

Facts prove that many abuses were made on Stalin's orders without reckoning with any norms of Party and Soviet legality. Stalin was a very distrustful man, sickly suspicious; we knew this from our work with him. He could look at a man and say: "Why are your eyes so shifty today?" or "Why are you turning so much today and avoiding to look me directly in the eyes?" This sickly suspicion created in him a general distrust even toward eminent party workers whom he had known for many years. Everywhere . . . he saw enemies, "two-facers," and "spies."

Possessing unlimited power, he indulged in great willfulness and choked a person morally and physically. A situation was created where one could not express one's own will.

When Stalin said that one or another should be arrested, it was necessary to accept on faith that he was an "enemy of the people." . . . And what proofs were offered? The confessions of the arrested, and the investigative judges accepted these "confessions." And how is it possible that a person confesses to crimes which he has not committed? Only in one way—because of application of physical measures of pressuring him, tortures, bringing him to a state of unconsciousness, deprivation of his judgment, taking away of his human dignity. In this manner were "confessions" acquired. . . .

During the war and after the war, Stalin put forward the thesis that the tragedy which our nation experienced in the first part of the war was the result of the "unexpected" attack of the Germans against the Soviet Union. But, comrades, this is completely untrue. . . . Documents which have now been published show that by April 3, 1941 Churchill, through his ambassador to the USSR Cripps, personally warned Stalin that the Germans had begun regrouping their armed units with the intent of attacking the Soviet Union. . . . Churchill stressed this repeatedly in his dispatches of April 18 and in the following days. However, Stalin took no heed of these warnings. . . . We must assert that information of this sort concerning the threat of German armed invasion . . . was coming in also from our own military and diplomatic sources. . . .

Despite these particularly grave warnings, the necessary steps were not taken to prepare the country properly for defense and prevent it from being caught unaware. . . .

Very grievous consequences, especially in . . . the beginning of the war, followed Stalin's annihilation of many military commanders and political workers during 1937–1941, because of his suspiciousness, and through slanderous accusations. During these years repressions were instituted against . . . military cadres beginning . . . at the company and battalion commander level and extending to the higher military centers; during this time the cadre of leaders who had gained military experience in Spain and the Far East was almost completely liquidated. The . . . large-scale repression against the military cadres led also to undermined military discipline, because for several years officers . . . were taught to unmask their superiors as hidden enemies. . . .

All this brought about the situation which existed at the beginning of the war and which was the great threat to our Fatherland. . . .

Even after the war began, the nervousness and hysteria which Stalin demonstrated, interfering with the actual military operation, caused our army serious damage. . . .

The tactics on which Stalin insisted without knowing the essence of the conduct of battle operations cost us much blood. . . . The military know that already by the end of 1941, instead of great operational maneuvers flanking the opponent and penetrating behind his back, Stalin demanded incessant frontal attacks and the capture of one village after another. Because of this, we paid with great losses. . . .

We must state that, after the war, the situation became even more complicated. Stalin became even more capricious, irritable, and brutal; in particular his suspicion grew. His persecution mania reached unbelievable dimensions. Many workers were becoming enemies before his very eyes. After the war, Stalin separated himself from the collective even more. Everything was decided by him alone without any consideration for anyone or anything. . . .

I recall the first days when the conflict between the Soviet Union and Yugoslavia began artificially to be blown up. Once, when I came from Kiev to Moscow, I was invited to visit Stalin who, pointing to the copy of a letter lately sent to Tito, asked me "Have you read this?" Not waiting for my reply, he answered, "I will shake my little finger and there will be no more Tito. He will fall."

. . . But this did not happen to Tito. No matter how much or how little Stalin shook, not only his little finger but everything else that he could shake, Tito did not fall. . . .

Let us also recall the affair of the doctor-plotters. Actually, there was no affair outside of the declaration of the woman doctor Timashuk, who was probably influenced or ordered by someone . . . to write Stalin a letter in which she declared that doctors were applying supposedly improper methods of medical treatment. Such a letter was sufficient for Stalin to reach an immediate conclusion that there are doctor-plotters in the Soviet Union. He issued orders to arrest a group of eminent Soviet medical specialists. He personally issued advice on the conduct of the investigation and the method of interrogation of the arrested persons . . . Stalin personally called the investigative judge, gave him instructions, and advised him on which investigative methods should be used. These methods were simple—beat, beat, and once again beat.

Shortly after the doctors were arrested, we members of the Political Bureau received protocols with the doctors' confessions of guilt. After distributing these protocols, Stalin told us, "You are blind like young kittens; what will happen without me? The country will perish because you do not know how to recognize enemies." . . .

Comrades, the cult of the individual acquired such monstrous size chiefly because Stalin himself, using all conceivable methods, supported the glorification of his own person. . . .

Comrades, we must abolish the cult of the individual decisively, once and for all. . . .

Comrades, the 20th Congress of the Communist Party of the Soviet Union has manifested with a new strength the unshakable unity of our party. . . . And the fact that we present in all their ramifications the basic problems of overcoming the cult of the individual . . . is an evidence of the great moral and political strength of our party. We are absolutely certain that our party, armed with the historical resolutions of the 20th Congress, will lead the Soviet people along the Leninist path to new successes, to new victories. . . .

DISCUSSION QUESTIONS

1. Why were outsiders excluded from the session at which Khrushchev gave this speech?
2. According to Khrushchev, what was wrong with a "cult of the individual"? What did Khrushchev say were Stalin's methods for dealing with those he distrusted?
3. Why did Khrushchev blame Stalin for massive Soviet suffering during World War II?
4. What were the benefits of giving this speech, and what were the risks involved?

30. The Hungarian Rebellion, 1956

Khrushchev's blunt denunciation of Stalin in the "Secret Speech" reverberated throughout the Soviet bloc. In October 1956, Budapest students demonstrated for the removal of Hungary's Stalinist rulers. Soviet forces were sent to restore order, but this only led to more uprisings, so popular reformer Imre Nagy was installed as premier to appease the people. The Soviets then began withdrawing their forces, but as demonstrations continued, Nagy announced his intent to remove Hungary from the Warsaw Pact, end the Communist power monopoly, and declare neutrality in the Cold War. Khrushchev could not permit this, so on the morning of 4 November, Soviet tanks rolled into Budapest. Nagy was removed and a new regime installed that was more to Soviet liking. The following excerpts provide insights into these tragic events.

A. Excerpts from Soviet Government Statement, 30 October 1956

. . . The Soviet Government regards it as indispensable to make a statement in connection with the events in Hungary.

The course of events has shown that the working people of Hungary, who have achieved great progress on the basis of the people's democratic order, are rightly raising the question of the necessity of eliminating serious shortcomings in the field of economic building, of the further raising of the material well-being of the population, and in the struggle against bureaucratic distortions in the state apparatus. However, this just and progressive movement of the working people was soon joined by forces of black reaction and counterrevolution, which are trying to take advantage of the discontent on the part of the working people in order to undermine the foundations of the people's democratic order in Hungary and to restore there the old landlords' and capitalists' order.

The Soviet Government, like the whole of the Soviet people, deeply regrets that the development of events in Hungary has led to bloodshed. At the request of the Hungarian people's government, the Soviet Government consented on the entry into Budapest of Soviet Army units for the purpose of assisting the Hungarian People's Army and the Hungarian organs of authority to establish order in the town.

Since it considers that the further presence of Soviet Army units in Hungary can serve as a cause for even greater deterioration of the situation, the Soviet Government has given an instruction to its military command to withdraw the Soviet Army units from Budapest as soon as this is recognized by the Hungarian Government to be necessary.

At the same time, the Soviet Government is ready to enter into corresponding negotiations with the Government of the Hungarian People's Republic and other participants of the Warsaw Treaty on the question of the presence of Soviet troops on the territory of Hungary. . . .

B. Hungarian Appeals for Help, 4 November 1956

Statement by Premier Imre Nagy Over Budapest Radio:

"Soviet troops have opened an attack on Budapest at dawn with the clear intention to overthrow the lawful, democratic government of the Hungarian people. Our troops are fighting the Soviets for right and freedom. The government is at its place! This we bring to the information of the Hungarian people and the entire world."

Teletype Message from Hungarian News Agency:

"Russian gangsters have betrayed us. The Russian troops suddenly attacked Budapest and the whole country. They opened fire on everybody in Hungary. It is a general attack. . . .

"I speak in the name of Imre Nagy. He asks help . . . Nagy and the whole government and the whole people ask help. . . .

"Long live Hungary and Europe! We shall die for Hungary and Europe. . . .

"Any news about help? Quickly, quickly, quickly. . . .

"The Russian attack was started at 4 A.M. Russian MiG fighters are over Budapest. . . .

"We have no time to lose, we have no time to lose. . . . "

Teletype Message From Budapest Newspaper:

"Since the early morning hours Russian troops are attacking Budapest and our population. . . .

"Please tell the world of the treacherous attack against our struggle for liberty. . . .

"Our troops are already engaged in fighting. . . .

"Help! Help! Help!

"S.O.S.! S.O.S.! S.O.S.!

"We have almost no weapons—only light machine guns, Russian-made long rifles and some carbines. We haven't any kind of heavy guns. The people are jumping at the tanks, throwing in hand grenades and closing the drivers' windows.

"The Hungarian people are not afraid of death. It is only a pity that we can't stand for long. . . .

"Now the firing is starting again. We are getting hits. . . .

"What is the United Nations doing? Give us a little encouragement. . . .

"The people have just turned over a streetcar to use as a barricade near the building. In the building, young people are making Molotov cocktails and hand grenades to fight the tanks. We are quiet, not afraid. . . .

"They just brought us a rumor that the American troops will be here within one or two hours. . . . We are well and fighting at 9:20 A.M."

C. Excerpts from the Proclamation of a New Hungarian Government, 4 November 1956

A Hungarian Workers and Peasants Government has been formed.

On October 23 a mass movement began in our country, whose noble purpose was to make good the anti-party and anti-national mistakes committed by Rakosi and his accomplices, and to defend the national independence and sovereignty of Hungary.

The weakness of Imre Nagy's government and the growing influence of counter-revolutionary elements in the revolutionary movement endangered our Socialist conquests, our people's state, our workers and peasants power, the very existence of our homeland.

This has led us, Hungarian patriots, to the creation of the Hungarian Revolutionary Workers and Peasants Government. . . .

The newly-formed Government addresses itself to the Hungarian people with the following appeal:

Brother Hungarians, workers, peasants, soldiers, comrades, our nation is living through hard times. The power of workers and peasants, the holy cause of socialism is in danger. Great danger hangs over the conquests of the last twelve years, which you Hungarian working people . . . have created with your hands by your heroic self-sacrificing labor.

The counter-revolutionary plotters are becoming increasingly daring. They are mercilessly persecuting the supporters of democracy. The Nihilists and other Fascist evil-doers are killing honest patriots and our best comrades. . . .

The reactionaries are working for their selfish aims. They have raised their hands against our people's democratic system. This signifies that they want to return the factories and works to the capitalists, and the land to the landlords. . . .

They would not have brought you freedom, prosperity and democracy had they won, but slavery, poverty, unemployment, and ruthless landlord exploitation. . . .

Exploiting the weakness of the Imre Nagy Government, the counter-revolutionary forces are marauding, murdering and robbing, and we must fear that their forces might get the upper hand. With deep sorrow and a heavy heart we see into what a terrible situation our beloved country has been dragged by counter-revolutionary elements, and often even by conscientious and progressive people, who consciously or unconsciously misused the slogans of democracy and freedom, and thus paved the road for the reactionaries.

Brothers, patriots, soldiers, and citizens. An end must be put to the misdeeds of the counter-revolutionary elements. The hour of action has struck.

We shall defend the powers of workers and peasants, the conquests of the people's democracy. We shall restore order, security and calm in our country. The interests of the people, the interests of our homeland demand that a stable and strong government be established, a government capable of bringing the country out of its present difficult position.

That is why we have formed the Hungarian Revolutionary Workers and Peasants Government . . .

DISCUSSION QUESTIONS

1. How did the 30 October Soviet statement hold out hopes for reconciliation? Why did the Soviets compromise in late October but then invade on 4 November?
2. Why were the 4 November broadcasts and dispatches from Budapest so frantic? Why might the Hungarians have expected outside help? Why did the West not come to their aid?
3. How did the new Hungarian government of 4 November justify taking power? What were the real reasons for its formation?

31. The Suez Crisis, 1956

In the 1950s, the Middle East emerged as a Cold War battleground. In July 1956, after Egypt's president Nasser denounced the State of Israel, aided Algerian rebels fighting against France, and recognized Communist China, the United States withdrew its funding for construction of the Aswan High Dam, a project dear to Nasser. Nasser responded by nationalizing the Suez Canal, whose tolls would help fund the dam project, and Moscow opportunistically offered financial and technical aid. Britain and France, dependent on the canal and Middle East oil, conspired with Israel to launch an attack on Egypt and seize the canal in late October 1956.

The attack misfired. Israel defeated key unit of Egypt's army, but British and French forces were unable to take the canal. Washington, fearing that the war would benefit the Soviets and Arab nationalists, obtained UN resolutions calling for withdrawal of all invading troops, while Moscow called for joint U.S.–Soviet action to end the hostilities. Lacking American support, and fearful of Soviet intervention, Britain and France were forced to withdrew their troops.

A. Withdrawal of U.S. Support for Aswan Dam Project, 19 July 1956

At the request of the Government of Egypt, the United States joined in December 1955 with the United Kingdom and with the World Bank in an offer to assist Egypt in the construction of a high dam on the Nile at Aswan. This project is one of great magnitude. It would require an estimated 12 to 16 years to complete at a total cost estimated at some $1,300,000,000. . . . It involves not merely the rights and interests of Egypt but of other states whose waters are contributory, including Sudan, Ethiopia, and Uganda . . .

Developments within the succeeding 7 months have not been favorable to the success of the project, and the US Government has concluded that it is not feasible in present circumstances to participate in the project. Agreement by the riparian states has not been achieved, and the ability of Egypt to devote adequate resources to assure the project's success has become more uncertain than at the time the offer was made.

This decision in no way reflects or involves any alteration in the friendly relations of the Government and people of the United States toward the Government and people of Egypt. . . .

B. President Nasser's Speech Nationalizing the Suez Canal Company, 26 July 1956

[Speaking of a meeting with Eugene R. Black, President of the International Bank for Reconstruction and Development, with which Egypt had been negotiating for a loan to help finance the construction of the Aswan Dam Project, President Nasser said:] I began to look at Mr. Black sitting in his chair imagining that I was sitting before Ferdinand De Lesseps. *[Ferdinand De Lesseps was the driving force behind the construction of the Suez Canal; the mention of his name in this speech was Nasser's prearranged signal to his troops to seize the Canal.]*

. . . In 1854, Ferdinand De Lesseps arrived in Egypt. He went to Mohamed Said Pasha, the Khedive. He sat beside him and told him, "We want to dig the Suez Canal. This project will greatly benefit you. It is a great project and will bring excellent returns to Egypt."

. . . The result of the words of De Lesseps in 1856, the result of friendship and loans, was the occupation of Egypt in 1882 . . .

We shall not repeat the past. We shall eradicate it by restoring our rights in the Suez Canal. This money is ours. This Canal is the property of Egypt because it is an Egyptian Joint Stock Company.

The Canal was dug by Egypt's sons and 120,000 of them died while working. The Suez Canal Company in Paris is an imposter company. It usurped our concessions . . .

But history will never repeat itself. On the contrary, we shall build the High Dam. We shall restore our usurped rights. We shall build the High Dam as we want it. We are determined to do it. Thirty-five million Egyptian pounds the company gets every year; let Egypt take it . . .

Therefore, I have signed today the following law which has been approved by the Cabinet: *[President Nasser then read the text of the Presidential decree on the Nationalization of the Suez Canal Company.]*

. . . Today, citizens, rights have been restored to their owners . . .

Today, we actually achieve true sovereignty, true dignity and true pride . . .

Today, when we regain our rights, I say in the name of the people of Egypt that we shall defend these rights and hold them fast. We shall sacrifice our lives and our blood in defending them. We shall make up for the past . . .

Today, citizens, the Suez Canal Company has been nationalized. This order has been published in the Official Journal. It has become a matter of fact . . .

Now, while I am speaking to you, fellow countrymen, brothers of yours are taking over the administration and the management of the Canal Company . . . for the direction of navigation in the Canal, the Canal which is situated in the territory of Egypt, cuts through the territory of Egypt, is a part of Egypt and belongs to Egypt. We now perform this task to compensate for the past and build up new edifices for pride and dignity.

May God guide you and peace be with you.

C. Excerpts from President Eisenhower's Address, 31 October 1956

. . . The United States, through all the years since the close of World War II, has labored tirelessly to bring peace and stability to [the Middle East]. We have considered it a basic matter of United States policy to support the new state of Israel and, at the same time, to strengthen our bonds both with Israel and the Arab countries. But, unfortunately, through all these years passion in the area threatened to prevail over peaceful purpose, and in one form or another there has been almost continuous fighting.

This situation recently was aggravated by Egyptian policy, including rearmament with Communist weapons. We felt this to be a misguided policy. . . . The state of Israel, at the same time, felt increasing anxiety for its safety. And Great Britain and France feared more and more that Egyptian policies threatened their lifeline of the Suez Canal.

These matters came to a crisis on July 26 of this year when the Egyptian Government seized the Universal Suez Canal Company. For ninety years, ever since the inauguration of the canal, that company has operated the canal—largely under British and French technical supervision.

Now, there were some among our allies who urged an immediate reaction to this event by use of force. We insistently urged otherwise, and our wish prevailed, through a long succession of conferences and negotiations. . . .

But the direct relations of Egypt with both Israel and France kept worsening to a point at which first Israel, then France—and Great Britain also—determined that in their judgment there could be no protection of their vital interests without resort to force.

Upon this decision events followed swiftly. On Sunday the Israeli Government ordered total mobilization. On Monday their armed forces penetrated deeply into Egypt and to the vicinity of the Suez Canal. . . . And on Tuesday the British and French Governments delivered a twelve-hour ultimatum to Israel and Egypt, now followed up by armed attack against Egypt.

The United States was not consulted in any way about any phase of these actions. . . .

We believe these actions to have been taken in error, for we do not accept the use of force as a wise or proper instrument for the settlement of international disputes. To say this . . . is in no way to minimize our friendship with these nations . . . And we are fully aware of the grave anxieties of Israel, of Britain, and of France. . . .

The present fact nonetheless seems clear. The action taken can scarcely be reconciled with the principles and purposes of the United Nations to which we have all subscribed. . . .

We took our first measure in this action yesterday. We went to the United Nations with a request that the forces of Israel return to their own line and that hostilities in the area be brought to a close. The proposal was not adopted because it was vetoed by Great Britain and by France. It is our hope and intent that this matter will be brought before the United Nations General Assembly. There, with no veto operating, the opinion of the world can be brought to bear in our quest for a just end to this tormenting problem. . . .

DISCUSSION QUESTIONS

1. What reasons did the Americans give for withdrawing from the Aswan Dam project? What other reasons did they have?
2. Why did Nasser link the financial benefits of nationalizing the Canal Company to Egyptian pride and dignity? Why did he emphasize Egypt's legal rights to the Canal?
3. What was Eisenhower's analysis of the Suez situation? What reasons did he give for not supporting Israel, Britain, and France? What other reasons did he have?
4. What did each of the participants gain from the Suez Crisis, and what did they lose?

32. The Eisenhower Doctrine, 1957

The United States managed to limit the damage from the Suez crisis, but President Eisenhower foresaw increased Communist pressure on Arab states in the wake of Nasser's moral victory. Hoping to forestall such pressure, he formulated the Eisenhower Doctrine, modeled on the Truman Doctrine (Document 7), to assure Middle Eastern nations threatened by Communist pressure that America would provide them with economic and military aid.

A. Excerpts from Eisenhower's Message to Congress on the Middle East, 5 January 1957

. . . It is nothing new for the President and the Congress to join to recognize that the national integrity of other free nations is directly related to our own security.

We have joined to create and support the security system of the United Nations. We have reinforced the collective security system of the United Nations by a series of collective defense arrangements. Today we have security treaties with 42 other nations which recognize that their, and our, peace and security are intertwined. We have joined to take decisive action in relation to Greece and Turkey and in relation to Taiwan.

Thus, the United States . . . has manifested in many endangered areas its purpose to support free and independent governments—and peace—against external menace, notably the menace of International Communism. Thereby we have helped to maintain peace and security during a period of great danger. It is now essential that the United States should manifest through joint action of the President and the Congress our determination to assist those nations of the Mid East area which desire that assistance.

The action which I propose would have the following features.

It would, first of all, authorize the United States to cooperate with and assist any nation or group of nations in the general area of the Middle East in the development of economic strength dedicated to the maintenance of national independence.

It would, in the second place, authorize the Executive to undertake in the same region programs of military assistance and cooperation with any nation or group of nations which desires such aid.

It would, in the third place, authorize such assistance and cooperation to include the employment of the armed forces of the United States to secure and protect the territorial integrity and political independence of such nations, requesting such aid, against overt armed aggression from any nation controlled by International Communism . . .

The present proposal would, in the fourth place, authorize the President to employ, for economic and defensive military purposes, sums available under the Mutual Security Act of 1954, as amended, without regard to existing limitations. . . .

B. Joint Congressional Resolution to Promote Peace and Stability in the Middle East, Approved by the President on 9 March 1957

Resolved by the Senate and House of Representatives of the United States of America in Congress assembled,

That the President be and hereby is authorized to cooperate with and assist any nation or group of nations in the general area of the Middle East desiring such assistance in the development of economic strength dedicated to the maintenance of national independence.

SEC. 2. The President is authorized to undertake, in the general area of the Middle East, military assistance programs with any nation or group of nations in that area desiring such assistance. Furthermore, the United States regards as vital to the national interest and world peace the preservation of the independence and integrity of the nations of the Middle East. To this end, if the President determines the necessity thereof, the United States is prepared to use armed forces to assist any such nation or group of such nations requesting assistance against armed aggression from any country controlled by international communism. . . .

SEC. 4. The President should continue to furnish facilities and military assistance, within the provisions of applicable law and established policies, to the United Nations Emergency Force in the Middle East, with a view to maintaining the truce in that region.

SEC. 6. This joint resolution shall expire when the President shall determine that the peace and security of the nations in the general area of the Middle East are reasonably assured by international conditions created by action of the United Nations or otherwise, except that it may be terminated earlier by a concurrent resolution of the two Houses of Congress.

DISCUSSION QUESTIONS

1. Why did Eisenhower stress "development of economic strength dedicated to the maintenance of national independence"? What earlier Cold War documents are echoed in that phrase?
2. Why did he consider it necessary to seek congressional support for this doctrine?
3. What problems might arise from Congress's authorization for the president to use armed forces to aid any nation requesting assistance against armed aggression?
4. What was the relationship between the Truman and Eisenhower doctrines and the gradual weakening of the British and French colonial empires?

33. Europe's Common Market: The Treaty of Rome, 1957

Seeing Western Europe's strength and stability as essential to combating Communism, the United States introduced the Marshall Plan in 1947 to aid Europe's economic recovery. Using this aid, nations such as West Germany, Italy, and France created "economic miracles" to regain prosperity between 1948 and 1951. Simultaneously, the Treaty of Brussels and the North Atlantic Treaty provided for military cooperation among Western European nations. As economic recovery continued, the merits of extending such cooperation to economic matters became apparent.

On 18 April 1951, six Western European nations (Belgium, Netherlands, Luxemburg, Italy,

France, and West Germany) signed a treaty establishing the European Coal and Steel Community. Since coal and steel were basic sinews of war, the signatories felt that a treaty binding them (especially France and West Germany) to peacetime cooperation in the production of these commodities would not only enhance their prosperity but also integrate their economies to make future war between them virtually impossible. Six years later, the same six nations met at Rome to create a European Economic Community (EEC) or "Common Market" covering all agricultural, industrial, and commercial production.

The 1957 Treaty of Rome had revolutionary implications. In 1833, the creation of the Zollverein, a customs union in Central Europe, foreshadowed the eventual unification of Germany. Now the creation of the EEC reflected hopes that a unified Europe could banish the scourge of war from that continent. Its anti-Soviet tone was obvious, particularly when Moscow responded to the Treaty of Rome with the creation of COMECON, a Common Market of the Communist bloc. Over the following decades, EEC would grow into the European Community and later the European Union, bringing in numerous new members and enhancing European unity. For the moment, European nations that had recently suffered through two world wars dared to hope that the Treaty of Rome would make a third war less likely.

Excerpts from the Treaty of Rome, 25 March 1957

Article 1

By the present Treaty, the HIGH CONTRACTING PARTIES establish among themselves a EUROPEAN ECONOMIC COMMUNITY.

Article 2

It shall be the aim of the Community, by establishing a Common Market and progressively approximating the economic policies of Member States, to promote throughout the Community a harmonious development of economic activities, a continuous and balanced expansion, an increased stability, an accelerated raising of the standard of living and closer relations between its Member States.

Article 3

For the purposes set out in the preceding Article, the activities of the Community shall include, under the conditions and with the timing provided for in this Treaty:

(a) The elimination, as between Member States, of customs duties and of quantitative restrictions in regard to the importation and exportation of goods . . . ,

(b) The establishment of a common customs tariff and a common commercial policy toward third countries;

(c) The abolition, as between Member States, of the obstacles to the free movement of persons, services and capital;

(d) The inauguration of a common agricultural policy;

(e) The inauguration of a common transport policy;

(f) The establishment of a system ensuring that competition shall not be distorted in the Common Market;

(g) The application of procedures which shall make it possible to coordinate the economic policies of Member States and to remedy disequilibria in their balances of payments;

(h) The approximation of their respective municipal law to the extent necessary for the functioning of the Common Market;

(i) The creation of a European Social Fund in order to improve the possibilities of employment for workers and to contribute to the raising of their standard of living;

(j) The establishment of a European Investment Bank intended to facilitate the economic expansion of the Community through the creation of new resources; and

(k) The association of overseas countries and territories with the Community with a view to increasing trade and to pursuing jointly their . . . economic and social development. . . .

Article 9

1. The Community shall be based upon a customs union covering the exchange of all goods and comprising both the prohibition, as between Member States, of customs duties on importation and exportation and all charges with equivalent effect and the adoption of a common customs tariff in their relations with third countries. . . .

Signed at Rome on March 25, 1957.

DISCUSSION QUESTIONS

1. Why was it so important to tie together the economies of France and West Germany following World War II?
2. How would the reduction of tariffs between member states and the establishment of a common external tariff against nonmembers benefit the signatories of the Treaty of Rome?
3. Which aspects of the treaty appear designed to appeal to left-wing political movements within the member states?
4. In what ways did the Treaty of Rome make eventual political unification possible in Europe?
5. Why would the USSR be unhappy about the Treaty of Rome?

34. The U–2 Affair, 1960

The Cold War began to thaw a bit in 1959. Soviet premier Khrushchev's September visit to the United States gave Americans their first close look at a man they would view henceforth as a human rather than an ogre. President Eisenhower, who had disliked Khrushchev when they first met at Geneva in 1955, now saw the Soviet leader as a man with whom he could cooperate to limit the nuclear arms race. Khrushchev invited Eisenhower to visit Russia in 1960, following a summit conference in Paris at which the two leaders expected to sign a treaty banning atmospheric nuclear tests. But shortly before that conference was to begin, an American spy plane crashed in Soviet territory, and its pilot, Francis Gary Powers, was captured.

The United States had been conducting espionage flights over the USSR since July 1956, using a high-altitude, top-secret aircraft called the U–2. When Khrushchev visited America in September 1959, Eisenhower suspended U–2 flights out of courtesy to his visitor and did not resume them until April 1960. At that time, Eisenhower authorized two flights in an attempt to gather as much information as possible concerning Soviet missile deployments before meeting with Khrushchev in Paris. It was the second of these flights, on 1 May, that was shot down over Sverdlovsk in the Soviet Union.

The U–2 incident placed both leaders in difficult positions. Eisenhower at first denied any knowledge of the flight, not realizing that the pilot had been captured alive. Then he admitted full responsibility, which enraged Khrushchev, who had been trying to persuade hard-liners in his government that Eisenhower was trustworthy. The Soviet premier demanded an apology, which Eisenhower refused to provide, and the Paris summit broke up in confusion.

A. Statement by U.S. Department of State, 5 May 1960

The Department has been informed by NASA [the National Aeronautics and Space Administration] that, as announced May 3, an unarmed plane, a U–2 weather research plane based at Adana, Turkey, piloted by a civilian, has been missing since May 1. During the flight of the plane, the pilot reported difficulty with his oxygen equipment. Mr. Khrushchev has announced that a U.S. plane has been shot down over the USSR on that date. It may be possible that this was the missing plane. It is entirely possible that, having failure in the oxygen equipment, which could result in the pilot losing consciousness, the plane continued on automatic pilot for a considerable distance and accidentally violated Soviet airspace. The United States is taking up the matter with the Soviet Government, with particular reference to the fate of the pilot.

B. Statement by U.S. Department of State, 7 May 1960

The Department has received the text of Mr. Khrushchev's further remarks about the unarmed plane which is reported to have been shot down in the Soviet Union. As previously announced, it was known that a U–2 plane was missing. As a result of the inquiry ordered by the President it has been established that insofar as the authorities in Washington are concerned there was no authorization for any such flight as described by Mr. Khrushchev.

Nevertheless it appears that in endeavoring to obtain information now concealed behind the Iron Curtain a flight over Soviet territory was probably undertaken by an unarmed civilian U–2 plane.

It is certainly no secret that, given the state of the world today, intelligence collection activities are practiced by all countries, and postwar history certainly reveals that the Soviet Union has not been lagging behind in this field.

The necessity for such activities as measures for legitimate national defense is enhanced by the excessive secrecy practiced by the Soviet Union in contrast to the free world. One of the things creating tension in the world today is apprehension over surprise attack with weapons of mass destruction. . . .

C. Soviet Note on the U–2 Incident, 10 May 1960

On May 1 of this year at 5 hours 36 minutes, Moscow time, a military aircraft violated the boundary of the Union of Soviet Socialist Republics and intruded across the borders of the Soviet Union for a distance of more than 2,000 kilometers. The government of the Union of Soviet Socialist Republics naturally could not leave unpunished such a flagrant violation of Soviet state boundaries. When the intentions of the violating aircraft became apparent, it was shot down by Soviet rocket troops in the area of Sverdlovsk.

Upon examination by experts of all data at the disposal of the Soviet side, it was incontrovertibly established that the intruder aircraft belonged to the United States of America, was permanently based in Turkey, and was sent through Pakistan into the Soviet Union with hostile purposes.

As Chairman of the USSR Council of Ministers N. S. Khrushchev made public on May 7 at the final session of the USSR Supreme Soviet, exact data from the investigation leave no doubts with respect to the purpose of the flight of the American aircraft which violated the USSR border on May 1. This aircraft was specially equipped for reconnaissance and diversionary flight over the territory of the Soviet Union. It had on board apparatus for aerial photography for detecting the Soviet radar network and other special radio-technical equipment which form part of USSR anti-aircraft defenses. . . .

Pilot Powers . . . is alive . . . and will be brought to account under the laws of the Soviet state. . . .

D. Excerpts from Khrushchev's Statement at Paris, 16 May 1960

As is generally known, a provocative act by the American air force against the Soviet Union has recently taken place. It consisted in the fact that on May 1 of this year a US military reconnaissance plane intruded into the USSR on a definite espionage mission of gathering intelligence about military and industrial installations on Soviet territory. After the aggressive purpose of the plane's flight became clear, it was shot down by a Soviet rocket unit. Unfortunately, this is not the only instance of aggressive and espionage actions by the US air force against the Soviet Union. . . .

At first the US State Department gave out an absurd version to the effect that the American plane had violated the frontiers of the Soviet Union by accident and had not had any spying or subversive assignment. When this version was shown with incontrovertible facts to be a manifest falsehood, the US State Department . . . declared on behalf of the US government that intrusions into the Soviet Union for purposes of military espionage were carried out by American aircraft in accordance with a programme approved by the US government and by the President in person. Two days later President Eisenhower himself confirmed that flights by American planes over the territory of the Soviet Union were and remained a calculated policy of the United States. . . .

The Soviet government and the entire people of the Soviet Union received with indignation these statements by the US government leaders, as did all honest people in the world who are concerned for peace. Now that the leaders of the governments of the Four Powers have come to Paris for their conference, the question arises: how is it possible to productively negotiate and examine the questions confronting the conference, when the US government and personally the President have not only failed to condemn the provocative intrusion of an American military plane into the Soviet Union, but, on the contrary, have declared that such actions remain official US policy towards the USSR? How can agreement be reached on this or that issue needing to be settled in order to lessen tension and remove suspicion and distrust between states, when the government of one of the Great Powers says outright that it is its policy to intrude into the confines of another Great Power for spying and subversive purposes, and consequently to heighten tension in the relations between the powers? Obviously, the proclamation of such a policy, which can only be adopted when nations are at war, dooms the Summit conference to total failure. . . .

E. Excerpts from Eisenhower's Broadcast Address, 25 May 1960

My fellow Americans—

Tonight I want to talk with you about the remarkable events last week in Paris, and their meaning to our future. . . .

You recall, of course, why I went to Paris ten days ago.

Last summer and fall I had many conversations with world leaders; some of these were with Chairman Khrushchev, here in America. Over those months a small improvement in relations between the Soviet Union and the West seemed discernible. A possibility developed that the Soviet leaders might at last be ready for serious talks about our most persistent problems—those of disarmament, mutual inspection, atomic control, and Germany, including Berlin. . . .

Our safety, and that of the free world, demand, of course, effective systems for gathering information about the military capabilities of other powerful nations, especially those that make a fetish of secrecy. This involves many techniques and methods. In these times of vast military machines and nuclear-tipped missiles, the ferreting out of this information is indispensable to free-world security. . . .

Moreover, as President, charged by the Constitution with the conduct of America's foreign relations, and as Commander-in-Chief, charged with the direction of the operations and activities of our Armed Forces . . . , I take full responsibility for approving all the various programs undertaken by our government to secure and evaluate military intelligence.

It was in the prosecution of one of these intelligence programs that the widely publicized U–2 incident occurred.

Aerial photography has been one of many methods we have used to keep ourselves and the free world abreast of major

Soviet military developments. The usefulness of this work has been well established through four years of effort. The Soviets were well aware of it. Chairman Khrushchev has stated that he became aware of these flights several years ago. Only last week, in his Paris press conference, Chairman Khrushchev confirmed that he knew of these flights when he visited the United States last September.

Incidentally, this raises the natural question—why all the furor concerning one particular flight? He did not, when in America last September, charge that these flights were any threat to Soviet safety. He did not then see any reason to refuse to confer with American representatives. This he did only about the flight that unfortunately failed, on May 1, far inside Russia.

Now, two questions have been raised about this particular flight; first, as to its timing, considering the imminence of the summit meeting; second, our initial statements when we learned the flight had failed.

As to the timing, the question was really whether to halt the program and thus forgo the gathering of important information that was essential and that was likely to be unavailable at a later date. The decision was that the program should not be halted.

The plain truth is this: when a nation needs intelligence activity, there is no time when vigilance can be relaxed. Incidentally, from Pearl Harbor we learned that even negotiation itself can be used to conceal preparations for a surprise attack.

Next, as to our government's initial statement about the flight, this was issued to protect the pilot, his mission, and our intelligence processes, at a time when the true facts were still undetermined.

Our first information about the failure of this mission did not disclose whether the pilot was still alive, was trying to escape, was avoiding interrogation, or whether both plane and pilot had been destroyed. Protection of our intelligence system and the pilot, and concealment of the plane's mission, seemed imperative. . . . For these reasons, what is known in intelligence circles as a "covering statement" was issued. It was issued on assumptions that were later proved incorrect. Consequently, when later the status of the pilot was definitely established, and there was no further possibility of avoiding exposure of the project, the factual details were set forth. . . .

At the four-power meeting on Monday morning, he [Khrushchev] demanded of the United States four things: First, condemnation of U–2 flights as a method of espionage; second, assurance that they would not be continued; third, a public apology on behalf of the United States; and, fourth, punishment of all those who had any responsibility respecting this particular mission.

I replied by advising the Soviet leader that I had, during the previous week, stopped these flights and that they would not be resumed. I offered also to discuss the matter with him in personal meetings, while the regular business of the summit might proceed. Obviously, I would not respond to his extreme demands. He knew, of course, by holding to those demands the Soviet Union was scuttling the summit conference.

In torpedoing the conference, Mr. Khrushchev claimed that he acted as the result of his own high moral indignation over alleged American acts of aggression. As I said earlier, he had known of these flights for a long time. It is apparent that the Soviets had decided even before the Soviet delegation left Moscow that my trip to the Soviet Union should be canceled and that nothing constructive from their viewpoint would come out of the Summit Conference. . . .

DISCUSSION QUESTIONS

1. Why did the Americans consider it necessary to conduct espionage flights over Soviet territory?
2. Why did the United States at first issue false statements concerning the U–2 flight? Why did it initially claim that there was "no authorization for any such flight"?
3. If Khrushchev had known of the U–2 flights for years, why had he been reluctant to expose them publicly?
4. Why was Khrushchev so angry about Eisenhower's refusal to disavow and apologize for these flights? What reasons did Khrushchev give for scuttling the Paris summit, and what other reasons might he have had?
5. Why did Eisenhower "take full responsibility" for approving such flights? How did he justify this decision?

35. The Congo Crisis, 1960

On 30 June 1960, the Belgian Congo became independent, with Joseph Kasavubu as president and Patrice Lumumba as prime minister. But Belgian officers still controlled the new nation's police force, and five days later Congolese police mutinied against those officers. Tens of thousands of Belgians still lived in the Congo, and violence quickly broke out on both sides. On 11 July, the mineral-rich province of Katanga declared its independence, plunging the nation into chaos and raising the possibility that more of its six provinces, which had been organized along tribal lines, would break away. In violation of its Treaty of Friendship with the Congo, Belgium sent paratroops and infantry into the country, both to defend white Belgians and to support Katanga in its bid for independence.

Faced with this upheaval, Kasavubu and Lumumba toured the country by plane in an effort to restore order. Their Belgian pilot refused to obey their orders, and at several stops, their lives were threatened. On 13 July, they appealed to the United Nations to send peacekeeping forces into the Congo but did not wait for that organization to act. On 14 July, fearing for their lives, they sent a hastily written telegram to Premier Khrushchev asking for Soviet intervention, thereby introducing the Cold War into central Africa. Khrushchev responded the following day, by which time the leaders were back in Leopoldville, the capital, and Prime Minister Lumumba was able to address the Congo's Chamber of Deputies and describe what had occurred.

All the documents reproduced below were originally written or spoken in French. In using them, students should understand several things. First, Document A was written in haste by two men in fear for their lives. French was not their native language, and their grammar and syntax are understandably shaky. They were also not highly educated, since Belgium denied university education to all but a very few Congolese. In addition, they appear to have realized near the end of the first sentence that the telegraph office charged by the word, and it was therefore less expensive to omit words like a, and, and the. This accounts for the choppy nature of the latter part of the document.

Second, Document B was dictated by Premier Khrushchev in his native language, Russian. He was a highly intelligent but not a well-educated man, and his spoken statements were sometimes ungrammatical. The Soviet Foreign Ministry cleaned up some but not all of his irregularities. His words then had to be translated into French, both because of politeness (since Kasavubu and Lumumba had written to him in French) and because in 1960 French was still the basic language of diplomacy. The translation was probably done by a Russian Foreign Ministry employee who was not a native French speaker.

Third, Document C is an English translation of the official stenographic record (in French) of Lumumba's 15 July speech. But that record was made in the midst of a turbulent legislative session, with deputies shouting at each other and frequently interrupting the prime minister as he tried to make himself heard. Its authenticity is unquestionable but its literal, word-for-word accuracy is open to debate.

None of this means that these documents should not be used. It means that they must be read and used with an understanding of the context in which they were written and spoken.

The Congo government's telegram and Khrushchev's response laid the foundation for one of the Cold War's most confusing crises. The mineral wealth of the provinces of Katanga and Kasai, particularly cobalt, chrome, and uranium, was valuable to the West, which feared that it might fall into Soviet hands. Moscow hoped for a foothold in the Congo as part of Khrushchev's strategy of encouraging the new states of Africa and Asia to turn to Communism. This East–West confrontation led to direct UN intervention (and the death of UN Secretary General Dag Hammarskjöld in a 1961 plane crash) in an internal Congolese power struggle that lasted more than two years. Eventually, the secession of Katanga was defeated by military force, and a pro-Western government under Mobutu Sese Seko emerged in 1965.

A. Telegram from President Kasasvubu and Prime Minister Lumumba to Premier Khrushchev, 14 July 1960

Kindu 14 July 1960.

In view of serious threats to the neutrality of the republic of the Congo on the part of Belgium and certain western nations supporting the conspiracy of Belgium against our independence, we ask you to kindly be willing to follow hour by hour unfolding situation in Congo stop we would be able to be agreeable to seek intervention of the Soviet Union if western camp does not put an end to act aggression against sovereignty republic of the Congo stop Congolese national territory to be this day militarily occupied by Belgian troops and life president of the republic and prime minister to be in danger full stop (Signed) the president of the republic Joseph Kasavubu.

The prime minister and minister of national defense Patrice Lumumba.

B. Reply of Premier Khrushchev to President Kasavubu and Prime Minister Lumumba, 15 July 1960

July 15, 1960

The Soviet Government, the peoples of the Soviet Union follow with attention the development of events in the Republic of the Congo, victim of an imperialist aggression. We understand the difficulties of your situation and we take heed of the enormous international impact of the heroic struggle of the Congolese people for the independence and territorial integrity of the Republic of the Congo.

The people are well acquainted with the colonialists, they know the innumerable atrocities that they have committed in the Congo as in the other regions of Africa, the millions of people that they have exterminated, their attempts to totally isolate the Congo from the outside world. For dozens of years, they spoke of their "civilizing mission" in the Congo, doing everything so that no Congolese could obtain higher education, nor rise to the rank of officer in the army. One can do nothing other than condemn the attitude of the ruling classes of Belgium: they signed a treaty of friendship with the independent Republic of the Congo and immediately afterwards they trampled it like a scrap of paper before the eyes of the entire world.

It is not difficult to see that those who set in motion the armed intervention against the Congo and those who pushed the Belgians to set this in motion wish to strike a blow at all the peoples of Africa, wish to preserve intact the medieval regime, the regime of slavery across a large area of the African continent. The hand raised by the aggressor against the independence of the Congo is raised at the same time against Nigeria, against Madagascar, Mali, Togo and the other countries of Africa which wish to gain independence or which should obtain it shortly.

Your struggle, is the struggle of hundreds and hundreds of millions of people in Africa, in Asia, in Latin America. Indochina, Algeria, Suez, Guatemala, Lebanon and Jordan, Guinea and Cuba, and now the Congo, they are all links in the same chain of the postwar imperialist policy . . .

The imperialist intervention against the Republic of the Congo is an attempt to apply the brakes to the process of total liberation of Africa and, if possible, to throw it into reverse . . . One knows that the former Congo was not only a Belgian colony. The bayonet was Belgian but the masters were the big American, Belgian, English, and West German monopolies. When the Congolese people rejected the Belgian yoke, it rejected the collective yoke of colonial imperialism on the Congo. That is the reason why the current aggression against the Congo, carried out by the Belgian units, is, at its roots, a collective imperialist aggression of powers which the big monopolies installed in the Congo and, first of all, in its rich province of Katanga.

The Soviet Union has already resolutely condemned the imperialist intervention against the Republic of the Congo. It has stated that the United Nations should take measures to end the aggression and reestablish entirely the sovereign rights of the independent Republic of the Congo.

In an atmosphere of increasing anger of peoples who have become indignant at the imperialist aggression in the Congo, the United Nations Security Council has done useful work in adopting a resolution inviting the government of Belgium to withdraw its troops from Congolese territory.

If aggression were to continue in spite of this resolution, the Soviet government declares that the necessity would arise for more effective measures to be taken, both within the framework of the United Nations and by the peace-loving states which sympathize with the Congo.

If the states which directly execute the imperialist aggression against the Republic of the Congo and those that have pushed them pursue their criminal activities, the Soviet Union will not hesitate to take resolute measures in order to put an end to the aggression . . . the cause of the Congo is that of all civilized humanity.

The demand of the Soviet Union is simple: Hands off the Republic of the Congo!

The government of the Congo may be assured that the Soviet government will grant the Republic of the Congo all the help that would be necessary for the triumph of your just cause . . .

C. Prime Minister Patrice Lumumba's Address to the Chamber of Deputies of the Congo, 15 July 1960

. . . After having received these reports, I decided that it was absolutely necessary for [President Kasavubu and myself] to go to Elisabethville [capital of secessionist Katanga] immediately, because the chief of state had publicly sworn, before this Chamber and before the entire nation, to protect and safeguard the integrity of the territory of the nation, and if he did not take steps, the nation would hold him responsible; this is also the duty of the government. It might mean our death, but if so we would die; as leaders responsible for the nation we had to go to Katanga.

We flew to Kamina [a military base in Katanga, occupied by Belgian forces] without notifying anyone beforehand; as we got off the plane, all the Belgian military personnel present and many European civilians who were at the airfield repeatedly called us "apes." They hurled unbelievable insults at us. The commandant of the base arrived, and I said to him: "Sir, we are in a sovereign country; I am accompanying the chief of state, who in your country is called the king. It is unthinkable that your officers and all these people here who are enjoying the hospitality of our country should permit themselves to insult our chief of state in such a shameful manner."

The Commandant replied: "You should have notified us that you were coming instead of just suddenly arriving at Kamina Base out of nowhere," whereupon he took us to the entrance of the airfield where these Europeans were standing. We went into a little office and he asked us not to leave the airfield. I asked why, and he replied that there was great tension in the city. We had gone there for the express purpose of relieving that tension . . .

The chief of state then asked the commandant of the base to put a plane from the base at our immediate disposal, along with an escort of Belgian soldiers to ensure our safety. "We are going directly to Elisabethville," the chief of state declared, and the commandant of the base replied that he could not put this plane at our disposal and would have to consult [Belgian officers in] Leopoldville.

We then said: "Sir, we have signed a treaty of friendship and cooperation with you. When the chief of state asks your help, don't waste time waiting for the approval of your government. If King Baudouin came to us to ask our help, do you think a member of our government would make him wait around for approval from the government? Where is the spirit of collaboration you have always made so much of?"

[Eventually they received a plane.] . . . We left Kamina at 8:00 P.M. for Elisabethville, and arrived there around 10:00 P.M. But the lights on the field were turned out before we could land. Why? Because Katanga was now independent. The chief of state and the prime minister were told that they would not be allowed to set foot in Katanga . . . We were forced to turn back . . .

Fifteen minutes after we had been refused permission to land, the [Belgian] pilot informed us that he had just received orders to take us directly to Luluabourg and not to go back to Kamina. We asked him who had any such right to order us around; we've left our plane and our pilot in Kamina and we have to go back there, we told him . . . The pilot took us to Luluabourg, against our will, as if we had been prisoners . . .

[The next day] we left for Stanleyville . . . The president went to ask the pilot again what time we would arrive in Stanleyville, since it was past the time he had said. The pilot replied that he had received orders to take us directly to Leopoldville. The president ordered him to land at Stanleyville immediately.

I then talked to the pilot too: "We know you are Belgian, but this plane now belongs to the chief of state and the Congolese government. You are in the service of the Congolese government and have no right to disregard the orders of the chief of state just because you have received orders from a foreign power, that is to say, Belgium. We are independent now; and Belgium is a separate country now, just as France and America and other countries are. What you are doing is an act of high treason."

The pilot pretended to obey then, and made a long detour to lead us to believe that we were returning to Stanleyville. Then suddenly we landed at Leopoldville, against our will as if we had been prisoners . . . We were met by a clique of the Belgian army under the command of General Cumont, who [insisted that we review a guard of Belgian troops that he had assembled].

"Sir, that is out of the question," I said. "You have brought these troops here to put our country under military occupation, in violation of our agreement, and you have the audacity to ask that the chief of state and the head of government review them? That would mean that we approve of the presence of these troops here."

General Cumont then said to the chief of state: "Are you aware that this airport is under my command and that I can take you prisoner?"

Here in Leopoldville yesterday, this Belgian general threatened to take the chief of state prisoner! I replied: "Sir, I should like you to know that you are not in your own country. You have arms and ammunition and we don't; we have only our bare hands." General Gheysen [another Belgian officer] retorted, "Sir, I should like you to know that I am in command of this airport. We are here to protect you." "We don't need your protection," I protested. "Go protect the Belgians in your own country . . . "

DISCUSSION QUESTIONS

1. Why did Kasavubu and Lumumba ask for Soviet intervention in the Congo? What condition did they put on their request?
2. How did Khrushchev's reply foreshadow his 6 January 1961 speech on the revolutionary situation in Africa and Asia (Document 37)? What sort of assistance did he promise to provide?
3. What is Khrushchev's opinion of the role played in the Congo Crisis by the United Nations?
4. In his speech to the Chamber, Lumumba did not mention the telegram sent to Khrushchev. What might explain this omission?
5. What might explain the arrogant conduct of Belgian officials toward Kasavubu and Lumumba?

36. Castro on the Cuban Revolution, 1960

In 1959, following a five-and-a-half year struggle against the corrupt, American-supported dictatorship of Fulgencio Batista, Fidel Castro established in Cuba a revolutionary regime. Before long it became apparent that his revolution was dedicated to diminished U.S. influence and presence on the island, and the purification of Cuban society from North American corruption. As time went on, he became increasingly outspoken about the Marxist nature of his revolution. By 1961 he had surrounded himself with Marxists and established close ties with Moscow, thus placing Cuba squarely in the midst of the Cold War.

The Eisenhower administration watched with alarm as the new Cuban government confiscated American property and executed many supporters of Batista (who had also been supporters of the United States). The U.S. government demanded payment in full for any land expropriated, and took various actions to increase economic pressure on Cuba, culminating in the suspension of the sugar quota, which had provided for American purchase of large amounts of Cuban sugar at prices above world market value. Castro responded by denouncing the United States and moving closer to Moscow, which subsequently agreed to buy Cuban sugar, and eventually even to defend the island with Soviet weapons. In September of 1960, the Cuban leader described the decline of relations between his country and the United States in a four-and-a-half hour address to the United Nations General Assembly.

Excerpts from Castro's Address to the UN General Assembly, 26 September 1960

. . . First of all, the revolution found that 600,000 Cubans, able and ready to work, were unemployed. An equal number, proportionately, to the number of unemployed in the United States at the time of the great depression that shook this country and almost produced a catastrophe in the United States. This is what we met with. Permanent unemployment in my country.

What alternative was there for the revolutionary government? Betray the people? As far as the President of the United States is concerned, what we have done for our people is treason to our people. . . .

The first . . . unfriendly act perpetrated by the Government of the United States was to throw open its doors to a gang of murderers, bloodthirsty criminals that had murdered hundreds of defenseless peasants, that never tired of torturing prisoners for many, many years, that killed right and left. These hordes were received by this country with open arms. . . .

When the revolutionary government reduced by 50 per cent the rents, there were many who were upset, . . . some who owned these buildings and apartment houses. But the people rushed into the streets, rejoicing.

Without an agrarian reform our country could not have taken its first tottering step toward development. And we were able, finally, to take that step. . . .

What did the American State Department put to us as its aspirations for its affected interests? They put three things to us: speedy payment, efficient payment, and just payment. Speedy, efficient and just! That means: "Pay! Now! Cash! On the spot! And what we ask, for our lands!"

We weren't 150 per cent Communists at that time. We were just pink at that time, slightly pink. We were not confiscating lands. We simply proposed to . . . pay for them over a period of twenty years. And the only way in which we could pay for them was by bonds, bonds which would mature in twenty years at four-and-a-half per cent and that would be amortized yearly.

How were we able to pay for this land in dollars? How were we going to pay cash on the spot, and how could we pay for them what they asked? It was ludicrous. It is obvious that at that time we had to choose between an agrarian reform and nothing.

By our honor we swear that we had then not even exchanged letters with the Prime Minister of the Soviet Union, Mr. Nikita Khrushchev. We had not even written one another. [However,] as far as the United States press was concerned . . . , Cuba then was a Red government—a Red danger ninety miles off the coast of the United States. . . .

But hysteria can reach any pitch. Hysteria can lead one to make the most unbelievable statements and the most absurd ones. Don't for one moment believe that we're going to intone a *mea culpa* here. We have to apologize to no one.

And the threats began—the threats on our sugar quota. And the cheap philosophy was spouted by imperialism.

Planes went and came back. . . . These planes were obviously leaving the United States. . . .

At least we expected the Organization of American States to condemn the political aggression against Cuba and . . . the economic aggressions of which we had been the victims.

The Government of the United States was not condemned . . . for the sixty overflights of pirate planes. The United States was not condemned for the economic and other aggressions of which we had been the victim. No. The Soviet Union was condemned.

Now this is really bizarre. We had not been attacked by the Soviet Union. We were not victims of aggression on the part of the Soviet Union. No Soviet plane had flown over our territory. . . . The Soviet Union had limited itself to saying that in the case of a military aggression against our country Soviet [artillerymen] . . . could support the victim with rockets . . .

What was yesterday a hopeless land, a land of misery and a land of illiterates, is gradually becoming one of the most enlightened and advanced and developed peoples of the continent. . . .

DISCUSSION QUESTIONS

1. According to Castro, what problems did he confront when he took power in Cuba? How did he deal with them?
2. According to Castro, why did the steps he took lead to conflict with the United States? What reasons did he provide to explain the hostility of the United States government toward the Cuban revolution?
3. How did Castro justify the expropriation of land owned by American companies? Why would U.S. corporations have been reluctant to accept Cuban government bonds in payment for the land taken from them?
4. How did Castro explain the developing relationship between Cuba and the Soviet Union?

37. KHRUSHCHEV ON "WARS OF NATIONAL LIBERATION," JANUARY 1961

Aware that direct military conflict with the West could be catastrophic, Soviet leader Khrushchev opted instead for indirect conflict by helping nations in Asia, Africa, and Latin America emerge from Western domination. Early in 1961, he spelled out his approach. Professing that his goal of "peaceful coexistence" meant avoiding wars between superpowers, he nonetheless promised to support "wars of national liberation." These wars, he asserted, were revolutionary struggles by oppressed peoples against "rotten reactionary" imperialist regimes. In aiding such struggles in Vietnam, Cuba, and elsewhere, he claimed, Communists could combat capitalist imperialism and deter U.S. intervention.

Excerpts from Address by Soviet Premier Khrushchev to a Meeting of Communist Party Organizations in Moscow, 6 January 1961

. . . In modern conditions the following categories of wars should be distinguished: World wars, local wars, liberation wars, and popular uprisings. This is necessary to work out the correct tactics with regard to these wars.

Let us begin with the question of world wars. Communists are the most determined opponents of world wars, just as they are generally opponents of wars among states. These wars are needed only by imperialists to seize the territories of others, and to enslave and plunder other peoples. . . .

Imperialists can unleash a war, but they must think hard about the consequences . . . In conditions where a mighty Socialist camp exists, possessing powerful armed forces, the peoples, by mobilization of all their forces for active struggle against the warmongering imperialist, can indisputably prevent war and thus insure peaceful coexistence.

A word or two about local wars . . . Certain imperialist circles, fearing that world war might end in the complete collapse of capitalism, are putting their money on unleashing local wars.

There have been local wars and they may occur again in the future, but opportunities for imperialists to unleash these wars too are becoming fewer and fewer. A small imperialist war, regardless of which imperialist begins it, may grow into a world thermonuclear rocket war. We must therefore combat both world wars and local wars . . .

Now a word about national liberation wars. The armed struggle by the Vietnamese people or the war of the Algerian people . . . serve as examples of such wars. These wars began as an uprising by the colonial peoples against their oppressors . . . Liberation wars will continue to exist as long as imperialism exists, as long as colonialism exists. These are revolutionary wars. Such wars are not only admissible but inevitable, since the colonialists do not grant independence voluntarily. Therefore, the peoples can attain their freedom and independence only by struggle, including armed struggle.

How is it that the US imperialists, while desirous of helping the French colonialists . . . , decided against direct intervention in the war in Vietnam? They did not intervene because they knew that if they did . . . , Vietnam would get relevant aid from China, the Soviet Union, and other Socialist countries, which could lead to a world war. . . .

At present, a similar war is taking place in Algeria . . . It is the uprising of the Arab people in Algeria against the French colonizers. . . . The imperialists in the United States and Britain render assistance to their French allies with arms. . . . The Algerian people, too, receive assistance from neighboring and other countries that sympathize with their peace-loving aspirations. But it is a liberation war of a people for its independence, it is a sacred war. We recognize such wars, we help and will help the peoples striving for their independence.

Or let us take the Cuban example. A war took place there too. But it also started as an uprising against the internal tyrannical regime supported by US imperialism . . . However, the United States did not interfere in that war directly with its armed forces. The Cuban people, under the leadership of Fidel Castro, have won.

Can such wars flare up in the future? They can. Can there be such uprisings? There can. But these are wars which are national uprisings. . . . What is the attitude of the Marxists toward such uprisings? A most positive one. These uprisings must not be identified with wars among states, with local wars, since in these uprisings the people are fighting for implementation of their right for self-determination, for independent social and national development. These are uprisings against rotten reactionary regimes, against the colonizers. The Communists fully support such just wars and march in the front rank with the peoples waging liberation struggles . . .

DISCUSSION QUESTIONS

1. Why and how did Khrushchev think Communists should support national liberation wars? Why did he think such wars were inevitable?
2. Why did he identify capitalism with imperialism? Why did he see socialists and national liberation movements as natural allies in a global struggle against capitalist imperialism?
3. What were the potential benefits and risks for the Soviets in supporting such wars?

38. Eisenhower's Farewell Address on the Military-Industrial Complex, 17 January 1961

On 17 January 1961, three days before leaving office, President Eisenhower delivered a televised farewell address to the American people. After extolling his nation's values and lamenting the threat to them posed by Soviet Communism, he warned Americans of a potential domestic threat to their freedom: the growing size and influence of America's massive "military-industrial complex." Noting the necessity of a powerful defense establishment and supportive arms industries, he nonetheless called for vigilance lest this potent combination acquire "unwarranted influence" that could "endanger our liberties or democratic processes." Then the former general, who had directly "witnessed the horrors of war," finished his address with an eloquent plea for peace among peoples of all races, faiths, and nations.

Excerpts from President Eisenhower's Televised Speech, 17 January 1961

My fellow Americans:

. . . This evening I come to you with a message of leave-taking and farewell, and to share a few final thoughts with you . . .

. . . America is today the strongest, the most influential and most productive nation in the world. Understandably proud of this pre-eminence, we yet realize that America's leadership and prestige depend, not merely upon our unmatched material progress, riches and military strength, but on how we use our power in the interests of world peace and human betterment.

Throughout America's adventure in free government, our basic purposes have been to keep the peace; to foster progress in human achievement, and to enhance liberty, dignity and integrity among people and among nations . . .

Progress toward these noble goals is persistently threatened by the conflict now engulfing the world. It commands our whole attention, absorbs our very beings. We face a hostile ideology—global in scope, atheistic in character, ruthless in purpose, and insidious in method. Unhappily the danger it poses promises to be of indefinite duration. To meet it successfully, there is called for, not so much the emotional and transitory sacrifices of crisis, but rather those which enable us to carry forward steadily, surely, and without complaint the burdens of a prolonged and complex struggle—with liberty the stake . . .

A vital element in keeping the peace is our military establishment. Our arms must be mighty, ready for instant action, so that no potential aggressor may be tempted to risk his own destruction.

Our military organization today bears little relation to that known by any of my predecessors in peacetime. . . .

Until the latest of our world conflicts, the United States had no armaments industry . . . But now . . . we have been compelled to create a permanent armaments industry of vast proportions. Added to this, three and a half million men and women are directly engaged in the defense establishment. We annually spend on military security more than the net income of all United States corporations.

This conjunction of an immense military establishment and a large arms industry is new in the American experience. The total influence—economic, political, even spiritual—is felt in every city, every State house, every office of the Federal government. We recognize the imperative need for this development. Yet we must not fail to comprehend its grave implications . . .

In the councils of government, we must guard against the acquisition of unwarranted influence, whether sought or unsought, by the military industrial complex. The potential for the disastrous rise of misplaced power exists and will persist.

We must never let the weight of this combination endanger our liberties or democratic processes. We should take nothing for granted. Only an alert and knowledgeable citizenry can compel the proper meshing of the huge industrial and military machinery of defense with our peaceful methods and goals, so that security and liberty may prosper together.

Disarmament, with mutual honor and confidence, is a continuing imperative. Together we must learn how to compose differences, not with arms, but with intellect and decent purpose. Because this need is so sharp and apparent I confess that I lay down my official responsibilities in this field with a definite sense of disappointment. As one who has witnessed the horror and the lingering sadness of war—as one who knows that another war could utterly destroy this civilization . . . —I wish I could say tonight that a lasting peace is in sight.

Happily, I can say that war has been avoided. Steady progress toward our ultimate goal has been made. But, so much remains to be done . . .

So—in this my last good night to you as your President—I thank you for the many opportunities you have given me for public service in war and peace . . .

To all the peoples of the world, I once more give expression to America's prayerful and continuing aspiration:

We pray that peoples of all faiths, all races, all nations, may have their great human needs satisfied; that those now denied opportunity shall come to enjoy it to the full; that all who yearn for freedom may experience its spiritual blessings; that those who have freedom will understand, also, its heavy responsibilities; that all who are insensitive to the needs of others will learn charity; that the scourges of poverty, disease and ignorance will be made to disappear from the earth, and that, in the goodness of time, all peoples will come to live together in a peace guaranteed by the binding force of mutual respect and love . . .

DISCUSSION QUESTIONS

1. What did Eisenhower see as America's main values and goals? Why did he think that Soviet Communist threatened those values and goals?
2. What did Eisenhower mean by the "military-industrial complex"? Why did he think it was necessary? Why did he think it was dangerous?
3. Why did he think that mutual disarmament by the superpowers was imperative? Why did he say he was leaving office with a "sense of disappointment"?

39. Kennedy's Inaugural Address, 1961

On 20 January 1961, three days after Eisenhower's farewell address, his youthful successor, John F. Kennedy, was sworn in as president of the United States. Kennedy's presidency corresponded roughly with the most perilous phase of the Cold War, highlighted by dangerous confrontations with the Soviet Union over Berlin and Cuba. He began his term with a ringing inaugural address, steeped in the rhetoric of the Cold War, yet calling for sacrifice both in the name of freedom and in the cause of peace. The address set the tone for his administration's approach to foreign affairs during the first two years of his presidency. Later, after the Cuban Missile Crisis, Kennedy would alter his rhetoric and his approach, most notably in his "Peace Speech" at American University in June 1963 (Document 42). But on the day he delivered his most famous and frequently quoted address, those changes lay in the future, hidden from the eyes and ears of the people who watched and listened in the bright, bitter cold.

Excerpts from Kennedy's Inaugural Address, 20 January 1961

We observe today not a victory of party but a celebration of freedom—symbolizing an end as well as a beginning—signifying renewal as well as change. For I have sworn before you and almighty God the same solemn oath our forebears prescribed nearly a century and three quarters ago.

The world is very different now. For man holds in his mortal hands the power to abolish all forms of human poverty and all forms of human life. And yet the same revolutionary beliefs for which our forebears fought are still at issue around the globe—the belief that the rights of man come not from the generosity of the state but from the hand of God. We dare not forget today that we are the heirs of that first revolution.

Let the word go forth, from this time and place, to friend and foe alike, that the torch has been passed to a new generation of Americans—born in this century, tempered by war, disciplined by a hard and bitter peace, proud of our ancient heritage—and unwilling to witness or permit the slow undoing of those human rights to which this nation has always been committed, and to which we are committed today, at home and around the world.

Let every nation know, whether it wishes us well or ill, that we shall pay any price, bear any burden, meet any hardship, support any friend, oppose any foe to assure the survival and success of liberty. This much we pledge—and more.

To those old allies whose cultural and spiritual origins we share, we pledge the loyalty of faithful friends. United, there is little we cannot do in a host of cooperative ventures. Divided, there is little we can do—for we dare not meet a powerful challenge at odds and split asunder.

To those new states whom we welcome to the ranks of the free, we pledge our word that one form of colonial control shall not have passed away merely to be replaced by a far more iron tyranny. . . .

To those peoples in the huts and villages of half the globe struggling to break the bonds of mass misery, we pledge our best efforts to help them help themselves, for whatever period is required—not because the communists may be doing it, but because it is right. If a free society cannot help the many who are poor, it cannot save the few who are rich.

To our sister republics south of our border, we offer a special pledge—to convert our good words into good deeds—in a new alliance for progress—to assist free men and free governments in casting off the chains of poverty. But this peaceful revolution of hope cannot become the prey of hostile powers. Let all our neighbors know that we shall join with them to oppose aggression or subversion anywhere in the Americas. And let every other power know that this Hemisphere intends to remain the master of its own house. . . .

Finally, to those nations who would make themselves our adversary, we offer not a pledge but a request: that both sides begin anew the quest for peace, before the dark powers of destruction unleashed by science engulf all humanity in planned or accidental self-destruction.

We dare not tempt them with weakness. For only when our arms are sufficient beyond doubt can we be certain beyond doubt that they will never be employed. But neither can two great and powerful groups of nations take comfort from our present course—both sides overburdened by the cost of modern weapons, both rightly alarmed by the steady spread of the deadly atom, yet both racing to alter the uncertain balance of terror that stays the hand of mankind's final war.

So let us begin anew—remembering on both sides that civility is not a sign of weakness, and sincerity is always subject to proof. Let us never negotiate out of fear. But let us never fear to negotiate. . . .

In your hands, my fellow citizens, more than mine, will rest the final success or failure of our course. Since this country was founded, each generation of Americans has been summoned to give testimony to its national loyalty. The graves of young Americans who answered the call to service surround the globe.

Now the trumpet summons us again—not as a call to bear arms, though arms we need—not as a call to battle, though embattled we are—but a call to bear the burden of a long twilight struggle, year in and year out, "rejoicing in hope, patient in tribulation"—a struggle against the common enemies of man: tyranny, poverty, disease and war itself. . . .

In the long history of the world, only a few generations have been granted the role of defending freedom in its hour of maximum danger. I do not shrink from this responsibility—I welcome it. I do not believe that any of us would exchange places with any other people or any other generation. The energy, the faith, the devotion which we bring to this endeavor will light our country and all who serve it—and the glow from that fire can truly light the world.

And so, my fellow Americans: ask not what your country can do for you—ask what you can do for your country.

My fellow citizens of the world: ask not what America will do for you, but what together we can do for the freedom of man.

Finally, whether you are citizens of America or citizens of the world, ask of us here the same high standards of strength and sacrifice which we ask of you. With a good conscience our only sure reward, with history the final judge of our deeds, let us go forth to lead the land we love, asking His blessing and His help, but knowing that here on earth God's work must truly be our own.

DISCUSSION QUESTIONS

1. Why did Kennedy begin by citing America's revolutionary heritage? What attitude did he adopt toward developing nations?
2. What messages did Kennedy's address send to America's allies? What messages did it send to the USSR and to Cuba?
3. Which parts of this address would you characterize as typical Cold War rhetoric? Why?
4. What dangers were inherent in Kennedy's pledge to "pay any price" and "bear any burden"?

40. The Berlin Crisis, 1961

In 1961, after Kennedy took office, Khrushchev again moved Berlin to the center of the Cold War stage. He proposed that it should become a "demilitarized city" and that the joint military occupation, in effect since the end of World War II, should end. At a summit meeting in June with Kennedy in Vienna, the Soviet leader tried to bully the young president, suggesting that failure to solve the Berlin problem could result in war and threatening to unilaterally turn the city over to East Germany.

Shaken by the summit, Kennedy addressed his nation on 25 July. Painting a somber picture of Khrushchev's intentions, he revealed plans for a

U.S. military buildup and depicted Berlin as "the great testing place of Western courage."

Meanwhile, the flow of East Berliners to the West, in progress since 1948, increased. Many East Berliners crossed every morning to work in West Berlin—by car, subway, bus, or on foot—and then returned home in the evening. As the crisis heated up during 1961, more and more of them simply did not go home. Since many of these were well-educated professionals, the exodus was devastating for East Germany (the German Democratic Republic).

Unable to drive the Western Powers out of West Berlin, the Soviet and East German governments finally decided to make the best of a bad situation and to seal off the border between East and West Berlin. Early in the morning of 13 August 1961, East German workers erected barriers and strung barbed wire across the border running through the center city. U.S. protests met a stiff Soviet response. Later these temporary fortifications would be replaced by the Berlin Wall, destined to become the Cold War's most enduring and recognizable symbol.

A. Kennedy's Report to the Nation on Berlin, 25 July 1961

Seven weeks ago tonight I returned from Europe to report on my meeting with Premier Khrushchev. . . . His grim warnings about the future of the world, his *aide mémoire* on Berlin, his subsequent speeches and threats . . . , and the increase in the Soviet military budget that he has announced have all prompted a series of decisions by the administration and a series of consultations with the members of the NATO organization. In Berlin, as you recall, he intends to bring to an end, through a stroke of the pen, first, our legal rights to be in West Berlin and, secondly, our ability to make good on our commitment to the 2 million free people of that city. That we cannot permit. . . .

The immediate threat to free men is in West Berlin. But that isolated outpost is not an isolated problem. The threat is worldwide. Our effort must be equally wide and strong. . . . We face a challenge in Berlin, but there is also a challenge in southeast Asia, where the borders are less guarded, the enemy harder to find, and the danger of communism less apparent to those who have so little. We face a challenge in our own hemisphere and indeed wherever else the freedom of human beings is at stake.

Let me remind you that the fortunes of war and diplomacy left the free people of West Berlin in 1945 110 miles behind the Iron Curtain. . . . West Berlin is 110 miles within the area which the Soviets now dominate—which is immediately controlled by the so-called East German regime.

We are there as a result of our victory over Nazi Germany, and our basic rights to be there deriving from that victory include both our presence in West Berlin and the enjoyment of access across East Germany. These rights have been repeatedly confirmed . . . in special agreements with the Soviet Union. Berlin is not a part of East Germany, but a separate territory under the control of the allied powers. Thus our rights there are clear and deep-rooted. But in addition to those rights is our commitment to sustain—and defend, if need be—the opportunity for more than 2 million people to determine their own future and choose their own way of life.

Thus our presence in West Berlin, and our access thereto, cannot be ended by any act of the Soviet Government. The NATO shield was long ago extended to cover West Berlin, and we have given our word that an attack in that city will be regarded as an attack upon us all.

For West Berlin, lying exposed 110 miles inside East Germany, surrounded by Soviet troops and close to Soviet supply lines, has many roles. It is more than a showcase of liberty, a symbol, an island of freedom in a Communist sea. It is even more than a link with the free world, a beacon of hope behind the Iron Curtain, an escape hatch for refugees.

West Berlin is all of that. But above all it has now become, as never before, the great testing place of Western courage and will, a focal point where our solemn commitments . . . and Soviet ambitions now meet in basic confrontation. . . .

We do not want to fight, but we have fought before. And others in earlier times have made the same dangerous mistake of assuming that the West was too selfish and too soft and too divided to resist invasions of freedom in other lands. Those who threaten to unleash the forces of war on a dispute over West Berlin should recall the words of the ancient philosopher: "A man who causes fear cannot be free from fear."

We cannot and will not permit the Communists to drive us out of Berlin, either gradually or by force. . . .

B. U.S. Note Protesting Closure of East Berlin Border, 17 August 1961

On August 13, East German authorities put into effect several measures regulating movement at the boundary of the western sectors and the Soviet sector of the city of Berlin. These measures have the effect of limiting, to a degree approaching complete prohibition, passage from the Soviet sector to the western sectors of the city. These measures were accompanied by the closing of the sector boundary by a sizable deployment of police forces and by military detachments brought into Berlin for this purpose.

All this is a flagrant, and particularly serious, violation of the quadripartite status of Berlin. Freedom of movement with respect to Berlin was reaffirmed by the quadripartite agreement of New York of May 4, 1949, and by the decision taken at Paris on June 20, 1949, by the Council of the Ministers of Foreign Affairs of the Four Powers. The United States Government has never accepted that limitations can be imposed on freedom of movement within Berlin. The boundary between the Soviet sector and the western sectors of Berlin is not a state frontier. The United States Government considers that the measures which the East German authorities have taken are illegal. It reiterates that it does not accept the pretension that the Soviet sector of Berlin forms a part of the so-called "German Democratic Republic" and that Berlin is situated on its territory. Such a pretension is in itself a violation of the solemnly pledged word of the USSR in the Agreement on the Zones of Occupation in Germany and the administration of Greater Berlin. Moreover, the United States Government cannot admit the right of the East German authorities to authorize their armed forces to enter the Soviet sector of Berlin.

By the very admission of the East German authorities, the measures which have just been taken are motivated by the fact that an ever increasing number of inhabitants of East Germany wish to leave this territory. The reasons for this exodus are known. They are simply the internal difficulties in East Germany. . . . .

The United States Government solemnly protests against the measures referred to above, for which it holds the Soviet Government responsible. The United States Government expects the Soviet Government to put an end to these illegal measures. This unilateral infringement of the quadripartite status of Berlin can only increase existing tension and dangers.

C. Soviet Response to the U.S. Protest, 18 August 1961

In connection with the note of the Government of the United States of America of August 17, 1961, the Government of the Union of Soviet Socialist Republics considers it necessary to state the following:

1. The Soviet Government fully understands and supports the actions of the Government of the German Democratic Republic which established effective control on the border with West Berlin in order to bar the way for subversive activity being carried out from West Berlin against the GDR and other countries of the socialist community. In its measures on the borders the Government of the GDR merely made sure the ordinary right of any sovereign state for the protection of its interests. Any state establishes on its borders with other states such regime as it deems necessary and responsive to its legitimate interests. As is known, the regime of state borders is one of the internal questions of any state, and its decision does not require recognition or approval on the part of other governments. Attempts by the Government of the USA to interfere in the internal affairs of the GDR are therefore completely unfounded and inappropriate.

2. Doubtless the reasons are well known to the Government of the USA which made necessary and even inevitable the introduction of control over movement across the border between the GDR and West Berlin. It expended no little effort itself to evoke these reasons. West Berlin has been transformed into a center of political and economic provocations against the GDR, the Soviet Union, and other socialist countries. Former and present West Berlin municipal leaders have cynically called West Berlin an "arrow in the living body of the German Democratic Republic," a "front city," a "violator of tranquility," the "cheapest atom bomb put in the center of a socialist state." The gates of West Berlin have been opened to international criminals and provocateurs of all kinds, if only to sharpen international tension and widen the dimensions of the provocations and subversive acts against the countries of the socialist community. . . .

DISCUSSION QUESTIONS

1. Why did Kennedy see Berlin as a testing ground for Western courage? How did he situate Berlin in the global struggle between Western democracy and Communism?
2. From an American perspective, what was wrong with Khrushchev's desire to change the status of Berlin? How did Kennedy justify his resistance to this change?
3. What similarities and differences do you see between Kennedy's approach to Berlin in 1961 and Truman's in 1948?
4. Why did the Soviets and East Germans decide to seal off the border? How did they expect this to help them?
5. In what ways might the construction of the Berlin Wall have helped the United States? In what ways might it be seen as a U.S. victory?

41. The Cuban Missile Crisis, October 1962

In April 1961, an American-sponsored effort to overthrow Cuba's Castro regime by landing a brigade of Cuban exiles on the island at a place called the "Bay of Pigs" failed miserably. Khrushchev assumed that the next invasion of Cuba would be led by U.S. combat troops—and probably succeed. In an effort to deter such an invasion, he beefed up Soviet forces on the island and, in a perilous move, decided to secretly install Soviet intermediate-range nuclear missiles in Cuba.

Khrushchev's aims went beyond defending Cuba. Faced with a growing U.S. lead in long-range (intercontinental) missiles, he hoped to avoid the great time and expense of building his own large fleet of them by placing existing intermediate weapons within range of America. He also hoped, once the missiles were in place, to use them to pry concessions from the West on Berlin.

Khrushchev's hopes rested on maintaining secrecy until the missiles were operational in November, but American U–2 planes detected them on 14 October. Before revealing their presence, Kennedy consulted for days with top advisors, rejecting both the option of negotiating with Moscow and the option of trying to take out the missiles with air strikes followed by invasion. Instead, in a televised address on 22 October, he announced that the United States would impose a naval blockade or "quarantine" of Cuba to prevent shipments of additional nuclear equipment and thus hopefully keep the missiles from becoming operational.

Following Kennedy's speech, the quarantine went into effect. Khrushchev decided not to try to break the blockade, but he refused to remove the missiles. Kennedy then considered an air attack on the missile sites, to be followed by an invasion. Since, unknown to Kennedy, many of the missiles were already operational, and since Soviet ground units were equipped with tactical nuclear weapons, such an attack could have sparked a nuclear war.

But on 26 October, Kennedy received a message from Khrushchev. Undiplomatic and emotional, it contained proposals that seemed to offer a path to a peaceful settlement. Astonishingly, the next day a second message from Khrushchev adopted a sterner tone and proposed that America remove its missiles from Turkey in return for removal of Soviet missiles from Cuba. Based on an advisor's suggestion, Kennedy's response ignored the second letter and suggested that the first be the basis for negotiations. Things got very tense on 27 October when a U–2 pilot was shot down over Cuba and killed, but Kennedy held off on retaliatory strikes, warning the Soviets through private channels that an invasion was imminent, while also pledging privately to remove U.S. missiles from Turkey. On 28 October, accepting Kennedy's assurance that the United States would not invade Cuba, Khrushchev agreed to remove the Soviet missiles, ending the missile crisis.

A. Highlights of Kennedy's Address to the Nation and the World, 22 October 1962

This Government, as promised, has maintained the closest surveillance of the Soviet military build-up on the island of Cuba. Within the past week unmistakable evidence has established the fact that a series of offensive missile sites is now in preparation on that imprisoned island. The purpose of these bases can be none other than to provide a nuclear strike capability against the Western hemisphere. . . .

This urgent transformation of Cuba into an important strategic base by the presence of these large, long-range, and clearly offensive weapons of sudden mass destruction constitutes an explicit threat to the peace and security of all the Americas. . . . This action also contradicts the repeated assurances of Soviet spokesmen . . . that the arms build-up in Cuba would retain its original defensive character and that the Soviet Union had no need or desire to station strategic missiles on the territory of any other nation. . . .

Neither the United States of America nor the world community of nations can tolerate deliberate deception and offensive threats on the part of any nation, large or small. We no longer live in a world where only the actual firing of weapons represents a sufficient challenge to a nation's security to constitute maximum peril. Nuclear weapons are so destructive and ballistic missiles are so swift that any substantially increased possibility of their use or any sudden change in their deployment may well be regarded as a definite threat to peace. . . .

Acting, therefore, in the defense of our own security and of the entire Western Hemisphere, and under the authority entrusted to me by the Constitution as endorsed by the resolution of the Congress, I have directed that the following initial steps be taken immediately:

First, to halt this offensive buildup, a strict quarantine on all offensive military equipment under shipment to Cuba is being initiated. All ships of any kind bound for Cuba from whatever nation or port will, where they are found to contain cargoes of offensive weapons, be turned back. . . .

Second, I have directed the continued and increased close surveillance of Cuba and its military build-up. . . . Should these offensive military preparations continue, thus increasing the threat to the hemisphere, further action will be justified. I have directed the Armed Forces to prepare for any eventualities, and I trust that, in the interest of both the Cuban people and the Soviet technicians at the sites, the hazards . . . of continuing this threat will be recognized.

Third, it shall be the policy of this nation to regard any nuclear missile launched from Cuba against any nation in the Western Hemisphere as an attack by the Soviet Union on the United States, requiring a full retaliatory response upon the Soviet Union. . . .

Sixth: Under the Charter of the United Nations, we are asking tonight that an emergency meeting of the Security Council be convoked—without delay to take action against this latest Soviet threat to world peace. . . .

Seventh and finally: I call upon Chairman Khrushchev to halt and eliminate this clandestine, reckless, and provocative threat to world peace and to stable relations between our two nations. . . .

Our goal is not the victory of might, but the vindication of right; not peace at the expense of freedom, but both peace and freedom here in this hemisphere, and we hope around the world. God willing, that goal will be achieved.

B. Excerpts from Khrushchev's Message to Kennedy, 26 October 1962

Dear Mr. President:

. . . In the name of the Soviet Government and the Soviet people, I assure you that your conclusions regarding offensive weapons in Cuba are groundless. . . .

All the means located there . . . have a defensive character, are on Cuba solely for the purpose of defense, and we have sent them to Cuba at the request of the Cuban government. . . .

You can regard us with distrust, but in any case you can be calm in this regard, that we are of sound mind and understand perfectly well that if we attack you, you will respond the same way. . . . Only lunatics or suicides, who themselves want to perish and to destroy the whole world before they die, could do this. We, however, want to live and do not at all want to destroy your country. We want something quite different: to compete with your country on a peaceful endeavor. . . .

I don't know whether you can understand me and believe me. But I should like to have you believe in yourself and agree that one cannot give way to passions; it is necessary to control them. . . .

If assurances were given by the President and the Government of the United States that the USA itself would not participate in an attack on Cuba and would restrain others from actions of this sort, if you would recall your fleet, this would immediately change everything. . . . Then, too, the question of armaments would disappear, since, if there is no threat, then armaments are a burden for every people. Then, too, the question of the destruction, not only of the armaments which you call offensive, but of all other armaments as well, would look different. . . .

Armaments bring only disasters. When one accumulates them, this damages the economy, and if one puts them to use, then they destroy people on both sides. Consequently, only a madman can believe that armaments are the principal means in the life of society. . . . If people do not show wisdom, then in the final analysis, they will come to a clash, like blind moles, and then reciprocal extermination will begin.

Let us therefore show statesmanlike wisdom. I propose: we, for our part, will declare that our ships, bound for Cuba, are not carrying any kind of armaments. You would declare that the United States will not invade Cuba with its forces and will not support any kind of forces that might intend to carry out an invasion of Cuba. Then the necessity for the presence of our military specialists in Cuba would disappear.

Mr. President, I appeal to you to weigh well what the aggressive, piratical actions, which you have declared the USA intends to carry out in international waters, would lead to. . . .

If you did this as the first step towards the unleashing of war, it is evident that nothing else is left to us but to accept this challenge of yours. If, however, you have not lost your self-control and sensibly conceive what this might lead to, then, Mr. President, we and you ought not now to pull on the ends of the rope in which you have tied the knot of war, because the more the two of us pull, the tighter that knot will be tied. And a moment may come when that knot will be tied so tight that even he who tied it will not have the strength to untie it, and then it would be necessary to cut that knot. And what that would mean is not for me to explain to you, because you yourself understand perfectly of what terrible forces our countries dispose.

Consequently, if there is no intention to tighten that knot and thereby doom the world to the catastrophe of thermonuclear war, then let us not only relax the forces pulling on the ends of the rope, let us take measures to untie the knot. We are ready for this. . . .

There, Mr. President, are my thoughts, which, if you agreed with them, could put an end to the tense situation which is disturbing all peoples. These thoughts are dictated by a sincere desire to relieve the situation, to remove the threat of war.

C. Excerpts from Khrushchev's Message to Kennedy, 27 October 1962

Dear Mr. President:

. . . I understand your concern for the security of the United States, Mr. President, because this is the primary duty of a President. But we, too, are disturbed about these same questions. . . . Our aim has been and is to help Cuba, and no one can dispute the humanity of our motives, which are oriented toward enabling Cuba to live peacefully and develop in the way its people desire.

You wish to ensure the security of your country, and this is understandable. But Cuba, too, wants the same thing; all countries want to maintain their security. But how are we . . . to assess your actions which are expressed in the fact that you have surrounded the Soviet Union with military bases; surrounded our allies with military bases; placed military bases literally around our country; and stationed your missile armaments there? . . . Your missiles are located in Britain, are located in Italy, and are aimed against us. Your missiles are located in Turkey.

You are disturbed over Cuba. You say that this disturbs you because it is 90 miles by sea from the coast of the United States of America. But Turkey adjoins us; our sentries patrol back and forth and see each other. Do you consider, then, that you have the right to demand security for your own country and the removal of the weapons you call offensive, but do not accord the same right to us? You have placed destructive missile weapons, which you call offensive, in Turkey, literally next to us. . . .

I think it would be possible to end the controversy quickly and normalize the situation. . . .

I therefore make this proposal: We are willing to remove from Cuba the means which you regard as offensive. We are willing to carry this out and to make this pledge in the United Nations. Your representatives will make a declaration to the effect that the United States, for its part, considering the uneasiness and anxiety of the Soviet State, will remove its analogous means from Turkey. Let us reach agreement as to the period of time needed by you and by us to bring this about. And, after that, persons entrusted by the United Nations Security Council could inspect on the spot the fulfillment of the pledges made. . . .

We, in making this pledge, in order to give satisfaction and hope to the peoples of Cuba and Turkey and to strengthen their confidence in their security, will make a statement within the framework of the Security Council to the effect that the Soviet Government gives a solemn promise to respect the inviolability of the borders and sovereignty of Turkey, not to interfere in its internal affairs, not to invade Turkey, not to make available our territory as a bridgehead for such an invasion, and that it would also restrain those who contemplate committing aggression against Turkey, either from the territory of the Soviet Union or from the territory of Turkey's other neighboring states.

The United States Government will make a similar statement within the framework of the Security Council regarding Cuba. . . .

D. Excerpt from Kennedy's Response to Khrushchev, 27 October 1962

Dear Mr. Chairman:

I have read your letter of October 26 with great care and welcomed the statement of your desire to seek a prompt solution to the problem. The first thing that needs to be done, however, is for work to cease on offensive missile bases in Cuba and for all weapons systems in Cuba capable of offensive use to be rendered inoperable, under effective United Nations arrangements.

Assuming this is done promptly, I have given my representatives in New York instructions that will permit them to work out this week . . . an arrangement for a permanent solution to the Cuban problem along the lines suggested in your letter of October 26. As I read your letter, the key elements of your proposals—which seem generally acceptable as I understand them—are as follows:

1. You would agree to remove these weapons systems from Cuba under appropriate United Nations observation and supervision; and undertake, with suitable safeguards, to halt the further introduction of such weapons systems into Cuba.

2. We, on our part, would agree—upon the establishment of adequate arrangements through the United Nations to ensure the carrying out and continuation of these commitments—(a) to remove promptly the quarantine measures now in effect and (b) to give assurances against an invasion of Cuba. I am confident that other nations of the Western Hemisphere would be prepared to do likewise.

If you will give your representatives similar instructions, there is no reason why we should not be able to complete these arrangements and announce them to the world within a couple of days. . . .

DISCUSSION QUESTIONS

1. Why did Kennedy stress that a nuclear attack launched from Cuba against any other nation would be considered equivalent to a Soviet attack upon the United States?
2. How did Kennedy justify his deployment of a naval quarantine against Cuba? What were the advantages of this approach over negotiations or invasion?
3. What did Kennedy mean when he said that, if the buildup of missiles in Cuba continued, "further action will be justified"?
4. How did Khrushchev justify the placement of missiles in Cuba? How did his two letters differ in the terms they proposed?
5. How did Kennedy's response clarify the issues and offer a basis for agreement that Khrushchev could accept?

42. Kennedy's "Peace Speech" at American University, June 1963

Kennedy emerged from the Cuban crisis relieved but sobered. The proximity of nuclear war weighed heavily on him. As Eisenhower had done, he renewed America's efforts to obtain a treaty with the USSR banning atmospheric testing of nuclear weapons. Levels of highly toxic radioactive elements, such as strontium–90 and cesium–139, had increased dramatically in the 1950s; cows ingested it on grass they ate and passed it to humans in their milk; fish absorbed dangerously high levels simply by living in the seas. A test ban treaty seemed essential, not necessarily to lessen the danger of nuclear war, but to halt the poisoning of the planet.

With Khrushchev also chastened by the near miss in Cuba, significant progress was made. The Soviet leader, eager for an agreement that would put his nation on an equal footing with the United States, was more than willing to negotiate. Kennedy made public his hopes in an eloquent commencement address at American University in Washington. Dubbed the "Peace Speech," it startled many with its abandonment of Cold War rhetoric and its conciliatory tone. John Kennedy had come a long way from the clarion calls of his inaugural address.

Excerpts from Kennedy's Commencement Address at American University, 10 June 1963

. . . What kind of peace do I mean and what kind of peace do we seek? Not a Pax Americana enforced on the world by American weapons of war. Not the peace of the grave or the security of the slave; I am talking about genuine peace—the kind of peace that makes life on earth worth living—and the kind that enables men and nations to grow and to hope and to build a better life for their children—not merely peace for Americans but peace for all men and women—not merely peace in our time but peace in all time.

I speak of peace because of the new face of war. Total war makes no sense in an age when great powers can maintain large and relatively invulnerable nuclear forces and refuse to surrender without resort to those forces. It makes no sense in an age when a single nuclear weapon contains almost ten times the explosive force delivered by all the Allied air forces in the second world war. It makes no sense in an age when the deadly poisons produced by a nuclear exchange would be carried by wind and water and soil and seed to the far corners of the globe and to generations yet unborn.

Today the expenditure of billions of dollars every year on weapons acquired for the purpose of making sure we never need them is essential to the keeping of peace. But surely the acquisition of such idle stockpiles—which can only destroy and can never create—is not the only . . . means of assuring peace.

I speak of peace, therefore, as the necessary rational end of rational men. I realize the pursuit of peace is not as dramatic as the pursuit of war—and frequently the words of the pursuer fall on deaf ears. But we have no more urgent task. . . .

No government or social system is so evil that its people must be considered as lacking in virtue. As Americans, we find Communism profoundly repugnant as a negation of personal freedom and dignity. But we can still hail the Russian people for their many achievements—in science and space, in economic and industrial growth, in culture and in acts of courage.

Among the many traits the peoples of our two countries have in common, none is stronger than our mutual abhorrence of war. Almost unique among the major world powers, we have never been at war with each other. And no nation in the history of battle ever suffered more than the Soviet Union in the second world war. At least 20,000,000 lost their lives. Countless millions of homes and families were burned or sacked. A third of the nation's territory, including two-thirds of its industrial base, was turned into a wasteland—a loss equivalent to the destruction of this country east of Chicago.

Today, should total war ever break out again—no matter how—our two countries will be the primary targets. It is an ironic but accurate fact that the two strongest powers are the two most in danger of devastation. All we have built, all we have worked for, would be destroyed in the first 24 hours. And even in the cold war—which brings burdens and dangers to so many countries, including this nation's closest allies—our two countries bear the heaviest burdens. For we are both devoting massive sums of money to weapons that could be better devoted to combat ignorance, poverty and disease.

We are both caught up in a vicious and dangerous cycle with suspicion on one side breeding suspicion on the other, and new weapons begetting counter-weapons.

In short, both the United States and its allies, and the Soviet Union and its allies, have a mutually deep interest in a just and genuine peace and in halting the arms race. Agreements to this end are in the interests of the Soviet Union as well as ours—and even the most hostile nations can be relied upon to accept and keep those treaty obligations . . . which are in their own interest.

So, let us not be blind to our differences—but let us also direct attention to our common interests and the means by which those differences can be resolved. And if we cannot end now our differences, at least we can help make the world safe for diversity. For, in the final analysis, our most basic common link is that we all inhabit this small planet. We all breathe the same air. We all cherish our children's future. And we are all mortal. . . .

I am taking this opportunity, therefore, to announce two important decisions:

First: Chairman Khrushchev, Prime Minister Macmillan and I have agreed that high-level discussions will shortly begin in Moscow toward early agreement on a comprehensive test ban treaty. Our hopes must be tempered with the caution of history— but with our hopes go the hopes of all mankind.

Second: To make clear our good faith and solemn convictions on the matter, I now declare that the United States does not propose to conduct nuclear tests in the atmosphere so long as other states do not do so. We will not be the first to resume. Such a declaration is no substitute for a formal binding treaty—but I hope it will help us achieve it. . . .

The United States, as the world knows, will never start a war. We do not want a war. We do not now expect a war. This generation of Americans has already had enough—more than enough—of war and hate and oppression. We shall be prepared if others wish it. We shall be alert to try to stop it. But we shall also do our part to build a world of peace where the weak are safe and the strong are just.

We are not helpless before that task or hopeless of its success. Confident and unafraid, we labor on—not toward a strategy of annihilation but toward a strategy of peace.

DISCUSSION QUESTIONS

1. How did the tone and substance of this speech differ from that of Kennedy's Inaugural Address? How do you account for the difference?
2. What conciliatory language can you find in Kennedy's speech? What Cold War rhetoric remains?
3. What reasoning did Kennedy use to persuade Americans of the need for a test ban treaty?
4. How did Kennedy explain his contention that Moscow would abide by such a treaty?
5. How did Kennedy demonstrate good faith in his proposal for a treaty?

43. Kennedy's Berlin Speech, June 1963: "Ich bin ein Berliner"

June 1963 was a tumultuous month for President Kennedy. His Peace Speech was followed the next day by a major address on civil rights. Three hours later Medgar Evers, a prominent black civil rights leader, was assassinated in his own driveway. In the midst of this tension, Kennedy flew to Europe and paid a visit to Berlin.

Speaking on a platform overlooking the Berlin Wall, surrounded by a huge crowd, Kennedy was in no mood to treat Moscow delicately. Hidden now was the conciliatory olive branch held out in the Peace Speech. Carried away by the drama of the occasion and his own inimitable rhetoric, Kennedy embellished the text crafted for him by his long-time speechwriter and *alter ego* Theodore Sorensen. The result was an emotional rallying cry that drove the crowd into a frenzy. More than a thousand people fainted during the brief address, and its impact astonished West German chancellor Konrad Adenauer and sobered Kennedy himself, who said later, "If I had told them to march on the wall and tear it down, they would have done it." It was not his greatest speech, but it would be among his most widely remembered.

Excerpts from Kennedy's Speech in Berlin, 26 June 1963

. . . Two thousand years ago the proudest boast was "civis Romanus sum [I am a Roman citizen]." Today in the world of freedom the proudest boast is "*Ich bin ein Berliner.*"

I appreciate my interpreter translating my German.

There are many people in the world who really don't understand . . . what is the great issue between the free world and the Communist world. Let them come to Berlin.

There are some who say that Communism is the wave of the future. Let them come to Berlin.

And there are some who say in Europe and elsewhere, "We can work with the Communists." Let them come to Berlin!

And there are even a few who say that it's true that Communism is an evil system but it permits us to make economic progress. Let them come to Berlin.

Freedom has many difficulties and democracy is not perfect. But we have never had to put a wall up to keep our people in, to prevent them from leaving us. . . .

I know of no town, no city that has been besieged for 18 years that still lives with the vitality and the force and the hope and the determination of the City of West Berlin.

While the wall is the most obvious and vivid demonstration of the failures of the Communist system, all the world can see we take no satisfaction in it, for it is, as your Mayor has said, an offense not only against history, but an offense against humanity, separating families, dividing husbands and wives and brothers and sisters and dividing a people who wish to be joined together. . . .

What is true of this city is true of Germany. Real lasting peace in Europe can never be assured as long as one German out of four is denied the elementary right of free men, and that is to make a free choice. . . .

You live in a defended island of freedom, but your life is part of the main. So let me ask you as I close to lift your eyes beyond the dangers of today to the hopes of tomorrow, beyond the freedom merely of this city of Berlin and all your country of Germany . . . to the advance of freedom everywhere, beyond the wall to the day of peace with justice, beyond yourselves and ourselves to all mankind.

Freedom is indivisible and when one man is enslaved, who are free? When all are free, then we can look forward to that day when this city will be joined as one with this country and this great continent of Europe in a peaceful and hopeful globe.

When that day finally comes, as it will, the people of West Berlin can take sober satisfaction in the fact that they were in the front lines for almost two decades.

All free men, wherever they may live, are citizens of Berlin. And therefore, as a free man, I take pride in the words "*Ich bin ein Berliner.*"

DISCUSSION QUESTIONS

1. How did the tone of Kennedy's Berlin address differ from that of his speech at American University? Why would Kennedy deliver so strident an anti-Communist address so soon after his "Peace Speech"?
2. In this address, how did Kennedy define the crucial issue preventing resolution of the German Question?
3. Listening to this speech only sixteen days after Kennedy's American University speech, what might Khrushchev have thought?
4. How did this address forecast the eventual solution of the German Question and the end of the Cold War?

44. The Nuclear Test Ban Treaty, August 1963

Kennedy's Berlin speech, strident as it was, did not undermine efforts to achieve a nuclear test ban treaty. These efforts, in fact, had been expedited by the United States when it decided to drop its earlier insistence upon on-site inspections. Since underground tests could not be easily detected without such inspections, given the technological limitations of the time, these tests were excluded from the agreement, making a *limited* test ban treaty.

The American action made a treaty possible by satisfying two key Soviet concerns: first, that Soviet facilities remain closed to outside inspection teams; and second, that some form of testing be permitted, since Soviet nuclear technology remained several years behind that of the United States. The treaty was signed by the Soviet Union, Great Britain, and the United States, but not by France, the only other power with atomic weapons in 1963.

Excerpts from the Limited Nuclear Test Ban Treaty, 5 August 1963

Article I

1. Each of the Parties to this Treaty undertakes to prohibit, to prevent, and not to carry out any nuclear weapon test explosion, or any other nuclear explosion, at any place under its jurisdiction or control:

(a) in the atmosphere; beyond its limits, including outer space; or underwater, including territorial waters or high seas; or

(b) in any other environment if such explosion causes radioactive debris to be present outside the territorial limits of the State under whose jurisdiction or control such explosion is conducted. It is understood in this connection that the provisions of this subparagraph are without prejudice to the conclusion of a treaty resulting in the permanent banning of all nuclear test explosions, including all such explosions underground. . . .

2. Each of the Parties to this Treaty undertakes furthermore to refrain from causing, encouraging, or in any way participating in, the carrying out of any nuclear weapon test explosion, or any other nuclear explosion, anywhere which would take place in any of the environments described, or have the effect referred to in paragraph 1 of this article.

Article II

1. Any Party may propose amendments to this Treaty. . . .

2. Any amendment to this Treaty must be approved by a majority of the votes of all Parties to this Treaty, including the votes of all the Original Parties.

Article III

1. This Treaty shall be open to all States for signature. . . .

2. This Treaty shall be subject to ratification by signatory States. . . .

3. This Treaty shall enter into force after its ratification by all the Original Parties. . . .

Article IV

This Treaty shall be of unlimited duration. . . .

DISCUSSION QUESTIONS

1. Why were underground tests not covered by the treaty? Why would the Soviets be pleased with their exclusion?
2. Why were outer space tests covered by the treaty, despite the fact that existing technology could not perform such tests?
3. What was paragraph 2 of Article I attempting to prevent?
4. Why did France refuse to sign the treaty? What potential problems might this refusal cause?

45. The Sino-Soviet Split, 1960–1963

Throughout the 1950s, despite increasing tensions between them, the USSR and Communist China maintained a façade of socialist solidarity. In 1960–1963, however, the dispute between the Communist giants became an open split. In 1960, the Soviets recalled their technicians from China and signed a generous treaty with India, and a Chinese publication called "Long Live Leninism" criticized the Soviet notion of peaceful coexistence and obliquely assailed the USSR by maligning Yugoslavia. Soon the Soviets retaliated with verbal attacks on China's close friend Albania. In 1961, when Khrushchev assaulted both Stalin and the Albanians at the 22nd Congress of the Soviet Communist Party, Chinese premier Zhou Enlai (Chou En-lai) objected and publicly laid a wreath at Stalin's tomb. In 1962, a bitter border dispute between Russia and China, combined with Chinese disgust at Khrushchev's backing down in the Cuban missile crisis and Soviet support for India in another border war with China, widened the breach still more. By 1963, the two nations were publicly assailing each other by name in open letters.

A. China's Publication of "Long Live Leninism," April 1960

In April of 1960, the editors of *Hongqi* (Red Flag), a journal published by the Central Committee of the Chinese Communist Party, issued an article called "Long Live Leninism" to mark the ninetieth anniversary of the birth of V. I. Lenin. Citing Lenin's identification of capitalism with imperialism as central to Leninist thought, the article criticized Communists who called for an end to war and pursued a path of peaceful cooperation with the capitalist West. According to the article, one of Leninism's basic tenets was that wars resulted inevitably from the actions of capitalist imperialists, whose relentless drive for markets, raw materials, and investment sources compelled them to seek military conquests and colonies to exploit. Wars would thus continue to occur as long as capitalist imperialist exploitation continued to exist.

Although the article was careful to praise the Soviet Union as the leader of the socialist camp, it vilified Yugoslav "revisionists," whom it accused of denying this basic truth by calling for peaceful cooperation with the capitalists, naively hoping that they would give up their colonies and wealth without a fight, and dreaming that capitalism would somehow peacefully transform itself into socialism. Stressing that Communist nations had a Leninist obligation to support socialist revolutions and wars of national liberation by colonized peoples against their imperialist oppressors, the Chinese editors insisted that attempts at peaceful cooperation with the West would merely perpetuate capitalist exploitation and imperialist oppression of the colonized peoples.

Although the article ostensibly targeted Yugoslav "revisionists," there was little doubt that, as its authors later tacitly admitted, its real targets were Nikita Khrushchev and the Soviet leadership, which had been seeking "peaceful coexistence" and better relations with the capitalist West. The article thus touched off an ideological war of words between the Soviet and Chinese Communists, as the Soviets responded first by criticizing China's Albanian allies, and later by openly and publicly disparaging the Chinese Communists themselves.

B. Excerpts from Khrushchev's Closing Remarks at the 22nd Party Congress, 27 October 1961*

. . .Some people attack us, charging that we seem to simplify or soften our assessment of the international situation when we stress the need for peaceful coexistence in present-day circumstances. They tell us that those who emphasize peaceful coexistence apparently underestimate the essence of imperialism. . . .

In our time the might of the world socialist system has grown as never before. It already unites more than a third of all humanity, and its

* *The Current Digest of the Soviet Press*, vol. XIII, No. 46 (December 13, 1961), 22–27.

forces are growing quickly; it is a great bastion of peace in our world. The principle of peaceful coexistence between countries with different social systems has attained vital significance in present-day circumstances.

This is not understood only by the hopeless dogmatists who, in repeating general formulas about imperialism, stubbornly turn away from life. . . .

Comrades! The report of the Central Committee, and also the remarks of delegates to the congress, spoke about the erroneous position of the leadership of the Albanian Labor Party, which set out to struggle against the tenets of the 20th Congress of our Party. . . .

It is clear that the Central Committee of our party had no choice but to tell the Congress the whole truth about the shameful position taken by the leadership of the Albanian Labor Party. If we had not done this, they would have continued to make it look as if the Central Committee of the Communist Party of the Soviet Union was afraid to inform the Party about its differences with the leadership of the Albanian Labor Party. . . .

At our Congress it has been emphasized that we are prepared to normalize relations with the Albanian Labor Party on the basis of Marxist-Leninist principles. How have the Albanian leaders responded to this? They have issued a brazen statement slinging mud at our party and its Central Committee.

The leader of the delegation of the Communist Party of China, Comrade Zhou Enlai, in his remarks expressed concern about the open consideration at our Congress of the question of Albanian-Soviet relations. As far as we can see, the main concern in his statement is that the current state of our relations with the Albanian Labor Party might affect the solidarity of the socialist camp.

We share the anxiety of our Chinese friends and appreciate their concern for the strengthening of unity. If our Chinese comrades wish to devote their energies to normalizing relations between the Albanian Labor Party and fraternal parties, it is doubtful that anyone could help accomplish this task better than the Communist Party of China. This would really work to the advantage of the Albanian Labor Party, and would serve the interests of the entire commonwealth of socialist countries. . . .

C. Excerpts from Open Letter of the Central Committee of the Soviet Communist Party to all Soviet Communists, 14 July 1963

The Central Committee of the CPSU [Communist Party of the Soviet Union] deems it necessary to address this open letter to you to set out our position on the fundamental questions of the international Communist movement in connection with the letter of the CPC (Communist Party of China) of June 14, 1963. . . .

For many years the relations between our parties were good. But some time ago, serious differences came to light between the CPC on the one hand and the CPSU and other fraternal parties on the other. . . .

For nearly half a century the Soviet country, under the leadership of the Communist Party, has been leading a struggle for the triumph of the ideas of Marxism-Leninism. . . .

The Soviet people generously shared with their Chinese brothers all their many years of long experience in Socialist construction, and their achievements in the field of science and technology. Our country has rendered and is rendering substantial aid to the development of the economy of People's China . . .

Our party—all Soviet people—rejoiced at the successes of the great Chinese people in the building of a new life, and took pride in them. . . .

This was how matters stood until the Chinese leaders began retreating from the general line of the world Communist movement.

In April 1960, the Chinese comrades openly disclosed their differences with the world Communist movement by publishing a collection of articles called "Long Live Leninism!" This collection, based on distortions—truncated and incorrectly interpreted theses of the well-known works of Lenin—contained propositions actually directed . . . against the policy of peaceful coexistence of states with different social systems, against the possibility of preventing a world war in the present day, against the use of both peaceful and non-peaceful roads of the development of Socialist revolutions.

The leaders of the CPC began imposing their views on all fraternal parties. . . . Furthermore, the Chinese comrades made their differences with the CPSU and other fraternal parties an object of open discussion in nonparty organizations. Such steps by the leadership of the CPC aroused and seriously troubled the fraternal parties. . . .

Unfortunately, the CPC leadership . . . continued pursuing its erroneous course and deepened its differences with the fraternal parties. . . .

In October 1961, the CPSU Central Committee undertook new attempts to normalize relations with the CPC. Comrades N. S. Khrushchev, F. R. Kozlov and A. I. Mikoyan had talks with Comrades Chou En-lai, Peng Cheng and other leading officials who arrived for the 22nd CPSU Congress. Comrade N. S. Khrushchev set forth to the Chinese delegation in detail the position of the CPSU Central Committee on the questions of principle which were discussed at the 22nd Congress, and stressed our invariable desire to strengthen friendship and cooperation with the Communist Party of China.

In its letters of February 22 and May 31, 1962, the CPSU Central Committee drew the attention of the CPC Central Committee to the dangerous consequences for our common cause that might be brought about by the weakening of the unity of the Communist movement. . . .

But the Chinese leaders, every time, ignored the comradely warnings of the CPSU, further exacerbating Chinese-Soviet relations. . . .

What is the gist of the differences between the CPC on the one hand, and the CPSU and the international Communist movement on the other hand? . . .

In point of fact . . . questions that bear on the vital interests of the peoples are in the center of the dispute. These are the questions of war and peace, the question of the role and development of the world Socialist system; these are the questions of struggle against the ideology and practice of the "personality cult"; these are the questions of strategy and tactics of the world labor movement and the national liberation struggle. . . .

Our party, in the decisions of the 20th and 22nd Congresses, . . . set before Communists as a task of extreme importance the task of struggling for peace, for averting a world thermonuclear catastrophe. . . . Suffice it to say that the explosion of only one powerful thermonuclear bomb surpasses the explosive force of all ammunition used during all previous wars, including World Wars I and II. And many thousands of such bombs have been accumulated! Do Communists have the right to ignore this danger? Do we have to tell the people all the truth about the consequences of thermonuclear war? We believe that undoubtedly we must. . . .

And what is the position of the CPC leadership? What do the theses that they propagate mean? An end cannot be put to wars as long as imperialism exists; peaceful coexistence is an illusion, . . . the struggle for peace hinders the revolutionary struggle? These theses mean that the Chinese comrades . . . do not believe in the possibility of preventing a new world war; they underestimate the forces of peace and Socialism and overestimate the forces of imperialism; they actually ignore the mobilization of the popular masses to the struggle with the war danger. . . .

The Chinese comrades obviously underestimate all the danger of thermonuclear war. "The atomic bomb is a paper tiger; it is not terrible at all," they contend. . . .

We would like to ask the Chinese comrades—who suggest building a bright future on the ruins of the old world destroyed by thermonuclear war—if they have consulted the working class of the countries where imperialism predominates. . . . The working class, the working people, will say to such "revolutionaries": "What right do you have to settle for us the questions of our existence and our class struggle? We are in favor of Socialism, but we want to gain it through the class struggle and not by unleashing a world war." . . .

The deep difference . . . on the questions of war, peace, and peaceful coexistence, was manifested with particular clarity during the 1962 crisis in the Caribbean Sea. . . . The Chinese comrades allege that in the period of the Caribbean crisis we made an "adventurist" mistake by introducing rockets in Cuba, and then "capitulated to American imperialism" when we removed the rockets from Cuba. . . . Such assertions utterly contradict the facts.

What was the actual state of affairs? The . . . Soviet Government possessed trustworthy information that an armed aggression of United States imperialism against Cuba was about to start. We realized . . . that the most resolute steps were needed to rebuff aggression, to defend the Cuban revolution effectively. . . .

The delivery of missiles to Cuba signified that an attack on her would meet resolute rebuff, with the employment of rocket weapons against the organizers of the aggression. . . .

Inasmuch as the point in question was not simply a conflict between the United States and Cuba but a clash between two major nuclear powers, . . . a real danger of world thermonuclear war arose. There was one alternative in the prevailing situation: either to . . . embark upon the road of unleashing a world thermonuclear war or, profiting by the opportunities offered by the delivery of missiles, to take all measures to reach an agreement on the peaceful solution of the crisis and prevent aggression against the Cuban Republic. We have chosen . . . the second road, and we are convinced that we have done the right thing. . . .

Agreement on the removal of missile weapons, in reply to the United States Government's commitment not to invade Cuba . . . have made possible the frustration of the plans of the extreme adventuristic circles of American imperialism, which were ready to go whole hog. As a result, it was possible to defend revolutionary Cuba and save peace. . . .

DISCUSSION QUESTIONS

1. What were the main issues involved in the Sino-Soviet dispute? Why were the Chinese upset about Soviet policies? How did the Soviets defend themselves against Chinese criticism?
2. Who were the actual "revisionists" referred to in "Long Live Leninism"? Why did the Chinese think it was harmful for Communists to pursue peaceful cooperation with the capitalist West?
3. At the 22nd Party Congress, why did Khrushchev attack Albania? Why did he not criticize China directly? Why did the Chinese object to the attack on Albania?
4. What were the implications of the Sino-Soviet split for both the Communist movement and the Cold War? What potential advantages and disadvantages did it provide the West?

46. THE GULF OF TONKIN RESOLUTION, 1964

During the early 1960s, in an effort to bolster the government of South Vietnam against a Communist insurgency, President Kennedy sent increasing numbers of American military advisors to that embattled land. After Kennedy's assassination in November 1963, his successor, Lyndon Johnson, continued to expand the U.S. role, especially after Communist North Vietnam began sending troops to join the fray in August 1964.

That same month, American surveillance ships in the Gulf of Tonkin, off the coast of North Vietnam, were reportedly attacked by North Vietnamese patrol boats. What actually occurred was not clear, but following the incident Johnson obtained congressional approval of a joint resolution giving him extensive authority to use military force in Southeast Asia.

This resolution became the main legal basis for American involvement in the Vietnam War. It enabled Johnson, who presented himself as a peace candidate in the 1964 elections, to avoid asking Congress for a declaration of war while gaining the powers he needed to fight one. Later, it allowed him to continue the war without having to jeopardize congressional support for his ambitious domestic agenda by seeking a formal declaration. So he used the resolution to fight an undeclared war, refusing to raise taxes or call up the reserves. The resulting economic and political pressures drove up the rate of inflation, weakened the U.S. economy, and helped convince Johnson not to seek reelection in 1968.

The Gulf of Tonkin Resolution, 10 August 1964

Whereas naval units of the Communist regime in Vietnam, in violation of the Charter of the United Nations and of international law, have deliberately and repeatedly attacked United States naval vessels lawfully present in international waters, and have thereby created a serious threat to international peace; and

Whereas these attacks are part of a deliberate and systematic campaign of aggression that the Communist regime in North Vietnam has been waging against its neighbors and the nations joined with them in the collective defense of their freedom; and

Whereas the United States is assisting the peoples of southeast Asia to protect their freedom and has no territorial, military or political ambitions in that area, but desires only that these peoples should be left in peace to work out their own destinies in their own way; Now, therefore, be it RESOLVED BY THE SENATE AND HOUSE OF REPRESENTATIVES OF THE UNITED STATES OF AMERICA IN CONGRESS ASSEMBLED, That the Congress approves and supports the determination of the President, as Commander in Chief, to take all necessary measures to repel any armed attack against the forces of the United States and to prevent further aggression.

SEC 2. The United States regards as vital to its national interest and to world peace the maintenance of international peace and security in Southeast Asia. Consonant with the Constitution and the Charter of the United Nations and in accordance with its obligations under the Southeast Asia Collective Defense Treaty, the United States is, therefore, prepared to take all necessary steps, including the use of armed force, to assist any member or protocol state of the Southeast Asia Collective Defense Treaty requesting assistance in defense of its freedom.

SEC. 3. This resolution shall expire when the President shall determine that the peace and security of the area is reasonably assured by international conditions created by action of the United Nations or otherwise, except that it may be terminated earlier by concurrent resolution of the Congress.

DISCUSSION QUESTIONS

1. What was so unusual about the way President Johnson used the Gulf of Tonkin Resolution?
2. What alleged events does the resolution use to justify American actions? Why?
3. To what external documents does the Resolution refer in providing a context for American actions? Why?
4. Why did Johnson decide to seek a congressional resolution rather than a declaration of war? What were the potential advantages and disadvantages of this decision?

47. Lin Biao, "Long Live the Victory of People's War," 1965

Lin Biao was the foremost military hero of China's Communist revolution. His skillfully orchestrated campaigns against the Nationalists in 1947–1949 were instrumental in bringing victory to the Communist People's Liberation Army (PLA). He grew in political stature throughout the 1950s and by 1965 was one of the closest confidants of Chairman Mao Zedong (Mao Tse-tung). Later, becoming impatient for the demise of the aging Mao and disagreeing with the decision of Mao and Zhou Enlai to seek better relations with the United States, Lin mounted an unsuccessful coup attempt in September1971. He was killed when his plane crashed as he fled toward exile in the Soviet Union.

In 1965, ostensibly to commemorate the twentieth anniversary of China's victory over Japan, Lin published a noteworthy article, "Long Live the Victory of People's War." It celebrated the crucial role of guerrilla warfare in bringing about the triumph of Communist revolution. But since guerrilla warfare had not played a decisive role in the defeat of Japan, his article was seen as having been motivated by the guerrilla war then raging in Vietnam. While carefully paying homage to the thought of Mao Zedong, Lin stressed the importance of unconventional combat in the emerging nations of Asia, Africa, and Latin America in assisting the inevitable triumph of Communism throughout the world.

Excerpts from "Long Live the Victory of People's War," 3 September 1965*

. . . If they are to defeat a formidable enemy, revolutionary armed forces should not fight with a reckless disregard for the consequences when there is a great disparity between their own strength and the enemy's. If they do, they will suffer serious losses and bring heavy setbacks to the revolution. Guerrilla warfare is the only way to mobilize and apply the whole strength of the people against the enemy, . . . to expand our forces in the course of the war, deplete and weaken the enemy, gradually change the balance of forces between the enemy and ourselves, switch from guerrilla to mobile warfare, and finally defeat the enemy. . . .

In order to annihilate the enemy, we must adopt the policy of luring him in deep and abandon some cities and districts of our own accord in a planned way, so as to let him in. It is only after letting the enemy in that the people can take part in the war in various ways and that the power of a people's war can be fully exerted. It is only after letting the enemy in that he can be compelled to divide up his forces, take on heavy burdens and commit mistakes. In other words, we must let the enemy become elated, stretch out all his ten fingers and become hopelessly bogged down. Thus, we can concentrate superior forces to destroy the enemy forces one by one, to eat them up mouthful by mouthful. Only by wiping out the enemy's effective strength can cities and localities be finally held or seized. We are firmly against dividing up our forces to defend all positions and putting up resistance at every place for fear that our territory might be lost. . . , since this can neither wipe out the enemy forces nor hold cities or localities.

Comrade Mao Tse-tung has provided a masterly summary of the strategy and tactics of people's war: You fight in your way and we fight in ours; we fight when we can win and move away when we can't.

In other words, you rely on modern weapons and we rely on highly conscious revolutionary people; you give full play to your superiority and we give full play to ours; you have your way of fighting and we have ours. When you want to fight us, we don't let you and you can't even find us. But when we want to fight you, we make sure that you can't get away and we hit you squarely on the chin and wipe you out. When we are able to wipe you out, we do so with a vengeance; when we can't, we see to it that you don't wipe us out. It is opportunism if one won't fight when one can['t] win. It is adventurism if one insists on fighting when one can't win. Fighting is the pivot of all our strategy and tactics. It is because of the necessity of fighting that we admit the necessity of moving away. The sole purpose of moving away is to fight and bring about the final and complete destruction of the enemy. This

* Lin Piao (Lin Biao), "Long Live the Victory of the People's War!" *Beijing Review*, Vol. XIII, No. 36 (September 3, 1965), pages 9–19, 22–30. Used by permission of *Beijing Review*.

strategy and these tactics can be applied only when one relies on the broad masses of the people, and such application brings the superiority of people's war into full play. However superior he may be in technical equipment and whatever tricks he may resort to, the enemy will find himself in the passive position of having to receive blows, and the initiative will always be in our hands. . . .

In order to make a revolution and to fight a people's war and be victorious, it is imperative to adhere to the policy of self-reliance, rely on the strength of the masses in one's own country and prepare to carry on the fight independently even when all material aid from outside is cut off. If one does not operate by one's own efforts, does not independently ponder and solve the problems of the revolution in one's own country and does not rely on the strength of the masses, but leans wholly on foreign aid—even though this be aid from socialist countries which persist in revolution—no victory can be won, or be consolidated even if it is won. . . .

The history of people's war in China and other countries provides conclusive evidence that the growth of the people's revolutionary forces from weak and small beginnings into strong and large forces is a universal law of development of class struggle, a universal law of development of people's war. A people's war inevitably meets with many difficulties, with many ups and downs and setbacks in the course of its development, but no force can alter its general trend toward inevitable triumph. . . .

Taking the entire globe, if North America and Western Europe can be called "the cities of the world," then Asia, Africa and Latin America constitute "the rural areas of the world." Since World War II, the proletarian revolutionary movement has . . . been temporarily held back in the North American and West European capitalist countries, while the people's revolutionary movement in Asia, Africa and Latin America has been growing vigorously. In a sense, the contemporary world revolution also presents a picture of the encirclement of cities by the rural areas. In the final analysis, the whole cause of world revolution hinges on the revolutionary struggles of the Asian, African and Latin American peoples who make up the overwhelming majority of the world's population. The socialist countries should regard it as their internationalist duty to support the people's revolutionary struggles in Asia, Africa and Latin America. . . .

Ours is the epoch in which world capitalism and imperialism are heading for their doom and socialism and communism are marching to victory. Comrade Mao Tse-tung's theory of people's war is not only a product of the Chinese revolution, but has also the characteristics of our epoch. The new experience gained in the people's revolutionary struggles in various countries since World War II has provided continuous evidence that Mao Tse-tung's thought is a common asset of the revolutionary people of the whole world. . . .

All peoples suffering from US imperialist aggression, oppression and plunder, unite! Hold aloft the just banner of people's war and fight for the cause of world peace, national liberation, people's democracy and socialism! Victory will certainly go to the people of the world! Long live the victory of people's war!

DISCUSSION QUESTIONS

1. For Lin Biao, what was the importance of "letting the enemy in"?
2. Why did Lin assert that the conventional military doctrine of defending all fixed positions was invalid under the conditions of people's war?
3. According to Lin Biao, what was the importance of self-reliance in a people's war?
4. What did Mao and Lin mean by the phrase, "You fight in your way and we fight in ours"?
5. How can you tell that this article was written by a Marxist?

48. Lyndon Johnson and the Vietnam War, 1965–1968

Following the Gulf of Tonkin resolution, U.S. involvement in the Vietnam War escalated as President Johnson sent in more and more troops. In April 1965, in a major speech at Johns Hopkins University, the president sought to explain and justify this conflict.

As time went on, however, increasing numbers of Americans began to question the U.S. role. Protest marches and demonstrations, at first isolated and small, gradually became larger and more significant. The Senate Foreign Relations Committee held a series of public hearings designed to cast doubt on the wisdom of war, and domestic protest escalated to serious proportions by spring 1968. Johnson made numerous overtures to North Vietnam to begin negotiations, but since his offers were predicated on the continued independence of South Vietnam (a condition Hanoi would not accept), his efforts were frustrating and futile.

In 1968, the American antiwar movement found a champion in Senator Eugene McCarthy of Minnesota, who challenged Johnson in the New Hampshire presidential primary. McCarthy won on absentee ballots, instantly legitimizing the political viability of the peace movement. Senator Robert F. Kennedy of New York, younger brother of the slain president, saw the implications of McCarthy's showing and entered the race himself; many who opposed the war but did not consider McCarthy presidential material switched to Kennedy. Meanwhile, Johnson came under pressure from his aides and from elder statesmen like Dean Acheson to pull America out of the war. Disillusioned and exhausted, he addressed the nation on Sunday evening, 31 March 1968, to proclaim a new peace initiative. Then, in a surprise ending that stunned many listeners, he announced that he was withdrawing from the presidential race. The war had claimed yet another victim: Johnson's political career.

A. Johnson's Speech at Johns Hopkins University, 7 April 1965

. . . Tonight Americans and Asians are dying for a world where each people may choose its own path to change. This is the principle for which our ancestors fought in the valleys of Pennsylvania. It is the principle for which our sons fight in the jungles of Vietnam.

Vietnam is far from this quiet campus. We have no territory there, nor do we seek any. The war is dirty and brutal and difficult. And some 400 young men—born into an America bursting with opportunity and promise—have ended their lives on Vietnam's steaming soil.

Why must we take this painful road? Why must this nation hazard its ease, its interest and its power for the sake of a people so far away? . . .

Why are we in South Vietnam? We are there because we have a promise to keep. Since 1954 every American President has offered support to the people of South Vietnam. We have helped to build and we have helped to defend. Thus, over many years, we have made a national pledge to help South Vietnam defend its independence. I intend to keep our promise. To dishonor that pledge, to abandon this small and brave nation to its enemy—and the terror that must follow—would be an unforgivable wrong.

We are also there to strengthen world order. Around the globe, from Berlin to Thailand, are people whose well-being rests, in part, on the belief that they can count on us if they are attacked. To leave Vietnam to its fate would shake the confidence of all these people in the value of American commitment. The result would be an increased unrest and instability, or even war.

We are also there because there are great stakes in the balance. Let no one think that retreat from Vietnam would bring an end to conflict. The battle would be renewed in one country and then another. The central lesson of our time is that the appetite of aggression is never satisfied. To withdraw from one battlefield means only to prepare for the next. We must say in Southeast Asia—as we did in Europe—in the words of the Bible: "Hitherto shalt thou come, but no further." . . .

Our objective is the independence of South Vietnam, and its freedom from attack. We want nothing for ourselves—only that the people of South Vietnam be allowed to guide their own country in their own way. We will do everything necessary to reach that objective. And we will do only what is necessary. . . . We will not be defeated. We will not grow tired. We will not withdraw, either openly or under the cloak of a meaningless agreement. . . .

B. Johnson's Address to the Nation, 31 March 1968

. . . Tonight, I renew the offer I made last August: to stop the bombardment of North Vietnam. We ask that talks begin promptly, that they be serious talks on the substance of peace. We assume that during those talks, Hanoi will not take advantage of our restraint.

We are prepared to move immediately toward peace through negotiations. So tonight, in the hope that this action will lead to early talks, I am taking the first step to de-escalate the conflict. We are reducing—substantially reducing—the present level of hostilities, and we are doing so unilaterally and at once.

Tonight I have ordered our aircraft and our naval vessels to make no attacks on North Vietnam except in the area north of the demilitarized zone where the continuing enemy build-up directly threatens allied forward positions and where the movement of their troops and supplies are clearly related to that threat. The area in which we are stopping our attacks includes almost 90 percent of North Vietnam's population, and most of its territory. Thus there will be no attacks around the principal populated areas, or in the food-producing areas of North Vietnam. . . .

Now let me give you my estimate of the chances for peace—the peace that will one day stop the bloodshed in South Vietnam [so that] all the Vietnamese people will be permitted to rebuild and develop their land. . . .

I cannot promise that the initiative that I have announced tonight will be completely successful in achieving peace any more than the thirty others that we have undertaken and agreed to in recent years. . . . But it is our fervent hope that North Vietnam, after years of fighting that has left the issue unresolved, will now cease its efforts to achieve a military victory and will join with us in moving toward the peace table. And there may come a time when . . . Vietnamese—on both sides—are able to work out a way to settle their own differences by free political choice rather than by war. . . .

During the past four and a half years, it has been my fate and my responsibility to be Commander-in-Chief. I have lived daily and nightly with the cost of this war. I know the pain that it has inflicted. I know perhaps better than anyone the misgivings it has aroused. And throughout this entire long period I have been sustained by a single principle: that what we are doing now in Vietnam is vital not only to the security of Southeast Asia but it is vital to the security of every American. . . .

And the larger purpose of our involvement has always been to help the nations of Southeast Asia become independent, and stand alone, self-sustaining as members of a great world community, at peace with themselves, at peace with others. And with such a nation our country—and the world—will be far more secure than it is tonight. . . .

With America's sons in the fields far away, with America's future under challenge right here at home, with our hopes and the world's hopes for peace in the balance every day, I do not believe that I should devote an hour or a day of my time to any personal partisan causes or to any duties other than the awesome duties of this office—the Presidency of your country.

Accordingly, I shall not seek, and I will not accept, the nomination of my party for another term as your President. But let men everywhere know, however, that a strong and a confident and a vigilant America stands ready tonight to seek an honorable peace; and stands ready tonight to defend an honored cause, whatever the price, whatever the burden, whatever the sacrifice that duty may require. . . .

DISCUSSION QUESTIONS

1. According to President Johnson's Johns Hopkins speech, what principle was America seeking to defend in Vietnam?
2. What were the three reasons he listed to explain American presence in Southeast Asia? How might Americans have differed in their perceptions of the validity of those three reasons?
3. Why would Johnson's stated objective—the independence of South Vietnam and its freedom from attack—be difficult to attain?
4. What evidence of President Johnson's frustration can you find in his address to the nation of 31 March 1968?
5. Why did Johnson decide to withdraw from the presidential race? How did he expect this to help his peace efforts?

49. CHINA'S GREAT PROLETARIAN CULTURAL REVOLUTION, 1966–1969

In 1966, China's Mao Zedong launched a spectacular campaign of mass mobilization called the Great Proletarian Cultural Revolution. Millions of young people heeded his call to form radical militias called Red Guards that disrupted businesses and closed universities, forcing managers and professors to labor in the fields with the peasants. For the next few years, the Chinese largely withdrew from world affairs as their energies focused inward. The Red Guards vilified not only capitalists but also the Soviet system, calling it bureaucratic and elitist, and even besieged the Soviet embassy in Beijing in 1967. They also held mass rallies to glorify their leader, waving copies of his "Little Red Book," *Quotations from Chairman Mao*, a collection of excerpts from his writings and sayings, which his youthful followers could recite by heart.

Excerpts from the "Little Red Book," *Quotations from Chairman Mao Tse-Tung*

A revolution is not a dinner party, or writing an essay, or painting a picture, or doing embroidery; it cannot be so refined, so leisurely and gentle, so temperate, kind, courteous, restrained and magnanimous. A revolution is an insurrection, an act of violence by which one class overthrows another.

Whoever sides with the revolutionary people is a revolutionary. Whoever sides with imperialism, feudalism and bureaucrat-capitalism is a counter-revolutionary . . .

Every Communist must grasp the truth, "Political power grows out of the barrel of a gun."

All reactionaries are paper tigers. In appearance, the reactionaries are terrifying, but in reality they are not so powerful. From a long-term point of view, it is not the reactionaries but the people who are really powerful.

. . . There are two winds in the world today, the East Wind and the West Wind. There is a Chinese saying, "Either the East Wind prevails over the West Wind or the West Wind prevails over the East Wind." I believe . . . that the East Wind is prevailing over the West Wind. That is to say, the forces of socialism have become overwhelmingly superior to the forces of imperialism.

The revolutionary war is a war of the masses; it can be waged only by mobilizing the masses and relying on them.

The people, and the people alone, are the motive force in the making of world history.

The masses are the real heroes, while we ourselves are often childish and ignorant . . .

The atom bomb is a paper tiger which the US reactionaries use to scare people. It looks terrible, but . . . the outcome of a war is decided by the people, not by . . . new types of weapon.

Every comrade must . . . understand that as long as we rely on the people, believe firmly in the inexhaustible creative power of the masses and hence trust and identify ourselves with them, we can surmount any difficulty, and no enemy can crush us while we can crush any enemy.

We should be modest and prudent, guard against arrogance and rashness, and serve the Chinese people heart and soul. . . .

Be resolute, fear no sacrifice and surmount every difficulty to win victory.

We Communists are like seeds and the people are like the soil. Wherever we go, we must unite with the people, take root and blossom among them.

You young people, full of vigour and vitality, are in the bloom of life, like the sun at eight or nine in the morning. Our hope is placed on you . . . The world belongs to you. China's future belongs to you.

The young people are the most active and vital force in society. They are the most eager to learn and the least conservative in their thinking . . .

DISCUSSION QUESTIONS

1. Why did the Cultural Revolution initially rely on the revolutionary fervor of young people? Why did so many Chinese youths respond to Mao's call to form and join Red Guards?
2. What benefits could China hope to gain from the Cultural Revolution? What potential dangers did it pose for Chinese society and national security?
3. Why did the Cultural Revolution and the Red Guards rely heavily on Mao's sayings? How did some of these sayings relate to the Cold War?

50. The Nuclear Non-Proliferation Treaty, July 1968

In 1964, China successfully tested an atomic bomb, thereby joining the "nuclear club" and frightening both the Soviets and the West. India and Pakistan were rumored to be developing such weapons, and Israel was believed to have secretly done so. In an effort to prevent the further spread of nuclear weapons, America, Britain, and the USSR began to discuss a treaty to halt nuclear proliferation, finally reaching agreement in 1968. Many other nations signed it, but France and China refused to do so until 1993, when the treaty was amended and renewed.

Treaty on the Non-Proliferation of Nuclear Weapons, 1 July 1968

The States concluding this Treaty, hereinafter referred to as the "Parties to the Treaty."

Considering the devastation that would be visited upon all mankind by a nuclear war and the consequent need to make every effort to avert the danger of such a war . . . ,

Believing that the proliferation of nuclear weapons would seriously enhance the danger of nuclear war,

In conformity with resolutions of the United Nations General Assembly calling for the conclusion of an agreement on the prevention of wider dissemination of nuclear weapons. . . .

Desiring to further the easing of international tension and the strengthening of trust between States in order to facilitate the cessation of the manufacture of nuclear weapons, the liquidation of all their existing stockpiles, and the elimination from national arsenals of nuclear weapons and the means of their delivery . . . ,

Have agreed as follows:

Article I

Each nuclear-weapon State Party to the Treaty undertakes not to transfer to any recipient whatsoever nuclear weapons or other nuclear explosive devices or control over such weapons or explosive devices directly, or indirectly; and not in any way to assist, encourage, or induce any non-nuclear-weapon State to manufacture or otherwise acquire nuclear weapons or other nuclear explosive devices, or control over such weapons or explosive devices.

Article II

Each non-nuclear-weapon State Party to the Treaty undertakes not to receive the transfer from any transferor whatsoever of nuclear weapons or other nuclear explosive devices or of control over such weapons or explosive devices directly, or indirectly; not to manufacture or otherwise acquire nuclear weapons or other nuclear explosive devices; and not to seek or receive any assistance in the manufacture of nuclear weapons or other nuclear explosive devices.

Article III

. . . 2. Each State Party to the Treaty undertakes not to provide: (a) source or special fissionable material, or (b) equipment or material especially designed or prepared for the processing, use or production of special fissionable material, to any non-nuclear weapon State for peaceful purposes, unless the source or special fissionable material shall be subject to the safeguards required by this article. . . .

Article IV

1. Nothing in this Treaty shall be interpreted as affecting the inalienable right of all the Parties to the Treaty to develop research, production and use of nuclear energy for peaceful purposes without discrimination and in conformity with Articles I and II of this Treaty . . .

DISCUSSION QUESTIONS

1. Why did the British, Americans, and Soviets all favor a nuclear nonproliferation treaty?
2. Why did France and China initially refused to sign it?
3. What was the treaty's potential effect on nuclear research and peaceful uses of atomic energy?
4. What did the treaty mean by "nuclear weapons or other nuclear explosive devices"?

51. The Soviet Invasion of Czechoslovakia, August 1968

In spring of 1968 Alexander Dubček, the new head of the Czechoslovak Communist Party, began enacting reforms designed to bring his nation a measure of freedom and democracy. For months Moscow closely watched the situation and tried to pressure Czech leaders to moderate their reforms. Finally, on the evening of 20–21 August, the USSR attacked its socialist ally with troops and tanks, eventually reversing the reforms and reasserting Soviet control. The invasion sparked international outrage, even in such Communist countries as Romania and Yugoslavia. Communist China, in particular, was frightened and appalled by Moscow's readiness to intervene in socialist countries that resisted Soviet control.

A. Statement of Czechoslovak Communist Party Presidium, 21 August 1968

. . . Yesterday . . . troops of the Soviet Union, Polish People's Republic, the GDR [East Germany], the Hungarian People's Republic, and the Bulgarian People's Republic crossed the frontiers of the Czechoslovak Socialist Republic.

This happened without the knowledge of the President of the Republic . . . or the First Secretary of the Czechoslovak Communist party Central Committee. . . .

The . . . Presidium appeals to all citizens of our republic to maintain calm and not to offer resistance to the troops on the march. Our army, security corps and people's militia have not received the command to defend the country.

The . . . Presidium regard this act as contrary not only to the fundamental principles of relations between Socialist states but also as contrary to the principles of international law. . . .

B. Statement of Soviet News Agency (TASS), 21 August 1968

Tass is authorized to state that party and Government leaders of the Czechoslovak Socialist Republic have asked the Soviet Union and other allied states to render the fraternal Czechoslovak people urgent assistance, including assistance with armed forces. This request was brought about by the threat . . . emanating from the counterrevolutionary forces which have entered into a collusion with foreign forces hostile to Socialism. . . .

The further aggravation of the situation in Czechoslovakia affects the vital interests of the Soviet Union and other Socialist states . . . [and] constitutes at the same time a threat to the mainstays of European peace. . . .

The actions which are being taken are not directed against any state and in no measure infringe state interests of anybody. They serve the purpose of peace and have been prompted by concern for its consolidation.

The fraternal countries firmly and resolutely counterpose their unbreakable solidarity to any threat from outside. Nobody will be ever allowed to wrest a single link from the community of socialist states.

DISCUSSION QUESTIONS

1. How did the Czechoslovak Presidium react to the Soviet invasion of Czechoslovakia?
2. What sort of resistance did it recommend?
3. How did the Soviet Union justify its invasion of Czechoslovakia?
4. Why would this invasion upset other Communist countries?

52. The Brezhnev Doctrine, 1968

In fall 1968, stung by the global outcry against its invasion of Czechoslovakia, the USSR sought to justify its actions. An article in *Pravda*, the Soviet Communist newspaper, declared that no Communists had the right to take actions detrimental to international socialism, implying that the Czechoslovaks had done so and that Moscow had been obliged to stop them. Later, in Poland, Soviet leader Brezhnev elaborated by asserting that a threat to socialism in any socialist nation was a threat to the security of the entire "socialist commonwealth." Implicit was the presumption, soon called the Brezhnev Doctrine, that as leader of the socialist commonwealth the USSR had a right to intervene in other Communist countries when it perceived their policies as detrimental to world socialism. Although Brezhnev denied its existence, this doctrine was not explicitly renounced by Moscow until 1989.

A. Excerpt from "Sovereignty and the International Obligations of Socialist Countries," *Pravda*, 26 September 1968*

. . . The peoples of the socialist countries and Communist parties certainly do have and should have freedom for determining the ways of advance of their respective countries. However, none of their decisions should damage either socialism in their country or the fundamental interests of other socialist countries, and the whole working class movement, which is working for socialism.

---

* "Sovereignty and International Duties of Socialist Countries," originally published in *Pravda* on September 26, 1968 and translated by Novosti, Soviet Press Agency. Reprinted in *The New York Times* September 27, 1968.

This means that each Communist party is responsible not only to its own people, but also to all the socialist countries, to the entire Communist movement. Whoever forgets this, in stressing only the independence of the Communist party, becomes one-sided. He deviates from his international duty. . . .

Each Communist party is free to apply the basic principles of Marxism-Leninism and of socialism in its country, but it cannot depart from these principles. . . .

Concretely, this means, first of all, that in its activity, each Communist party cannot but take into account such a decisive fact of our time as the struggle between two opposing social systems—capitalism and socialism. . . .

The system of socialism exists in concrete form in some countries, which have their own definite state boundaries; this system is developing according to the specific conditions of each country. Furthermore, nobody interferes in the concrete measures taken to improve the socialist system in the different socialist countries.

However, the picture changes fundamentally when a danger arises to socialism itself in a particular country. As a social system world socialism is the common gain of the working people of all lands; it is indivisible and its defense is the common cause of all Communists and all progressives in the world, in the first place, the working folk of the socialist countries. . . .

The interests of the socialist community and of the whole revolutionary movement, the interests of socialism in Czechoslovakia demand complete exposure and political isolation of the reactionary forces in that country, consolidation of the working people and consistent implementation of the Moscow agreement between the Soviet and Czechoslovak leaders. . . .

B. Excerpt From Brezhnev's Remarks to the Polish Party Congress, 12 November 1968*

. . . It is well known that the Soviet Union has done much to really strengthen the sovereignty and independence of socialist countries. The CPSU has always asserted that every socialist country must determine the concrete forms of its own development on the path to socialism, in accordance with the specific features of its national circumstances. But it is also known, comrades, that there exist general laws of socialist development, deviation from which could lead to deviation from socialism as such. And when internal and external forces hostile to socialism seek to turn the development of any socialist country toward restoring the capitalist order, when there arises a threat to the cause of socialism in that country—a threat to the security of the socialist commonwealth as a whole—this already becomes not only a problem for the people of that country, but also a common problem, the concern of all socialist countries.

Clearly, such action as military aid to a fraternal country to suppress a threat to the socialist order—this is an extraordinary, forced measure which can be provoked only by the direct activity of the enemies of socialism inside the country and beyond its borders, actions which create a threat to the general interests of the socialist camp. . . .

DISCUSSION QUESTIONS

1. Why did Moscow feel compelled to justify its actions in Czechoslovakia? Why did *Pravda* say that all Communist parties were responsible to the entire communist movement?
2. Why did Brezhnev say that a threat to socialism in any socialist country was a threat to whole socialist commonwealth? Under what conditions did he think that one socialist country should intervene in the affairs of another?
3. Why would the Brezhnev Doctrine increase tensions between the USSR and the China?
4. What were the similarities and differences between the Brezhnev Doctrine and the Truman Doctrine (Document 7)?

---

* *The Current Digest of the Soviet Press*, vol. XX, No. 46 (December 4, 1968), 3–5.

53. The Soviet–Chinese Border Conflict, 1969

On 2 March 1969, a clash occurred between Chinese and Soviet troops over an island in the river separating Russia from Manchuria. More than thirty Soviet soldiers were killed, eventually prompting Moscow to launch a powerful counter-attack. The documents excerpted here provide two very different accounts of what happened. By frightening both sides and inducing both to seek better relations with the West, these events had a profound impact on the Cold War.

A. Note from the Chinese Ministry of Foreign Affairs to the Soviet Embassy in China, 2 March 1969*

On the morning of March 2, 1969, Soviet frontier guards intruded into the area of Chenpao [Zhen Bao] Island, Heilunkiang Province, China, and killed and wounded many Chinese frontier guards by opening fire on them, thus creating an extremely grave border armed conflict. Against this, the Ministry of Foreign Affairs of the People's Republic of China is instructed to lodge the strongest protest with the Soviet Government.

At 0917 hours on March 2, large numbers of fully armed soldiers, together with four armored vehicles and cars, sent out by the Soviet frontier authorities, flagrantly intruded into the area of Chenpao Island which is indisputable Chinese territory, carried out blatant provocations against the Chinese frontier guards on normal patrol duty and were the first to open cannon and gun fire, killing and wounding many Chinese frontier guards. The Chinese frontier guards were compelled to fight back in self-defence when they reached the end of their forbearance after their repeated warnings to the Soviet frontier guards had produced no effect. This grave incident of bloodshed was entirely and solely created by the Soviet authorities. . . which have long been deliberately encroaching upon China's territory, carrying out armed provocations and creating ceaseless incidents of bloodshed.

The Chinese Government firmly demands that the Soviet Government punish the culprits of this incident and immediately stop its encroachment upon China's territory and its armed provocations, and reserves the right to demand compensation from the Soviet side for all the losses suffered by the Chinese side. The Chinese Government once again sternly warns the Soviet Government: China's sacred territory brooks no violation; if you should willfully cling to your reckless course and continue to provoke armed conflicts along the Sino-Soviet border, you will certainly receive resolute counterblows from the Chinese people; and it is the Soviet Government that must bear full responsibility for all the grave consequences arising therefrom.

B. Statement by Soviet Government, 29 March 1969**

Recently on the Ussuri River in the region of Damanskii [Zhen Bao] Island there have occurred armed border incidents provoked by the Chinese side. The Chinese authorities did not and cannot have any justification for the organization of these incidents or for the resulting clashes and bloodshed. Such events can only gladden those who want by any means to dig an abyss of enmity between the Soviet Union and the People's Republic of China. They have nothing in common with the basic interests of the Soviet and Chinese peoples.

The circumstances of the armed attacks on Soviet border guards on the Ussuri River are well

---

* "Note of the Ministry of Foreign Affairs of the People's Republic of China to the Soviet Embassy in China, March 2, 1969," *Beijing Review*, Vol. 12, No. 10 (March 7, 1969), pages 5, 7. Used by permission of *Beijing Review*.

** "Statement of USSR Government (*Pravda*, March 30, p. 1, *Izvestia*, pp. 1–2)," *The Current Digest of the Soviet Press*, vol. XXI, No. 13 (April 16, 1969), 3–5.

known. These were premeditated and previously planned actions.

On the morning of 2 March of this year, an observation post detected a transgression of the Soviet border at Damanskii Island by approximately 30 Chinese soldiers. A group of Soviet border guards headed by an officer made their way toward the transgressors with the aim of filing a protest . . . and insisting that they leave Soviet territory. The Chinese soldiers allowed the Soviet border guards to approach within several meters and then suddenly, without any warning, opened fire at them from pointblank range.

At the same time, from an ambush on Damanskii Island where the Chinese soldiers had earlier secretly moved under cover of darkness, and from the Chinese shore, artillery guns, mortars, and automatic weapons opened fire on another group of Soviet border guards located near the Soviet shore. They joined the battle and, with the support of a neighboring border post, drove the transgressors out of Soviet territory. As a result of this treacherous attack there were dead and wounded on both sides.

In spite of a warning from the Soviet government and a call to refrain from such provocations, on 14–15 March in this same region the Chinese side launched new attempts at armed intrusion into the Soviet Union. Elements of the regular Chinese army, supported by artillery and mortar fire, attacked the Soviet border troops protecting Damanskii Island. The attack was decisively repelled, and the transgressors were driven from Soviet territory. This provocation by the Chinese side generated new casualties.

Now the Chinese authorities in their statements are trying to avoid responsibility for the armed clashes. They claim that it was not the Chinese but the Soviet border guards who transgressed the state frontier, and that this island supposedly does not belong to the Soviet Union. The Chinese side does not dispute the fact that its military personnel acted according to a prepared plan, although by having recourse to a false assertion, it presents the use of arms by the Chinese transgressors as a "necessary measure." . . .

DISCUSSION QUESTIONS

1. In what ways do the Soviet and Chinese versions of this episode differ? How do you account for these differences?
2. Why did these border clashes become such important international incidents?
3. In the long run, why were the Chinese and the Soviets each anxious to avoid war?
4. Why did these border clashes lead each side to seek better relations with the West?

54. THE NIXON DOCTRINE, 1969

When Richard Nixon became president in January 1969, the United States was in the midst of a disastrous and unpopular conflict. The Vietnam War, and the growing realization that America was not winning, had sapped the people's morale and left them deeply divided. In line with his campaign promises, Nixon was eager to end the war and avoid the involvement of U.S. troops in any more such ventures. But as a staunch anti-Communist and devout Cold Warrior, he was also determined to protect U.S. interests and prevent Communist expansion.

One aspect of his approach was the Nixon Doctrine, which he first put forth in July 1969 while conversing with reporters on the island of Guam during a trip to Asia. Ruminating on America's role in Asia once the war in Vietnam was over, he speculated that the increasing independence and nationalism of Asian nations portended a more limited and less visible

American presence. Then, in response to a question, he set forth the heart of his new doctrine: The United States would expect its friends and clients in Asia to take increasing responsibility for their own internal security and military defense.

In November of that year, in a major speech on the Vietnam War, he spelled out this new approach. The United States would continue to uphold its treaty commitments and provide a nuclear shield for its allies and friends. However, in the event of conflict, although America would still supply extensive economic aid and military equipment, it would henceforth expect the nation involved to provide the troops and personnel for its own defense. This was embodied in his Vietnamization program, designed to gradually turn over the actual fighting in Southeast Asia to the forces of South Vietnam. But it was also intended as a general policy principle to preclude Vietnam-type debacles elsewhere in the future.

A. Excerpts from Nixon's Remarks at Guam, 25 July 1969

The United States is going to be facing, we hope before too long . . . a major decision: What will be its role in Asia and in the Pacific after the end of the war in Vietnam? We will be facing that decision, but also the Asian nations will be wondering about what that decision is. . . .

This is a decision that will have to be made, of course, as the war comes to an end. But the time to develop the thinking which will go into that decision is now. I think that one of the weaknesses in American foreign policy is that too often we react rather precipitately to events as they occur. We fail to have the perspective and the long range view which is essential for a policy that will be viable. . . .

Now, one other point I would make very briefly . . . as far as the role we should play, we must recognize that there are two great, new factors which you will see, . . . particularly when you arrive in the Philippines—something . . . that we didn't see in 1953, to show you how quickly it has changed: a very great growth of nationalism, nationalism . . . vis-a-vis the United States, as well as other countries in the world. And, also, at the same time that national pride is becoming a major factor, regional pride is becoming a major factor.

The second factor is one that is going to . . . have a major impact on the future of Asia. . . . Asians will say in every country that we visit that they do not want to be dictated to from the outside, Asia for the Asians. And that is what we want, and that is the role we should play. We should assist, but we should not dictate.

At this time, the political and economic plans that they are gradually developing are very hopeful. We will give assistance to those plans. We, of course, will keep the treaty commitments that we have. But as far as our role is concerned, we must avoid that kind of policy that will make countries in Asia so dependent upon us that we are dragged into conflicts such as the one that we have in Vietnam. . . .

. . . I believe that the time has come when the United States, in our relations with all of our Asian friends, [must] be quite emphatic on two points: One, that we will keep our treaty commitments, our treaty commitments, for example, with Thailand under SEATO; but, two, that as far as the problems of internal security are concerned, as far as the problems of military defense, except for the threat of a major power involving nuclear weapons, that the United States is going to encourage and has a right to expect that this problem will be increasingly handled by . . . the Asian nations themselves.

I believe, incidentally, from my preliminary conversations with several Asian leaders over the past few months that they are going to be willing to undertake this responsibility. It will not be easy. But if the United States just continues down the road of responding to requests for assistance, of assuming the primary responsibility for defending these countries when they have internal problems or external problems, they are never going to take care of themselves.

B. Excerpts from Nixon's Address to the Nation, 3 November 1969

At the time we launched our search for peace I recognized we might not succeed in bringing an end to the war through negotiation. I, therefore, put into effect another plan to bring peace—a plan which will bring the war to an end regardless of what happens on the negotiating front.

It is in line with a major shift in US foreign policy which I described in my press conference at Guam on July 25. Let me briefly explain what has been described as the Nixon Doctrine—a policy which not only will help end the war in Vietnam, but which is an essential element of our program to prevent future Vietnams.

We Americans are a do-it-yourself people. We are an impatient people. Instead of teaching someone else to do a job, we like to do it ourselves. And this trait has been carried over into our foreign policy. In Korea and again in Vietnam, the United States furnished most of the money, most of the arms, and most of the men to help the people of those countries defend their freedom against Communist aggression.

Before any American troops were committed to Vietnam, a leader of another Asian country expressed this opinion to me when I was traveling in Asia as a private citizen. He said: "When you are trying to assist another nation to defend its freedom, US policy should be to help them fight the war but not to fight the war for them."

Well, in accordance with this wise counsel, I laid down in Guam three principles as guidelines for future American policy toward Asia:

- First, the United States will keep all of its treaty commitments.
- Second, we shall provide a shield if a nuclear power threatens the freedom of a nation allied with us or of a nation whose survival we consider vital to our security.
- Third, in cases involving other types of aggression, we shall furnish military and economic assistance when requested in accordance with our treaty commitments. But we shall look to the nation directly threatened to assume the primary responsibility of providing the manpower for its defense.

After I announced this policy, I found that the leaders of the Philippines, Thailand, Vietnam, South Korea, and other nations which might be threatened by Communist aggression, welcomed this new direction in American foreign policy.

The defense of freedom is everybody's business—not just America's business. And it is particularly the responsibility of the people whose freedom is threatened. . . .

DISCUSSION QUESTIONS

1. Why did Nixon first float his new approach in a meeting with reporters, rather than proclaiming it at once as a basic policy doctrine?
2. According to Nixon, what was wrong with U.S. policy in Asia prior to the Nixon Doctrine?
3. What reasons did he give for the promulgation of the Nixon Doctrine? What other reasons might he have had that he did not mention?
4. How did Nixon expect the Asian nations to respond to his new doctrine? How did he expect the American people to respond?

55. The Berlin Accords, September 1971

After becoming West German chancellor in 1969, Willy Brandt set about to regularize relations with the Warsaw Pact, negotiating with Poland and the USSR as part of his "Eastern Policy" or *Ostpolitik*. He also opened discussions with East Germany in an effort to reduce the misery caused by the Berlin Wall. In 1971, his labors paid off when the four powers occupying Germany—the United States, Britain, France, and the USSR—signed an agreement on the status of West Berlin. The Berlin Accords removed the threat of East German harassment of traffic on highways linking West Berlin to West Germany, thus lessening the prospects of a repetition of the 1948–1949 Berlin Blockade (Document 14). In return for this restriction on its sovereignty over access routes, East Germany received *de facto* Western recognition as an independent state when its name appeared seven times in the document.

Quadripartite Agreement on Berlin, 3 September 1971

The Governments of the United States of America, the French Republic, the Union of Soviet Socialist Republics, and the United Kingdom of Great Britain and Northern Ireland,

Represented by their Ambassadors, who held a series of meetings in the building formerly occupied by the Allied Control Council in the American sector of Berlin,

Acting on the basis of their quadripartite rights and responsibilities, and of the corresponding wartime and postwar agreements and decisions of the four powers, which are not affected,

Taking into account the existing situation in the relevant area,

Guided by the desire to contribute to practical improvements of the situation,

Without prejudice to their legal positions,

Have agreed on the following. . . .

Part II: Provisions Relating to the Western Sectors of Berlin

A. The Government of the Union of Soviet Socialist Republics declares that transit traffic by road, rail and waterways through the territory of the German Democratic Republic [East Germany] of civilian persons and goods between the western sectors of Berlin and the Federal Republic of Germany [West Germany] will be unimpeded; that such traffic will be facilitated so as to take place in the most simple and expeditious manner; and that it will receive preferential treatment. . . .

B. The Governments of the French Republic, the United Kingdom and the United States of America declare that the ties between the Western sectors of Berlin and the Federal Republic of Germany will be maintained and developed, taking into account that these sectors continue not to be a constituent part of the Federal Republic of Germany and not to be governed by it. . . .

C. The Government of the Union of Soviet Socialist Republics declares that communications between the Western sectors of Berlin and areas bordering on these sectors and those areas of the German Democratic Republic which do not border on these sectors will be improved. Permanent residents of the Western sectors of Berlin will be able to travel to and visit such areas for compassionate, family, religious, cultural or commercial reasons, or as tourists, under conditions comparable to those applying to other persons entering these areas. . . .

DISCUSSION QUESTIONS

1. What did West Berlin gain from the Berlin Accords? What did East Germany gain?
2. Why did the treaty reassert that West Berlin was not a constituent part of West Germany?
3. How did the treaty seek to prevent a repetition of the Berlin Blockade?
4. Why would the USSR be willing to accept this agreement?

56. Nixon's China Visit: The Shanghai Communique, February 1972

President Nixon's visit to China in February 1972 created enormous excitement. With the world looking on, Nixon met with Premier Zhou and Chairman Mao, visited China's Great Wall, and was entertained by his Chinese hosts. In private discussions, however, it became clear that continued U.S. support for the Nationalist regime on Taiwan would preclude full normalization of relations between Washington and Beijing. On 27 February as Nixon prepared to leave, the two governments issued a joint communique outlining their agreements and differences (especially regarding Taiwan) and pledging to work together to improve relations and relax tensions.

Excerpts from Communique Issued at Shanghai, 27 February 1972

. . . There are essential differences between China and the United States in their social systems and foreign policies. However, the two sides agreed that countries, regardless of their social systems, should conduct their relations on the principles of respect for the sovereignty and territorial integrity of all states, nonaggression against other states, noninterference in the internal affairs of other states, equality and mutual benefit, and peaceful coexistence. International disputes should be settled on this basis, without resorting to the use or threat of force. The United States and the People's Republic of China are prepared to apply these principles to their mutual relations.

With these principles of international relations in mind the two sides stated that:

- Progress toward the normalization of relations between China and the United States is in the interests of all countries.
- Both wish to reduce the danger of international military conflict.
- Neither should seek hegemony in the Asia-Pacific region and each is opposed to the efforts by any other country or group of countries to establish such hegemony; and
- Neither is prepared to negotiate on behalf of any third party or to enter into agreements or understandings with the other directed at other states.

Both sides are of the view that it would be against the interests of the peoples of the world for any major country to collude with another against other countries, or for major countries to divide up the world into spheres of interest.

The sides reviewed the long-standing serious disputes between China and the United States.

The Chinese side reaffirmed its position: the Taiwan question is the crucial question obstructing the normalization of relations between China and the United States; the Government of the People's Republic of China is the sole legal government of China; Taiwan is a province of China which has long been returned to the motherland; the liberation of Taiwan is China's internal affair in which no other country has the right to interfere; and all US forces and military installations must be withdrawn from Taiwan. The Chinese government firmly opposes any activities which aim at the creation of "one China, one Taiwan," "one China, two governments," "two Chinas," and "independent Taiwan" or advocate that "the status of Taiwan remains to be determined."

The US side declared: The United States acknowledges that all Chinese on either side of the Taiwan Strait maintain there is but one China and that Taiwan is a part of China. The United States Government does not challenge that position. It reaffirms its interest in a peaceful settlement of the Taiwan question by the Chinese themselves. With this prospect in mind, it affirms the ultimate objective of the withdrawal of all US forces and military installations from Taiwan. In the meantime, it will progressively reduce its forces and military installations on Taiwan as the tension in the area diminishes.

The two sides agreed that it is desirable to broaden the understanding between the two peoples. To this end, they discussed specific areas in such fields as science, technology, culture, sports, and journalism, in which people-to-people contacts and exchanges would be mutually beneficial. Each side undertakes to facilitate the further development of such contacts and exchanges.

Both sides view bilateral trade as another area from which mutual benefits can be derived, and agree that economic relations based on equality and mutual benefit are in the interest of the peoples of the two countries. They agree to facilitate the progressive development of trade between their two countries.

The two sides agree that they will stay in contact through various channels, including the sending of a senior US representative to Peking [Beijing] from time to time for concrete consultations to further the normalization of relations between the two countries and continue to exchange views on issues of common interest.

The two sides expressed the hope that the gains achieved during this visit would open up new prospects for the relations between the two countries. They believe that the normalization of relations between the two countries is not only in the interest of the Chinese and American peoples, but also contributes to the relaxation of tension in Asia and the world. . . .

DISCUSSION QUESTIONS

1. What factors prompted the Americans and Chinese to seek improved relations? Why was Nixon in a better position to take this step than other U.S. leaders?
2. Why did the two sides issue this communique at the end of Nixon's visit? What implicit message did it contain for the USSR?
3. Why was the Taiwan issue so important to China and such an obstacle to normalized relations with America? How did the two sides differ on this issue?
4. What steps did the two sides agree could be taken to improve relations between them?

57. The ABM Treaty and SALT I, 1972

In May 1972, President Nixon flew to Moscow for a summit conference with Soviet leader Brezhnev, marking the onset of the era of détente. There, on 26 May, the superpower leaders signed two landmark agreements: the ABM Treaty, which restricted each side to two missile-defense systems (one to protect its capital and one to defend a missile site), and the Interim SALT I Agreement, which sought to freeze strategic missiles at 1972 levels for five years.

A. Treaty on the Limitation of Anti-Ballistic Missile Systems, 26 May 1972

Article I

1. Each Party undertakes to limit anti-ballistic missile (ABM) systems and to adopt other measures in accordance with the provisions of this Treaty.
2. Each Party undertakes not to deploy ABM systems for a defense of the territory of its country and not to provide a base for such a defense, and not to deploy ABM systems for defense of an individual region except as provided for in Article III of this Treaty. . . .

Article III

Each Party undertakes not to deploy ABM systems or their components except that:

(a) within one ABM system deployment area having a radius of 150 kilometers and centered on the Party's national capital, a Party may deploy:

- **(1)** no more than one hundred ABM launchers and no more than 100 ABM interceptor missiles at launch sites, and
- **(2)** ABM radars within no more than six ABM radar complexes, the area of each complex being circular and having a diameter of no more than three kilometers; and

(b) within one ABM system deployment area having a radius of 150 kilometers and containing ICBM silo launchers, a Party may deploy:

- **(1)** no more than one hundred ABM launchers and no more than 100 ABM interceptor missiles at launch sites,
- **(2)** two large phased-array ABM radars operational or under construction on the date of signature of the Treaty in an ABM system deployment area containing ICBM silo launchers, and
- **(3)** no more than eighteen ABM radars each having a potential less than the potential of the smaller of the above-mentioned two large phased-array ABM radars. . . .

Article V

1. Each Party undertakes not to develop, test, or deploy ABM systems or components which are sea-based, air-based, space-based, or mobile land-based.
2. Each Party undertakes not to develop, test, or deploy ABM launchers for launching more than one ABM interceptor missile at a time from each launcher . . . , nor to develop, test, or deploy automatic or semi-automatic or other similar systems for rapid reload of ABM launchers. . . .

Article XII

1. For the purpose of providing assurance of compliance with the provisions of this Treaty, each Party shall use national technical means of verification at its disposal in a manner consistent with generally recognized principles of international law.
2. Each Party undertakes not to interfere with the national technical means of verification of the other Party operating in accordance with paragraph 1 of this Article.
3. Each Party undertakes not to use deliberate concealment measures which impede verification by national technical means of compliance with the provisions of this Treaty. . . .

Article XV

1. This Treaty shall be of unlimited duration.
2. Each Party shall, in exercising its national sovereignty, have the right to withdraw from this Treaty if it decides that extraordinary events related to the subject matter of this Treaty have jeopardized its supreme interests. It shall give notice of its decision to the other Party six months prior to withdrawal from the Treaty. Such notice shall include a statement of the extraordinary events the notifying Party regards as having jeopardized its supreme interests. . . .

B. Interim Agreement on Certain Measures with Respect to the Limitation of Strategic Offensive Arms (SALT I), 26 May 1972

Article I

The Parties undertake not to start construction of additional fixed land-based intercontinental ballistic missile (ICBM) launchers after July 1, 1972. . . .

Article III

The Parties undertake to limit submarine-launched ballistic missile (SLBM) launchers and modern ballistic missile submarines to the numbers operational and under construction on the date of signature of this Interim Agreement, and in addition to launchers and submarines constructed under procedures established by the Parties as replacements for an equal number of ICBM launchers of older types deployed prior to 1964 or for launchers on older submarines.

Article IV

Subject to the provisions of this Interim Agreement, modernization and replacement of strategic offensive ballistic missiles and launchers covered by this Interim Agreement may be undertaken.

Article V

[This article repeats verbatim the provisions of Article XII of the ABM Treaty, above.]

Article VII

The Parties undertake to continue active negotiations for limitations on strategic offensive arms. The obligations provided for in this Interim Agreement shall not prejudice the scope or terms of the limitations on strategic offensive arms which may be worked out in the course of further negotiations.

Article VIII

1. This Interim Agreement shall enter into force upon exchange of written notices of acceptance by each Party, which exchange shall take place simultaneously with the exchange of instruments of ratification of the Treaty on the Limitation of Anti-Ballistic Missile Systems.
2. This Interim Agreement shall remain in force for a period of five years unless replaced earlier by an agreement on more complete measures limiting strategic offensive arms. It is the objective of the Parties to conduct active follow-on negotiations with the aim of concluding such an agreement as soon as possible.
3. Each Party shall, in exercising its national sovereignty, have the right to withdraw from this Interim Agreement if it decides that extraordinary events related to the subject matter of this Interim Agreement have jeopardized its supreme interest. It shall give notice of its decision to the other Party six months prior to withdrawal from this Interim Agreement. . . .

Protocol to the Interim Agreement

. . . The Parties understand that, under Article III of the Interim Agreement for the period during which that Agreement remains in force:

The US may have no more than 710 ballistic missiles launchers on submarines (SLBMs) and no more than 44 modern ballistic missile submarines. The Soviet Union may have no more than 950 ballistic missile launchers on submarines and no more than 62 modern ballistic missile submarines.

Additional ballistic missile launchers on submarines up to the above-mentioned levels, in the US—over 656 ballistic missile launchers on nuclear-powered submarines, and in the USSR—over 740 ballistic missile launchers on nuclear-powered submarines, operational and under construction, may become operational as replacements for equal numbers of ballistic missile launchers of older types deployed prior to 1964 or of ballistic missile launchers on older submarines.

The deployment of modern SLBMs on any submarine, regardless of type, will be counted against the total level of SLBMs permitted for the US and the USSR.

DISCUSSION QUESTIONS

1. Why were the Americans eager to restrict ABM development? Why was the ABM treaty considered essential to controlling the arms race?
2. Why did the treaty permit each side to construct two ABM sites?
3. What was the main significance of the SALT I agreement? What were its main shortcomings?
4. How did the development and use of spy satellites (referred to in the treaties under "national technical means") help make these treaties possible?

58. The U.S. Withdrawal from Vietnam, January 1973

After President Nixon took office in 1969, he began searching for an honorable way out of the Vietnam War through a backstairs deal with the Soviets or the Chinese, the two main suppliers of arms to the Vietnamese Communists. Meanwhile national security advisor Henry Kissinger began meeting secretly in Paris with Le Duc Tho, a special emissary of North Vietnam. By October 1972, it appeared that a deal was close, but North Vietnamese recalcitrance following Nixon's reelection in November led Nixon to order a massive bombing campaign in December. This "Christmas bombing" caused widespread damage to North Vietnamese cities and ports, and to Nixon's standing at home, making clear to both sides the cost of further combat. Kissinger and Le Duc Tho continued to negotiate and soon reached agreement. In a nationwide address on 23 January, Nixon announced that "peace with honor" had been achieved. Four days later, the Paris Peace Accords were signed, ending U.S. involvement in Vietnam.

A. Nixon's Address to the Nation, 23 January 1973

Good evening. I have asked for this radio and television time tonight for the purpose of announcing that we today have concluded an agreement to end the war and bring peace with honor in Vietnam and Southeast Asia. . . .

In my addresses to the nation . . . on January 25 and May 8, I set forth the goals that we considered essential for peace with honor. In the settlement that has now been agreed to, all the conditions that I laid down then have been met. A cease-fire internationally supervised will begin at 7 P.M. this Saturday, January 27, Washington time. Within 60 days from this Saturday all Americans held prisoners of war throughout Indochina will be released.

There will be the fullest possible accounting for all of those who are missing in action. During the same 60-day period all American forces will be withdrawn from South Vietnam.

The people of South Vietnam have been guaranteed the right to determine their own future without outside interference. . . .

The United States will continue to recognize the Government of the Republic of Vietnam as the sole legitimate government of South Vietnam. We shall continue to aid South Vietnam within the terms of the agreement, and we shall support efforts for the people of South Vietnam to settle their problems peacefully among themselves.

We must recognize that ending the war is only the first step toward building the peace. All parties must now see to it that this is a peace that lasts and also a peace that heals, and a peace that not only ends the war in Southeast Asia but contributes to the prospects of peace in the whole world. This will mean that the terms of the agreement must be scrupulously adhered to. We shall do everything the agreement requires of us, and we shall expect the other parties to do everything it requires of them. We shall also expect other interested nations to help insure that the agreement is carried out and peace is maintained. . . .

Now that we have achieved an honorable agreement, let us be proud that America did not settle for a peace that would have betrayed our allies, that would have abandoned our prisoners of war or that would have ended the war for us but would have continued the war for the 50 million people of Indochina.

Let us be proud of the two and a half million young Americans who served in Vietnam, who served with honor and distinction in one of the most selfless enterprises in the history of nations.

And let us be proud of those who sacrificed, who gave their lives, so that the people of South Vietnam might live in freedom, and so that the world might live in peace. . . .

B. The Paris Peace Accords, 27 January 1973

Article 1

The United States and all other countries respect the independence, sovereignty, unity and territorial integrity of Vietnam as recognized by the 1954 Geneva Agreements on Vietnam.

Article 2

A cease-fire shall be observed throughout South Vietnam as of 2400 hours G.M.T. on Jan. 27, 1973. At the same hour, the United States will stop all its military activities against the territory of the Democratic Republic of Vietnam [North Vietnam] by ground, air and naval forces . . . , and end the mining of the territorial waters, ports, harbors and waterways of the Democratic Republic of Vietnam. The United States will remove, permanently deactivate or destroy all the mines in the territorial waters, ports, harbors and waterways of North Vietnam as soon as this agreement goes into effect.

The complete cessation of hostilities mentioned in this article shall be durable and without limit of time. . . .

Article 4

The United States will not continue its military involvement or intervene in the internal affairs of South Vietnam.

Article 5

Within 60 days of the signing of this agreement, there will be a total withdrawal from South Vietnam of troops, military personnel, including technical military personnel and military personnel associated with the pacification program, armaments, munitions and war material of the United States. . . .

Article 6

The dismantlement of all military bases in South Vietnam of the United States and . . . other foreign countries . . . shall be completed within 60 days of the signing of this agreement. . . .

Article 8

(a) The return of captured military personnel and foreign civilians of the parties shall be carried out simultaneously with and completed not later than the same day as the troop withdrawal mentioned in Article 5. . . .

(b) The parties shall help each other to get information about those military personnel and foreign civilians of the parties missing in action. . . .

Article 9

The Government of the United States of America and the Government of the Democratic Republic of Vietnam undertake to respect the following principles for the exercise of the South Vietnamese people's right to self-determination:

(a) The South Vietnamese people's right to self-determination is sacred, inalienable and shall be respected by all countries.

(b) The South Vietnamese people shall decide themselves the political future of South Vietnam through genuinely free and democratic general elections under international supervision.

(c) Foreign countries shall not impose any political tendency or personality on the South Vietnamese people. . . .

Article 15

The reunification of Vietnam shall be carried out step by step through peaceful means on the basis of discussions and agreements between North and South Vietnam, without coercion or annexation by either party, and without foreign interference. The time for reunification will be agreed upon by North and South Vietnam. . . .

DISCUSSION QUESTIONS

1. How did Nixon define "peace with honor"? What sort of settlement would he have seen as dishonorable? What U.S. commitments to South Vietnam are reaffirmed in the speech?
2. What did Nixon expect North Vietnam to do after the Paris Peace Accords?
3. Which articles of the Paris accords reflected American interests, and which reflected North Vietnamese interests? How and why did they do so?
4. How did the Paris accords handle the question of Vietnam's eventual reunification?

59. The Yom Kippur/Ramadan War, 1973

On 6 October 1973, coinciding with the Jewish feast of Yom Kippur and Islamic holy month of Ramadan, Egypt and Syria launched a surprise attack on Israel. From the start, this conflict had serious Cold War implications. Egypt won the early battles, forcing Israel to ask for massive supplies of weapons from America. This enabled Israel to reverse the momentum, which in turn led Egypt to complain to Moscow that U.S. aid was unfairly affecting the war. Soviet leader Brezhnev responded by asking U.S. secretary of state Kissinger to fly to Moscow, where the two sides agreed on cease-fire language that became UN Security Council Resolution 338.

But the crisis was not over. Although Israel and Egypt accepted the cease-fire, both violated it, so on 24 October Brezhnev placed Soviet airborne divisions on alert and proposed a joint U.S.–Soviet military intervention, failing which Moscow might intervene alone. Washington responded by alerting its military forces to move to DEF CON 3, "the highest state of readiness for essentially peacetime conditions." The alert had an immediate effect: the Egyptians and Soviets accepted a large UN observer force to separate the warring sides, and the U.S. ended its alert at midnight on 25 October, after pressing the Israelis to observe the cease-fire.

A. United Nations Security Council Resolution 338, Passed on 22 October 1973

The Security Council,

1. Calls upon all parties to the present fighting to cease all firing and terminate all military activity immediately, no later than 12 hours after the moment of the adoption of this decision, in the positions they now occupy . . .

3. Decides that immediately and concurrently with the cease-fire, negotiations start between the parties concerned under appropriate auspices aimed at establishing a just and durable peace in the Middle East.

B. Israel Accepts the Cease-Fire, 22 October 1973

At its meeting this morning (Monday), the Cabinet decided unanimously to accept the proposal of the US Government and President Nixon, and to announce its readiness to agree to a cease-fire in accordance with proposed Security Council Resolution 338.

Under the terms of this proposed Resolution, the military forces will remain in the positions they occupy upon the coming into effect of the cease-fire. Israel will insist on an exchange of prisoners.

The implementation of the cease-fire is conditional upon reciprocity . . .

The Minister of Defence and the Chief of Staff reported on the situation on the battle fronts.

At 4 P.M. the Government issued the following statement: The Government of Israel has been informed that the Government of Egypt has instructed the armed forces of Egypt to cease hostilities in accordance with the Security Council Resolution concerning the cease-fire.

Following upon this, the Government of Israel has issued orders to the Israeli Defence Forces on the Egyptian front to stop firing at 1850 hours Israeli time today, 22 October, provided it is confirmed that the Egyptians have indeed ceased hostilities.

The cease-fire will therefore come into effect at the end of the 12-hour period stipulated by the Security Council Resolution.

C. Egypt Accepts the Cease-Fire, 22 October 1973

President Sadat has studied with great care the Security Council resolution adopted this morning, calling for a cease-fire within a 12-hour delay and immediate and full implementation of the UN Resolution of 22 November 1967.

The Arab armed forces have confirmed their courage, skill, and martyrdom on the battlefield and it was this great action alone that has broken the deadlock in the crisis.

President Sadat also has studied with great care details of the Security Council debate and noted the following points:

1. The draft Resolution debated by the Security Council was submitted by the two super Powers, the Soviet Union and the United States, after intensive contacts between them at the highest levels and bearing in mind their special responsibility toward current international situations.
2. The Security Council adopted the draft Resolution without objections from any of its members.
3. The debate which took place in the Council was of great importance and shed necessary light on its attitudes. In this connection the statements of the French and Indian delegates were of particular importance.

Other important factors to be taken into consideration include the following:

1. The peace plan which President Sadat broadcast to the nation and the world in his speech to the People's Assembly and the Central Committee of the Arab Socialist Union on October 16, in which the President made complete Israeli withdrawal a basic point of any political action.
2. Talks held by President Sadat and Soviet Premier Alexei Kosygin in Cairo on 16–19 October, when five working sessions were held.
3. Assurances which President Sadat received from Soviet Leader Leonid Brezhnev and which were conveyed to Sadat in a special message by the Soviet ambassador to Cairo on the night of October 21.
4. Contacts which took place with a number of Arab capitals directly concerned in the battle.

President Sadat also took into consideration that the powerful factor which has changed the nature and circumstances of the entire Middle East crisis was highlighted and strengthened by the great action in which the Arab armed forces have carried out and are carrying out, and in which they confirmed their courage, skill and martyrdom on the field of battle.

This great action alone has broken the deadlock in the crisis, changed the fait accompli and the whole map of the Middle East crisis and ended for ever the arrogance and power which the Israeli enemy had been displaying for the past 25 years.

In accordance with the above considerations, President Sadat, in his capacity as Supreme Commander of the Armed Forces, has issued an order to the general command to observe a cease-fire at the time laid down by the Security Council Resolution, provided the enemy is also committed to observe it.

President Sadat, in taking this decision on his own historic responsibility, considers that the main credit in this first stage of a decisive phase in the pan-Arab and Egyptian struggle is due to the firm stand taken by the whole Arab nation and to the deep awareness of its peoples as well as, above all, to the heroism of the men who accepted the challenge of fire and blood on the battlefield. God's victory for them was certain.

DISCUSSION QUESTIONS

1. Why did Israel cite "the US Government and President Nixon" in accepting Resolution 338?
2. Why did Egypt refer to Soviet leaders Brezhnev and Kosygin in accepting Resolution 338?
3. Why did Sadat emphasize the courage and skill of his armies, which were losing the war?
4. How did the language of Sadat's acceptance demonstrate his eagerness to work toward a long-term solution of the Middle East crisis?

60. Deng Xiaoping's "Three Worlds" Speech, April 1974

By the 1970s, it was obvious that the Cold War was far more complex than the "two worlds" image of Communist East versus capitalist West portrayed in Stalin's 1946 "election speech" (Document 4). The Communist world had split wide apart, deep divisions had emerged in the capitalist West, and many developing "Third World" nations remained nonaligned. In a notable address to the UN General Assembly in April 1974, China's vice premier Deng Xiaoping asserted that this "drastic division and realignment" had created "three worlds," deftly depicting both the Soviets and Americans as exploiters and oppressors seeking "world hegemony," while adroitly identifying China with the Third World.

Highlights of Speech by Chinese Vice Premier Deng Xiaoping to the UN General Assembly, 10 April 1974

. . . At present, the international situation is most favourable to the developing countries and the peoples of the world. More and more, the old order based on colonialism, imperialism and hegemonism is being undermined and shaken to its foundations. International relations are changing drastically. The whole world is in turbulence and unrest. The situation is one of "great disorder under heaven," as we Chinese put it . . .

In this situation of "great disorder under heaven," all the political forces in the world have undergone drastic division and realignment . . . A large number of Asian, African and Latin American countries have achieved independence one after another and they are playing an ever greater role in international affairs. As a result of the emergence of social-imperialism, the socialist camp which existed for a time after World War II is no longer in existence. Owing to the law of the uneven development of capitalism, the Western imperialist bloc, too, is disintegrating. Judging from the changes in international relations, the world today actually consists of three parts, or three worlds, that are both interconnected and in contradiction to one another. The United States and the Soviet Union make up the First World. The developing countries in Asia, Africa, Latin America and other regions make up the Third World. The developed countries between the two make up the Second World.

The two superpowers, the United States and the Soviet Union, are vainly seeking world hegemony. Each in its own way attempts to bring the developing countries of Asia, Africa and Latin America under its control and, at the same time, to bully the developed countries that are not their match in strength.

The two superpowers are the biggest international exploiters and oppressors of today. They are the source of a new world war. They both possess large numbers of nuclear weapons. They carry on a keenly contested arms race, station massive forces abroad and set up military bases everywhere, threatening the independence and security of all nations. They both keep subjecting other countries to their control, subversion, interference or aggression. They both exploit other countries economically, plundering their wealth and grabbing their resources . . .

The numerous developing countries have long suffered from colonialist and imperialist oppression and exploitation. They have won political independence, yet all of them still face the historic task of clearing out the remnant forces of colonialism, developing the national economy and consolidating national independence. These countries cover vast territories, encompass a large population and abound in natural resources. Having suffered the heaviest oppression, they have the strongest desire to oppose oppression and seek liberation and development . . .

Since the two superpowers are contending for world hegemony, the contradiction between them is irreconcilable . . . Their compromise and collusion can only be partial, temporary and relative, while their contention is all-embracing, permanent and absolute. In the final analysis, the so-called "balanced reduction of forces" and "strategic arms limitation" are nothing but empty talk . . . Every day, they talk about disarmament but are actually engaged in arms expansion. Every day, they talk about "detente" but are actually creating tension. Wherever they contend, turbulence occurs. So long as imperialism and social-imperialism exist, there definitely will be no tranquility in the world . . .

The two superpowers have created their own antithesis. Acting in the way of the big bullying the small, the strong domineering over the weak and the rich oppressing the poor, they have aroused strong resistance among the Third World and the people of the whole world. The people of Asia, Africa and Latin America have been winning new victories in their struggles against colonialism, imperialism, and particularly hegemonism. . . . The struggles of the Asian, African and Latin American countries and people, advancing wave upon wave, have exposed the essential weakness of imperialism, and particularly the superpowers, which are outwardly strong but inwardly feeble, and dealt heavy blows at their wild ambitions to dominate the world.

Innumerable facts show that all views that overestimate the strength of the two hegemonic powers and underestimate the strength of the people are groundless. It is not the one or two superpowers that are really powerful; the really powerful are the Third World and the people of all countries uniting together and daring to fight and daring to win . . .

China is a socialist country, and a developing country as well. China belongs to the Third World. Consistently following Chairman Mao's teachings, the Chinese Government and people firmly support all oppressed peoples and oppressed nations in their struggle to win or defend national independence, develop the national economy and oppose colonialism, imperialism and hegemonism . . . We are convinced that, so long as the Third World countries and people strengthen their unity, ally themselves with all forces that can be allied with and persist in a protracted struggle, they are sure to win continuous new victories.

DISCUSSION QUESTIONS

1. What did Deng Xiaoping mean by "great disorder under heaven"? Why did he say the world situation favored developing countries?
2. Why did he lump the Soviets and Americans together as exploiters and oppressors? Why did he dismiss their efforts at détente as "temporary and relative"?
3. Why did he identify China with the Third World?
4. In what ways was his address an accurate analysis of the world situation, and in what ways was it a clever bit of anti-Soviet, anti-American, and pro-Chinese propaganda?

61. The Vladivostok Summit, 1974

By 1974, the spirit of détente had begun to fade. The SALT II discussions, designed to replace the interim five-year SALT I accord with a long-term agreement, had drifted into deadlock, and the Middle East crisis of October 1973 had exposed the limits of superpower cooperation. In August 1974, Richard Nixon, one of détente's key architects, was forced by the Watergate scandal to resign as U.S. president.

Soon after Nixon left office, a summit conference was arranged between his successor, Gerald R. Ford, and Soviet leader Brezhnev. Their meeting, at Vladivostok in Soviet East Asia, exceeded most expectations and breathed new life into détente. The two leaders, assisted by Soviet foreign minister Gromyko and U.S. secretary of state Kissinger, managed to overcome the SALT impasse by agreeing to establish "ceilings" for the sum total of missiles and bombers each side could have and for the number of these that could be fitted with multiple warheads. They also discussed many other issues and agreed to meet again the next year.

A. Agreement Concluded at Vladivostok, November 24, 1974

During their working meeting in the area of Vladivostok on Nov. 23–24, 1974, the President of the USA, Gerald R. Ford, and General Secretary of the Central Committee of the CPSU, L. I. Brezhnev, discussed in detail the question of further limitations of strategic offensive arms.

They reaffirmed the great significance that both the United States and the USSR attach to the limitation of strategic offensive arms. They are convinced that a long-term agreement on this question would be a significant contribution to improving relations between the US and the USSR, to reducing the danger of war and to enhancing world peace. Having noted the value of previous agreements on this question, including the interim agreement of May 26, 1972, they reaffirm the intention to conclude a new agreement on the limitation of strategic offensive arms to last through 1985.

As a result of the exchange of views on the substance of such a new agreement, the President . . . and the General Secretary . . . concluded that favorable prospects exist for completing the work on this agreement in 1975.

Agreement was reached that further negotiations will be based on the following provisions:

1. The new agreement will incorporate the relevant provisions of the interim agreement of May 26, 1972, which will remain in force until October, 1977.
2. The new agreement will cover the period from October, 1977, through Dec. 31, 1985.
3. Based on the principle of equality and equal security, the new agreement will include the following limitations:
   - **A.** Both sides will be entitled to have a certain agreed aggregate number of strategic delivery vehicles.
   - **B.** Both sides will be entitled to have a certain agreed aggregate number of ICBM's [intercontinental ballistics missiles] and SLBM's [submarine-launched ballistics missiles] equipped with multiple independently targetable warheads (MIRV's).
4. The new agreement will include a provision for further negotiations beginning no later than 1980–1981 on the question of further limitations and possible reductions of strategic arms in the period after 1985.
5. Negotiations between the delegations of the US and USSR to work out the new agreement incorporating the foregoing points will resume in Geneva in January, 1975.

B. Excerpt from President Ford's Statement, 2 December 1974

My meetings at Vladivostok with General Secretary Brezhnev were a valuable opportunity to review Soviet-American relations and chart their future course. Although this was our original purpose, Secretary Brezhnev and I found it possible to go beyond this get-acquainted stage. Building on the achievements of the past three years we agreed that prospects were favorable for more substantial, and may I say, very intensive negotiations on the primary issue of limitation of strategic arms. In the end, we agreed on the general framework for a new agreement that will last through 1985.

We agreed it is realistic to aim at completing this agreement next year. This is possible because we made major breakthroughs on two critical issues.

(1) We agreed to put a ceiling of 2,400 each on the total number of intercontinental ballistic missiles, submarine-launched missiles and heavy bombers.

(2) We agreed to limit the number of missiles that can be armed with multiple warheads (MIRV's). Of each side's total of 2,400, 1,320 can be so armed.

These ceilings are well below the force levels which would otherwise have been expected over the next 10 years, and very substantially below the forces which would result from an all-out arms race over that same period.

What we have done is to set firm and equal limits on the strategic forces of each side, thus preventing an arms race with all its terror, instability, war-breeding tension and economic waste. We have in addition created the solid basis from which future arms reductions can be . . . and hopefully will be . . . negotiated.

It will take more detailed negotiations to convert this agreed framework into a comprehensive accord. But we have made a long step forward toward peace, on a basis of equality, the only basis on which agreement was possible. . . .

DISCUSSION QUESTIONS

1. Why were Soviet leaders eager to restore détente's momentum after Nixon's resignation? Why were U.S. leaders eager to continue their dialogue with Moscow?
2. What were the basic conditions agreed to at Vladivostok? How did they differ from SALT I?
3. Why did agreement lump together ICBMs, SLBMs, and long-range bombers, rather than establishing separate ceilings for each?
4. According to President Ford, what expectations did he have going into this meeting? What expectations did he have as a result of it?

62. The Helsinki Final Act, 1975

In summer 1975, leaders of 35 nations gathered in Helsinki, Finland, to sign the Helsinki Final Act. It was a crowning achievement of the Conference on Security and Cooperation in Europe (CSCE), which had begun in 1973. It represented the centerpiece of European détente, the final peace settlement of World War II in Europe, and the culmination of Moscow's efforts to gain international recognition of its territorial gains. Along with its provisions on European security, economic cooperation, and scientific collaboration, the Final Act also established guidelines regarding human rights. These guidelines, grouped together in "Basket Three," provided specific standards concerning freedom of emigration and freedom of information. In future years, Soviet failure to comply with these standards would be monitored by Western governments, human rights advocates, and dissident groups in the USSR, creating serious headaches for Moscow.

Excerpts from Declaration Signed at Helsinki, 1 August 1975

Questions Relating to Security in Europe

The states participating in the Conference on Security and Cooperation in Europe. . . .

Declare their determination to respect and put into practice the following principles, which all are of primary significance, guiding their mutual relations:

The participating states will respect each other's sovereign equality and individuality as well as all the rights inherent in and encompassed by its sovereignty, including in particular the right of every state to juridical equality, to territorial integrity and to freedom and political independence. They will also respect each other's right freely to choose and develop its political, social, economic and cultural systems as well as its right to determine its laws and regulations. . . .

The participating states will refrain in their mutual relations, as well as in their international relations in general, from the threat or use of force against the territorial integrity or political independence of any state. . . .

The participating states regard as inviolable all one another's frontiers as well as the frontiers of all states in Europe, and therefore they will refrain now and in the future from assaulting these frontiers. . . .

The participating states will settle disputes among them by peaceful means in such a manner as not to endanger international peace and security and justice. They will endeavor in good faith and a spirit of cooperation to reach a rapid and equitable solution on the basis of international law. . . .

The participating states will refrain from any intervention, direct or indirect, individual or collective, in the internal or external affairs falling within the domestic jurisdiction of another participating state, regardless of their mutual relations.

The participating states will refrain from direct or indirect assistance to terrorist activities or to subversive or other activities directed towards the violent overthrow of the regime of another participating state.

The participating states will respect human rights and fundamental freedoms, including the freedom of thought, conscience, religion or belief, for all without distinction as to race, sex, language or religion.

Within this framework the participating states will recognize and respect the freedom of the individual to profess and practice, alone or in community with others, religion or belief acting in accordance with the dictates of his own conscience.

The participating states on whose territory national minorities exist will respect the right of persons belonging to such minorities to equality before the law, will afford them the full opportunity for the actual enjoyment of human rights and fundamental freedoms and will, in this manner, protect their legitimate interests in this sphere.

The participating states recognize the universal significance of human rights and fundamental freedoms, respect for which is an essential factor for the peace, justice and well-being necessary to insure the development of friendly relations and cooperation among themselves as among all states. They will constantly respect these rights and freedoms in their mutual relations. . . .

Documents On Confidence-Building Measures and Certain Aspects of Security and Disarmament

The participating states . . .

Recognizing the need to contribute to reducing the dangers of armed conflict and of misunderstanding or miscalculation of military activities which could give rise to apprehension, particularly in a situation where the participating states lack clear and timely information about the nature of such activities . . . , have adopted the following:

They will notify their major military maneuvers to all other participating states through usual diplomatic channels in accordance with the following provisions:

Notification will be given of major military maneuvers exceeding a total of 25,000 troops, independently or combined with any possible air or naval components. . . .

Notification will be given of major military maneuvers which take place on the territory, in Europe, of any participating state as well as, if applicable, in the adjoining sea area and airspace. . . .

Notification will be given 21 days or more in advance of the start of the maneuver, or in the case of a maneuver arranged at shorter notice, at the earliest possible opportunity prior to its starting date.

Notification will contain information of the designation, if any, of the general purpose of and the states involved in the maneuver, the type or types and numerical strength of the forces engaged, the area and estimated time frame of its conduct. . . . .

The participating states will invite other participating states, voluntarily and on a bilateral basis . . . , to send observers to attend military maneuvers. . . .

Cooperation in the Field of Economics, of Science and Technology, and of the Environment

The participating states will encourage the expansion of trade on as broad a multilateral basis as possible, thereby endeavoring to utilize the various economic and commercial possibilities.

They will endeavor to reduce or progressively eliminate all kinds of obstacles to the development of trade; will foster a steady growth of trade while avoiding as far as possible abrupt fluctuations in their trade.

The participating states will promote the publication and dissemination of economic and commercial information at regular intervals and as quickly as possible. . . .

Cooperation in Humanitarian and Other Fields

The participating states,

Will make it their aim to facilitate freer movement and contacts . . . among persons, institutions and organizations of the participating states.

In order to promote further development of contacts on the basis of family ties the participating states will favorably consider applications for travel with the purpose of allowing persons to enter or leave their territory temporarily and on a regular basis if desired, in order to visit members of their families. . . .

The participating states will deal in a positive and humanitarian spirit with the applications of persons who wish to be reunited with members of their family, with special attention given to requests of an urgent character. They will deal with applications in this field as expeditiously as possible. . . .

The participating states will examine favorably and on the basis of humanitarian considerations requests for exit or entry permits from persons who have decided to marry a citizen from another participating state. . . .

The participating states intend to facilitate wider travel by their citizens for personal or professional reasons and to this end they intend in particular:

- Gradually to simplify and to administer flexibly the procedures for exit and entry;
- To ease regulations concerning movement of citizens from the other participating states in their territory with due regard to security requirements. . . .

By way of further developing contacts among governmental institutions and non-governmental organizations and associations, including women's organizations, the participating states will facilitate the convening of meetings as well as travel by delegations, groups and individuals.

The participating states,

Make it their aim to facilitate the freer and wider dissemination of information of all kinds, to encourage cooperation in the field of information and the exchange of information with other countries, and to improve the conditions under which journalists from one participating state exercise their professions in another participating state, and express their intention in particular:

- To facilitate the dissemination of oral information through the encouragement of lectures and lecture tours by personalities and specialists from the other participating states, as well as exchanges of opinions at round-table meetings, seminars, symposia, summer schools, congresses and other bilateral and multilateral meetings.
- To facilitate the improvement of the dissemination, on their territory, of newspapers and printed publications, periodical and non-periodical, from the other participating states. For this purpose they will encourage their competent firms and organizations to conclude agreements and contracts designed gradually to increase

the quantities and the number of titles of newspapers and publications imported from the other participating states.

The participating states express the intention to promote the improvement of the dissemination of filmed and broadcast information.

The participating states note the experience in the dissemination of information broadcast by radio and express the hope for the continuation of this process so as to meet the interest of mutual understanding among peoples and the aims set forth by this conference.

To encourage cooperation in the field of information on the basis of short or long term agreements or arrangements, in particular:

They will favor increased cooperation among mass media organizations, including press agencies, as well as among publishing houses and organizations.

They will favor cooperation among public or private national or international radio and television organizations, in particular through the exchange of both live and recorded radio and television programs. . . .

The participating states are disposed to increase substantially their cultural exchanges, with regard both to persons and to cultural works, and to develop among them an active cooperation, both at the bilateral and the multilateral level, in all fields of culture.

The participating states express their intention to promote wider dissemination of books and artistic works, in particular by facilitating . . . international contacts and communications between authors and publishing houses as well as other cultural institutions, with a view to a more complete mutual access to cultural achievements.

The participating states express their intention to contribute, by appropriate means, to the development of contacts and cooperation in the various fields of culture, especially among creative artists and people engaged in cultural activities.

DISCUSSION QUESTIONS

1. In what sense was the Helsinki Final Act the final peace settlement of World War II in Europe?
2. How did it seek to improve European security and cooperation?
3. Why was the USSR eager to have Europe's current frontiers recognized as permanent? Why would Moscow have reason to be pleased with the Final Act?
4. Why did its provisions on human rights present potential problems for Moscow?

63. Carter on Human Rights, 1977

In pursuing détente the Soviet leaders worked reasonably well with Presidents Nixon and Ford. Despite his strident anti-Communism, Nixon was a realistic politician who put pragmatism above principle. When Nixon resigned in 1974, Moscow was at first alarmed but was quickly reassured when Nixon's successor, Gerald Ford, proved equally practical. But Jimmy Carter's election in 1976 changed the rules and left the Soviets uncertain of how to proceed.

Carter, an enigma to many in America and around the world, was a born-again Christian peanut farmer from Georgia with a degree in nuclear engineering from the U.S. Naval Academy. As if his background was not sufficiently unusual, he proceeded to introduce a new variable into American foreign policy. Since the Declaration of Independence in 1776, American politics had often been filled with references to human rights, but those rights were not always honored at home and rarely emphasized in Washington's dealings abroad. Now, as Americans finished celebrating the bicentennial of their independence, Carter proposed to create a "human rights" standard by which the United States would judge other nations. A government wishing to remain friendly with Washington would have to meet that standard. The USSR was both perplexed and annoyed, given its problems with the human rights provisions of the Helsinki Final Act.

Carter's Address to the United Nations, 17 March 1977

. . . It's now eight weeks since I became President. I've brought to office a firm commitment to a more open foreign policy. And I believe that the American people expect me to speak frankly about the policies that we intend to pursue and it is in that spirit that I speak to you tonight about our own hopes for the future.

I see a hopeful world, a world dominated by increasing demands for basic freedoms, for fundamental rights, for higher standards of human existence. We are eager to take part in the shaping of that world.

But in seeking such a better world, we are not blind to the reality of disagreement nor to the persisting dangers that confront us all. Every headline reminds us of bitter divisions, of national hostilities, of territorial conflicts, of ideological competition. In the Middle East peace is a quarter century overdue. A gathering racial conflict threatens Southern Africa, new tensions are rising in the horn of Africa; disputes in the eastern Mediterranean remain to be resolved.

Perhaps even more ominous is the staggering arms race. The Soviet Union and the United States have accumulated thousands of nuclear weapons. Our two nations have almost five times as many missile warheads today as we had eight years ago. Yet we are not five times more secure! On the contrary, the arms race has only increased the risk of conflict.

We can only improve this world if we are realistic about its complexities. The disagreements we face are deeply rooted, and they often raise difficult philosophical as well as territorial issues. They will not be solved easily; they will not be solved quickly. The arms race is now embedded in the very fabric of international affairs and can only be contained with the greatest difficulty. Poverty, inequality are of such monumental scope that it will take decades of deliberate and determined effort even to improve the situation substantially.

I stress these dangers and these difficulties because I want all of us to dedicate ourselves to a prolonged and persistent effort designed:

First, to maintain peace and to reduce the arms race;

Second, to build a better and more cooperative international economic system;

And third, to work with potential adversaries as well as our close friends to advance the cause of human rights. . . .

The search for peace and justice also means respect for human dignity. All the signatories of the UN Charter have pledged themselves to observe and to respect basic human rights. Thus, no member of the United Nations can claim that mistreatment of its citizens is solely its own business. Equally, no member can avoid its responsibilities to review and to speak when torture or unwarranted deprivation occurs in any part of the world.

The basic thrust of human affairs points toward a more universal demand for fundamental human rights. The United States has a historical birthright to be associated with this process.

We in the United States accept this responsibility in the fullest and the most constructive sense. Ours is a commitment, and not just a political posture. I know . . . that our own ideals in the area of human rights have not always been attained in the United States, but the American people have an abiding commitment to the full realization of these ideals. We are determined, therefore, to deal with our deficiencies quickly and openly. We have nothing to conceal. . . .

The United Nations is the global forum dedicated to the peace and well-being of every individual—no matter how weak or how poor. But we have allowed its human rights machinery to be ignored and sometimes politicized. There is much that can be done to strengthen it. . . .

Strengthened international machinery will help us to close the gap between promise and performance in protecting human rights. When gross or widespread violation takes place—contrary to international commitments—it is of concern to all. The solemn commitments of the UN Charter, of the UN's Universal Declaration of Human Rights, of the Helsinki Accords and of many other international instruments must be taken just as seriously as commercial or security agreements. . . .

These then are our basic priorities as we work with other members to strengthen and improve the United Nations:

First, we will strive for peace in the troubled areas of the world.

Second, we will aggressively seek to control the weaponry of war.

Third, we will promote a new system of international economic progress and cooperation.

And fourth, we will be steadfast in our dedication to the dignity and well-being of people throughout the world. . . .

DISCUSSION QUESTIONS

1. President Carter asserted that no nation could claim that "mistreatment of its citizens is solely its own business." Why not?
2. What did he mean by claiming that the United States had a "historical birthright to be associated with this process"?
3. When Carter said that the United States had not always lived up to its human rights ideals, to what might he have been referring?
4. What counterarguments might other UN members have used against Carter?

64. Peace Between Egypt and Israel, 1977–1979

Although he signed a Treaty of Peace and Friendship with Moscow in 1971 and accepted large amounts of Soviet aid in preparation for the Arab–Israeli War of 1973, Egypt's president Anwar el-Sadat grew increasingly dissatisfied with Soviet support and concluded that only Washington had enough clout to pressure Israel into making real concessions. In 1972, he expelled Soviet advisors from Egypt, and in 1976, he abrogated the treaty with the USSR. The following year, in a dramatic break with precedent, he flew to Israel and made a historic speech on 20 November to the Israeli parliament (the Knesset).

It is difficult to exaggerate the impact of Sadat's action. No leader of an Arab state had ever visited Israel. No Arab state had granted diplomatic recognition to Israel. Since 1948, most Arabs had refused to recognize Israel's right to exist. Sadat's bold gesture astounded Israelis and enraged much of the Arab world.

His initiative led to a return visit by Israeli prime minister Menachem Begin to Egypt later that year. Extensive diplomatic contacts then took place behind the scenes. In September 1978, President Carter invited both Sadat and Begin to the United States to negotiate a framework for an eventual treaty, underscoring America's importance as a power broker in the Middle East.

Sadat and Begin met for twelve days at Camp David, the presidential retreat in Maryland's Catoctin Mountains. Carter was present for much of that period and saved the conference from collapse on 16 September, when he prevailed on the two men to make one last attempt to reach agreement with himself as mediator. The effort proved successful, and the historic Camp David Agreements were announced the next day.

Although the Camp David Framework envisioned a treaty within three months, several issues, including that of the Palestinian Arabs living in Israeli-occupied territory on the West Bank and in the Gaza Strip, delayed its conclusion until March 1979. Finally the two parties agreed to leave the Palestinian problem for another day and were able to reach agreement on issues affecting themselves. The final document, signed on a bright spring day in Washington, afforded one of the great photo opportunities of the twentieth century, with Sadat and Begin joining hands that were clasped by a beaming Jimmy Carter, as the flags of Egypt, Israel, and the United States rippled in a stiff breeze. It remained to be seen if this treaty would lead to a general Middle East peace or remain an isolated example of what can be accomplished when statesmen set out to break the chains of past ideas and animosities.

A. Excerpt from Sadat's Speech in Israel, 20 November 1977

I have chosen to set aside all precedents and traditions known by warring countries. In spite of the fact that occupation of Arab territory is still there, the declaration of my readiness to proceed to Israel came as a great surprise that stirred many feelings and confounded many minds. Some of them even doubted its intent. . . .

I have chosen to come to you with an open heart and an open mind. I have chosen to give this great impetus to all international efforts exerted for peace. I have chosen to present you in your own home, the realities, devoid of any scheme or whim. Not to maneuver, to win a round, but for us to win together, the most dangerous of rounds embattled in modern history, the battle of permanent peace based on justice.

It is not my battle alone. Nor is it the battle of the leadership in Israel alone. It is the battle of all and every citizen in our territories, whose right it is to live in peace. It is the commitment of conscience and responsibility in the hearts of millions.

When I put forward this initiative, many asked what is it that I conceived as possible to achieve during this visit and what my expectations were. And as I answer these questions, I announce before you that I have not thought of carrying out this initiative from the precepts of what could be achieved during this visit. I have come here to deliver a message. I have delivered the message and may God be my witness.

I repeat with Zacharia: Love right and justice. From the holy Qu'ran I quote the following verses: "We believe in God and in what has been revealed to us and what was revealed to Abraham, Ishmael, Isaac, Jacob and the 13 Jewish tribes. And in the books given to Moses and Jesus and the prophets from their Lord, who made no distinction between them." So we agree, Salam Aleikum—peace be upon you.

B. Framework for Peace Agreed to at Camp David, 17 September 1978

Muhammad Anwar el-Sadat, president of the Arab Republic of Egypt, and Menachem Begin, prime minister of Israel, met with Jimmy Carter, President of the United States of America, at Camp David from September 5 to September 17, 1978, and have agreed on the following framework for peace in the Middle East. They invite other parties to the Arab-Israeli conflict to adhere to it.

. . . The parties are determined to reach a just, comprehensive, and durable settlement of the Middle East conflict. . . . Their purpose is to achieve peace and good neighborly relations. They recognize that for peace to endure, it must involve all those who have been most deeply affected by the conflict. They therefore agree that this framework as appropriate is intended by them to constitute a basis for peace not only between Egypt and Israel, but also between Israel and each of its other neighbors which is prepared to negotiate peace with Israel on this basis. With that objective in mind, they have agreed to proceed as follows:

A. West Bank and Gaza

1. Egypt, Israel, Jordan and the representatives of the Palestinian people should participate in negotiations on the resolution of the Palestinian problem in all its aspects. . . .

(a) Egypt and Israel agree that, in order to ensure a peaceful and orderly transfer of authority, and taking into account the security concerns of all the parties, there should be transitional arrangements for the West Bank and Gaza for a period not exceeding five years. In order to provide full autonomy to the inhabitants, under these arrangements the Israeli military government and its civilian administration will be withdrawn as soon as a self-governing authority has been freely elected by the inhabitants of these areas to replace the existing military government. To negotiate the details of a transitional arrangement, the government of Jordan will be invited to join the negotiations on the basis of this framework. These new arrangements should give due consideration both to the principle of self-government by the inhabitants of these territories and to the legitimate security concerns of the parties involved. . . .

B. Egypt-Israel

1. Egypt and Israel undertake not to resort to the threat or the use of force to settle disputes. Any disputes shall be settled by peaceful means in accordance with the provisions of Article 33 of the Charter of the United Nations.
2. In order to achieve peace between them, the parties agree to negotiate in good faith with a goal of concluding within three months from the signing of this framework a peace treaty between them, while inviting the other parties to the conflict to proceed simultaneously to negotiate and conclude similar peace treaties with a view to achieving a comprehensive peace in the area. The Framework for the Conclusion of a Peace Treaty Between Egypt and Israel will govern the peace negotiations between them. The parties will agree on the modalities and the timetable for the implementation of their obligations under the treaty.

C. Associated Principles

1. Egypt and Israel state that the principles and provisions described below should apply to peace treaties between Israel and each of its neighbors—Egypt, Jordan, Syria and Lebanon.
2. Signatories shall establish among themselves relationships normal to states at peace with one another. To this end, they should undertake to abide by all the provisions of the Charter of the United Nations. Steps to be taken in this respect include:
   (a) full recognition;
   (b) abolishing economic boycotts;
   (c) guaranteeing that under their jurisdiction the citizens of the other parties shall enjoy the protection of the due process of law. . . .

Signed by Sadat and Begin, with Carter signing as a witness.

C. Treaty Between Egypt and Israel, 26 March 1979

Article I

1. The state of war between the parties will be terminated and peace will be established between them upon the exchange of instruments of ratification of this treaty.
2. Israel will withdraw all its armed forces and civilians from the Sinai behind the international boundary between Egypt and mandated Palestine . . . , and Egypt will resume the exercise of its full sovereignty over the Sinai.
3. Upon completion of the interim withdrawal . . . , the parties will establish normal and friendly relations, in accordance with Article III (3).

Article II

The permanent boundary between Egypt and Israel is the recognized international boundary between Egypt and the former mandated territory of Palestine . . . without prejudice to the issue of the status of the Gaza Strip. The parties recognize this boundary as inviolable. Each will respect the territorial integrity of the other, including their territorial waters and airspace.

Article III

1. The parties will apply between them the provisions of the Charter of the United Nations and the principles of international

law governing relations among states in time of peace. In particular:

A. They recognize and will respect each other's sovereignty, territorial integrity and political independence.

B. They recognize and will respect each other's right to live in peace within their secure and recognized boundaries.

C. They will refrain from the threat or use of force, directly or indirectly, against each other and will settle all disputes between them by peaceful means.

2. Each party undertakes to insure that acts or threats of belligerency, hostility or violence do not originate from and are not committed from within its territory, or by any forces subject to its control or by any other forces stationed on its territory, against the population, citizens or property of the other party. Each party also undertakes to refrain from organizing, instigating, inciting, assisting or participating in acts or threats of belligerency, hostility, subversion or violence against the other party, anywhere, and undertakes to insure that perpetrators of such acts are brought to justice.

3. The parties agree that the normal relationship established between them will include full recognition, diplomatic, economic and cultural relations, termination of economic boycotts and discriminatory barriers to the free movement of people and goods, and will guarantee the mutual enjoyment by citizens of the due process of law. . . .

DISCUSSION QUESTIONS

1. Why would many Israelis distrust Sadat? How did Sadat attempt to overcome this distrust?
2. Why did Sadat conclude that Soviet support was less valuable to him than U.S. support?
3. Why did Carter work so hard for peace between Egypt and Israel? What benefits might such a peace bring to the United States?
4. Why were the West Bank and Gaza such difficult situations for Egypt and Israel to settle? How did the treaty deal with the issue of Gaza?
5. What concessions did Israel make to Egypt? What concessions did Egypt make to Israel?

65. The Normalization of U.S.–Chinese Relations, 1978–1979

In December 1978, President Carter made the dramatic announcement that, as of 1 January 1979, the United States would establish formal diplomatic relations with the People's Republic of China. This event marked the culmination of the process that had begun with President Nixon's trip to China in 1972. It also represented a decision by the Carter administration to strengthen its hand against Moscow by improving U.S. ties with Beijing.

From the time of Nixon's visit, the main obstacle to normalized relations had been the Taiwan issue. For decades the United States had maintained close ties with the Nationalist regime ("Republic of China"), and had continued to recognize it as China's official government, even though since 1949 it had controlled only Taiwan. From Beijing's perspective, however, Taiwan was part of China, and U.S. support for the Nationalists was blatant interference in Chinese internal affairs. In the Shanghai Communique of 1972, the Nixon administration acknowledged that Taiwan was considered part of China by both Communists and Nationalists and gradually decreased the U.S. military presence there. But it had been unwilling to terminate U.S. diplomatic relations with the Taiwan government.

By 1978, however, the Carter administration was willing to take that step. Nationalist leader Chiang Kai-shek (Jiang Jieshi), America's old wartime ally, had died in 1975, and was followed to the grave the next year by Mao Zedong. Since then, led by Deng Xiaoping, the Chinese Communists had moved away from Mao's frenetic radicalism and had adopted a more pragmatic approach to domestic and foreign affairs. They also had joined the United States in vehement denunciations of the USSR. So, in return for unspecified assurances from Beijing that the Taiwan issue would be resolved by peaceful means, the United States agreed to cut diplomatic ties with Taiwan and formally recognize the People's Republic.

A. Carter's Statement on Opening Ties with China, 15 December 1978

Good evening. I would like to read a joint communique which is being simultaneously issued . . . at this very moment by the leaders of the People's Republic of China:

> *A Joint Communique on the Establishment of Diplomatic Relations Between the United States of America and the People's Republic of China, January 1, 1979.*
>
> The United States of America and the People's Republic of China have agreed to recognize each other and to establish diplomatic relations as of January 1, 1979. The United States recognizes the Government of the People's Republic of China as the sole legal Government of China. Within this context the people of the United States will maintain cultural, commercial and other unofficial relations with the people of Taiwan.
>
> The United States of America and the People's Republic of China reaffirm the principles agreed on by the two sides in the Shanghai Communique of 1972 and emphasize once again that both sides wish to reduce the danger of international military conflict. Neither should seek hegemony—that is the dominance of one nation over others—in the Asia-Pacific region or in any other region of the world and each is opposed to efforts by any other country or group of countries to establish such hegemony. Neither is prepared to negotiate on behalf of any other third party or to enter into agreements or understandings with the other directed at other states.
>
> The Government of the United States of America acknowledges the Chinese position that there is but one China and Taiwan is part of China. Both believe that normalization of Sino-American relations is not only in the interest of the Chinese and American people but also contributes to the cause of peace in Asia and in the world. The United States of America and the People's Republic of China will exchange ambassadors and establish embassies on March 1, 1979.

Yesterday, our country and the People's Republic of China reached this final historic agreement. On Jan. 1, 1979, a little more than two weeks from now, our two Governments will implement full normalization of diplomatic relations.

As a nation of gifted people who comprise about one-fourth of the total population of the Earth, China plays, already, an important role in world affairs—a role that can only grow more important in the years ahead.

We do not undertake this important step for transient tactical or expedient reasons. In recognizing the People's Republic of China—that it is a single Government of China, we're recognizing simple reality. But far more is involved in this decision than just the recognition of a fact. . . .

The change that I'm announcing tonight will be of great long-term benefit to the peoples of both our country and China and I believe for all the peoples of the world.

Normalization and expanded commercial and cultural relations that it will bring will contribute to the well-being of our nation to our own national interest. And it will also enhance the stability of Asia.

These more positive relations with China can beneficially affect the world in which we live and the world in which our children will live.

We have already begun to inform our allies and other nations and the members of the Congress of the details of our intended action, but I wish also tonight to convey a special message to the people of Taiwan.

I have already communicated with the leaders in Taiwan, with whom the American people have had, and will have, extensive, close and friendly relations. This is important between our two peoples. As the United States asserted in the Shanghai Communique of 1972, issued on President Nixon's historic visit, we will continue to have an interest in the peaceful resolution of the Taiwan issue.

I have paid special attention to insuring that normalization of relations between our country and the People's Republic will not jeopardize the well-being of the people of Taiwan.

The people of our country will maintain our current commercial, cultural, trade and other relations with Taiwan through nongovernmental means. Many other countries of the world are already successfully doing this.

These decisions and these actions open a new and important chapter in our country's history and also in world affairs. To strengthen and to expedite the benefits of this new relationship between China and the United States, I am pleased to announce that Vice Premier Teng [Deng Xiaoping] has accepted my invitation and will visit Washington at the end of January. His visit will give our Governments the opportunity to consult with each other on global issues and to begin working together to enhance the cause of world peace.

These events are the final result of long and serious negotiations begun by President Nixon in 1972 and continued under the leadership of President Ford. The results bear witness to the steady, determined, bipartisan effort of our own country to build a world in which peace will be the goal and the responsibility of all nations.

The normalization of relations between the United States and China has no other purpose than the advancement of peace. It is in this spirit, at this season of peace, that I take special pride in sharing this good news with you tonight.

B. Statement by the People's Republic of China

As of Jan. 1, 1979, the People's Republic of China and the United States of America recognize each other and establish diplomatic relations, thereby ending the prolonged abnormal relationship between them. This is an historic event in Sino-United States relations.

As is known to all, the Government of the People's Republic of China is the sole legal Government of China and Taiwan is a part of China. The question of Taiwan was the crucial issue obstructing the normalization of relations between China and the United States. It has now been resolved between the two countries in the spirit of the Shanghai Communique and through their joint efforts, thus enabling the normalization of relations so ardently desired by the people of the two countries.

As for the way of bringing Taiwan back to the embrace of the motherland and reunifying the country, it is entirely China's internal affair.

At the invitation of the US Government, Teng Hsiao-ping [Deng Xiaoping], Deputy Prime Minister of the State Council of the People's Republic of China, will pay an official visit to the United States in January 1979, with a view to further promoting the friendship between the two peoples and good relations between the two countries.

DISCUSSION QUESTIONS

1. What reasons did Carter give for establishing diplomatic relations with China? What other reasons might he have had?
2. Why were the Chinese interested in establishing diplomatic relations with the United States?
3. What concessions did the Americans make in order to establish ties with China? What concessions did the Chinese make?
4. Why was the Taiwan issue so important to the Chinese?
5. Why was it difficult for the U.S. government to break off diplomatic relations with Taiwan?

66. The SALT II Agreement, 1979

The SALT I agreement signed by Nixon and Brezhnev in 1972 was an interim treaty, intended only to restrain the arms race for five years, during which the superpowers would negotiate a more comprehensive accord. After the 1974 Vladivostok summit, at which agreement was reached on the main issues, it seemed that a new treaty was within reach. However, due to the worsening international climate and the complexity of the remaining issues, things took longer than expected. They were further delayed in 1977, when President Carter took office and insisted on pushing for extensive arms reductions, far beyond what was agreed at Vladivostok. As a result, the treaty was not completed until 1979.

The SALT II agreement, signed by Carter and Brezhnev during their Vienna summit meeting of June 1979, followed the Vladivostok guidelines. It placed a ceiling of 2,400 (to be reduced to 2,250 in 1981) on the overall number of strategic missiles and bombers each side could possess, with a sublimit of 1,320 on the number that could have multiple warheads. As a result, although the arms race was slowed, each side retained vast quantities of ICBMs (intercontinental ballistics missiles), SLBMs (submarine-launched ballistics missiles), ASBMs (air-to-surface ballistics missiles), and MIRVs (multiple independently-targeted reentry vehicles).

The SALT II accord was destined to remain unratified. In the U.S. Senate, a determined opposition was led by Senator Henry Jackson of Washington, who had blasted the treaty as "appeasement" even before it was signed. Moscow's continuing deployment of its new SS–20, a mobile triple-warhead intermediate-range missile that was not covered under SALT (because it could not reach the United States and was thus not considered "strategic"), raised concerns among many senators. So did the 1979 revolution in Iran, which cost the United States some of its best facilities for monitoring Russian compliance. In January 1980, following the Soviet invasion of Afghanistan, Carter asked the Senate to postpone further action on the treaty. Still, although it did not have Senate approval, both Washington and Moscow professed to abide by it up to and beyond its stated expiration at the end of 1985.

Treaty on the Limitation of Strategic Offensive Arms (SALT II), 18 June 1979

Article I

Each Party undertakes, in accordance with the provisions of this Treaty, to limit strategic offensive arms quantitatively and qualitatively, to exercise restraint in the development of new types of strategic offensive arms, and to adopt other measures provided for in this Treaty. . . .

Article III

1. Upon entry into force of this Treaty, each Party undertakes to limit ICBM launchers, SLBM launchers, heavy bombers, and ASBMs to an aggregate number not to exceed 2,400.
2. Each Party undertakes to limit, from January 1, 1981, strategic offensive arms referred to in paragraph 1 of this Article to an aggregate number not to exceed 2,250, and to initiate reductions of those arms which as of that date would be in excess of this aggregate number.
3. Within the aggregate numbers provided for in paragraphs 1 and 2 of this Article . . . , each Party has the right to determine the composition of these aggregates. . . .

Article V

1. Within the aggregate numbers provided for in paragraphs 1 and 2 of Article III, each Party undertakes to limit launchers of ICBMs and SLBMs equipped with MIRVs, ASBMs equipped with MIRVs, and heavy bombers equipped for cruise missiles capable of a range in excess of 600 kilometers to an aggregate number not to exceed 1,320.
2. Within the aggregate number provided for in paragraph 1 of this Article, each Party undertakes to limit launchers of ICBMs and

SLBMs equipped with MIRVs and ASBMs equipped with MIRVs to an aggregate number not to exceed 1,200.

3. Within the aggregate number provided for in paragraph 2 of this Article, each Party undertakes to limit launchers of ICBMs equipped with MIRVs to an aggregate number not to exceed 820. . . .

Article XIV

The Parties undertake to begin, promptly after the entry into force of this Treaty, active negotiations with the objective of achieving, as soon as possible, agreement on further measures for the limitation and reduction of strategic arms. It is also the objective of the Parties to conclude well in advance of 1985 an agreement limiting strategic offensive arms to replace this Treaty upon its expiration.

Article XV

1. For the purpose of providing assurance of compliance with the provisions of this Treaty, each Party shall use national technical means of verification at its disposal in a manner consistent with generally recognized principles of international law.
2. Each Party undertakes not to interfere with the national technical means of verification of the other Party operating in accordance with paragraph 1 of this Article.
3. Each Party undertakes not to use deliberate concealment measures which impede verification by national technical means of compliance with the provisions of this Treaty. . . .

Article XVI

1. Each Party undertakes, before conducting each planned ICBM launch, to notify the other Party well in advance on a case-by-case basis that such a launch will occur, except for single ICBM launches from test ranges or from ICBM launcher deployment areas, which are not planned to extend beyond its national territory . . .

DISCUSSION QUESTIONS

1. Why did it take so long to negotiate the SALT II agreement?
2. What were the similarities and differences between this treaty and the SALT I treaty?
3. What impact would this treaty have on the arms race? What impact would it have on the size of the arsenals of the superpowers?
4. Why was there so much opposition to this treaty in the United States?
5. Why did the U.S. Senate not ratify the SALT II treaty? Why would both superpowers adhere to the treaty even though it was not ratified?

67. The Euromissile Controversy, 1979

In 1977, the strategic balance of forces in Europe was tested when the USSR deployed new SS–20 nuclear missiles. These intermediate-range missiles carried three warheads each and could be moved from place to place and fired at Western European targets from mobile launchers. Since the SS–20 could not reach the United States, Moscow contended that its deployment did nothing to alter the balance of forces between the superpowers. Privately, many American leaders agreed. But the Soviet move alarmed Europeans who might be the targets of those missiles, and this gave Washington an opportunity to reassert its leadership of NATO after more than a decade of U.S. absorption in Southeast Asian affairs. The United States suggested that outmoded Pershing IA missiles deployed in West Germany be replaced by modern two-stage Pershing IIs and Tomahawk cruise missiles, both of which could reach targets in the USSR.

The Soviet reaction was negative and swift. From Moscow's perspective, a NATO decision to station missiles in West Germany that could reach the USSR in 6–12 minutes would destabilize the strategic balance. NATO might argue that since both SS–20s and Pershing IIs were intermediate-range missiles, the balance remained, but to the Soviets, this ignored the fact that Pershing missiles in Germany would be able to hit them, while their SS–20s could not hit America. Soviet leader Brezhnev denounced the impending NATO deployment in a speech in East Berlin in October 1979. Two months later NATO announced a "dual track" policy: The missiles would be deployed as planned, but not until 1983; in the meantime, negotiations could begin with the objective of reducing not only intermediate range but intercontinental nuclear systems. However, in the hostile climate engendered by the Soviet invasion of Afghanistan (Document 68), those talks went nowhere, and the NATO missiles were deployed in 1983.

A. Brezhnev's Condemnation of NATO's Plans, 6 October 1979

The dangerous plans for the deployment of new types of American missile nuclear weapons in the territory of Western Europe—about which Western propaganda is trumpeting already now—give cause for serious concern. To put it straight, implementation of these designs would change essentially the strategic situation on the continent. Their aim is to upset the balance of forces that has taken shape in Europe and to try to insure military superiority for the NATO bloc.

As to military superiority—that we shall see. The Socialist countries would not, of course, watch indifferently the efforts of the NATO militarists. We would have in such a case to take the necessary extra steps to strengthen our security. There would be no other way out left for us. But one thing is absolutely clear: realization of NATO plans would inevitably aggravate the situation in Europe and vitiate in many respects the international atmosphere in general.

It is no secret that the Federal Republic of Germany, alongside of the USA, is assigned not the least part in the preparation of these dangerous plans.

Frankly speaking, those who shape the policy of that country are facing a very dangerous choice. They will have to decide which is the best for the FRG: to help strengthen peace in Europe and develop peaceful, mutually beneficial cooperation among European states in the spirit of good neighborliness and growing mutual confidence, or to contribute to a new aggravation of the situation in Europe and the world by deploying in its territory American missile nuclear arms spearheaded against the USSR and its allies.

It is clear that in this latter case, the position of the FRG itself would considerably worsen. It is not hard to see what consequences the FRG would have in store for itself if these new weapons were to be put to use by their owners one day.

The above said also applies, of course, to other European NATO countries which would be "lucky" enough to have American medium-range missile nuclear arms deployed in their territories.

As for the Soviet Union, I repeat again and again that we do not seek military superiority. We have never intended and do not intend to threaten any state or a group of states. Our strategic doctrine is purely defensive in nature. The assertions that the Soviet Union is building up its military might in the European continent above its defense needs have nothing in common with reality. This is a deliberate deception of the broad public.

As chairman of the Defense Council of the USSR, I am most definitely stating that the number of medium-range carriers of nuclear arms on the territory of the European part of the Soviet Union has not been increased by a single missile, by a single plane during the past 10 years. On the contrary, the number of launchers of medium-range missiles and also the yield of the nuclear charges of these missiles have even been somewhat decreased. The number of medium-range bombers, too, has diminished. As to the territory of other states, the Soviet Union does not deploy such means there at all. It is already for a number of years that we are not increasing the number of our troops stationed in Central Europe as well.

I will say more. We are prepared to reduce the number of medium-range nuclear means deployed in western areas of the Soviet Union as compared to the present level, but of course, only in the event if no additional medium-range nuclear means are deployed in Western Europe.

I also want to confirm solemnly that the Soviet Union will never use nuclear arms against those states that renounce the production and acquisition of such arms and do not have them on their territory.

Motivated by a sincere desire to take out of the impasse the efforts of many years to achieve military détente in Europe, to show an example of transition from words to real deeds, we have decided, in agreement with the leadership of the GDR and after consultations with other member-states of the Warsaw Treaty, to unilaterally reduce the number of Soviet troops in Central Europe. Up to 20,000 Soviet servicemen, 1,000 tanks and also a certain amount of other military hardware will be withdrawn from the territory of the German Democratic Republic in the course of the next 12 months.

We are convinced that this new concrete manifestation of the peaceableness and good will of the Soviet Union and its allies will be approved by the peoples of Europe and the whole world. We call upon the governments of NATO countries to properly assess the initiatives of Socialist states and to follow our good example.

The Soviet Union comes out for a further expansion of measures of trust in Europe. In particular, we are prepared to reach agreement that notification about big exercises of ground forces, provided for by the Helsinki Final Act, be made even earlier and not from the level of 25,000 men, as is the case now, but from a smaller one, for instance, from the level of 20,000 men. We also are prepared, on the basis of reciprocity, not to conduct military exercises involving more than 40,000 to 50,000 men. . . .

Consideration could be given also to other ideas directed at strengthening trust between states, at lessening the danger of the outbreak of war in Europe. We continue to regard a European conference held on the political level as the most suitable place for discussing a broad complex of measures of military détente in Europe. . . .

Lying ahead, as is known, are also important talks on SALT III. We are for commencing them immediately after the entry into force of the SALT II treaty. Within the framework of these talks we agree to discuss the possibilities of limiting not only intercontinental but also other types of armaments, but with due account, of course, for all related factors and strict observance of the principle of the equal security of the sides.

B. NATO Communique on "Dual Track" Approach, 12 December 1979

1. At a special meeting of the Foreign and Defense Ministers in Brussels on 12 December 1979:
2. Ministers recalled the May 1978 Summit where governments expressed the political resolve to meet the challenges to their security posed by the continuing momentum of the Warsaw Pact military build-up.
3. The Warsaw Pact has over the years developed a large and growing capability in nuclear systems that directly threaten Western Europe and have a strategic significance for the Alliance in Europe. This situation has been especially aggravated over the last few years by Soviet decisions to implement programs modernizing and expanding their long-range nuclear capability substantially. In particular, they have developed the SS–20 missile, which offers significant improvements over previous systems in providing greater accuracy, more mobility, and greater range, as well as having multiple warheads, and the Backfire bomber, which has a much better performance than other Soviet aircraft deployed hitherto in a theater role. During this period, while the Soviet Union has been reinforcing its superiority in LRTNF [long range theatre nuclear forces] both quantitatively and qualitatively, Western LRTNF

capabilities have remained static. Indeed these forces are increasing in age and vulnerability and do not include land-based, long-range theater nuclear missile systems.

4. At the same time, the Soviets have also undertaken a modernization and expansion of their shorter-range TNF [theatre nuclear forces] and greatly improved the overall quality of their conventional forces. These developments took place against the background of increasing Soviet inter-continental capabilities and achievement of parity in inter-continental capability with the United States.

5. These trends have prompted serious concern within the Alliance, because, if they were to continue, Soviet superiority in theater nuclear systems could undermine the stability achieved in inter-continental systems and cast doubt on the credibility of the Alliance's deterrent strategy by highlighting the gap in the spectrum of NATO's available nuclear response to aggression.

6. Ministers noted that these recent developments require concrete actions on the part of the Alliance if NATO's strategy of flexible response is to remain credible. After intensive consideration . . . , Ministers concluded that the overall interest of the Alliance would best be served by pursuing two parallel and complementary approaches of TNF modernization and arms control.

7. Accordingly Ministers have decided to modernize NATO's LRTNF by the deployment in Europe of US ground-launched systems comprising 108 Pershing II launchers, which would replace existing US Pershing I–A, and 464 Ground Launched Cruise Missiles (GLCM), all with single warheads. . . .

9. Ministers consider that . . . , taking account of the expansion of Soviet LRTNF capabilities of concern to NATO, arms control efforts to achieve a more stable overall nuclear balance at lower levels of nuclear weapons on both sides should therefore now include certain US and Soviet long-range theater nuclear systems. This would reflect previous Western suggestions to include such Soviet and US systems in arms control negotiations and more recent expressions by Soviet President Brezhnev of willingness to do so. Ministers fully support the decision taken by the United States following consultations within the Alliance to negotiate arms limitations on LRTNF and to propose to the USSR to begin negotiations as soon as possible along the following lines . . .

A. Any future limitations on US systems principally designed for theater missions should be accompanied by appropriate limitations on Soviet theater systems.

B. Limitations on US and Soviet long-range theater nuclear systems should be negotiated bilaterally in the SALT III framework in a step-by-step approach.

C. The immediate objective of these negotiations should be the establishment of agreed limitations on US and Soviet land-based long-range theater nuclear missile systems.

D. Any agreed limitations on these systems must be consistent with the principle of equality between the sides. . . .

E. Any agreed limitations must be adequately verifiable. . . .

11. The Ministers have decided to pursue these two parallel and complementary approaches in order to avert an arms race in Europe caused by the Soviet TNF buildup, yet preserve the viability of NATO's strategy of deterrence and defense and thus maintain the security of its member states. A modernization decision, including a commitment to deployments, is necessary to meet NATO's deterrence and defense needs, to provide a credible response to unilateral Soviet TNF deployments, and to provide the foundation for the pursuit of serious negotiations on TNF. Success of arms control in constraining the Soviet build-up can enhance Alliance security, modify the scale of NATO's TNF requirements, and promote stability and détente in Europe . . .

DISCUSSION QUESTIONS

1. Did Soviet deployment of SS–20s alter of the strategic balance between the USSR and the United States? Why or why not?
2. Moscow considered the NATO deployment equivalent to Khrushchev's decision to place missiles in Cuba in 1962. Is this a reasonable comparison? Why or why not?
3. What did Brezhnev mean when he spoke of possible "consequences" for West Germany?
4. What did Brezhnev offer in return for a NATO decision not to deploy Pershing II missiles?
5. What reasons did NATO give in support of its contention that the SS-20 deployment altered the strategic balance?

68. The Soviet Invasion of Afghanistan, December 1979

In December 1979, faced with a rebellion in neighboring Afghanistan against its new radical Communist regime, the USSR invaded that country, replaced the radical regime with moderate Communists, and sought to crush the rebellion with overwhelming force. President Carter, who had dedicated much effort to improving relations with Moscow, felt outraged and betrayed. First, he issued a statement denouncing the invasion and dispatched a protest note to Soviet leader Brezhnev. Then, in a revealing interview, he declared that events in Afghanistan had caused him to rethink his entire attitude toward the USSR. In January 1980, he effectively withdrew the SALT II agreement from Senate consideration and announced an embargo on shipments of grain and transfers of electronic technology to the USSR. His actions and words, and Brezhnev's angry response, left little doubt that the era of détente was over.

A. Carter's Statement on Iran and Afghanistan, 28 December 1979

Thank you. Secretary of State Vance will proceed to the United Nations tomorrow to press the world's case against Iran in order to obtain the speediest possible release of American hostages in accordance with demands which have already been made earlier by the United Nations Security Council and the International Court of Justice. . . .

Another serious development which has caused increased concern about peace and stability in the same region of the world is the recent Soviet military intervention in Afghanistan, which has now resulted in the overthrow of the established Government and the execution of the President of that country.

Such gross interference in the internal affairs of Afghanistan is in blatant violation of accepted international rules of behavior. This is the third occasion since World War II that the Soviet Union has moved militarily to assert control over one of its neighbors, and this is the first such venture into a Moslem country by the Soviet Union since the Soviet occupation of Iranian Azerbaijan in the 1940's. The Soviet action is a major matter of concern to the entire international community.

Soviet efforts to justify this action on the basis of the United Nations Charter are a perversion of the United Nations. They should be rejected immediately by all its members. I have discussed this serious matter personally today with several other heads of government, all of whom agree that the Soviet action is a grave threat to peace. I will be sending the Deputy Secretary of State to Europe this weekend to meet with representatives of several other nations to discuss how the world community might respond to this unwarranted Soviet behavior.

Soviet military action beyond its own borders gives rise to the most fundamental questions pertaining to international stability, and such close and extensive consultation[s] between ourselves and with our allies are urgently needed. Thank you very much.

B. Carter's Interview Concerning the Soviet Response to his Protest Note on the Invasion of Afghanistan, 31 December 1979

A. He [Brezhnev] responded in what I consider to be an inadequate way. He claimed that he had been invited by the Afghan Government to come in and protect Afghanistan from some outside third nation threat. This was obviously false because the person that he claimed invited him in, President Amin, was murdered or assassinated after the Soviets pulled their coup. He also claimed that they would remove their forces from Afghanistan as soon as the situation should be stabilized and the outside threat to Afghanistan was eliminated. So that was the tone of his message to me, which, as I say, was completely inadequate and completely misleading.

Q. Well, he's lying, isn't he, Mr. President?

A. He is not telling the facts accurately, that's correct.

Q. Have you changed your perception of the Russians in the time that you've been here? You started out, it seemed to a great many people, believing that if you expressed your good will and demonstrated it that they would reciprocate.

A. My opinion of the Russians has changed most drastically in the last week than even the previous two and a half years before that. It's only now dawning on the world the magnitude of the action that the Soviets undertook in invading Afghanistan. This is a circumstance that I think is now causing even former close friends and allies of the Soviet Union to re-examine their opinion of what the Soviets might have in mind.

And I think it's imperative . . . that in the next few days when we, after we consult with one another, that the leaders of the world make it clear to the Soviets that they cannot have taken this action to violate world peace not only in that region but throughout the world without paying severe political consequences. And what we will do about it I cannot yet say.

But to repeat myself, this action of the Soviets has made a more dramatic change in my own opinion of what the Soviets' ultimate goals are than anything they've done in the previous time I've been in office.

Q. But what we and the other nations allied with us do will involve more than stiff notes of protest?

A. Yes it will.

Q. It will? Action will be taken?

A. Yes. . . .

C. Brezhnev's Explanation of the Soviet Role in Afghanistan, 12 January 1980

It has been clear for some time that the leading circles of the United States and of some other NATO countries have embarked on a course hostile to the cause of détente, a course of spiraling the arms race and leading to a growth of the war danger. . . .

Today the opponents of peace and détente are trying to speculate on the events in Afghanistan. Mountains of lies are being built up around these events and a shameless anti-Soviet campaign is being mounted. What has really happened in Afghanistan?

A revolution took place there in April 1978. The Afghan people took its destiny into its hands and embarked on the road of independence and freedom. As it has always been in history, the forces of the past ganged up against the revolution. The people of Afghanistan, of course, could have coped with them itself. But from the very first days of the revolution it encountered an external aggression, rude interference from outside into its internal affairs.

Thousands and tens of thousands of insurgents, armed and trained abroad, whole armed units were sent into the territory of Afghanistan. In effect, imperialism together with its accomplices launched an undeclared war against revolutionary Afghanistan.

Afghanistan persistently demanded an end to the aggression, that it be allowed to build its new life in peace. Resisting the external aggression, the Afghan leadership . . . repeatedly asked the Soviet Union for assistance. On our part, we warned those concerned that if the aggression would not be stopped we would not abandon the Afghan people at a time of trial. As is known, we stand by what we say . . .

The unceasing armed intervention, the well advanced plot by external forces of reaction created a real threat that Afghanistan would lose its independence and be turned into an imperialist military bridgehead on our country's southern border.

In other words, the time came when we no longer could fail to respond to the friendly request of the Government of friendly Afghanistan. To have acted otherwise would have meant leaving Afghanistan a prey to imperialism, allowing the aggressive forces to repeat in that country what they had succeeded in doing, for instance, in Chile where the people's freedom was drowned in blood. To act otherwise would have meant to watch passively the origination on our southern border of a seat of serious danger to the security of the Soviet state. . . .

It was no simple decision for us to send Soviet military contingents to Afghanistan. But the Party's Central Committee and the Soviet Government acted in full awareness of their responsibility and took into account the entire sum total of circumstances. The only task set to the Soviet contingents is to assist the Afghans in repulsing the aggression from outside. They will be fully withdrawn from Afghanistan once the causes that made the Afghan leadership request their introduction disappear.

It goes without saying that there has been no Soviet "intervention" or "aggression" at all. There is another thing: we are helping the new Afghanistan on the request of its Government to defend the national independence, freedom and honor of its country from armed aggressive actions from outside. . . .

Finally, the entire sum total of the American Administration's steps in connection with the events in Afghanistan—the freezing of the SALT II treaty, refusal to deliver to the USSR a whole number of commodities, including grain, in accordance with some already concluded contracts, the termination of talks with the Soviet Union on a number of questions of bilateral relations, and so on, shows that Washington again, like decades ago, is trying to speak with us in the language of the Cold War. . . .

DISCUSSION QUESTIONS

1. Why was Carter outraged by the Soviet invasion of Afghanistan? What impact did it have on his attitude toward the USSR?
2. Why did Carter respond so forcefully? To what extent were his actions justified?
3. What reasons did Brezhnev give for Soviet actions? What other reasons might he have had? How did his description of events in Afghanistan contrast with Carter's?
4. Why was the invasion of Afghanistan a fatal blow to détente?

69. The Carter Doctrine, January 1980

President Carter's response to the Soviet invasion of Afghanistan was dictated, not only by his personal outrage but also by his fear that Moscow was moving to establish a presence on the Indian Ocean near the Persian Gulf, where it could threaten the vital oil shipments on which the West depended. Sensitive to anything that might endanger America's energy supplies, he moved resolutely to preclude Soviet expansion into this region. On 23 January 1980, in his state of the union address, he declared that the Persian Gulf would henceforth be considered a vital U.S. interest and that America would use military force if necessary to prevent an outside power from gaining control there. This declaration was soon called the Carter Doctrine.

Excerpt from Carter's State of the Union Address, 23 January 1980

. . . Since the end of the Second World War, America has led other nations in meeting the challenge of mounting Soviet power. This has not been a simple or a static relationship. Between us there has been cooperation—there has been competition—and at times there has been confrontation. . . .

But now the Soviet Union has taken a radical and an aggressive new step. It's using its great military power against a relatively defenseless nation. The implications of the Soviet invasion of Afghanistan could pose the most serious threat to the peace since the second World War.

The vast majority of nations on earth have condemned this latest Soviet attempt to extend its colonial domination of others and have demanded the immediate withdrawal of Soviet troops. The Moslem world is especially and justifiably outraged by this aggression against an Islamic people. No action of a world power has ever been so quickly and so overwhelmingly condemned.

But verbal condemnation is not enough. The Soviet Union must pay a concrete price for their aggression. While this invasion continues, we and the other nations of the world cannot continue business as usual with the Soviet Union.

That's why the United States has imposed stiff economic penalties on the Soviet Union. I will not issue any permits for Soviet ships to fish in the coastal waters of the United States. I've cut Soviet access to high technology equipment and to agricultural products. I've limited other commerce with the Soviet Union, and I've asked our allies and friends to join with us in restraining their own trade with the Soviets and not to replace our own embargoed items. And I have notified the Olympic Committee that with Soviet invading forces in Afghanistan, neither the American people nor I will support sending an Olympic team to Moscow.

The Soviet Union is going to have to answer some basic questions: Will it help promote a more stable international environment in which its own legitimate, peaceful concerns can be pursued? Or will it continue to expand its military power far beyond its genuine security needs, and use that power for colonial conquest?

The Soviet Union must realize that its decision to use military force in Afghanistan will be costly to every political and economic relationship it values.

The region which is now threatened by Soviet troops in Afghanistan is of great strategic importance. It contains more than two-thirds of the world's exportable oil. The Soviet effort to dominate Afghanistan has brought Soviet military forces to within 300 miles of the Indian Ocean and close to the Straits of Hormuz—a waterway through which most of the world's oil must flow. The Soviet Union is now attempting to consolidate a strategic position therefore that poses a grave threat to the free movement of Middle East oil.

The situation demands careful thought, steady nerves and resolute action— not only for this year, but for many years to come. It demands collective efforts to meet this new threat to security in the Persian Gulf and in Southwest Asia. It demands the participation of those who rely on oil from the Middle East and who are concerned with global peace and stability. And it demands consultation and close cooperation with countries in the area which might be threatened.

Meeting this challenge will take national will, diplomatic and political wisdom, economic sacrifice and, of course, military capability. We must call on the best that is in us to preserve the security of this crucial region.

Let our position be absolutely clear: An attempt by any outside force to gain control of the Persian Gulf region will be regarded as an assault on the vital interests of the United States of America. And such an assault will be repelled by any means necessary, including military force. . . .

DISCUSSION QUESTIONS

1. What motives did Carter see behind the Soviet invasion of Afghanistan? What justification did he give for the steps he was taking?
2. Why was Carter so concerned about a threat to the Persian Gulf? Why did he consider it a vital American interest?
3. How would you expect the USSR to react to the measures announced by Carter? Why?

70. Reagan's Anti-Soviet Rhetoric, 1981–1983

The inauguration of Ronald Reagan in January 1981 brought to power a man who was not only passionately anti-Communist, but who also characterized the Cold War as a conflict between good and evil. Deeply distrustful of Moscow, the new president intensified the arms race and used his rhetorical skills to depict the U.S. buildup as a crusade against the powers of darkness. In his first press conference, Reagan complained that Americans were at a disadvantage because the Soviets were ready to "commit any crime; to lie; to cheat" in order to advance their cause. Two years later, in the most widely quoted speech of his presidency, directed to a group of Protestant ministers, he characterized the USSR as an "evil empire" and the "focus of evil in the modern world." He went on to proclaim, prophetically, that "Communism is another sad, bizarre chapter in history whose last pages even now are being written. . . ."

A. Excerpt from President Reagan's First Press Conference, 29 January 1981

Q. Mr. President, what do you see as the long-range intentions of the Soviet Union? Do you think . . . the Kremlin is bent on world domination that might lead to a continuation of the cold war? Or do you think that under other circumstances détente is possible?

A. Well, so far détente's been a one-way street the Soviet Union has used to pursue its own aims. I don't have to think of an answer as to what I think their intentions are: They have repeated it. I know of no leader of the Soviet Union, since the revolution and including the present leadership, that has not more than once repeated . . . their determination that their goal must be the promotion of world revolution and a one world Socialist or Communist state—whichever word you want to use.

Now, as long as they do that and as long as they, at the same time, have openly and publicly declared that the only morality they recognize is what will further their cause: meaning they reserve unto themselves the right to commit any crime; to lie; to cheat, in order to obtain that and that is moral, not immoral, and we operate on a different set of standards, I think when you do business with them—even at a détente—you keep that in mind.

B. Excerpt from Reagan's "Evil Empire" Speech, 8 March 1983

During my first press conference as president . . . I pointed out that as good Marxist-Leninists the Soviet leaders have openly and publicly declared that the only morality they recognize is that which will further their cause, which is world revolution. I think I should point out I was only quoting Lenin, their guiding spirit, who said in 1920 that they repudiate all morality that proceeds from supernatural ideas or ideas that are outside class conceptions; morality is entirely subordinate to the interests of class war; and everything is moral that is necessary for the annihilation of the old exploiting social order and for uniting the proletariat.

I think the refusal of many influential people to accept this elementary fact of Soviet doctrine illustrates a historical reluctance to see totalitarian powers for what they are. We saw this phenomenon in the 1930s; we see it too often today.

This does not mean we should isolate ourselves and refuse to seek an understanding with them. I intend to do everything I can to persuade them of our peaceful intent; to remind them that it was the West that refused to use its nuclear monopoly in the forties and fifties for territorial gain and which now proposes fifty percent cuts in strategic ballistic missiles and the elimination of an entire class of land-based, intermediate-range nuclear missiles.

At the same time, however, they must be made to understand we will never compromise our principles and standards. We will never give away our freedom. We will never abandon our belief in God. And we will never stop searching for a genuine peace. But we can assure none of these things America stands for through the so-called nuclear freeze solutions proposed by some. The truth is that a freeze now would be a very dangerous fraud, for that is merely the illusion of peace. The reality is that we must find peace through strength. . . .

Let us pray for the salvation of all those who live in totalitarian darkness, pray they will discover the joy of knowing God. But until they do, let us be aware that while they preach the supremacy of the state, declare its omnipotence over individual man, and predict its eventual domination of all peoples of the earth—they are the focus of evil in the modern world. . . .

If history teaches anything, it teaches: simple-minded appeasement or wishful thinking about our adversaries is folly—it means the betrayal of our past, the squandering of our freedom. So, I urge you to speak out against those who would place the United States in a position of military and moral inferiority. . . . In your discussions of the nuclear freeze proposals, I urge you to beware the temptation of pride—the temptation of blithely declaring yourselves above it all and label both sides equally at fault, to ignore the facts of history and the aggressive impulses of an evil empire, to simply call the arms race a giant misunderstanding and thereby remove yourself from the struggle between right and wrong, good and evil. . . .

I believe we shall rise to the challenge. I believe that Communism is another sad, bizarre chapter in history whose last pages even now are being written. . . .

DISCUSSION QUESTIONS

1. How did Reagan's Cold War approach differ from that of the previous three presidents? From Reagan's perspective, what had been wrong with détente?
2. Why was Reagan's rhetoric so appealing to many Americans?
3. According to Reagan, why were Americans at a disadvantage in dealing with the USSR? What might they do to overcome this?
4. What were the advantages and disadvantages of Reagan's anti-Soviet rhetoric? What implications did Reagan's rhetoric have for U.S. foreign policy?

71. Reagan's Arms Control Proposals, November 1981

Arms control was not one of Reagan's priorities when he first took office. He focused instead on enlarging the U.S. arsenal, investing billions in new weapons systems. The resulting escalation of the arms race, however, combined with the president's strident rhetoric, heightened anxieties and led to widespread criticism. In November 1981, to alleviate such fears and objections, he put forth his own arms proposals. In the arena of intermediate-range nuclear forces (INF), he offered what came to be called the "zero option": NATO would cancel its installation of new missiles in Europe if Moscow would eliminate all its intermediate-range missiles. In the realm of strategic arms, he proposed replacing SALT with START (strategic arms *reduction* talks), thus changing the focus from mere limitation to deep and sweeping cuts. Both the Kremlin and Reagan's critics saw these as public relations gimmicks rather than serious proposals, but in the long run, they helped pave the way for major arms reduction treaties.

Excerpt from Reagan's Address on Arms Reduction, 18 November 1981

. . . Now let me turn now to our hopes for arms control negotiations. There's a tendency to make this entire subject overly complex; I want to be clear and concise. I told you of the letter I wrote to President Brezhnev last April? Well, I've just sent another message to the Soviet leadership.

It's a simple, straightforward yet historic message. The United States proposes the mutual reduction of conventional, intermediate-range nuclear and strategic forces. Specifically, I have proposed a four-point agenda to achieve this objective. . . .

The first and most important point concerns the Geneva negotiations. As part of the 1979 two-track decision, NATO made a commitment to seek arms control negotiations with the Soviet Union on intermediate-range nuclear forces. . . . We're now ready to set forth our proposal.

I have informed President Brezhnev that when our delegation travels to the negotiations on intermediate-range land-based nuclear missiles in Geneva on the 30th of this month, my representatives will present the following proposal:

The United States is prepared to cancel its deployment of Pershing 2 and ground-launched missiles if the Soviets will dismantle their SS–20, SS–4 and SS–5 missiles. This would be an historic step. With Soviet agreement, we could together substantially reduce the dread threat of nuclear war which hangs over the people of Europe. This, like the first footstep on the moon, would be a giant step for mankind.

Now we intend to negotiate in good faith and go to Geneva willing to listen to and consider the proposals of our Soviet counterparts. But let me call to your attention the background against which our proposal is made. During the past six years, while the United States deployed no new intermediate-range missiles and withdrew 1,000 nuclear warheads from Europe, the Soviet Union deployed 750 warheads on mobile, accurate ballistic missiles. They now have 1,100 warheads on the SS-20's, SS-4's and 5's. And the United States has no comparable missiles. . . .

As we look to the future of the negotiations, it's also important to address certain Soviet claims which, left unrefuted, could become critical barriers to real progress in arms control. The Soviets assert that a balance of intermediate-range nuclear forces already exists; that assertion is wrong. By any objective measure . . . the Soviet Union has developed an increasing, overwhelming advantage. They now enjoy a superiority on the order of 6 to 1. . . .

Now Soviet spokesmen have suggested that moving their SS–20's behind the Ural Mountains will remove the threat to Europe. Well, . . . the SS–20's, even if deployed behind the Urals, will have a range that puts almost all of Western Europe . . . , all of the Middle East, all of Northern Africa—all within range of these missiles, which, incidentally, are mobile and can be moved on shorter notice. . . .

The second proposal that I've made to President Brezhnev concerns strategic weapons. . . .

. . . I have informed President Brezhnev that we will seek to negotiate substantial reductions in nuclear arms, which would result in levels that are equal and verifiable. Our approach with verification will be to emphasize openness and creativity rather than the secrecy and suspicion which have undermined confidence in arms control in the past.

While we can hope to benefit from work done over the past decade in strategic arms negotiations, let us agree to do more than simply begin where these previous efforts left off. We can and should attempt major qualitative and quantitative progress. Only such progress can fulfill the hopes of our own people and the rest of the world. And let us see how far we can go in achieving truly substantial reductions in our strategic arsenals.

To symbolize this fundamental change in direction, we will call these negotiations START—Strategic Arms Reduction Talks.

The third proposal I've made to the Soviet Union is that we act to achieve equality at lower levels of conventional forces in Europe. The defense needs of the Soviet Union hardly call for maintaining more combat divisions in East Germany today than were in the whole allied invasion force that landed in Normandy on D-Day. The Soviet Union could make no more convincing contribution to peace in Europe and in the world than by agreeing to reduce its conventional forces significantly and constrain the potential for sudden aggression.

Finally, I have pointed out to President Brezhnev that to maintain peace we must reduce the risks of surprise attack and the chance of war arising out of uncertainty or miscalculation. I am renewing our proposal for a conference to develop effective measures that would reduce these dangers.

At the current Madrid meeting of the Conference on Security and Cooperation in Europe we're laying the foundation for a western-proposed conference on disarmament in Europe. This conference would discuss new measures to enhance stability and security in Europe. . . . I urge the Soviet Union to join us and many other nations who are ready to launch this important enterprise.

All of these proposals are based on the same fair-minded principles: substantial, militarily significant reduction in forces, equal ceiling for similar types of forces, and adequate provisions for verification.

My Administration, our country and I are committed to achieving arms reductions agreements based on these principles.

DISCUSSION QUESTIONS

1. Why was Reagan reluctant to enter arms control talks with Moscow? Why did he want to build up the U.S. arsenal before holding such talks?
2. How did Reagan's approach to arms control differ from that of his predecessors?
3. Why did he advance the "zero-option"? Why did he change SALT to START? Why would Moscow object to these proposals?
4. Why did he propose deep cuts in conventional forces in Europe? Why would Moscow object?

72. The Polish Imposition of Martial Law, December 1981

In 1980 in Poland, a series of strikes, triggered by severe economic crisis, led to formation of a independent worker's trade union movement called Solidarity. In 1981, as the union grew in size and audacity, it organized mass demonstrations and pushed for political as well as economic changes. As the situation deteriorated and the Communist government began to lose control, the Soviet military started staging maneuvers near the Polish border. For awhile it looked as if the USSR would invade, as it had in Hungary in 1956 and Czechoslovakia in 1968. But in December the Polish regime, led by General Wojciech Jaruzelski, took matters into its own hands and declared martial law. It imposed curfews, suspended liberties, banned public demonstrations, arrested Solidarity leaders, and eventually outlawed the union.

A. General Jaruzelski's Radio Address, 13 December 1981

Citizens of the Polish People's Republic, I address you today as a soldier, as the chief of the Polish Government. I address you on the most important matters.

Our country is on the edge of the abyss. Achievements of many generations, raised from the ashes, are collapsing into ruin. State structures no longer function. New blows are struck each day at our flickering economy. Living conditions are burdening people more and more.

Through each place of work, many Polish people's homes, there is a line of painful division. The atmosphere of unending conflict, misunderstanding and hatred sows mental devastation and damages the tradition of tolerance.

Strikes, strike alerts, protest actions have become standard. Even students are dragged into it.

Last night, many public institutions were occupied. There are calls for physical debate with "Reds," with people of different opinions. There are more and more examples of terror, threats, moral lynching and direct assaults. Crimes, robberies and break-ins are spreading like a wave through the country. Fortunes of millions are being made by the sharks of the economic underground.

Chaos and demoralization have reached the level of defeat. The nation has reached the borderline of mental endurance, many people are desperate. Now, not days but hours separate us from a nationwide catastrophe. . . .

We have to declare today, when we know the forthcoming day of mass political demonstrations, including the ones in the center of Warsaw called in connection with the anniversary of the December events—that tragedy cannot be repeated. It must not. We cannot let these demonstrations be a spark causing a fire in the country.

The self-preservation instinct of the nation must be taken into account. We must bind the hands of adventurers before they push the country into civil war. Citizens of Poland, heavy is the burden of responsibility which lies upon me at this very dramatic moment in Polish history. But it is my duty to take it. . . .

I declare that today the Martial Council for National Redemption has been constituted, and the Council of State obeying the Polish Constitution declared a state of emergency at midnight on the territory of Poland.

I want everybody to understand my motives and aims for action. We do not aim at a military takeover, a military dictatorship. The nation is strong and wise enough to develop a democratic system of socialist government. And in such a system, military forces could stay where their place is. None of Poland's problems can be solved by force.

The Martial Council for National Redemption is not a substitute for the constitutional government. Its only task is to protect law in the country, to guarantee reestablishment of order and discipline. That is the way to start coming out of the crisis, to save the country from collapsing. . . .

. . . The declaration of the Martial Council for National Redemption and other decrees published today define the terms and standards of public order for the duration of the state of emergency. The military council would be disbanded when law governs the country and when the conditions for the functioning of civilian administration and representative bodies are created. As the situation stabilizes itself gradually, the limits on freedom in public life will be overruled. But nobody can count on weakness or indecision. . . .

In the name of national interests, a group of people threatening the safety of the country has been interned. The extremists of Solidarity are included in this group as well as other members of illegal organizations.

On the demand of the military council, several people responsible personally for pushing the country into crisis during the 1970's and abusing the posts for personal profit have been interned. . . . The full list will be published. We will consequently clean Polish life from evil no matter where it arises. . . .

B. Excerpts from the Decree Imposing Martial Law

The convening and holding of all kinds of gatherings, processions and demonstrations is banned, as well as the organizing and conducting of public gatherings and artistic, entertainment and sports events without first obtaining the consent of the appropriate regional organ of the state administration. Excepted are religious services and rites taking place on the premises of churches, chapels or other places designated exclusively for these purposes.

The dissemination of all kinds of publications or information by any means is banned. The public performance of works of art and the use of any kind of printing equipment, without first obtaining the permission of the appropriate organ is also banned.

In connection with the introduction of martial law, the Interior Minister has introduced a ban on movement by citizens in public places during the hours from 2200 to 0600. The curfew has been introduced throughout the country. Persons who spend the daytime in public places must carry personal identity documents.

People wanting to change their permanent residence or their temporary residence for a period longer than 48 hours must first obtain permission from the regional authorities. On arrival in a given locality they must report to the authorities within 12 hours. . . .

All citizens are asked to restrict to a minimum their movements in public places so as to prevent violations of public order.

Civil, military and other public-order officials may use direct coercion with regard to persons failing to observe the above restrictions.

The introduction of martial law entails the temporary suspension of basic civil rights defined in the Polish Constitution, in particular those of personal liberty.

Polish citizens over the age of 17 whose behavior in the past gives rise to the justified suspicion that, if left free, they would not observe the legal order or that they would engage in activity that threatens the interest, security or defense of the state, may be interned at centers of isolation for the duration of martial law. . . .

In connection with the exacerbation of the political situation caused by forces hostile to the socialist state seeking to take over the radio and television, conditions arose that made it impossible to carry out normal work and that endangered the safety of the employees of Polish radio and television. In order to insure the correct and essential functioning of the radio and television, the Council of Ministers orders the following:

1. One central radio program and one central television program will be broadcast.
2. The remaining radio programs and the second television channel will cease broadcasting.
3. The regional broadcasting stations and regional television centers will be switched off and the activity of the television center and the central radio station in Warsaw will be restricted to the essential minimum. . . .

All firearms, ammunition and explosives must be handed in to the civic militia within 24 hours. The carrying of all potentially dangerous weapons is banned. . . .

State organs are also authorized to introduce limitation of freedom of movement of inhabitants in specified times and places through the introduction of a curfew or prohibition of movement to and from specified provinces, towns and parishes. . . .

From today the sale of engine fuels is suspended immediately at all public fuel stations for all private motor vehicles. All users of private cars are asked not to drive up to fuel stations because these stations will not fill tanks for an indefinite period.

DISCUSSION QUESTIONS

1. What reasons did Jaruzelski give for declaring martial law? What other reasons did he have? Why did he not mention them?
2. Why were the Soviets pleased by the imposition of martial law? Why did they want to avoid an invasion of Poland?
3. What restrictions did martial law entail? How were they intended to ease the crisis?
4. Why were the Solidarity leaders arrested? How did Jaruzelski justify this action?

73. Andropov's Peace Offensive, 1982

Yuri V. Andropov, who succeeded Brezhnev as Soviet leader in November 1982, believed that new insights and approaches were needed. Apprehensive about the increasing risk of nuclear war since the collapse of détente, and mindful that global concern about that danger was mounting, he embarked on a skillful public relations campaign aimed not only at America but also at its allies in Europe. In December 1982, as part of this "peace offensive," he delivered a speech calling for measures to reduce the threat of nuclear war, including substantial reductions in the numbers of missiles deployed by both sides in Europe.

Excerpts from Andropov's Speech on Reductions in Nuclear Missiles, 21 December 1982

A nuclear war, whether big or small, whether limited or total, must not be allowed to break out. That is why the unilateral commitment of the Soviet Union not to use nuclear weapons first was received with approval and hope all over the world. If our example is followed by the other nuclear powers, this will be a truly momentous contribution to . . . preventing nuclear war. . . .

Of course, one of the main avenues leading to a real scaling down of the threat of nuclear war is that of reaching a Soviet-American agreement on limitation and reduction of strategic nuclear armaments. . . .

We are prepared to reduce our strategic arms by more than 25 percent. US arms, too, must be reduced accordingly, so that the two states have the same number of strategic delivery vehicles. We also propose that the number of nuclear warheads should be substantially lowered and that improvement of nuclear weapons should be maximally restricted. . . .

And, while the negotiations are under way, we offer what is suggested by common sense: to freeze the strategic arsenals of the two sides. The US Government does not want this and now everyone can understand why: it has embarked on a new, considerable buildup of nuclear armaments. . . .

The Soviet Union is prepared to go very far. As everybody knows, we have suggested an agreement renouncing all types of nuclear weapons . . . designed to strike targets in Europe. But this proposal has come up against a solid wall of silence. Evidently they do not want to accept it, but are afraid to reject it openly. . . .

We have also suggested . . . that the USSR and the NATO countries reduce their medium-range weaponry by more than two-thirds. So far, the United States will not have it. For its part, it has submitted a proposal that, as if in mockery, is called a "zero option." It envisages elimination of all Soviet medium-range missiles not only in the European but also in the Asiatic part of the Soviet Union, while NATO's nuclear missile arsenal in Europe is to remain intact and may even be increased. Does anyone really think that the Soviet Union can agree to this? . . .

We are prepared, among other things, to agree that the Soviet Union should retain in Europe only as many missiles as are kept there by Britain and France—and not a single one more. This means that the Soviet Union would reduce hundreds of missiles, including dozens of the latest missiles known in the West as SS–20. In the case of the USSR and the USA this would be a really honest "zero option" as regards medium-range missiles. . . .

Along with this there must also be an accord on reducing to equal levels on both sides the number of medium-range nuclear-delivery aircraft stationed in this region by the USSR and the NATO countries.

We call on the other side to accept these clear and fair terms, to take this opportunity while it still exists. But let no one delude himself: we will never let our security or the security of our allies be jeopardized. It would also be a good thing if thought were given to the grave consequences that the stationing of new US medium-range weapons in Europe would entail for all further efforts to limit nuclear armaments in general. In short, the ball is now in the court of the USA.

DISCUSSION QUESTIONS

1. Why did Andropov launch a "peace offensive"? How did his proposals differ from Reagan's (Document 71)? Why did he object to Reagan's "zero option"?
2. Why did Andropov stress the Soviet pledge not to use nuclear weapons first? Why might the Americans not want to make such a pledge?
3. Why did he propose freezing strategic arsenals at current levels during negotiations? Why might the Americans refuse to go along?
4. Why did he suggest that the USSR should retain in Europe "only as many missiles as are kept there by Britain and France"? What objections might Washington raise to this proposal?

74. Reagan's "Star Wars" Speech, 1983

In March 1983, as Andropov pursued his peace offensive, Ronald Reagan announced his own unique peace program. Rather than basing U.S. security on negotiations with a foe he deeply distrusted or on the deterrent threat of nuclear war, he placed his faith in American technology. In a televised address that surprised even some of his advisors, he announced a program to develop a space-based "shield" that would protect America from Soviet attack by shooting down incoming missiles. Reagan called it his Strategic Defense Initiative (SDI), but it was widely known as "Star Wars." Although SDI would severely complicate arms negotiations, it enabled Reagan to portray himself as a man of peace working to reduce the threat of nuclear war.

Excerpts from Reagan's Televised Speech, 23 March 1983

My fellow Americans, thank you for sharing your time with me tonight. The subject I want to discuss with you, peace and national security, is both timely and important—timely because I have reached a decision that offers new hope for our children in the 21st century. . . .

We are engaged right now in several negotiations with the Soviet Union to bring about a mutual reduction of weapons. . . . If the Soviet Union will join us in our effort to achieve major arms reduction we will have succeeded in stabilizing the nuclear balance. Nevertheless, it will be necessary to rely on the specter of retaliation—on mutual threat, and that is a sad commentary on the human condition.

Wouldn't it be better to save lives than to avenge them? Are we not capable of demonstrating our peaceful intentions by applying all our abilities and our ingenuity to achieving a truly lasting stability? I think we are—indeed, we must!

After careful consultation with my advisors, including the Joint Chiefs of Staff, I believe there is a way. Let me share with you a vision of the future which offers hope. It is that we embark on a program to counter the awesome Soviet missile threat with measures that are defensive. Let us turn to the very strengths in technology that spawned our great industrial base and that have given us the quality of life we enjoy today.

What if free people could live secure in the knowledge that their security did not rest upon the threat of instant US retaliation to deter a Soviet attack; that we could intercept and destroy strategic ballistic missiles before they reached our own soil or that of our allies?

I know this is a formidable, technical task, one that may not be accomplished before the end of this century. Yet, current technology has attained a level of sophistication where it is reasonable for us to begin the effort. It will take years, probably decades, of effort on many fronts. There will be failures and setbacks just as there will be successes and breakthroughs. And as we proceed, we must remain constant in preserving the nuclear deterrent and maintaining a solid capability for flexible response. But isn't it worth every investment necessary to free the world from the threat of nuclear war? We know it is. . . .

I clearly recognize that defensive systems have limitations and raise certain problems and ambiguities. If paired with offensive systems, they can be viewed as fostering an aggressive policy, and no one wants that.

But with these considerations in mind, I call upon the scientific community in our country, those who gave us nuclear weapons, to turn their great talents now to the cause of mankind and world peace: to give us the means of rendering these nuclear weapons impotent and obsolete.

Tonight, consistent with our obligations under the ABM Treaty and recognizing the need for closer consultation with our allies, I am taking an important first step. I am directing a comprehensive and intensive effort to define a long-term research and development program to begin to achieve our ultimate goal of eliminating the threat posed by strategic nuclear missiles. This could pave the way for arms control measures to eliminate the weapons themselves. We seek neither military superiority nor political advantage. Our only purpose—one all people share—is to search for ways to reduce the danger of nuclear war.

DISCUSSION QUESTIONS

1. What was the essence of Reagan's "Star Wars" vision? Why was it so appealing?
2. What were the potential advantages and disadvantages of SDI for the United States? Why might some be skeptical of its value?
3. What political benefits might Reagan derive from initiating SDI?
4. Why would Soviet leaders respond negatively to SDI? What concerns did it arouse in them?

75. The Nuclear Freeze Resolution, 1983

In the early 1980s, as the nuclear arms race intensified, a "nuclear freeze" movement emerged in Europe and America. Proposing to end the arms race by negotiating a prompt cessation of all weapons testing and production, it called for an "immediate, mutual and verifiable freeze" on the arsenals of both sides. As the movement picked up steam, politicians climbed on board. Despite Reagan's efforts to counter it, a nuclear freeze resolution was approved by the U.S. House of Representatives in May 1983. Although it was not binding, it served as a public call to Reagan to moderate his policies and reach an agreement with Moscow.

Highlights of the Nuclear Weapons Freeze Resolution Passed by the House of Representatives, 4 May 1983

Resolved by the Senate and House of Representatives of the United States of America in Congress assembled, that, consistent with the maintenance of essential equivalence in overall nuclear capabilities now and in the future, the Strategic Arms Reduction Talks between the United States and the Soviet Union should have the following objectives:

1. Pursuing the objective of negotiating an immediate, mutual and verifiable freeze, then pursuing the objective of negotiating immediate, mutual and verifiable reductions in nuclear weapons.
2. Deciding when and how to achieve a mutual verifiable freeze on testing, production, and further deployment of nuclear warheads, missiles, and other delivery systems, and systems which would threaten the viability of sea-based nuclear deterrent forces, and to include all air defense systems designed to stop nuclear bombers. Submarines are not delivery systems as used herein.

3. Consistent with pursuing the objective of negotiating an immediate, mutual and verifiable freeze, giving special attention to destabilizing weapons, especially those which give either nation capabilities which confer upon it even the hypothetical advantage of a first strike.
4. Providing the cooperative measures of verification, including provisions for on-site inspection as appropriate to complement national technical means of verification and to ensure compliance.
5. Proceeding from this mutual and verifiable freeze, pursuing substantial, equitable and verifiable reductions through numerical ceilings, annual percentages, or any other equally effective and verifiable means of strengthening strategic stability. . . .
6. Preserving present limitations and controls on nuclear weapons and nuclear delivery systems.
7. Incorporating ongoing negotiations in Geneva on intermediate-range nuclear systems into the START negotiations.
8. Discussing the impact of comprehensive defensive systems consistent with all provisions of the Treaty on the Limitation of Anti Ballistic-Missile Systems.

In those negotiations, the United States shall make every effort to reach a common position with our North Atlantic Treaty Organization allies on any element of an agreement which would be inconsistent with existing United States commitments to those allies.

DISCUSSION QUESTIONS

1. Why did the freeze movement become so popular in America in 1983? Why would Andropov be supportive of this movement?
2. How did Reagan's policies and rhetoric contribute to the growth of this movement?
3. What were the key provisions of the freeze resolution? Which provisions would Reagan object to and why?
4. What did its sponsors hope to accomplish in getting congressional approval?

76. The KAL 007 Incident, 1983

In September 1983, as the Cold War climate worsened, a tragic incident damaged relations still further. A South Korean Airliner, on a flight from New York to Korea (KAL flight 007), went off course and flew through Soviet air space for a few hours, passing over sensitive military sites. As it was about to leave Soviet air space, it was shot down with a missile fired by a Soviet pilot, killing all 269 persons aboard. The event resulted in international outrage against the USSR, and in charges and countercharges that brought superpower relations to an impasse.

Statement by Secretary of State George Shultz on Soviet Downing of Korean Jetliner, 1 September 1983

At 1400 hours Greenwich mean time yesterday, a Korean Air Lines Boeing 747 en route from New York to Seoul, Korea, departed Anchorage, Alaska. Two-hundred sixty-nine passengers and crew were on board, including Congressman Lawrence P. McDonald.

At approximately 1600 hours Greenwich mean time, the aircraft came to the attention of Soviet radar. It was tracked constantly by the Soviets from that time.

The aircraft strayed into Soviet airspace over the Kamchatka Peninsula and over the Sea of

Okhotsk and over the Sakhalin Islands. The Soviets tracked the commercial airliner for some two and a half hours.

A Soviet pilot reported visual contact with the aircraft at 1812 hours. The Soviet plane was, we know, in constant contact with its ground control.

At 1821 hours the Korean aircraft was reported by the Soviet pilot at 10,000 meters. At 1826 hours the Soviet pilot reported that he fired a missile and the target was destroyed. At 1830 hours the Korean aircraft was reported by radar at 5,000 meters. At 1838 hours the Korean plane disappeared from the radar screen.

We know that at least eight Soviet fighters reacted at one time or another to the airliner. The pilot who shot the aircraft down reported after the attack that he had in fact fired a missile, that he had destroyed the target, and that he was breaking away.

About an hour later, the Soviet controllers ordered a number of their search aircraft to conduct search and rescue activities in the vicinity of the last position of the Korean airliner as reflected by Soviet tracking. One of these aircraft reported finding kerosene on the surface of the seas in that area.

During Wednesday night, United States State Department officials . . . were in contact with Soviet officials seeking information concerning the airliner's fate. The Soviets offered no information.

As soon as US sources had confirmed the shooting down of the aircraft, the US on its own behalf and on behalf of the Republic of Korea called in the Soviet chargé d'affaires in Washington this morning to express our grave concern over the shooting down of an unarmed civilian plane carrying passengers with a number of nationalities. We also urgently demanded an explanation from the Soviet Union.

The United States reacts with revulsion to this attack. Loss of life appears to be heavy. We can see no excuse whatsoever for this appalling act.

DISCUSSION QUESTIONS

1. Why would the Soviets shoot down a foreign aircraft that flew over their territory?
2. Why did Shultz provide precise detail about the time and circumstances of the incident?
3. Why would Moscow accuse the United States of purposely provoking this incident? Why did it have such a devastating impact on international relations?

77. The Geneva Summit, 1985

When Gorbachev emerged as Soviet leader, President Reagan invited him to America for a summit conference. Gorbachev preferred a neutral setting, so the two men met at Geneva, Switzerland, in November 1985. Their summit meeting produced no major breakthroughs, but it did generate real progress in personal relations. During a break in the formal talks, Gorbachev and Reagan held a private discussion, with no advisors present, by a fireplace in a beach house near Lake Geneva. The dynamic young Communist and the aging Cold Warrior, so different in background and beliefs, shared with each other their hopes and concerns and developed a rapport that would help them make real headway in the next few years.

A. Excerpts from Joint Soviet-American Statement on the Geneva Summit, 21 November 1985

By mutual agreement, the President of the United States, Ronald Reagan, and the General Secretary of the Central Committee of the Communist Party of the Soviet Union, Mikhail S. Gorbachev, met in Geneva November 19–21. . . .

While acknowledging the differences in their systems and approaches to international issues, some greater understanding of each side's view was achieved by the two leaders. They agreed about the need to improve US-Soviet relations and the international situation as a whole.

In this connection the two sides have confirmed the importance of an ongoing dialogue, reflecting their strong desire to seek common ground on existing problems. They agreed to meet again in the nearest future. The General Secretary accepted an invitation by the President . . . to visit the United States of America, and the President . . . accepted an invitation by the General Secretary . . . to visit the Soviet Union. Arrangements for the timing of the visits will be agreed upon through diplomatic channels.

In their meetings, agreement was reached on a number of specific issues. . . .

> ***SECURITY.*** The sides . . . have agreed that a nuclear war cannot be won and must never be fought. Recognizing that any conflict between the USSR and the US could have catastrophic consequences, they emphasized the importance of preventing any war between them, whether nuclear or conventional. They will not seek to achieve military superiority.
>
> ***NUCLEAR AND SPACE TALKS.*** The President and the General Secretary discussed the negotiations on nuclear and space arms. They agreed to accelerate the work at these negotiations, with a view to . . . prevent an arms race in space and to terminate it on earth, to limit and reduce nuclear arms and enhance strategic stability. Noting the proposals recently tabled by the US and the Soviet Union, they called for early progress . . . in areas where there is common ground, including the principle of 50 percent reductions in the nuclear arms of the US and the USSR . . . , as well as the idea of an interim I.N.F. agreement. During the negotiation of these agreements, effective measures for verification . . . will be agreed upon.
>
> ***RISK REDUCTION CENTERS.*** The sides agreed to study the question at the expert level of centers to reduce nuclear risk. . . . They took satisfaction in such recent steps in this direction as the modernization of the Soviet-US hot line.
>
> ***NUCLEAR NONPROLIFERATION.*** General Secretary Gorbachev and President Reagan reaffirmed the commitment of the USSR and the US to the Treaty on the Nonproliferation of Nuclear Weapons and their interest in strengthening together with other countries the nonproliferation regime, and in further enhancing the . . . treaty . . . by enlarging its membership. . . .
>
> ***CHEMICAL WEAPONS.*** . . . [T]he two sides reaffirmed that they are in favor of a general and complete prohibition of chemical weapons and the destruction of existing stockpiles of such weapons. They agreed to accelerate efforts to conclude an effective and verifiable international convention on this matter. . . .
>
> ***PROCESS OF DIALOGUE.*** President Reagan and General Secretary Gorbachev agreed . . . to place on a regular basis . . . dialogue at various levels. Along with meetings between the leaders of the two countries, this envisages regular meetings between the USSR Minister of Foreign Affairs and the US Secretary of State, as well as between the heads of other ministries and agencies. . . . Recognizing that exchanges of views on regional issues on the expert level have proven useful, they agreed to continue such exchanges on a regular basis. The sides intend to expand the programs of bilateral cultural, educational and scientific-technical exchanges, and also to develop trade and economic ties. . . . They agreed on the importance of resolving humanitarian cases in the spirit of cooperation. They believe that there should be greater understanding among our peoples and that to this end they will encourage greater travel and people-to-people contact. . . .
>
> ***ENVIRONMENTAL PROTECTION.*** Both sides agreed to contribute to the preservation of the environment—a global task—through joint research and practical measures. In accordance with the existing US-Soviet agreement in this

area, consultations will be held next year in Moscow and Washington on specific programs of cooperation. . . .

FUSION RESEARCH. The two leaders emphasized the potential importance of the work aimed at utilizing controlled thermo-nuclear fusion for peaceful purposes and . . . advocated the widest practicable development of international cooperation in obtaining this source of energy, which is essentially inexhaustible, for the benefit for all mankind.

B. Remarks by General Secretary Gorbachev

. . . The President and I have done a huge amount of work. We've gone into great detail; we've really done it in depth. And we've done it totally openly and frankly.

We've discussed several most important issues. The relations between our two countries and the situations in the world in general today—these are issues and problems the solving of which in the most concrete way is of concern both to our countries and to the peoples of other countries in the world. We discussed these issues basing our discussions on both sides' determination to improve relations between the Soviet Union and the United States of America. We decided that we must help to decrease the threat of nuclear war. We must not allow the arms race to move off into space and we must cut it down on earth.

It goes without saying that discussions of these sorts we consider to be very useful, and in its results you find a clear reflection of what the two sides have agreed together. We have to be realistic and straightforward, and therefore the solving of the most important problems concerning the arms race and increasing hopes of peace we didn't succeed in reaching at this meeting. So of course there are important disagreements on matters of principle that remain between us. However, the President and I have agreed that this work . . . will be continued here in Geneva by our representatives.

We're also going to seek new kinds of developing bilateral Soviet-American relations. And also we're going to have further consultations on several important questions where, for the most part, our positions again are completely different. . . .

But the significance of everything which we have agreed with the President can only, of course, be reflected if we carry it on into concrete measures. If we really want to succeed in something, then both sides are going to have to do an awful lot of work. . . . I would like to announce that the Soviet Union, for its part, will do all it can in this cooperation with the United States of America . . . to cut down the arms race, to cut down the arsenals which we've piled up and . . . produce the conditions which will be necessary for peace on earth and in space.

We make this announcement perfectly aware of our responsibility both to our own people and to the other peoples of the earth. And we would very much hope that we can have the same approach from the Administration of the United States of America. If that can be so, then the work that has been done in these days in Geneva will not have been done in vain. . . .

C. Remarks by President Reagan

. . . We've packed a lot into the last two days. I came to Geneva to seek a fresh start in relations between the United States and the Soviet Union and we have done this. General Secretary Gorbachev and I have held comprehensive discussions covering all elements of our relationship. I'm convinced that we are heading in the right direction. We've reached some useful interim results which are described in the joint statement that is being issued this morning.

In agreeing to accelerate the work of our nuclear arms negotiators, Mr. Gorbachev and I have addressed our common responsibility to strengthen peace. I believe that we have established a process for more intensive contacts between the United States and the Soviet Union. These two days of talks should inject a certain momentum into our work . . . a momentum we can continue at the meeting that we have agreed on for next year.

Before coming to Geneva, I spoke often of the need to build confidence in our dealings with each other. Frank and forthright conversation at the summit are part of this process. But I'm certain General Secretary Gorbachev would agree that real confidence in each other must be built on deeds, not simply words. This is the thought that ties together all the proposals that the United States has put on the table in the past, and this is the criteria by which our meetings will be judged in the future.

The real report card on Geneva will not come in for months or even years. But we know the questions that must be answered.

Will we join together in sharply reducing offensive nuclear arms and moving to nonnuclear defensive strengths for systems to make this a safer world? Will we join together to help bring about a peaceful resolution of conflicts in Asia, Africa and Central America, so that the peoples there can freely determine their own destiny without outside interference? Will the cause of liberty be advanced, and will the treaties and agreements signed—past and future—be fulfilled? The people of America, the Soviet Union and throughout the world are ready to answer yes.

I leave Geneva today and our fireside summit determined to pursue every opportunity to build a safer world of peace and freedom. There's hard work ahead, but we're ready for it. General Secretary Gorbachev, we ask you to join us in getting the job done, as I'm sure you will. Thank you.

DISCUSSION QUESTIONS

1. Why did Gorbachev prefer to meet Reagan in Geneva rather than America?
2. Why was the establishment of personal rapport between these two men so important?
3. What was the nature and significance of the formal agreements reached at Geneva?
4. Why did Gorbachev insist that "we must not allow the arms race to move off into space"? Why did Reagan call for "a peaceful resolution of conflicts in Asia, Africa and Central America"?

78. The Reykjavik Summit, 1986

Although Gorbachev agreed at the Geneva summit to visit the United States, he refused to do so until the arms talks made some headway. Eventually, however, he agreed to preliminary talks with Reagan in the fall of 1986 at Reykjavik, Iceland. The Reagan team saw it as a preparatory meeting to discuss a Washington summit, but Gorbachev came ready to talk turkey, bringing sweeping proposals for a 50 percent cut in all strategic arms, the elimination of intermediate-range weapons from Europe, talks on a total test ban, and mutual agreement to abide by the ABM treaty for ten more years. Struck by the scope of these proposals, the Americans eventually replied with a counterproposal to abolish all strategic missiles in the next ten years. Not to be outdone, Gorbachev came back with a plan to eliminate *all* nuclear weapons, not just missiles, by 1996. Excitement grew as the two sides worked to hammer out an accord. But the talks collapsed when Reagan refused to confine his Strategic Defense Initiative (SDI) to laboratory testing during that period. Bitterly disappointed, the two sides blamed each other, and Gorbachev made the following remarks while still in Iceland.

Excerpts from Gorbachev's Statement in Reykjavik, 12 October 1986

About one hour has passed since our meeting with the President of the United States of America ended. . . . And sometimes they say when you stand face to face with somebody you cannot see his face. So I have just left . . . that meeting and particularly at the last stages of that meeting, the debates were very pointed and I'm still very much under the influence of those debates.

The atmosphere at the meeting was friendly. We could discuss things freely and without limitation, outlining our views as to various problems and this has made it possible for us to have a more in-depth understanding of many major issues of international politics, bilateral relations and above all, the questions of war and peace, of ending the nuclear arms race and the entire range of problems within that broad topic. . . .

We brought here a whole package of major proposals which . . . could genuinely within a short period of time make it possible to genuinely avert the threat of nuclear war and would also make it possible to begin movement toward a non-nuclear world. I proposed to the President that we should here in Reykjavik issue instructions to the agencies involved to prepare three draft agreements that we could then sign during my visit to the United States.

On strategic weapons, we proposed that they should be reduced by 50 percent, so that before the end of this century, this most deadly type of weapon would be completely eliminated. It was our belief that the world was looking for major steps, that it was expecting deep cuts rather than some cosmetic reductions, that bold and responsible decisions were necessary. . . .

But when we began discussing that question, we felt in response that the proposals which were given to us were not adequate. They were not really relevant because they only repeated what is already being bandied about, limits, sub-limits, arithmetic that only makes the substance of the question very confusing.

We said, we have this recognition of the triad of strategic offensive weapons: ICBMs, missiles carried by submarines and strategic missiles on bombers. Now let us reduce that by one half, a 50 percent reduction in land-based missiles, including the heavy missiles that so concerned the United States, a 50 percent reduction in submarine- launched missiles and 50 percent reduction in missiles on strategic aircraft. The American delegation agreed to that. We had an accord there.

We put forward a proposal to instruct delegations to prepare an agreement on medium-range missiles. I proposed to the President to give up all the options that had been discussed until then, and to really go back to the American proposals of complete elimination of US medium-range missiles in Europe and to eliminate also the Soviet medium-range missiles in Europe. At this meeting, we decided to remove from the agenda altogether the question of British and French nuclear missiles. Let them remain, let them be upgraded.

The Americans did not expect that we would make such proposals. That was not acceptable. The US side again wanted us to accept interim solutions that would preserve some American missiles in Europe and some Soviet missiles.

In the end, we made that last step. We said, in Europe we will eliminate US and Soviet medium-range missiles. In Asia, 100 warheads on missiles each. We agreed that an agreement to that effect could be signed.

In this situation, when we are entering the stage of genuine cuts, [we proposed] that in 10 years the nuclear arsenals of the Soviet Union and the United States would be eliminated altogether. We said that within that period, the treaties that exist, like the ABM treaty, should not only be preserved, but they should be strengthened. We proposed that the ABM treaty should be strengthened, that both sides should undertake within the next 10 years not to use their right to withdraw from that treaty. . . . We said in our proposals that . . . within those 10 years, all the requirements of the ABM treaty would be strictly preserved, that the development and testing of space weapons would be banned and that only research within laboratories would be permitted.

We know the commitment of the US Administration and the President to SDI. Our agreement to the possibility of lab testing makes possible for the President to go through with the research and to see what is SDI and what it's all about. And this is really where the real fight began. The President insisted until the end that the United States retained the right to . . . test things relating to SDI not only in the laboratories but also out of the laboratories, including in space.

I said to the President that we were missing a historic chance. Never had our positions been so close together. When we were saying goodbye, the President said he was disappointed and that from the very beginning I, that is to say Gorbachev, had come to Reykjavik with no willingness to reach agreement. Why, he said, because of just one word are you so intransigent in your approach to SDI and as regards testing?

No, it's not one word that is the point here. It is the substance that is the key to what the Administration really intends. If you make an inventory of things that have happened, you will see that we have made very serious, unprecedented concessions and compromises. . . . And still there has been no agreement. The Americans came to this meeting empty-handed, with an entire set of mothballed proposals that made the situation so bad, so stuffy at the Geneva negotiations.

DISCUSSION QUESTIONS

1. Why was Gorbachev so eager to move forward with sweeping arms cuts? What conditions in the USSR may have contributed to his haste?
2. Why was the Reagan team reluctant to move so quickly?
3. Why did the Soviets dislike the U.S. proposal to abolish all strategic missiles in ten years? Why did Gorbachev up the ante and propose elimination of *all* nuclear weapons in ten years?
4. Why did Gorbachev insist that both sides must agree to adhere to the ABM treaty for those ten years? Why did Reagan refuse to limit SDI testing to the laboratory during this period? Why was this refusal unacceptable to Gorbachev?

79. Reagan's 1987 Berlin Speech: "Tear Down This Wall"

In 1987, as Cold War tensions eased, Ronald Reagan made a trip to West Berlin. There, in a stunning speech in the shadow of the Berlin Wall, evoking memories of Kennedy's 1963 Berlin speech (Document 43), he challenged Mr. Gorbachev to "tear down this wall." The wall stood for two more years, but Reagan's speech was a harbinger of its collapse.

Highlights of Reagan's Berlin Wall Speech, 12 June 1987

Behind me stands a wall that encircles the free sectors of this city, part of a vast system of barriers that divides the entire continent of Europe. From the Baltic south, those barriers cut across Germany in a gash of barbed wire, concrete, dog runs and guard towers. Farther south, there may be no visible, no obvious, wall. But there remain armed guards and checkpoints all the same—still a restriction on the right to travel, still an instrument to impose upon ordinary men and women the will of a totalitarian state.

Yet it is here in Berlin where the wall emerges most clearly; here, cutting across your city, where the news photo and the television screen have imprinted this brutal division of a continent upon the mind of the world. Standing before the Brandenburg Gate, every man is a German, separated from his fellow men. Every man is a Berliner, forced to look upon a scar.

[West German] President von Weizsäcker has said: The German Question is open as long as the Brandenburg Gate is closed. Today I say: As long as this gate is closed, as long as this scar of a wall is permitted to stand, it is not the German Question alone that remains open, but the question of freedom for all mankind. Yet I do not come here to lament. For I find in Berlin a message of hope—even, in the shadow of this wall, a message of triumph. . . .

From devastation—from utter ruin—you Berliners have in freedom rebuilt a city that once again ranks as one of the greatest on earth. . . .

In the 1950s, Khrushchev predicted, "We will bury you." But in the West today, we see a free world that has achieved a level of prosperity and well-being unprecedented in all human history. In the Communist world, we see failure. Technological backwardness. Declining standards of health. Even want of the most basic kind—too little food. Even today, the Soviet Union still cannot feed itself.

After these four decades, then, there stands before the entire world one great and inescapable conclusion. Freedom leads to prosperity. Freedom replaces the ancient hatreds among the nations with comity and peace. Freedom is the victor.

Now the Soviets themselves may in a limited way be coming to understand the importance of freedom. We hear much from Moscow about a new policy of reform and openness. Some political prisoners have been released. Certain foreign news broadcasts are no longer being jammed. Some economic enterprises have been permitted to operate with greater freedom from state control.

Are these the beginnings of profound changes in the Soviet state? Or are they token gestures, intended to raise false hopes in the West or to strengthen the Soviet system without changing it? We welcome change and openness. For we believe freedom and security go together—that the advance of human liberty can only strengthen the cause of world peace. There is one sign the Soviets can make that would be unmistakable, that would advance dramatically the cause of freedom and peace.

General Secretary Gorbachev, if you seek peace—if you seek prosperity for the Soviet Union and Eastern Europe—if you seek liberalization, come here, to this gate.

Mr. Gorbachev, open this gate.

Mr. Gorbachev, tear down this wall.

I understand the fear of war and the pain of division that afflict this continent—and I pledge to you my country's efforts to help overcome these burdens. To be sure, we in the West must resist Soviet expansion. So we must maintain defenses of unassailable strength. Yet we seek peace. So we must strive to reduce arms on both sides.

Beginning 10 years ago, the Soviets challenged the Western alliance with a grave new threat: hundreds of new and more deadly SS–20 nuclear missiles, capable of striking every capital in Europe. The Western alliance responded by committing itself to a counterdeployment unless the Soviets agreed to negotiate a better solution—namely, the elimination of such weapons on both sides.

For many months, the Soviets refused to bargain in earnestness. As the alliance in turn prepared to go forward with its counterdeployment, there were difficult days—days of protests like those during my 1982 visit to this city—and the Soviets later walked away from the table.

But through it all, the alliance held firm. And I invite those who protested then—I invite those who protest today—to mark this fact: Because we remained strong, the Soviets came back to the table. Because we remained strong, today we have within reach the possibility, not merely of limiting the growth of arms, but of eliminating, for the first time, an entire class of nuclear weapons from the face of the earth. . . .

Today, thus, represents a moment of hope. We in the West stand ready to cooperate with the East to promote true openness—to break down the barriers that separate people, to create a safer, freer world. And surely there is no better place than Berlin, the meeting place of East and West, to make a start. . . .

As I looked out a moment ago from the Reichstag, that embodiment of German unity, I noticed words crudely spray-painted upon the wall—perhaps by a young Berliner. "This wall will fall. Beliefs become reality." Yes, across Europe, this wall will fall. For it cannot withstand faith. It cannot withstand truth. The wall cannot withstand freedom.

DISCUSSION QUESTIONS

1. In what ways was Reagan's speech reminiscent of Churchill's Iron Curtain speech (Document 5) and Kennedy's Berlin speech (Document 43)? In what ways did it differ?
2. To which aspects of Soviet liberalization did Reagan call attention? To what basic human desire did he link the idea of freedom?
3. How did Reagan support his conviction that Europe's division was coming to an end?
4. Why did he issue a personal appeal to Gorbachev? What impact might this appeal have had on the Soviet leader?

80. Gorbachev's New Thinking on International Relations

As Soviet leader, Gorbachev articulated a viewpoint very much at odds with traditional Soviet behavior. He encouraged *glasnost*, or openness and candor, in political and cultural activities. He introduced *perestroika*, restructuring of the Soviet system to decentralize decision making, institute profit incentives, and create a more open economy. And he called for *new thinking*, an outlook that said war was no longer winnable, military solutions were no longer acceptable, and the security of all nations was intertwined. In 1987, to elaborate and advance his ideas, he published a book titled *Perestroika: New Thinking for Our Country and the World.* Reproduced below are highlights from the section on "New Political Thinking."

Excerpts from "New Political Thinking," from *Perestroika* by Mikhail Gorbachev*

In the two and a half years which have passed since April 1985, we have gone a long way in comprehending the world situation and ways to change it for the better. . . .

Yes, we remain different as far as our social system, ideological and religious views and way of life are concerned. To be sure, distinctions will remain. But should we duel because of them? Would it not be more correct to step over the things that divide us for the sake of the interests of all mankind, for the sake of life on Earth? . . .

I realize that everything cannot change overnight. I also realize that the West and we shall continue to have different approaches to specific situations. And still . . . the nations of the world resemble today a pack of mountaineers tied together by a climbing rope. They can either climb on together to the mountain peak or fall together into an abyss. In order to prevent disaster, political leaders should rise above their narrow interests and realize the drama of the situation. That is why the need for a new comprehension of the situation and of its complacent factors is so urgent today.

It is no longer possible to draft a policy on the premises of the year 1947, the Truman doctrine and Churchill's Fulton speech. It is necessary to think and act in a new way. What is more, history cannot wait; people cannot afford to waste time. It may be too late tomorrow, and the day after tomorrow may never come.

The fundamental principle of the new political outlook is very simple: *nuclear war cannot be a means of achieving political, economic, ideological or any other goals.* This conclusion is truly revolutionary, for it means discarding the traditional notions of war and peace. It is the political function of war that has always been a justification for war, a "rational" explanation. Nuclear war is

---

* Mikhail Gorbachev, "New Political Thinking," in *Perestroika: New Thinking for Our Country and the World* (New York, NY: HarperCollins, 1987), 139–144.

senseless; it is irrational. There would be neither winners nor losers in a global nuclear conflict: world civilization would inevitably perish. It is a suicide, rather than a war in the conventional sense of the word. . . .

For the first time in history, basing international politics on moral and ethical norms that are common to all humankind, as well as humanizing interstate relations, has become a vital requirement.

A new dialectic of strength and security follows from the impossibility of a military—that is, nuclear—solution to international differences. Security can no longer be assured by military means—neither by the use of arms or deterrence, nor by continued perfection of the "sword" and the "shield." Attempts to achieve military superiority are preposterous. Now such attempts are being made in space. It is an astonishing anachronism which persists due to the inflated role played by militarists in politics. From the security point of view the arms race has become an absurdity because its very logic leads to the destabilization of international relations and eventually to a nuclear conflict. Diverting huge resources from other priorities, the arms race is lowering the level of security, impairing it. It is in itself an enemy of peace.

The only way to security is through political decisions and disarmament. In our age genuine and equal security can be guaranteed by constantly lowering the level of the strategic balance from which nuclear and other weapons of mass destruction should be completely eliminated. . . .

The new political outlook calls for the recognition of one more simple axiom: security is indivisible. It is either equal security for all or none at all. The only solid foundation for security is the recognition of the interests of all peoples and countries and of their equality in international affairs. The security of each nation should be coupled with the security for all members of the world community. Would it, for instance, be in the interest of the United States if the Soviet Union found itself in a situation whereby it considered it had less security than the USA? Or would we benefit by a reverse situation? I can say firmly that we would not like this. So, adversaries must become partners and start looking jointly for a way to achieve universal security.

We can see the first signs of new thinking in many countries, in different strata of society. And this is only natural, because it is the way of mutually advantageous agreements and reciprocal compromises on the basis of the supreme common interest—preventing a nuclear catastrophe. Consequently, there should be no striving for security for oneself at the expense of others. . . .

Universal security in our time rests on the recognition of the right of every nation to choose its own path of social development, on the renunciation of interference in the domestic affairs of other states, on respect for others in combination with an objective self-critical view of one's own society. A nation may choose either capitalism or socialism. This is its sovereign right. Nations cannot and should not pattern their life either after the United States or the Soviet Union. Hence, political positions should be devoid of ideological intolerance.

Ideological differences should not be transferred to the sphere of interstate relations, nor should foreign policy be subordinate to them, for ideologies may be poles apart, whereas the interest of survival and prevention of war stand universal and supreme.

On a par with the nuclear threat, the new political mode of thinking considers the solution of other global problems, including those of economic development and ecology, as an indispensable condition for assuring a lasting and just peace. To think in a new way also means to see a direct link between disarmament and development. . . .

There are serious signs that the new way of thinking is taking shape, that people are coming to understand what brink the world has approached. But this process is a very difficult one. And the most difficult thing is to ensure that this understanding is reflected in the actions of the policy-makers. . . . But I believe that the new political mentality will force its way through, for it was born of the realities of our time.

DISCUSSION QUESTIONS

1. According to Gorbachev, what was the central reality of the world situation in the 1980s? What steps did he suggest to deal with this reality?
2. How did Gorbachev's approach differ from that of previous Soviet leaders? Why did he insist that Soviet security and U.S. security were interconnected?
3. Why did he call for "renunciation of interference in the internal affairs of other states"? Why did he say that ideology should not be part of international relations?
4. What sort of a world did Gorbachev envision? What might he gain by explaining his ideas in a book for ordinary people in the West?

81. THE INF TREATY, DECEMBER 1987

In early 1987, frustrated by the impasse over SDI that paralyzed the strategic arms reduction talks (START) , Gorbachev unexpectedly announced that, no matter what happened with SDI or START, Moscow was ready to discuss the elimination of U.S. and Soviet intermediate-range missiles in Europe. Since Reagan had already urged such a deal, it now seemed within reach. But Washington, concerned that the Soviets would still have many intermediate-range missiles in Asia, pressed for a broader accord: Why not abolish all such weapons, wherever they were located? This breathtaking proposal, known as "global zero-zero," would form the basis for the INF treaty, worked out through negotiations during 1987 and signed by Gorbachev and Reagan in Washington in December. For the first time ever, the superpowers agreed not just to limit the arms race but actually to abolish a whole class of weapons.

Treaty on Intermediate and Shorter Range Nuclear Forces, 8 December 1987

Article I

In accordance with the provisions of this Treaty . . . each Party shall eliminate its intermediate range and shorter-range missiles, not have such systems thereafter, and carry out the other obligations set forth in this Treaty. . . .

Article II

For the purposes of this treaty:

(1) The term "ballistic missile" means a missile that has a ballistic trajectory over most of its flight path. The term "ground launched ballistic missile (GLBM)" means a ground launched ballistic missile that is a weapon-delivery vehicle.

(2) The term "cruise missile" means an unmanned, self-propelled vehicle that sustains flight through the use of aerodynamic lift over most of its flight path. The term "ground launched cruise missile (GLCM)" means a ground launched cruise missile that is a weapon-delivery vehicle. . . .

(5) The term "intermediate-range missile" means a GLBM or GLCM having a range capacity in excess of 1000 kilometers but not in excess of 5500 kilometers.

(6) The term "shorter-range missile" means a GLBM or GLCM having a range capacity equal to or in excess of 500 kilometers but not in excess of 1000 kilometers. . . .

Article IV

(1) Each Party shall eliminate all its intermediate-range missiles and launchers of such missiles, and all support structures and support equipment . . . associated with such missiles and launchers, so that no later than three years after entry into force of this Treaty and thereafter no such missiles, launchers, support structures or support equipment shall be possessed by either Party.

(2) To implement paragraph 1 of this Article, upon entry into force of this Treaty, both parties shall begin and continue throughout the duration of each phase, the reduction of all types of their deployed and non-deployed intermediate-range missiles and deployed and non-deployed launchers of such missiles and support structures and support equipment associated with such missiles and launchers. . . . These reductions shall be implemented in two phases so that:

(a) by the end of the first phase, that is, no later than 29 months after entry into force of this treaty . . .

(ii) the number of deployed intermediate-range missiles for each Party shall not exceed the number of such missiles . . . to carry 180 warheads. . . .

(iv) the aggregate number of deployed and non-deployed intermediate-range missiles for each Party shall not exceed the number of such missiles . . . to carry 200 warheads. . . .

(b) by the end of the second phase, that is, no later than three years after entry into force of this Treaty, all intermediate-range missiles of each Party, launchers of such missiles and all support structures and support equipment . . . shall be eliminated.

Article V

(1) Each Party shall eliminate all its shorter-range missiles and launchers of such missiles, and all support equipment . . . so that no later than 18 months after entry into force of the Treaty and thereafter no such missiles, launchers or support equipment shall be possessed by either Party.

(2) No later than 90 days after entry into force of the Treaty, each Party shall complete the removal of all its deployed shorter-range missiles and deployed and non-deployed launchers of such missiles to elimination facilities and shall retain them at those locations until they are eliminated. . . . No later than 12 months after entry into force of the Treaty, each Party shall complete the removal of all its non-deployed shorter-range missiles until they are eliminated. . . .

Article XI

(1) For the purpose of ensuring verification of compliance with the provisions of this Treaty, each Party shall have the right to conduct on-site inspections. . . .

(2) . . . both within the territory of the other Party and within the territories of basing countries. . . .

Article XII

(1) For the purpose of ensuring verification of compliance with the provisions of the Treaty, each Party shall use national technical means of verification at its disposal in a manner consistent with . . . international law.

(2) Neither Party shall:

(a) interfere with national technical means of verification of the other party . . . ; or

(b) use concealment measures which impede verification of compliance with the provisions of the Treaty by national technical means of verification. . . .

Article XV

(1) This Treaty shall be of unlimited duration.

(2) Each Party shall, in exercising its national sovereignty, have the right to withdraw from this Treaty if it decides that extraordinary events related to the subject matter of this Treaty have jeopardized its supreme interests. It shall give notice of its decision to withdraw to the other Party six months prior to withdrawal from this Treaty. . . .

DISCUSSION QUESTIONS

1. Why was Gorbachev willing to negotiate an INF treaty, but not a START treaty, without progress on SDI?
2. Why did the treaty call for the phased elimination of intermediate-range weapons, rather than their immediate destruction?
3. Why did the treaty place so much emphasis on verification procedures?
4. What was the most important accomplishment of the INF treaty? Why did its signing create such excitement?

82. The Soviet Withdrawal from Afghanistan, 1988–1989

A few months after the INF treaty signing came another very hopeful development. The USSR, frustrated by an unwinnable war that was draining its resources and sapping its soldiers' morale, decided to cut its losses and withdraw from Afghanistan. In a statement excerpted below, Gorbachev announced that, as long as an agreement was reached barring outside interference, Soviet troops would begin pulling out in May. Despite problems caused by U.S. insistence on continuing aid to the rebels, the withdrawal proceeded on schedule.

Gorbachev's Statement on Soviet Withdrawal from Afghanistan, 8 February 1988

The military conflict in Afghanistan has been going on for a long time now. It is one of the most bitter and painful regional conflicts. Judging by everything, certain prerequisites have now emerged for its political settlement. In this context the Soviet leadership considers it necessary to . . . make its position totally clear.

In the near future, a new round of talks conducted by Afghanistan and Pakistan through the personal representative of the United Nations Secretary General will be held in Geneva. There are considerable chances that this round will become a final one.

By now documents covering all aspects of a settlement have been almost fully worked out. . . . They include agreements between Afghanistan and Pakistan on non-interference in each other's internal affairs and on the return of Afghan refugees from Pakistan; international guarantees of non-interference in Afghanistan's internal affairs; a document on the interrelationship of all elements of political settlement. There is also agreement on establishing a verification mechanism.

So what remains to be done? It is to establish a time frame for the withdrawal of Soviet troops from Afghanistan that would be acceptable to all. Precisely that—a time frame, since the fundamental political decision to withdraw Soviet troops from Afghanistan was adopted by us, in agreement with the Afghan leadership, some time ago, and announced at that same time.

The question of time frame has both a technical and a political aspect. As for the technical aspect, it is clear that the actual withdrawal of troops will take a certain amount of time. . . . As for the political aspect of the matter, it is that the withdrawal of Soviet troops is, quite naturally, linked with precluding interference in Afghanistan's internal affairs. Prerequisites for that have now been created to a mutual satisfaction.

Seeking to facilitate a speedy and successful conclusion of the Geneva talks between Afghanistan and Pakistan, the Government of the USSR and the Republic of Afghanistan have agreed to set a specific date for beginning the withdrawal of Soviet troops—May 15, 1988—and to complete their withdrawal within 10 months. The date is set based on the assumption that agreements on the settlement would be signed no later than March 15, 1988, and that, accordingly, they would all enter into force simultaneously two months after that. If the agreements are signed before March 15, the withdrawal of troops will, accordingly, begin earlier. . . .

And now about our boys, our soldiers in Afghanistan. They have been doing their duty honestly, performing acts of self-denial and heroism.

Our people profoundly respect those who were called to serve in Afghanistan. The state provides for them, as a matter of priority, good educational opportunities and a chance to get interesting, worthy work.

The memory of those who have died a hero's death in Afghanistan is sacred to us. It is the duty of party and Soviet authorities to make sure that their families and relatives are taken care of with concern, attention and kindness.

And, finally, when the Afghan knot is untied, it will have the most profound impact on other regional conflicts too.

Whereas the arms race, which we are working so hard—and with some success—to stop, is mankind's mad race to the abyss, regional conflicts are bleeding wounds which can result in gangrenous growth on the body of mankind.

The earth is literally spotted with such wounds. Each of them means pain not only for the nations directly involved but for all—whether in Afghanistan, in the Middle East, in connection with the Iran-Iraq war, in southern Africa, in Kampuchea, or in Central America.

Who gains from those conflicts? No one except the arms merchants and various reactionary expansionist circles who are used to exploiting and turning a profit on people's misfortunes and tragedies.

Implementing political settlement in Afghanistan will be an important rupture in the chain of regional conflicts.

Just as the agreement to eliminate intermediate- and short-range missiles is to be followed by a series of further major steps towards disarmament, with negotiations on them already underway or being planned, likewise behind the political settlement in Afghanistan already looms a question: which conflict will be settled next? And it is certain that more is to follow.

States and nations have sufficient reserves of responsibility, political will and determination to put an end to all regional conflicts within a few years. This is worth working for. The Soviet Union will spare no effort in this most important cause.

DISCUSSION QUESTIONS

1. Why was Gorbachev anxious to end Soviet involvement in the Afghan war? Why did he wish to preclude outside interference?
2. What impact might his announcement be expected to have on superpower relations?
3. Why did he think Soviet withdrawal from Afghanistan could help end other regional conflicts?
4. What factors might account for Soviet failure to win the Afghan war?

83. Gorbachev's UN Address, December 1988

In December 1988, Gorbachev visited New York to address the UN General Assembly. In his remarkable speech, reflecting a momentous shift in Soviet behavior, he emphatically declared that all nations must be free to choose their own destiny, that ideology had no place in foreign affairs, and that great powers should renounce the use of force in international relations. He went on to pledge substantial cuts in Soviet troops and tanks, especially those stationed in Eastern Europe. His speech would soon reverberate throughout the Soviet bloc.

Excerpts From Gorbachev's Speech to the United Nations, 7 December 1988

. . . The world in which we live today is radically different from what it was at the beginning or even in the middle of this century. And it continues to change as do all its components. The advent of nuclear weapons was just another tragic reminder of the fundamental nature of that change. A material symbol and expression of absolute military power, nuclear weapons at the same time revealed the absolute limits of that power. The problem of mankind's survival and self-preservation came to the fore. . . .

It is obvious, for instance, that the use or threat of force no longer can or must be an instrument of foreign policy. This applies above all to nuclear arms, but that is not the only thing that matters. All of us, and primarily the stronger of us, must exercise self-restraint and totally rule out any outward-oriented use of force. . . .

The new phase also requires de-ideologizing relations among states. We are not abandoning our convictions, our philosophy or traditions, nor do we urge anyone to abandon theirs. But neither do we have any intention to be hemmed in by our values. That would result in intellectual impoverishment, for it would mean rejecting a powerful source of development—the exchange of everything original that each nation has independently created.

In the course of such exchange, let everyone show the advantages of their social system, way of life or values—and not just by words or propaganda, but by real deeds. That would be a fair rivalry of ideologies. But it should not be extended to relations among states.

We are, of course, far from claiming to be in possession of the ultimate truth. But, on the basis of a thorough analysis of the past and newly emerging realities, we have concluded that . . . we should jointly seek the way leading to the supremacy of the universal human idea over the endless multitude of centrifugal forces, the way to preserve the vitality of this civilization, possibly the only one in the entire universe.

Could this view be a little too romantic? Are we not overestimating the potential and the maturity of the world's social consciousness? We have heard such doubts and such questions both in our country and from some of our Western partners. I am convinced that we are not floating above reality. . . .

Now let me turn to the main issue—disarmament, without which none of the problems of the coming century can be solved. . . .

Today, I can report to you that the Soviet Union has taken a decision to reduce its armed forces. Within the next two years their numerical strength will be reduced by 500,000 men. The numbers of conventional armaments will also be substantially reduced. This will be done unilaterally, without relation to the talks on the mandate of the Vienna meeting.

By agreement with our Warsaw Treaty allies, we have decided to withdraw by 1991 six tank divisions from East Germany, Czechoslovakia and Hungary, and to disband them. Assault landing troops and several other formations and units, . . . with their weapons and combat equipment, will also be withdrawn. Soviet forces stationed in those countries will be reduced by 50,000 men and their armaments, by 5,000 tanks.

All Soviet divisions remaining for the time being in the territory of our allies are being reorganized. Their structure will be different from what it is now; after a major cutback of their tanks it will become clearly defensive. At the same time, we shall reduce the numerical strength of the armed forces and the numbers of armaments stationed in the European part of the Soviet Union. In total, Soviet armed forces in this part of our country and in the territories of our European allies will be reduced by 10,000 tanks, 8,500 artillery systems and 800 combat aircraft.

Over these two years we intend to reduce significantly our armed forces in the Asian part of our country, too. By agreement with the government of the Mongolian People's Republic a major portion of Soviet troops temporarily stationed there will return home.

In taking this fundamental decision the Soviet leadership expresses the will of the people, who have undertaken a profound renewal of their entire socialist society. We shall maintain our country's defense capability at a level of reasonable and reliable sufficiency so that no one might be tempted to encroach on the security of the Soviet Union and our allies.

By this action, and by all our activities in favor of demilitarizing international relations, we wish to draw the attention of the international community to yet another pressing problem—the problem of transition from the economy of armaments to an economy of disarmament. Is conversion of military production a realistic idea? . . . We think that, indeed, it is realistic. For its part, the Soviet Union is prepared to do these things:

- In the framework of our economic reform we are ready to draw up and make public our internal plan of conversion;
- In the course of 1989 to draw up, as an experiment, conversion plans for two or three defense plants;
- To make public our experience in providing employment for specialists from military industry and in using its equipment, buildings and structures in civilian production.

It is desirable that all states, in the first place major military powers, should submit to the United Nations their national conversion plans. It would also be useful to set up a group of scientists to undertake a thorough analysis of the problem of conversion as a whole and as applied to individual countries and regions and report to the secretary-general of the United Nations, and, subsequently, to have this matter considered at a session of the General Assembly.

And finally, since I am here on American soil . . . , I have to turn to the subject of our relations with this great country. I had a chance to appreciate the full measure of its hospitality during my memorable visit to Washington exactly a year ago.

The relations between the Soviet Union and the United States of America have a history of five and a half decades. As the world changed, so did the nature, role and place of those relations in world politics. For too long a time they developed along the lines of confrontation and sometimes animosity. . . . But in the last few years the entire world could breathe a sigh of relief thanks to the changes for the better . . . in the relationship between Moscow and Washington.

No one intends to underestimate the seriousness of our differences and the toughness of outstanding problems. We have, however, already graduated from the primary school of learning to understand each other and seek solutions in both our own and common interests. The Soviet Union and the United States have built the largest nuclear and missile arsenals. But it is those two countries that, having become specifically aware of their responsibility, were the first to conclude a treaty on the reduction and physical elimination of a portion of their armaments which posed a threat to both of them and to all others. Both countries possess the greatest and the most sophisticated military secrets. But it is those two countries that have laid a basis for and are further developing a system of mutual verification both of the elimination of armaments and of the reduction and prohibition of their production. It is those two countries that are accumulating the experience for future bilateral and multilateral agreements.

We value this. We acknowledge and appreciate the contribution made by President Ronald Reagan and by the members of his administration, particularly Mr. George Shultz. All this is our joint investment in a venture of historic importance. We must not lose this investment, or leave it idle.

The next US administration, headed by President-elect George Bush, will find in us a partner who is ready—without long pauses or backtracking—to continue the dialogue in a spirit of realism, openness and good will, with a willingness to achieve concrete results working on the agenda which covers the main issues of Soviet-US relations and world politics. I have in mind, above all, these things:

- Consistent movement toward a treaty on 50 percent reductions in strategic offensive arms while preserving the ABM treaty;

- Working out a convention on the elimination of chemical weapons . . .
- And negotiations on the reduction of conventional arms and armed forces in Europe.

I also have in mind economic, environmental and humanistic problems . . .

I would like to believe that our hopes will be matched by our joint effort to put an end to an era of wars, confrontation and regional conflicts, to aggressions against nature, to the terror of hunger and poverty as well as to political terrorism. This is our common goal and we can only reach it together. Thank you.

DISCUSSION QUESTIONS

1. Why did Gorbachev choose the UN as his forum for this speech? How did the ideas expressed in it reflect his "new thinking" (Document 80)?
2. Why did he say that "force no longer can . . . be an instrument of foreign policy"? What implications did this have for the Soviet bloc?
3. What did he mean by "transition . . . to an economy of disarmament"? How did he foresee that such a transition could occur?
4. Why did he announce specific Soviet force and weapons reductions in this speech? What did he foresee as the future role of the superpowers?

84. The Tienanmen Square Massacre, June 1989

In 1989, as Cold War tensions were subsiding, a crisis developed in China. A dozen years of modernization, including capitalist-style economic freedoms and growing commerce with the West, had raised hopes among Chinese youths for more political freedom. Beginning in April, thousands of student protesters and others camped out in Beijing's vast Tiananmen Square, staging demonstrations and demanding more freedom and an end to official corruption. As the protests increased, Chinese premier Li Peng called for "decisive measures" to restore order, including the use of armed force. Deng Xiaoping, China's main leader, eventually sided with Li Peng. On 19 May, Li Peng demanded resolute action in a starkly worded address, and on 20 May, he declared martial law in Beijing. On 3–4 June, martial law units of the Chinese army forcefully cleared the square, killing hundreds of protesters. On 9 June, in a speech to these units, Deng Xiaoping lauded their efforts and blamed the massacre on a "rebellious clique" that wanted to "topple our country and overthrow our party." Stability was restored and economic modernization continued, but hopes for greater freedom in China were dashed.

A. Li Peng's Speech on Behalf of the Chinese Communist Party Central Committee and State Council, 19 May 1989

Comrades, . . . the party Central Committee and the State Council have convened a meeting here . . . calling on everyone to mobilize in this emergency and to adopt resolute and effective measures to curb turmoil in a clear-cut manner, to restore normal order in society, and to maintain stability and unity . . .

. . . [T]he current situation in the capital is quite grim. The anarchic state is going from bad to worse. Law and discipline have been undermined . . . More and more students and other people have been involved in demonstrations. Many institutions of higher learning have come to a standstill. Traffic jams have taken place everywhere. The party and government leading organs have been affected, and public security has been rapidly deteriorating. All this has seriously disturbed and undermined the normal order of production, work, study, and everyday life of the people . . .

The activities of some of the students on hunger strike at Tiananmen Square have not yet been stopped completely. Their health is seriously deteriorating and some of their lives are still in imminent danger. In fact, a handful of persons are using the hunger strikers as hostages to coerce and force the party and the government to yield to their political demands . . .

. . . The square is packed with extremely excited crowds who keep shouting demagogic slogans. Right now, representatives of the hunger striking students say that they can no longer control the situation. If we fail to promptly put an end to such a state of affairs and let it go unchecked, it will very likely lead to serious consequences which none of us want to see.

The situation in Beijing is still developing, and has already affected many other cities in the country. In many places, the number of demonstrators and protesters is increasing. In some places, there have been many incidents of people breaking into local party and government organs, along with beating, smashing, looting, burning, and other undermining activities that seriously violated the law . . .

All these incidents demonstrate that we will have nationwide major turmoil if no quick action is taken to turn and stabilize the situation . . .

. . . At present, it has become more and more clear that the very, very few people who attempt to create turmoil want to achieve, under the conditions of turmoil, precisely their political goals which they could not achieve through normal democratic and legal channels . . .

One important reason for us to take a clear-cut stand in opposing the turmoil and exposing the political conspiracy of a handful of people is to distinguish the masses of young students from the handful of people who incited the turmoil. For almost a month, we adopted an extremely tolerant and restrained attitude in handling the student unrest. No government in the world would be so tolerant . . . However, the handful of behind-the-scenes people, who were plotting and inciting the turmoil, . . . took the tolerance as weakness on the part of the party and government. They continued to cook up stories to confuse and poison the masses, in an attempt to worsen the situation. This has caused the situation in the capital and many localities across the country to become increasingly acute. Under such circumstances, the CPC . . . is forced to take resolute and decisive measures to put an end to the turmoil . . .

. . . Now, to check the turmoil with a firm hand and quickly restore order, I urgently appeal on behalf of the party Central Committee and the State Council: First, to those students now on hunger strike at Tiananmen Square to end the fasting immediately, leave the square, receive medical treatment, and recover their health as soon as possible. Second, to the masses of students and people in all walks of life to immediately stop all parades and demonstrations, and give no more so-called support to the fasting students in the interest of humanitarianism . . .

Comrades, on behalf of the party Central Committee and the State Council, I now . . . call on the whole party, the entire army, and people of all nationalities throughout the country to unite, to pull together, and to act immediately at all their posts in an effort to stop the turmoil and stabilize the situation . . .

B. Deng Xiaoping's Speech to Martial Law Units, 9 June 1989

Comrades, you have been working very hard. First, I express my profound condolences to the commanders and fighters of the People's Liberation Army [PLA], commanders and fighters of the armed police force, and public security officers and men who died a heroic death . . . , and cordial regards to all commanders and fighters of the PLA, commanders and fighters of the armed police force, and public security officers and men who took part in this struggle. I propose that we all rise and stand in silent tribute to the martyrs.

The main difficulty in handling this incident has been that we have never experienced such a situation before, where a handful of bad people mixed with so many young students and onlookers. For a while we could not distinguish them, and as a result, it was difficult for us to be certain of the correct action that we should take . . .

. . . Actually, what we face is not simply ordinary people who are unable to distinguish between right and wrong. We also face a rebellious clique and a large number of the dregs of society, who want to topple our country and overthrow our party . . . They have two main slogans: One is to topple the Communist Party, and the other is to overthrow the socialist system . . .

In the course of quelling this rebellion, many of our comrades were injured or even sacrificed their lives. Their weapons were also taken from them. Why was this? It also was because bad people mingled with the good, which made it difficult to take the drastic measures we should take.

Handling this matter amounted to a very severe political test for our army, and what happened shows that our PLA passed muster. . . . Even though the losses are regrettable, this has enabled us to win over the people and made it possible for those people who can't tell right from wrong to change their viewpoint. This has made it possible for everyone to see for themselves what kind of people the PLA are, whether there was bloodbath at Tiananmen, and who were the people who shed blood.

. . . Although it is very saddening to have sacrificed so many comrades, if the . . . incident is analyzed objectively, people cannot but recognize that the PLA are the sons and brothers of the people. This will also help the people to understand the measures we used in the course of the struggle. In the future, the PLA will have the people's support for whatever measures it takes to deal with whatever problem it faces . . .

America has criticized us for suppressing students. In handling its internal student strikes and unrest, didn't America mobilize police and troops, arrest people, and shed blood? They are suppressing students and the people, but we are quelling a counterrevolutionary rebellion. What qualifications do they have to criticize us? From now on, we should pay attention when handling such problems. As soon as a trend emerges, we should not allow it to spread . . .

DISCUSSION QUESTIONS

1. Why did China's economic modernization and trade with the West lead Chinese students to hope for more political freedom? Why did China's leaders take so long to act against them?
2. Why did Li Peng consider the situation so dangerous? Why did he advocate forceful steps to restore order? What dangers did he see in letting the protests continue?
3. What did Deng Xiaoping give as reasons why the crisis arose? Was his speech an accurate analysis or a self-serving justification for the actions of the Chinese leaders?
4. How did Deng justify the violent crackdown? Why did he portray the martial law units as heroes? Why did he refer to actions earlier taken in America against student protesters?

85. The Opening of the Berlin Wall, November 1989

On 9 November 1989, faced with a mass exodus of people and demonstrations throughout East Germany, that country's Communist regime took a desperate gamble. Hoping to ease the crisis, the regime announced that it was lifting almost all restrictions on travel and emigration to the West. Within hours the Berlin Wall was opened, and Berliners exuberantly began dismantling the Cold War's most powerful symbol. Before long, inspired by these events, revolutions would overthrow Communist regimes throughout Eastern Europe. Gorbachev and the Soviets chose not to intervene, as the empire that Stalin built crumbled.

Statement Allowing East Germans to Travel Abroad or Emigrate, 9 November 1989

. . . The Council of Ministers of East Germany has decided immediately to set in force the following stipulations for private journeys and permanent emigration until a corresponding parliamentary law comes into effect:

1. Private journeys into foreign countries can be applied for without fulfilling preconditions (reasons for travel, relatives). Permission will be given at short notice.
2. The relevant passport and registration offices of the regional offices of the People's Police in East Germany have been ordered to issue visas for permanent emigration immediately without the present preconditions for permanent emigration having been fulfilled. Application for permanent emigration is also possible as before at departments of internal affairs.
3. Permanent emigration is allowed across all border crossing points between East Germany and West Germany and West Berlin.
4. Because of this the temporary issuing of permits in East German missions abroad and permanent emigration using East German identity cards through third countries will no longer apply.

DISCUSSION QUESTIONS

1. What did East German leaders hope to accomplish by issuing this statement?
2. What was its significance for Berliners? Why did it lead to the fall of the Berlin Wall?
3. How did the Berlin events help open the way for revolutions throughout Eastern Europe?
4. How did these events help pave the way for reunification of Germany?

86. NATO's London Declaration on the End of the Cold War, July 1990

On 6 July 1990, a NATO conference in London issued a statement in response to the liberation of Central and Eastern Europe from Soviet control. Asserting that Europe had entered a new era, it effectively declared that the Cold War was over.

The London Declaration, 6 July 1990

Europe has entered a new, promising era. Central and Eastern Europe is liberating itself. The Soviet Union has embarked on the long journey toward a free society. The walls that once confined people and ideas are collapsing. Europeans are determining their own destiny. They are choosing freedom. They are choosing economic liberty. They are choosing peace. They are choosing a Europe whole and free. As a consequence, this Alliance must and will adapt.

The North Atlantic alliance has been the most successful defensive alliance in history. As our alliance enters its fifth decade and looks ahead to a new century, it must continue to provide for the common defense. . . . Yet our alliance must be even more an agent of change. It can help build the structures of a more united continent, supporting security and stability with the strength of our shared faith in democracy, the rights of the individual, and the peaceful resolution of disputes. . . .

We recognize that, in the new Europe, the security of every state is inseparably linked to the security of its neighbors. NATO must become an institution where Europeans, Canadians and Americans work together not only for the common defense, but to build new partnerships with all the nations of Europe. The Atlantic Community must reach out to the countries of the East which were our adversaries in the cold war, and extend to them the hand of friendship.

We will remain a defensive alliance and will continue to defend all the territory of all of our members. We have no aggressive intentions and we commit ourselves to the peaceful resolution of all disputes. We will never in any circumstance be the first to use force.

The member states of the North Atlantic Alliance propose to the member states of the Warsaw Treaty Organization a joint declaration in which we solemnly state that we are no longer adversaries and reaffirm our intention to refrain from the threat or use of force against the territorial integrity or political independence of any state, or from acting in any other manner inconsistent with the purpose and principles of the United Nations Charter and with the CSCE [Conference on Security and Cooperation in Europe] Final Act. We invite all other CSCE member states to join us in this commitment to non-aggression.

In that spirit, and to reflect the changing political role of the Alliance, we today invite President Gorbachev on behalf of the Soviet Union, and representatives of the other Central and Eastern European countries, to come to Brussels and address the North Atlantic Council. We today also invite the Governments of the Union of Soviet Socialist Republics, the Czech and Slovak Federal Republic, the Hungarian Republic, the Republic of Poland, the People's Republic of Bulgaria and Romania to come to NATO, not just to visit, but to establish regular diplomatic liaison with NATO. This will make it possible for us to share with them our thinking and deliberations in this historic period of change.

Our alliance will do its share to overcome the legacy of decades of suspicion. We are ready to intensify military contacts, including those of NATO Military Commanders, with Moscow and other Central and Eastern European capitals.

We welcome the invitation to NATO Secretary General Manfred Wörmer to visit Moscow and meet with Soviet leaders. . . .

The significant presence of North American conventional and US nuclear forces in Europe demonstrates the underlying political compact that binds North America's fate to Europe's democracies. But, as Europe changes, we must profoundly alter the way we think about defense.

To reduce our military requirements, sound arms control agreements are essential. That is why we put the highest priority on completing this year the first treaty to reduce and limit conventional armed forces in Europe. . . .

As Soviet troops leave Eastern Europe and a treaty limiting conventional armed forces is implemented, the Alliance's integrated force structure and its strategy will change fundamentally to include the following elements:

- NATO will field smaller and restructured active forces. These forces will be highly mobile and versatile so that Allied leaders will have maximum flexibility in deciding how to respond to a crisis. It will rely increasingly on multinational corps made up of national units.
- NATO will scale back the readiness of its active units reducing training requirements and the number of exercises.
- NATO will rely more heavily on the ability to build up larger forces if and when they might be needed.

To keep the peace, the Alliance must maintain for the foreseeable future an appropriate mix of nuclear and conventional forces, based in Europe, and kept up to date where necessary. But, as a defensive Alliance, NATO has always stressed that none of its weapons will ever be used except in self-defense and that we seek the lowest and most stable level of nuclear forces needed to secure the prevention of war.

The political and military changes in Europe, and the prospects of further changes, now allow the Allies concerned to go further. They will thus modify the size and adapt the tasks of their nuclear deterrent forces. They have concluded that, as a result of the new political and military conditions in Europe, there will be a significantly reduced role for sub-strategic nuclear systems of the shortest range. They have decided specifically that, once negotiations begin on short-range nuclear forces, the Alliance will propose, in return for reciprocal action by the Soviet Union, the elimination of all its nuclear artillery shells from Europe. . . .

Today, our Alliance begins a major transformation. Working with all the countries of Europe, we are determined to create enduring peace on this continent.

DISCUSSION QUESTIONS

1. Why did NATO need to redefine its mission in 1990? What did it expect the "new NATO" would become?
2. Why did the London Declaration invite Warsaw Pact members to visit NATO headquarters? Why did NATO feel that further arms control agreements were still needed?
3. How was NATO ready to respond to the withdrawal of Soviet forces from Eastern Europe?
4. What sort of Europe did NATO envision in the aftermath of the Cold War?

87. The Kohl–Gorbachev Agreement on German Unification, July 1990

After the fall of the Berlin Wall and liberation of Eastern Europe removed the main obstacles to German unification, Germans pressed the four powers that had divided their country (America, Britain, France, and the USSR) to let them reunite. After some initial hesitance, a framework for discussions was approved. But the West envisioned a unified Germany that was part of NATO, while Soviets insisted that it must be neutral. In July 1990, in an effort to break the impasse, West German chancellor Helmut Kohl traveled to the USSR and persuaded Gorbachev to accept NATO membership for a united Germany, in return for major economic concessions and a pledge that the NATO military structure would not expand into eastern Germany until Soviet troops had left. This agreement removed the last major hurdle and, once appropriate treaties were completed and signed, 3 October 1990 was proclaimed the "Day of German Unity."

A. Statement by Helmut Kohl, 16 July 1990

The . . . significance of our meeting lies in the results: We have agreed that significant progress could be made in central questions. This breakthrough was possible because both sides are aware that in Europe, in Germany and in the Soviet Union historic changes are taking place that give us a special responsibility. . . .

President Gorbachev and I have agreed that we have to face this historic challenge and that we have to try to be worthy of it. And we understand this task out of a special duty to our own generation, which consciously saw and witnessed the war and its consequences, and which has the great, maybe unique, chance to durably create the future of our Continent and our countries peacefully, securely and freely.

It is clear to President Gorbachev and to me that German-Soviet relations have a central significance for the future of our peoples and for the fate of Europe. We want to express this and have agreed to conclude an all-encompassing bilateral treaty immediately after unification, which shall organize our relations durably and in good-neighborliness. . . .

Today I can state the following with satisfaction and in agreement with President Gorbachev:

- The unification of Germany encompasses the Federal Republic, the GDR and Berlin.
- When unification is brought about, all the rights and responsibilities of the Four Powers will end. With that, the unified Germany, at the point of its unification, receives its full and unrestricted sovereignty.
- The unified Germany may . . . decide freely and by itself if and which alliance it wants to be a member of. . . . I have declared as the opinion of the West German Government that the unified Germany wants to be a member of the Atlantic Alliance, and I am certain that this also complies with the opinion of the Government of the GDR.
- The unified Germany concludes a bilateral treaty with the Soviet Union for the reorganization of the troop withdrawal from the GDR, which shall be ended within three to four years. . . .
- As long as Soviet troops will remain stationed on the territory of the GDR, NATO structures will not be expanded to this part of Germany. . . .
- A unified Germany will refrain from producing, holding or commanding of atomic, biological and chemical weapons and will remain a member of the Non-Proliferation Treaty. . . .

B. Statement by Mikhail Gorbachev, 16 July 1990

Chancellor Kohl has said a great deal about the great work we have done together. . . .

We could work so fruitfully because . . . our relations are already marked by a very high level of dialogue, and the meetings on highest levels, the telephone calls, the mutual visits have contributed to this intensive dialogue.

We have expected that there will be . . . changes, for example in the area of NATO.

The Warsaw Pact has already, as you know, changed its doctrine at its last session. That was a challenge, a call to change the structures of the blocs, from military blocs to more political ones.

We have received a very important impulse from the conference in London, NATO's most recent conference, which brought very important positive steps. . . .

If the . . . step of London had not been made, then it would have been difficult to make headway at our meeting. I want to characterize the two last days with a German expression: we made realpolitik. We have taken as a basis today's reality, the significance for Europe and the world.

We have reached agreement over the fact that the NATO structure is not going to be expanded to the territory of the former GDR. And if on the basis of our agreement the Soviet troops will be withdrawn in a time frame of, let us say, three to four years, then we take it that after this time period this territory will also be part of a Germany that has full sovereignty. We take it that no other foreign troops appear there; here we have trust and are aware of the responsibility of this step.

Mr. Chancellor, it was you most of all who developed this idea at this meeting. We cannot talk yet about a unified Germany, it is still an idea yet, but an idea that I welcome. . . .

DISCUSSION QUESTIONS

1. Why would Kohl and his NATO allies insist that a unified Germany be part of NATO? Why would the Soviets oppose this?
2. Why was Gorbachev so sensitive to the military status of East Germany (the GDR)?
3. How did Kohl reassure Gorbachev about NATO's role in a reunified Germany? As reflected in their statements, how did Kohl's and Gorbachev's positions differ?
4. What was the historic significance of the Kohl–Gorbachev agreement?

88. The START Treaty, July 1991

In summer of 1991, at a summit meeting in Moscow, Presidents Bush and Gorbachev signed the Strategic Arms Reduction (START) treaty, culminating over two decades of arms control negotiations. Within seven years, according to its terms, the Soviets would eliminate half of their deployed nuclear warheads, and the Americans would cut theirs by over a third. The nuclear arms race, which had terrified the world for over four decades, was over.

Treaty on the Reduction and Limitation of Strategic Offensive Arms, 31 July 1991

Article I

Each Party shall reduce and limit its strategic offensive arms in accordance with the provisions of this Treaty. . . .

Article II

1. Each Party shall reduce and limit its ICBMs and ICBM launchers, SLBMs and SLBM launchers, heavy bombers, ICBM warheads, SLBM warheads, and heavy bomber armaments, so that seven years after entry into force of this Treaty and thereafter, the aggregate numbers, as counted in accordance with Article III of this Treaty, do not exceed:
   (a) 1600, for deployed ICBMs and their associated launchers, deployed SLBMs and their associated launchers, and deployed heavy bombers, including 154 for deployed heavy ICBMs and their associated launchers;
   (b) 6000, for warheads attributed to deployed ICBMs, deployed SLBMs, and deployed heavy bombers, including: (i) 4900, for warheads attributed to deployed ICBMs and deployed SLBMs; (ii) 1100, for warheads attributed to deployed ICBMs on mobile launchers of ICBMs; (iii) 1540, for warheads attributed to deployed heavy ICBMs.
2. Each Party shall implement the reductions pursuant to paragraph 1 of this Article in three phases, so that its strategic offensive arms do not exceed:
   (a) by the end of the first phase, that is, no later than 36 months after entry into force of this Treaty, and thereafter, the following aggregate numbers: (i) 2100, for deployed ICBMs and their associated launchers, deployed SLBMs and their associated launchers, and deployed heavy bombers; (ii) 9150, for warheads attributed to deployed ICBMs, deployed SLBMs, and deployed heavy bombers; (iii) 8050, for warheads attributed to deployed ICBMs and deployed SLBMs;
   (b) by the end of the second phase, that is, no later than 60 months after entry into force of this Treaty, and thereafter, the following aggregate numbers: (i) 1900, for deployed ICBMs and their associated launchers, deployed SLBMs and their associated launchers, and deployed heavy bombers; (ii) 7950, for warheads attributed to deployed ICBMs, deployed SLBMs, and deployed heavy bombers; (iii) 6750, for warheads attributed to deployed ICBMs and deployed SLBMs;
   (c) by the end of the third phase, that is, no later than 84 months after entry into force of this Treaty: the aggregate numbers provided for in paragraph 1 of this Article.
3. Each Party shall limit the aggregate throw-weight of its deployed ICBMs and deployed SLBMs so that seven years after entry into force of this Treaty and thereafter such aggregate throw-weight does not exceed 3600 metric tons. . . .

Article IX

1. For the purpose of ensuring verification of compliance with the provisions of this Treaty, each Party shall use national technical means

of verification at its disposal in a manner consistent with . . . international law.

2. Each Party undertakes not to interfere with the national technical means of verification of the other Party operating in accordance with paragraph 1 of this Article.
3. Each Party undertakes not to use concealment measures that impede verification, by national technical means of verification, of compliance with the provisions of this Treaty. . . .

Article XI

1. For the purpose of ensuring verification of compliance with the provisions of this Treaty, each Party shall have the right to conduct inspections and continuous monitoring activities. . . .

Article XVII

1. This Treaty . . . shall be subject to ratification in accordance with the constitutional procedures of each Party. . . .
2. This Treaty shall remain in force for 15 years unless superseded earlier by a subsequent agreement on the reduction and limitation of strategic offensive arms. . . .
3. Each Party shall, in exercising its national sovereignty, have the right to withdraw from this Treaty if it decides that extraordinary events related to the subject matter of this Treaty have jeopardized its supreme interests. It shall give notice of its decision to the other party six months prior to withdrawal from this Treaty. . . .

DISCUSSION QUESTIONS

1. Why was Gorbachev so anxious for an arms reduction treaty? How did the replacement of Reagan by Bush help pave the way for this treaty?
2. In what sense did the provision for equal ceilings of 1600 delivery systems and 6000 deployed warheads represent a U.S. victory?
3. Why were the provisions for inspection and monitoring so important?
4. Why did the treaty phase in the force reductions over a seven-year period?

89. THE ATTEMPTED *Coup* IN THE USSR, AUGUST 1991

Only three weeks after the signing of the START treaty in Moscow, a group of Soviet officials, disturbed by the deterioration of Soviet power under Gorbachev's regime, attempted to remove him from power. Detaining him at his vacation home, they set up an emergency committee to run the country and sent troops and tanks into Moscow and other major cities. But their plans unraveled when Boris Yeltsin, the flamboyant president of the Russian republic, issued an appeal for massive popular resistance, and the troops refused to move against huge crowds that gathered around his Moscow headquarters. Within a few days, the coup collapsed and Gorbachev returned to Moscow, but it soon became clear that real power had shifted to Yeltsin.

A. Announcement on Gorbachev's Removal and Formation of Emergency Committee, 19 August 1991

In view of Mikhail Sergeyevich Gorbachev's inability, for health reasons, to perform the duties of the USSR President and of the transfer of the USSR President's powers, in keeping with . . . the USSR Constitution, to USSR Vice President Gennady Ivanovich Yanayev,

With the aim of overcoming the profound and comprehensive crisis, political, ethnic and civil strife, chaos and anarchy that threaten the lives and security of the Soviet Union's citizens and the sovereignty, territory integrity, freedom and independence of our fatherland,

Proceeding from the results of the nationwide referendum on the preservation of the Union of Soviet Socialist Republics, and

Guided by the vital interests of all ethnic groups living in our fatherland and all Soviet people,

We Resolve:

1. In accordance with . . . the USSR law "on the legal regime of a state of emergency," and with demands by broad popular masses to adopt the most decisive measures to prevent society from sliding into national catastrophe and insure law and order, to declare a state of emergency in some parts of the Soviet Union for six months from 04:00 Moscow time on Aug. 19, 1991.
2. To establish that the Constitution and laws of the USSR have unconditional priority throughout the territory of the USSR.
3. To form a State Committee for the State of Emergency in the USSR in order to run the country and effectively exercise the state-of-emergency regime, consisting of:
   O. D. Baklanov, First Deputy Chairman of the USSR Defense Council
   V. A. Kryuchkov, chairman of the KGB
   V. S. Pavlov, Prime Minister of the USSR
   B. K. Pugo, Interior Minister of the USSR
   V. A. Starodubtsev, chairman of the Farmers' Union of the USSR
   A. I. Tizyakov, president of the USSR Association of State Enterprises and Industrial, Construction, Transport and Communications Facilities
   D. T. Yazov, Defense Minister of the USSR
   G. I. Yanayev, Acting President of the USSR
4. To establish that the USSR State Committee for the State of Emergency's decisions are mandatory for unswerving fulfillment by all agencies of power and administration, officials and citizens throughout the territory of the USSR.

B. Yeltsin's Call to Resist the *Coup* Attempt, 19 August 1991

Citizens of Russia: On the night of 18–19 August 1991, the legally elected President of the country was removed from power.

Regardless of the reasons given for his removal, we are dealing with a rightist, reactionary, anti-constitutional coup. Despite all the difficulties and severe trials being experienced by the people, the democratic process in the country is acquiring an increasingly broad sweep and an irreversible character.

The peoples of Russia are becoming masters of their destiny. The uncontrolled powers of unconstitutional organs have been considerably limited, and this includes party organs.

The leadership of Russia has adopted a resolute position toward the union treaty striving for the unity of the Soviet Union and unity of Russia. Our position on this issue permitted a considerable acceleration of the preparation of this treaty, to coordinate it with all the republics and to determine the date of signing as Aug. 20. Tomorrow's signing has been cancelled.

These developments gave rise to angry reactionary forces, pushed them to irresponsible and adventurist attempts to solve the most complicated political and economic problems by methods of force. Attempts to realize a coup have been tried earlier. We considered and consider that such methods of force are unacceptable. They discredit the union in the eyes of the whole world, undermine our prestige in the world community, and return us to the cold-war era along with the Soviet Union's isolation in the world community. All of this forces us to proclaim that the so-called committee's ascendancy to power is unlawful.

Accordingly we proclaim all decisions and instructions of this committee to be unlawful. We are confident that the organs of local power will unswervingly adhere to constitutional laws and decrees of the President of Russia. We appeal to citizens of Russia to give a fitting rebuff to the putschists and demand a return of the country to normal constitutional development.

Undoubtedly it is essential to give the country's President, Gorbachev, an opportunity to address the people. Today he has been blockaded. I have been denied communications with him. We demand an immediate convocation of an extraordinary Congress of People's Deputies of the Union. We are absolutely confident that our countrymen will not permit the sanctioning of the tyranny and lawlessness of the putschists, who have lost all shame and conscience. We address an appeal to servicemen to manifest lofty civic duty and not take part in the reactionary coup. Until these demands are met, we appeal for a universal unlimited strike.

C. President Bush's Statement on the Soviet *Coup*, 19 August 1991

We are deeply disturbed by the events of the last hours in the Soviet Union and condemn the unconstitutional resort to force. While the situation continues to evolve and information remains incomplete, the apparent unconstitutional removal of President Gorbachev, the declaration of a state of emergency, and the deployment of Soviet military forces in Moscow and other cities raise the most serious questions about the future course of the Soviet Union. This misguided and illegitimate effort bypasses both Soviet law and the will of the Soviet peoples.

Accordingly, we support President Yeltsin's call for "restoration of the legally elected organs of power and the reaffirmation of the post of USSR President M. S. Gorbachev."

Greater democracy and openness in Soviet society, including steps toward implementation of Soviet obligations under the Helsinki Final Act and the Charter of Paris, have made a crucial contribution to the welcome improvement in East-West relations during the past few years.

In these circumstances, US policy will be based on the following guidelines:

We believe the policies of reform in the Soviet Union must continue, including democratization, the process of peaceful reconciliation between the center and the republics and economic transformation.

We support all constitutionally elected leaders and oppose the use of force or intimidation [to] suppress them or restrict their right to free speech.

We oppose the use of force in the Baltic states or against any republics to suppress or replace democratically elected governments.

We call upon the USSR to abide by its international treaties and commitments, including its commitments to respect basic human rights and democratic practices under the Helsinki Accords, and the Charter of Paris.

We will avoid in every possible way actions that would lend legitimacy or support to this coup effort.

We have no interest in a new cold war or in the exacerbation of East-West tensions.

At the same time, we will not support economic aid programs if adherence to extra-constitutional means continues.

D. Excerpts from Soviet Television Report, 21 August 1991

Good evening, Comrades. Television viewers, an hour ago, the President of the USSR, Mikhail Gorbachev, made a statement for the country's radio and television. He stays fully in command of the situation and the connections which have been interrupted by the activities of the group of the emergency council have now been restored.

The President of the USSR had a telephone conversation with Comrades Yeltsin, Nazarbayev, Karimov and others. All of them totally denounced the attempt at a *coup d'etat* or the interruption in the legal activities of the country's Government. They stated that these anti-constitutional actions were not supported by the higher authorities of the country nor by the peoples of the country. These adventurists will bear full responsibility, liability for their illegal actions.

Mikhail Gorbachev gave directions to the general staff and the Minister of Defense Moiseyev to remove all troops presently in the cities of the country.

Today Mikhail Gorbachev had a telephone conversation with the President of the United States, Bush. The President of the United States expressed his very profound satisfaction at the fact that the extremely dangerous situation which arose because of these unconstitutional acts of this group of individuals have ended. In turn, President Gorbachev stated that the society and Government of the country had rebuffed this adventure. And the Presidents agreed to maintain continuing contact with one another and continuing cooperation in accordance with agreements reached already.

DISCUSSION QUESTIONS

1. Why did the coup organizers depose Gorbachev? What did they hope to accomplish?
2. Why did Yeltsin appeal for a universal strike? Why was his resistance so effective?
3. Why did Bush denounce the coup and threaten to cut off economic aid? What risks did he take in doing so?
4. Why did the coup fail? How did it help undermine Gorbachev and empower Yeltsin?

90. Gorbachev's Resignation Speech, December 1991

After the abortive August 1991 coup, Gorbachev sought vainly to hold onto power and keep the Soviet Union together. But Yeltsin's role in foiling the coup had strengthened him and his Russian republic, enabling him and the heads of other republics to ignore Gorbachev and his badly weakened Soviet regime. On 8 December, Yeltsin and the leaders of Ukraine and Belarus decided to replace the USSR with a loose association called the Commonwealth of Independent States. When most of the other republics agreed to join it, Gorbachev's cause was lost. On 25 December 1991, he formally relinquished his duties and resigned as Soviet president. A short time later, the Soviet flag was lowered from its place atop the Kremlin, and the USSR—one of history's largest and most powerful empires—officially ceased to exist.

Highlights of Gorbachev's Resignation Speech, 25 December 1991*

Dear follow countrymen, compatriots. Due to the situation which has evolved as a result of the formation of the Commonwealth of Independent States, I hereby discontinue my activities at the post of President of the Union of Soviet Socialist Republics. I am making this decision on considerations of principle. I firmly came out in favor of the independence of nations and sovereignty for the republics. At the same time, I support the preservation of the union state and the integrity of this country. The developments took a different course. The policy prevailed of dismembering this country and disuniting the state, which is something I cannot subscribe to. . . .

This being my last opportunity to address you as President of the USSR, I find it necessary to inform you of what I think of the road that has been trodden by us since 1985. I find it important because there have been a lot of controversial, superficial, and biased judgments made on this score.

---

* Transcript of Mikhail S. Gorbachev's resignation speech in Moscow, as recorded through the facilities of CNN and translated by CNN from the Russian. Reprinted in *The New York Times*, December 26, 1991, A12. Reprinted courtesy CNN.

Destiny so ruled that when I found myself at the helm of this state it already was clear that something was wrong in this country. We had a lot of everything—land, oil and gas, other natural resources—and there was intellect and talent in abundance. However, we were living much worse than people in the industrialized countries were living and we were increasingly lagging behind them. The reason was obvious even then. This country was suffocating in the shackles of the bureaucratic command system. Doomed to cater to ideology, and suffer and carry the onerous burden of the arms race, it found itself at the breaking point. . . . This country was going nowhere and we couldn't possibly live the way we did. We had to change everything radically.

It is for this reason that I have never had any regrets . . . that I did not use the capacity of General Secretary just to reign in this country for several years. I would have considered it an irresponsible and immoral decision. I was also aware that to embark on reform of this caliber and in a society like ours was an extremely difficult and even risky undertaking. But even now, I am convinced that the democratic reform that we launched in the spring of 1985 was historically correct.

The process of renovating this country and bringing about drastic change in the international community has proven to be much more complicated than anyone could imagine. However, let us give its due to what has been done so far.

This society has acquired freedom. It has been freed politically and spiritually, and this is the most important achievement that we have [not] yet fully come to grips with. And we haven't, because we haven't learned to use freedom yet. However, an effort of historical importance has been carried out. The totalitarian system has been eliminated, which prevented this country from becoming a prosperous and well-to-do country. . . . A breakthrough has been effected on the road of democratic change.

Free elections have become a reality. Free press, freedom of worship, representative legislatures and a multi-party system have all become reality. Human rights are being treated as the supreme principle and top priority. Movement has been started toward a multi-tier economy and the equality of all forms of ownership. . . .

We're now living in a new world. An end has been put to the cold war and to the arms race, as well as to the mad militarization of the country, which has crippled our economy, public attitudes and morals. The threat of nuclear war has been removed.

Once again, I would like to stress that during this transitional period, I did everything that needed to be done to insure that there was reliable control of nuclear weapons. We opened up ourselves to the rest of the world, abandoned the practices of interfering in others' internal affairs and using troops outside this country, and we were reciprocated with trust, solidarity, and respect.

We have become one of the key strongholds in terms of restructuring modern civilization on a peaceful democratic basis. The nations and peoples of this country have acquired the right to freely choose their format for self-determination. . . .

I consider it vitally important to preserve the democratic achievements which have been attained in the last few years. We have paid with all our history and tragic experience for these democratic achievements, and they are not to be abandoned, whatever the circumstances, and whatever the pretexts. Otherwise, all our hopes for the best will be buried. . . .

Of course, there were mistakes made that could have been avoided, and many of the things that we did could have been done better. But I am positive that sooner or later, some day our common efforts will bear fruit and our nations will live in a prosperous, democratic society.

I wish everyone all the best.

DISCUSSION QUESTIONS

1. Why did Gorbachev resign as Soviet president?
2. According to Gorbachev, what was wrong with the USSR when he took over as leader?
3. Why did he insist that his reforms were necessary, despite the fact that they had helped to enable the USSR's dismemberment?
4. What did Gorbachev consider to be his main achievements and legacy?

INDEX

Note: '*illus*' following the page number indicates an illustration in the text.

O

P

Q

R